THE SUNDAY READINGS

THE SUNDAY READINGS

"Cycle A" (1)

An Explanation and Application of the Sunday Readings

KEVIN O'SULLIVAN, O.F.M. D.D. L.SS.

FRANCISCAN HERALD PRESS
CHICAGO
COSTELLO PUBLISHING CO. INC.
NEW YORK

NIHIL OBSTAT:
    VERY REVEREND CANON M. MCDONOUGH
        Censor Deputatus

IMPRIMATUR:
    ✠MICHAEL
    Episcopus Galviensis

GALVIAE 16 Maii 1971

©REV. KEVIN O'SULLIVAN, O.F.M.

Library of Congress Catalog Card Number: 74–141766
ISBN: 8199–0436–8

PRINTED AND BOUND BY CAHILL & CO. LIMITED
    DUBLIN, IRELAND.

FOREWORD

by Most Rev. Dr. Michael Browne, D.D. D.C.L. LL.D., Bishop of Galway.

The Sunday Readings by Fr. Kevin O'Sullivan, O.F.M., in three volumes, gives the readings for the Masses of Sundays and Holydays of Obligation following the three-year cycle of the lectionary. The author is a biblical scholar of deep learning and long years of teaching and pastoral experience. After each reading he gives an explanation of the text—first giving the historical and literary background of the author and then elucidating particular words or phrases. Next he gives an application of the reading to the lives and problems of modern Catholics. These are always deeply spiritual and soul-searching. Priests will find them a valuable help in preparing their homily or sermon : they will easily be able to apply them to the concrete problems or needs of the congregation. The author follows this plan for each of the three volumes and the reader will find his explanation of the biblical texts most helpful and illuminating.

These volumes will be a great help to the pastoral priest : they provide him with the biblical data on each reading which he would otherwise be able to obtain only from searching through text-books and commentaries—if he had them. They give him the exact meaning of the sacred text and of God's message and they provide very valuable ideas and suggestions for preaching.

It is a book for priests, but also for the laity. It will help them to follow and appreciate the message of the liturgy, which they might otherwise miss.

I recommend these three volumes most warmly not only to priests but to all Catholic convents and homes.

16th May, 1971.   ✠ MICHAEL.

CONTENTS

LENTEN SEASON

EASTER SEASON

FIRST SUNDAY OF ADVENT

FIRST READING : Is. 2 : 1–5. The word which Isaiah the son of Amoz saw concerning Judah and Jerusalem.

It shall come to pass in the latter days that the mountain of the house of the Lord shall be established as the highest of the mountains, and shall be raised above the hills; and all the nations shall flow to it, and many peoples shall come, and say : "Come, let us go up to the mountain of the Lord, to the house of the God of Jacob; that he may teach us his ways and that we may walk in his paths. For out of Zion shall go forth the law, and the word of the Lord from Jerusalem. He shall judge between the nations, and shall decide for many peoples; and they shall beat their swords into ploughshares, and their spears into pruning hooks; nation shall not lift up sword against nation, neither shall they learn war any more. O house of Jacob, come, let us walk in the light of the Lord."

EXPLANATION : Isaiah, the greatest of the Old Testament prophets, whose writings are extant, preached in Jerusalem from 742 to 700 B.C. This was one of the most critical periods of the Chosen People's history. The northern tribes (Israel) were subjugated by Assyria in 722, and disappeared as a people. Judah began to rely on political alliances rather than on Yahweh. Isaiah condemned this betrayal, and foretold the doom which awaited Judah, if they did not return to God. He was ignored, and the people of Judah ended in the exile and slavery of Babylon. The prophet nonetheless makes many messianic prophecies, that is, many references to a glorious age in the future, when God will fulfill his promises to the patriarchs . . . God will yet have a Chosen People who will be loyal to him. Today's reading is one of these messianic references.

In the latter days : In the future days of the Messiah.

mountain . . . of the Lord : The temple was built on Mount Zion in Jerusalem.

raised above the hills : Because the Lord's house is there, Zion will, in those future days, be raised above all mountains and hills, not physically but in the esteem in which it will be held.

all nations . . . to it : This new Jerusalem or Zion will be the center of attraction for all *nations,* not only for Jews.

come . . . go up : The Gentiles will be exhorting one another to come to the house of the God of Jacob, to the God of the Jews.

teach . . . his ways : They come to learn his ways, his message of truth and salvation.

walk in his paths : In order to follow his teaching and his rule of life.

Zion . . . law : In that future day the new law, the word of God, the gospel message of salvation, shall spread to the world from Zion.

He shall . . . nations : The new law and the new legislator shall not be for the Jews alone but also for all nations.

beat their . . . spears : This new law will make all men brothers, men of peace; there shall be an end to hatred and warfare. There shall be "peace on earth to all who are God's friends," to all those who will accept the Messiah and his gospel of love.

come let us walk : The prophet now turns to his own people, the "house of Jacob" and exhorts them not to be outdone by the Gentile nations. They should accept the Messiah sent by God and the new form of life—the "light of the Lord"—which he is bringing with him.

APPLICATION : Today, the first Sunday of Advent, is the ecclesiastical New Year's day. The Church begins her annual liturgical cycle of feasts, with a period of four weeks' preparation for Christmas—the great feast of Christ's coming on earth. The readings selected for today, and the following three Sundays, are chosen to help us prepare for this, the greatest event that ever happened on our planet.

The Son of God took our human nature and "dwelt among us" for a while on earth, in order to bring us to heaven, where we shall dwell forever with the Blessed Trinity.

The whole of the Old Testament—the story of God's dealings with the Chosen People—describes God's long preparation for this, almost incredible, act of divine love and mercy, the Incarnation. God sent his Son in our lowly human nature, in order to raise us, mere creatures, to the dignity of adopted sons of God, brothers of Christ, and thus, heirs of the eternal life with him in heaven.

Today's lesson from Isaiah contains one of the encouraging speeches which God's great prophet addressed to his fellow-Jews, to help them persevere in their faith in God. Days of distress and tribulation lay ahead. Jerusalem, their beloved and holy city, the site of the temple where the true God manifested his power and his mercy among them, was to be razed one day to the ground, because of their sins. But when the great day came and God fulfilled his promises to them, Jerusalem would once more be the glory and the pride, not only of the Jews, but of all nations.

The "Word of the Lord," the true Son of Man made flesh, would rebuild their temple, not with stones and mortar, but with living, human beings who would form his Church: the members of his mystical body on earth. His message, and his means of salvation for man, would go forth from Jerusalem to the ends of the earth.

This prophecy of Isaiah, spoken 700 years before the coming of Christ, has been fulfilled. "The Word was made flesh and dwelt among us." And we today, thousands of miles from Jerusalem, and almost two thousand years after his coming among us, are preparing ourselves for the annual commemoration of that greatest event of history.

To do so, let the basic meaning and messages of the Incarnation, which Christmas commemorates, sink deeply into our minds : we were not created by

God in order to live fifty, seventy, or even a hundred years in this world; we were created to be citizens of heaven for all eternity. This is God's plan for us, and to bring it about, he chose that his divine Son should share in our humanity, so that we could share forever in his divinity.

What words of ours could express our gratitude for this stupendous act of God's love? What sacrifices could we offer—even that of life itself—which could make us worthy of this divine generosity? But Christ has acted on our behalf, he has graciously shared his merits with us, and his merits were infinite because he was true God as well as true man.

SECOND READING : Romans 13 : 11-14. You know what hour it is, how it is full time now for you to wake from sleep. For salvation is nearer to us now than when we first believed; the night is far gone, the day is at hand. Let us then cast off the works of darkness and put on the armor of light; let us conduct ourselves becomingly as in the day, not in reveling and drunkenness, not in debauchery and licentiousness, not in quarreling and jealousy. But put on the Lord Jesus Christ, and make no provision for the flesh, to gratify its desires.

EXPLANATION : This Epistle to the Romans is the longest of St. Paul's epistles, and the only one written to a church he has founded personally, or through one of his disciples (e.g. Colossians). Perhaps because of this, it is more a treatise on the basic gospel of Christ, as preached by Paul, than an epistle or letter. It was written about 58 A.D. It was partly a preparation for the visit he intended to pay the Christians of Rome, after he had delivered the alms he had collected from the faithful of the churches of Macedonia and Achaia, to the poor Christians of Jerusalem (15 : 22–29). He did eventually visit Rome, but as a prisoner, and not as a free Apostle. But even as a prisoner, he did much to help the spread of the gospel in the capital of the empire, even in the very household of Caesar (Ph. 1 : 12–14).

In the verses chosen for today's second reading, St. Paul urges the Roman Christians to keep the purpose of their conversion, of their acceptance of the gospel, of true salvation, always before their eyes. They had accepted Christ in order to merit eternal salvation; for this reason, they must "cast off the works of darkness," in which they indulged before their conversion. **full time . . . sleep :** As far as salvation, their eternal life, was concerned, their past life was like that of one who sleeps and does nothing. This has all changed now, they must be active, up and doing what the Gospel prescribes.

salvation is nearer : Each day brings nearer the judgement, which will decide their eternal fate.

night . . . far gone . . . hand : Their life before their conversion, whether they were Jews or Gentiles, is compared to the night, because they could do, or in fact did, nothing towards earning their eternal salvation. Things are now changed, the era of salvation has come with Christ, who brought salvation for all mankind.

cast off works of darkness : They must give up all evil habits of their past lives.

put on . . . light : To St. Paul, the Christian is a soldier of Christ. Therefore, he frequently uses military metaphors to describe the Christian virtues, which are the defensive and offensive weapons that the Christian must use. The "armor of light" are the spiritual weapons which Christ has placed at our disposal, namely : prayer, self-sacrifice, the sacraments and the commandments.

reveling . . . licentiousness : Having urged them to practice the Christian virtues, he now tells them to avoid the evil practices so prevalent then in the pagan world.

quarreling and jealousy : These were sins fairly common among the first Christian converts, made up as they were of Jews and Gentiles. The Jewish converts were inclined to regard themselves as superior to the Gentiles, because they had been the Chosen People of the pre-Christian era. The Gentiles reacted, perhaps not always with proper humility, to this presumption, because Christianity had leveled all barriers. There was no longer "question of Greek or Jew, circumcised and uncircumcised, slave and freeman, but Christ is all and is in all," as St. Paul wrote to the Colossians (3 : 11).

make . . . flesh : The unlawful desires of the flesh must be curbed.

APPLICATION : These words of St. Paul to the Roman Christians of the year 58 A.D., are words that each one of us should apply to himself today. Advent begins today. We must prepare ourselves to celebrate worthily the commemoration of the greatest act of love and condescension which the God of infinite love deigned to do for us creatures. He sent his divine Son to become man, to become one of us, so that we could become his adopted sons, sharers in his divine life. This is what our annual feast of Christmas commemorates.

The fact that we are in existence, that we are alive here on earth, is a free gift of God to us. We had no hand, act or part in it. Life of itself is a wonderful gift, a gift we share with the beasts of the field and the birds of the air, and the fish of the sea. But we humans are far superior to these other creatures of God, because we have the extra gift of intelligence and free will. And because

of these gifts, we have ambitions and desires which other creatures have not got. We have in our make-up a spiritual element which raises us above mere matter and makes us want to continue to live.

The cow in the field does not know that it is certain to die, and it does not care, but man knows and has a natural abhorrence of death. Should I, with all the gifts the Creator has given me, and all the reasonable ambitions and desires which these gifts arouse in me, end like the cow in the field : a mere handful of clay, finished with life forever?

Christmas gives an emphatic No to that frightening thought. The infinitely merciful and loving God planned from all eternity for man, the recipient of these superior gifts, a share in his own eternal life, once his short sojourn on this earth was over. The Incarnation—his divine Son sharing in our human nature—was the mysterious, but loving way God ordained to bring this about.

Because of this decree of God, our true and unending life begins after our earthly death.

But we must do our part to earn this divine gift. All men are destined by God for eternal life, but to attain it each man must follow the path laid down by God. St. Paul tells us today some of the things we must avoid, and some of the things we must do, if we want to reach the eternal happiness planned for us. "We must," he says, "put on the Lord Jesus Christ." He made himself our brother, we must live as true brothers of his.

Advent is a glorious opportunity for each one of us to look into his own life and see if he is living as a true brother of Christ, as a true Christian. Few of us can honestly claim that we are doing this, but there is none among us who cannot improve and do better.

Think this morning, and think during the week, of all God has done, and is still doing, in order to give you an eternal life of happiness. Think also, that you could be unfortunate enough to lose this eternal happiness, if you were so foolish as to choose the "works of darkness" instead of the "armor of light," which Christ has offered to you.

GOSPEL : Matt. 24 : 37–44. Jesus said to his disciples, "As were the days of Noah, so will be the coming of the Son of man. For as in those days before the flood they were eating and drinking, marrying and giving in marriage, until the day when Noah entered the ark, and they did not know until the flood came and swept them all away so will be the coming of the Son of man. Then two men will be in the field; one is taken and one is left. Two women will be grinding at the mill; one is taken and one is left. Watch therefore, for you do not know on what day your Lord is coming. But know this, that if the householder had known in what part of the night the thief was coming, he would have watched and would not have let his house be broken into. Therefore you also must be ready; for the Son of man is coming at an hour you do not expect."

EXPLANATION : In chapter 24 of his Gospel, St. Matthew gives us a discourse which our Lord held with his disciples, concerning the destruction of the temple of Jerusalem and the *Parousia*, or the second coming of Christ as judge of the world. In the verses we read today Christ is speaking of his second coming, and emphasizes its unexpectedness and suddenness.

As were . . . Noah : Christ says that his coming as judge will be for most people as unexpected as was the Flood. Only Noah and his family had foreknowledge of the coming Flood, they prepared for it and were saved in the Ark.

eating . . . marrying : The rest of the people where Noah lived went on with their daily tasks and enjoyments, too fully occupied with their own earthly interests to have any time to think of the sudden end that was approaching them.

So will . . . Son of man : It will be the

same with many when Christ the judge comes. They will be taken completely by surprise.

two men in the field . . . two . . . mill: In both cases, the men and women will be occupied with their necessary daily tasks, but of each pair one will be unprepared because he and she will be found working for purely worldly motives, while the other two will have sanctified their daily labor, and made it meritorious for heaven.

watch therefore: The only way to be prepared for the moment of judgement is to be always prepared.

if the householder: Christ now uses a parable or example to prove his point. The man who knows when and where a thief is going to break into his house will be there ready and prepared to repel him.

at an hour you do not expect: Just as thieves do not inform their prospective victims of the hour of their proposed raid so neither will we be informed of the exact day or hour of our death and judgement. It will come unexpectedly.

APPLICATION: During this holy season of Advent we are all being called on and exhorted by the Church to prepare ourselves to commemorate worthily the first coming of Christ as our Brother and Savior. If we do that each year; if we let the full meaning of this great festival of Christmas enter into our innermost being, welcoming the Son of God in the form of the Babe of Bethlehem with a clean, sincere and grateful heart, then each year of our lives will be sanctified and a big step will be taken towards our eternal goal. Christmas each year should be a mile-stone on the road to heaven for every true Christian. It is a festival which vividly recalls to our minds the length our heavenly Father has gone to in order to make us adopted sons and sharers in his everlasting happiness.

If God cares so much for our true welfare—and the Incarnation surely proves that he does—we should surely have enough interest in our own future to cooperate with him in this affair of our eternal salvation.

In today's gospel lesson it is Christ himself who is asking each one of us so to live our lives that no matter when we are called to judgement we shall not be found wanting. This does not mean that we must always be praying. Nor does it mean that we must take no interest in the affairs of this life. Of the two men working in the field and of the two women grinding corn, one of each was found unworthy, not because of the work he or she was doing, but because that work had for them wrongly excluded God and his purpose in life. The two found worthy had room for God and their own eternal welfare in their hearts—their work was part of their loyal service to God and was a means towards their salvation.

In this town (or city) of ours all adults are occupied one way or another with earthly affairs and necessarily so. But while these earthly affairs may, and do alas, become cruel task-masters for some and tie down their whole attention to the things of this earth, for others, thank God, their daily tasks are stepping stones to heaven. The day of reckoning will come, suddenly like a thief in the night for the former, and for the others it will not be a thief breaking in but the Master knocking at their door to take them to himself.

Christmas comes but once a year but its meaning, its lesson, must remain in our hearts and minds all the year round. God wants us in heaven forever. He sent his Son on earth to bring us there. Aided by God's grace we resolve today so to live our lives that when death claims us we shall meet Christ, not as a condemning judge, but as a loving brother.

SECOND SUNDAY OF ADVENT

FIRST READING : Isaiah 11 : 1–10. There shall come forth a shoot from the stump of Jesse, and a branch shall grow out of his roots. And the Spirit of the Lord shall rest upon him, the spirit of wisdom and understanding, the spirit of counsel and might, the spirit of knowledge and the fear of the Lord. And his delight shall be in the fear of the Lord.

He shall not judge by what his eyes see, or decide by what his ears hear; but with righteousness he shall judge the poor, and decide with equity for the meek of the earth; and he shall smite the earth with the rod of his mouth, and with the breath of his lips he shall slay the wicked. Righteousness shall be the girdle of his waist, and faithfulness the girdle of his loins.

The wolf shall dwell with the lamb, and the leopard shall lie down with the kid, and the calf and the lion and the fatling together, and a little child shall lead them. The cow and the bear shall feed; their young shall lie down together; and the lion shall eat straw like the ox. The sucking child shall play over the hole of the asp, and the weaned child shall put his hand on the adder's den. They shall not hurt or destroy in all my holy mountain; for the earth shall be full of the knowledge of the Lord as the waters cover the sea.

In that day the root of Jesse shall stand as an ensign to the people; him shall the nations seek, and his dwellings shall be glorious.

EXPLANATION : To help us prepare for the coming of Christ at Christmas, the Church recalls the prophecies of the great Isaiah on each of the four Sundays of Advent. To encourage the Chosen People who, because of the bad example of their worldly leaders, were wavering in their loyalty to Yahweh their true God, the prophet reminds them of him who is to come. This was 700 years before Christ came, but it was a reminder that God, who had called Abraham and had made him the father and founder of the Chosen People some thousand years previously, had not forgotten his promises. He would fulfill his word. He would one day send them a ruler, a king, who would rule and judge with justice because he would have the true spirit of the Lord. He who was to come would set up a kingdom of peace, not only for the Chosen People but for all men. The kingdom he was to establish would be for Jew and Gentile.

a shoot from the stump of Jesse: Jesse was King David's father. From him descended the line of kings that ruled Judah for 500 years. The infidelities of the kings who followed David caused that line almost to disappear. Only a stump—the remains of an apparently dead tree—would remain, but from that stump a shoot, or sprig, would come forth and become a new tree, far superior to the original one. This shoot was the Messiah, the son of Mary, a descendant of David.

Spirit . . . him: The prophet indicates that it is to the expected Messiah that he is referring. He describes the marvelous gifts of God that he will possess in his human nature.

fear . . . Lord: That is, veneration and respect, filial obedience, not fear in its English meaning. One who feared the Lord in the Old Testament was a true worshipper of God.

He shall not judge: The gifts he shall have from God will enable him to practice absolute justice towards all, especially towards those who are most in need, the poor and the meek.

the earth . . . wicked: The earth contaminated by sin, and the wicked, will receive their just punishment also.

righteousness . . . faithfulness: Justice and fidelity in his relationship with God and with mankind were to be as much part of him as the clothes he wore.

the wolf . . . the lion: Perfect peace will reign in his kingdom, not only between men but between irrational creatures. This is a poetic, not a factual, description as far as the animal world is concerned. As far as man is concerned, the conditions for peace are laid down in the teaching of the Messiah, but it is only in his future kingdom in heaven that they will have their complete fulfillment.

In that day . . . ensign: This descendant of Jesse, this new Davidic king, will be a standard around which Jews and Gentiles will gather.

his dwellings: Wherever people rally to this standard (the Messiah), honor and glory will follow. He is the source and cause of eternal glory for all who will receive him.

APPLICATION: In the eighth century B.C., when Isaiah spoke these prophetic words, many of his contemporaries were in the depths of despair. Because of the sad state of the true religion and the return to idolatry and paganism then so prevalent among them, many of Yahweh's loyal followers were afraid that Yahweh had forgotten his promises to the Patriarchs, their ancestors. Isaiah dispels their fears and their despair, by his definite promise that a new Davidic King would come who would establish peace and a glorious kingdom of justice on earth. His kingdom would be a return to the peace of Paradise, before sin entered the world.

Today, twenty-seven centuries later, we too need to listen to this prophet of hope. We are living in a world where disloyalty to God among those who believe in him, and the denial of his very existence by many more, are prevalent. The natural and logical result of these two positions is that justice and peace among men do not and cannot exist. If men deny that God has any rights or claims over them or act as if he has not, then they cannot admit that their fellowman has any claims on them, or any right to demand justice from them. There can be no true love of neighbor, and no true respect for his rights, where there is no love for God and respect for his rights.

This explains the chaotic state of our world today. But an explanation is not a solution. Diagnosis of a disease is not its cure. We must strive to give God his rightful place in our daily lives, and follow the only path that leads to justice and peace on earth. This is the path laid down by Christ, the true son of God, who came on earth, as man, to teach us that we should love God, and love our neighbor because God loves us. Through the coming of Christ he has made us all his own adopted children.

Many will shrug their shoulders and say: what can I do about this, what effect can any action of mine have in bringing sanity (i.e. true religion), back to this mad world of ours? Yet, you can do a lot, and far more than you could expect. If you put your own conscience straight with God and with your neighbor, God has one more loyal son on earth, one more channel through which he can send his grace to men, one more ray of light, which will help dispel the darkness of despair which surrounds us.

To prepare yourself to welcome Christ at Christmas take an honest look at yourself. How do you stand in relation to God and your neighbor? Are you doing your part to keep peace and love in the home and in your neighborhood? In your place of work are you an example of justice, of peace, of respect for the things of God? Are your language and your conduct truly Christian? Can your fellow-workers say of you : "that man's religion really means something to him, I wish I were like him"? If you can say "yes," to these soul-questions, then thank God for it and strive to do even more. If your honest answer is "No," then begin today to change your life. Your true happiness on earth, and the guarantee of your eternal happiness after death, will depend on this change. Not only that, but the true happiness of many others on earth, and the chance of their eternal happiness hereafter, will depend on it too. Is this too much to ask of any sensible man, who knows where he came from and knows where he is going?

SECOND READING : Romans 15 : 4–9. Whatever was written in former days was written for our instruction, that by steadfastness and by the encouragement of the scriptures we might have hope. May the God of steadfastness and encouragement grant you to live in such harmony with one another, in accord with Christ Jesus, that together you may with one voice glorify the God and Father of our Lord Jesus Christ.

Welcome one another, therefore, as Christ has welcomed you, for the glory of God. For I tell you that Christ became a servant to the circumcised to show God's truthfulness, in order to confirm the promises given to the patriarchs, and in order that the Gentiles might glorify God for his mercy. As it is written, "Therefore I will praise thee among the Gentiles, and sing to thy name."

EXPLANATION : St. Paul is telling the newly-converted Christians of Rome, many of whom were Jews, that the sacred Scriptures of the Old Testament are still a source of instruction, encouragement, and hope. The call of Abraham and the promises made to him, and to his descendants, were fulfilled in the coming of Christ. Christ was the glory of the Chosen People— the fruit of centuries of preparation and expectation—but he brought the knowledge and blessings of the true God to the Gentile pagans also. Henceforth, all men are brothers of Christ.

whatever was written . . . hope : The Old Testament was not only a preparation for the New. It will remain for all time a source of encouragement and hope for Christians.

live in harmony : The Jewish converts were inclined to look down on the Gentile converts because, until then, they alone knew the true God, they alone had this revelation in their Scriptures. But St. Paul tells them that Jew and Gentile are now one in Christ, who has broken down the wall which separated Jew from Gentile.

with one voice . . . our Lord : They must together give glory and thanks to God the Father who sent his divine Son on earth to make all men his adopted sons. Note how the true divinity and the true humanity of Christ are the basis of the Christian religion.

welcome . . . therefore : They must all be one therefore as Christ has made them all one.

for the glory of God : The purpose of the Incarnation : Christ, the Son of God, became man so that men could become sons of God by adoption and be capable of giving external glory to God for all eternity.

a servant . . . circumcised : Christ took human nature among the Jews, as God had promised Abraham, but the effects of this act of love, and self-humiliation ("Christ became a servant"), were intended not only for Abraham's descendants but for all peoples : "All the communities of the earth shall find blessings in you" was part of God's promise to Abraham (Gen. 12 : 3).

As it is written : To confirm what he has said regarding the Gentiles' place in God's plan of salvation, Paul quotes Psalm 18 : 55, which foretells that God will be praised and glorified among the Gentiles.

APPLICATION : "Whatever was written in former days was written for our instruction." St. Paul is referring to the inspired books of the Old Testament in this sentence, and how true this statement is. From these books we learn of the existence of the true God, from whom all things came to be. And not only do we learn of the existence of God, who is our Creator, but we learn that he is our Father, that he has a paternal interest in us, that he has put us on earth in order to share his heaven with us later. It was for this purpose that he revealed himself to Abraham, and made him the father of the Chosen People : from him he had planned that his Son would take his human nature and become one of us, in order to make us brothers and sons of the eternal Father.

All God's dealings with Abraham and his descendants—the Jews—as described in the books of the Old Testament, were part of and preparation for this great central act of God's love for men—the Incarnation.

In these dealings, we learn of another most consoling fact about God—his infinite mercy and his unbounded gift of forgiveness for sinful, unworthy men. His Chosen People, the Jews, were sinful and stubborn, yet he put up with them for centuries, came to their aid again and again, when their own sins had brought misfortunes and catastrophes upon them. Like a recurring decimal, we have, in their whole history of eighteen hundred years, the following theme : sin and disloyalty to their good God, punishment generally from pagan neighbors, their return to God, when in extreme and dire straits, God's forgiveness and a new start.

For most of us Christians, who should know better and should love God more sincerely, for we are witnesses of his supreme act of love in the Incarnation, the knowledge that we are dealing with a God of infinite mercy and patience is a source of strength and encouragement. For we too, unfortunately, are too apt to imitate the Jews in our dealings with God. There are few of us who cannot see in our past lives something similar to the recurring decimal of the Jewish history. However, God is still the God of infinite mercy. He does not, and cannot, change. He is ever ready to forgive and pardon; the prodigal will still get the fatted calf, and the newest garment, if he really returns to his Father.

Yes, whatever was written in former days was written for our instruction. Add to this what has been written concerning Christ's coming among us, with his teaching and promises, and we Christians surely have an inexhaustible source of encouragement and hope. To help us prepare ourselves to welcome Christ at Christmas, the Church brings before our minds sections of the Old and New Testaments, which should inspire us with new faith, hope and charity. Faith in God, who always fulfills his promises, hope for our eventual salvation, and charity, or love for God, who has done, and is still doing, such wonderful things for us unworthy men. This charity and love of God múst spill over on our neighbor, if it is sincere, for as St. John tells us, the man who says he loves God and yet hates his neighbor is a liar (2 Jn. 4 : 20).

GOSPEL : Matthew 3 : 1–12. John the Baptist came preaching in the wilderness of Judea, "Repent, for the kingdom of heaven is at hand." For this is he who was spoken of by the prophet Isaiah when he said,

"The voice of one crying in the wilderness :
Prepare the way of the Lord, make his paths straight."

Now John wore a garment of camel's hair, and a leather girdle around his waist; and his food was locusts and wild honey. Then went out to him Jerusalem and all Judea and all the region about the Jordan, and they were baptized by him in the river Jordan, confessing their sins.

But when he saw many of the Pharisees and Sadducees coming for baptism, he said to them, "You brood of vipers! Who warned you to flee from the wrath to come? Bear fruit that befits repentance, and do not presume to say to yourselves, 'We have Abraham as our father'; for I tell you, God is able from these stones to raise up children to Abraham. Even now the axe is laid to the root of the trees; every tree therefore that does not bear good fruit is cut down and thrown into the fire.

"I baptize you with water for repentance, but he who is coming after me is mightier than I, whose sandals I am not worthy to carry; he will baptize you with the Holy Spirit and with fire. His winnowing fork is in his hand, and he will clear his threshing floor and gather his wheat into the granary, but the chaff he will burn with unquenchable fire."

EXPLANATION: About 30 years previous to the event described in to-day's Gospel, an angel announced to Zechariah, a priest of the temple, that he would have a son (even though his wife Elizabeth was barren and advanced in years). This son was destined to be the Precursor who would announce the proximate arrival of the long-expected Messiah.

John, the name given him by the angel even before his conception, spent his youth and early manhood as a hermit in the desert of Judea, preparing himself for his exalted office. When God revealed to him that the Messiah was soon to begin his public life, John set out for the bank of the Jordan, where he began to preach repentance, in order to prepare the people for "him who was to come."

Kingdom of heaven: That is, the Messianic kingdom which would begin on earth but have its completion and perfection in heaven.

one crying . . . wilderness: John quotes a text from second-Isaiah (40:3), in which the prophet is telling the Jews to prepare a royal road through the desert for the future Messianic king.

camel's hair: John is still dressed as a hermit and eats as a hermit.

Jerusalem . . . Judea: Word of John's arrival at the Jordan went around quickly, and people flocked to hear him.

baptized by him: Not the sacrament of baptism, later instituted by Christ, but a symbolic washing, to indicate repentance and the resolution to avoid sin, is what is indicated here.

Pharisees and Sadducees: The two main religious groups of Jews at that time. The Pharisees were strict observers of the Law of Moses, but their good works were ruined by their pride (see Lk. 18: 9–14). The Sadducees were more political than religious. They denied the resurrection of man, and other beliefs, held by the Pharisees and the majority of Jews.

brood of vipers: John did not mince his words when addressing them.

Abraham as our father: Descent from Abraham and membership of the chosen race would not save them unless they truly repented. God would find a new Chosen People, which he did.

who is . . . me: John realizes that he is only the Precursor. His baptism has no effective power, its value coming from the personal repentance of those who received it. But the one he is preparing for will truly cleanse from sins, and give the Spirit of God to those who accept him. John, in true humility, feels he is not worthy to be even a menial servant of the Messiah.

wheat . . . chaff : The Messiah will separate the wheat from the chaff, the good from the bad, and each will receive what he deserves.

APPLICATION : In this holy season of Advent, as we prepare to welcome Christ at Christmas, John the Baptist has words of advice and warnings for each one of us. He advises us to "prepare the way of the Lord," by true repentance of our past sins and a firm resolution to straighten "the ways of the Lord," that is, not to deviate from the true Christian way of life in the future. Please God, none of us deserves the reproaches he addressed to the Pharisees and Sadducees, but most of us perhaps can find traces of some predominant vices in our innermost selves. The pride and self-righteousness of the Pharisees ruined their otherwise good lives. The worldliness of the Sadducees made them lose interest in the future life, until they went so far as to deny any future existence after death.

Of these two vices, that of the Sadducees is the more prevalent today, and it is to be found in the best of us, in a greater or lesser degree. While all true Christians repudiate atheistic Communism, with its denial of the existence of God and of a future life, many become so immersed in the things of this world that they have no time or thought for the world that is to come. While, theoretically, they reject Communism, they themselves, like the "brood of vipers" of whom the Baptist spoke, are full of the poison of materialism, and are injecting this poison into those whom they influence.

A sincere examination of our outlook on life *and death*, and of our way of life up to today, will tell us how we stand in relation to Christ. Let each one of us ask himself : if Christ, for whose coming as the Divine Babe of Bethlehem we are preparing, were to come to him before Christmas as his just judge, how would he fare? Would he be gathered with the wheat into the granary, or be bundled with the chaff into the unquenchable fire? Each one of us has the decision in his own hands. We can, by true repentance, change ourselves from chaff into wheat, but once we draw our last breath, not even the infinitely merciful God can do that for us.

THIRD SUNDAY OF ADVENT

FIRST READING: Isaiah 35:1–6, 10. The wilderness and the dry land shall be glad, the desert shall rejoice and blossom; like the crocus it shall blossom abundantly, and rejoice with joy and singing. The glory of Lebanon shall be given to it, the majesty of Carmel and Sharon. They shall see the glory of the Lord, the majesty of our God.

Strengthen the weak hands, and make firm the feeble knees. Say to those who are of a fearful heart, "Be strong, fear not! Behold your God will come with vengeance, with the recompense of God. He will come and save you."

Then the eyes of the blind shall be opened, and the ears of the deaf unstopped; then shall the lame man leap like a hart, and the tongue of the dumb sing for joy.

And the ransomed of the Lord shall return, and come to Zion with singing; everlasting joy shall be upon their heads; they shall obtain joy and gladness, and sorrow and sighing shall flee away.

EXPLANATION: The Exodus, or the liberation of Abraham's descendants from the slavery of Egypt, which the "mighty hand of Yahweh" brought about, and their establishment in the land of Canaan, promised to Abraham four centuries previously, were the greatest events in the history of the Jews. It was then that they really became the Chosen People, a nation set apart to serve the true God. There was a second Exodus eight centuries later, the liberation from the Babylonian exile. Through their disloyalty to God, they lost their nation and their liberty, and were taken as slaves to Babylon, where they lived in servitude for sixty years (598–538 B.C.).

But the merciful God came to their rescue once more. The Jews were set free by Cyrus (who had captured Babylon), and were allowed to return to their native land, rebuild Jerusalem and the temple, and serve God once more as his Chosen People. It is this liberation of which Isaiah speaks in today's reading. It is chosen for Advent, because both Exoduses were only foreshadowings of the coming of the Messiah to liberate the human race, and make it not only God's "Chosen People," but his adopted family.

the wilderness . . . glad . . . rejoice: This liberation from slavery of Babylon will be such a source of joy that the very desert, which separates Babylon from Jerusalem, will blossom forth in flower and foliage and "rejoice with joy and singing."

glory of Lebanon . . . Sharon: It will become fertile and wooded like Lebanon, Carmel and Sharon.

glory . . . of God : The hand of God will be visible in all of this.

Be strong . . . save you : This evident presence of their God, in this great act of mercy, should make the weakest strong and courageous. God has come to save them.

blind . . . deaf . . . dumb : Those suffering from human defects will be cured. This did not happen at the liberation from Babylon, but it happened when the true liberation came (see today's gospel, Mt. 11 : 5, where our Lord applies this prophecy to himself), which proves that while Isaiah was speaking in the literal sense of the Babylonian liberation, his prophecy included the greater messianic liberation of which the others were a foreshadowing.

ransomed . . . Lord : Those set free by God's mercy rejoice with an everlasting joy, when they return to Jerusalem. Again this was only partially fulfilled in 538, but it will be literally fulfilled when the ransomed of the Lord reach the "Jerusalem which is above."

APPLICATION : Even if we took this prophecy of Isaiah as relating to the return from Babylon only, it would still be a source of consolation to us, and a reason for thanking our good God who, in this return of the Jews from Babylon, was preparing the way for the coming of his divine Son among us. The Exodus from Egypt in the 13th century, and the liberation from Babylon in the 6th, were big steps taken by God on the road to our eternal liberation.

But as we know from our Lord's own interpretation (Mt. 11 : 5), these words of the prophet referred also to God's greatest act of love and mercy— the Incarnation of his divine Son, which was to liberate all mankind from the slavery of sin and worldliness, and make men citizens of an everlasting homeland, heaven.

How can we ever thank God for this act of infinite love for us? The answer is that we cannot. All eternity itself will not be long enough for us to praise and thank God. Just as our creation was an act of sheer generosity, so this greater gift, our elevation to adopted sonship, is an act of infinite generosity, for which all that he expects in return, is our true appreciation of the gift and honor conferred on us.

Christmas, each year, brings vividly before our minds this proof of God's infinite love. Every time a sincere Jew saw the rebuilt Temple and city of Jerusalem, he must surely have thanked God for having released his people from the slavery of Babylon, and for having given them, once more, a homeland of their own, and a temple where they could worship him freely. How much greater should be our gratitude when the Christmas crib reminds us of all that God has done for us? The statue of the small Baby, lying on a wad of straw in a stable, is but a feeble representation of the self-humiliation willingly accepted by the Son of God, when he assumed our human nature, in order to raise us up to the dizzy heights of divine sonship. All we can say is, "thank you, God, you have surely shown your love for us, would that we could show you some real love in return."

Jerusalem with its temple, God's earthly abode, and the land of Canaan, were God's gifts to the Chosen People of old. They were but symbols of the reality he has promised to us. God grant we may all inherit that reality.

SECOND READING: James 5 : 7–10. Be patient, brethren, until the coming of the Lord. Behold, the farmer waits for the precious fruit of the earth, being patient over it until it receives the early and the late rain. You also be patient. Establish your hearts, for the coming of the Lord is at hand. Do not grumble, brethren, against one another, that you may not be judged; behold, the Judge is standing at the doors. As an example of suffering and patience, brethren, take the prophets who spoke in the name of the Lord.

EXPLANATION: It is generally admitted today, that the James who wrote this Epistle, was not one of the two of that name who were Apostles, but James "the brother (cousin) of the Lord" (Mt. 13 : 55). He was prominent as leader of the Judaeo-Christian church in Jerusalem, from the beginning (see Acts 12 : 17; 15 : 13; 21 : 18; 1 Cor. 15 : 7; Gal. 1 : 19; 2 : 9–12), and remained head of that church until his martyrdom in 62 A.D.

He addresses his letter, which is really a collection of exhortations to live the Christian life, not merely profess it, to the "twelve tribes of the Dispersions," that is to Jewish converts to Christianity living outside of Palestine. The theme dealt with in the verses read today—the second coming of Christ as judge of the world—was very topical in the early years of Christianity.

Be patient brethren: From the very beginning of the Church, all Christians recognized one another as "brothers," i.e. brothers in the Lord, members of the one household. Christ himself gave the title to all "those who do the will of his Father" (Mk. 3 : 35), to his Apostles and disciples (Jn. 20 : 17), and to all whom he has redeemed (Heb. 2 : 11). Therefore St. Paul calls him "the first-born among many brothers" (Rom. 8 : 29). St. James exhorts his Christian brothers to wait in patience, "until the coming of the Lord." That he would

return, soon after his Ascension, seems to have been a fairly widespread idea among the first generation of Christians (see 1 Th. 4 : 13–18; 2 Th. 2 : 1–12; 1 Cor. 1 : 7), perhaps because of their ardor and fervent desire to be united forever with him. But Christ himself had stated very explicitly that the day of his coming, as judge, was a secret known to God only (see Mt. 24 : 36).

Behold the farmer: Jesus uses a very homely example—the farmer plants his seeds and then waits patiently, without anxiety, for the result of his labor in its due season.

establish your hearts: "do not lose heart" (J. Bible) or "be slow hearted" (N.E.B.). Some were evidently inclined to grow tired, leading the strict Christian life, and possibly were suffering persecution from their non-converted fellow-Jews. James, therefore, tells them to have courage, the end was near, they would not have to suffer much longer. This was true, because each would meet Christ as judge at his or her death, even though the general judgement was still far off.

do not grumble: Be charitable, do not find fault with your neighbors, if you want Christ to find no fault with you when your moment of judgement comes. **standing at the doors:** This, your judgement, is nearer than you think. **example . . . patience:** James takes it for granted that they know the Old

Testament. Most of God's prophets suffered, and many were put to death (see Mt. 23 : 29–37), for speaking in God's name.

APPLICATION : "The coming of the Lord is at hand." These words of St. James are true for all of us, in two senses. His first coming, which we shall be commemorating in ten days or so, is very near. I am sure you are all busy already, making preparations for this great family feast—buying presents and greeting cards, putting your homes in order, getting ready to welcome and entertain relatives, friends and neighbors—all of which is becoming and right. The sincere Christian is, or should also be, busy putting his spiritual home in order, so that he may be able to welcome and entertain the greatest friend man could ever have. Christmas is the anniversary feast of his friend's coming among us, to become one of the family, and enable us to become, for evermore, members of his.

The sincere Christian, who prepares thus, need have no fear of the second coming of Christ, as his judge—the coming of which St. James speaks today. One of the hardest things, even for a devout Christian, is to convince himself that death—the moment when eternal destiny is decided—is not yet years and years away. Not one among us will deny the existence of such escapism. Death, therefore, for all of us will be unexpected when it comes. Even for the vast majority of those who die after a long illness the end is not in fact expected.

But death need not be unexpected, that is, unprepared for. This is really what matters. The man, or woman, who heeds the words of our Lord : "stand ready because the Son of Man is coming at an hour you do not expect" (Lk. 12 : 40) will strive to be always ready, by attempting to live always at peace with God.

Ours is a God of mercy. He will never try to catch, in one of their moments of weakness, those who are striving to live in his love and grace. Nor does he fail to send forewarnings, even to those who not only forget him but continually offend him. Those warnings can, of course, fall on deaf ears. St. James' words today are such a warning. If anyone among you has hitherto neglected his duties to God, let him listen now to that warning and put his conscience right with God. The sinner who will do so, will have a holy and happy Christmas. He will welcome Christ becomingly at his first coming, and Christ's second coming will have no terrors for him.

GOSPEL : Matthew 11 : 2–11. When John heard in prison about the deeds of the Christ, he sent word by his disciples and said to him, "Are you he who is to come, or shall we look for another?" And Jesus answered them, "Go and tell John what you hear and see : the blind receive their sight and the lame walk, lepers are cleansed and the deaf hear, and the dead are raised up, and the poor have good news preached to them. And blessed is he who takes no offense at me."

As they went away, Jesus began to speak to the crowds concerning John: "What did you go out into the wilderness to behold? A reed shaken by the wind? Why then did you go out? To see a man clothed in soft raiment? Behold, those who wear soft raiment are in kings' houses. Why then did you go out? To see a prophet? Yes, I tell you, and more than a prophet. This is he of whom it is written,

'Behold, I send my messenger before thy face,
who shall prepare thy way before thee.'

Truly, I say to you, among those born of women there has risen no one greater than John the Baptist; yet he who is least in the kingdom of heaven is greater than he."

EXPLANATION: John the Baptist, who had announced the arrival of the Messiah and had pointed him out as "the Lamb of God who takes away the sin of the world" (Jn. 1:29), was now imprisoned by the Tetrarch Herod, because he had publicly denounced Herod's adulterous union with Herodias. While in prison, he had heard of the missionary activity of Jesus in which love, mercy and understanding for sinners predominated. This merciful and loving approach did not quite fit in with the "fire and judgement" aspect of the Messiah's mission, which he himself had foretold (Mt. 2:7-12), and so he is now wondering if Jesus is really the Messiah. To solve his doubts, he sends a delegation to Jesus to ask:

Are you he who is to come: Are you the Messiah, the promised one for whom we have been waiting?

tell John what you hear and see: The reports of Jesus' miracles had already spread far and wide, and Luke adds that our Lord worked miracles of healing in the presence of John's delegates (Lk. 7:19-23).

blind . . . deaf: These acts of compassionate use of his power are cited by Jesus, as proof that he is the true Messiah and is fulfilling the prophecies (see his application of Is. 61:1-2 to himself—a parallel to his answer here Lk. 4:16-19). His coming as judge and punisher, as John described him, will be on the last day.

takes . . . me: Jesus' gentleness towards all, his compassion, and even friendship for sinners, his stress on the mercy rather than the justice of God, caused scandal, not only to the Pharisees but even to some of his close followers. This is evident in the subsequent gospel story. John the Evangelist and James, his brother, devout though they were, wanted Jesus to call fire down from heaven on a Samaritan village that refused hospitality to the apostolic group (Lk. 9:54).

speak . . . John: Our Lord then praises John the Baptist. The people went to hear him preach at the Jordan because he was not:

a reed . . . wind: Instead he was a man of principle. He spoke the truth and was ready, as he proved later, to give his life in defense of truth and moral principles. He lived a life of mortification (not in "soft garments"), unlike the worldly and pampered princes (Herod and Herodias, for example).

more . . . prophet : He was the last, and the most important, of all the prophets of the Old Testament.

Behold I . . . messenger : He was the immediate Precursor of Christ the one foretold by the prophet Malachi (3 : 1).

no one . . . Baptist : He was the greatest, the closest to God, of all the great personages of the Old Testament; a gift of God, in fact, to his parents and to mankind.

yet . . . heaven : The Baptist only stood at the threshold of the new era, the kingdom of God, which was just beginning on earth, and would have its glorious culmination in heaven. The lowliest Christian, therefore, who would follow Christ and receive his gifts and graces, would, because of his elevation to sonship of God, be capable of rendering far greater honor to God than John the Baptist ever could. This does not mean that the Baptist has not a very high place among the saints of heaven, for the merits of the Incarnation were retro-active for all those who had acted according to their knowledge and conscience before Christ's death and resurrection.

APPLICATION : The Church brings John the Baptist, the man who prepared the people for Christ's public mission, before our minds today, as an example that we should follow, even if only from afar. John prepared himself for the task of welcoming and introducing Christ to others, by a life of self-mortification and penance. He told the people that the first essential for meeting Christ, and profiting by his coming, was that they should turn away from sin and give up any evil ways, which hitherto they had followed. He himself practiced what he preached and his preaching, therefore, bore fruit among many of his hearers. Four of the twelve Apostles became followers of Christ because of the Baptist's example and preaching.

John is calling on us too today, to prepare ourselves for Christ's coming this Christmas, by turning away from sin, and by the mortification of ourselves in many ways. We are not expected to wear the rough camel-hair dress he wore, and eat nothing but locusts and wild honey. But each one of us can restrain the excessive luxuries of the palate, in which we often indulge, and use the money, thus saved, to help those who are short of the necessities of life, in far too many parts of today's world. Many of us, too, could look through our wardrobes and find garments we can well do without. These could help to keep the wintry blasts from our poor, shivering fellowmen or women this Christmas.

Most of us feel touched, when we see the Baby Christ lying, half-naked, on the rough straw in the stable. But to do something for him, we need not wish we were there on that first Christmas. We can do it for his suffering brothers this Christmas, and he himself tells us if we do that we are doing it for him.

In repenting of our sins, the first necessary step if we want to welcome Christ into a pure heart and into our Christian homes, let our conversion and resolutions be firm, as was the resolute stand of John the Baptist. He was not a reed that was shaken by every wind, and we too must stand firm against the temptations of the world, the flesh and the devil, if we are to remain worthy of the name of Christian. John the Baptist suffered martyrdom for his faith and convictions. Few, if any, of us will be called on to lay down our lives for our faith, but we are all called on to live for it, and with it, every day of our lives.

This may demand sacrifice nowadays, when our permissive society derides and looks down on those still trying to live according to the old-fashioned ten commandments. But we must not only be ready to accept this derision; we must do all in our power, by word, prayer and example, to get our erring neighbor to see that virtue does pay in the end.

We have much in this story of John the Baptist which should help us to welcome Christ properly this Christmas. Think of the Baptist today, and listen to the message he has for you. If you do your best to put it into practice, the good, merciful Lord himself will do the rest for you. He came to save sinners. He came to save you. If you co-operate and do your part, you will hear, on your judgement day, the joyful words of Christ : "You are more than a prophet, you are a citizen of heaven—a saint."

FOURTH SUNDAY OF ADVENT

FIRST READING : Isaiah 7 : 10–14. The Lord spoke to Ahaz, "Ask a sign of the Lord your God; let it be deep as Sheol or high as heaven." But Ahaz said, "I will not ask, and I will not put the Lord to the test." And he said, "Hear then, O house of David! Is it too little for you to weary men, that you weary my God also? Therefore the Lord himself will give you a sign. Behold, a young woman shall conceive and bear a son, and shall call his name Immanuel (which means, God with us)."

EXPLANATION : These words of Isaiah form one of his most descriptive and definite prophecies foretelling the future messianic king, Christ. Judah, separated from Israel (the northern part of Palestine), since the revolt of 931, was in dire straits when Isaiah uttered those words. King Ahaz, who ruled Judah from 736 to 716, was expecting an attack from the combined forces of Israel and Syria. Instead of trusting in God, he had asked for help from the pagan Assyrian king, a request which later led to the overthrow of the kingdom of Judah. The prophet tried to persuade Ahaz not to take this fatal step, but instead to put his trust in Yahweh, his God, who was ready to give him any proof, any sign, in the heavens or under the earth, "as deep as Sheol or as high as heaven," to convince him, the king, that Yahweh was on his side. Ahaz stubbornly refused—he had no faith in Yahweh—and then Isaiah gave him the following sign:

Hear . . . David: The mention of the dynasty of David, of whom Ahaz was a direct descendant, was a reminder to the king that the kingdom of Judah was always under Yahweh's protection, because of his messianic plan. The future king, whose reign would be universal and eternal, would descend from David, as God had promised through the prophet Nathan (2 Sm. 7:12–16). Therefore, Judah would not be wiped out; Syria and Israel would not succeed.

weary men . . . God also: Ahaz distrusted his subjects, and wore out their patience, the prophet Isaiah included, but now he is clearly distrusting Yahweh, and "wearing out" his patience.

Therefore . . . himself: The sign to be given will indicate punishment for Ahaz, but encouragement and hope for the people. God's promise to David will be fulfilled. A son of David will yet come, but not through the male line, as the kingdom was handed down, but through a young virgin—here was the sign, the miracle—and this descendant of David would be more than a king of Judah, he would be God among us.

a young woman: The Hebrew word used here "Alma," means a girl of marriageable age, but in the circumstances of the time this would also imply virginity. Besides, the fact that this future event is to be a "sign," a miracle of God, indicates the virginity of the mother in question. A young married girl, bearing a child through normal intercourse with her husband, had nothing in the nature of a "sign" or miracle about it. Furthermore, the Greek translators of Isaiah 150 years B.C., translated Alma as "parthenes" meaning "virgin," and St. Matthew leaves no doubt as to the virginal conception of Christ, as the context (Mt. 1:18–25) indicates, when he says this is the fulfillment of this prophecy of Isaiah (1:22–23).

she shall . . . name: It was the father's privilege, and right, to name his son. The fact that it is the mother who will name her son here is another indication of the virginal conception. In St. Luke's account of the Annunciation, the Angel tells Mary she is to "name her child Jesus" (Lk. 1:31). The fact that Joseph, having been informed by an angel of the divine intervention in the case, is told to name the child to be born "Jesus," is not a contradiction of Isaiah and Luke, but an external sign of Joseph's acceptance of his role as foster-father.

Immanuel: That is, God with us. The prince of the house of David who was to come, was to be God living among us. As St. John puts it: "The Word (the Son of God) became flesh and dwelt among us" (Jn. 1:14).

APPLICATION: In today's prophecy, Isaiah gives us the most important detail concerning the Messiah, Christ. He was to be God as well as man. This is what Christ was, as he claimed and as he proved by his miracles and by his resurrection. What a stunning, and at the same time, what an inspiring fact this knowledge is for us! We call the Incarnation, the coming of the Son of God among us in human nature, a mystery. It is one of the basic mysteries of our Christian religion, but the mystery lies not so much in how it was done ("with God all things are possible"), but rather in the infinite, mysterious love of God for us, who are so much below him and so unworthy of his love.

It would be waste of time for us mortals, with our small, limited capacity for real love, even to try to fathom this depth of God's love. All we can do is to be grateful for it, while we wonder at its immensity. God loved man from all eternity and decided to give him gifts of intellect and will, far beyond the gifts given to all other earthly creatures. Because of these gifts, he made man capable of enjoying an eternity of happiness, and decreed to give this eternal enjoyment to him.

The Incarnation was the means chosen by God to attain this purpose of his. He would send his divine Son to live among us, for a short time, on earth. Because his Son became real man, he became our brother, and thereby we were raised to the dignity of sons of his heavenly Father.

· Man had sinned in the meantime, and had refused the obedience and reverence his intellect told him he owed to his Creator and Benefactor. This, God had foreseen, of course, but the perfect obedience and reverence rendered to the Father by his incarnate Son, "an obedience even unto the death on the cross," made atonement and satisfaction for all the sins of all men that ever had lived or would live, and, therefore, removed the obstacle that could prevent man reaching the end God had planned for him.

Redemption from sin, in order to make man fit for heaven, was a necessary effect of the Incarnation, but the prime and principal purpose of this act of God's love was, precisely, to show love for us, and to give effect to his intention to make us his adopted sons, and thus heirs of heaven. How can man ever forget this love which God has shown him? How can I forget that I am no longer a mere man but an adopted son of God, that every day that passes brings me a day nearer to my entry into the inheritance God has planned for me? I have difficulties and troubles during my years on this earth, but these are the very means God is putting at my disposal to enable me to prepare myself for the life of eternal happiness that awaits me.

Christmas, especially, should remind me that he who came on earth, to make me fit for heaven, had trials and troubles far greater and bigger than mine. He in no way deserved these trials; he bore them and accepted them gladly, so that I could, one day, enter into the life where troubles and trials will be no more, "because the Lamb of God who is at the throne . . . will lead me to springs of living water and God will wipe away all tears" (Rev. 7 : 17).

SECOND READING: Romans 1:1–7. Paul, a servant of Jesus Christ, called to be an Apostle, set apart for the gospel of God which he promised beforehand through his prophets in the holy scriptures, the gospel concerning his Son, who was descended from David according to the flesh and designated Son of God in power according to the Spirit of holiness by his resurrection from the dead, Jesus Christ our Lord, through whom we have received grace and apostleship to bring about the obedience of faith for the sake of his name among all the nations, including yourselves who are called to belong to Jesus Christ;

To all God's beloved in Rome, who are called to be saints:

Grace to you and peace from God our Father and the Lord Jesus Christ.

EXPLANATION: On St. Paul's letter to the Romans, see First Sunday of Advent. In today's reading, we have the opening verses of that Epistle. In it, he calls himself a servant of Christ, an Apostle, set apart (chosen) to preach the gospel of God. This gospel is the news of the Incarnation, through which and by which, all men are called to follow Christ and become his brothers, and thus sons of God destined to be saints in heaven.

called . . . Apostle: The story of Paul's (Saul then) conversion, and his call to the apostolate, is found in Acts 9:1–19. He was the latest, but also one of the greatest, of Christ's Apostles.

promised beforehand: The coming of Christ was foretold in the Old Testament. In fact the whole history of the Chosen People, from Abraham (1800 B.C.) to John the Baptist, was a preparation and a foreshadowing of his coming.

from David . . . flesh: David, the second and greatest of Israel's kings, was promised by Nathan that he would have a descendant on his throne whose kingdom would be universal and eternal. This prophecy is here interpreted of Christ, and it was only in him that it was fulfilled.

Son . . . resurrection: It was by his resurrection from the dead that Christ, the man who died on the cross, was recognized for what he always was, the Son of God in human form, the Son who took his human nature from a descendant of David (Mary).

in power: Because he was divine—the Son of God—he raised his human nature from the grave. The Father and Holy Spirit cooperated in this action, and from then on Christ reassumed both the divine glory, "of which he had emptied himself" during his earthly sojourn (see Phil. 2:5–11), and the mission to sanctify all men with a new life through the sending of the Holy Spirit.

Jesus . . . Lord: Lord is a translation of *Adonai,* the name usually used by the Jews for Yahweh, a holy name that they did not dare to pronounce. There is no doubt in Paul's mind, nor among any of the early Christian writers, that the Christ who lived, died and rose from the dead in Palestine was God the Son.

obedience of faith: It was not enough, theoretically, to profess belief in Christ. His Gospel had to be *lived*.

for . . . name: Paul was chosen to call all nations to the knowledge of Christ

B

and his gospel. It was on Christ's behalf that he labored ("we are ambassadors for Christ"—2 Cor. 5 : 20).

peace . . . Christ: Again, he equates Jesus with God the Father.

APPLICATION: Paul opens his letter to the Jewish and Gentile converts of Rome, the first generation of Christians in the capital city of the empire, by stating that he is an Apostle chosen by Christ to spread the good news of the Incarnation. He calls this news the "Gospel of God," for it is an account of that almost incredible act of God's love for us. God sent his divine Son, as man, among us in this world, in order that we might be with the three divine Persons for all eternity in the next world.

God does not need us: the Blessed Trinity is all-perfect and all-glorious in itself. He did not have to create the universe or its inhabitants: they add nothing to his internal perfection. But, as the nature of a burning coal is to spread its heat, so the nature of the God, who is love, is to distribute his love among others outside of him. Hence creation.

Having created the universe, God brought one species of its inhabitants, human beings, to the height of created perfection. He gave man the spiritual faculties of intelligence and free-will, faculties which he himself possesses in an infinite degree. Even though these powers are limited in man, because of his limited, created nature, yet because of them, man is somewhat "like unto God."

This was not the limit of God's goodness. As a result of the spiritual gifts he has received, man is capable of knowing and loving God. The benevolent God decided to give him the possibility of doing this, not only for his short spell on earth, but for all eternity. Hence the Incarnation. That God could have found other ways of doing this we can hardly doubt, but the way he did it cannot be surpassed as a demonstration of his infinite love for us.

The Son of God became man. The Creator became as one of his creatures. The master took on the form of his slave. Only supreme love and benevolence could invent such a humiliation for himself. Add to this, the sufferings, the insults, the hatreds, which culminated in the humiliating and most painful of deaths on the cross, which the sins and the ingratitude of those he had come to raise up brought on him during his earthly life among us, and we have some idea of the debt we owe the God of love.

We can never repay it, but God will accept the little gratitude we can render him. From the bottom of our hearts, let us all thank our Father in heaven, this Christmas, for sending us his Son, so that we could have God himself as our Father. And let our heartfelt thanks to God overflow into acts of love for our neighbor, for it's only thus that we can really prove to God that we love him. This is "the obedience of faith," the putting of the "Gospel of God" into practice, which St. Paul demands.

GOSPEL : Matt. 1 : 18–24. The birth of Jesus took place in this way. When his mother Mary had been betrothed to Joseph, before they came together she was found to be with child of the Holy Spirit; and her husband Joseph, being a just man and unwilling to put her to shame, resolved to send her away quietly. But as he considered this, behold, an angel of the Lord appeared to him in a dream, saying, "Joseph, son of David, do not fear to take Mary your wife, for that which is conceived in her is of the Holy Spirit; she will bear a son, and you shall call his name Jesus, for he will save his people from their sins." All this took place to fulfill what the Lord had spoken by the prophet : "Behold, a virgin shall conceive and bear a son, and his name shall be called Emmanuel" (which means, God with us). When Joseph woke from sleep, he did as the angel of the Lord commanded him; he took his wife.

EXPLANATION : St. Matthew begins his gospel in a typical Hebrew fashion, by giving the genealogical table of Jesus, who was born of Mary (1 : 1–16). He does not mention the Annunciation, nor Mary's problem of preserving virginity while becoming a mother. But the revelation given to Joseph, Mary's betrothed, which Matthew here describes, brings out the fact of the virginal conception of Jesus, and his messianic mission of salvation. Matthew then adds that Christ was the Messiah, to be born of a virgin, of whom the prophet Isaiah spoke, seven centuries earlier.

Jesus Christ : This was the double name by which our Lord was known to all Christians, by the time Matthew's gospel was written.

betrothed to Joseph : She was engaged to Joseph. This may seem strange, when we realize her intention of preserving her virginity, but marriages were arranged by parents in those days, and Mary was an obedient daughter. Most likely she had not informed her parents of the unusual resolve, inspired by God, which she had taken.

before . . . together : The actual marriage took place when the groom took his betrothed to his own home. In Mary's case, this did not take place until some five or six months after the Annunciation.

she was found . . . child : Most probably it was Joseph himself who discovered this because Mary confided in him.

of the Holy Spirit : Mary alone knew this, and most probably she had told Joseph. Matthew adds this explanation of the virginal conception (Luke gives much more detail), for the benefit of his readers.

her husband Joseph : He is called husband even though the actual marriage had not yet taken place. The act of betrothal, which was a very solemn contract among the Jews, legally made the betrothed pair husband and wife, in all things, except the actual use of marriage. Should one of the betrothed pair die before the actual marriage took place, the other person was regarded as a widow or widower. Should a girl, who was betrothed, behave unchastely with another man, she was deemed guilty of adultery, just as a married woman would be. The man to whom she was betrothed was then bound to denounce her, and give her a bill of divorce.

Joseph . . . just man : As a just man

Joseph would have been bound to denounce an unfaithful spouse. He did not, because he must have known of her innocence, and must have been aware of the Annunciation story. But he began to feel that he was unworthy to have any part in this divine plan, and therefore he was about to dissolve the betrothal contract, quietly and secretly, so that the good name of Mary would be saved.

behold an angel: Revelation given through dreams was fairly common in the Old Testament.

Joseph, son of David: Joseph is addressed as son of David, to remind him of the messianic prophecy, and that he was to have a part in God's messianic plans.

do not fear: This message of the angel confirms what was suggested above. Joseph was afraid. He felt himself utterly unworthy, but God now tells him to accept the honor offered to him.

you shall . . . Jesus: It was the father's right to name his child. Joseph is fully aware that he is not the real father of this child to be born, but he is ordered by the angel to adopt him as his own, by naming him.

all this took place: Matthew now goes on to show that the birth of Christ from a virgin mother, without human father, was the fulfillment of Isaiah's prophecy (see the First Reading for today).

Joseph did . . . commanded him: He took Mary to his home, and humbly accepted the divine charge of foster-father of the Messiah, the Son of God made man.

APPLICATION: "How unsearchable are the judgements of God and how inscrutable his ways!" as St. Paul says to the Romans (11:33). If God had preserved the kingdom of Judah (which he could so easily have done), and if the Messiah, the son of David, were to be born in the royal palace in Jerusalem, it would be natural and we would almost say, more fitting the dignity of the Messiah. Instead, God allowed the kingly line, and the throne of Judah, to disappear, and he chose a humble carpenter of Nazareth, a true descendant of David but a lowly one, to be the foster-father of his divine Son, when he took human nature and came on earth to "dwell among us." But God's ways are not our ways. It is not by their social standing, nor by their bank-accounts, that God values men. Virtue is the scale he uses when weighing men. In God's eyes, no king sat on the throne of Judah, not even David himself, who was more acceptable to God as foster-father for his Son, than the carpenter of Nazareth.

This is the last Sunday of our preparation for Christmas, the anniversary of Christ's birth. Like Joseph, we can all feel unworthy of the honor of welcoming him into our hearts and our homes. We are indeed unworthy, not because we have little of this world's goods, but because we have so little humility, so little charity, so little faith and trust in God's goodness. Let us try to imitate Joseph and Mary, the humblest of the humble, the kindliest of the kindly, and the greatest-ever believers in God's goodness and mercy. We can never hope to equal them, but we can follow them humbly, from afar.

The feast of Christmas should draw the hearts of every child of God towards the furnace of divine love. In the manger, the infinite love of God for us miserable sinners is dramatically and forcefully portrayed before our eyes. In that helpless Baby, represented by a statue, we know that the person, and the power, of the omnipotent Creator and sustainer of the universe lie hidden "He emptied himself, taking the form of a slave" for us. He became a creature, like ourselves, so that he would make us sharers in his divine nature. He came on earth to bring us to heaven. He hid his divine nature so that he could cover us with it.

"Unsearchable indeed are the judgements of God, and inscrutable his ways." But though we are unworthy of his infinite love, it nevertheless stands out as clear as the noonday sun in the Incarnation. We realize that we can never make ourselves worthy of this infinite love, but let us imitate Joseph and accept the honor which God is giving us, as we trust that he will continue to make us daily less unworthy.

CHRISTMAS : MIDNIGHT MASS

FIRST READING : Isaiah 9 : 2–7. The people who walked in darkness have seen a great light; those who dwelt in a land of deep darkness, on them has light shined. Thou hast multiplied the nation, thou hast increased its joy; they rejoice before thee as with joy at the harvest, as men rejoice when they divide the spoil. For the yoke of his burden, and the staff for his shoulder, the rod of his oppressor, thou hast broken as on the day of Midian. For every boot of the tramping warrior in battle tumult and every garment rolled in blood will be burned as fuel for the fire. For to us a child is born, to us a son is given; and the government will be upon his shoulder, and his name will be called "Wonderful Counsellor, Mighty God, Everlasting Father, Prince of Peace." Of the increase of his government and of peace there will be no end, upon the throne of David, and over his kingdom, to establish it, and to uphold it with justice and with righteousness from this time forth and for evermore. The zeal of the Lord of hosts will do this.

EXPLANATION : The prophet Isaiah (765-700 B.C.) has many references to the future Messiah. This prophecy, just read, was spoken very probably soon after the northern kingdom Israel had been destroyed and its inhabitants taken prisoner to Assyria (722 B.C.). The words of the prophet were intended to console the "remnant," those who were left behind. Even though things looked dismal and depressing, a day would come when God would bring joy and happiness once more to the land and to its people—that would be the day of the Messiah.

seen a great light : A complete change has (will) come—the people will rejoice like the farmer rejoices when harvest is plentiful or like soldiers who have won and are dividing the spoils they captured.

yoke . . . oppressor : They will be slaves no longer; they will be free.

day of Midian : As narrated in the book of Judges (7 : 1–8; 28) the Judge Gedeon inflicted a crushing defeat on the Midianites who had been harassing the Chosen People. This victory was remembered and spoken of for centuries.

boot . . . garment : There will be an end to wars.

for . . . a child is born to us : The cause of the great change that will come over the land and its people is the birth of a new King—the birth of a son of David who will establish David's throne forever as the prophet Nathan had foretold (2 Sm. 7 : 14).

Wonderful Counselor : The titles given to the new-born King imply that he will have the wisdom of Solomon, the valor of David and the virtues of Moses and the Patriarchs. In other words, he is the ideal King, the last and true representative of David's line. The description could not apply to any earthly king who held the throne of David; it was fulfilled in the Messiah only.

peace . . . no end : He will bring peace among men and peace between man and God. His Kingdom will be vast.

justice . . . righteousness : The qualities and prerogatives of a wise king.

Lord of hosts : His coming and his gifts will be the work of the all-powerful God—the "God of hosts," who is moved by his love and fidelity to his promises, "his zeal" to do this for us. It is for "us he is born," it is to "us he is given."

APPLICATION : What Isaiah foresaw some 700 years before it happened we are commemorating tonight nearly 2,000 years after it happened, and it will still be commemorated 2,000 years from today if this world will still be in existence. God came on our earth, became one of us so that we could become one with God. This is incomparably greater than any other historical event that ever happened or ever could happen on our planet.

Yet unfortunately there are millions of people who have not yet heard this good news, but its good effects will reach them if their ignorance is not their fault. There are millions of others who have heard this good news but refuse to believe it. The basic reason for their disbelief is not that it couldn't be true, but that it is too good to be true. It is indeed hard to believe that the infinite, all-perfect God should bother with such imperfect, such mean creatures, as we are. But it is because he is infinite and his love is infinite that he can and did go to such lengths for us his unworthy creatures.

While we thank God tonight with true sincerity and heartfelt gratitude, for all he has done for us, and while we promise faithfully to try to make ourselves less unworthy of the infinite love he has shown us in the Incarnation, let us remember all those millions of our brothers who do not really know him yet. Let us beg God to send them the good news and the grace to accept this great gift of infinite love, so that all his children on earth may know and thank him too. And let us strive by the example of a truly Christian life to make God's love for us known not only to our fellow-Christians but to all men.

SECOND READING: Epistle to Titus 2:11-4. The grace of God has appeared for the salvation of all men, training us to renounce irreligion and worldly passions, and to live sober, upright, and godly lives in this world, awaiting our blessed hope, the appearing of the glory of our great God and Savior Jesus Christ, who gave himself for us to redeem us from all iniquity and to purify for himself a people of his own who are zealous for good deeds.

EXPLANATION: Titus was a Gentile convert of St. Paul to whom he then became a faithful companion and fellow-worker in his missionary labors. Some years after his conversion he was appointed in charge of the church in Crete, its first overseer or Bishop. While there Paul wrote this letter to him calling him his "beloved son in the common faith." In the letter he exhorts him to be zealous for the spread of the faith and gives him counsels and instructions to guide him in his episcopal office. Titus and his Christians must be an example in all things for:

the grace of God: Translations differ here, but the basic meaning is the same, namely, salvation has been given to all men through God's merciful love (his grace) for us. It was Christ who brought us this free gift of God.

renounce irreligion: The following of Christ's teaching forbids the converts to imitate the practices and sexual abberations of the pagan world; instead the Christian was expected to use the things of this world temperately and justly, that is, with respect for neighbor, and piously, that is, being faithful to God.

awaiting our blessed hope: Keeping an eye fixed firmly on the great day that was to come.

glory . . . Christ: The day of reward when Christ comes in glory to judge the world. St. Paul, since the day of his conversion on the road to Damascus, had never the slightest doubt as to the divinity of Christ. Here as in all his Epistles he expressly calls Christ God.

gave himself for us: This same Jesus Christ who was God was also true man and offered himself (his human nature) as a sacrifice for us on Calvary.

a people of his own: a Chosen People. The Jews were the Chosen People of the Old Covenant. Christians, whether of Jewish or Gentile origin, are the Chosen People of the New Covenant.

zealous for good deeds: The essence of the Christian life.

APPLICATION: Christmas is an occasion for rejoicing, a season of goodwill, a time of joy even for those who unfortunately do not know or realize its true meaning. For us Christians it is the second of our greatest annual feasts (next after Easter) in which we call to mind God's infinite love for us and his infinite mercy towards us mortals.

We surely have reason to rejoice and be glad. Christ, the true Son of God, the Second Person of the Blessed Trinity, took to himself our lowly human nature and became one with us in order to raise us up to the dignity of adopted sons of his heavenly Father. If some earthly king or nobleman took the son of one of his servants into his palace, clothed him in costly robes and made him his heir, the world would gasp in amazement. God has taken us, his lowly creatures; has clothed us in the divine garments of grace; has made us one of his family by making his Son one of us, and has made us heirs of an eternal kingdom.

And yet mankind can ignore or forget such an act of benevolence, such a proof of divine love! Of course, we Christians do not ignore or forget this divine benevolence but we just do not remember it as much as we should; we do not thank God often enough for all he has done for us; too often we are ungrateful children.

Tonight, as we call to mind the infinite love of God which sent his Son on earth to be born of the virgin Mary in a stable in Bethlehem so that we could spend our eternity in the mansions of heaven, let us show our gratitude, our appreciation, by resolving to live as adopted sons of God are expected to live.

St. Paul's letter to Titus tells us how. We must reject ungodliness and worldly lusts by living temperately, justly and piously, using the things of this world as stepping-stones to heaven. God has made us his Chosen People; nay more! he has made us his adopted sons. Let us show our true gratitude by striving to live a life worthy of such a sublime vocation.

GOSPEL : Luke, 2 : 1–14. A decree went out from Caesar Augustus that all the world should be enrolled. This was the first enrollment, when Quirinius was governor of Syria. And all went to be enrolled, each to his own city. And Joseph also went up from Galilee, from the city of Nazareth, to Judea, to the city of David, which is called Bethlehem, because he was of the house and lineage of David, to be enrolled with Mary, his betrothed, who was with child. And while they were there, the time came for her to be delivered. And she gave birth to her first-born son and wrapped him in swaddling cloths, and laid him in a manger, because there was no place for them in the inn.

And in that region there were shepherds out in the field, keeping watch over their flock by night. And an angel of the Lord appeared to them, and the glory of the Lord shone around them, and they were filled with fear. And the angel said to them, "Be not afraid; for behold, I bring you good news of a great joy which will come to all the people; for to you is born this day in the city of David a Savior, who is Christ the Lord. And this will be a sign for you : you will find a babe wrapped in swaddling cloths and lying in a manger." And suddenly there was with the angel a multitude of the heavenly host praising God and saying, "Glory to God in the highest, and on earth peace among men with whom he is pleased!"

EXPLANATION :

world . . . enrolled : The Roman Emperor Augustus ordered a general census of his empire; this was the whole world in his eyes.

Joseph . . . went . . . Bethlehem : The Jewish family records were kept in the ancestral town or village. As Joseph was descended from David, Bethlehem was the ancestral home.

with Mary : It was only the father of the household who had to register, but Joseph could not leave Mary alone in Nazareth at this critical time for her; besides it was God's will that she should go to Bethlehem (whether she realized this or not) for Bethlehem was to be the birthplace of her Son, Christ.

first-born son : It does not follow from this that there were other children later. The first-born was a title which emphasized the dignity and rights of the child.

no place for them : Most likely because they were too poor to pay the innkeeper or when they arrived the inn was already full. They found shelter in a stable, and there Christ was born.

shepherds ... in the fields : These humble men who live close to nature were evidently close to God too for it was to them and not the learned or wealthy of Bethlehem that he sent his messenger.

be not afraid : The sudden appearance of this divine messenger, in human form evidently, naturally caused them to be alarmed.

news of a great joy : The shepherds, like all Jews of the time, and perhaps more so than most Jews, were anxiously awaiting the Messiah.

city of David : The divine messenger emphasizes the Davidic descent of the newly-born, for thus the prophecies were fulfilled.

in a manger : The long-promised heir to the throne of David, the royal descendant of the great king was born in a stable and was resting on a bed of straw in a manger! What a test for the faith of anyone who judges by earthly standards. But a greater test was still to come.

Christ the Lord : This baby in these lowly circumstances, poorer even than the poorest who had some little hovel and some poor cradle of his own, was not only the expected Messiah, the heir of the royal David, but he was also the Lord—a title reserved to God in the Old Testament.

Glory to God : Praise and thanksgiving to the great God who is the supreme ruler of all things.

peace . . . pleased : peace to men who are God's friends—who have God's benevolence, "good-will." Here we have the first verse of the hymn of praise and thanksgiving which is sung or said at every Mass, given to us by the messengers God sent to the shepherds of Bethlehem that first Christmas night. The coming of the Messiah was the beginning of the era in which true praise and thanks could be offered to God. Man alone of his own powers could not offer praise worthy of God, but united to the God-man Christ his acts of praise would have a divine value, for they would be offered in union with Christ. Peace was another consequence of the coming of Christ—man could now be at peace with God and would be at peace with his neighbor if he followed Christ's teaching.

APPLICATION : Tonight as we kneel before the Baby in the Manger in praise and thanksgiving to the Son of infinite love and mercy let not our amazement at the humility and poverty of the stable and manger, touching though they be, prevent us from seeing the greater, the almost incredible, humiliation of the Incarnation itself. Had our Savior been born in Herod's marble palace in Jerusalem and laid on a gilded cot with covers of the finest silk, his becoming man would yet have been a humbling, a lowering of himself, which would stagger the human mind. There are those who puzzle over and try to explain the mystery of the Incarnation—how Christ, namely, could be God and man at the same time, how one Person could have two natures. But mystery though this is, and fully intelligible to God only, the mystery of the love of God who did this *for us* is a greater mystery still and more of a puzzle to our finite human minds. "What is man that God should be mindful of him?" What have we ever done or what could we ever do to merit such love, such mercy, such condescension? No, we did not merit such love but the infinitely unselfish generosity of God, which no human mind is capable of grasping, has done this. We are his creatures who are capable of sharing his own happiness with him for all eternity and he has arranged it that we shall do so.

All we can do is to say from our heart a humble, thank you God, and to resolve to have the sense to avail ourselves of this almost incredible offer. We are "God's friends." He has called us so, then let us do our best to retain this friendship than which there is nothing greater for us on earth or in heaven. If we do, and if we do the little he asks of us, he will do his part; he will give us our share in the eternal happiness the Incarnation has won for us.

MASS AT DAWN

FIRST READING : Isaiah 62 : 11–12. Behold, the Lord has proclaimed to the end of the earth : Say to the daughter of Zion, "Behold, your salvation comes; behold, his reward is with him, and his recompense before him." And they shall be called the holy people, the redeemed of the Lord; and you shall be called Sought out, a city not forsaken.

EXPLANATION : This second section of the book of Isaiah was written after the return from the Babylonian exile. The lot of the returned exiles was sad, the country desolate, most of Jerusalem still in ruins, the people depressed almost to despair. The writer has words of consolation and encouragement for his compatriots. They must trust in God's promise and pray for its fulfillment. There are great things in store for Judah and Jerusalem.

the Lord . . . proclaimed : Through the prophet God is making known not only to the Jews but to all people what he is about to do for his Chosen People. This work of his, therefore, was not only for the Jews but for all nations.

daughter of Zion : Zion is another name for Jerusalem. Its citizens, the Chosen People, were God's spouse, their capital city his daughter.

your salvation comes : To the mind of the prophet the Savior, the promised

Messiah, is already on the point of coming.

his reward . . . his recompense : He will come as a conqueror carrying the "prize of his victory" and "his trophies" (in Hebrew); his battle already won. It is understood this victory is for his people. **They shall be called :** Those for whom he comes will be

holy people . . . redeemed . . . Lord : His victory for them is a spiritual victory now brought (or bought) back to the Lord, to God.

not forsaken : People will throng to the new Jerusalem. It will no longer be deserted, it will be renowned, not forsaken.

APPLICATION : These few lines from the book of Isaiah have been chosen to remind us of the blessings the promised Messiah of the Old Testament brought us when he came and formed the New. He redeemed us by his death on the cross. He has made a new covenant with us, an everlasting covenant unlike the old which was only preparatory and therefore temporary. He has made us the new Chosen People, chosen so that we could be holy and near to God. He has won for us and promised to us, not the holy land of Palestine which the first covenant promised, but the abode of eternal happiness, heaven, the new Jerusalem which will be renowned and

glorious forever.

We surely have reason to thank God for sending us our Savior and for having made us members of his Chosen People, the mystical body of Christ, his church. We can never be worthy of such an honor, but let each one of us examine himself and see if he is trying to be less unworthy, trying to get rid of the attractions of this earth which impede his heavenward journey.

Our welcome for Christ this Christmas Day and our thanks to him for coming and doing what he did for us will be sincere if we are sincerely trying to live up to our high vocation as the holy Chosen People of the new covenant.

SECOND READING : Titus 3 : 4–7. When the goodness and loving kindness of God our Savior appeared, he saved us, not because of deeds done by us in righteousness, but in virtue of his own mercy, by the washing of regeneration and renewal in the Holy Spirit, which he poured out upon us richly through Jesus Christ our Savior, so that we might be justified by his grace and become heirs in hope of eternal life.

EXPLANATION : For Titus and this Epistle see above in Second Reading of Midnight Mass.

When . . . kindness . . . our Savior appeared : The coming of the Savior, Christ, and his redemptive work on our behalf, is equated to the "goodness and

kindness of God," this is the only explanation for the infinite love which the Incarnation applies.

not . . . deeds : We did not, we could not, merit such kindness, it was a free gift of God's mercy.

washing of regeneration : The sacrament

of Baptism regenerates us—we are given a new life, we share in God's life, for we become members of Christ's body who is God and man.

renewal in the Holy Spirit : In our Baptism the Holy Spirit enters into us and gives us the gifts of faith, hope and charity (see Romans 5 : 5) together with "abundant grace."

through Jesus Christ : All this Christ has merited for us through his life, death and resurrection. St. Paul in these few lines tells us how each person of the Blessed Trinity plays a part in our sanctification. The Father sends the Son in our human nature to merit heaven for us, the Holy Spirit applies his merits to us in Baptism (and later in the other sacraments).

we . . . heirs : Through Baptism and the grace of the Holy Spirit we are made capable of attaining to heaven, we are made heirs and sons of God. But we must cooperate with God's grace if our "hope of eternal life" is to be fulfilled.

APPLICATION : Christmas is the season of good-will—the season when every Christian worthy of the name strives to be good and kind to all his fellowmen. But this spirit of good-will, of love and kindness, should be active in our hearts all the year round and all our lives. It would be thus if only we reminded ourselves more frequently of the mystery of Christmas, the mystery of the Incarnation which was, and is, the gift of God's goodness and kindness to us. When he created us God gave us existence—he gave existence, life, to the plants and the animals too, but he gave us more than plant or animal life; he gave us the gift of intelligence and free-will which we call our soul, a gift which raises us above all other earthly creatures, makes us the masterpiece of God's creation and in a way, a finite way, like unto himself.

This is surely something we could never be too grateful for, but would it be enough to justify and satisfy these very gifts he has given us? Would sixty, seventy, even a hundred years of peace and plenty on this earth satisfy all our desires, would we want nothing more, would we have made full use of the spiritual powers within us in that short period? And if the answer is "no" even for those whose earthly span was lived in peace and plenty, what of the ninety-nine per cent of the human race whose lot on earth is one of struggle and strain, of hardship and heartbreak? Would their ambitions and desires be fulfilled? The answer of course is no, and the one who says the earthly grave is the end of man is not true to his intelligence and is denying intelligence to his Creator.

God's goodness and kindness in creating us had more in view for us than our span on this earth. He gave us gifts capable of knowing and understanding him and capable of enjoying a share in his own divine happiness. That we could share in that happiness forever, he provided for through his plan of the Incarnation—man could share in the eternal joy of the Trinity because God the Son shared our humanity with us. He raised up, regenerated our human nature, and thereby made us heirs of the everlasting life.

Our real purpose on earth is to get to heaven. This is God's plan for us and the only true explanation of our wonderful human nature. Christmas—the Incarnation of the Son of God—has given us the means and has shown us the way to get to heaven. Would we, could we, be so foolish as to refuse to go there?

GOSPEL: Luke 2:15–20. When the angels went away from them into heaven, the shepherds said to one another, "Let us go over to Bethlehem and see this thing that has happened, which the Lord has made known to us." And they went with haste, and found Mary and Joseph, and the babe lying in a manger. And when they saw it they made known the saying which had been told them concerning this child; and all who heard it wondered at what the shepherds told them. But Mary kept all these things, pondering them in her heart. And the shepherds returned, glorifying and praising God for all they had heard and seen, as it had been told them.

EXPLANATION:
when the angels: See Gospel of Midnight Mass.

let us go over: They accepted the word of the angel as the word of God and did not hesitate to do as they were told.

found Mary and Joseph: Luke puts Mary the wife before Joseph because he has already, in his account of the Annunciation (1:26–38), narrated the privileged position of Mary in the Incarnation and Joseph's secondary position as foster-father.

when they saw . . . known: The angel had told them they would find the Messiah—the promised Savior, descendant of King David, as a baby laid in a manger, but this baby was also the Lord. They now are convinced of the truth of the angel's good news.

All who heard: There was nothing marvelous about a baby being born, or a baby resting in a manger in those days of poverty. The shepherds had something more to tell that made the people marvel and that was, as the angel had said, that this baby was more than human, that he was divine as well—the Son of God.

Mary kept all . . . in her heart: Luke is hinting here as to the source of his information for the events he is narrating. Who else but Mary, whom he could, and almost certainly did, meet during the years 58-60 when he was in Palestine (while Paul was a prisoner in Caesarea— see Acts 21:15), could have known these facts? And was it likely that she could ever forget them?

Glorifying and praising God: Simple, honest, devout men, they returned to their daily task of minding their flocks but they returned, new men, full of praise and thanksgiving to God for the marvelous things he had done for them.

APPLICATION: These simple, uneducated shepherds show us what we should do today when thinking of Christmas and of God's marvelous kindness to us mortal men. They couldn't read or write but they could and did use their natural intelligence. They believed in God, the Creator of the universe;

they believed he would fulfill the promises he had made to Abraham and to the Chosen People down through the centuries. They were told now by God's messenger that God had fulfilled his promise and, through grace given them, they saw how far the fulfillment exceeded the hopes of Abraham and of the Chosen People. The Babe in Bethlehem was greater than Abraham, greater than David, greater than all the prophets God had sent them down through the ages, for he was God as well as man. "They returned glorifying and praising God for all they had heard and seen."

Let us imitate those humble shepherds this morning. Let us too return after Mass to our homes, to our ordinary daily tasks, but with renewed spiritual strength, keeping ever before our minds what great things God has done for us. He has raised us up above and beyond our natural human selves. He has given us a supernatural life and a supernatural end and purpose, which is, eternal happiness. Our years on this earth may be short or long, pleasant or difficult, for the vast majority more difficult than pleasant. Whatever they may be, if we but keep our eye fixed on the glorious future that he has prepared for us, we'll use these years as the stepping-stones to get us across the river of life to our everlasting home.

Thank you, Jesus, Son of God, for becoming a Baby in Bethlehem so that I could become a fully-grown supernatural man as God's adopted son in heaven.

CHRISTMAS DAY : MASS

FIRST READING : Isaiah 52 : 7–10. How beautiful upon the mountains are the feet of him who brings good tidings, who publishes peace, who brings good tidings of good, who publishes salvation, who says to Zion, "Your God reigns." Hark, your watchmen lift up their voice, together they sing for joy; for eye to eye they see the return of the Lord to Zion. Break forth together into singing, you waste places of Jerusalem; for the Lord has comforted his people, he has redeemed Jerusalem. The Lord has bared his holy arm before the eyes of all the nations; and all the ends of the earth shall see the salvation of our God.

EXPLANATION : These words were written by a disciple of the great Isaiah, most probably in Babylon, to encourage the exiles. Their God would set them free and return them once more to a clean and purified Jerusalem. But this return, like the Exodus from Egypt centuries earlier, was a type of a foreshadowing of the greater redemption that was to come. The possession of the land of Canaan for a few years; the restoring of Jerusalem and Judah, were but pale shadows of the great restoration and the possession of our eternal "promised land" which were to be given in the days to come, not only to Israel but to all nations.

How beautiful . . . the feet . . . good tidings : The person who brings good tidings is always welcome. The writer sees the announcer of the good news as already present. His good news is that salvation is at hand, that peace has come, that war and exiles are over. The exiles in Babylon would naturally understand this of their return to Jerusalem, but there was much more than that in this message.

Zion, your God reigns : Many of the exiles expected the Davidic monarchy to be restored, because of the promise given to David (2 Sm. 7 : 14). But the returned exiles had no king until the true descendant of David, the promised Messiah, came. He was King as he admitted to Pilate and as the title on his cross proclaimed, but his kingdom "was not of this world."

Hark . . . voice : There were no watchmen on the walls of Jerusalem at the time as there were no walls and no city, but the prophet sees the future day when God will "redeem Jerusalem and comfort his people."

Lord has bared his holy arm : God has shown his power to all the nations.

the ends of the earth : The salvation which the prophet foresees is not just the return from Babylon which was for the Jews alone and did not interest the nations, but the universal redemption of all men in the messianic age.

APPLICATION : Today, Christmas Day, is the day when we commemorate the greatest, the mightiest, the most far-reaching event which ever took place in human history. No wonder we date our years from that event—the period that preceded it we call B.C., "before Christ's coming," the years since as "Anni Domini," the years of the Lord, the years which have elapsed since Christ came to assume the kingship of the world.

The good tidings—the gospel—of peace has been brought to us by no less a person than the Son of God himself. And he came not as a mighty prince in the prime of life, as he could have done, but he came into this world like one of ourselves born of a human mother, "taking the form of a slave," as St. Paul says, "like us in all things save sin." Not alone that but he chose the poorest (though holiest) of mothers who had to give birth to him in a stable. He could have been born in a palace—God could easily have arranged that, but he wanted it this way. He wanted to show us that it is not the things of this world that matter. Wealth and power, the goal and the god of so many foolish men, are empty baubles. We can have them and *perhaps* enjoy them for a few short years but what then? Naked we came into the world and naked we shall go out of it.

Thank God, true Christians, and you are among them, have accepted the good news Christ brought to the world, and are showing their joy and thankfulness for it by following it daily as well as they are able. We fail, yes, maybe often, but we are dealing with a merciful God who sees our good intentions and accepts them often for the good deeds we should have done. We need God's mercy, all of us, but this great and mighty act of God, the Incarnation, which we are celebrating today is such a proof of his love for man and his mercy for us, that we could never and should never despair of receiving that mercy, no matter how black our record, no matter how seriously we have sinned.

Let us therefore "shout for joy and break out in song" as the prophet tells us, together with all the Christians of the earth on this great festival. It is the festival of God's infinite love and mercy, the festival of our salvation and elevation to sonship with God. Nothing greater could have happened to human nature. The Incarnation is *the* event of human history.

SECOND READING : Hebr. 1 : 1–6. In many and various ways God spoke of old to our fathers by the prophets; but in these last days he has spoken to us by a Son, whom he appointed the heir of all things, through whom also he created the world. He reflects the glory of God and bears the very stamp of his nature, upholding the universe by his word of power. When he had made purification for sins, he sat down at the right hand of the Majesty on high, having become as much superior to angels as the name he has obtained is more excellent than theirs. For to what angel did God ever say, "Thou art my Son, today I have begotten thee?" Or again, "I will be to him a father, and he shall be to me a son?" And again, when he brings the firstborn into the world, "Let all God's angels worship him."

EXPLANATION :

God . . . spoke : On the Epistle to the Hebrews see Cycle C (3) above—the 4th Sunday of Advent.

Down through almost two thousand years God spoke to the Chosen People through his deeds and through his mouthpieces—the patriarchs and the prophets.

in . . . various ways : At various times and in various ways. The author is thus bringing out the imperfection of the old revelation when compared with the new which was given *once and for all* by *one* person.

by a son : For the author, following his master and model St. Paul, Christ was unquestionably the Son of God.

heir of all things : In his human nature, after his resurrection, Christ was made heir of all things. As God in his divine nature he was from eternity heir of all things, Son of God.

through whom . . . world : The pre-existence of Christ is stated here, namely, in his divine nature. He cooperated with the Father and the Holy Spirit in the act of creation. In the Old Testament (Wisdom books), wisdom cooperated with God in creation; wisdom is personified and is really the Son (see Prov. 8 : 30. Wis. 7 : 22).

reflects the glory : Here the author is possibly using a more ancient liturgical hymn to give some idea of the divine nature of the Son in relation to the Father. He is the reflection, the reflected glory of the Father, as one's face is reflected in a mirror.

bears . . . very stamp : The Greek word translated "representation" is "character," the imprint of a seal, the mark of one thing found on something else. This stresses the exact similarity but at the same time the distinction of one from the other.

upholding . . . universe : The Son maintains all creation in existence and directs their courses "by his word of power," i.e. powerful word. All this stresses his divinity in which he is equal to the Father.

he . . . purification : Through his death in his human nature, the Son, Christ, has redeemed mankind and

sat . . . at the right hand : After his resurrection he has the place of honor in heaven in his human nature.

superior to . . . angels : The aim of the writer of this Epistle was to show the superiority of the new covenant over the old. It was superior because it was given by the Son of God who is superior not only to the prophets, priests and patriarchs but to the angels, the heavenly messengers sent from heaven in the old dispensation.

Thou art my son : The words of Ps. 2 : 7 and of 2 Sm. 7 : 14 refer directly to the king, but in their fuller sense they are fulfilled only in Christ. This is the inspired interpretation of the author of Hebrews.

let all . . . angels worship him : If the angels must adore the Son they are inferior to him (see Dt. 32 : 43).

APPLICATION : The Epistle to the Hebrews was written to show how superior the new covenant was to the old. It was written most probably to converts from Judaism who, because of persecution from Judaizers who were numerous at the time, were tempted to change back to the old law and religion. These six verses of its first chapter were chosen for today's reading because of the clear, definite and emphatic declaration of the divinity of Christ which they contain. The baby who was born in a stable in Bethlehem, lived and died in Palestine, rose the third day from the grave and ascended to heaven forty days later, was also God, equal to the Father in all things. This is a mystery beyond our human comprehension, yet it is a fact, stated by Christ himself, believed and preached by the Apostles and accepted by the Church for almost two thousand years.

To admit the fact of this mystery is no difficulty for anyone who believes in God. If God had no mysteries, if our finite minds could sound the depths of his nature, then he would not be God but a finite being like ourselves. We believe, and we know, because God has revealed it to us, that there are three persons in our one God, and that the Second Person, the Son, became man for our sakes. This may be a mystery to our limited intellectual powers, but it is a consoling fact and a source of joy and rejoicing to us this morning. It is also the basis of our hope of a great future— the Son of God, through his humanity and because of his infinite divine love for us, has made it possible for us to reach heaven when our earthly days are over.

While thanking God this morning for the privilege that is ours, let us not forget our unfortunate fellowmen who are redeemed by the God-man. He wishes them all to share in this great blessing which his Incarnation brought to mankind. Our prayers can help to bring the light of faith to them. Let us be generous with this help—it will be one very effective way of showing God this morning that we realize how generous he was towards us and that we are truly grateful for his divine generosity.

GOSPEL: Jn. 1:1–18. In the beginning was the Word, and the Word was with God, and the Word was God. He was in the beginning with God; all things were made through him, and without him was not anything made that was made. In him was life, and the life was the light of men. The light shines in the darkness, and the darkness has not overcome it.

There was a man sent from God, whose name was John. He came for testimony, to bear witness to the light, that all might believe through him. He was not the light, but came to bear witness to the light.

The true light that enlightens every man was coming into the world. He was in the world, and the world was made through him, yet the world knew him not. He came to his own home and his own people received him not. But to all who received him, who believed in his name, he gave power to become children of God; who were born, not of blood nor of the will of the flesh nor of the will of man, but of God.

And the Word became flesh and dwelt among us, full of grace and truth; we have beheld his glory, glory as of the only Son from the Father. (John bore witness to him, and cried, "This was he of whom I said, 'He who comes after me ranks before me, for he was before me.'") And from his fullness have we all received, grace upon grace. For the law was given through Moses; grace and truth came through Jesus Christ. No one has ever seen God; the only Son, who is in the bosom of the Father, he has made him known.

EXPLANATION: The gospel according to St. John was written long after the other three gospels. The essentials of the Christian faith had already been preached and accepted by thousands of Jews and Gentiles throughout the then-known world—the Roman Empire. The basic doctrine of the faith, that Christ who lived and died in Palestine, rose from the dead and ascended to heaven, was not a mere man but was the Son of God who took human nature for our salvation—this basic doctrine had been preached and believed for over sixty years before John's gospel was written. The other three Evangelists had already given a written synopsis of the faith that had been preached—they too had as their basic tenet the Incarnation. But John's gospel gives a more profoundly theological vision of Christ, the result of years of preaching and of meditating on this wondrous mystery of God's love. And while stressing the divinity of Christ he leaves no doubt as to the reality of his human nature. It was the God-man on whose breast he leaned at the Last Supper of whom he wrote.

In the beginning: While Mark begins with Christ's public life and Matthew and Luke go back to the birth in Bethlehem, John goes back to the beginning of time, when creation began and

was the Word: Christ already was. The Greek imperfect translated "was" means continuous, timeless existence.

the Word: John uses this Greek term "logos"=word to describe the Son as the emanation, the reproduction, the utterance of God. In the Old Testament the word of God meant the revelation of himself in power, in grace, in prophecy.

was with God: This "word" who was divine, was from eternity, was at the same time distinct from the Father (God with the article=Father in New Testament), so there are two persons (at least), two distinct individuals in the Godhead.

Word was God : God here, without the article, means the divinity. A clear statement that this Word was divine.

all things . . . made : This Second Person in the Godhead cooperated in the creation of all things, so he is not only distinct from creatures : he is their cocreator.

In him . . . life : The reference is to the supernatural life and light of revelation. The act of creation mentioned, referred to the natural life given us.

a man . . . name was John : This refers to the Baptist whose preaching prepared for the public ministry of Christ. He spoke of the revelation (the light) of the expected Messiah which was imminent.

He was in the world . . . made : God should have been known through his creatures (see Rom. 1 : 18–23) if men used their intelligence but they did not.

he came to his own : He came in the Incarnation to his own Chosen People and told them who he was, the Messiah and the Son of God, but they (that is, their leaders especially) received him not.

become children of God : The purpose of the Incarnation was to raise humanity to the supernatural level of adopted sons of God—those who accept Christ and keep his doctrine are capable of this divine sonship.

believed in his name : Name stands for person—belief in Christ is belief that he is the Son of God and therefore the source of all *grace* and *truth*.

not of blood . . . God : Those who accept Christ are re-born, regenerated, in a way that is not like the natural conception and birth—it is spiritual, it is "of God."

This verse can possibly refer to the human birth of Christ, too, namely, his birth from a virgin without human father (Jerusalem Bible).

Word became flesh : The Word was divine and continued to be divine, but at a particular moment in history (Greek aorist) it assumed human nature. The word "flesh" which St. John uses here was used in the Old Testament to signify all that was transitory, mortal, lowly and imperfect. John is here stressing the humiliation (the emptying of himself as St. Paul—Phil. 2 : 6—puts it) of Christ in the Incarnation.

dwelt among us : Pitched his tent (in Greek), became one of our tribe, one with us.

beheld his glory : John was one of the first four disciples who followed Christ. He was therefore a witness to Christ's public life from the Jordan to the Ascension.

only Son . . . Father : Having brought the hymn of the Incarnation to its climax —the Word taking flesh, John does not use this term Word any more—he speaks of Jesus Christ, the Son of God.

was before me : Evidently the Baptist knew by revelation of the divinity of Christ. The Baptist was senior to Christ in age—but Christ was (God) from the beginning.

from his fullness . . . received : Of the fullness of "grace and truth" which the God-man brought us, we have all received in the sacraments and in the Church he set up for us.

grace . . . upon grace : One grace brings another, or possibly : the new covenant which replaces the old as the following verse clearly states.

no one . . . seen God : He is not visible to earthly human eyes but

who . . . him known : God is made known to us through Christ; we can grasp the infinite love and mercy of God —his compassion, his understanding of us weak mortals through Christ's loving dealings with us and his gospel of mercy. Christ is God and is in intimate union with the Father, "in the bosom of the Father," hence even in his human nature he reflects the divinity.

APPLICATION : The message the Church wishes us to hear from the readings that are read at the Sunday Masses of Advent and at the three Christmas Masses is surely this : "God so loved the world (i.e. us) that he gave his only-begotten son for us." He gave his divine Son a human nature, to dwell among us, to teach us, and finally to die for us. And "who or what are we that he should be mindful of us?" Why did he go to such lengths for us? This is one of the questions to which we shall, please God, get the answer in heaven.

In the meantime all we can do is admit the fact that God loved us, that he has done wondrous things for us because of that love. One of these things, the greatest of them, is what today's gospel puts so clearly before us : it is the fact of the Incarnation which joined our human nature with the divinity in the Person of Christ, and thereby made us heirs of heaven.

We have forgotten this privilege, this gift, too often in the past and instead of being grateful to God we have insulted and offended him. Through our sinful acts we have told him we did not want him to be our Father, we did not want the eternal heaven his Son earned for us —we did not want his love.

This morning let us tell him we didn't really mean that. We want to love him and we want to go to heaven and with the help of his grace we shall endeavor in the future to be obedient and grateful children of his.

Today's fervor, of course, may not last—but our loving Father foresaw our weaknesses and left us the means of returning to him any time we fail. Let not our frailty then or our fickleness frighten us. We are dealing with the God of love, among whose sons there is no prodigal who is not welcome back, if he takes the simple steps on the return journey.

SUNDAY IN THE OCTAVE OF CHRISTMAS.

FEAST OF THE HOLY FAMILY

FIRST READING: Sirach 3:2-6; 12-14. The Lord honored the father above the children, and he confirmed the right of the mother over her sons. Whoever honors his father atones for sins, and whoever glorifies his mother is like one who lays up treasure. Whoever honors his father will be gladdened by his own children, and when he prays he will be heard.

Whoever glorifies his father will have long life, and whoever obeys the Lord will refresh his mother.

O son, help your father in his old age, and do not grieve him as long as he lives; even if he is lacking in understanding, show forbearance, in all your strength do not despise him. For kindness to a father will not be forgotten, and against your sins it will be credited to you.

EXPLANATION: The author of this book was a pious Jew who lived in the second century B.C. He had made a deep study of the law and the revealed religion of his people, and moved by the love of God, of his Law, and of his religion, he wrote a collection of wise maxims to help others live a life pleasing to God. In the verses read today he speaks of the family:

the Lord . . . the father: In God's plan for the spread of the human race, the family unit has its foundation. The father has the place of honor and the right to respect and obedience.

right of the mother: The mother shares the authority with the father in the home. It is God's will and decree that their authority be respected by the children.

honors his father . . . glorifies his mother:

The children who respect and obey their parents are doing God's will and are thereby giving glory to God and storing up spiritual reward for themselves.

gladdened by . . . children: The son (or daughter) who respects his parents will in turn be respected by his own children. God will bless him or her with children who will be dutiful and respectful in turn.

when he prays: Because he is pleasing to God, his prayers will be answered.

glorifies . . . long life: A long life was looked on as a divine blessing. It is that, if properly lived. The longer we can work for God (and neighbor) in this life the greater the reward in heaven.

will refresh his mother: The obedient child is a comfort and a source of joy for his mother (and father). He will be obedient to his parents if he is obedient to God—this is one of God's commandments.

help your father in . . . age : It is in his later days a father needs the loving care of his children. Natural instinct and decency would demand this of children, but a greater authority still—the divine will—demands this of them.

do not grieve him : What greater grief could a father have in his old age than to have raised a son of whom he has to be ashamed. The child who has learned to respect his parents is respecting God, and will never cause his parents to be ashamed of him.

if . . . understanding : No matter how feeble, mentally or physically, one's parents may become, it is the children's duty to care for them. Those parents, when they had their health and strength, devoted their energies to their children— the children must now do their part.

kindness . . . not forgotten : God will repay the dutiful child. The kindness he shows his parents in their need is as good as, and better than any sacrifice he can offer in the temple. If he displeases God by neglecting his duty to his parents, no sacrifice of his can be acceptable to God.

credited to you : The full effects of obedience and respect for parents will have a lasting effect on the character of the child and its reward will be everlasting.

APPLICATION : Although all the emphasis, in these verses of holy Scripture just read to us, seems to be on the obligation of children to their parents, there is a profound lesson here for parents too. "Like father like son" is an old and a true saying very often. If the parents fail to do what is right and just in the sight of God they can hardly complain if their children turn out disobedient to God and to them. The young learn more from example than from precept. If parents give their children the example of a life of obedience to the laws of God, and their country—the children will in turn carry out their duties to God, to their parents and to their fellowman. There have been and there will be exceptions, of course, to this rule but they are exceptions; the vast majority follow the pattern laid down for them by their parents.

As you heard during your marriage ceremony: "children are a gift from God to you," a gift for this life to be the joy of your young years and a help and comfort in your old age; but above and beyond that, they are a gift which you must do all in your power to return to God when their hour comes. You must not only strive to make them good citizens of this world but you must never forget that God gave them to you primarily so that you would make them citizens of heaven. You may fail, in spite of your best intentions and endeavors, but God will reward you nonetheless— the failure will not be laid to your door.

Today, on the feast-day of the only perfect family that ever lived on this earth, I would ask all parents to examine themselves and see how they are fulfilling this grave responsibility—which God has placed on them. Are they preparing their children by word and example, especially by example, to be worthy citizens of heaven where they will be their parents' crown and glory?

SECOND READING : Colossians 3 :12–21. Put on then, as God's chosen ones, holy and beloved, compassion, kindness, lowliness, meekness, and patience, forbearing one another and, if one has a complaint against another, forgiving each other; as the Lord has forgiven you, so you also must forgive. And above all these put on love, which binds everything together in perfect harmony. And let the peace of Christ rule in your hearts, to which indeed you were called in the one body. And be thankful. Let the word of Christ dwell in you richly, as you teach and admonish one another in all wisdom, and as you sing psalms and hymns and spiritual songs with thankfulness in your hearts to God. And whatever you do, in word or deed, do everything in the name of the Lord Jesus, giving thanks to God the Father through him.

Wives, be subject to your husbands, as is fitting in the Lord. Husbands, love your wives, and do not be harsh with them. Children, obey your parents in everything, for this pleases the Lord. Fathers, do not provoke your children, lest they become discouraged.

EXPLANATION : It was Epaphras, a disciple of St. Paul, who preached the Christian message in the town of Colossae. Paul took a keen interest in the work of his disciples. While a prisoner in Rome, Epaphras came to visit him and told him his converts were being disturbed by false teachers. Paul wrote a letter to the Colossians encouraging them to persevere in the true faith, based on the solid foundation of Christ's divinity, and to keep on living a true Christian life according to the teaching of Christ—preached to them by Epaphras. He gave them some very practical rules for an ideal Christian life, a few of which have been read to us today.

put on then . . . patience : These Christian virtues so necessary in a community must be in their heart—part and parcel of themselves. In accepting Christianity they accepted a new life.

forgiving each other : Even Christians could forget their Christian obligations and injure their neighbor but the injured one must always be ready to forgive the offender.

as the Lord has forgiven you : The Lord wiped out all their sins in Baptism and is ever ready to wash away the sins of a repentant sinner. The true Christian must imitate God in this and quickly and willingly forgive a repentant brother.

love . . . perfect : The virtues mentioned above are compared to new garments which are *put on*, but the final outer garment which binds and keeps the others in place is charity—true Christian, brotherly love.

peace of Christ . . . hearts : Christ is the source of unity, harmony and peace. His followers form one compact community —one body, with Christ as its head.

word of Christ . . . you : Christians must not only know the doctrine of Christ, they must live it and produce fruits worthy of it.

teach . . . one another : One member must help the other as in the human body.

in the name of the Lord Jesus : Because they are members of Christ's Body, their every act has a divine value. It is as members of Christ's body that they honor God the Father, their acts give special honor to him.

wives, be subject : Paul gets down to details now. The Christian faith is lived in the Christian home by each member doing his or her duty. It is duty that is stressed here not rights. As "the husband is head of the wife, as Christ is head of the Church" (Eph. 5 : 23), the wife must be subject to him—but in no servile way—it is a loving subjection for the good of the family.

husbands, love your wives : This may sound commonplace today but in the pagan world of St. Paul's time wives were little more than chattels; they were the "property" of the husband and were often treated cruelly and harshly. Christianity changed all that.

children, obey your parents : The family circle is God's place for the spread of the human race. He could have created, and could continue to create, human beings in the prime of life, each one capable of running his own life. He chose the better way, we can rest assured. Parents have the responsibility of preparing their children to take their place in life, and what wonderful virtues are developed in parents because of this responsibility! Children on the other hand, have their obligations as soon as they come to the use of reason, the basic obligation of which is obedience to their parents. Through this obedience they will learn to take their place in life and more important still it is through this obedience that they will learn to obey God and reach eternal life.

do not provoke . . . discouraged : Fathers (and mothers too) must teach their children to obey not out of fear but out of love and respect. Obedience given out of fear is not true obedience and is not a training for the child's future life. A loving interest in the child's true welfare must be the motive behind every command and every reprimand.

APPLICATION : Ninety per cent of the first readers of St. Paul's letter—the first Christian converts of the town of Colossae—were pagans before their conversion. To practice the new Christian virtues was no easy task for people reared in the laxity and license of the paganism of their day. Yet they did practice these virtues and produced many saints and martyrs. After twenty centuries of Christianity one would expect that to live a full Christian life today should be less difficult but unfortunately it is not so. For the fact is : our world is rapidly sinking back again into paganism—a paganism more inimical to truth and morality than the paganism of St. Paul's day. The pagans of the Roman Empire were tired of vice and worldliness—they were looking for the truth and the real purpose of life. They found it in Christianity and cherished it. Today's neo-pagans are tired of Christianity—they have found it wanting, because they are found wanting in its observance.

What was once the Christian world is today divided into two opposing factions, on one side those who openly deny the existence of God and of a future world; on the other, those who for all practical purposes care not whether God exists and whose only care is for the wealth, pleasure and power of this world. These factions are not in opposition because of any creed or doctrine; it is not dogma that divides them. Both parties have the same idols, *themselves*; their temples are identical, their banks and their stock-exchanges.

No wonder then that true Christians find the practice of their Christian life difficult today, no wonder that the youth of the world is bewildered and baffled, the winds of falsehood are blowing on them from all sides.

But it is not by banner-waving and protest-marching that our world can be saved from itself. Nothing but a return to the gospel of Christ and to the virtues that gospel demands of us can bring saints back to the world. Where God is forgotten there is no happiness for man. Where the peace of Christ does not reign there is nothing but strife and hostility among men. Where there is no faith and hope in a future life, the present world is already hell.

Let us begin in our own family circle to bring sanity back to our world. Let us have the true peace of Christ in our hearts and in our home, each one carrying out the task God has allotted to him. We shall not convert the world immediately but we shall have made a start. The world is the sum-total of its individual families.

GOSPEL : Matthew 2 : 13–15; 19–23. When the wise men had departed, behold, an angel of the Lord appeared to Joseph in a dream and said, "Rise, take the child and his mother, and flee to Egypt, and remain there till I tell you; for Herod is about to search for the child, to destroy him." And he rose and took the child and his mother by night, and departed to Egypt, and remained there until the death of Herod. This was to fulfill what the Lord had spoken by the prophet, "Out of Egypt have I called my son."

But when Herod died, behold, an angel of the Lord appeared in a dream to Joseph in Egypt, saying, "Rise, take the child and his mother, and go to the land of Israel, for those who sought the child's life are dead." And he rose and took the child and his mother, and went to the land of Israel. But when he heard that Archelaus reigned over Judea in place of his father Herod, he was afraid to go there, and being warned in a dream he withdrew to the district of Galilee. And he went and dwelt in a city called Nazareth, that what was spoken by the prophets might be fulfilled, "He shall be called a Nazarene."

EXPLANATION : Herod, the King in Jerusalem, had heard from the Magi that the Messiah, the "King of the Jews," was born. Unpopular though he was, he saw in this birth a danger to his own position. So, he determined that this newly-born Messiah would never reach the throne. Through an angel God told Joseph to take the Holy Family to Egypt to escape his evil clutches. Then when Herod died, Joseph was told once more to return to Israel. He returned to Nazareth and there the Holy Family settled, living a humble life with Joseph the carpenter, their bread-winner. It is not known when St. Joseph died, but Mary and Jesus continued to live in Nazareth until the time had come for Jesus to begin his public life, when he was about 30 years of age (Lk. 3 : 23).

Herod . . . him : The massacre of the Holy Innocents proved Herod's intentions, but God knew this and got the Holy Child away in time together with his blessed Mother and St. Joseph.

He rose . . . child : Joseph accepted the angel's command without hesitation, knowing that it came from God. He knew already that this child was someone very special, as is clear from Matthew 1 : 18–21. He headed for Egypt, a journey of ten to twelve days over desolate lands, without a word or murmur of complaint.

Out of Egypt . . . Son : Matthew, writing his gospel for Jewish converts, and possible converts, loses no opportunity to show that the Old Testament prophecies were fulfilled in Christ. Here the return of the Holy Family from Egypt is said to fulfill the prophecy in Hosea 11 : 1. This prophet was actually referring to the Exodus, when God brought the Israelites out of Egypt and made them his Chosen People and his children. The coming of Christ was the second and the real Exodus and the founding of the true Chosen People, because it made all men really sons of God.

Archelaus reigned : Archelaus had a reputation somewhat like his father. Joseph therefore did not return to Bethlehem but to Nazareth, his original home-town and also Mary's. They had not returned there after the birth of our Lord because Joseph, a carpenter, had most probably found better employment in Bethlehem and decided to settle there.

called a Nazarene : Again Matthew finds a fulfillment of an Old Testament prophecy in the fact that Jesus grew to manhood in Nazareth. There is no evident prophecy to this effect, but Isaiah's description of the Messiah as "a root from the stump of Jesse," may have been in Matthew's mind as he wrote his gospel. The Hebrew word for "root" is "*Neser*," from which Matthew may have thought "Nazarene" and "Nazareth" were derived.

APPLICATION : During this holy season of Christmas, Jesus, Mary and Joseph should be remembered frequently by every Christian. To help us to remember them and above all to strive to imitate them, the Church has dedicated this Sunday to the memory of the Holy Family. Although they were God's closest friends, and although they were the holiest family that ever lived, or ever will live, on earth, they had more than their share of this world's troubles and cares.

Today's gospel story tells us of some of these earthly woes and sufferings. They had just settled in Bethlehem, and the Baby Jesus was only a few months old when, to avoid his murder at the hands of the murderous and jealous Herod, they had to flee from Bethlehem and become displaced persons in a foreign and pagan land.

The journey itself, some 300 miles across a desert, was a frightening, exhausting and dangerous experience. The search for some place to live in a foreign land, the difficulty for Joseph in finding employment in an unfriendly land, so that they could have the bare necessities of life, and the constant fear for the welfare and survival of the blessed child committed to their care, must have been experiences that Joseph and Mary never could forget.

Why, we may well ask, did God allow this to happen to his dearest and nearest friends on earth? The answer is : he did it for our sakes. He sent his divine Son, as one of us, on earth to bring us to heaven and he chose a life for Christ, as well as for his blessed Mother and his foster-father St. Joseph, which would be a model and source of encouragement for the lowliest, and the poorest, and the most persecuted of all those who would ever be his followers.

With the example of the sufferings and poverty of the Holy Family of Nazareth before their minds, no Christian family can ever say that their sufferings and hardships are more than God can demand of them. No believing Christian can ever say that Christ is asking of him more than he demanded of himself, and of his beloved Mother

and foster-father. There are few, if any, families in this world who do not have to face troubles and trials of one kind or another. But our Christian faith, and our firm conviction, that our few short years on this earth are only a proving ground, a preparation, for a life of endless peace and happiness to come, should give us the necessary strength to bear with them.

The message of today's gospel story is a message of encouragement and consolation for every one of us. If the holiest and greatest family that ever lived on earth, suffered such trials and hardships all for our salvation, surely we should be ready and willing to suffer and bear with the trials that God sends us for our own eternal welfare.

OCTAVE OF CHRISTMAS : FEAST OF MARY, MOTHER OF GOD

FIRST READING : Numbers 6 : 22–27. The Lord said to Moses, "Say to Aaron and his sons, thus you shall bless the people of Israel : you shall say to them : The Lord bless you and keep you; the Lord make his face to shine upon you, and be gracious to you; the Lord lift up his countenance upon you, and give you peace. So shall they put my name upon the people of Israel, and I will bless them."

EXPLANATION : After the Exodus (or coming out of Egypt) and after God had made a covenant on Mount Sinai with the Chosen People, Moses, on God's instructions, set the tribe of Levi apart so that they would offer the sacrifices and carry out the liturgy in the name of, and for, the rest of the tribes. The direct line of Aaron, head of the tribe of Levi, were to be the priests who would have

the principal part in the offering of the sacrifices and in the other liturgical acts. The other male members of the tribe were the Levites whose duty it was to assist the priests. One of the liturgical acts of the priests was to bless the people after the daily sacrifices and on other solemn occasions. The blessing was a reward for the keeping of the covenant by the people, and a guarantee that the blessing promised to all nations through Abraham would be fulfilled one day.

The words of this blessing given by God to Moses are recorded in these verses of the book of Numbers read at today's Mass.

The Lord bless you and keep you : The blessing of God meant peace and temporal prosperity and a renewal of the hope of the great future blessing which was to come.

face shine upon you : May God smile on you, that is, may he be your friend.

be gracious to you : May he grant you his favors.

lift . . . upon you . . . give you peace : May you continue to be his favorites and may he protect you from all enemies so you can live in peace.

I will bless them : This is not just a wish which the priests make on behalf of the people. God promises that he will grant their request which he commands them to make.

APPLICATION : All God's dealings with the Chosen People of the Old Testament, the call of Abraham, the Exodus, the liturgy, this special blessing were part of God's plan of preparation for his greatest act of infinite blessing which was to come in the Incarnation. God's Son was to take our human nature in order to unite us with God. All God's promises, all God's fatherly care for the Chosen People, down through the centuries, all his blessings had their perfect fulfillment and culmination in the coming of Christ on earth.

And the one human being who received the fullness of these promises and blessings was the Virgin Mary when she said: "Be it done unto me according to thy word," for at that very moment she conceived the Christ, the Son of God in her womb. As proof of this we have the Angel Gabriel's words on the occasion of the Annunciation. He salutes her as "full of grace," that is, she has the full friendship of God. He is truly gracious to her, his "face shines on her," he is actually with her as the closest of friends: "the Lord is with thee." He adds : "blessed art thou among women" to show that no woman (or man either) ever received the fullness of God's blessing until now.

The title the Church has always given her, a title confirmed by the Council of Ephesus (431) : "Mother of God," aptly expresses all this. She became the Mother of Christ who was the Messiah and the Son of God, an honor and a dignity which no human imagination could have thought possible. But nothing is impossible to God. As she says herself in her Magnificat : "He who is mighty has done great things for me." And let us not forget it : in honoring Mary, *one of us,* he has honored us all. Through that act of divine love and condescension which brought about the Incarnation, we, the whole human race, with Mary as the most perfect example, have been raised up to a new status, a new supernatural condition—we have been made children of God, brothers of Christ and heirs of heaven.

Let us thank God today for all the graces conferred upon Mary, graces through which we all profit. Being the Mother of Christ, she is our Mother too. She will not forget us—she has a greater interest in our true welfare than any earthly mother could have—she will help us on the road to heaven if we place ourselves under her motherly care.

SECOND READING: Galatians 4:4–7. When the time had fully come, God sent forth his Son, born of woman, born under the law, to redeem those who were under the law, so that we might receive adoption as sons. And because you are sons, God sent the Spirit of his Son into our hearts, crying, "Abba! Father!" So through God you are no longer a slave but a son, and if a son then an heir.

EXPLANATION: The people of Galatia, a town in Asia Minor (part of Turkey today), were converted by St. Paul during his second missionary journey (50-52). They accepted the Christian faith gladly and practiced it faithfully until some Judaizers came among them telling them that Paul's doctrine was wrong, that the old law was still in force and must be accepted by Christians. To refute this heresy Paul wrote this letter from Ephesus, showing that the coming of Christ had fulfilled the old law and annulled it. The shadow was removed by the reality. Christians are freed from the slavery of the old law for they have been made children of God.

When . . . time . . . come: The whole history of man on earth, the period of the Old Testament in particular, was a period of promises and preparation. The hour appointed by God from all eternity for fulfilling these promises came when:

God sent . . . his Son: Ever since that day on the road to Damascus (Acts 9: 1–19), when the risen Christ appeared to him, Paul had not the slightest doubt that the Christ who had lived in Palestine and had died on the cross, was the true Son of God, as well as the promised Messiah.

born of woman: Paul does not mention Mary. He is not concerned with details here which are known to his converts. What he is stressing is the reality of the human nature of Christ. He has already mentioned his divinity. And especially he is stressing the self-humiliation of the Son of God who deigned to be born of a mother like any human child.

born . . . under the law: Another humiliation. He was the maker of the law but in order to fulfill all the Old Testament prophecies, he took human nature from a descendant of Abraham, and became one of the Chosen Race.

to redeem . . . were under the law: The promises had been given to "those under the law," the Chosen People, so therefore the gospel of redemption was offered to them first.

we . . . adoption . . . sons: The result of Christ's coming was that all men, Jew and Gentile, could become adopted sons of God. All those who accept Christ are by Baptism raised to a new status, a new supernatural life.

Abba (Father): We are adopted sons and can truly call God our Father, as Christ taught his disciples to do. It is the Spirit of his Son, the Holy Spirit given at Baptism, which gives us this privilege.

through God . . . heir: This privilege of sonship which as a consequence makes us heirs of his happiness, i.e. of heaven, is a free gift of God's love and goodness. As human beings we could never earn such a privilege for ourselves. But the Incarnation has earned it for us, and the Incarnation is an act of pure love on God's part.

APPLICATION: The Galatians—pagans recently converted to Christianity by Paul—were being disturbed in their faith by Judaizers, that is, by Jews who pretended to be Christians but were not. These were telling the new converts that Christianity was not something really new, but only a new form of Judaism, and therefore the converts must accept circumcision and other practices of the old law. Paul in his letter reacts strongly to this falsehood. Christianity is not a reform of Judaism, he states, but is its replacement. Judaism was only a preparation, Christianity is the fulfillment; the old law was but a shadow of things to come, Christianity is the reality.

The "fullness of time has come," the period of preparation and promise has ended. Men are no longer slaves of the law or slaves of their past pagan polytheism and its practices. They are now free men and new men, sons of God. They can now truly call God "Abba Father," "for God sent his Son born of a woman." The Incarnation has taken place, men are no longer mere human beings, they have a new life given them in Baptism. They now share in the divine life because Christ has shared their human life with them.

Do we Christians of today really appreciate the privileges the Incarnation has brought to us? Do we really realize what our Christianity means to us? When we say the "Our Father who art in heaven" do we understand even vaguely what we are saying? If we were allowed to salute God as our Creator it would be a reminder of all we owe him, and our duty, but to have the right to call him our Father, the Father who loves us so much, that he has made us his

sons, and is gladly ready to share his eternal happiness with us, is so great a privilege that we almost find it hard to believe it.

Yet this is the result and consequence of that great mystery of God's love—the Incarnation, the basic tenet of our Christianity. Today's feast-day—the feast of Mary, Mother of God—recalls to our minds this fundamental truth of our faith. "God sent his son born of a woman"—the woman was Mary "our tainted nature's solitary boast" as Wordsworth describes her. She, among all the daughters and sons of men, was the most closely connected with God's gift of the Incarnation to us. She conceived Christ in his human nature, in her womb. She bore him within her for nine months, she gave birth to him in Bethlehem, she fed him at her breast in his infancy—she provided and cared for him in his boyhood and youth. She finally offered him for us on Calvary. And this son of hers was the Son of God from all eternity.

We Christians are privileged to have been made sons of God by the Incarnation. But how much greater was and is the privilege of the one who was made the Mother of God, and his nearest and dearest human assistant in this mystery of his love for us! God loves us, of that we can have no doubt; Mary too loves us, for we are brothers of the Son of God whom she loves so dearly. She wants us to reap the reward of the Incarnation, in which she played such a privileged part, whose reward is to share in the happiness of God for all eternity. This reward she will obtain for us when our moment of judgement comes, if we have tried to love and respect her in life. If we say devoutly, thoughtfully and frequently that simple prayer the Church has taught us: "Holy Mary, Mother of God, pray for us sinners now" we can face "the hour of our death" with confidence. Amen.

GOSPEL : Luke 2 : 21. At the end of eight days, when he was circumcised, he was called Jesus, the name given by the angel before he was conceived in the womb.

EXPLANATION : See the gospel of the "Dawn Mass on Christmas Day" for the explanation of verses 15–20.

At the end of eight days : Circumcision was the outward sign of the covenant God made with Abraham and his descendants (see Gen. 17 : 12, renewed in Lev. 12 : 3). Every male child had to be circumcised on the eighth day after his birth in order to become a member of the Chosen People. It was at this ceremony that the child was given his name.

called Jesus : Joshuah, in Hebrew, which means Yahweh (or God) saves. In Matthew's Gospel the angel explains the meaning of the name to Joseph : "he is the one who is to save his people from their sins" (Mt. 1 : 21).

name . . . the angel . . . in the womb : The angel Gabriel had told Mary that the child who was to be born of her was to be called Jesus, and goes on to state that he will be the Messiah, the Savior of the people (Lk. 1 : 30–33).

APPLICATION : This story of the humble shepherds of Bethlehem coming to find Jesus "in the manger wrapped in swaddling clothes" already read at the Dawn Mass on Christmas Day, is repeated today because of the feast we are celebrating, the Divine Motherhood of Mary. It is the feast of Christmas again, the feast of the Incarnation and birth of our Savior, but it is Mary's part in this wonderful mystery of God's love for men that the Church is stressing today.

There have been Christians who could see no importance in the part played by Mary in our redemption, yet it was God himself who chose her from all eternity for this role and it was God's messenger at the Annunciation who proclaimed she was "full of grace" and that she was God's special friend—"The Lord was with her." The humble shepherds searching for the Savior whose birth "God had made known to them" found Mary first, then Joseph (the one after Mary who had a very important part in God's plan) and then "the babe lying in the manger."

In following the inspired words of the gospels of Matthew and Luke who stress the importance of Mary's role in the Incarnation, and the constant teaching of the Catholic Church ever since, we need have no fear of taking anything from the honor, glory and gratitude we owe to God, when we honor, as our Mother, the Virgin he first honored by making her the Mother of his Son. Furthermore the last act of our Savior, before dying on the cross, was to make his Mother our Mother, through our representative St. John, to whom he said: "behold thy Mother" (Jn. 1 : 27). It would be disloyalty to Christ not to accept her as our Mother, and it would be disloyalty to the revealed word of God if we denied her divine maternity. God made her Mother of the Messiah, the Savior, who was his divine Son.

Mary was, and is, a human creature, a mere human creature but a human creature selected by God to be the mother of the Savior's human nature, the human nature his divine sonship assumed in order to redeem man and raise him up. It was through no merit of her own that Mary earned this dignity—this honor given her was a sheer gift of God. She was the first to realize and declare this when she said God had "regarded the lowliness of his handmaid" (Lk. 1 : 48). When we honor her therefore we are in fact and in intention honoring and thanking God for the marvelous gifts and privilege he conferred on one of us.

God could have sent his Son on earth without the help of a human mother. He could have created directly for him a human nature in the prime of manhood. He chose instead to make the Son "like unto us in all things except sin" and as man he was born of a human mother, "born of a woman," as St. Paul puts it. That woman was Mary ever-Virgin, she was God's privileged handmaid. And when we honor that privilege of hers we are honoring the loving condescension of God who not only deigned to send us his Son to be our Savior, but deigned that he should be born of one of our own weak human nature to whom he had given and continued to give the necessary graces.

Thank you God, for the Incarnation, thank you God, for the honorable part you gave to "one of us" to play in that drama of divine love. May we ever be worthy of your gifts of infinite love to us!

SECOND SUNDAY AFTER CHRISTMAS

FIRST READING : Sirach (Ecclesiasticus), 24 : 1–2; 8–12. Wisdom will praise herself, and will glory in the midst of her people. In the assembly of the Most High she will open her mouth, and in the presence of his host she will glory : "The Creator of all things gave me a commandment, and the one who created me assigned a place for my tent. And he said, 'Make your dwelling in Jacob, and in Israel receive your inheritance.' From eternity, in the beginning, he created me, and for eternity I shall not cease to exist. In the holy tabernacle I ministered before him, and so I was established in Zion. In the beloved city likewise he gave me a resting place, and in Jerusalem was my dominion. So I took root in an honored people, in the portion of the Lord, who is their inheritance."

EXPLANATION : On Sirach, the author of this book, see page 43. In the verses read today we have the author's eulogy of Wisdom. Personified Wisdom declares herself as being in union with God and yet distinct from him. She came forth from the mouth of the Most High. She has an important part in the divine council and dwells in the highest heavens. She pre-existed with God and participated in all the works of creation, and will exist for all eternity. From this it is easy to see in personified Wisdom a pre-figuring of St. John's doctrine of the "Logos," the Word which "was with God, was God, and became man and pitched his tent among us" (Jn. 1 : 1–14).

Wisdom will praise herself : No finite mind could describe the infinite eternal Wisdom. She had revealed herself (partially) to her Chosen People.

In the assembly of the Most High : In the divine council she speaks with authority. All the heavenly hosts recognize her importance.

The creator . . . gave . . . commandment : Wisdom was then sent to men on this earth by the creator, by God, saying :

In Jacob . . . your dwelling : God sends Wisdom to the Chosen People—the children of Israel. Sirach now sees Wisdom on earth in the Thorah—the covenant and law given to Moses. He did not see the fuller and true meaning of his words, which became evident only when the "Word of God came on earth and dwelt among us."

from eternity . . . for eternity : Wisdom now declares she is eternal, everlasting, in other words, divine.

In the holy Tabernacle . . . Zion : Ever since David brought the Ark of the Covenant into that city (about 100 B.C.),

C

Jerusalem had been God's earthly dwelling place among his people.

I took root . . . people . . . inheritance : He came to stay among his Chosen People. Unfortunately, they did not remain loyal to him. Jerusalem was destroyed but God's hand was not shortened by their defects. He set up a new Chosen People, a new Jerusalem which would be everlasting, for its real culmination was to be in heaven.

APPLICATION : St. Augustine truly says : "The New Testament is hidden in the Old, the Old Testament is made clear in the New." These verses we have read today from Sirach, an inspired writer of the Old Testament, makes this evident to us. He describes Wisdom—the knowledge and power of God—as someone distinct from God yet equal to God. This was a daring innovation on the part of a Jewish writer for whom the unicity or oneness of God was the basic tenet of the true religion. The doctrine of the Blessed Trinity—three distinct but equal persons in the *One God*—was not openly revealed in the Old Testament. The people of the old dispensation were not ready yet to accept this divine mystery.

But the all-wise God, author of the Old and New Testaments, moves Sirach (as also the writers of the Books of Proverbs and Wisdom) to prepare the minds of the future generations of Chosen People to whom he was to reveal this basic doctrine of the New Testament, for the mysterious but glorious doctrine of the Blessed Trinity, three persons in the One God.

We are surely fortunate. We are truly God's Chosen People, for he has deigned to reveal to us this basic essence of his divine nature, this essential foundation of our Christian faith. Unless we knew of, and believed in, the doctrine of the Trinity our following of Christ would be folly and futile. If Christ was not God,

he did not redeem us men; he did not raise us up to give us a share in the divine nature; he could not and did not make us sons of the Father and heirs of heaven; he did not send us the Holy Spirit, a divine person distinct from the Father and the Son, to sanctify and direct his Church and to help us on our road to heaven.

But he did all this because he was true God and true man. He is true God because he is the Second Person of the Blessed Trinity. He is true man because, carrying out the Father's plan for man's glorification, he took real human nature in order to raise us up to the supernatural, divine status God willed for us.

We know, because God has said it, that there are three Persons in the One God. We, with our very limited, finite minds, cannot grasp the full meaning of this mystery—if we could, God would be limited and finite like ourselves. But we can accept it on God's word, and Christ's life and teaching among us confirms this word of God for us. We can therefore rest assured that our Christian faith is on the solid basis of God's truth, that the three Persons of the Blessed Trinity are not only there in some remote heaven, but that they are close beside us, deeply interested and involved in our salvation. The infinite, divine love of the Father for man—the masterpiece of his creation—has sent his Son to become man so that men could become sons of God. The Holy Spirit, continuing the work of the Son among us, is helping us on the road to heaven through his gifts and his inspirations. It is there, please God, in heaven, that the greatest joy of our heavenly existence will be the contemplation of the most Blessed Trinity—the Father, the Son and the Holy Spirit to whom be honor and glory forever. Amen.

SECOND READING : Ephesians 1 : 3–6; 15–18. Blessed be the God and Father of our Lord Jesus Christ, who has blessed us in Christ with every spiritual blessing in the heavenly places, even as he chose us in him before the foundation of the world, that we should be holy and blameless before him. He destined us in love to be his sons through Jesus Christ, according to the purpose of his will, to the praise of his glorious grace which he freely bestowed on us in the Beloved.

For this reason, because I have heard of your faith in the Lord Jesus and your love toward all the saints, I do not cease to give thanks, for you, remembering you in my prayers, that the God of our Lord Jesus Christ, the Father of glory, may give you a spirit of wisdom and of revelation in the knowledge of him, having the eyes of your hearts enlightened, that you may know what is the hope to which he has called you, what are the riches of his glorious inheritance in the saints.

EXPLANATION : This letter was written by St. Paul from his prison in Rome (about 63 A.D.) to his converts in Ephesus. He had already taught them the full Christian doctrine. This letter is a reminder to them to continue as faithful followers of Christ.

blessed be the God and Father : St. Paul has taught the doctrine of the Blessed Trinity to his converts (Jews and Gentiles) who have accepted it without question, although for Jewish converts especially this was not easy.

of our Lord Jesus Christ : The Jesus who had lived and died recently in Palestine was "Christ," that is, the promised Messiah, and was furthermore Lord, i.e. God. We have, therefore, in this single verse the doctrine of the Trinity,

the Father and Son (the Holy Spirit is mentioned later), two distinct persons yet one God, and the doctrine of the Incarnation. Jesus, who was the man about whom they all knew, was also the Son of the Father, God.

blessed . . . blessing : The blessings of Christianity have come to them from the Father through (in) the Son, Christ.

before . . . of the world : God's plan for our elevation to sonship with him, through the Incarnation, was from all eternity, as Scotus teaches, and not merely as a remedy necessary because of men's sins.

destined us ... sons through Jesus : This was God's eternal plan : man would be elevated to the status of adopted son of God through Christ's, his Son's, adoption or assumption of man's human nature.

praise . . . glorious grace : His own glory is God's principal motive in the Incarnation, the secondary motive is our eternal glorification.

APPLICATION : St. Paul in his dungeon prison in Rome could find time to pray for his Ephesian converts. Now that he is in the glorious halls of heaven, he must surely be praying for us too today. And what he prayed and asked God for them is exactly what we need today and need even more so than the Ephesians. He asked God to enlighten their minds so that they would understand the full meaning of their vocation. Do we not all need enlightenment on this very important matter? How often do we stop and think of what being a Christian means? It means we are brothers of Christ, sons of God, and heirs to the eternal kingdom of heaven. We are, as St. Peter (1 Pet. 2 : 9) tells us : "a chosen race, a royal priesthood, a holy nation, a purchased people." Do we realize how privileged we are, do we try to live up to our noble calling? We would all be shocked if the son of a king or the son of a president behaved like a thug or gangster, if he forgot his father's and his own dignity and acted like a criminal. Yet our dignity is higher than that of any earthly king's or potentate's sons, we are sons of God, heirs of heaven. And we do forget that dignity of ours, and bring dishonor on our heavenly Father (in as far as we can) when we break his commandments and refuse to do his will.

Another gift Paul asked for his Ephesian converts was that they should learn to realize the riches of the glory of the inheritance God has prepared for his saints. Would that we too could realize this and think often on it! Heaven is ours for the taking, an everlasting home in which there will be nothing but perfect happiness and contentment. There will be no more pains of mind or body—no more strife or quarreling, no shortage of anything that delights us—no more partings from friends, death will be no more. And over and above and infinitely beyond all this, there will be our vision of the Blessed Trinity, the source of all joy and happiness.

Is there a man so foolish who would, even for a moment, run the risk of losing this inheritance, which God has prepared for him, because of some earthly, passing, pleasure or gain?

Let us give ourselves a few moments during today to think seriously on the glorious future which awaits us, and let us see if we are really on the right road towards that inheritance which the Blessed Trinity, the Father, the Son and the Holy Spirit, has prepared for us. These few moments of serious meditation will perhaps mean for some of us here present the turning point in a life that was heading in a wrong, in a fatal, direction.

GOSPEL : Jn. 1 : 1–18. In the beginning was the Word, and the Word was with God, and the Word was God. He was in the beginning with God; all things were made through him, and without him was not anything made that was made. In him was life, and the life was the light of men. The light shines in the darkness, and the darkness has not overcome it.

There was a man sent from God, whose name was John. He came for testimony, to bear witness to the light, that all might believe through him. He was not the light, but came to bear witness to the light.

The true light that enlightens every man was coming into the world. He was in the world, and the world was made through him, yet the world knew him not. He came to his own home, and his own people received him not. But to all who received him, who believed in his name, he gave power to become children of God; who were born, not of blood nor of the will of the flesh nor of the will of man, but of God.

And the Word became flesh and dwelt among us, full of grace and truth; we have beheld his glory, glory as of the only Son from the Father. (John bore witness to him and cried, "This was he of whom I said, 'He who comes after me ranks before me, for he was before me.'") And from his fullness have we all received, grace upon grace. For the law was given through Moses; grace and truth came through Jesus Christ. No one has ever seen God; the only Son, who is in the bosom of the Father, he has made him known.

EXPLANATION : These verses of St. John's Gospel have already been explained in the Third Mass on Christmas Day (see above). A brief summary will suffice here. St. John "the beloved disciple," wrote his Gospel about sixty years after the Ascension of Christ. The other three Gospels had already been for many years in circulation, and the facts concerning Jesus—his doings and sayings—had already been preached to, and lived by, two generations of Christians. The principal purpose John had in writing his Gospel was not to retell the story already well-known (though he does occasionally repeat some miracles and sayings of Jesus given by the Synoptics) but to emphasize those elements of Christianity most relevant to the Christians of his day and to put them in a language comprehensible to the people of that day.

One of the basic elements of Christianity, of course, was the Incarnation : that the Son of God, who was co-eternal with the Father, took a true human nature and lived among us. The Son of God became the Son of Man. He did this to raise us up and to enlighten us—that is, he, by uniting the human with the divine in his own person, united all of the human race with God; and he "enlightened" us, he gave us the power to see God in him and through him. He who is with the Father and who has pitched his tent among us is the bridge that spans the infinite divide that separates mere man from God.

God had revealed himself in a limited, partial way, to the Chosen People in the law of Moses. But Jesus Christ has brought us "grace," the intimate friendship of God; and "truth," all the knowledge of God and of our relationship with him, which our finite minds can grasp on earth, and which is sufficient for us to enable us to reach our heavenly home where we will see him "face to face."

APPLICATION : We can never fully appreciate the infinite love and condescension God has shown towards us in the Incarnation, but we can and should realize sufficient of its magnitude to move us to do the little he demands of us in return. And that little he demands is more for our benefit than for his. He wants us to earn an eternal life of happiness with him in heaven, by living the few years he gives us in this life, as true Christians, as true followers of his Son whom he sent among us.

Imagine for a moment, the case of an earthly king or nobleman who so loves the family of one of his subjects that he decides to bring them to live with him in his mansion. He sends his own son to live with them in their lowly cottage in order to teach them and prepare them for the day when his father will call them to take up their abode with him and share in all his earthly wealth and comfort. What would you think of their folly, if some or all of that family refused to be taught, and preferred their hovel, their poverty, and their rags to the comforts and honors offered them?

And yet, this is what Christians do who refuse to carry out the law laid down for them by Christ and prefer instead to cling to their earthly attractions, and thus lose their place in the heavenly mansions of their loving Father!

There is no sane man living, of course, who does not want eternal happiness. There is no one (outside of the mental homes) who would wish all his gifts, all his mental abilities, desires and hopes, to end forever in the grave. But there are many, normally sane men, who are so immersed, so taken up, with the fleeting things of this life that they cannot spare the time to think of their final end. Our Lord tells of two such men (there were many others), in the stories of "Dives and Lazarus" and in that of the man building bigger and better barns to store his earthly wealth. He died the night he finished his biggest barn!

We are not forbidden to enjoy and use the gifts God has put in this world for our use. He made man master of all other created things. Man fails in his duty to God and to his own best interest, not while he masters and uses these gifts of God, but when he lets these created things master him and use him.

Let us think again today of the two greatest mysteries and truths of our Christian religion, the Blessed Trinity and the Incarnation. God has raised us by the latter mystery, the Incarnation, so that we could forever enjoy the company of the former—the company of the Father, Son and Holy Spirit in heaven.

FEAST OF THE EPIPHANY

FIRST READING : Isaiah 60 : 1–6. Arise, shine; for your light has come, and the glory of the Lord has risen upon you. For behold, darkness shall cover the earth, and thick darkness the peoples; but the Lord will arise upon you, and his glory will be seen upon you. And nations shall come to your light, and kings to the brightness of your rising. Lift up your eyes round about, and see; they all gather together, they come to you; your sons shall come from far, and your daughters shall be carried in the arms.

Then you shall see and be radiant, your heart shall thrill and rejoice; because the abundance of the sea shall be turned to you, the wealth of the nations shall come to you. A multitude of camels shall cover you, the young camels of Midian and Ephah; all those from Sheba shall come. They shall bring gold and frankincense, and shall proclaim the praise of the Lord.

EXPLANATION : The prophet (second-Isaiah probably) is trying to cheer the exiles by foretelling the glorious future of the new Jerusalem which is not yet rebuilt. The special radiance of God will illuminate it. Gentiles (who once despised it) will bring their riches to it. From East and West peoples will flock to it.

glory of the Lord : The gloom of sadness and despair which enveloped the derelict Jerusalem during the exile will give way to a heavenly brightness, for God will dwell within it once more.

darkness . . . covers the earth : This divine brightness is first and foremost for the Chosen People.

nations shall come to your light : The Gentiles will partake of this divine blessing—their kings will come to share in the light of Zion.

all gather . . . come to you : The glory of Jerusalem will be such that all nations will come to it, and the scattered children of Israel will return home also (see 49 : 22).

abundance . . . sea : The nations of the West (the sea, the Mediterranean) will bring their riches in ships.

Midian, Ephah and Sheba : The eastern nations will come in camel caravans, the usual way of travel through the desert, bearing their gifts.

gold and frankincense : Two of the most valuable means of barter-trading of the time.

proclaim the praise of the Lord : They will come with their gifts to honor the God of Israel, forsaking their pagan idols for the true God.

APPLICATION : The feast of the Epiphany is the feast which commemorates the manifestation of God to the Gentiles. This manifestation began when the Wise Men from the East came to Bethlehem to pay their respects and offer their gifts to the newly-born king of the Jews (see Mt. 2 in today's Gospel). Though the words of second-Isaiah were not understood by his hearers as referring to this event, it was only in the coming of the Magi, to welcome Christ, that they were really fulfilled. Jerusalem was in no sense an attraction for the nations in the intervening centuries. But the Magi at Bethlehem were the first-fruits of the thousands and millions of Gentiles who have since then seen the glory of God in the Babe of Bethlehem and who have figuratively come to Jerusalem from the West and from the East to form the new Chosen People, the new Kingdom of God.

Let us thank God today for having called us, Gentiles, to his kingdom, his Church, and for giving us the means to reach heaven. Let us never imitate the Chosen People of the Old Testament who so often forgot how good God was to them, and who often so provoked him, that he allowed them to be taken into exile as slaves of a pagan nation. We too could bring exile on ourselves, an exile much more fatal than the Babylonian one. Whatever else may be my lot, whatever hardships I may have to suffer during the few years I am on earth, God forbid that I should ever, through my unfaithfulness, cause myself to be excluded from my true home, heaven, where "the glory of the Lord will shine" forever.

SECOND READING : Eph. 3 : 2-3; 5-6. I assume that you have heard of the stewardship of God's grace that was given to me for you, how the mystery was made known to me by revelation, which was not made known to the sons of men in other generations as it has now been revealed to his holy Apostles and prophets by the Spirit; that is, how the Gentiles are fellow-heirs, members of the same body, and partakers of the promise in Christ Jesus through the gospel.

EXPLANATION :
stewardship . . . grace : Paul, writing from a prison in Rome to the Ephesians, whom he had converted to Christianity about 53-56, reminds them of the fact that he was "the Apostle of the Gentiles."
to me for you : This mission to bring the knowledge of Christ to the Gentiles Paul counted as a special grace from God, which it was, both for him and for his converts (see also Rm. 1 : 5; 15 : 15; Gal. 2 : 9).

by revelation : His mission was revealed to him when Christ appeared to him on the road to Damascus (see Acts 9 : 15; 22 : 21).
in . . . generations : The expected Messiah of the Old Testament was understood to be for the Jews only— this was the common opinion of the Jewish people. Even the prophets, many of whom referred to the Gentiles in relation to the Messiah, had no clear understanding of him.
revealed . . . Apostles and prophets :

That Christ the Messiah had come for the Gentiles as well as for the Jews was revealed to the Apostles and prophets—those Christians who in the early Church had special revelations from God for the community. To the Apostles Christ gave the command after his resurrection: "Go therefore and make disciples of all nations" (Mt. 28 : 19; see Mk. 16 : 15; 24 : 47).

members of the same body: The Gentiles are equal members with the Jewish converts in the mystical body of Christ, the Church.

the promise . . . through the gospel: The eternal reward promised by Christ to his followers, in the gospel, and through living up to its teaching.

APPLICATION: St. Paul's thoughts in his prison in Rome are not for himself nor for the fate that awaits him. He is thinking instead of the mission Christ gave him, to evangelize the Gentile nations. He has done much already, and even in prison he does all he can to continue the good work. He writes to his Gentile converts from Rome, to remind them of their great privilege in being called to the Christian faith. They are now God's new Chosen People, they are now members of Christ's mystical body, they are now guaranteed heaven if they appreciate and live up to their vocation.

Today, on the feast of the Epiphany, we are celebrating the coming of the first Gentiles to the feet of Christ. They were the first of the long stream of Gentile peoples and nations that flowed steadily toward Christ's mystical body, the Church, down through the years. We have the privilege of being part of that stream, and St. Paul, who today in heaven is as interested in us as he was in his Ephesian converts, is exhorting us, through these words of his, to appreciate the privilege which is ours. Through the grace of God and not through any merits of our own, we are Christians and are on the road to heaven. "Rejoice and persevere" is St. Paul's advice to us today. If we truly rejoice it means we truly appreciate what the gift of the true faith means. We know where we came from, we know where we are going, and we are certain there is a place, a wonderful, eternal place, to go to. We know too how to get there. This is no mean knowledge in the world of today, where so many seem content to make this world their heaven, and let the future look after itself—if there be a future (and logically to ease their consciences they must hope there isn't one).

Thank God, our faith and our ordinary intelligence tell us there has to be a future life—God would be a cruel joker if he gave us the nature we possess with its spiritual gifts and desires only to have them end in a grave after a few short years. We can rejoice then because we appreciate the great privilege given us, and if we appreciate it we shall hold on to it and follow the path it indicates. We may have to climb some hills and they may look as steep as Calvary, but after Calvary comes the Mount of Olives, the mount of the Ascension.

GOSPEL : Mt. 2 : 1–12. When Jesus was born in Bethlehem of Judea in the days of Herod the king, behold, wise men from the East came to Jerusalem, saying, "Where is he who has been born king of the Jews? For we have seen his star in the East, and have come to worship him." When Herod the king heard this, he was troubled, and all Jerusalem with him; and assembling all the chief priests and scribes of the people, he inquired of them where the Christ was to be born. They told him, "In Bethlehem of Judea; for so it is written by the prophet : 'And you, O Bethlehem, in the land of Judah, are by no means least among the rulers of Judah; for from you shall come a ruler who will govern my people Israel.' "

Then Herod summoned the wise men secretly and ascertained from them what time the star appeared; and he sent them to Bethlehem, saying, "Go and search diligently for the child, and when you have found him bring me word, that I too may come and worship him." When they had heard the king they went their way; and lo, the star which they had seen in the East went before them, till it came to rest over the place where the child was. When they saw the star, they rejoiced exceedingly with great joy; and going into the house they saw the child with Mary his mother, and they fell down and worshipped him. Then, opening their treasures, they offered him gifts, gold and frankincense and myrrh. And being warned in a dream not to return to Herod, they departed to their own country by another way.

EXPLANATION :

Wise men : The term was usually reserved for men learned in the sciences, and among the Persians these were especially the priestly caste.

from the East : From Mesopotamia, of which Persia was the only country of any importance then.

to Jerusalem : Evidently God had revealed to them that a new King of the Jews had been born, and they understood from God that he was a special King; they did not come when Herod or Herod's son was born.

we have seen his star : Astrology was one of the sciences studied by Magi. There was a firm conviction that each human being had his own star and that his fate in life was governed by that star. This was not and is not so, but God made use of their superstition to teach them truth. Some unusual light in the sky

aroused their interest; God did the rest.

Herod . . . troubled : He knew the Magi had not come to honor his son—all his sons were grown up at the time, so he immediately thought of an opponent who would oust him from the throne.

all Jerusalem with him : Not because Herod might lose his throne, but for fear of what excess Herod would go to if any opposition arose.

Christ was to be born : Herod, who was a pagan, may have had some idea of the messianic promises which were the kernel of the Old Testament. But when the question of a *special* king of the Jews arose, some of his household must have told him that this must be the expected Messiah (a Hebrew word meaning the Anointed, or the Christ).

the priests and scribes : They knew their bible, they remembered the prophecy of Micah (see Cycle C (3) 4th

Sunday of Advent), and so informed Herod that Bethlehem was to be the birthplace of the Christ.

time the star appeared : Herod had already formed his plans—he would destroy that infant. The Magi had probably spent months on their journey. The star may have appeared some months before they left. The Baby could possibly be a year old. But Herod took no chances : when ordering the murder of all the male children of Bethlehem (3 : 16), he said : "from two years and under."

I may . . . come and worship : He may have deceived the Magi but could not deceive God.

star . . . over the place : This heavenly light directed them to the place (not the stable, as it says, they "entered the house") where they found the Child.

with Mary his mother : The omission of Joseph may be due to the simple fact that he was absent because he had found employment in Bethlehem as a carpenter. It is, however, more likely that Matthew who has already (1 : 18-25) told of the virginal conception of Christ, is emphasizing here the fact that Joseph was only the foster-father of Christ.

worshiped him : That is, they paid him reverence by prostrating themselves before him. It does not prove they recognized him as God but they did recognize him as a special King.

gold . . . myrrh : Precious gifts to show their respect and esteem.

departed . . . another way : Herod had told them to return to him but God had other plans—the Magi were instructed to return not via Jerusalem but by another route. This gave time to Joseph to remove the Child before Herod could lay hands on him.

APPLICATION : The Magi are the central personages in today's feast of Epiphany. They were pagans who did not know the true God of the Jews. Yet that true God revealed to them that the King he had promised to the Jews had come. The expected Prince was born. They came to Jerusalem, the capital of Judah, expecting, of course, to find the city and the whole country rejoicing. Instead they found suspicion and hatred in the reigning king—a hatred which in a few days turned to murder. Among the religious leaders they found knowledge of their past history, but utter indifference as regards the present and the future. These leaders knew the Messiah would be born in Bethlehem; they must have realized that the Magi were very sure of the truth revealed to them—they would not have come such a long journey on a "fool's errand." In spite of that, the thought of going to Bethlehem with the Magi never entered their minds. These were the leaders who some years later refused to listen to Christ and in spite of his miracles refused to admit his claim that he was not only the promised Messiah, but the true Son of God. These were the men who rejected him because he had mercy on sinners, and spoke of a future life. What they wanted from their Messiah was political power and earthly freedom and prosperity. Like Herod they ended with murder—the crucifixion of the "King of the Jews." The pagan king was not much worse than the indifferent leaders of God's Chosen People.

We too know the true facts concerning Christ, his mission, and his present and future kingdom. Like the leaders of the Jews of his day, we also could become absorbed in the affairs of this life and the quest for wealth, pleasure and power. We could become so totally absorbed in such things as to have neither the interest nor the time to pay our respects to Christ or to welcome him into our homes and our hearts, as our true Lord. God forbid it should ever be thus with us. Rather let us resolve this morning to make the Magi our models, to follow them to Bethlehem and offer him all that we have and are. He will accept our offering and we will return by another way, wiser and better men.

FIRST SUNDAY OF THE YEAR

FEAST OF THE BAPTISM OF OUR LORD

FIRST READING: Is. 42 : 1–4; 6–7. Thus says the Lord; Behold my servant, whom I uphold, my chosen, in whom my soul delights; I have put my Spirit upon him, he will bring forth justice to the nations. He will not cry or lift up his voice, or make it heard in the street; a bruised reed he will not break, and a dimly burning wick he will not quench; he will faithfully bring forth justice. He will not fail or be discouraged till he has established justice in the earth; and the coastlands wait for his law.

"I am the Lord, I have called you in righteousness, I have taken you by the hand and kept you; I have given you as a covenant to the people, a light to the nations, to open the eyes that are blind, to bring out the prisoners from the dungeon, from the prison those who sit in darkness."

EXPLANATION : In second-Isaiah (40–55) there are a series of oracles which describe a "servant of Yahweh" who is to come. He will have the qualities of a king, priest and prophet but to a greater degree. He will suffer for his people and be put to death because he carries out the will of (Yahweh) God to the letter. But God will again raise him up and give him numerous spiritual offspring. The New Testament and Christian tradition have always seen these oracles as messianic prophecies. They were fulfilled in Jesus Christ and in him only.

whom I uphold : God is his support and strength for it is God who has "chosen" him and in him God is "pleased." St. Matthew and St. Mark and St. Luke say these words were repeated from heaven when Christ was baptized by John in the Jordan : "Thou art my beloved (chosen) servant (son, in Greek, can be translated son or servant, like boy in English) in whom I am well pleased." (Lk. 3 : 22; Mk. 1 : 11; Mt. 3 : 17).

I have put my Spirit : In the Old Testament the spirit of God was bestowed on kings, priests and prophets. It is given to the servant because

he will . . . justice to the nations : He shall proclaim the will, the law of God, not only to the Jews but to all nations—his jurisdiction will be universal.

not cry . . . or lift . . . voice : Unlike oriental despots, he will accomplish his missions quietly and kindly.

bruised reed . . . burning wick : Nothing is more useless than a broken reed, nothing more loathsome than a smoking wick as used in the lamps of those days. Yet this servant can and will make something of them—his mercy and power can reach to the very dregs of humanity. Our Lord speaking of "mercy" applies these verses of Isaiah to himself (Mt. 12 : 15–21).

Justice in the earth : To establish the justice, that is, the will of God on earth, is his mission—he will persevere, come what may, until he has done this.

the coastlands : The nations will anxiously wait until he comes to bring them his teaching, i.e. the law of God. The Jews have some knowledge of it already.

I . . . Lord have called you : His mission is from God; his power is from God, "I have grasped you by the hand," and **I . . . the hand :** refers to Christ's human nature. The words used are those used in describing Adam's creation.

covenant . . . light : The Jews had already a covenant, a pact with God, but the servant will make a new one and the nations will share in it; they too will have his light.

Blind . . . prisoners . . . darkness : His work is to open the spiritual eyes of people, to free them from the captivity and the darkness of sin and ignorance of God.

APPLICATION : This prophecy of second-Isaiah was chosen for today, the feast which commemorates the baptism of Christ in the Jordan, because on that occasion the Father's voice from heaven proclaimed that Christ was "his beloved servant in whom he was well pleased." Following the interpretation of the inspired Evangelists and of the ancient and constant tradition of the Church, we can have no hesitation in seeing in these words of second-Isaiah, written five centuries or so before Christ, a description of the Savior who came on earth to teach Jew and Gentile the new law of God, the law of love and mercy.

He who was the Son of God took our human nature in order to represent us, and *as one of us* to give *our* heavenly Father the perfect obedience and service which no mere man had done ever since the creation, and which no mere man could ever do. This perfect obedience or service of God which Christ, the perfect servant, gave the Father, went as far as the acceptance of the shameful and excruciating death on a cross. But all this he accepted gladly for us—it was in our name he did it—and because he did it, we are all raised to a new relationship with God. He has made us all, Jew and Gentile, the whole human race, adopted sons of his heavenly Father.

As members of his mystical body we can now, because he is our Head, give a service to God worthy of our new status, a service which God accepts from us because it is given to him and through "Christ our Lord."

Today, as we offer the Mass, the sacrifice of Christ renewed before our eyes, let us try to realize the privilege that is ours. We are able, through Christ, to offer a sacrifice which gives infinite honor to God. We are able in spite of all our weaknesses and all our faults to give a service that is pleasing to God and to make some return for all he has done for us. We have become "good and faithful servants" because Christ the Son of God became the perfect servant of God for our sakes.

SECOND READING : Acts 10 : 34–38. Peter opened his mouth and said : "Truly I perceive that God shows no partiality, but in every nation anyone who fears him and does what is right is acceptable to him. You know the word which he sent to Israel, preaching good news of peace by Jesus Christ (he is Lord of all), the word which was proclaimed throughout all Judea, beginning from Galilee after the baptism which John preached : how God anointed Jesus of Nazareth with the Holy Spirit and with power; how he went about doing good and healing all that were oppressed by the devil, for God was with him."

EXPLANATION : These verses of Acts are read for us today because they contain a reference to our Lord's baptism. This reference occurs in a very interesting event which took place soon after the Ascension and is described in Acts 10 : 1; 11 : 18. Cornelius, a pagan Roman officer stationed in Caesarea in Palestine, a devout man who admires the God of the Jews and the religion of the Jews, is told by an angel to send for Peter. Peter in the meantime has seen a vision from which he learns that the Gentile is as welcome into the fold as the Jew. He comes to Cornelius and baptizes him and his household—the first Gentile family to be accepted into the Christian Church and by none other than by the Prince of the Apostles, Peter himself. Having heard Cornelius's story, Peter has these words to say :

God shows no partiality : Because of the vision he saw and because of the words of Cornelius he has just heard, from which it is evident that Cornelius is dear to God, Peter understands that Christ's salvation is not only for Jews but for Gentiles too.

who fears him . . . to him : He who accepts and respects God does God's will.

the word to . . . Israel : Christ preached to the Jews only, but he gave the order to his Apostles to preach to all nations.

preach . . . by Jesus Christ : This is the essence of the gospel : peace with God and peace between all men brought about by Christ's sojourn on earth.

Galilee . . . John preached : Peter gives a brief summary of Christ's public life in Palestine.

God anointed Jesus : This refers to the descent of the spirit in visible form on Jesus at his baptism in the Jordan, and to the words of the Father proclaiming him his beloved servant—the Messiah. He was the Messiah from the moment of his conception but this was first made evident on the occasion of his baptism and proved apodictically at his resurrection. This was his anointing, i.e. the moment of his inauguration, as the kings and priests were anointed when they actually took on their office.

doing good . . . healing : A reference to the miracles of Jesus of which Cornelius must have heard.

oppressed . . . devil : Epilepsy, madness and most mental illnesses as well as many bodily defects, were attributed directly to the devil at that time. By healing the sufferers, Christ showed his power over the demons.

God was with him : He had the divine power which miracles demand, only God can alter the laws of nature, which he has made. Prophets and holy men in the Old Testament worked miracles by calling on God to give them this power; Christ was God; through his own power he worked his miracles.

APPLICATION : That day, nearly two thousand years ago, when Christ by his baptism in the Jordan, began his public preaching of salvation for all men, is a day—a feastday—no true Christian can ever forget. The baptism of John was for sinners—a sign of change of heart and a turning to God. Christ had no sin, he had never turned away from God, he was God—but he was the representative of sinful humanity. He represented us sinners that day and opened the door of salvation for us. In that ceremony Christ was proclaimed by the heavenly Father to be his son and faithful servant, and the power of the Holy Spirit came upon him.

But this was all for us; as God he already had all things in common with the Father and the Holy Spirit. But in his human nature—our weak human nature which he took on himself in order to be one of us, and our representative—he was on that day proclaimed God's true and faithful servant. At the same moment we human beings were accepted *in him* and *through him* (i.e. through his perfect obedience even unto the death on the cross) as God's adopted children.

The mission of Christ was for us. The Incarnation took place because God's infinite love wanted man, the masterpiece of his whole creation, to have a share in the divine gifts of the Blessed Trinity. God united the divine with the human nature in Christ. We mortal men were raised above our human nature; we would become immortal, not that we would never die on this earth—Christ himself died in his human nature—but "he would raise us up on the last day" to share forever with the Father, the Holy Spirit and the Incarnate Son the eternal bliss of heaven.

How could a Christian, one who knows all this, ever refuse to do the little part he is called on to do—"to fear God, that is, to reverence and respect him and to do what is right"? Reverence and respect for God should come easily from anyone who realizes what God has done for him. But true respect for God is not proved by a few distracted prayers and a grudging attendance at Sunday Mass. It is proved by striving to keep the laws Christ gave us, i.e. doing what is right, every day of our lives. This is difficult at times but if we keep our eternity—the unending life—before our eyes, the few short years of hardship and training on earth, will seem very short indeed. There is no comparison between what God has prepared for us, and promises us, and the trifling conditions he asks us to fulfill in order to earn his promised reward.

GOSPEL : Matthew 3 : 13–17. Jesus came from Galilee to the Jordan to John, to be baptized by him. John would have prevented him, saying, "I need to be baptized by you, and do you come to me?" But Jesus answered him, "Let it be so now; for thus it is fitting for us to fulfill all righteousness." Then he consented. And when Jesus was baptized, he went up immediately from the water, and behold, the heavens were opened and he saw the Spirit of God descending like a dove, and alighting on him; and lo, a voice from heaven, saying, "This is my beloved Son, with whom I am well pleased."

EXPLANATION : John's mission was to prepare his fellow-Jews for the inauguration of the messianic kingdom, expected and eagerly awaited, for centuries. His baptism, a washing of the people in the Jordan waters, was an outward sign of their inner repentance, and a turning of their hearts to God. Jesus had no sins of which to repent, and his heart was always with God. He was God in human nature, but he wished to be associated with all pious Jews, and so, like them, to be baptized by John. This was his way of inaugurating the messianic era. God's revelation to the Baptist and to the bystanders, which immediately followed the baptism, showed that it was the inaugural act of Christ's messianic mission.

Jesus . . . Galilee : Nazareth was a town of Galilee, and there Christ had lived as a humble carpenter for nearly thirty years. He had given no indication of what he truly was, except for his devout life of obedience to God's law and to his parents. A rabbi, or teacher of religion, had to have reached full manhood according to the Jewish custom before he was allowed to teach. Jesus obeyed this custom, even though he could have begun to teach as early as the age of twelve, as we know from the incident in the temple related by St. Luke (2 : 41–48). He faithfully obeyed all the legitimate customs of his fellow-Jews of the time.

he saw . . . dove : The Baptist (and the bystanders also, as the visible form of a dove would imply) saw the Spirit of God alighting on him, to signify the beginning of his mission as Messiah. In the Old Testament the Spirit of God is always given for a specific task (see Jg. 3 : 10; 6 : 34; Num. 11 : 7 etc.). Christ's task, already indicated by the Baptist, may be deduced clearly from the words of the voice from heaven :

This is . . . pleased : It is generally admitted that these words are a declaration that Jesus is in truth the "servant," foretold by Isaiah (cf. Is. 42 : 1–9; 49 : 1–6; 50 : 4–11; 52 : 13—53 : 12), but the substitution of "Son" for servant (the Greek word *pais* has both meanings), was a result of the firm conviction which the Apostles and the first Christians had, that Christ was indeed the Son of God. But it is his messianic role which is emphasized here, a role so clearly foretold in the texts of Isaiah, on the "suffering servant," quoted above.

APPLICATION : Christ, our beloved Savior, began his messianic mission, the mission of enabling the whole human race to be sons of God and heirs of heaven, with an act of self-humiliation. He insisted on going through John's baptismal rite, which was only for sinners, even though he had no sin to repent of. He did this, firstly, because he was the representative of all sinners, and had come "to take away the sin of the world," and secondly, in order to set sinners of all time an example of true humility and true repentance.

During the Christmastide just ended, the Sunday lessons from holy Scripture have reminded us, again and again, of the humiliations Christ endured on earth for our sakes. The greatest of these, of course, was the Incarnation, God taking the nature of man, the Creator becoming a creature, the master making himself a slave. Add to this, the reception he got when he came among us, his birth in a stable, his cradle a manger, his forced flight into Egypt, his life of poverty in the despised town of Nazareth, where he earned his meager livelihood by the sweat of his brow like the most ordinary of men.

All this was for me and for you! He suffered all of this, and much more, notwithstanding the fact that, as God, he foresaw the ingratitude he would receive in return, from the vast majority of those for whom he suffered. All of us here today, you and I, have shown him our share of this ingratitude. We have not only forgotten to thank him, but we have positively offended him by our sins. We have grumbled and complained, and perhaps openly rebelled, when he asked us to follow him on the path of humiliation and suffering, which he trod before us for our sakes.

What human benefactor, what fellow-man, who had put himself to great inconvenience, and caused himself humiliation and personal suffering in order to help us, would not wash his hands of us, forever, if our return was forgetfulness, thanklessness, ingratitude and even insult, in return for all he had done for us? And could we blame him? But God is not a human benefactor. His love, his mercy, his understanding and sympathy, are not finite and limited like those of men. His love is for sinners, as well as for saints. It is reaching out to us every day and every hour of the day, recalling us to a sense of duty, a sense of gratitude, and indeed a sense of self-interest in our eternal welfare.

Meditate for a few moments today on the lesson of this Gospel reading. Think of the magnitude of the humiliations and the sufferings that Christ, God's Son, endured in order that you could have eternal happiness. Your own earthly troubles, your worldly aches and pains, will then appear small in comparison. Instead of upbraiding God for letting them happen to you, you will welcome them as his means of making you more like his beloved Son, and so more worthy to be among the brothers of Christ who will share his heaven with him for all eternity.

SECOND SUNDAY OF THE YEAR

FIRST READING : Isaiah 49 : 3, 5–6. The Lord said to me, "You are my servant, Israel, in whom I will be glorified." And now the Lord says, who formed me from the womb to be his servant, to bring Jacob back to him, and that Israel might be gathered to him, for I am honored in the eyes of the Lord, and my God has become my strength—he says : "It is too light a thing that you should be my servant to raise up the tribes of Jacob and to restore the preserved of Israel; I will give you as a light to the nations, that my salvation may reach to the end of the earth."

EXPLANATION : We have here a messianic prophecy, which is the second of the "servant of Yahweh" or "suffering servant" prophecies, found in second-Isaiah, chapters 42–53. These were prophecies uttered during the Babylonian exile to encourage the Jewish exiles to persevere in their trust in Yahweh, who would soon liberate them from Babylon, and eventually send them the long-expected Messiah, promised to Abraham. This "one who is to come," will give perfect obedience to God, will bear severe hardship, will be "a man of sorrows," and because of this he will bring back all men, Jew and Gentile, to God. He will represent the whole human race, and earn for it the true friendship of God.

The Lord . . . glorified : The "servant," the Messiah, says God has appointed him as his (faithful) servant who will bring all men to reverence and glorify God. The insertion of Israel after "my servant," is very probably a later gloss.

In verse 5, the servant will bring back *Israel* to God, so he can hardly be identified with Israel.

formed . . . womb : He was predestined before his birth for this office. He is to be in human nature, formed in his mother's womb by God. The full implication of these words can be seen in their fulfillment, as described in Luke's Gospel : "the angel answered (Mary's question regarding her virginity) : 'the Holy Spirit will come upon you and the power of the Most High will cover you with its shadow and so the child will . . . be called the Son of God' " (Lk. 1 : 34–36; see Mt. 1 : 18–22).

to bring back . . . Israel : The Chosen People were to be the first to whom the Messiah and his message would come.

light . . . nations : This was only a small part of God's purpose in sending his Son. The salvation which the Messiah brought was for the Gentiles too, "even to the end of the earth."

APPLICATION : That these prophecies were remembered and studied by devout Jews is evident from the words of Simeon, who because of his saintly life, had been promised that he would live to see the promised Messiah. The promise was fulfilled. He was inspired to come to the temple on the very day the Blessed Mother brought the Infant Jesus for his presentation, as the Mosaic law prescribed. Simeon recognized in the Infant Jesus the promised Messiah. He took him in his arms, and sang his "Nunc dimittis" . . . "My eyes have seen the salvation you have prepared for all the nations, a light to enlighten the pagans and the glory of your people Israel" (Lk. 2 : 27–32).

We too today, twenty centuries later, can sing that "Nunc dimittis" with heartfelt joy and gratitude, for we can see, and have seen with the eyes of faith, that our Savior, the Son of God, has come among us, and has enlightened us with the true knowledge of our real purpose in life.

Because of our Christian faith, life has an entirely different meaning for us from what it had for our pagan ancestors. The real pagans today—those who never heard of Christ, or of his all-loving divine Father—and especially the self-made pagans, who have heard of God and of his divine Son who became man, but do not believe in his divinity or his message, must and should, look at human life on earth as a torture invented by some cruel sadistic joker. If they happen to have many of this world's goods they may be able to avoid some of life's hardships. But wealth cannot guarantee them good health and peace of mind; in fact, its possession adds to the torture that the thought of having to die very soon must constantly cause them. They must leave it all and end in a hole in the ground, like their pet dog or any other dumb beast of the field.

If, instead, the neo-pagan has little of this world's possessions, his few years on earth are but a purgatory in preparation for NOTHING.

Let us thank and bless God, with the saintly Simeon and with the millions of devout Christians down through the centuries, for having given us the light of faith, and the source of that light, his beloved Son who came among us. Because of Christ's coming on earth, and because of the gospel of peace and hope that he has left to us, we know the purpose of life. We know why we are here, we know why we must expect and accept trials and troubles, because we know where we are going, and understand that life's tribulations, as well as its joys and consolations, are the road which leads us to the true life.

Thank you, God of love, for sending your divine Son to make heaven available to us! Thank you for having given us the Christian faith, which shows us what path to follow in our journey to that real heaven. Please forgive our past forgetfulness of your goodness, and give us the grace to follow our loving Savior more closely in future, so that when death calls us we may be worthy of the eternal life he earned for us. Amen.

SECOND READING : 1 Cor. 1 : 1–3. Paul, called by the will of God to be an apostle of Christ Jesus, and our brother Sosthenes.

To the church of God which is at Corinth, to those sanctified in Christ Jesus, called to be saints together with all those who in every place call on the name of our Lord Jesus Christ, both their Lord and ours :

Grace to you and peace from God our Father and the Lord Jesus Christ.

EXPLANATION : Corinth, an important port-town and a Roman colony, was materially prosperous but morally corrupt. In the year 50 A.D., St. Paul went there to preach the gospel. He made some converts among his fellow-Jews, and many among the Gentiles, during his two years' stay there. He left for Ephesus in 52 A.D., and from there he wrote this Epistle to the church of Corinth, correcting some of the abuses that had crept in, and adding further explanations to the gospel message he had already taught them.

The opening verses of this letter have been chosen for our reading today, because they show the prophecy, read in the first lesson, as fulfilled among the pagans, as well as emphasizing the purpose of the Messiah's coming : the sanctification and true enlightenment of all nations.

Paul . . . Jesus : Paul rightly attributes his vocation, to be an apostle of Christ, to the direct intervention of God. He had done nothing to deserve it. In fact, he had done everything to make himself unworthy of it. Of the bitter opponents of the early Christians in Jerusalem, he was the most bitter. A vision of the risen, glorified Christ, seen on the road to Damascus, had changed his outlook, and his way of life (see Acts 9 : 1–19).

our . . . Sosthenes : Paul, in his letters, usually mentions one or more of his assistants in the apostolate, who are with him at the time of writing. Evidently, Sosthenes was known to the Corinthian Christians. Most probably he was the Sosthenes mentioned in Acts 18 : 17, who was the president of the Jewish synagog and was beaten up by the Jews who opposed Paul, because most probably, he had favored Paul and was about to join him.

church of God : This is a translation (coming through the Greek LXX) of the Hebrew phrase *Qahal Yahweh,* that is, the assembly of Yahweh, meaning God's Chosen People. It shows that from the earliest days the Christian Church saw itself as God's Chosen People of the new covenant.

called . . . saints : Called to be Christians and eventually saints.

call . . . name : Accept and reverence :

our Lord . . . Christ : The basis of Christianity is the divinity of Jesus Christ, the man who had lived and died in Palestine (our Lord=our God).

their Lord and ours : He is God, not only of the Corinthians but of all nations.

grace and peace : Two of the usual blessings found in the openings or the endings of the Christian letters. Peace, in St. Paul, has a fuller meaning through the Hebrew *shalom,* which meant well-being. Christian peace, especially in St. Paul, means reconciliation with God (see Col. 1 : 20; Rom. 5 : 1), and unity among the brotherhood (Col. 3 : 15).

APPLICATION : The conversion of Paul on the road to Damascus—the changing of the arch-enemy of Christianity into an apostle of Christ Jesus —was, after the descent of the Holy Spirit on Pentecost day, the greatest benefit God conferred on the infant Church. From the moment he began his apostolate, he devoted himself wholeheartedly and exclusively to the spreading of Christianity among the Gentiles. Every thought of his mind, every bodily energy, and every gift of grace and nature which he possessed, were given to that one end : to make Christ and his message of salvation known to all men. He did not forget his fellow-Jews, but when they rejected him and his master Christ, he turned to the Gentiles.

During the 34 years of his missionary activity, he founded flourishing Christian churches in the principal towns of Asia Minor and Greece. In Rome itself he played a big part in the spread of the faith, from his prison cell. After his release in 62 from his first imprisonment, he spent another four or five years preaching in Spain and Italy, and revisiting his earlier converts. Finally, in the year 67 or thereabouts, he laid down his life in Rome for the faith for which he had lived.

His apostolate did not end with his death. He has left to the Church a collection of letters, which are a source of encouragement and instruction for all who would live a true Christian life.

Today, he reminds each one of us that being Christians means we are called to be saints in heaven, when our years on earth come to an end. In heaven we shall certainly be, if we appreciate properly our Christian vocation, and live as true Christians, each day of our earthly lives. This does not mean that we must not take any interest in the affairs of this world, nor does it mean that we should neglect the earthly duties, which our own particular walk in life imposes on us. On the contrary living a truly Christian life means that we carry out faithfully and honestly our daily tasks. Our week-days are as important as our Sundays. In fact, if our week-days are dishonestly, that is sinfully, spent, our Sunday display of "Christian devotion" is not only a sham, it is an attempt at deceiving God. In reality, we are deceiving only ourselves.

Paul is still praying and wishing for us that grace and peace which he wished for the Corinthians. We need God's grace, and his divine help, to live in peace and union with him, and with our fellowmen. Paul's prayer for us will be heard. Christ our Lord will not refuse his most devoted apostle if, but only if, we heed Paul's words, and try every day to follow the path of faith which he preached to the Corinthians, and is still preaching to us today.

GOSPEL : John 1 : 29–34. John saw Jesus coming toward him, and said, "Behold, the Lamb of God, who takes away the sin of the world! This is he of whom I said, 'After me comes a man who ranks before me, for he was before me.' I myself did not know him; but for this I came baptizing with water, that he might be revealed to Israel." And John bore witness, "I saw the Spirit descend as a dove from heaven, and it remained on him. I myself did not know him; but he who sent me to baptize with water said to me, 'He on whom you see the Spirit descend and remain, this is he who baptizes with the Holy Spirit.' And I have seen and have borne witness that this is the Son of God."

EXPLANATION : All four Evangelists narrate the part played by John the Baptist to prepare the people for the proximate arrival, in their midst, of the promised and long-expected Messiah. The Baptist had spent his youth, and early manhood, living as a hermit in the desert of Judah. God revealed to him that the time had come for him to go to the Jordan riverside, to bring the glad tidings to the Chosen People.

Many thought the Baptist was himself the Messiah, but he vehemently denied this and said he was not even worthy to be his lowliest slave. On the previous day, recognizing the Lord's superiority, he had reluctantly baptized Jesus in the Jordan. During that washing with water, the Baptist saw the Holy Spirit descend on Jesus, and heard the voice from heaven proclaiming him to be his chosen servant foretold by Isaiah (see Gospel of last Sunday—Feast of the Baptism of our Lord).

Jesus coming . . . him : Jesus remained for a few days (see Jn. 1 : 33–45), near the Jordan region where John was preaching.

Behold . . . God : The Baptist points out Jesus to the people as the Messiah, the "servant of God" of whom Isaiah spoke. John spoke in Aramaic, and in that language the same word *Thalya* can mean lamb or servant. The "pass-over lamb" (Ex. 12 : 7) had no part in taking away sin, but the servant of God, in Isaiah 53 : 7, is compared to a "lamb led to the slaughter," and suffering for the sins of his people.

he . . . I said : This is, on the previous day (Jn. 1 : 27; Mt. 3 : 6).

he was . . . me : Not in his human nature, because the Baptist was born six months before Christ, but in his divine nature (see Jn. 1 : 1). Whether the Baptist understood the full meaning of his words or not is doubtful, but when John the Evangelist was writing his gospel the real meaning of these words was clear to all Christians.

revealed to Israel : The Baptist's mission to prepare the Chosen People for the proximate arrival of the Messiah.

Spirit descend . . . dove : See last Sunday's gospel regarding this fact.

he . . . said : John the Baptist had evidently never met Christ. This is understandable : they lived about 80 miles apart, a long distance in those days. Besides, John spent his days in the desert.

baptizes . . . Spirit : John's baptism was only a type, or symbol, of the real baptism with which Christ would baptize men. He would confer on them not only "grace," friendship with God, but sonship of God.

witness . . . God : The Baptist's witness was, that the man he had baptized and on whom he had seen the Spirit descend (the sign of identification given him by God—"he who sent me"), was the expected Messiah, the servant described in Isaiah. At that time, his divinity was not yet recognized, nor was it made manifest, but by the time the Evangelists wrote, it was the basic teaching and belief of the Church.

APPLICATION : At last the promise, made to Abraham when God commanded him to leave his home, his country, and his kin (Gen. 12 : 1–3), was fulfilled. The Messiah who would bring blessings to Jew and Gentile (to all mankind) had arrived. Eighteen hundred years of expectation had at last come to an end. During these long years of waiting, God had, through his prophets and through his prophetic actions, renewed the hope in the hearts of his Chosen People. These prophecies and prophetic actions had given indications that the expected one would be someone very close to God, someone who was more than a mere man. Yet, who among the Chosen People could ever have thought that the "Promised One" would be the very Son of God in human nature?

His contemporaries, when he came, refused to believe this truth even though Christ had, during his public ministry, made claims to equality with God the Father, and had proved these claims by miracles (see, for example, the story of the paralytic : "Your sins are forgiven you . . . who can forgive sins but God alone? . . . to prove to you . . . he said to the sick man ' get up . . . and go home,' " Lk. 5 : 17–25).

But we must try to understand how difficult for a strict monotheistic Jew were the thought of three persons in God (the Trinity), and the idea that the infinite God could be in a limited, finite, human nature (the Incarnation). Our Lord himself showed that he understood their lack of faith, when he said on the cross : "Father, forgive them for they know not what they do" (Lk. 23 : 24).

We, however, have no reason for any such doubts or scruples. The full story of Christ's conception, birth, life, preaching and miracles, crowned by his death on the cross and his glorious resurrection, is in itself sufficient guarantee and proof that he was indeed the Son of God-made-man for our sakes. The spread of his Church among the Jews and Gentiles is another convincing proof. What sane man would accept self-mortification, undergo trials and hardships, even martyrdom, or give up all the attractions and pleasures of the body, if he were not convinced that the story of Christ, and therefore his gospel-message, were true?

The sad part is that, while we have every reason, in this world and the next, to believe in Christ and follow his teaching, so many nominal Christians live as if Christ himself had never lived and died for them. Their hearts are centered in the pleasures, the power and the wealth of this earth. These are passing things, which they will have to bid goodbye very soon. They devote their energies to getting all this world can give them. Its final gift to them will be a six-feet-by-three hole in the earth.

If we neglect our vocation as Christians, if we forget God's infinite love for us, as shown in the Incarnation, and if we fail to learn the lesson he taught us: that our purpose in this short life is to earn the eternal life after death, we, too, could become renegades to Christianity, traitors to Christ and our own greatest enemy.

Christ came to make us his brothers and children of the heavenly Father. He came to die for us so that we could live forever. We can deny our heaven-sent brother, we can leave our father's home, we can lose the eternal happiness that Christ has won for us. God forbid that we should ever be so foolish, so ungrateful to God and Christ, and so inimical to our own real self-interest.

THIRD SUNDAY OF THE YEAR

FIRST READING: Isaiah 9:1–4. In the former time God brought into contempt the land of Zebulun and the land of Naphtali, but in the latter time he will make glorious the way of the sea, the land beyond the Jordan, Galilee of the nations.

The people who walked in darkness have seen a great light; those who dwelt in a land of deep darkness, on them has light shined. Thou hast multiplied the nation, thou hast increased its joy; they rejoice before thee as with joy at the harvest, as men rejoice when they divide the spoil. For the yoke of his burden, and the staff for his shoulder, the rod of his oppressor, thou hast broken as on the day of Midian.

EXPLANATION: This reading for today's Mass is another prophecy, concerning the messianic days, given by Isaiah in the eighth century B.C. It describes the new era of liberty and joy, which the future Messiah will usher in. Galilee, the north-eastern corner of Palestine, had been populated for the most part by pagan Assyrian settlers, who had been brought in there after the fall of the northern kingdom (Israel) in 722. Paganism had control, and the few Chosen People, thinly scattered in the region, found it difficult to retain their faith in the true God, and more difficult still, to practice it. All that will be changed, the prophet says.

Zebulun and Naphtali: These were two of the 12 Tribes who settled in the region of Galilee after the Exodus from Egypt (Jos. 29:21–39).

brought into contempt: In other words, disappeared practically after the Assyrian invasion.

way of the sea: The route from the East (Syria, Assyria and Babylon) to Egypt passed through Galilee, and then down by the Mediterranean coast.

God . . . glorious : "In the latter time," that is, in the messianic days, the new era as opposed to the old, Galilee will play a great part. It was there that Christ spent most of his public life, and from there, eleven of his twelve Apostles came (see Mt. 4 : 12–16 in today's gospel, where he considered this prophecy of Isaiah fulfilled when Jesus began to preach in Galilee).

darkness . . . light : The darkness of paganism and slavery will be changed into the bright noon-day light of Christianity and real freedom.

multiplied . . . joy : Numerous believers in the true God will inhabit this territory, and serve him with joy in the great era that is to come.

joy . . . spoil : Their joy, because of their real liberation, is compared to that of the farmer when he collects an abundant harvest, or a conquering army dividing the spoils of a victorious battle.

yoke . . . rod : All the instruments and symbols of the oppressor will be removed.

as on . . . Midian : That future day will be a day of victory, like the day Gideon defeated the Midianites, one of the greatest victories of the period of the Judges (Jgs. 7 : 16–25).

APPLICATION : " The people who walked in darkness have seen a great light." Before the coming of Christ 98 per cent of the human race lived in the darkness and hopelessness of paganism. They knew nothing of the good God who made them; they knew nothing of their real purpose in this life, and did not know that there was a future life to look forward to. The two per cent, or less, of Jews had a knowledge of the true God. But it was a limited knowledge and their service of him was motivated by fear rather than by love. Their belief in a future, endless life was weak in the best of them, and was not accepted at all by many.

The Incarnation has changed all that. The darkness of paganism, and ignorance of the true nature of the God who created us, has been banished forever by the coming of the Son of God among us as man. From it we have learned not only that God loves us, and that he is interested in every one of us, but that he loves us with an infinite, unlimited love, and wants each one of us to share in his own eternal kingdom of happiness forever. For this reason he has raised us up to adopted sonship, through the Incarnation in which his real Son took on himself our lowly created nature and became our brother.

This was God's plan for mankind for all eternity. Sin had entered the world of men in the meantime. Man became so proud of the gifts he possessed, that he forgot the giver of those gifts, and not only refused to thank his benefactor, but turned against him and made for himself false gods. This, however, did not change God's plan nor his infinite love for man. Christ, the son of God in our human nature, was the representative of all men. He gave perfect obedience to his heavenly Father in the name of us all. Because he was God, as well as man, he made a perfect atonement for the sins of all men, of all time. No mere human being could ever have done this.

We, Christians today, are walking in the full light of the knowledge of God's infinite love for us, of God's eternal plan for our unending happiness, of the almost incredible mystery of that divine love for us sinners, which was shown in the Incarnation. If an earthly king should leave his palace, and go among his peasants, and dress and live like one of them, in order to educate them and clothe them in royal robes, and then bring them to his palace to live with him as his adopted children, what an amazing act of benevolence and love this would be. Yet, the Creator of all things, the King of the universe, did this and more for us.

Does anyone among us really appreciate what God has done for him? Does he realize what the privilege of being a Christian means? Does he ever thank God sufficiently for the benefits he has conferred on him? We have all seen the great light which expelled all darkness. We are living under its heavenly illumination. But are we all benefiting from that light as we should? Will it lead us to the eternal, everlasting light —the purpose for which it was given to us?

This is a question each one of us must ask himself today, and the future fate of every one of us will depend on the answer we can honestly give to this question.

SECOND READING: 1 Cor. 1:10–13; 17. I appeal to you, brethren, by the name of our Lord Jesus Christ, that all of you agree that there be no dissensions among you, but that you be united in the same mind and the same judgement. For it has been reported to me by Chloe's people that there is quarreling among you, my brethren. What I mean is that each one of you says, "I belong to Paul," or "I belong to Apollos," or "I belong to Cephas," or "I belong to Christ." Is Christ divided? Was Paul crucified for you? Or were you baptized in the name of Paul? Christ did not send me to baptize but to preach the Gospel, and not with eloquent wisdom, lest the cross of Christ be emptied of its power.

EXPLANATION: St. Paul not only preached the gospel, and set up Christian communities in the principal towns of the Roman Empire, but he kept a life-long interest in their spiritual welfare. He revisited the principal churches which he had founded, and if he could not do so, he kept himself informed of their progress, and wrote letters to them to praise them, or correct them, if things were not as they should have been. The section of one of these letters, which we read today, is an example of such a correction.

I appeal . . . Lord: Paul calls them his brothers, and begs them to be truly brothers to one another, to preserve unity among themselves. This appeal is not just the wish of Paul, but it is Christ's commandment, who put loving neighbor as oneself next to the command to love God (Mt. 22:36). Hence it is in the name of the Lord Jesus Christ that he makes this appeal.

it has . . . me: See how he kept in touch with his converts!

I belong . . . Christ: Some divisions, or factions, began to be set up in the church of Corinth since he had left them. These were, most likely, caused by the arrival of some converts from outside. Apollos, an Alexandrian Jewish convert, was an eloquent preacher and some may have thought him a greater apostle than Paul, even though he was not an apostle. Others preferred their first teacher, Paul. Jewish converts from Palestine who would have been converted by Peter (Cephas=the Rock, the head and fountain of the Church), were all for Peter, while some declared that their loyalty was to Christ, rather than to any of his messengers.

Is Christ divided? : All are brothers of Christ and in Christ. Christ wishes all to be one, as does Paul.

Paul crucified : It was Christ who died for them. It was Christ who made them members of his body, the Church, through baptism. Paul did no more than bring this good news to them.

not send . . . baptize : Evidently, Paul's whole time was spent teaching the faith to the people. His helpers baptized those whom he had prepared to become members of Christ's mystical body—the Church.

not eloquent . . . power : It was not by human persuasion, or human eloquence, that Paul converted the people—this was done by the power of Christ. The people were convinced that God loved them, and that he had proved that love by sending his divine Son to live among them and die on the cross for them.

APPLICATION : Human nature has changed little through all the centuries. When it has, it has often been a change for the worse not for the better. In today's lesson, we are a bit shocked to hear that the first generation of Christians were beginning to form factions and divisions in the church of Corinth. Three years had barely passed since they had dedicated their lives to Christ, their one ambition and desire being to follow Christ on the road to heaven. Now, already, personal pride was entering in. Some were looking down on others, because it was the great Paul who instructed and converted them. The others resisted this, and claimed a greater superiority, because they had a more eloquent teacher, Apollos of Alexandria, while others, again, began to despise both of these parties, because they were instructed by the head of the Apostles, the Rock, Peter.

How silly it may seem to us! What does it matter who taught them, if they have learned the truth about Christ and God's great love for them? To St. Paul it did not seem silly, but very dangerous, because it showed that human pride, the basic sin, and the first sin of human nature, was beginning to revive once more among them.

This letter of St. Paul, recalling to their minds who their true master and teacher was, very likely put an end to this trouble in Corinth, but it did not banish foolish pride from among men, nor worse still from among Christians who profess to be followers of the humble Christ.

Do we need examples to show the dreadful damage that pride has inflicted on the Church of Christ? The long-standing divisions and separated sects in the Church—a scandal to the followers of Christ and an impediment to the conversion of unbelievers—are the direct result of the actions of proud men. It is not necessary here to apportion blame—Paul did not when reproving the divisions in Corinth—but what is necessary is that all Christians should take to heart Paul's reminder that it was Christ who died for us all and that Christ is not and must not be divided.

Thank God, and thanks to the saintly Pope John, Christians are today taking active steps to reunite the Church of Christ once more, to bring together once again the separated members of Christ's mystical body. The Roman soldiers nailed his human body to the cross. We, his professed lovers and followers, have torn his mystical body apart. We have been more cruel to him than the ignorant pagan soldiers.

In this essential and urgent work of reunion each one of us, even the humblest and least educated, can play an important part. First, by fervent prayer that God will give all Christians, ourselves included, the grace to come together in true love of God, and true love of our Christian neighbor, no matter what his interpretation or even misrepresentation of Christ's teaching may have hitherto been. Secondly, by showing in our daily actions that we recognize all men, not alone Christians, as our brothers. We have all been raised to sonship with God, we have all been redeemed by Christ. We must, if we

love God and appreciate what God has done for the human race, want all men to avail themselves of this marvelous supernatural gift that he has intended for them.

The most effective and convincing way, in which we can prove our true concern for the eternal welfare of all our fellowmen, is by living a true Christian life ourselves. If we have burning within us the fire of God's love, its heat will spread and warm the hearts and minds of all those with whom we come in contact.

The leaders and theologians of all the Christian bodies will have their very important part to play in this sincere attempt at reunifying the Church of Christ. But unless we, ordinary Christians, bring down the fire of God's love on earth, by our prayers and good works, their task will be ever so difficult, if not nearly impossible. We'll begin to put our own Christian faith into daily and hourly practice and start to storm heaven for the success of this most necessary endeavor. God will not be deaf to the requests in word and deed that come from his humble servants.

GOSPEL : Matt. 4 : 12–23. When Jesus heard that John had been arrested, he withdrew into Galilee; and leaving Nazareth he went and dwelt in Capernaum by the sea, in the territory of Zebulun and Naphtali, that what was spoken by the prophet Isaiah might be fulfilled :

"The land of Zebulun and the land of Naphtali, toward the sea, across the Jordan, Galilee of the Gentiles—the people who sat in darkness have seen a great light, and for those who sat in the region and shadow of death light has dawned."

From that time Jesus began to preach, saying, "Repent, for the kingdom of heaven is at hand."

As he walked by the Sea of Galilee, he saw two brothers, Simon who is called Peter and Andrew his brother, casting a net into the sea; for they were fishermen. And he said to them, "Follow me, and I will make you fishers of men." Immediately they left their nets and followed him. And going on from there he saw two other brothers, James the son of Zebedee and John his brother, in the boat with Zebedee their father, mending their nets, and he called them. Immediately they left the boat and their father, and followed him.

And he went about all Galilee, teaching in their synagogs and preaching the gospel of the kingdom and healing every disease and every infirmity among the people.

EXPLANATION: The Baptist's mission, of proximate preparation for the Messiah, ended when John was arrested by Herod, because he had publicly denounced the king's adulterous association with his brother's wife. Jesus then began his own mission, and moved from near the Jordan in Judea up to Galilee. He continued John's call to repentance, "for the kingdom of heaven is at hand." He chose his first four disciples near Capernaum and worked many miracles around Galilee. In this missionary activity of Jesus in Galilee, Matthew sees fulfilled the prophecy of Isaiah, given over 700 years before. True freedom, and the true light of faith, have come to that once oppressed region.

leaving Nazareth: From the Jordan, Jesus went to Nazareth and remained there for a short while. The wedding feast at Cana, near Nazareth, described by John (2:1–12), and the preaching of Christ in the synagog of Nazareth, which resulted in his rejection as described by Luke (4:16–30), can be fitted in here. Matthew and Mark do not mention these events, but both of them mention a visit of our Lord to Nazareth later.

Capernaum: A small town on the northern shore of Lake Genesareth. It was the home-town of Peter and Andrew and, probably for that reason, it became Christ's base or second home-town during his missionary journeys around Galilee and the neighboring districts.

Zebulun . . . dawned: On the prophecy of Isaiah which Matthew now sees fulfilled, see today's first reading.

Simon . . . Peter: Simon, son of Jonah, was the original name. This name was replaced by Peter (*Cephas* in Aramaic, which means a rock, which in turn became *Petros* in Greek, the masculine form of *petra*), when Christ appointed him the foundation and head of the Church (Mt. 16:18): "Thou art Rock and on this rock I will build my Church."

Andrew . . . James . . . John: Peter and Andrew were blood brothers, so were James and John. All four earned their livelihood fishing in the Lake of Genesareth, a good source of living at that time.

Immediately . . . father: All four had listened to the Baptist's preaching, and were probably disciples of John. But on hearing John's declarations, and having probably heard the words from heaven, they left John and followed Jesus of their own accord. The three synoptic Gospels do not mention this voluntary following of Jesus by the first disciples, but all three mention this official call to the apostolate. This official call does not deny the earlier, personal attraction toward, and belief in, Jesus as the Messiah which they had received through the Baptist.

teaching . . . synagog : The Jews attended their synagog in large numbers on the Sabbath day. This was a suitable occasion for Christ to meet them and explain his message in person to them.

gospel . . . kingdom : The messianic kingdom, or new era in the relationship between God and men. It is also called the kingdom of heaven for, though it would begin on earth, its culmination and perfection would be in heaven.

healing . . . disease : These were acts of compassion and mercy, rather than proofs of his claims. However, he did occasionally work miracles to prove his divine claims (see the case of the paralytic and the power to forgive sins— Lk. 5 : 17–25).

APPLICATION : The true freedom, and the true light which Christ brought to Galilee nearly 2,000 years ago, were brought on earth for us too. The Christian faith, and the Christian knowledge of God's love for us and his infinite interest in our real welfare, are his gift to us and to all men of goodwill, who will accept it. Thanks be to God for this marvelous gift of faith, which frees us from the slavery of paganism and sin, and lights the road to heaven for us, amidst the darkness and drudgery of this life.

The lot of the insensitive tree in the forest, and of the dumb beast of the field, would be far and away a better one than the lot of rational man, who knew neither God nor any plan that God had for him. Man with his superior gifts, which raise him above all the other earthly creatures, can experience and enjoy happiness and well-being. The joy of living, the gift of life, is the greatest source and the basis of all his other earthly joys. His short life on earth may be frequently interspersed with troubles and trials, aches and pains, yet to stay alive is so innate a desire, and so strong a determination, that the common opinion of men is that it is only a mentally deranged person who can commit suicide.

But there is a shadow, the shadow of death, over the very greatest of our earthly pleasures. Through our gift of intellect, and the experience of our race, we all know that life on this earth has to end, and no matter how many more years we may think we still have left to us, death will be too soon, far too soon, when it comes. The neo-pagan (the real pagans, who have not heard of the true God, have some god or gods in whom they hope and trust) will do all in his power to forget this dreadful thought of death, but he is reminded of it everyday of his earthly life. To live with this thought that all he shall be in eighty years' time is a bucket of lifeless and useless dust, must be an anticipation of the hell he may also have to face after his death.

We love life, we too want to live on, we too know that this cannot be on this earth, but thanks to the merciful revelation given us in our faith, we know that the infinite love of God has prepared a future life for us. We know that Christ, by his life and death as man among us, has made us adopted sons of God. We know we have an eternal life awaiting us, when we depart from this life, and that for the Christian who did his best to be a true follower and disciple of Christ, death is not the end but the beginning of our real life. The grave is not our goal forever, but the key which opens the door to eternal life and eternal happiness for us.

With this divine knowledge revealed to us by and through Christ, everything falls into place in our earthly sojourn. We have our joys and our sorrows, our births and our burials, but we know, with the certainty of God's word, that these are but sign-posts that mark our stages toward, and direct our steps to, our eternal home. We are superior to the tree of the forest therefore, and to the beast of the field, not only because of our earthly gifts of intelligence and will, but because we know that our end on earth will not be like theirs. It will be, instead, the great awakening to a joy and happiness of which, at present, we can only form a very limited and vague idea. We Christians have indeed seen a great, a heaven-sent light.

FOURTH SUNDAY OF THE YEAR

FIRST READING: Zephaniah 2:3; 3:12–13. Seek the Lord, all you humble of the land, who do his commands; seek righteousness, seek humility; perhaps you may be hidden on the day of the wrath of the Lord. For I will leave in the midst of you a people humble and lowly. They shall seek refuge in the name of the Lord, those who are left in Israel; they shall do no wrong and utter no lies, nor shall there be found in their mouth a deceitful tongue. For they shall pasture and lie down, and none shall make them afraid.

EXPLANATION: Zephaniah, one of the twelve minor prophets, preached during the days before King Josiah (640–609) introduced a religious reform into Judah. Under Manasseh and Amon (687–640), Yahweh was abandoned and almost forgotten by the leaders of the Chosen People, and even by very many of the ordinary people. But the "day of Yahweh" was coming, the day when God would come to punish not only the pagan nations, but also Judah for her pride and rebelliousness. However, a remnant, a small percentage of God's people, would survive the day of wrath, if they continued to be humble and obedient to God's commands. It is this section of Zephaniah's prophecy that is read for us today.

seek ... commands: The people in high positions, and the rich merchants had forsaken their God (1:1–18), and would suffer for this. Here the prophet turns to the poor, the "humble of the land who do his commands" and exhorts them to continue to be faithful—to keep

on seeking him in justice and humility.
day of the wrath . . . Lord : Some future day, in which God would intervene in a special way in human affairs. That day, according to Zephaniah, would be a day of punishment for those who had deserted God.
I will . . . you : God promises that he will preserve a remnant, a small portion of his Chosen People, who will re-main loyal to him, who will continue to trust in him until he fulfills his age-old promises.
those . . . Israel : This remnant will keep God's commandments and be honest and truthful.
none . . . afraid : God will be their shepherd; he will pasture and protect them, as a true shepherd provides for and protects his flock.

APPLICATION : How truly this prophecy was fulfilled is evident from the history of the Chosen People. The northern ten tribes had already disappeared from the pages of sacred history, when Zephaniah lived, because of their desertion of Yahweh. Judah (and Benjamin) were taken as exiles to Babylon in 587. Although allowed to return some 50 years later, many remained in Babylon because they had managed to become wealthy there, and had forgotten Yahweh and their special vocation. Of those who returned, many soon forgot things spiritual, and set their hearts on a new, temporal kingdom which would rule the nations (thus misinterpreting the messianic prophecies).

Hence, when the Messiah came among them and proclaimed a kingdom not of this world, but of preparation for their eternal welfare, the true kingdom of God, they had no time for him. They rejected him, and forced the pagan Romans to condemn him to the death of the cross.

But "the remnant" had still been preserved by God. The "humble of the land" welcomed him and believed in him. Though his crucifixion stunned them for a moment, his glorious resurrection proved to them that he was what he claimed to be—the Son of God, in human nature. The cross became the banner around which the few faithful Jews and the Gentiles, in their thousands, rallied. His kingdom on earth, the Church, was established and spread rapidly, and mankind had the road to the eternal kingdom of heaven marked out for them. The Good Shepherd, who truly laid down his life for his sheep, had come. Henceforth his flock—the community of his faithful followers—could feel that their life, their future, was in the safe hands of one who had proved his love for them.

We, Christians of today, are the successors of that chosen remnant. We realize how unworthy we are of such an honor. We have too often proved ourselves unworthy in the past. We are still in the fold. We still have the Good Shepherd as our leader; a Shepherd who has infinite compassion and mercy, because he is God as well as man. He is still the Shepherd who leaves the ninety-nine ones in the pen, and goes after the lost sheep and brings it back on his shoulders rejoicing. Day after day, and hour after hour, he is still doing just that for his wayward followers. Is there one among us who has not experienced this infinite mercy and this divine compassion, not once, but many times in his life?

Let us thank God today, for having preserved a remnant among his thankless Chosen People, through whom he sent us his divine Son to be our Good Shepherd. Let us humbly say that we are sorry for all the times we were wayward, erring sheep in the past, who caused him so much extra pain and labor. And above all, let us sincerely promise him that, with the help of his divine grace, we will endeavor to be more worthy members of his chosen flock in the future.

SECOND READING : 1 Cor. 1 : 26–31. Consider your call, brethren; not many of you were wise according to worldly standards, not many were powerful, not many were of noble birth; but God chose what is foolish in the world to shame the wise, God chose what is weak in the world to shame the strong, God chose what is low and despised in the world, even things that are not, to bring to nothing things that are, so that no human being might boast in the presence of God. He is the source of your life in Christ Jesus, whom God made our wisdom, our righteousness and sanctification and redemption; therefore, as it is written, "Let him who boasts, boast of the Lord."

EXPLANATION : See last Sunday's second reading, on St. Paul's care for his converts.

consider . . . brethren : The Corinthian Christians have been called by God to be members of Christ's kingdom on earth, in order to be members of God's heavenly kingdom in the hereafter. This is something they must never forget.

wise . . . birth : Their worldly standing had nothing to do with this Christian call. Most of them were from what the worldly would consider the lower classes, but they were high in God's esteem.

foolish . . . despised : God's standards are the very opposite of worldly standards. The wise ones of this world, that is, those who use all their intellectual and other gifts, to acquire power and privilege for themselves here below; the strong ones of this world who lord it over others; the nobles (in their own esteem) who despise those of lower rank

—all of these are already surpassed and left behind (put to shame) by the very ordinary people whom God has chosen as his own.

no human . . . boast : It was not because of any worldly supereminence that Christians received their call. They have nothing personal to boast of in God's presence, and his judgement is truth itself.

he is . . . Jesus : It is from God, through the Incarnation of his divine Son— " through Christ Jesus," that they have received the Christian faith, which brings with it :

wisdom . . . redemption : True wisdom governs men's whole life from birth to the beatific Vision; in true righteousness they serve God as he ought to be served; sanctification and redemption are the result of the Incarnation. Christ atoned for, and took away, all the sins of the world, and gave to men the power and the means to be saints and the adopted

D

sons of God in heaven with him.

Let . . . boasts : The true Christian has marvelous gifts and privileges, but they are from God. It is God only, and not himself, that man must thank, and to him alone must he give the credit.

APPLICATION : In these words which St. Paul wrote to his recent converts centuries ago, he is speaking, today, to you and to me also. He is reminding us of the immense debt of gratitude that we owe to the loving God, for the divine gift of the Incarnation. The Son of God shared our human nature with us, so that we could share his divinity with him. He not only atoned for the sins of all men, by his earthly life and death, but by taking our nature and uniting it with his divinity, he raised all men up to the sublime status of adopted sonship with God.

This was God's plan from all eternity. Hence the wonderful spiritual powers given to man, powers that raise him above all other earthly creatures, and make him capable of enjoying divine sonship. There is only one obstacle that can keep any man, Christian or pagan (that is, the pagan who through no fault of his own has not heard of God or of Christ his Incarnate Son), from losing the eternal enjoyment of this sonship. That one obstacle is serious sin of which one does not repent.

No sane Christian, and no honest pagan who obeys the dictates of his conscience, could hardly be so foolish as to let this obstacle block the road to his eternal welfare. We Christians, especially, have so many reminders of God's infinite love for us and of his eternal interest in our welfare, that it would seem impossible for us ever to forget all we owe him. But the fact is that there is sin in the world and Christians too can, and do, offend their loving Father. There are Christians who go on living in a state of sin. Doing this, they are risking the eternal life of happiness that Christ won for them at such cost, should their hour of judgement come on them while in that state. God forbid that we should ever be so foolish as to take this risk, the greatest and the most fatal risk that any man could take on earth.

Instead, today let us think once more of the great gifts God has given us. Above and beyond the gift of human life with all its noble qualities, a gift we have in common with all men, we Christians have a knowledge, through the Incarnation, of what God has planned for us and of what God intends to make of us. We have also the supernatural help of the teaching Church and of the sacraments. Christ knows how weak our human nature is and, therefore, he left us ways and means to help us to overcome our weaknesses.

If we fail to use the remedies and the helps he has left to us in his Church we are not only guilty of gross ingratitude to God and to Christ but we are proving to be our own worst enemies,

GOSPEL: Matthew 5:1–12. Seeing the crowds, Jesus went up on the mountain, and when he sat down his disciples came to him. And he opened his mouth and taught them, saying: "Blessed are the poor in spirit, for theirs is the kingdom of heaven. Blessed are those who mourn, for they shall be comforted. Blessed are the meek, for they shall inherit the earth. Blessed are those who hunger and thirst for righteousness, for they shall be satisfied. Blessed are the merciful, for they shall obtain mercy. Blessed are the pure in heart, for they shall see God. Blessed are the peacemakers, for they shall be called sons of God. Blessed are those who are persecuted for righteousness' sake, for theirs is the kingdom of heaven. Blessed are you when men revile you and persecute you and utter all kinds of evil against you falsely on my account. Rejoice and be glad, for your reward is great in heaven."

EXPLANATION: In the first two readings for today, the lowly state, the poverty, the meekness of Christ's followers, is contrasted with the wealth, the power, the worldly wisdom of those who will ignore him. In the third reading, the Gospel, we have the word of Christ himself, describing the qualities or dispositions which he expects his followers to possess in this life, if they hope to be with him in heaven hereafter. The theme is very similar in all three readings. St. Matthew gives us here what are commonly known as the Eight Beatitudes.

the mountain: As Moses proclaimed the Old Law on a mountain so Christ announces the New Law on a mountain.

opened his mouth: A formula to stress the importance of his declarations. In the Old Testament, God opened the mouths of the prophets to teach the people.

Blessed: In Latin *Beatus* or *beatitudo* hence the English "beatitudes." It means "fortunate," "happy."

poor in spirit: That is, the real poor: those who are poor, not only through want of this world's goods, but because of their total subjection to their masters, to whom they were slaves in fact or at least in practice. This was the status of the vast majority of the then known world. These poor people suffer now, but in the kingdom that is to come they will be the possessors of supreme happiness (provided they follow Christ and his teaching).

mourn . . . comforted: Not those who have earthly sorrows and every reason to be sad (these are already mentioned in the first beatitude and again in the third), but most probably those who bewail the sad state of the Chosen People, caused by their disloyalty to God; such sincere people will soon have the comfort and consolation of the long-awaited, messianic kingdom.

meek . . . land: Very similar to the first group, the dispossessed who have to suffer in silence. But it is they and not their oppressors, their masters, who will enter into the true promised land, heaven, of which the land of Canaan was but an earnest and a symbol.

hunger . . . righteousness: The hunger and thirst is spiritual rather than corporal. Those who are whole-heartedly wishing that God will fulfill his promises, and indicate the truth of his word given to Abraham, and repeated down through the centuries. Jesus tells these people their desires are about to be fulfilled.

merciful . . . mercy : The Incarnation was the supreme act of divine mercy. Man, a mere creature and a sinful creature at that, was adopted by God as a son, and promised a part in the divine, eternal inheritance. So every true follower of Christ must be merciful to his fellowman. If he is, he will have a share in God's merciful plan, and if he has failings God will treat him with mercy. Mercy and true love of neighbor are closely akin. The man who has no compassion for his neighbor does not love him.

pure . . . God : The purity of heart mentioned here, is not only chastity, but a sincere cleansing of the heart from all sin as opposed to the many levitical forms of external cleansing to which the Pharisees of the time were so addicted (see Mt. 23 : 27, where our Lord compares the Pharisees to white-washed sepulchres; externally they looked clean and pure, but internally full of decaying corpses). Those who are free from sin at the moment of their judgement will enter God's household, they will be forevermore in his presence.

peacemakers . . . God : The peacemaker is one who not only is at peace and fraternal harmony with all men, but one who assumes the task of reconciling neighbors who have quarreled. This is a specific virtue of the messianic kingdom, and therefore a virtue by which every true follower of Christ can be recognized. Such Christians are the true Israelites, who can rightly claim the title of "sons of God" in a much more realistic sense than that in which the Israelites claimed it.

persecuted . . . heaven : Jesus promises those who will suffer for his sake (and he therefore foretells that persecution will be the lot of many because of their adherence to the messianic kingdom), that their reward will be great in heaven.

APPLICATION : We all learned these eight beatitudes by heart during our early school days, and we have all tried, let's hope, to take them to heart in the intervening years, and put them into practice. Our world has changed a lot since our Lord proclaimed these words of divine wisdom in Galilee, but unfortunately, for the vast majority of mankind, life on this world is still a struggle against poverty, privation and persecution. In this respect it has changed very little, if at all, for the greater part of the human race.

The slaves and the serfs of our Lord's day had sufficient food to keep them fit for work because their masters needed their labor; today, there are millions in the underdeveloped continents who are not slaves but who are continually on the borderline of starvation through no fault of theirs. And in the developed countries there are many thousands who are in dire need because of the injustices of their fellowmen.

The early Christians suffered tortures and death for professing the faith of Christ, but they felt privileged to be called on to imitate their divine master. Today, there are millions of Christians who are suffering a long-drawn-out, and therefore a more difficult persecution, for the same cause.

To all of these, to the poor, the despised, the persecuted, Christ gave the promise of an eternal reward which would repay a thousand-fold the short-lived sufferings of this life. It was this promise that gave the strength to so many, and is still giving the strength to thousands, to persevere in their faith and in their trust in God, no matter what their earthly lot may be.

While consoling the underprivileged, Christ has positive commands for those of his followers who are in a position to carry them out. "Blessed are the merciful," he says. That is to say: those who will show mercy and compassion to their suffering, needy fellowmen, can rest assured that God will be merciful to them, when they meet him on their judgement day. The contrary is equally true and certain. The man who shuts his eyes and his heart to the hungry, the oppressed, the naked among his fellowmen need not, and cannot, expect mercy and forgiveness, when he has to render an account of his life's work. This is a thought that should make many of us examine our consciences more closely.

A second command which would do so much to make life on this earth more tolerable for all, if only all Christians and all other men of goodwill carried it out, is: "Blessed are the peacemakers." The vast majority of men of all creeds and colors desire peace. They hate war, which brings nothing but misfortune and sufferings to all sides. If only the peace-loving people of the earth could make their voices heard, life's journey would be made so much easier for all. Christians, surely, should give the lead here; it is Christ himself who

told us that it is one of the principal means to happiness, not only in the next life but in this. Life for all of us has enough of sadness, trials and catastrophes without adding the man-made sufferings and afflictions of war.

What can I do?, you may well ask. You can begin by eradicating from your own heart every racial, national or other prejudice. You can then spread this leaven among your fellowmen, whenever you associate with them. You can become active in forming and promoting societies for national and international peace. Peaceful means will alone breed peace. Violence can only breed violence and is a miniature war. It is true that the masters on both sides of a divided nation, or divided groups of nations, are doing all in their power to prevent their "slaves," those over whom they exercise control, from meeting and fraternizing. But their power is limited, they are not one-tenth in number of the people whom they seek to control. The nine-tenths will eventually prevail, if they persevere in their good intentions.

It is true that the real, the eternal, beatitude or happiness can be found by men only in heaven, but a certain portion of it could be found by us on this earth if mercy and peace-making were practiced by all Christians and non-Christians of goodwill.

FIFTH SUNDAY OF THE YEAR

FIRST READING: Isaiah 58 : 7–10. Thus says the Lord: "Share your bread with the hungry, and bring the homeless poor into your house; when you see the naked, cover him, and do not hide yourself from your own flesh. Then shall your light break forth like the dawn, and your healing shall spring up speedily; your righteousness shall go before you, the glory of the Lord shall be your rear guard. Then you shall call, and the Lord will answer; you shall cry, and he will say, Here I am. If you take away from the midst of you the yoke, the pointing of the finger, and speaking wickedness, if you pour yourself out for the hungry and satisfy the desire of the afflicted, then shall your light rise in the darkness and your gloom be as the noonday."

EXPLANATION : The prophet is here telling his fellow-Jews that God commands them to practice charity towards their needy neighbors. It is only by so doing, that they can prove their love and loyalty to their God and expect favors from him in return.

share . . . cover him : The faithful Jew is urged by God, through his prophet, to provide the three basic necessities of life for a fellow-Jew: food, clothing and shelter. This was already commanded through Moses (Let. 19 : 17): "You shall love your neighbor as yourself," but was often forgotten, alas! That a fellow-Jew only was a neighbor was necessitated by the prohibition to mix with the idolatrous nations.

light . . . healing : If they practice true charity their hope for the future, namely, that God will send the Messiah, will grow strong and bright; and the healing of the wound, that is, the offences to God which caused the exile (this part of Isaiah is post-exile), will be swift and sure.

righteousness . . . Lord : True charity for neighbor will prove their true loyalty to God, and God in his turn will be their light and their security. They can trust in him.

call . . . answer : Then their prayers and their other religious practices will be answered by God.

take . . . yoke : If they cease to oppose their weaker neighbors :

pointing . . . wickedness : "The pointing finger" is better translated as "the clenched fist" (J.B.) or "oppression" (CCD New American version); it is the same as "yoke" above.

speaking wickedness : cursing and abusing their neighbors.

pour . . . out : If they undertake charitable works, with a sincere heart, they can look forward to a bright and happy future.

APPLICATION : Charity, true love of neighbor which produces good deeds of kindness, is equated with love of God, by Christ himself (Mt. 22 : 39), and is the proof of one's true love for God, according to St. John (1 Jn. 4 : 20). All our protestations that we love God, and all our devotions and prayers are not only useless, but are lies to God, if we hate one of our neighbors or refuse to help a needy one, when we are able to do so.

This is a truth that should make us all stop and think. We may wonder sometimes, if God has forgotten us when all the prayers for something we need so badly, are left unanswered. Perhaps it's because we have been liars to God's face, or have professed that we loved him and trusted in his goodness while we hated one of his children—our neighbor.

It is true, there are so many calls on our charity today. So many are in dire need at home and abroad, that we can grow tired of sharing our bread or our clothes. But God does not expect, or demand of us, to help everybody, but only as many as we can. However, the obligation of forgiving a neighbor who has offended us, or of ridding ourselves of any racial, color or religious bias, which we hold, costs us only a wee bit of personal pride. Are we so important that nobody should dare ever offend us, or rather do we act as if an offense were meant? Nearly always a friendly word from the one who was offended, or who thought that he was offended, will put the record straight and mutual charity will be restored. Are we so superior because of our color, or our creed, that we can behave insultingly, that is uncharitably, towards a neighbor who hasn't got these same gifts that we have the good fortune to possess?

Charity begins at home, but it must not end there. Be peaceful, forgiving, cheerful, helpful in the home and you will find how quickly the other members of the family will react and begin to imitate you. Outside of the home our nearest neighbors must be the first to feel the warmth of our charity. Without prying into their private affairs, which is the opposite of charity, we can easily learn, from casual conversation, if any of them are in need of some of the spiritual or corporal works of mercy.

Remember this : he who loves his neighbor with a Christian love, which means that he is always ready to help any neighbor in need, is thereby proving his true love for God. Should the time come when he himself should be in need of help, he is assured of God's help, and his neighbors will not be found wanting either.

SECOND READING : 1 Cor. 2 : 1–5. When I came to you, brethren, I did not come proclaiming to you the testimony of God in lofty words or wisdom. For I decided to know nothing among you except Jesus Christ and him crucified. And I was with you in weakness and in much fear and trembling; and my speech and my message were not in plausible words of wisdom, but in demonstration of the Spirit and power, that your faith might not rest in the wisdom of men but in the power of God.

EXPLANATION : On last Sunday, we heard St. Paul telling his Corinthian converts that they had not been called by God to become members of Christ's Church, because of any worldly nobility or power or wealth which they had. They were called from, what the world would call them today, the "lower classes." But they were high in God's esteem. Today, he tells them that his success among them was not due to any great gifts of body or mind which he had, or displayed. Their conversion was due not to his earthly wisdom or rhetorical powers, but to the spirit and the power of God which was made manifest among them. It is to God's power alone that they owe their faith.

testimony of God : The divinity of Christ, proved by the Father's raising him from the dead, was the basic doctrine of the Christian faith. This was God's testimony to the truth of Christ's claims and Christ's teaching.

lofty . . . wisdom : Paul did not convince the converts of the truth of Christianity by human wisdom or great oratory.

Christ . . . crucified : This was the burden of his preaching : Christ was the Son of God who took human nature for our sakes, died nailed to a cross, but rose again conquering death for all of us.

with you . . . trembling : From the human point of view he felt he was a most unsuitable teacher for such a sublime message but :

the Spirit and power : What he lacked was amply compensated for by the Holy Spirit, whose gifts were showered on the church of Corinth in great abundance and variety (see 1 Cor. 12 : 1–11).

that your faith . . . not rest : It was through the power of God, manifested in the gifts of the Holy Spirit, and not through any human eloquence or powers of persuasion, that the church of Corinth was founded and spread so rapidly and so successfully.

APPLICATION : The movie, "The Song of Bernadette," which gives the story of Lourdes and its miracles, begins with the following words which are displayed across the screen : "For him who does not believe in God no explanation is possible; for him who believes in God no explanation is necessary." These words very aptly describe the lesson to be drawn from today's reading from St. Paul's first letter to his Corinthian converts. These had not become Christians, they had not changed their mode of life and their outlook on life, because of any human or earthly influence.

Their conversion was due, exclusively, to the divine power which convinced them that there was a God—a God of power and majesty, but especially a God of love, who so loved mankind that he sent his divine Son on earth to bring all men to heaven. The facts of the Incarnation, of Christ's life, death and resurrection were told to them by Paul, but the gift of faith which enabled them to accept these facts as objective reality and truth was given them by God.

Worldly wisdom had no part in getting the Corinthians to give up their pagan life of easy morality and loose living, to take on themselves the restrictions and obligations of the Christian faith. Today, more perhaps than in any previous age in the Church's history, there are Christians who are looking for human reasons, that they think will justify them in giving up the restrictions and obligations of the faith of Christ, to return to the freedom and self-indulgence of neo-paganism.

Human reasoning alone cannot give one an adequate and sufficient knowledge of God, but it does give us a basis on which God's gift of faith can solidly rest. But there is no human logic, no human reasoning, which can disprove the existence of God, or the fact that he has revealed to us sufficient knowledge of himself, to enable us to reach the end he has planned for us.

It was "the power of God," and the merciful kindness of God, that brought the gift of faith to the Corinthians. Paul was but the weak, fragile vessel in which that gift came to them. It was the same power, and the same merciful goodness of God, which also brought the gift of faith to each one of us through fragile and weak, human vessels. We freely and gladly accepted it, when we came to the age when we were able to appreciate its value, not only for the after-life, but also for our years on earth. Our faith has been called, by the irreverent, the "opium of the people." If peace of mind, consolation in sorrow, a knowledge of whither we are going, an understanding of the meaning of suffering, as well as the explanation of true joy, can be called an "opium," then the more of that opium which this world gets the more human, as well as the more divine, it will become.

May God make his gift of faith grow stronger in each one of us, so that we may learn daily more and more about the infinite love God has for us; about the humiliations the Son of God suffered in his Incarnation for our sakes; and about the great eternal future the Father, Son and Holy Spirit have prepared for us.

GOSPEL : Matthew 5 : 13–16. Jesus said to his disciples, "You are the salt of the earth; but if salt has lost its taste, how shall its saltness be restored? It is no longer good for anything except to be thrown out and trodden under foot by men.

"You are the light of the world. A city set on a hill cannot be hid. Nor do men light a lamp and put it under a bushel, but on a stand, and it gives light to all in the house. Let your light so shine before men, that they may see your good works and give glory to your Father who is in heaven."

EXPLANATION : This is part of the Sermon on the Mount, part of which we heard last Sunday also, in the beatitudes. This Sermon, as it now appears in Matthew (5–7), was not delivered by Christ on one occasion. Matthew, as is his wont, has collected here many sayings and teachings of Jesus, uttered on different occasions, and formed them into one complete unit. The Sermon, as we find it in Matthew, is a synopsis or the substance of the new dispensation —the new order of salvation which Christ established. The primacy of the interior spirit (in contrast to the external observance of the Mosaic law), detachment from the wealth and goods of this world, and a love of all men as brothers under the universal fatherhood of God, are its essential doctrines.

said . . . disciples : His disciples include not only the Apostles but all those who, among the crowds following him, were anxious to learn his message—the messianic message of salvation which they believed he had come to give.

salt of the earth : As usual, Christ uses everyday similes to bring his teaching home to his hearers. Salt was essential for preserving and savoring meat and other foods. If it ceased to have the power and the flavor of salt, it was no longer of any use. In fact, it was a deception and deceiver, and deserved to be crushed into the ground. So, also, the true Christian must become the preserver and promoter of the true religion, the true service of God on earth.

if salt . . . taste : It becomes not only useless but harmful; the man who uses it, will find his meat not only unpalatable but unfit for human consumption —it will have become putrid and decomposed. So, likewise, will be the evil effects of the lapsed Christian on his neighbors.

saltness be restored : The mineral, salt, can do nothing to bring back the natural qualities it once possessed, but the Christian, who allows the power of God to work in him, can return to his former state, provided, of course, that God so designs and that the pervert's pride will allow him to admit his error. But these are provisos nobody can presume on.

light . . . world : True Christians, living as true followers of Christ, are the light that will banish the darkness of paganism and of the external formalism of the pharisaic followers of the old law.

under a bushel : The bushel was a wooden vessel for measuring and containing grain. To light a lamp, and cover it with this container, was to render the lamp-light invisible and useless.

Let . . . shine : The Christian must not hide the faith, and the true knowledge of God and of his love for men, which he has received. It is not a gift for himself alone, but its effects must spread out to his neighbors, as the lamp's light spreads around the room.

see . . . works : It is through their truly Christian way of living, doing good to all men as the beatitudes bring out, and keeping the commandments of God, every day of their lives, that Christians can enlighten their non-Christian neighbors.

Father in heaven : The true followers of Christ will give external glory to God by their own saintly lives, and their example will bring in many others to the acknowledgement of God. They will thank this true God, who is not only their creator but their loving father.

APPLICATION : No less an authority than Christ himself calls his true followers the "salt of the earth," and the "light of the world." These are titles of honor, surely, and of the greatest distinction. Christ is putting his true follower on almost a level with himself. He *was* the light of the world; he *was* the salt of the earth. He it was who gave men the knowledge of the true nature of God, as shown by the Incarnation. He it was who gave this life its flavor, who gave this life its meaning, its preservation. By his death and resurrection he took away the sting of death, and removed its eternal corruption, by the guarantee and promise of a resurrection to an eternal life.

This very Christian knows, and this knowledge every Christian helps to bring to those who are ignorant of it, if he lives his life daily and sincerely. The Christian who does this, is really another Christ; he is continuing his work of salvation during his years on earth. He is the salt of the earth and the light of the world. How many of us here present this morning, can truly say that these honorable titles, which Christ gives to his followers, are given to us?

In true humility, we can all say that we are far from worthy of any such honorable titles. Yet in all sincerity too, many if not the majority among us, are doing their little bit of Christ's work, in cultivating their own small corner of his vineyard. The parents who teach the Christian way of life to their children by word, and especially by example, are spreading the Christian faith. The workmen, whether in office or factory, who show that they are Christians by their honesty, charity for their fellowmen, their respect for God, and the things of God, in their speech, are spreading their Christian faith. All those who show moderation in their personal expenditures, and donate some of their savings to help their brothers, their fellowmen who are in need, these are true disciples of Christ and are co-operating with him in bringing God's children back to their Father who is in heaven.

Unlike the salt that has lost its flavor, and the light that is kept under the bushel, the Christian who has thus behaved can change his attitude, provided he is aided by God's grace which is never refused. He can become once more what he ought to be—a life-preserver for his neighbor.

Life on earth is short. The demands of our Christian life may not always be easy, but we know that if we live up to them, we are other Christs. We are continuing his great work by our own good example to our neighbor, and we are giving glory to God, and are earning for ourselves the eternal light of heaven.

SIXTH SUNDAY OF THE YEAR

FIRST READING : Sirach 15 : 15–20. If you will, you can keep the commandments, and to act faithfully is a matter of your own choice. He has placed before you fire and water : stretch out your hand for whichever you wish. Before a man are life and death, and whichever he chooses will be given to him. For great is the wisdom of the Lord; he is mighty in power and sees everything; his eyes are on those who fear him, and he knows every deed of man. He has not commanded anyone to be ungodly, and he has not given anyone permission to sin.

EXPLANATION : The book of Sirach (which used to be called Ecclesiasticus), is one of the Wisdom books of the Old Testament. It treats of good morals and the true religious philosophy of life. It was written in Hebrew, about 180 B.C., by a man who called himself Joshua ben Eleazer ben Sirach. His grandson translated it into Greek, in Egypt in the year 132 B.C., so that his fellow-Jews, who lived in Egypt and had forgotten their native language (Hebrew), could learn from it much practical wisdom to help them live according to the Mosaic law. This book has still much practical wisdom for us Christians, and today's reading from it is a proof of this.

If you . . . commandments : Sirach has no doubts whatsoever that man has a free will. He is responsible for his deliberate actions. God gave the ten commandments through Moses. They are obligatory on those who know them, and no man can say that he was forced by any circumstances to disobey them.

to act faithfully : A parallelism, a Hebrew method of emphasis. You act faithfully, you keep God's law, when you choose to do so and the choice is yours to make. You are a free agent.

fire . . . wish : God wants a free, willing service. Fire and water represent what is destructive : sin; and what is good and useful : virtue. God gives each man the freedom to choose.

life and death : Another parallelism. Life and death are like water and fire : the latter destroys, the former vivifies. It is not, probably, that the author was here referring to eternal life and eternal death, but rather to true life on earth, that is, the willing service of God as opposed to disloyalty to God which was a form of death—a useless life.

wisdom . . . Lord : He now extols the mighty wisdom of the Lord; through it he can do all things and knows all things.

eyes . . . him : He takes account of those who reverence him and keep his law. "Fear of the Lord," in the Old Testament, means reverence and respect for his infinite wisdom and majesty.

knows every deed : Nothing is hidden from him, and the actions of men are especially noted (unlike the actions of the lower creatures) for reward or punishment.

commanded . . . to be ungodly : Nobody can claim that his ungodly acts are done because God wanted it so. No one has permission from God to sin. The sinner has only himself to blame, and he must realize that God too will blame him, for he was free to avoid sin.

APPLICATION : Any Christian parent or teacher could give us these words of truth and wisdom, and they would be of great value if we heeded them. But this same advice comes to us today not from any human authority but from God himself, who inspired and moved the man called Sirach to write these words of wisdom, which were to last and have value, for all ages and generations of men. We might question a parent's or a teacher's wisdom, or their right, to tell us of our personal responsibility for our actions, but who can question or challenge God's wisdom, or God's right, to teach us the truth concerning ourselves?

We have received the gift of free-will from God. We know that we can serve God by keeping his commandments, or that we can disrespect his authority and refuse to keep his law. Having given us free-will, he cannot force us to be loyal or grateful to him. But if we had not free-will, we should be like the beast of the field who can neither honor nor dishonor God. From the dumb beast God does not expect, nor much less demand, obedience. But from us men, to whom he gave the gifts which put us above all earthly creatures, intelligence and free-will, he does expect and demand obedience and loyal service.

Let us listen to this man Sirach today who speaks to us in God's name. We can keep God's commandments, and we know we can. We can choose to do good or to do evil, but if we choose evil we cannot say we could not help doing so.

We might fool a fellowman by this false line of defense, but the all-wise God who "sees everything" and "knows every deed of man" cannot be deceived. But what decent man and especially what decent Christian, who knows the lengths the good God has gone to in order to give us eternal life, would want to deceive him or be disloyal to him?

Ours is a religion of love, we do not and ought not, avoid sin because we should thereby bring sufferings, and perhaps eternal death, upon ourselves. We avoid sin because it is an insult to our loving Father in heaven, who sent his divine Son on earth to live, suffer and die for us, in order to give us eternal life with the Blessed Trinity in heaven. It should be hard for any true Christian deliberately to offend such a kind, loving Father.

For those among us, who may have forgotten God's love for them, and may have broken his commandments, let them thank God that their hour of reckoning is not already upon them. They may have written many shameful pages in their life's story, but they have not yet finished writing it. There is still time to tear out, or erase from their biography, those pages they should not have written. The loving Father is also the all-merciful, all-forgiving Father. No sinner, no matter how sordid and shameful his actions and his disrespect for God may have been, will turn to him asking for pardon and find his request was in vain. But the sinner who keeps on postponing this return to God and continues to offend him, may find himself in the presence of the just judge when he least expects it.

God's mercy is infinite, but he cannot pardon the free agent who does not want pardon. Notwithstanding his infinite love for all men, he cannot welcome home the prodigals who will not return home.

SECOND READING: 1 Cor. 2:6–10. Among the mature we do impart wisdom, although it is not a wisdom of this age or of the rulers of this age, who are doomed to pass away. But we impart a secret and hidden wisdom of God, which God decreed before the ages for our glorification. None of the rulers of this age understood this; for if they had, they would not have crucified the Lord of glory. But, as it is written, "What no eye has seen, nor ear heard, nor the heart of man conceived, what God has prepared for those who love him," God has revealed to us through the Spirit. For the Spirit searches everything, even the depths of God.

EXPLANATION: Today's reading is a continuation of last Sunday's, in which St. Paul impressed on his converts of Corinth that the Christian faith they had received was a gift from God. They were converted from Judaism and (for the most part) from paganism, not by any oratorical gifts of Paul, nor by any earthly wisdom or philosophy, but by the grace and power of God. In today's pericope he says he has true wisdom to give to those capable of receiving it, but it is a very different wisdom of God, now being revealed to those who are willing to learn it.

among . . . mature: Mature, not only in age but in progress and practice of the Christian faith—spiritual men as opposed to the materially-minded (see 3:1).

rulers . . . age: He is referring to the pagan (Roman) and Jewish authorities of that time. Their wisdom is of this world. It prevented the pagan Romans from recognizing God in his works as Creator (Rom. 1:19–20), and it blinded the Jewish leaders so that they could not recognize the Messiah in Christ Jesus, notwithstanding all the proofs he gave them.

doomed . . . pass away: Their power will come to an end. That of the Jews ended some fourteen years later in 70 A.D. The Roman empire ended some centuries afterwards.

secret . . . God: God's eternal plan for man's glorification and elevation to sonship, to be brought about by the Incarnation of his divine Son, Christ (see Eph. 3:10; Col. 1:15). This divine eternal plan is now being revealed fully in the Christian religion, which St. Paul and his fellow-apostles are preaching. The Jews had an inkling of this plan of God in their messianic prophecies, but the vast majority of them refused to believe it possible.

they . . . glory: It was not Pilate, the Roman authority whose hand was forced by the Jewish leaders, but these very leaders who crucified Christ, because they looked on him as a blasphemer who claimed to be God. St. Paul says he was God: "the Lord of glory" was a Jewish title for Yahweh, the true God.

as it is written : Paul is citing no explicit text of Scripture, but what he says is reminiscent of Is. 64 : 3 and 65 : 16.

no eye . . . men : What God has prepared for those who love him surpasses all human comprehension. Our finite, limited minds, and powers in this life are incapable of forming any concept of what the bounty of the infinite God is like, and what the nature of the eternal happiness he has prepared for us is.

God . . . Spirit : Christians, says St. Paul, have been fortunate in that God's eternal plan for man's elevation and final glorification has been revealed to them, partially by Christ himself, but especially by the Holy Spirit whom he sent, as he had promised, on Pentecost day. On that day the spreading of the Good News of God's infinite love for men began with Peter's first sermon to the multitude of Jews, who had gathered outside the Upper Room (see Acts 2 : 14–40).

APPLICATION : The mental outlook of the world of today is little changed from that of St. Paul's day. The philosophy and the wisdom of the rulers of this age, and unfortunately not only of those rulers, is still earth-bound and worldly. The things of God are openly denied in a large section of our world, while he is shamefully ignored and neglected in the remaining sections which nominally believe in him. Nations, and most of their citizens, are bending all their energies to obtain more and more of the passing, perishable wealth and power of this miserable planet. We are living in a welter of international, limited wars, while all the time the threat of global war, and universal destruction, is hanging like a dark thunder cloud on our horizon.

We have advanced technically beyond the wildest dreams of our forebears, but every technical advance which could and should be a boon for humanity, is turned instead into a possible instrument of human extermination. The brotherhood of man is no longer accepted as a basic human tenet, and it is little wonder, since the fatherhood of God is denied in practice as well as in theory. And it is not only in apartheid and color-prejudiced countries that segregation and suppression of the weaker brethren is practiced, but also, and maybe more so, in the so-called free democracies.

The big business tycoons of today are the counterparts of the Roman slave-drivers. Their shares and their bank accounts are their household gods. Their workers and their poorer neighbors are far less concern to them than their cadillacs, their yachts and their racehorses. They hold solemn funeral rites for their pet dogs, and erect tombstones over their graves, but their charwomen, living in squalor, are not given a spare thought nor a spare dime. But what is worse, this pagan and inhuman worldly philosophy spreads down like a poison gas through the ranks of the less successful middle and lower-middle classes.

This is the direct result of our forgetfulness of, or rather our ignoring, the only true wisdom of life. The eternal happiness of man, planned by God's wisdom and love from all eternity, and effected and revealed in the Incarnation, has been forgotten. Modern man, like the pagans of old, thinks his home and his true happiness are on this earth, hence he rides roughshod over his weaker neighbor, to get all he can out of the few years he realizes he has to enjoy himself.

A return to sanity in our world can be brought about only by a return to a recognition of God's plan for us. Our time on earth is a journey to heaven. The less we load ourselves with this world's goods or interests, the easier our journey will be. The more we help our fellow-travellers on this journey (and this includes all men), the safer and the smoother will be our own travel. Our true happiness, our everlasting happiness, will begin only when we arrive at our earthly journey's end. If we keep on the path marked out for us by our loving heavenly Father, and if we practice true brotherly love on the way, we can rest assured that our journey will not have been in vain.

GOSPEL : Matt. 5 : 20–22; 27–28; 33–34; 37. Shorter Form. Jesus said to his disciples, "I tell you, unless your righteousness exceeds that of the scribes and Pharisees, you will never enter the kingdom of heaven. "You have heard that it was said to the men of old, 'You shall not kill; and whoever kills shall be liable to judgement.' But I say to you that everyone who is angry with his brother shall be liable to judgement. You have heard that it was said, 'You shall not commit adultery.' But I say to you that everyone who looks at a woman lustfully has already committed adultery with her in his heart. Again you have heard that it was said to the men of old, 'You shall not swear falsely, but shall perform to the Lord what you have sworn.' But I say to you, Do not swear at all. Let what you say be simply 'Yes' or 'No'; anything more than this comes from evil."

EXPLANATION : We are still in St. Matthew's Sermon on the Mount. In today's section of it, we find our Lord quoting some of the ten commandments, given by God to Moses, and adding to them. This he does on his own authority : "I say to you," thus putting himself on a level with God, which, as he was God, he could do.

Unless . . . exceeds : The scribes and Pharisees were most rigorous in their external observance of the law of Moses, but this observance of the law lacked true sincerity of heart, and was not done out of charity. They sought the praise of their fellowmen, and thus vitiated all their good actions (see the parable of the Pharisee and the publican in the temple, Lk. 18 : 10–14). Christ tells his disciples and followers that their observance, their religion, must be better than that—they must obey God's commands out of love and true sincerity, or they will not be worthy of heaven.

You . . . kill : Our Lord not only confirms this commandment but adds to it. Murder begins in the mind. Anger unchecked, or worse still, nourished with brooding over one's real or imaginary injuries, can and often does lead to murder.

not . . . adultery : Again he stresses the need for internal self-restraint. Lustful thoughts, looks and desires, will not always lead to an external act, but they are already sinful in themselves and are conducive to the external act.

not swear ... sworn : Calling God as a witness that what one says is true, when it is not, or as a guarantor of one's false promise or vow, is a direct and serious insult to the God of truth and justice.

Christ demands more. One should be so truthful, and so faithful in keeping one's promises, that to swear by God should not be necessary. A yes or a no, a simple promise, should be enough if one is honest with God, with his neighbor, and with his own conscience.

APPLICATION : In this Sermon on the Mount, we have various sayings of Christ, actually spoken on different occasions. Matthew, in his systematic manner, has gathered these sayings into one continuous discourse here. This makes it easier for his readers, who were Jewish converts, to grasp the new order of salvation as inaugurated by Christ. They knew the ten commandments, but they knew them as their rabbis had taught them. These rabbis, for the most part Pharisees, put all the stress on the letter of the law and on its external observance. Christ's opening statement, that the attitude of his followers towards the commandments (and other precepts of the law) must be different, and superior to that of the scribes and Pharisees, clearly indicates how Christianity must differ from, and supersede, Judaism.

Christ is not abolishing the ten commandments, but he is demanding of his followers a more perfect, a more sincere, fulfillment of them. The whole moral value of any legal observance (the Mosaic law included), comes from the interior disposition of him who observes or keeps the law. No man serves or honors God by any exterior acts, be they ever so arduous or continuous, unless these acts proceed from an intention and a will to honor and please God. This is the charter, the constitution, of the new law, Christianity. The

old law is not abolished, but deepened and given a new life.

Avoiding murder therefore is not enough; the true Christian must remove any inclination to murder by building up true, brotherly love for all men in his heart. We must not only not injure our neighbor or fellowman in his person, or in his character, but we must be ever ready to help him and prevent injury to him, whenever and wherever we can.

We must not only not commit adultery, but must also develop a Christian respect and esteem for purity, the virtue which will preserve us not only from adultery but even from thoughts of adultery, or any other abuse of our sexual gifts given us by God for his sublime purpose.

We must be truthful always, and men of our word. This virtue is not only necessary for man's salvation, but is the basis of rational intercourse between men in civilized society. While our civil courts still deem it necessary to impose oaths on contestants and witnesses (since they have, unfortunately, to take account of the liars and deceivers who still are a menace to society), the truthful man need not be afraid of insulting or dishonoring God by calling him as his guarantor, if asked to do so.

True and loyal service of God therefore begins in the heart, and has its value from this interior disposition. Keeping the ten commandments is our way of proving to God that we are grateful, obedient and loyal to him who gave us all we have and who has promised us future gifts infinitely greater still. And just as our love for God is proved by our true love for our neighbor, so the last seven of the commandments impose on us obligations regarding our neighbor. It is only by fulfilling these seven that we can fulfill the first three which govern our relations with God.

This truth is expressed by our Lord in the words : If you are offering your gift at the altar, and remember that your brother has something against you, leave your gift there . . . first be reconciled to your brother and then come and offer your gift.

FIRST SUNDAY OF LENT

FIRST READING : Gen. 2 : 7–9; 3 : 1–7. The Lord God formed man of dust from the ground, and breathed into his nostrils the breath of life; and man became a living being. And the Lord God planted a garden in Eden, in the east; and there he put the man whom he had formed. And out of the ground the Lord God made to grow every tree that is pleasant to the sight and good for food, the tree of life also in the midst of the garden, and the tree of the knowledge of good and evil.

Now the serpent was more subtle than any other wild creature that the Lord God had made. He said to the woman, "Did God say, 'You shall not eat of any tree of the garden'?" And the woman said to the serpent, "We may eat of the fruit of the trees of the garden; but God said, 'You shall not eat of the fruit of the tree which is in the midst of the garden, neither shall you touch it, lest you die.' " But the serpent said to the woman, "You will not die. For God knows that when you eat of it your eyes will be opened, and you will be like God, knowing good and evil." So when the woman saw that the tree was good for food, and that it was a delight to the eyes, and that the tree was to be desired to make one wise, she took of its fruit and ate; and she also gave some to her husband, and he ate. Then the eyes of both were opened, and they knew that they were naked; and they sewed fig leaves together and made themselves aprons.

EXPLANATION : Today, as we begin the liturgical season of Lent, a period of preparation for the sufferings and death of Christ for us, our first and second readings give us the reason why that suffering and death were necessary.

God created man, "male and female he created them" (Gen. 1 : 27). He gave man powers superior to all the other earthly creatures, and expected of him in return obedience and reverence. Man, because of his pride in the gift given him, refused that obedience—with disastrous results that would have everlasting effects on himself and his descendants, had not the mercy of God intervened.

man . . . ground : This description of the creation and fall of man, as given in chapters 2 and 3 of Genesis, dates from about the tenth century B.C. The first eleven chapters of Genesis were written in order to explain why Abraham was called by God to form the Chosen People. The writer of these early chapters had some oral, and perhaps even some written, traditions which were centuries older. They deal with "facts," however, which happened millions of years previously, but the basic truths they contain—namely, the existence of one only God, all-powerful, all-knowing, all-loving, who created, by a simple word of command, the whole universe with all its inhabitants including man—the masterpiece "made to God's image and likeness" and the master of all the other creatures—are truths which could only have been known from divine revelation. Apart from these basic truths, the literary settings in which the author or authors tell their story, need not be taken literally in all their details.

into . . . life : That man was made from dust, like a vase is made by a potter, is one such detail. This was but a poetic way of saying God formed or made him. Experience taught that a dead man turns eventually into a heap of dust, so it seemed natural that he came from dust. Likewise a man breathes through his nostrils, and it's a sign that he lives; while life leaves him through his nostrils when he ceases to breathe; therefore life was "put into him" through his nostrils.

a garden in Eden : A poetic description of the happy life of man before he sinned.

tree of life : A symbol of the everlasting life he would have after he had ended his life on this earth, if he had remained faithful.

tree . . . evil : To know good and evil means to experience in act what is good and what is evil. The tree is a symbol for man's conduct in relation to God. While man respected and reverenced God he experienced what was good; when he refused to serve God and followed his own desires he experienced evil.

the serpent : That the world was full of sin was self-evident; not only did all the nations of the author's day ignore the true God, but even the people he had chosen to prepare for the great event of the Incarnation, disobeyed and disrespected him continually. How then did it happen that God's masterpiece and image had not only forgotten him but positively disobeyed him? The serpent, representing some intelligent *creature* already an enemy of God, induced the first human beings to disobey.

you . . . God : This was the bait offered : "You need not be subject to God, you need not obey or reverence him, you shall be his equals." Independence, equality, freedom to do as they wished, in other words, the sin of pride.

eyes were opened : No sooner had they given their consent to this act of pride than they realized their terrible mistake. The loss of their state of grace, of friendship with God, brought with it numerous disorders of body and mind which resulted in the sins of the world, which are still with us.

APPLICATION : In recent years theologians have been discussing and arguing about the nature of what is called "Original sin," and how it is transmitted from generation to generation. The patent fact is that sin abounds, and has abounded in our world from the earliest days of man on earth. The reason why the Church recalls to our minds today the basic facts that God, out of sheer goodness, created man and gave him marvelous gifts, and man in his meanness and foolish pride refused obedience and loyalty to his divine benefactor, is simply to remind us that we are all sinners and descendants of sinners.

While theologians may, and should, try to discover the real nature of original sin and its mode of transmission, the fact that we men of today, centuries and millennia later, are still sinners, still proud, still so often disloyal and ungrateful to the good God, who made us what we are, is and should be our chief preoccupation during this season of Lent.

While we have every reason to regret that our first parents acted so foolishly and so ungratefully, the fact that we ourselves, with far more knowledge of God's goodness to mankind can and do act even more foolishly and more ungratefully every time we disobey God, should be a greater cause for shame and regret to each one of us.

We know that God sent his Son on earth in human nature, in order to earn for us a share in God's own divine happiness. And God did this, even though the human race had proved itself so unworthy of this divine favor. His divine Son had to suffer, not only the humiliation of taking on himself the nature of a mere creature—our human nature, but he had to suffer insults and injuries in that human nature, which reached their climax in his crucifixion on Calvary.

That God would deign to share his heaven with the saintly and the good who had never offended him, even though they were mere creatures, would be an act of divine love indeed, but that he should want to grant eternal happiness to sinners, at the cost of the torments and sufferings of his beloved Son, is surely a mystery of love beyond our human comprehension. Yet, this is one of the basic truths of our Christian faith. What sinner—and we are all sinners—could dare to hope that God would forgive his sins; what right could he have, after his own mean behavior toward the God who gave him everything he has, to expect any pardon? But one sincere look at a crucifix should be enough to dispel any thought of despair or despondency.

Christ took on himself the sins of the world. He nailed them to the cross, in order to open the door to heaven for all men. Through his Incarnation he raised us up to the status of adopted sons of God; through his sufferings and crucifixion he made atonement to his Father for the sins of all men, thus removing the impediment that could prevent us from reaching the reward of sonship, membership in the eternal kingdom of God.

But even God cannot remove our sins unless we do our part; Christ's sufferings and death for us will be in vain, unless we cooperate. This is just what Lent means for us. It is a period of penance and repentance. We regret the many disobediences and disloyalties we have shown to God up to now, and we try to make some personal atonement for them, by some special acts of mortification and devotion during this holy season.

We want to go to heaven when our life here ends. God wants us in heaven and has proved this beyond a shadow of doubt. Satan—the serpent mentioned in today's reading—does not want us to go there. He deceived our first parents; could we possibly be so foolish as to let him deceive us too?

SECOND READING : Romans 5 : 12–19.   Sin came into the world through one man and death through sin, and so death spread to all men because all men sinned—sin indeed was in the world before the law was given, but sin is not counted where there is no law. Yet death reigned from Adam to Moses, even over those whose sins were not like the transgressions of Adam, who was a type of the one who was to come.

But the free gift is not like the trespass. For if many died through one man's trespass, much more have the grace of God and the free gift in the grace of that one man Jesus Christ abounded for many. And the free gift is not like the effect of that one man's sin. For the judgement following one trespass brought condemnation, but the free gift following many trespasses brings justification. If, because of one man's trespass, death reigned through that one man, much more will those who receive the abundance of grace and the free gift of righteousness reign in life through the one man Jesus Christ.

Then as one man's trespass led to condemnation for all men, so one man's act of righteousness leads to acquittal and life for all men. For as by one man's disobedience many were made sinners, so by one man's obedience many will be made righteous.

EXPLANATION : In chapters 5–8 (inclusive) of his letter to the Romans, St. Paul is speaking of some of the immediate effects of Christian salvation, as brought to mankind by Christ. Sin has been conquered; eternal life has been won for all who will follow Christ. All who die with Christ through baptism will rise with Christ to an everlasting life of glory; they are sons of God, they are entitled to call God their father, "Abba." They are therefore God's heirs and Christ's fellow-heirs if they continue to follow him.

In today's reading (5 : 12–19), St. Paul is stressing the fact that Christ through his death not only conquered sin but poured out divine grace so abundantly and lavishly on mankind, making them his brothers and therefore sons of God, that there is no comparison between the world redeemed by Christ's death and the world of sin which prevailed up to then.

sin . . . man : Paul is referring to the pride and folly of our first parents, as described in chapters 2 and 3 of Genesis (see first reading for today). As he is contrasting Christ, the founder of the new redeemed and exalted human race, with the founder of the sinful, fallen human race, he speaks of Adam as the one individual who brought sin into this world.

death . . . sin : That is, spiritual death or sin, because sin alienated man from

God and made it impossible for man to reach the goal which God had planned for him—eternal life with God.

spread . . . sinned : This spiritual death or alienation from God, infected all men. How this happened is a much disputed question. It is sufficient for our purpose to admit the fact as St. Paul states it.

sin . . . law : The law given to Moses contained all the precepts and commands God wished his Chosen People to keep. To break one of these precepts was to sin. And such a sin was like that of Adam, as *literally* described in Genesis, for Adam had been given an explicit command. But St. Paul says that in the long period between Adam and Moses, when men had no explicit commands from God, sin still abounded because man's reason could and did inform men of the sinfulness of certain acts. By violating what we call the "natural law" men sinned.

sin . . . counted : These sins were not violations of God's formally expressed commands; but still they were violations of God's law "written in men's hearts" and as such merited eternal death.

free gift . . . trespass : This is the point St. Paul wants to stress : the grace, the favor of God, brought to men through the Incarnation, exceeds beyond measure the evil that sin brought into the world. For, by the Incarnation Christ not only took away the sins of men but made all men adopted sons of God and heirs to eternal life.

condemnation . . . justification : The condemnation which sin brought on man was estrangement from God in this life, to be followed by eternal separation from him in the next. The justification brought to us by Christ, not only means the renewal of our friendship with God, but it gives us the new status of adopted sonship.

death . . . man : Many, perhaps, refused to repent of their personal sins and so merited exclusion from God's eternal kingdom, but compared with the millions who would gain eternal life, because of Christ, their number was very small.

trespass . . . righteousness : Again the same contrast between the relatively small consequence of the original sin, and the superabundance of the effects of the Incarnation. It has made life eternal available to all men.

APPLICATION : The message that should come over "loud and clear" to each one of us today, from these words of St. Paul, is that we are dealing with a God of infinite mercy and infinite love. He created man and gave him gifts which raised him above all other earthly creatures. Through these gifts, man was able to recognize that he was a mere creature, that he owed all he was and had to a generous Creator, and that therefore he was in duty bound to respect and reverence his benefactor (see Rom. 1 : 19–23). But man, moved by pride in the higher gifts he possessed, which were not his own, turned his back on God and refused to revere and obey him. Man sinned and thereby excluded himself from the eternal reward God had planned for him.

What human benefactor would stand for such ingratitude, and would not turn his back on such an ungrateful creature for evermore? But God is infinite in mercy and in love; he is not a human, limited being. He would still carry out his plan to make men his adopted sons, and thus give them a share in his eternal inheritance. The Incarnation as planned from the beginning would still take place. The Son of God would take our human nature, would come down to our level, so that we could share in his divine nature, and be raised up to sonship with God. The Incarnation—this almost incredible act of God's infinite love for us—was not a "second thought" on God's part when man sinned, but was willed by God from all eternity as a means of uniting all men with himself and with each other.

The sins of the generations that preceded Christ's coming were therefore, in comparison, but tiny shadows which brought out all the more strongly the brilliance of divine love as seen in the Incarnation. The effects of the Incarnation were retroactive—sinners who repented before the Incarnation took place, became heirs of heaven, as will also all repentant sinners who have lived and died since Christ came on earth.

Learning the lesson Paul teaches us today, let us thank God for his infinite mercy and love, as proved by his making us brothers of Christ and co-heirs with Christ to heaven. Let us also beg pardon with heartfelt contrition for the many times we have forgotten his goodness to us, and in our pride have followed our own will rather than his. He will forgive and forget our sins if we sincerely seek his pardon. He has prepared heaven for us and wants us there; let us all use this holy season of Lent to help us to get there.

GOSPEL : Matt. 4 : 1–11. Jesus was led up by the Spirit into the wilderness to be tempted by the devil. And he fasted forty days and forty nights, and afterwards he was hungry. And the tempter came and said to him, "If you are the son of God, command these stones to become loaves of bread." But he answered, "It is written, 'Man shall not live by bread alone, but by every word that proceeds from the mouth of God.'"

Then the devil took him to the holy city, and set him on the pinnacle of the temple, and said to him, "If you are the Son of God, throw yourself down; for it is written, 'He will give his angels charge of you,' and 'On their hands they will bear you up, let you strike your foot against a stone.'" Jesus said to him, "Again it is written, 'You shall not tempt the Lord your God.'"

Again, the devil took him to a very high mountain, and showed him all the kingdoms of the world and the glory of them; and he said to him, "All these I will give you, if you will fall down and worship me." Then Jesus said to him, "Begone, Satan! for it is written, 'You shall worship the Lord your God and him only shall you serve.'" Then the devil left him, and behold, angels came and ministered to him.

EXPLANATION : It was God's purpose that the devil should tempt Christ and be conquered in the contest. As the Fathers of the Church aptly remark, there was nothing unbecoming in the fact that Christ allowed the devil to tempt him and to touch him in his human nature. He had assumed that human nature in order to suffer in it, through Satan and his agents, and thus redeem and elevate all human nature.

Jesus . . . Spirit : After his baptism by John in the Jordan, Jesus was led by the Holy Spirit into a desert place (near the Jordan). This was a voluntary act under the guidance of the Holy Spirit, through which he would set an example to all his followers.

tempted by the devil : This was a humiliation surely for the Son of God, but only one of the many Christ underwent for our sakes.

forty . . . nights : The length of his period of fasting, 40 days, and the desert, would seem to indicate that Christ, the founder of the New Israel, was reproducing at the beginning of his messianic mission, the trials and temptations of the old Chosen People during their 40 years wandering in the desert. They failed miserably in their tests, they murmured and rebelled against God, but Christ gave a decisive "no" to the tempter's suggestions. Christ's answers are couched in words taken from Deuteronomy 6–8, the section of the Old Testament which summarizes the trials and the failures of the old Israel in the desert (see Dt. 8 : 1–6).

he was hungry : Christ was really human, and he used no divine power to prevent the natural effects of want of food on a human body. This gave the tempter his opportunity.

If you . . . God : Satan, the tempter, suspected or knew that Christ was the promised Messiah, that is, the "Son of God," in the sense of an agent or close friend of God. The kings of Israel and the Chosen People were also called "sons of God."

command . . . stones : In all three

temptations, the tempter wants him to use his messianic power for his own benefit. Here he is asked to turn stones into loaves of bread, just to satisfy his own hunger.

It is written : Christ's answer is a quotation from Deuteronomy 8 : 3, where God tells the Chosen People, who had bitterly complained of hunger and whom he had fed miraculously with the "manna," that bread alone was not the sustenance or source of life, but the will of God their Creator and sustainer.

pinnacle . . . temple : Probably the south-eastern corner of the wall which surrounded the temple, where there was a drop of 120 feet into the Kedron valley.

for it is written : Shakespeare says : "the devil can quote scripture for his own purpose." Again the attempt is to make Christ abuse his messianic power and tempt God.

again . . . written : Christ answers with another quotaton from scripture (Dt. 6 : 16) in its true sense. The texts quoted by Satan were falsely interpreted. God would protect his faithful one, but the faithful servant of God must not put himself deliberately in danger—this would be tempting God. The reference in Dt. 6 : 16, is to the rebellious Israelites who accused God of bringing them out of Egypt to die of thirst in the desert (Ex. 17 : 1–7).

all . . . world : Here is a final temptation to use his messianic power for his own aggrandizement and glorification, not for the glory of God. Also, it is a foolish attempt to lead Christ into idolatry.

Begone Satan : The tempter is named and dismissed. And Christ reminds him that God alone must be worshipped and served "as it is written" (Dt. 6 : 13). The Israelites, on getting possession of the Promised Land, frequently forgot God in their desire for earthly wealth and power, and thus frequently turned to idolatry. This eventually made them slaves of the pagan nations whose false gods they had adored instead of Yahweh the real God.

angels . . . him : God sent his messengers to provide for his bodily needs after the long fast.

APPLICATION : This incident in our Lord's life, his forty days and nights of fasting followed by temptations, has been chosen as a reading for this first Sunday of Lent for our edification and encouragement. Lent is a period of preparation for the central Christian events of Good Friday and Easter Sunday. Christ, the Son of God in human nature, died the excruciating death of crucifixion on Good Friday, because of the sins of the human race. By this supreme act of obedience to his heavenly Father he made atonement for all our disobediences, and set us free from the slavery of Satan and of sin. In his resurrection his human nature was glorified by God the Father, and in that glorification we are all offered a share and given the right to an eternal life of glory, if we follow Christ faithfully in this life.

For every sincere Christian therefore, who appreciates what Good Friday and Easter Sunday mean for her or him, this period of preparation should be a welcome opportunity. The Church no longer imposes on us any obligatory fasting from food, but it urges us to find other means of mortifying ourselves, so as to show that we realize what Christ has done for us and what he has earned for us through his passion, death and resurrection. The example of Christ fasting from food for forty days, should move even the coldest Christian heart to try to do something to make reparation for past negligence and sins. Christ had no sin to atone for; it was for our sins that he mortified himself. We all have much to atone for. If, because of the demands of our present way of life, we cannot fast rigorously as our grandparents did, we can find many other less noticeable, but maybe nonetheless difficult, ways of subduing our human worldly inclinations. Where there is a will there is a way; the willing Christian will find ready substitutes for fasting.

The temptations, to which our Lord allowed himself to be submitted, are for us a source of encouragement and consolation. If our Lord and master underwent temptation, we cannot and must not expect to live a Christian life without experiencing similar tests and trials. The three temptations Satan put to our Lord were suggestions to forget his purpose in life—his messianic mission of redemption. He was urged to get all the bodily comforts of life, all the self-glory which men could give him, and all the possessions and power this world has to offer.

Our basic temptations in life are the same : bodily comforts and pleasure, the empty esteem of our fellowmen, wealth and power. There are millions of men and women on earth today—many of them nominal Christians—who have given in to these temptations and are wasting their lives chasing after these unattainable shadows. But even should they manage to catch up with some of them, they soon find out that they are empty baubles. They will have to leave them so very soon.

Today, let each one of us look into

his heart and honestly examine his reaction to these temptations. Do we imitate our Savior and leader, and say "begone Satan"? Our purpose in life is not to collect its treasures, its honors or its pleasures. We are here for a few short years, to merit the unending life which Christ has won for us. Would we be so foolish as to swap our inheritance for a mere mess of pottage (see Gen. 25 : 29-34)?

Lent is a golden opportunity to review our past and make sensible resolutions for our future.

SECOND SUNDAY OF LENT

FIRST READING : Genesis 12 : 1-4. The Lord said to Abram, "Go from your country and your kindred and your father's house to the land that I will show you. And I will make of you a great nation, and I will bless you, and make your name great, so that you will be a blessing. I will bless those who bless you, and him who curses you I will curse; and by you all the families of the earth shall bless themselves."

So Abram went, as the Lord had told him.

EXPLANATION : God's plan for man, when he created this world and made man the principal being in it, was to share his own eternal happiness with him. The Incarnation was the means chosen for this act of gracious love. By taking our human nature, and uniting it to his divinity, the Son of God raised all human nature to the honor of adopted sonship of God. Before this took place, before the time preordained by God, or "the fulness of time" as St. Paul calls it, arrived, men had forgotten God and their purpose in life.

In their sinful disloyalty to their maker they had made idols or false gods for themselves—gods who demanded little, if any, service of them. But God's plan was unchanged and unchangeable. In due time he began the remote preparation for the Incarnation. Almost 2,000 years before Christ was to come, he selected Abram to be the father of a people who would be his special friends, his "Chosen People," and to them he would reveal himself, and through them, the fulness of his revelation, Christ, would come to all men. This is the divine event read for us today.

Lord . . . Abram : Abram was a pagan when called by God. At the time of his call he was living in Haran in northern Mesopotamia; his father Thare had come there from "Ur of the Chaldees."

Evidently, God convinced him that he alone was the true God, and that he alone should be served.

Go . . . country : Even today this command could not be called easy to fulfillment, but in the days of Abram to leave one's tribe and one's relatives was to risk one's life.

go . . . show you : He was commanded to emigrate to some foreign land, the very name of which was kept secret from him.

I will make . . . nation : God promises Abram that he will be the father and founder of a numerous following. He will be blessed by God and will be a blessing for many, for all mankind in fact.

I will . . . curse : A Hebrew parallelism. God will bless those who help Abram; he will *not* bless those who oppose him.

all . . . earth : All the human race will be blessed and will bless Abram, because God chose him as the ancestor of Christ.

Abram . . . him : Abram trusted implicitly and whole-heartedly in the true God who had so recently revealed himself to him. He did as God told him, without question or hesitation.

APPLICATION : God's mercy and love for us men is the first lesson this call of Abram should teach us. Over 3,800 years ago God began the proximate preparations for opening heaven to us. He converted the pagan Abram and got him to leave his idol-worshiping family, kinsmen and country. He set him up in Canaan and promised him a great posterity, numerous descendants, who would eventually possess that land. His purpose in doing this was to preserve the knowledge of the true God, and continually enlarge on that knowledge, until the "fulness of time" and the fulness of his knowledge would come to all men in the Incarnation.

The story of God's infinite patience in his dealings with the descendants of Abram, as narrated in the Old Testament, is another convincing proof of his infinite love for us. Only infinite love could have persevered in the face of the stubborn hard-heartedness, repeated ingratitude and infidelities of his Chosen People. But infinite love prevailed; a remnant of that people was preserved until the promised one, the Messiah, through whom all the nations of the earth would be blessed, came on earth.

Another lesson which every Christian should learn from the call of Abram, is that each and every one of us, no matter what our state in life may be, is called like Abram to preserve the knowledge of God in our own life, and to do all in our power to bring that knowledge to our neighbors. Some are asked to leave their home and their country and go to a land that God chooses for their apostolate. These are the missionaries, who are called on to do more than the rest of us. Their task is more arduous; their vocation makes greater demands on human nature; but God is with them and their reward is great.

But those of us, the vast majority of Christians, who are not called to the mission-fields, are still called to the apostolate. Every one of us has the call and the obligation to share his knowledge of God with his neighbors. We are adopted sons of God, true sons of Abram. We are a small part of the whole human race which God wants in heaven. As he looked to the Chosen

People of old to help him in bringing eternal life to all nations, so he looks to us now to continue the same divine task.

The Incarnation has made all men sons of God, brothers of Christ and true brothers of one another. Am I really a brother of Christ if I have no interest in the true welfare of my neighbor, my brother? If I shrug my shoulders and say that I have enough to do to try to get to heaven myself, without having to bother with my neighbor, this is a sure sign that I am not trying to get to heaven. If my Christian life does not include the good example of true Christian living, a word of advice for a brother who needs it, a daily prayer for the salvation of all my fellow-travellers to heaven, I am not on the road to heaven myself.

Lent is a very suitable occasion to examine my past conduct in this regard. Christ suffered and died on the cross to open heaven for all men. He rose from the dead—"the first-fruits" of the millions of those who will one day rise from the dead and enter into a new and everlasting life. That some, and maybe many, of my fellowmen will reap the reward of what Christ did for them, will and does depend on my true charity. If I fail in this duty, if I turn a deaf ear to this Christian vocation, I am gravely endangering my own participation in the eternal happiness won for me by Christ.

SECOND READING: 2 Tim. 1:8–10. Take your share of suffering for the gospel in the power of God, who saved us and called us with a holy calling, not in virtue of our works but in virtue of his own purpose and the grace which he gave us in Christ Jesus ages ago, and now has manifested through the appearance of our Savior Jesus Christ, who abolished death and brought life and immortality to light through the gospel.

EXPLANATION: Timothy, son of a pagan father and a Jewish mother, became a Christian, together with his mother Eunice and his grandmother Lois (2 Tim. 1:5), on St. Paul's first visit to Lystra. When Paul returned to Lystra on his second missionary journey, Timothy joined him and became his "fellow-worker" for the gospel. He remained with Paul all through his second and third missionary journeys, during which time Paul sent him on several special missions. Later, Paul appointed him head of the church at Ephesus (1 Tim. 1:3), as he had made Titus bishop in Crete (Tit. 1:5). It is pretty certain that Paul appointed other such bishops, or "overseers," in the larger communities which he founded, but their names are unknown. We know of Titus and of Timothy because of the letters Paul wrote to them. These epistles are called the Pastoral Epistles, because they are principally concerned with the pastoral duties of these men whom he placed over the churches. These were the duties of pastors or shepherds of the communities.

Take . . . suffering: In the preceding verses, Paul had reminded Timothy of the gift, the power, God had given him through the laying of Paul's hands on him (ordination). He must use that gift for the spread of the gospel, even if it will cause him suffering and humiliation, which it did.

God . . . us : The call to follow Christ and become Christians in Baptism, is always attributed by Paul to God; the Christian faith is a free gift of God.

a holy calling : It is a call to holiness not only in this life but to an eternal participation in the divine sanctity and happiness.

not in . . . works : Nothing men could do of themselves could make them heirs to heaven; this was a free gift of God.

in Christ . . . ago : The divine plan from all eternity; the literal translation of the Greek (pro cheonon aionion) is : " before eternal times " (see Eph. 1 : 4).

now has manifested : This eternal plan of God for us has been made known to us in our day, Paul says, through the coming of Christ, that is, through the Incarnation.

who abolished death : Physical death would and should be the natural end of man if God had not decreed otherwise. But God had so decreed : physical death would be the doorway to a new eternal life. Sin would have prevented man from attaining to this divine gift, but here again Christ's physical death made absolute atonement for all men's sins, and so abolished the spiritual death brought upon themselves by men.

life and immortality : This is the gift which the Incarnation, death and resurrection of Christ brought to all men —eternal life. This is the " good news," the gospel that Timothy must preach and gladly suffer for.

APPLICATION : The old saying, "familiarity breeds contempt," can be true of spiritual as well as material things. We Christians often so take our faith, with all it means for us, for granted, that we fail to appreciate it as we should. If St. Paul felt it necessary to remind Timothy, his faithful co-worker, of vigilance, how much more necessary are his words of exhortation for each one of us today!

Even the holiest of us can get into a rut and forget what our real purpose in life is. We were created by God and given marvelous gifts to make our way through this life. This is already something for which we should be most grateful. But, as God saw, what good would 90 or 100 years of happiness be for a human being on this earth, if he would have to leave it all and end as a little pile of dust in a cemetery?

So, the all-wise and all-loving God decreed that we should not end in the grave, but that instead our real life would begin after our physical death on earth. We would be taken into the eternal life of the Trinity, through the privilege of adoption, which the Incarnation would earn for us. This is the basis of our Christian faith and hope. This is the end and purpose of our Christian way of living while here on earth. This end and purpose we should never forget.

It is true that we have many earthly occupations and concerns, many passing sources of worry and distraction, but these should not, and need not, be a hindrance in our daily cares and crosses to lift us up above our earthly status. We must make them aids on our journey, rather than let them be impediments. To do this, we must never forget the plan God has for us. We must never forget what the coming of Christ in our human nature means for us. He has "abolished death" and brought us immortality. Physical death is no longer to be feared; it is not the end for us but the beginning, provided we do the relatively little that is expected of us.

Are we all doing the little that the Christian gospel demands of us? Don't wait until tomorrow, or next week, to give yourself an honest answer to this question. There may be no tomorrow, no next week, for you. Thank God, that you have *today*; use it as if it were your last day on earth. It will be the last day for over 100,000—you could easily be one of that large number.

GOSPEL : Matt. 17 : 1–9. Jesus took with him Peter and James and John his brother, and led them up a high mountain apart. And he was transfigured before them, and his face shone like the sun, and his garments became white as light. And behold, there appeared to them Moses and Elijah, talking with him. And Peter said to Jesus, "Lord, it is well that we are here; if you wish, I will make three booths here, one for you and one for Moses and one for Elijah." He was still speaking, when lo, a bright cloud overshadowed them, and a voice from the cloud said, "This is my beloved Son, with whom I am well pleased; listen to him." When the disciples heard this, they fell on their faces, and were filled with awe. But Jesus came and touched them, saying, "Rise, and have no fear." And when they lifted up their eyes, they saw no one but Jesus only.

And as they were coming down the mountain, Jesus commanded them, "Tell no one the vision, until the Son of man is raised from the dead."

EXPLANATION : In the two preceding readings, we have been reminded today of the necessity of suffering, and self-mortification, during this season of Lent. Abram had to leave his home and his country, and face the dangers and difficulties of setting up a home among "strangers," that is, enemies at that time. Timothy is reminded of the necessity of suffering for the gospel, if he is to preach it effectively. Our third reading from Matthew's gospel is, instead, a source of encouragement—an incitement to be willing to suffer for a brief period because of the glory that will be ours

later on. In 16 : 21–25, Jesus has warned his disciples that Christ must suffer and be humiliated. This was something they could not easily accept—who could humiliate or cause suffering to one who had such miraculous powers? In order to strengthen them for the scandal of the cross, and his apparent failure, Christ now gives the three leading disciples a brief glimpse of his future glory. This vision is a contrast to the agony in the garden on Holy Thursday night, of which the same three disciples were witnesses. The transfiguration they witnessed on the mountain could not have been forgotten and must have been a source of strength to them in the Garden of Gethsemani.

he was transfigured . . . them : Peter, James and John were the only witnesses on this "mountain apart"—Mount Thabor probably. The transfiguration meant that they got a brief glimpse of his future glory.

His face . . . sun : His human appearance took on something of the divine, his garments became bright as light. This is an attempt to describe a heavenly vision, a divine revelation (see Is. 6; Ez. 1 : 26–28; Dan. 10 : 5–10 for similar visions).

Moses and Elijah : These two great men of the Old Testament represent the law and the prophets, who are testifying that Christ is the Messiah promised of old, he whom they had already prophesied.

Peter . . . Jesus : Peter is not yet overwhelmed by the vision, and he declares how blessed he and his two companions are to witness it. He would like this moment of joy to be prolonged, and so he suggests setting up three tents in which Christ, Moses and Elijah could sojourn. The feast of Tents or Tabernacles—a feast of lights and illuminations—was looked on in later Jewish history as a representation of God's final kingship of the world. This thought was probably in Peter's mind.

a bright . . . cloud : A manifestation of Yahweh, God the Father. He appeared to Moses on Mount Horeb in a cloud (Ex. 24 : 12–16). His presence in the Tent of Meeting is manifested by the cloud which covered it (Ex. 40 : 34); as also in the newly-erected temple— Jerusalem (1 Kgs. 8 : 10).

my beloved . . . him : A repetition of the words heard at Christ's baptism in the Jordan, an echo of the messianic "Servant of Yahweh," as foretold in Isaias (42 : 1). "Listen to him"—he is the revealer, he has the true message of salvation. He is the new Moses, the prophet promised by Yahweh to Moses (Dt. 18 : 15–18).

fell on their faces : They knew they were in God's presence.

Rise . . . fear : According to the Old Testament, to see God was to die; hence their fear, but Jesus tells them there is no reason for fear.

Jesus only : The vision had ended. Jesus was alone in his natural form once more.

until . . . dead : "Son of man" was a title given to Jesus by himself only. It was a half-hidden messianic title, taken from Daniel (7 : 13), and also a stressing of his real human nature. In the semitic languages "Son of man" equals "a man." The three disciples were not to reveal this vision until Christ had been raised from the dead. It was only then that the true messiahship, as well as the true divinity, of Christ came to be accepted by the Apostles. The Transfiguration on Mount Thabor was but a grief glimpse of it, to help these three Apostles especially.

APPLICATION : This momentary vision of Christ, in his glory, was given in order to strengthen the three principal Apostles to face the trials to their faith, which the sufferings and crucifixion of their beloved master would bring on them. For the very same reason it is retold to us today, in the early part of Lent, to encourage us to persevere in our lenten mortifications. It reminds us that, very soon, the Easter bells will be ringing out their message of joy once more. If we are sharers with Christ in his sufferings, we shall be sharers with him in his glory as St. Paul reminds us.

This is a truth we all too easily forget, namely, that we cannot and do not get to heaven in a limousine. Our spell on earth is the chance given us by our heavenly Father to earn an eternal reward. This reward surpasses even the wildest imagination of man. We could never earn it, but God accepts the little we can do and provides the balance of his infinite mercy. And yet there are many, far too many, who refuse even that little bit that is asked of them, and are thus running the risk of not partaking in God's scheme for their eternal happiness.

And are they any happier during their few years on this earth by acting thus towards the God of mercy? Can they, by ignoring God and their duties towards him, remove all pain, all sorrow, all sufferings, from their daily lives? Death, which means a total separation from all we possessed and cherished in this world, is waiting around the corner for all of us. Who can face it more calmly and confidently —the man who is firmly convinced that it is the gateway to a new life, and who has done his best to earn admission through that gateway, or the man who has acted all his life as if death did not exist for him, and who has done everything to have the gate to the new life shut forever in his face?

Illnesses and troubles and disappointments are the lot of all men. They respect neither wealth, nor power, nor position. The man who knows his purpose in life, and is ever striving to reach the goal God's goodness has planned for him, can and will see in these trials of life the hand of a kind father who is preparing him for greater things. His sufferings become understandable and more bearable because of his attitude to life and its meaning. The man who ignores God and tries to close the eyes of his mind to the real facts of life has nothing to uphold him or console him in his hours of sorrow and pain. Yet, sorrow and pain will dog his footsteps, strive as he will to avoid them, and he can see no value, no divine purpose in these, for him, misfortunes.

Christ has asked us to follow him, carrying our daily cross, and the end of our journey is not Calvary but resurrection, the entrance to a life of glory with our risen Savior. The Christian who grasps his cross closely and willingly, knowing its value for his real life, will find it becomes lighter and often not a burden but a pleasure. The man who tries to shuffle off his cross, and who curses and rebels against him who sent it, will find it doubles its weight and loses all the value it was intended to have for his true welfare.

Let the thought of the Transfiguration encourage each one of us today, to do the little God demands of us, so that when we pass out of this life we may be assured of seeing Christ in his glory, ready to welcome us into his everlasting, glorious kingdom.

THIRD SUNDAY OF LENT

FIRST READING : Exodus : 17 : 3–7. The people thirsted for water, and murmured against Moses, and said, "Why did you bring us up out of Egypt, to kill us and our children and our cattle with thirst?" So Moses cried to the Lord, "What shall I do with this people? They are almost ready to stone me." And the Lord said to Moses, "Pass on before the people, taking with you some of the elders of Israel; and take in your hand the rod with which you struck the Nile, and go. Behold, I will stand before you there on the rock at Horeb; and you shall strike the rock, and water shall come out of it, that the people may drink." And Moses did so, in the sight of the elders of Israel. And he called the name of the place Massah and Meribah, because of the fault-finding of the children of Israel, and because they put the Lord to the proof by saying, "Is the Lord among us or not?"

EXPLANATION : The Israelites, the Chosen People of God, were suffering slavery and the threat of total extermination in Egypt; God miraculously set them free and, with Moses as their leader, he led them towards the promised land of Canaan. But they soon forgot what God had done for them and began to murmur and rebel because of the difficulties of the long desert journey.

One of these rebellious murmurings is put before us today, for a purpose which we shall see.

murmured . . . Moses : They knew that Moses was God's representative, so it was really against God that they murmured.

to kill . . . thirst : A desert journey has its difficulties; the scarcity of wells or oases is one of these. It necessitated taking supplies of water from one watering place to the next. The Israelites knew this and should have been ready to put up with a certain amount of difficulty, but this they were unwilling to do. Instead they accused the kind God, who had brought them out of Egypt, of wishing to let them die of thirst.

strike the rock : Moses appealed to God. And, notwithstanding the ingratitude and the mistrust of the people, God gave him the power to bring water from a rock.

Massah and Meribah : Two names which mean "testing-place." They were probably two separate places where the doubting Israelites lost confidence in God, but both are joined together here. The exact location of these places cannot be identified.

Is the Lord among us? : This shows the weakness of their faith : the little trust they had in God, in spite of all he had already done for them.

APPLICATION : This incident, which happened over 3,000 years ago and which brings out the ingratitude and the inborn mistrust of the Israelites, is put before us today, not that we should criticize them, but rather that we should look into our own consciences and see how solid and how true is our own trust in God, and how sincere our gratitude to him is for all his past favors.

Unfortunately, we have to admit that many among us are fair-weather Christians. While their ship of life is sailing peacefully on smooth seas they respect God and trust him, because this puts no great strain on their energies. In times like these, to be a good Christian seems very easy; they don't have to give it much thought. But when storms blow up, and the winds and the waves of life are tossing and throwing them about and threatening to engulf them, it is then that their true faith and sincerity is put to the test.

Like the thirsty Israelites in the desert, they then begin to doubt if God is really there, if he has any interest in them or is not rather a cruel, merciless, far-away being who delights in their misfortunes. All the past favors, all the days of good health and prosperity, are immediately forgotten, because these past benefits were rarely or never attributed to God with any real sincerity.

Such Christians, and there are more of them today perhaps than ever before, have forgotten that their earthly life is but a journey, not from the cradle to the grave, but from baptism to the beatific vision in heaven. Anyone, who realizes that he is on a journey, will expect inconveniences and difficulties and will accept them as such, knowing that they are of the essence of a journey. But the man who foolishly, against all the proofs and evidence of human history, thinks he can build an abode of permanent happiness for himself on this earth, is preparing himself for a rude and shocking awakening.

Yet, millions of our fellowmen are today feverishly building an earthly Utopia, and are enticing others to join them and help find once more the earthly garden of Eden. Get rid of all governments, including the divine Ruler; get rid of all authority from above, including the ten commandments and the teaching Church; and then peace and brotherhood and plenty for all will flood the earth! These are the slogans of the new saviors of the human race.

The truth is very different : God created us and made us what we are. God gives each one of us a short period on this world during which, aided by the Incarnate Son of God, and by the means of grace and reconciliation he left us in his Church, we can wend our way to the true Utopia, eternal life with God. To reach this end that God has in store for us, the trials and tests of life are as important, and as useful, as the moments of quiet calm and earthly well-being. In many cases they may be far more useful, as they may be just what we need to reawaken in our drowsy minds the purpose for which we are on earth.

When next tempted to imitate the murmuring and ungrateful Israelites in the desert, think instead of the loving God who brought you out of the Egypt of nothingness and who is, through these very trials and sufferings, getting you ready to enter the promised land, not of Canaan, but of heaven.

SECOND READING : Romans 5 : 1–2; 5–8. Since we are justified by faith, we have peace with God through our Lord Jesus Christ. Through him we have obtained access to this grace in which we stand, and we rejoice in our hope of sharing the glory of God, and our hope does not disappoint us, because God's love has been poured into our hearts through the Holy Spirit who has been given to us.

While we were yet helpless, at the right time Christ died for the ungodly. Why, one will hardly die for a righteous man—though perhaps for a good man one will dare even to die. But God shows his love for us in that while we were yet sinners Christ died for us.

EXPLANATION : This brief section from St. Paul's letter to the Romans is an encouragement to all who have been given the gift of the Christian faith to persevere in spite of adversity (verses 3 & 4 which mention sufferings and their value, are strangely omitted here). It is the infinite love of God which is the basis of their hope—how could it grow weak? Christ was sent by the Father when we were most unworthy—full of sin; how much more so will he now show his love for us once we have been reconciled to him and have been made sharers in his glory as adopted sons?
since . . . faith : Justification for St. Paul is not merely the remission of personal sins but is an especially positive quality which makes us friends of God, adopted sons in fact, and therefore heirs to God's eternal glory. This special gift, together with the remission of our sins, has come to us, who have accepted the Christian faith, through:
our Lord Jesus Christ : The incarnation, death and resurrection of Christ, who is God, "Lord," as well as man, were the means God used to make us Christians what we are.
hope of sharing : We have every reason to rejoice, for we are promised a share in the eternal glory of God.
through . . . Spirit : Since our baptism, we have within us the Holy Spirit, God's most special gift to us, the sure basis of our unflinching hope.
While . . . helpless : Mere man could not, of his own created nature, take one step towards friendship, much less sonship with God.
Christ died . . . ungodly : At the right time—that is, at the time preordained by God—Christ became man to raise us up to a new status. This he did even though we were not only mere creatures, but sinful ones. We were "ungodly," far from meriting any special love or consideration from God.
one . . . man : The sinfulness of mankind brings out all the more strongly the depths of divine love for us.
Christ died for us : In the eternal plan of the Incarnation, the future sins of the world were foreseen; also the consequences of these sins for the Incarnate Christ, namely, his cruel sufferings and death on the cross. But this did not hinder God's love for us. He carried out the eternal plan for our elevation and redemption.

APPLICATION : The uppermost thought in any mind today must be gratitude, a heartfelt thankfulness, to the all-good, all-merciful God, who deigned to send his Son down to earth in order to raise us up and make us heirs to heaven. This seems almost too good to be true, because our finite minds are incapable of grasping what infinite love is. We all have a bit of true love for our neighbor in us, but how limited, how fickle it is! If we honestly try to help a neighbor, who is in great spiritual or temporal need, but find he is abusing our generosity and lapsing back into the same spiritual or worldly faults, how quickly we can grow tired of him! How easily we can persuade ourselves that we are wasting our efforts, that he has really proved himself unworthy of any claim on our charity!

Yet, God conferred the greatest benefit that even he could confer on a creature, when he adopted us as his sons, even though the whole human race almost had abused the gifts he had already given them, and even though he foresaw that many who would at first appreciate this, his greatest gift, would forget and abuse it later.

Many of us are among the latter; we have often sinned and strayed from the high road to heaven, marked out for us by him. It's a cause for shame and confusion, and indeed a cause for the deepest despair, were it not that we know his mercy and love in our regard are infinite. He is like the father in the parable of the Prodigal Son, ever waiting for the return of the sinner. But, much as he would love to, he cannot welcome us back unless we return. He gave us our free-will and he will not force us to any unwilling act. Who is there among us who would say the Prodigal Son was foolish to return home to such love and luxury? Yet, all those among us who prefer to continue in their sinful ways are saying just that about themselves. They say that they prefer the swineherd's job, and the husks fed to the swine, to being a respected and beloved son in their father's home.

We would all deny that we are making any such foolish choice. But unless we abandon sin, and return to God with a sincere heart, we are excluding ourselves from the eternal home Christ won for us, and becoming instead eternal prodigals. Granted God's mercy to be infinite, our human life is not. And the man who tries to convince himself that he will put all things right with God when his end is nearer, is only adding the sin of presumption to his other actual and habitual sins.

Eternity is too long to take any foolish chances with it. Human life on earth is too short and too uncertain to count on even an extra day, one extra hour. Let us use this holy season of Lent to put ourselves right with God. Nobody else can do this for us, not even the all-merciful God unless we cooperate with him.

GOSPEL : John 4 : 5–42. Jesus came to a city of Samaria, called Sychar, near the field that Jacob gave to his son Joseph. Jacob's well was there, and so Jesus, wearied as he was with his journey, sat down beside the well. It was about the sixth hour.

There came a woman of Samaria to draw water. Jesus said to her, "Give me a drink." For his disciples had gone away into the city to buy food. The Samaritan woman said to him, "How is it that you, a Jew, ask a drink of me, a woman of Samaria?" For Jews have no dealings with Samaritans. Jesus answered her, "If you knew the gift of God, and who it is that is saying to you, 'Give me a drink,' you would have asked him, and he would have given you living water." The woman said to him, "Sir, you have nothing to draw with, and the well is deep; where do you get that living water? Are you greater than our father Jacob, who gave us the well, and drank from it himself, and his sons, and his cattle?" Jesus said to her, "Everyone who drinks of this water will thirst again, but whoever drinks of the water that I shall give him will never thirst; the water that I shall give him will become in him a spring of water welling up to eternal life." The woman said to him, "Sir, give me this water, that I may not thirst, nor come here to draw."

Jesus said to her, "Go, call your husband, and come here." The woman answered him, "I have no husband." Jesus said to her, "You are right in saying, 'I have no husband;' for you have had five husbands, and he whom you now have is not your husband; this you said truly.' The woman said to him, "Sir, I perceive that you are a prophet. Our fathers worshiped on this mountain; and you say that in Jerusalem is the place where men ought to worship." Jesus said to her, "Woman, believe me, the hour is coming when neither on this mountain nor in Jerusalem will you worship the Father. You worship what you do not know; we worship what we know, for salvation is from the Jews. But the hour is coming, and now is, when the true worshipers will worship the Father in spirit and truth, for such the Father seeks to worship him. God is spirit, and those who worship him must worship in spirit and truth." The woman said to him, "I know that Messiah is coming (he who is called Christ); when he comes, he will show us all things." Jesus said to her, "I who speak to you am he."

Just then his disciples came. They marveled that he was talking with a woman, but none said, "What do you wish?" or, "Why are you talking with her?" So the woman left her water jar, and went away into the city, and said to the people, "Come, see a man who told me all that I ever did. Can this be the Christ?" They went out of the city and were coming to him.

Meanwhile the disciples besought him, saying, "Rabbi, eat." But he said to them, "I have food to eat of which you do not know." So the disciples said to one another, "Has anyone brought him food?" Jesus said to them, "My food is to do the will of him who sent me, and to accomplish his work. Do you not say, 'There are yet four months, then comes the harvest'? I tell you, lift up your eyes, and see how the fields are already white for harvest. He who reaps receives wages, and gathers fruit for eternal life, so that sower and reaper may rejoice together. For here the saying holds true, 'One sows and another reaps.' I sent you to reap that for which you did not labor; others have labored, and you have entered into their labor."

Many Samaritans from that city believed in him because of the woman's testimony, "He told me all that I ever did." So when the Samaritans came to him, they asked him to stay with them; and he stayed there two days. And many more believed because of his word. They said to the woman, "It is no longer because of your words that we believe, for we have heard for ourselves, and we know that this is indeed the Savior of the world."

EXPLANATION: The incident, described here, happened as our Lord and his disciples were on their way from Judea to Galilee. They were passing through Samaria, a region which was inhabited, ever since 722 B.C., by a people mostly pagan and very anti-Jewish, but who had some knowledge of the true God of the Jews, for they retained the first five books of the Old Testament. The woman with whom our Lord spoke, and many of her compatriots as later events show, were expecting the same Messiah as the Jews. She would seem to be referring to the promise given to Moses, as narrated in Dt. 18:15.

How . . . Jew: The woman was surprised that a Jew would speak to a Samaritan and ask a favor of her. This shows the relationship that existed between the two peoples.

If you . . . is: If she knew who Jesus was she would ask him for living water, that is, the life-giving water of grace, "welling up to eternal life."

give . . . water: She understands him to speak of natural water, which would end all bodily thirst and save her the daily task of coming to Jacob's well.

call your husband: Jesus thus indirectly shows her that he knows all about her, though he had never seen her before this.

I perceive . . . prophet: She is intelligent, and concludes that he is one who has knowledge from God—a prophet.

our fathers worshiped: She raises the question of the false temple built on Mount Garizim when Samaria (the ten northern tribes) broke away from Judah, about 931 B.C. The temple in Jerusalem was the only place of worship authorized by God; the Jews therefore rightly considered Mount Garizim as a pagan temple.

the hour is coming: Jesus tells her that this question is no longer of any importance. In the messianic kingdom he is setting up, God will be worshiped, not with mere external ceremonies in some particular place, but throughout the world, and this universal worship will be given by men of all nations "in spirit and in truth." It will be true worship, because it will come from convinced hearts moved by the Holy Spirit—the "living water" given by the Messiah. It will not exclude external rites, but the internal sincerity is what will give it value.

salvation . . . Jews : The Jews, in spite of their sinfulness, have preserved the knowledge of the true God, and the Messiah promised to Abraham, Isaac, Jacob and Judah comes from them.

God is spirit : Jesus emphasizes again that the worship God wants is the true dedication and service of the interior man. A service of love, not the *mere* performance of some external rites.

I who . . . he : When the woman states her belief and hope in a Messiah who is to come, Jesus openly declares his identity to her. As there was no danger of a political upheaval in Samaria (unlike Judea), he could proclaim his Messiahship here.

The fields . . . harvest : Using a familiar metaphor, he tells the astonished disciples, when they returned from the town to which they had gone to buy food, that the world was ready for the messianic message.

Samaritans . . . them : The woman hastened back to the town and told the people that it was most probably the Messiah who was at Jacob's well. They came out to hear him and became convinced that he was the Savior of the world, that is, the promised Messiah. And he remained there two days instructing them. They became the first-fruits of the non-Jewish world to accept him as Messiah.

APPLICATION : In the first reading today, we saw the Israelites rebelling against God and calling him a murderer, because they thought they were in danger of dying of bodily thirst in the desert. He mercifully forgave their blasphemies and gave them an abundance of water. In the gospel just read, Christ tells the Samaritan woman, and through her all mankind, that the "spiritual drink" he has come to give men is not primarily given to preserve bodily life, but rather to give eternal life to those who will drink of it. Not only will they know and serve the true God in this life, but they will be given a right to an everlasting life with God if they serve him "in spirit and in truth" during their earthly life.

This is the kernel, the essence of our Christian religion. In baptism we have been made sons of God, heirs of heaven, and directed towards our eternal destination. Christ, in his divine mercy, has given to his Church all the means and all the helps we need on that journey.

We have the road-maps clearly drawn for us in the infallible, dogmatic and moral teaching of the Church. We have the first-aid stations along the route, where those who injure themselves by sin, can be medicated and made sound once more. We have, above all, the miraculous nourishment of the Eucharist—the manna of the New Testament—Christ himself, who so lovingly and condescendingly arranged to be our spiritual food and sustenance during life's journey.

Could even God have done any more for us in order to bring us to heaven? Can there exist a thinking Christian who would be so neglectful of his own true and lasting welfare—not to mention the ingratitude to the one who has done so much for him—that he would ignore the divine guidance and graces given him, and be content to sit by the wayside in spiritual rags and misery? It is almost unthinkable that such a man could exist.

There is another secondary lesson—

but a very practical and urgent one, especially in our day—to be learned from this incident at Jacob's well. It is the lesson that condemns racialism. St. Paul (and the other Apostles), insisted that the gospel of Christ and the brotherhood of Christ were for all men. There was neither "Jew nor Gentile, Greek nor barbarian," Paul said, as far as Christianity was concerned. No less an authority than Christ himself had first taught that truth, and he taught it at Jacob's well as told in today's gospel.

For centuries, Jews and Samaritans were bitter enemies. Even individuals were not on speaking terms. That day at Jacob's well Christ broke down this separating wall. While admitting that their knowledge, up to now, of the true God was faulty, they too were acceptable to God, as his adopted children. They too could and would become members of his earthly and eternal kingdom.

Have we not all a lesson to learn from our Lord's mercy and kindness, which broke through racial and national barriers on that day in Samaria? Has not something very basic gone wrong with our Christianity, or rather with our application of it to our own daily lives, when our world is torn to pieces by fraternal strife? Not only is one nation against or threatening another, but groups and factions, classes, creeds and colors are fighting one another within the one nation. We may well be surprised when we learn that the family next door is at loggerheads. Why, we say, aren't they one family? Why can't they live in love and harmony as a family should? But what is our country —what is this planet on which we live, but the home of one family—the family of God, the human race? Why are we quarreling, why do we hate one another, why cannot we live in peace?

We can, and we will, if and when each one of us recognizes his fellowmen as his brothers. It is the charity of Christ, practiced as Christ practiced it towards us, and not demonstrations, or protests, or force of arms, that will make this earth once more the true (if temporal) home of the whole human family.

FOURTH SUNDAY OF LENT

FIRST READING : 1 Sam. 16 : 1; 6–7; 10–13. The Lord said to Samuel, "Fill your horn with oil, and go; I will send you to Jesse the Bethlehemite, for I have provided for myself a king among his sons."

When he came, he looked on Eliab and thought, "Surely the Lord's anointed is before him." But the Lord said to Samuel, "Do not look on his appearance or on the height of his stature, because I have rejected him; for the Lord sees not as man sees; man looks on the outward appearance, but the Lord looks on the heart." And Jesse made seven of his sons pass before Samuel. And Samuel said to Jesse, "The Lord has not chosen these." And Samuel said to Jesse, "Are all your sons here?" And he said, "There remains yet the youngest, but behold, he is keeping the sheep." And Samuel said to Jesse, "Send and fetch him; for we will not sit down till he comes here." And he sent, and brought him in. Now he was ruddy, and had beautiful eyes, and was handsome. And the Lord said, "Arise, anoint him; for this is he." Then Samuel took the horn of oil, and anointed him in the midst of his brothers; and the Spirit of the Lord came mightily upon David from that day forward.

EXPLANATION : The Israelites, ever since their liberation from Egypt and their entry into the Promised Land, lived more or less as separate tribes. They had no central government. When one of the twelve tribes was in danger from a neighboring pagan nation, God raised up a leader, called a "Judge," who led the tribe to victory in most cases. Samuel was the last of these Judges, and towards the end of his life he had more or less succeeded in forming a loose confederation among the twelve tribes. But the people were displeased with the lack of unity and political security. The pagan nations which surrounded them were ruled by kings who led them to battle and who organized their territories on a sound, political basis.

The Israelites therefore appealed to Samuel to give them a king with a hereditary kingship, and thus secure national government and a guarantee of survival. Saul, on the advice of God, yielded, if reluctantly, to their request. Saul was appointed the first king of all Israel (1030 B.C.), but though successful in many battles, he offended God and the kingship was taken from him and his descendants.

David, a shepherd boy of Bethlehem, was privately anointed king, at God's command, to replace Saul. His dynasty lasted 500 years (until the Babylonian exile), and his direct descendants survived until the promised Messiah, the Son of Mary and adopted son of Joseph, finally came and changed the Chosen People of the Old Testament—the Israelites—into the new people of God which comprised the men of all nations. Today's first reading describes the selection and anointing of King David.

Fill . . . oil : Anointing with olive oil had a special significance among the Chosen People, ever since the Exodus. The High Priests were consecrated to God's service in the Temple by this sacred anointing (Lev. 8 : 12). The Kings, beginning with Saul, were anointed to signify that they were God's representatives and now invested with a sacred character. They were henceforth called "God's anointed" and were revered by all.

I have . . . myself : When told to go to Bethlehem to the house of Jesse, Samuel did not know whom he was to anoint king. God simply tells him that he has chosen for himself a king from that household.

He looked on Eliab : Because of the eldest son's stature and fine appearance, Samuel felt "here is God's chosen one," but God told him otherwise. God sees the inner man, the true man, and therefore can judge rightly.

seven . . . Samuel : What happened to Eliab happened to the next six sons. They were not chosen by God.

youngest . . . sheep : The youngest son was so unimportant in his father's eyes that he had not even thought of calling him in from the fields.

this is he : God tells Samuel to anoint him, for this is the young man he has chosen as his king.

spirit . . . David : The young shepherd-boy received the power of God in that anointing—his later deeds of valor and wisdom proved this. He had still many sufferings and trials to undergo at the hands of the rejected Saul before he became king of Israel, but he received God's mandate and God's divine assistance from that day forward.

APPLICATION : The selection of David, an unimportant shepherd-boy of little Bethlehem, as second King of Israel, was an event which happened over 3,000 years ago, and may at first sight appear to be of little importance for us Christians of the 20th century. Yet it has many important lessons to teach us. First and foremost, it shows us how little years and centuries mean to God in his eternal plans. In choosing David he was choosing the royal ancestor of the King of Kings, a thousand years before he came on earth. The day he sent Samuel to Bethlehem, he was planning in advance for you and for me. His thoughts were on us from eternity.

The choice of David, the least likely of Jesse's sons, is another lesson for us, a lesson to make us humble by admitting our limitations. The whole book of man's life is open before God; we can see only the cover and the title. In that book, together with his good deeds, God saw the very serious offences David would commit against him in later years, but he also saw his sincere repentance— he still chose David, a consolation surely and an encouragement for all of us sinners, provided our repentance (like David's) is sincere. And also a lesson for even the holiest of us to avoid rash judgement of our neighbours and of those placed over us.

Another and a very important truth which needs stressing today, perhaps more than ever before, is that all legitimate power exercised by men over their fellowmen comes from God. It is part of God's plan for men's existence on this earth. Because of the special gifts he has given us, God intends us to live in society, to live together in smaller or greater groups for the benefit of all. For such a group, let it be a tribe or a nation or group of nations, there must be an authority which will regulate the dealings of individuals with one another and with the appointed lawful authority. This authority, provided it is lawfully conferred and lawfully exercised, comes from God and must be accepted, revered and obeyed as such.

And what holds for civil or secular authority holds for authority in the Church also. Christ founded a society in which all the members of his mystical body would live in mutual love and fraternal cooperation. To lead and direct these members Christ appointed leaders to whom he promised his divine assistance. The first leaders were the Apostles, with Peter as their head. Their direct successors are with us still (and will be till the end of time) in the persons of the Pope and the bishops of the Church. To these we owe obedience in all matters that concern our Christian welfare, because this is God's will and purpose for us.

While those who hold authority in state or Church must exercise that authority with justice and prudence, never forgetting that the power they wield is not their own personal prerogative but is given to them by God, so in like manner must their subjects accept their directives and their laws as coming from God, not from a fellowman.

SECOND READING: Ephesians 5:8–14. Once you were darkness, but now you are light in the Lord; walk as children of light (for the fruit of light is found in all that is good and right and true), and try to learn what is pleasing to the Lord. Take no part in the unfruitful works of darkness, but instead expose them. For it is a shame even to speak of the things that they do in secret; but when anything is exposed by the light it becomes visible, for anything that becomes visible is light. Therefore it is said, "Awake, O sleeper, and arise from the dead, and Christ shall give you light."

EXPLANATION: Ephesus (now a heap of ruins) was on the coast of Asia Minor. It was a flourishing port and city (in St. Paul's day). The Apostle preached in Ephesus during his second missionary journey (Acts 18:19–21), and during the third journey he stayed there for almost three years (Acts 19:1—20:1). This letter to the Ephesians (probably intended as a circular letter for the churches of that part of Asia Minor) was written by Paul while a prisoner in Rome. In it he stresses the doctrine of the Church as mystical body of Christ: all men, Jews and Gentiles, become members of Christ's body of which he is the head. He also uses the metaphor of marriage to describe this relationship: Christ is the Bridegroom, the Church his Bride (5:22–32).

darkness . . . light : The majority of the new Christians of Ephesus were converts from paganism. Paganism was darkness; it shed no light on man's purpose in life. The pagan knew not whither he came from, where he was going, or how he could get there. This has all changed for the converts. They have the truth of the Lord, the true facts of the Incarnation, and all it means for them, so they must :

walk . . . light : Their daily life must be lived according to the truths of the Christian faith they have received, trying always to please God by doing his will.

unfruitful . . . darkness : Apart from the immorality and vices which were rife among the pagans of that time, their religious rites or services were unfruitful—they were offered to false gods, who could not reward or help them.

instead expose them : Not only must they not think of going back to these pagan practices, but they must do all they can to show their pagan neighbors how sinful and how unfruitful they are.

shame . . . speak : The immoralities practiced by the pagans, not only in their daily lives, but frequently in their so-called religious rites were not fit even to be mentioned by a Christian.

exposed by the light : It is the duty of the newly-converted Christians to bring home to their pagan neighbors the contrast that exists between their pagan way of life and the light of truth and virtue which they now possess as Christians.

it is said : The light of glory and revelation which the Messiah would bring into the world is mentioned in Is. 9:1 and 60 : 1–3 (see also John 1 : 7–9, 14).

awake . . . dead : This is probably part of a baptismal hymn. Baptism by immersion, as practiced in the early Church, represented the convert as dying to his old self and being buried with Christ and then rising from the waters to live with Christ "the light of the world."

APPLICATION : These words of St. Paul to the Ephesians are applicable to every one of us, especially during this season of Lent. We too have the great blessing of the light of the Christian faith. We, too, have died with Christ in our baptism and have been set on the road to the eternal life. We, too, know "all that is good and right and true," and we know that if we live according to this knowledge, we will be "pleasing to the Lord" and will be moving steadily towards the destination God in his love and mercy has prepared for us.

That destination is heaven, a place of everlasting happiness which God has planned for us before time began and which is the only place which will satisfy all the desires of the human heart.

Knowing this, one wonders why we need reminders to keep us on our toes : that the purpose of today's lesson should be to awaken us from the sleep of laziness and forgetfulness of our real purpose in life. But the sad fact is, that, apart from the few truly devoted Christians who never forget what their Christian faith means to them, the vast majority of us are very apt to let the passing pleasures and interests of this life take hold on us and blot out ninety-nine per cent of the Christian light which should illuminate all our daily actions.

Many of us today also are asleep, and need this call to awaken us to a sense of our obligations as Christians. This does not mean that we must change our occupation or cut ourselves off from all our relatives and friends, but that we must change our outlook on life and eternity. We must still carry out our daily, worldly tasks whatever they may be, but we must do these tasks from the Christian motive of pleasing God.

The light which Christ has brought to us shows us the true meaning of life. Our short sojourn on earth is our training ground and preparation for the everlasting life which will be ours after death, if we use the few years we are given on this earth properly. If any of us have been sleeping—that is, wasting the valuable time God is giving us—now is the time to wake up to the reality of life. There is still time to roll up our sleeves and get to work. We know not how much time is left, but this we do know, that if we use that time as St. Paul tells us today, if we "walk as children of light," living our Christian life to the full, we can still earn the resurrection from the dead and receive eternal light from Christ, our brother and our Savior.

GOSPEL : John 9 : 1–41. As Jesus passed by, he saw a man blind from his birth. And his disciples asked him, "Rabbi, who sinned, this man or his parents, that he was born blind?" Jesus answered, "It was not that this man sinned, or his parents, but that the works of God might be made manifest in him. We must work the works of him who sent me, while it is day; night comes, when no one can work. As long as I am in the world, I am the light of the world." As he said this, he spat on the ground and made clay of the spittle and anointed the man's eyes with the clay, saying to him, "Go, wash in the pool of Siloam" (which means Sent). So he went and washed and came back seeing. The neighbors and those who had seen him before as a beggar, said, "Is not this the man who used to sit and beg?" Some said, "It is he;" others said, "No, but he is like him." He said, "I am the man." They said to him, "Then how were your eyes opened?" He answered, "The man called Jesus made clay and anointed my eyes and said to me, 'Go to Siloam and wash;' so I went and washed and received my sight." They said to him, "Where is he?" He said "I do not know."

They brought to the Pharisees the man who had formerly been blind. Now it was a Sabbath day when Jesus made the clay and opened his eyes. The Pharisees again asked him how he had received his sight. And he said to them, "He put clay on my eyes, and I washed, and I see." Some of the Pharisees said, "This man is not from God, for he does not keep the Sabbath." But others said, "How can a man who is a sinner do such signs?" There was a division among them. So they again said to the blind man, "What do you say about him, since he has opened your eyes?" He said, "He is a prophet."

The Jews did not believe that he had been blind and had received his sight, until they called the parents of the man who had received his sight, and asked them, "Is this your son, who you say was born blind? How then does he now see?" His parents answered, "We know that this is our son, and that he was born blind; but how he now sees we do not know, nor do we know who opened his eyes. Ask him; he is of age, he will speak for himself." His parents said this because they feared the Jews, for the Jews had already agreed that if anyone should confess him to be Christ, he was to be put out of the synagog. Therefore his parents said, "He is of age, ask him."

So for the second time they called the man who had been blind, and said to him, "Give God the praise; we know that this man is a sinner." He answered, "Whether he is a sinner, I do not know; one thing I know, that though I was blind, now I see." They said to him, "What did he do to you? How did he open your eyes?" He answered them, "I have told you already, and you would not listen. Why do you want to hear it again? Do you too want to become his disciples?" And they reviled him, saying, "You are his disciple, but we are disciples of Moses. We know that God has spoken to Moses, but as for this man, we do not know where he comes from." The man answered, "Why, this is a marvel! You do not know where he comes from, and yet he opened my eyes. We know that God does not listen to sinners, but if anyone is a worshipper of God and does his will, God listens to him. Never since the world began has it been heard that anyone opened the eyes of a man born blind. If this man were not from God, he could do nothing." They answered him, "You were born in utter sin, and would you teach us?" And they cast him out.

Jesus heard that they had cast him out, and having found him he said, "Do you believe in the Son of man?" He answered, "And who is he, sir, that I may believe in him?" Jesus said to him, "You have seen him, and it is he who speaks to you." He said, "Lord, I believe;" and he worshiped him. Jesus said, "For judgement I came into this world, that those who do not see may see, and that those who see may become blind." Some of the Pharisees near him heard this, and they said to him, "Are we also blind?" Jesus said to them, "If you were blind, you would have no guilt; but now that you say, 'We see,' your guilt remains."

EXPLANATION: This miracle, worked by our Lord in Jerusalem, and so dramatically told by St. John, brings out the merciful kindness of Jesus "the light of the world," who gives to a blind beggar not only his bodily light or eyesight but also the light of faith. It also shows the stubborn pride of the Pharisees which prevented them, not only from seeing in the humble "son of man" the long-expected Messiah, but made them incapable of seeing a miracle which was evident to everybody else in the neighborhood.

who . . . parents: The disciples' question arose from the common conviction among the Jews that all physical defects and all pain was a punishment for sin. Our Lord tells them this is not so.

works . . . him: That this man was born

blind was not caused by God, but his physical defect gave Christ an opportunity to prove to the Pharisees that he was from God.

night . . . work : Christ had to fulfill his messianic mission during the span of life allotted him on this earth.

clay . . . Siloam : Jesus tested the man's faith and obedience. Clay mixed with spittle was an unlikely cure for blindness, but the man did as he was told and returned from the pool "seeing."

some said . . . no : It was customary for the disabled to sit near one of the gates leading to the temple court, and beg for alms. This man was well-known to all temple-goers, but some could not believe their own eyes when they saw him with his eyes open for the first time. Hence the arguments.

the Pharisees : Now the Pharisees dispute among themselves. If Jesus mixed clay with spittle on the Sabbath day he was a sinner. But if he worked this miracle he could not be a sinner, for miracles come from God.

He is a prophet : The beggar agrees with the latter statement. Christ must be from God, a prophet.

called the parents : Now the Pharisees began to deny the man was born blind. They called his parents, who testified that this man was their son and was born blind. However, to avoid any trouble the Pharisees could cause them, they wisely said their son was of age and could speak for himself.

for the second time : During this second interrogation the man born blind throws the Pharisees into greater confusion. He asks them if they too wished to become Jesus' disciples. This is, to them, an insult—they are disciples of Moses, they keep and expound Moses' law, they know nothing of this newcomer. The man tells them this is a marvel; with all their knowledge and authority they do not know this man who worked such a marvelous miracle! If he were not from God he could not do this.

you were . . . sin : They now admit the man was born blind, which is a proof of sin, and how dare he teach them. "And they cast him out."

Jesus . . . him : After he had been cast out by the Pharisees, Jesus asked him if he believed in the Son of man, that is, in the Messiah.

it is . . . you : Jesus tells him he himself is the Messiah, and the man answered : "Lord, I believe, and he worshiped him." He had now the gift of faith as well as the gift of his sight.

For judgement I came : Not to condemn the world, but by the acceptance or the rejection of him, would each man decide his own eternal fate.

are we also blind : The Pharisees understood rightly that they were included in those who condemned themselves.

If . . . blind : If it were ignorance that prevented them from recognizing and accepting him, they would be excused, but it was their pride and prejudice which had brought an incurable blindness of mind to them and led them to reject him and eventually crucify him.

APPLICATION : St. John was an eyewitness of this story. He was one of our Lord's first disciples and was with him in Jerusalem when this incident took place. That the behavior of the Pharisees made a deep impression on his young mind is evident from the minute details he is able to give when writing his gospel, sixty years later. The Pharisees were opposed to Jesus from the very beginning of his public life (see Jn. 3 & 7). He mixed with publicans and sinners; he preached mercy and forgiveness. Many of the common people all over the country and in Jerusalem itself were becoming his disciples, and this meant that the Pharisees were losing followers and temple revenue. Their personal pride was being hurt and their privileges being weakened. They would have long since put an end to his mission, but "his hour had not yet come" (Jn. 7 : 30).

Today's story shows up this pride and prejudice. They at first refuse to admit a miracle occurred. When the parents convince them that the cured man is their son who was born blind, they attribute the miracle to a sinner, one in league with Satan, but the cured man shows them this is impossible. They then excommunicate the man but they remain convinced that the worker of this miracle is not from God, not the Messiah, but an impostor.

The Pharisees have long since disappeared from history, but there are thousands still among us who, blinded by the same pharisaical pride and prejudice, refuse to see the truths of God's revelation as made known to mankind in its fulness by the Incarnation and the teaching of Christ. They refuse to admit that God exists or that Christ existed, or that if he did he was the Son of God, who became man in order to make us sons of God and heirs of heaven. In their pride they claim to be absolute masters of their own fate, and they seem or pretend to be content that that fate will end in the death of the body.

Like the fox who lost his tail, they are not content to keep their irrational unbelief to themselves, but want others to join them. They are ever ready to propagate their errors and to accuse believers of childish credulity and folly. We accept their accusations; we are thankful to God and to his beloved Son, Christ, that we have been given the light of faith. Our reason tells us that the marvelous gifts we have are not from ourselves but were given us by a loving God who by the act of creation shared his own goodness with all creatures, but especially with man whom he made "in his own image and likeness." These gifts of intellect and will we possess are such that they could never be satisfied in the few years we are given in this life. God's revelation through Christ informs us that there is a future life awaiting us where our spiritual faculties, and our transformed bodies as well, will be fully and fittingly satisfied.

Christ, "the light of the world," to whom the Pharisees and their modern followers shut their eyes lest they see, is our light and our delight. Through the gift of faith, he has given us a spiritual eyesight, which, while it cannot dispel all the shadows and discomforts of this life, opens up to us a glorious unending future where our God-given gifts will at last find their true purpose, their true satisfaction.

May God shed some of this light on those who in their folly ignore and deny him, and may he never let us falter in our faith and in our fidelity to the baptismal promises which we made to him when, through his grace and generosity, we became his chosen children of light.

FIFTH SUNDAY OF LENT

FIRST READING : Ezekiel 37 : 12–14.   Thus says the Lord God : Behold, I will open your graves, and raise you from your graves, O my people; and I will bring you home into the land of Israel. And you shall know that I am the Lord, when I open your graves, and raise you from your graves, O my people. And I will put my Spirit within you, and you shall live, and I will place you in your own land; then you shall know that I, the Lord, have spoken, and I have done it, says the Lord.

EXPLANATION : Ezekiel was a priest of the temple of Jerusalem up to 597 B.C., when he was deported to Babylon with the king Joachim and the first deportees. Among the exiles in Babylon he denounced the sins of the people which brought about the exile, and foretold greater misfortunes still for Judah. Jerusalem and its temple would be destroyed by the Babylonians, and the remainder of the people taken into captivity. They had deserted Yahweh; he would now desert them for a while. But Ezekiel, like Jeremiah and second-Isaiah his contemporaries, had words of encouragement also. Better days were to come, when Yahweh would take back his people once more and dwell in their midst forever (37 : 25). The verses taken from Ezekiel today are part of this encouragement.

Thus . . . God : The prophet is speaking for the Lord.

I will . . . graves : In the eleven verses preceding this pericope the prophet has described how God, through him, spoke to the dry bones of the Israelites and raised them up and gave them life once more. As is clear from verse 11, there is no question of resurrection of the body here : the dry bones are the exiled Israelites who say "our bones are dried up, and our hope is lost, we are clean cut off." Now God tells these despairing Israelites that all is not lost. He will give them a real life, not that of slavery, once more.

O my people : They are still his chosen people in spite of their neglect of him.

My spirit . . . you : He will give them a new spirit, a spirit of obedience once more.

and you shall live : Living in slavery in a foreign land was not life.

place . . . land : He will bring them back from exile and establish them in Judah again.

then . . . shall know : They will then realize that nothing short of the power of Yahweh could have done this for them.

APPLICATION : God revealed himself and his true nature to his Chosen People in the Old Testament by his actions more than by his words. They were a stubborn, stiff-necked people—they were so often ungrateful for all the benefits he conferred on them. They forgot him in material prosperity and only turned to him in need. The idolatry and misconduct of their kings ever since Solomon (with a few notable exceptions), and the no-less-pagan outlook of the majority of the people, brought on them the destruction of Jerusalem with its temple, the centre of their life and religion, in the year 587. They had been warned by God's prophets but they turned a deaf ear to all remonstrances and warnings. When the foretold calamity fell they turned to Yahweh, but too late.

However, when they had done their penance in Babylon, Yahweh came to their aid once more and brought them back to Judah and Jerusalem, where they eventually rebuilt the city and their temple and where they remained until the promised Messiah came.

In all of this we have the merciful, forgiving God, revealing himself, while using this very ungrateful people to carry out his plan for raising the whole human race to adopted divine sonship through the loving mystery of the Incarnation.

We Christians have seen that plan fulfilled. We know we have been adopted by God and made heirs of heaven because Christ made himself our brother. We know too that we shall rise again from the dead and be brought back not to Judah or Jerusalem, but to the land of eternal happiness—to "the Jerusalem that is above." God revealed much of his divine qualities to the Jews, but how incomparably greater is the revelation we have received from him through the coming of Christ among us!

The Jews of that day had but a very vague idea of life after death; we are certain that our physical death is not the end for us but rather the beginning of our true life. The Jews called God their "father" but because of their infidelity the father-son relationship was a cold one, built more on fear than on love. We call God our Father, but we use the term with sincerity and love for we have become his children through the brotherhood of Christ, his real, divine Son.

God helped the Jews often in their temporal needs, they seldom sought spiritual aid from him. We have in the mystical body of Christ, his Church, all the spiritual helps we need for our journey to heaven, and temporal favors on innumerable occasions, during our stay on earth. God said of his Chosen People : "What more was there to do for my vineyard that I have not done for it? When I looked for it to yield grapes, what did it yield—wild grapes?"

Unfortunately, he has to make the same complaint of many in his Christian vineyard, and how much more has he done for them than he ever did for the Jews? God forbid that any one of us should be deserving of this complaint. When we meet him on the day of judgement let us hope and pray that we will have the true grapes of a virtuous life to offer him.

SECOND READING : Romans 8 : 8–11. Those who are in the flesh cannot please God. But you are not in the flesh, you are in the Spirit, if the Spirit of God really dwells in you. Anyone who does not have the Spirit of Christ does not belong to him. But if Christ is in you, although your bodies are dead because of sin, your spirits are alive because of righteousness. If the Spirit of him who raised Jesus from the dead dwells in you, he who raised Christ Jesus from the dead will give life to your mortal bodies also through his Spirit who dwells in you.

EXPLANATION : On the Epistle to the Romans, see First Sunday of Advent above.

in the flesh . . . God : St. Paul nearly always uses the word "flesh" for those tendencies in man which incline him to sin and to the things of this earth in opposition to things spiritual. The man who follows these inclinations (who lives according to the flesh) cannot please God, but rather offends him.

You are . . . flesh : He is addressing Christians who have died (to all their evil inclinations) with Christ in baptism. "Do you not know," Paul says (in Rom. 6:3–4), "that all of us who have been baptized into Christ Jesus were baptized into his death? We were buried therefore with him by baptism into death . . ."

you are . . . Spirit : The Holy Spirit has been given to the baptized. Through their union with Christ the Spirit is within believers, transforming their rational faculties; they live a new life.

Anyone . . . Christ : Paul uses the terms "Spirit of God," the "Spirit," the "Spirit of Christ" and "Christ" as interchangeable terms to express the indwelling of God in the baptized. The man who has not this indwelling Spirit does not belong to Christ. He is not a Christian.

bodies . . . sin : Because the Christian has Christ dwelling in him (even though the Christian lives in a body which can be called "dead" because of its inclination to sin), he is alive with a true spiritual life because of the uprightness and divine grace which Christ brings to him.

spirit . . . Jesus : It was God the Father who raised Jesus from the dead. The Christian who has the Spirit of God dwelling in him will be raised from the dead by the same Spirit. His body doomed to die will be given a new mode of life—the risen Christian, like the risen Christ, will be given a new mode of existence, an unending life.

APPLICATION : The three readings for today, the Fifth Sunday of Lent, have a common theme—resurrection. In Ezekiel the release of the Jews from the captivity and slavery of Babylon is described as a rising from their graves to return to a new life in their own homeland. This is a metaphor, a type of the true resurrection which will come later. In the third reading—the gospel—we have the story of the raising of Lazarus from the tomb, which proves the power Jesus had of raising the dead.

In this second reading, in St. Paul's instruction to the Roman Christians, we have a direct reference to the future resurrection to a life of unending glory for all those who during their time on earth, were loyal to God and Christ. This resurrection in a new body, which will never again be subject to death or pain or suffering, has been won for us by Christ who, having died for our sins, was raised by the Father on Easter morning.

Only the munificence of an infinitely loving God could plan and provide such a marvelous future for us. "What is man that you are mindful of him?", the Psalmist says to God. What are we indeed—mere creatures, finite, limited beings, in comparison with the infinite Godhead! Yet, when creating us he gave us the spiritual faculties which enable us to appreciate the good, the beautiful and the perfect. He knew that in this life these powers could never be satisfied, and so he ordained that after "working our passage" through this valley of tears, a new life would await us, an unending life in which, in company with the Blessed Trinity, our blessed Mother and the millions of fellow-saints, we would have eternal contentment and happiness.

The thought of this glorious future should never be far from our minds. It was this thought that enabled the martyrs to face their executioners with joy in their hearts. It was this thought that made the saints rejoice in their bodily sufferings and mortifications. It was this hope of eternal happiness which spurred on the millions of ordinary men and women like ourselves, whose life on earth was a monotonous sequence of one drudgery after another, one misfortune following on the heels of the previous one.

It is by imitating these people that we too will join them when our call will come. It is by bearing the burdens of each day, by welcoming, and seeing God's will in all the ups and downs of our very ordinary lives, that we can join them. Listen again to these solemn words of St. Paul: "Anyone who does not have the spirit of Christ does not belong to him." You have the Spirit of Christ in you, if you are striving to live a Christian life. This means taking each day as it comes, offering to God its joys and its sorrows, its honest pleasures and its pains, its sunshine and its showers. All this means: living in peace with God and with your neighbor. This may sound easy but it is not so; it will mean much self-denial, but then think of what awaits us at the end of our road—a resurrection to a new life, an unending life of happiness. God grant that we may all have this happy ending to our earthly journey.

GOSPEL: John 11:3–7; 17; 20–27; 33–45. The sisters of Lazarus sent to Jesus, saying "Lord, he whom you love is ill." But when Jesus heard it he said, "This illness is not unto death; it is for the glory of God, so that the Son of God may be glorified by means of it."

Now Jesus loved Martha and her sister and Lazarus. So when he heard that he was ill, he stayed two days longer in the place where he was. Then after this he said to the disciples, "Let us go into Judea again."

Now when Jesus came, he found that Lazarus had already been in the tomb four days. When Martha heard that Jesus was coming, she went and met him, while Mary sat in the house. Martha said to Jesus, "Lord, if you had been here, my brother would not have died. And even now I know that whatever you ask from God, God will give you." Jesus said to her, "Your brother will rise again." Martha said to him, "I know that he will rise again in the resurrection at the last day." Jesus said to her, "I am the resurrection and the life; he who believes in me, though he die, yet shall he live, and whoever lives and believes in me shall never die. Do you believe this?" She said to him, "Yes, Lord; I believe that you are the Christ, the Son of God, he who is coming into the world." Jesus was deeply moved in spirit and troubled, and he said, "Where have you laid him?" They said to him, "Lord, come and see." Jesus wept. So the Jews said, "See how he loved him!" But some of them said, "Could not he who opened the eyes of the blind man have kept this man from dying?"

Then Jesus, deeply moved again, came to the tomb; it was a cave, and a stone lay upon it. Jesus said, "Take away the stone." Martha, the sister of the dead man, said to him, "Lord, by this time there will be an odor, for he has been dead four days." Jesus said to her, "Did I not tell you that if you would believe you would see the glory of God?" So they took away the stone. And Jesus lifted up his eyes and said, "Father, I thank thee that thou hast heard me. I knew that thou hearest me always, but I have said this on account of the people standing by, that they may believe that thou didst send me." When he had said this, he cried with a loud voice, "Lazarus, come out." The dead man came out, his hands and feet bound with bandages, and his face wrapped with a cloth. Jesus said to them, "Unbind him, and let him go."

Many of the Jews therefore, who had come with Mary and had seen what he did, believed in him.

EXPLANATION: St. John gives us here the last and the greatest of the miracles worked by our Lord. It had two purposes: first, to prove that Christ was the Messiah, the Son of God to whom the Father was now testifying publicly by this miracle and secondly, to move the chief priests and Pharisees to carry out the plan they long since contemplated. This miracle took place a few miles from Jerusalem—within a few hours the Pharisees had news of it (11:46); they called a meeting and decided that Christ must be put to death.

It was his Father's will that he should die at the Passover feast which was drawing near: he had completed his work; his "hour" had come and so in working this miracle, he gave them the extra motive and excuse for carrying out their wicked designs. Christ's death, like the illness of Lazarus, would be for the glory of God, manifested in him. His raising of Lazarus was but for a short extra period of earthly life; his own resurrection would be the first fruits of the eternal resurrection which he would win for all those who would follow him.

this illness . . . death: Its result was death, but the illness and death were intended in order that Christ's messiahship would be finally and convincingly proved by means of it.

already . . . days: Lazarus must have died the day the messengers came from Martha and Mary. Jesus stayed two days more, east of the Jordan; the return journey to Bethany took a full day and as burial took place on the day of death, Lazarus was already four days buried.

if you . . . here: Both sisters believed Christ could have cured their brother had he been present; they did not think he could do so from a distance. Nor did they think he could now raise him from the dead. Yet, Martha still shows her strong faith in Jesus' influence when she says: "Even now I know that whatever you ask from God, God will give you," but this evidently did not include the possibility of his calling Lazarus from the tomb, as her objection to removing the stone later shows.

Your brother . . . again: Martha believed in the future resurrection of the dead as did many, but not all, of her contemporaries, and she understands Jesus' words to refer to this general resurrection.

I am . . . life: Jesus confirms this belief and adds that it is he himself who is the cause of the resurrection and the eternal life which will follow it.

whoever . . . never die: All who believe in Christ and live according to that faith will live forever. While they must pass through the gates of physical death—the lot of all mankind—they only pass into eternal life.

Christ . . . God: Martha answers that she believes he is the Messiah so long expected. "Son of God" in opposition to "the Christ," that is, the Messiah, is not used in its strict sense.

deeply . . . troubled: Christ in his human nature suffered anguish and pain to a greater degree than any mere human being. His agony in the garden as his passion approached is evidence of this (see Heb. 5:7). He knew that this present miracle was to precipitate his passion and death, as the sequel shows.

Take . . . stone: Martha, thinking he wanted to see his dead friend, objected as corruption would already have set in.

You . . . God: Jesus tells her that had she believed, trusted in him she would see a miracle—"the glory of God." God would glorify himself and his Son.

people . . . sent one: He had thanked his Father aloud for having heard his request—to raise Lazarus. He was the Son of God and his, and the Father's, power were one, but the people could not grasp the truth of his divinity yet—what he wants is that they will accept him as the promised Messiah.

Lazarus, come out: The miracle takes place, the dead man rose and:

many of the Jews: Not all of them believed his claim that he was the Messiah *whom God had sent*, notwithstanding this extraordinary miracle.

APPLICATION : On hearing this story of the resurrection of Lazarus, the question which will arise in the minds of most people is this : why did Jesus allow his best and most faithful friends to suffer anguish for four days? He could have cured Lazarus of his illness the moment he heard of it. Yet he delayed and allowed the sisters to suffer the death of their beloved brother. We have already given the answer above. He wanted to make this, his last recorded miracle, a convincing proof of his claim to be what he was—the Messiah, sent by God to give a new life, an eternal life, to mankind. He also wanted to give his enemies a great impulse and motive to carry out his condemnation and crucifixion, which was the debt he "the suffering servant" of God, was to pay for the sins of mankind.

That his closest friends had to suffer for a while, in order to cooperate with him in his plans was therefore an unavoidable necessity. Is there not here an answer to the questionings of divine providence which we hear so often from otherwise devout followers of Christ? Drowned in their own personal sorrow and grief they cannot see that this very sorrow and grief is part of Christ's plan for the salvation of men. And the fact that they are loyal, true friends of Christ is the very reason they are chosen to carry this particularly heavy cross. Less faithful friends would not help him, so in his mercy he does not put that extra load on their unwilling shoulders.

Martha and Mary had to live through four sad days, while their friend seemed to forget them. But how great was the reward for their sufferings, when their beloved brother returned to the family circle—a brother they thought they had lost forever! We can well imagine the rejoicings that took place in that home in Bethany (not only that night but for years to follow).

We all have our sorrows and separations from our loved ones. But as in the case of the Bethany family, they are temporary separations. Our dear ones who are taken from us are not lost to us—they are perhaps closer to us and more helpful to us than they ever could have been in this life. And our faith convinces us that we will be reunited soon with them. Christ, by his death, has conquered death. He has won eternal life for all men. His resurrection was the prelude ("the first-fruits," as St. Paul calls it) to the resurrection of all mankind—a resurrection to an eternal life of happiness where families, friends and neighbors will rejoice together in the presence of God for all eternity. The years of sorrow we have to endure here below will look small and trifling indeed when viewed from eternity.

But—and this is a capital but—though Christ has won a new, eternal life of adopted sonship with God for all men, each man must do his part to earn that sonship, to merit the eternal happiness which Christ came to win for us. "God created us without our consent," says St. Augustine, "but he cannot save us without our cooperation." We must live our lives then as Christ has taught us.

For every thought we give to death, and we are reminded of it hourly and daily, let us think three times on what will follow after it. If we do, we will never die unprepared. We will have made sure of a happy eternity.

PASSION SUNDAY

FIRST READING : Isaiah 50 : 4–7. The Lord God has given me the tongue of those who are taught, that I may know how to sustain with a word him that is weary. Morning by morning he wakens, he wakens my ear to hear as those who are taught. The Lord God has opened my ear, and I was not rebellious, I turned not backward. I gave my back to the smiters, and my cheeks to those who pulled out the beard; I hid not my face from shame and spitting. For the Lord God helps me; therefore I have not been confounded; therefore I have set my face like a flint, and I know that I shall not be put to shame.

EXPLANATION : The second-Isaiah describes in these verses how the suffering servant—the Messiah—accepts the role of suffering which the Father had designated for him. He is to preach the message of God's mercy to men. Many will reject him and torture him, but God is on his side and he will not be moved from his resolute purpose by their insults and injuries.

The Lord has given me : It is God who has appointed him teacher of the people and has given him "a well-trained tongue," the gift necessary for his task.

how . . . word : His preaching will touch both friend and foe. The former will be moved to listen and obey—the latter will grow stronger in their opposition.

morning by morning : His was a daily task, a difficult task, but :

I . . . rebellious : He continued notwithstanding the difficulties.

I gave my back . . . my cheeks : Literally fulfilled in the scourging at the pillar and the mocking of the Roman soldiers.

shame and spitting : In the presence of Caiphas (see Mt. 26 : 67–68).

The Lord God . . . me : The source of his strength.

set my face like a flint : No insult or suffering would weaken his resolve (see Ez. 3 : 8, when God promises the same strength to Ezekiel).

I shall not be put to shame : All their insults and injuries (even crucifixion) will be in vain. He will triumph in the end.

APPLICATION : The sufferings and crucifixion of our divine Lord in his humanity are the Christian's source of strength and encouragement in his daily struggles against the enemies of God and of his own spiritual progress. Because of our earthly bodies, and because of the close grip that this world of the senses has on us, to keep free from sin and to keep close to God on our journey to heaven is a daily struggle for even the best among us. But we have the example before our eyes, the example of our true brother. He was one of ourselves, the truly human Christ. He not only traveled the road before us and made the journey to heaven possible for us, but he is with us every day, close beside us, to encourage and help us on the way.

We need to remind ourselves daily of this. We have the crucifix in our Christian homes, on our rosary beads, on our altars, on the very steeples of our churches. These crucifixes are not ornaments, but stark reminders that our Savior's path to heaven led through Calvary and through all that preceded Calvary. They are also stern reminders to us that the carrying of our crosses on the road to heaven is not an unbearable burden for us, but an essential aid to our progress.

When you are tried by temptations, when you are tested by bodily pain or mental suffering, worried to death perhaps by the bodily needs of yourself or your family or by the disobedience and insults of ungrateful children, stop and think on the Leader and his humiliations and sufferings. He came to open the road to heaven for us, to make us all sons of God, to preach the message of divine forgiveness and mercy to mankind. What did he get in return? He was scourged, tied to a pillar, spat upon and insulted, jeered at and mocked. He was nailed to a cross on Calvary between two thieves!

How light is my cross in comparison, how easy my Calvary. But he was sinless; his obedience, as man, to the Father was perfect. Can we or should we complain, we whose life up to now has often been far from perfect? Stop, think and listen to today's lesson.

SECOND READING : Philippians 2 : 6–11. Christ Jesus, though he was in the form of God, did not count equality with God a thing to be grasped, but emptied himself, taking the form of a servant, being born in the likeness of men. And being found in human form he humbled himself and became obedient unto death, even death on a cross. Therefore God has highly exalted him and bestowed on him the name which is above every name, that at the name of Jesus every knee should bow, in heaven and on earth and under the earth, and every tongue confess that Jesus Christ is Lord, to the glory of God the Father.

EXPLANATION : It is generally admitted that Paul is here quoting an earlier liturgical hymn in which the Judeo-Christian Church expressed its faith in the true humanity and the true divinity of Jesus Christ. He who was God, humbled himself to become a man like us, hiding his divine glory but receiving it back at his resurrection, or exaltation.

Because of this, everyone must confess and adore his equality in divine glory with his Father.

in the form of God : He was divine and did not cease to be divine when he became man but :

emptied himself : He did not let the divine glory appear. Instead his humanity, the same as that possessed by all men, was what was evident. He was a truly obedient servant (slave) of God however, as all men should be, but were not. This true obedience led him to the humiliating death on a cross (see Isaiah in first reading).

God exalted him : By raising him from the dead on Easter morning God restored to him the glory of the divinity that he had hidden during his earthly life (see Eph. 1:21), and glorified his human nature.

name above every other name : Name stands for "person." He is exalted to the right hand of the Father in his humanity as well as in his divinity, the chief place in heaven after God the Father.

at Jesus' name : The man who walked the roads and hills of Palestine, who ended his life on a cross, is none other than the Lord. Adonai is the name for God used by the Jews to avoid saying the sacred name Yahweh. It is God the Father who has proclaimed this, who "bestowed upon him the name" therefore :

every knee must bend : All men are bound to pay him reverence as God and :

every tongue confess : To proclaim their faith in the divinity of Christ the Savior is the basis of their Christian faith and the only hope of salvation for all.

to the glory of God the Father : His human nature also is sharing in the divine glory in heaven, the guarantee that our finite human nature can partake in some measure in this same divine glory if we have been his faithful brothers on earth.

APPLICATION : As Christians we have no doubt as to the two natures of our Savior. He was the God-man. He humbled himself so low in order to represent us before his Father and by his perfect obedience ("even unto the death on a cross") earn for us not only God's forgiveness but a sharing in the divinity, through his being our brother but also the Son of God. These words of Paul, or rather of the early Christian hymn he is quoting, are for us today a consolation and an encouragement.

Surely every sincere Christian must be consoled by the thought of God's infinite love for him, as shown in the Incarnation. We are not dealing with some distant, cold, legal God of justice who spends his time marking up our sins and failures against us. We are dealing with a loving Father who sent his own beloved Son to live among us and die for us in order to bring home to us the greatness of divine love. Could any human mind, even the minds of the greatest of this world's philosophers, have invented such a humanly incredible story of true love? No, it was only in the infinite mind of God that such a proof of love could have its source.

What encouragement this should and does give to every sincere Christian. We know we are weak. We can and do sin often. We know we are mean and ungrateful and that we seldom stop to thank God for the love he has shown us. If we were dealing with a human, narrow-visioned God, we should have reason to despair, but when our Judge is the all-loving, all-merciful God how can even the worst sinner ever lose hope?

No, there is no place for despair in the Christian faith. But there is room for gratitude and confidence. We can never thank God sufficiently for all that he has done for us. Eternity itself will not be long enough for this, but we must do the little we can. Let us face this coming Holy Week with hearts full of thanks to God and to his divine Son for all they have done for us. When meditating on the passion of Christ on Good Friday let us look with gratitude and confidence on the Son of God who died on the cross in order to earn eternal life for us.

He did not die to lose us but to save us. He has done ninety per cent of the work of our salvation. And, even as regards the remaining ten per cent that he asks us to do, he is with us helping us to do it. Could we be so mean and so foolish as to refuse the little he asks of us?

GOSPEL : Matthew 26:14–27:66.

EXPLANATION : Because of the length of this gospel (127 verses) the text is not printed here—it is easily available to any reader. Nor shall we give any detailed explanation, as the story of the passion is well known to all Christians; a brief summary must suffice.

St. Matthew begins with the story of Judas, *"one of the twelve,"* promising to betray Jesus to the chief priests, the arch-enemies of Christ, for thirty pieces of silver. Then comes the Passover meal on Thursday night, followed by the institution of the Blessed Eucharist. In the utterance : "I shall not drink wine until I drink the new wine with you in the kingdom of my Father," Jesus tells his disciples his next supper with them will be in the eschatological kingdom—the future life, where *the new wine* of that kingdom will be drunk (see 8:11; 22:1–14).

Jesus foretells that they will all desert him in his hour of trial, and to Peter, who feels his faith would never waver, he foretells his threefold denial. Then comes the Agony in the Garden, where the human nature of Jesus shrinks from the sufferings he foresees, but yet he accepts the Father's will. He allows himself to be arrested by a gang of armed men, led by Judas who betrayed him with a kiss. The disciples scatter in fear. He is led before the Sanhedrin. Challenged on oath, he openly admits he is not only the Messiah, but is next to Yahweh, "the Power," in heaven. In this the Sanhedrin see that he is claiming a divine nature; hence he is condemned for blasphemy.

On the morning of Friday he is brought, bound as a prisoner, before Pilate, the pagan Roman governor, to have the Sanhedrin's sentence of death officially confirmed. Pilate judges Jesus to be innocent and tries to convince his accusers of this, but fails. Fearing a riot, and anxious for his own position, he condemns Jesus to crucifixion, while washing his hands to show he is not responsible for his injustice. Having been scourged, a Roman prelude to crucifixion, Christ is then mocked by the soldiers.

He is led out to Golgotha (Calvary) carrying his cross and is crucified between two thieves. While he is dying slowly on the cross his enemies jeer at him and challenge him to come down from it if he is king of Israel : "He saved others, now let him save himself." "He puts his trust in God, he said I am the Son of God, now let God rescue him if he wants him."

Certain signs occurred : darkness suddenly covered the land, there was an earthquake, the veil of the temple (which separated the sanctuary from the Holy of Holies) was rent from top to bottom. Seeing these signs the pagan Roman centurion and the soldiers under him, were terrified and said : "In truth this was the Son of God."

Joseph of Arimathea, having asked Pilate for permission, had the dead body of Jesus buried in his own new tomb.

The Jews, remembering Jesus' prophecies that he would rise from the dead, got permission from Pilate to put a guard of soldiers around the tomb lest the disciples should steal him away and pretend he had risen. But the thought of Christ's resurrection was far from the disciples' minds—they had forgotten or disbelieved these prophecies while his enemies remembered them! The stone at the door of the tomb was sealed and a guard mounted to prevent what was unpreventable. Christ rose the third day.

APPLICATION : Is there any human being, not to mention any Christian, whose heart is so hard and so callous, that he could read or hear of the torments Christ endured during his last twelve hours on earth without being moved to pity and to tears? Even if the victim of this, the cruellest form of execution, crucifixion, were guilty of crimes against humanity, as were the two robbers crucified with him, our hearts should be filled with sympathy for him.

But in the case of Christ we are dealing with a victim who not only had committed no crime, but was incapable of even a venial fault. He had come to save the whole human race—to make all men his brothers and thus co-heirs of an eternal life. To do this he had taken human nature in order to become our brother, and because of the sins of the world he had to die this excruciating death in order to save mankind from the effects of their sins, which would have been eternal death.

Lest we might think that his being divine as well as human might have eased his sufferings in any way, we have proof of the opposite in his agony in the garden, and his pitiful call to his Father as he was dying painfully and slowly on the cross : " My God, my God, why hast thou forsaken me?" His human nature had to bear the full effects of the torments inflicted on him. This was the will of his Father, which Christ willingly accepted as the prophet Isaiah had foretold centuries before, when he described the Messiah as the "suffering servant" of God.

Looking back today, on that sorrow-laden first Good Friday, there is not one of us who would not gladly have done everything in his power to ease the pains and the sufferings of our loving Savior if he had been there. But, mindful of any past loyalty or lack of loyalty to this Jesus who suffered for us, are we honest with ourselves when we express this sentiment? Did we never imitate Judas and betray Christ and his commandments for the sake of some few unjustly gained pieces of silver? Did we never let our pride and prejudice condemn, offend and unjustly injure our neighbor, just as the pride and prejudice of the chief priests and the Sanhedrin condemned Christ unjustly? Did we never crown him with thorns, and mockingly call him our king when we posed as loyal subjects of his while living lives of sin? Did we never imitate Pilate, who condemned an innocent man—a man he declared innocent—because he feared for his own future comforts and honors? Was our position in politics and power, or possessions, ever more important to us than the true following of Christ and his teaching?

We could go on with our examination of conscience, but surely each one of us can see that he played, in a greater or lesser degree, the part not of a comforter or consoler of Jesus in his torments, but the part of one or other of the wicked actors in the tragedy of Calvary. However, we have the great consolation of knowing that Christ prayed for his tormentors on the cross (Lk. 23:34), and that he included us in this solemn request to his Father. We can still repent of our past sins and turn with confidence to him, assured that he will forgive and forget, and give us a new start.

Let each one of us return from Calvary today, beating our breasts in sorrow for the pains and sufferings we have caused our loving Savior. He died an excruciating death so that we might live an unending life of happiness. We shall live that eternal life if we die now to our sins, our passions, and our weaknesses.

EASTER SUNDAY

FIRST READING : Acts 10 : 34; 37–43. Peter opened his mouth and said: "You know the word which was proclaimed throughout all Judea, beginning from Galilee after the baptism which John preached : how God anointed Jesus of Nazareth with the Holy Spirit and with power; how he went about doing good and healing all that were oppressed by the devil, for God was with him. And we are witnesses to all that he did both in the country of the Jews and in Jerusalem. They put him to death by hanging him on a tree; but God raised him on the third day and made him manifest; not to all the people but to us who were chosen by God as witnesses, who ate and drank with him after he rose from the dead. And he commanded us to preach to the people, and to testify that he is the one ordained by God to be judge of the living and the dead. To him all the prophets bear witness that everyone who believes in him receives forgiveness of sins through his name."

EXPLANATION : These verses are part of the story of the conversion of Cornelius, a Roman army officer. Stationed in Caesarea, Cornelius believed the God of the Jews was the true God, but though a good-living man, he had not become a Jew. Advised by a divine messenger, he sent to Joppa for St. Peter, whose antipathy to pagans had been corrected by a vision seen that same day. Peter came to Caesarea and, contrary to his life-long custom, entered the pagan home of Cornelius, who explained to him why he had been asked to come (10 : 1–33). Peter then speaks :

You know . . . which was proclaimed : Peter gives a synopsis of Christ's public life and mission in Palestine, of which Cornelius, a man in a position of authority, must have heard already.

anointed . . . with the Holy Spirit : a reference to the descent of the Holy Spirit on Jesus during his baptism by the Baptist in the Jordan.

and . . . power : proved by his many miracles and by his teaching.

God was with him : In his human nature divine power was given him. He was God the Son, but in his human nature, as man, he emptied himself of his divine glory, as St. Paul tells us (Phil. 2 : 6; see last Sunday).

"hanging him on a tree" : a figurative expression for crucifixion (see Dt. 21 : 23).

only to have God raise him . . . third day : The resurrection of Jesus is attributed to the Father in almost all the texts that refer to it in the New Testament. The verb in Greek is passive "was raised." St. Jerome translated this with the active voice *surrexit* "he rose." As the Father and Son are one God, there is no theological difference.

not to all . . . witnesses : He appeared to the Apostles, disciples and others (see 1 Cor. 15 : 1–8), during forty days after his resurrection.

and drank with him : Jesus had eaten with the Apostles—not that the risen, glorified body needed food but to convince them of the reality of his risen human body.

to preach to the people : The commission given to the Apostles on Ascension Day.

judge of the living and the dead : Judge of all men. This will be the role of Christ the God-man (see 17 : 31).

prophets . . . witnesses : No prophets are quoted, but in a true sense the whole Old Testament was a preparation, and a prophecy in fact, concerning him who was to come (see 3 : 19–26).

through his name : The purpose of the Incarnation was to make men not only friends but sons of God. Where sin had intervened, its remission was necessary and available for all who believed in Christ (see 3 : 19–26).

APPLICATION : This passage from Acts has been selected for Easter Sunday not only because the resurrection is mentioned in it, but especially because St. Peter in his first discourse to a Gentile makes the resurrection the basic doctrine and the crowning proof of the truth of the Christian faith. As St. Paul says : "If Christ has not risen vain is our preaching, vain too is your faith" (1 Cor. 15 : 14). And like Paul, St. Peter stresses the truth of the resurrection by citing

witnesses, including himself, who had not only seen the risen Jesus but had spoken to him and actually eaten with him.

There is little doubt but that the Apostles and disciples had thought that the sad events of Good Friday had put an end forever to the mission of love and mercy of their beloved Master. In spite of his previous references to his resurrection, they had completely forgotten it and were convinced that the tomb near Calvary was the end of all their hopes. They had locked themselves into the room of the Last Supper for fear of the Jews—two of them had set off for home on the Sunday morning, down-hearted at the Master's failure; the others were waiting for an opportunity to slip out of the city quietly. But the resurrection changed all this. The unexpected, the unhoped-for happened. Even the most skeptical of them all, doubting Thomas, was eventually convinced of its reality. Had they been hoping for it, or even thinking of it, there might be some reason to suspect it was only an hallucination, the result of their "wishful thinking," but the very opposite was the case. They were hard to convince even when it happened.

All this was intended by God—the basis of our Christian faith was proved beyond doubt. Christ, who had died on the cross on Good Friday, was raised from the dead by his Father on Easter morning. He returned to heaven in the full glory of the divinity which he had hidden while on earth, together with his human body, now also glorified. There (in heaven), as God and Man, he pleads for us at the right hand of the Father until the day when he who redeemed all men will come to judge them all.

The Alleluia is repeated often during the Easter ceremonies. It is a Hebrew word which means "praise ye the Lord." It is our attempt to give verbal expression to our joy and gratitude for all that God has done for us. We are no longer mere humans living on this planet for a few short years. We are citizens of heaven, made children of God the Father by Christ our Brother. And he has gone before us to his and our kingdom to prepare a place for us. He conquered death. Our earthly death has, therefore, now no real fears for us : it is not the end but the beginning of our true lives. It is only after our earthly death that we truly begin to live.

There is only one death now which we can fear—the spiritual death of serious sin which can keep us from our true heavenly life. But while this is a possibility for all of us, it is only a possibility. The sincere Christian who realizes what God has done for him and what is in store for him, will never be so ungrateful to God or so forgetful of his own best interests as to let some temporal and passing pleasure, pride, or profit, come between him and the eternal home which God's love has prepared and planned for him.

SECOND READING : Colossians 3 : 1–4. If you have been raised with Christ, seek the things that are above, where Christ is, seated at the right hand of God. Set your mind on things that are above, not on things that are on earth. For you have died, and your life is hid with Christ in God. When Christ who is our life appears, then you also will appear with him in glory.

EXPLANATION : The method of administering Baptism in the apostolic days was by immersion. Those who heard the story of the gospel and were ready to believe in the one true God, the Father, the Son and the Holy Spirit who had cooperated in man's redemption and elevation to divine sonship, were immersed in water to be cleansed from their sins and their previous worldliness. Immersion in water symbolized being buried in the tomb with Christ. By immersion, therefore, the new Christian died with Christ to all earthly attachments and desires. He was raised again from the water (the tomb) to be with the Risen Christ.

If you have been raised . . . Christ: The physical act of immersion and rising again from the baptismal bath was not enough unless the convert meant what he was doing. The Christian life was a **new life,** a life of unity with Christ. Therefore, the new Christian must:

set your mind . . . things above: His thoughts must now be on the things of the spirit, the everlasting truths which he has just learned. His past evil practices must be forgotten.

where Christ is seated: He must strive to earn heaven where Christ is now in glory, having gone through death and resurrection to make heaven available to us.

not on things that are on earth: The things of earth insofar as they are sinful, or occasions of sin, are now forbidden. Insofar as they are necessary for the sustenance of earthly life they are not forbidden, but they must always be used so that they do not impede the journey to heaven.

You have died . . . your life . . . Christ: The Christian has died in baptism to all sinful earthly concerns. He is now living a new life; it is hidden because it is a spiritual life. Externally, in bodily appearance, he has not changed, but since his baptism, he is a *new man.* He is with God, a brother of Christ and a member of God's family.

When Christ . . . appears: Christ lives in the Christian. The Christian lives in Christ and through Christ. Christ is the source of our new life, and the essence of it, by faith and the sacraments, especially the Eucharist.

you shall appear . . . glory: Christ will appear in glory at the particular and the general judgements. The loyal Christian will appear, will return with Christ from the grave, in the glorified state which will be his for all eternity.

APPLICATION: Children at boarding schools draw up calendars and mark off each day which brings them one nearer to the end of the term. Fiancés mark off the months, the weeks, the days that separate them from the great day when they will be united forever, they say, to their beloved one. Seminarians count the years, months, weeks to the great day when they will be ordained and say their first Masses. Parents look forward anxiously to the day when their children will be educated and safely settled in life. In fact, we are all always looking forward to a happier day which is to come some time. All this is very natural and very human, because our present life is not our permanent life; our present home, this earth, is not the real home destined for us by our loving Creator.

We were created for unending happiness in heaven, and it is only when we get there that our desire and our quest for some greater happiness will end. From then on, we will always enjoy and possess that all-satisfying happiness.

Today, Easter Sunday, St. Paul reminds us that we have this happiness within our grasp. We are moving steadily and more quickly than we realize toward it. The Holy Trinity, God the Father, the Son and the Holy Spirit, have already done, and are daily continuing to do for us, all within their power. All that is needed is that we do the little that is asked of us.

St. Paul tells us we must "mind the things that are above not the things that are on earth." We must never let the "things of earth," the pleasures, the power, the possessions which we can or could have in this life, block or impede us on our upward journey. Does this mean that we must all return to the deserts of Egypt, as some early Christians did? By no means. We are not forbidden to have the lawful pleasures of life. We are not forbidden possessions or power if they are used justly. All we are forbidden is the unlawful use of the things of this world.

And as regards minding the things that are above, this is not something calling for extraordinary self-sacrifice or unnatural mental activity. All we are asked to do is to try to stay in God's grace, and do our daily chores whatever they be, as well and as diligently as we can. We are expected to recognize our natural weakness and to turn to God frequently for pardon and for help.

Whilst there are saints in heaven who lived lives of extreme self-mortification and did extraordinary things for God and for their neighbor, it is an encouraging and consoling thought that there are millions of unknown saints in heaven who lived normal lives, unnoticed by the world and maybe even by themselves. They are people who kept God's friendship all their lives, or got back quickly to it, if they sometimes forgot or offended their heavenly Father.

What millions of others have done we can do too. We are aided by God's grace as they were. God wants us in heaven. He has an Easter resurrection planned for us.

GOSPEL : John 20 : 1–9. On the first day of the week Mary Magdalene came to the tomb early, while it was still dark, and saw that the stone had been taken away from the tomb. So she ran, and went to Simon Peter and the other disciple, the one whom Jesus loved, and said to them, "They have taken the Lord out of the tomb, and we do not know where they have laid him." Peter then came out with the other disciple, and they went toward the tomb. They both ran, but the other disciple outran Peter and reached the tomb first; and stooping to look in, he saw the linen cloths lying there, but he did not go in. Then Simon Peter came, following him, and went into the tomb; he saw the linen cloths lying, and the napkin, which had been on his head, not lying with the linen cloths but rolled up in a place by itself. Then the other disciple, who reached the tomb first, also went in, and he saw and believed for as yet they did not know the scripture, that he must rise from the dead.

EXPLANATION : The accounts of Christ's resurrection on Easter morning as given by the four Evangelists vary in details but agree on the essential points. Some women, the leader among them being Mary Magdalene, came to the

F

tomb early on Sunday morning to anoint the dead body with spices, in order to help preserve it. This anointing had been done very hastily on the Friday because of the Sabbath which began at sundown. The tomb was found open and empty. The first thought of the women was that somebody had stolen the corpse. This shows how far resurrection was from their minds. They went in haste to tell the disciples. Peter and John ran to the tomb. Later that day Christ appeared to Mary Magdalene, to ten of the Apostles, to Peter separately (according to St. Paul, 1 Cor. 15 : 5), to two disciples on the road to Emmaus (Lk. 24 : 13); and, later on, he appeared often to the Apostles and disciples in Galilee, for a period of days.

First day of the week : The Sabbath was the last day of the Jewish week, so the first day corresponds to what is now called Sunday.

Mary Magdalene : John mentions only Magdalene by name but the "we don't know" in verse 2 implies there were others with her.

stone had been moved away : The tomb was raised above the ground and its entrance was closed by rolling a large stone, cut for the purpose, across the entrance (see Mk. 16 : 3).

they . . . the Lord : This was Magdalene's only possible explanation of the absence of the body.

Peter and the other disciple : Peter and John ran to the tomb. When they found the winding sheet and the cloth that covered the head lying there, they realized that the body had not been stolen or taken away : why should the linen coverings have been removed?

He saw and believed : That Peter had been the first to believe and then John, seems to be the meaning here, not that John believed in contrast to Peter.

as yet they did not understand : Until this moment they had not understood the scriptures which had foretold his resurrection. In fact neither had they believed Christ's own prophecies of his resurrection—it seemed to be something which could not happen.

APPLICATION : As we said above, the accounts of the resurrection of Christ differ in many details in the different writings of the New Testament, but the fact of the resurrection stressed in all of them, was the basis of the new Christian Faith. Had it not happened, Christianity would have been stillborn. It would have disappeared from Jerusalem and the world on that first Easter Sunday. Peter and his companions would have returned to their fishing-nets and boats on Lake Genesareth, and Christ the good and the kind man who had helped so many, would have been forgotten in half a generation.

But Christ was no mere man of kindly acts and words of wisdom. He was the Messiah promised for centuries. He was the suffering servant foretold by Isaiah, whose perfect obedience to his Father had led him to the Cross and the grave. But above all, he was the Son of God who had emptied himself (St. Paul) of his divine glory in order to be the perfect human servant of the Father, and who was now raised by the Father, with his divine glory restored, and his glorified resurrected body sharing in that glory. This was the divine plan of God for mankind: through Christ, and because of Christ's (the new Adam's) perfect obedience, all mankind would be made worthy of divine sonship, and worthy of one day rising like Christ from the grave in glorified bodies.

Is all this too good to be true? It is, if we make God to our image and likeness, as so many opponents of Christianity do. He is God and his love is infinite and incomprehensible to us. What God can see in me and my fellowmen will always be a mystery to me, but then I have not the mind of God. All I know and all I need to know is that I have sufficient proofs that God loves all men. The Incarnation, death and resurrection of his Divine Son for man's sake is the greatest proof of love for us that even the omnipotent God could give. He has given it. As a necessary consequence from this act of divine love, we are guaranteed our resurrection from the dead to a life of unending happiness and glory if we do not, in extreme folly, reject God's offer.

Today, let us thank God once more for Easter and for all it means for us. Our personal Easter morning is not far away from even the youngest among us. We have a few Calvaries to climb perhaps in the meantime but what are they when we see our glorious Easter on the horizon?

SECOND SUNDAY OF EASTER

FIRST READING : Acts 2 : 42–47. The brethren devoted themselves to the Apostles' teaching and fellowship, to the breaking of bread and the prayers.

And fear came upon every soul; and many wonders and signs were done through the Apostles. And all who believed were together and had all things in common; and they sold their possessions and goods and distributed them to all, as any had need. And day by day, attending the temple together and breaking bread in their homes, they partook of food with glad and generous hearts, praising God and having favor with all the people. And the Lord added to their number day by day those who were being saved.

EXPLANATION : On Pentecost Sunday the Holy Spirit, as promised by Christ, descended on the Apostles with external signs which brought the people of Jerusalem in their hundreds to the Upper Room where the Apostles lived. St. Peter addressed them and explained what had happened, with the result that "about three thousand souls were baptized and added that day" (Acts 2:41) to the Apostles and disciples, who formed the nucleus of the Christian Church.

In a few brief verses St. Luke tells us in today's reading how they lived their new Christian life.

The brethren : Jesus himself had already given the title of "Brothers" to all those who do the will of his Father (Mk. 3:23). The Jews were accustomed, from early times, to call their fellow-Israelites "brothers." So, from the very beginning the Christians looked on one another as brothers in Christ, fellow sons of God.

Apostles . . . fellowship : The newly converted eagerly learned from the Apostles all they could about the life of Christ and his teaching. Thus the first Christian doctrine began to be systematized, and became the basis of the written gospels.

breaking of bread : Although this expression in the Old Testament meant partaking of a meal in common, and at the Last Supper our Lord ate a meal with his disciples before instituting the Eucharist, the term "breaking of bread" became, from the earliest days of the Church, a technical term for celebrating the Eucharist. Associated with "the prayers," as it is here, it almost certainly refers to the Eucharistic meal.

fear . . . soul : This statement does not fit in very well here, and is probably taken from 5:11, after the incident of Ananias and Sapphira.

many . . . signs : Luke is giving a brief summary of the life of the infant Church in Jerusalem. The signs and wonders worked by the Apostles are described in later chapters of the Acts.

all things in common : The ideal form of Christian life. But as the Church grew in numbers it became impossible—there would be always Ananiases and Sapphiras.

attending . . . together : As yet the Christians had no special place of worship of their own. Our Lord himself went to the temple and used it as a place for teaching his message. The Apostles continued to do so, and the early Christians gathered in the temple to pray until under Saul's persecution, they were driven from the city (Acts 8:1–4).

breaking . . . homes : Partaking of a community meal and the Eucharist.

praising God : They were all full of gratitude for the Christian faith which they had received, and continually thanked God for it.

favor . . . people : Their lives of holiness and brotherly love could not but be noticed by all unprejudiced Jews.

Lord . . . number : The result was that the number of converts went on increasing daily. This was the work of the Lord; he alone could call men to salvation, to brotherhood with Christ.

APPLICATION : In these six short verses of the second chapter of the Acts we are given a picture of the fervent religious life of the first Christian community. As would be expected, these Jerusalem Christians, having the Apostles still among them, and the memory of the resurrection and the descent of the Holy Spirit still fresh in their memories, were animated and moved by a deep religious fervor.

Apart from its noble ideal of true brotherhood, which moved those who possessed property to sell their possessions and divide the proceeds among the community—an ideal which could not continue, because of the selfishness in human nature, of which he was well aware—our Lord himself had recommended it only to a chosen few. We Christians today have in this first Christian Church of Jerusalem a model which we must strive to follow.

"They devoted themselves to the

Apostles' teaching and fellowship, to the breaking of bread and the prayers." While the Church has always and everywhere endeavored to instruct its members in the teaching of the Apostles, and encouraged them to take part in the celebration of the Eucharist and in community and private prayers, we present-day Catholics have, thanks to Pope John and his second Vatican Council, a better opportunity than ever before of imitating more closely the early Christians of Jerusalem.

The introduction of the vernacular language in place of Latin in the liturgy, gives even the humblest and least educated among us the chance not only of following what is taking place at the altar, but of taking an active part in it. While it is still the priest, through the power which comes to him from Christ through the Apostles in the sacrament of orders, who brings Christ present on the altar, it is the whole community present to whom he comes, and who offer him with the priest as the atonement for the sins of the world.

The congregation are no longer silent spectators at a rite performed on their behalf; they are co-offerers with the celebrant in this miraculous mystery of divine love. The prayers they say are not their own private petitions to God, but are the public expression of the Christian community's acts of adoration, thanksgiving, atonement and petition. In this liturgical renewal, therefore, the present generation, if they play the part expected of them, resemble more closely the first Christian community in Jerusalem. Hitherto, through no fault of their own, our Christian congregations let the priest at the altar carry out the liturgical action for them; they were content with their personal private prayers, while the public, community, liturgical service was performed in their name. Now, however, let us hope that all true Christians who appreciate what the "breaking of bread" or the Eucharistic sacrifice means for them, will appreciate also they have an active part to perform in this community service.

Christ in his loving mercy comes on our altar under the form of bread, to be our spiritual nourishment and our strength on the hard road to heaven. We should prove ourselves ungrateful indeed, were we to refuse this divine gift, which only divine love could think of giving us and which only divine power could give. If we feel unworthy of this great honor, remember he has given us also the sacrament which will remove anything which is really displeasing in us, and if we have but the passing, human failings, remember how he loved the publicans and sinners in Palestine and daily mixed with them.

The new liturgy gives us a better opportunity also of imitating the first Jerusalem Christians in devoting ourselves to the Apostles' teaching. In the three-year cycle of scripture readings which form the introduction to the Eucharistic sacrifice and communion, we have a wealth of instructive excerpts from the Bible, chosen especially to help us get a better knowledge of God and his love for us, and of the meaning of our Christian vocation. Every sincere Christian should not only listen carefully to these readings but should study them privately in the quiet of the home, and try to let their message influence their daily lives.

If we devote ourselves in this way to the Apostles' teaching, if we take an active, devout part in the weekly community celebration of the sacrament of

God's infinite love, and attend daily when possible, we will, like the first Jerusalem Christians, give true praise and glory to God and earn not only the favor but the following of our non-Christian neighbors.

SECOND READING : 1 Peter 1 : 3–9. Blessed be the God and Father of our Lord Jesus Christ! By his great mercy we have been born anew to a living hope through the resurrection of Jesus Christ from the dead, and to an inheritance which is imperishable, undefiled, and unfading, kept in heaven for you, who by God's power are guarded through faith for a salvation ready to be revealed in the last time. In this you rejoice, though now for a little while you may have to suffer various trials, so that the genuineness of your faith, more precious than gold which though perishable is tested by fire, may redound to praise and glory and honor at the revelation of Jesus Christ. Without having seen him you love him; though you do not now see him you believe in him and rejoice with unutterable and exalted joy. As the outcome of your faith you obtain the salvation of your souls.

EXPLANATION : This first epistle of St. Peter has always been accepted as authentic, that is, it was written by St. Peter and most probably from Rome which he calls "Babylon." Tradition says he died a martyr there in 64 or 67. The letter, therefore, was written before 67 at the latest. It is in the form of an encyclical letter to the numerous churches of Asia Minor. Its purpose was to recall to the minds of these converts to the Church the basic doctrines of Christianity and to encourage them to endure any persecution that the faithful observance of their new religion might bring on them from their pagan or Jewish neighbors.

Blessed . . . Father : The opening words are an expression of praise and thanksgiving to God the Father.

our . . . Christ : The doctrine of the blessed Trinity and the divinity of Christ is taken as known by his readers, which of course it was.

By his . . . anew : It was the infinite mercy of God which from all eternity had planned for mankind a new life, beyond this earthly life.

through . . . Christ : God the Father, in raising the human nature of Christ from his earthly death, proved beyond doubt that Christ was the Incarnate Son of God who had taken human nature in order to raise us up to sonship with the Father.

inheritance . . . unfading : Our second life, our new life, will be eternal and unchangeable.

kept . . . for you : That new life destined for mankind will be with God in his own eternal kingdom.

are . . . faith : It was God's power which gave us not only the possibility and knowledge of this supra-natural life, but which keeps us living the Christian faith so that we will be prepared and worthy to receive it when this life ends.

though . . . while : St. Peter reminds them of the joy and consolation this merciful act of God brings them. The thought of the happy ending which awaits them should make the trials and troubles of this passing life easy to bear.

genuineness . . . tested : As gold is purified of all dross in fire, so their faith—much more precious—will be tested and purified by these trials, so that their steadfastness in the faith will "redound to the glory and honor of Jesus Christ" who revealed it to them.

without . . . him : Peter admires their love for Christ whom they had not seen. Christ himself says in today's Gospel (Jn. 20:29): Blessed are "those who have not seen and yet believe." Peter himself had been a disciple and friend of Christ and probably still regrets his own cowardly denials on that fatal Thursday night in Jerusalem, though he had made up for that weakness later.

as the outcome of your faith : They are firmly convinced of the truth of the Christian faith, and rejoice in the hope of the eternal future (the eternal salvation) where death and pain and trials will no longer have any part in their new mode of existence.

APPLICATION : We have just celebrated the feast of the resurrection, and St. Peter's words today are intended to remind us again of what that unique event means to us and to the Christian faith which we profess. It is the final and convincing proof of the truth of the Incarnation. The Christ who had been born as a baby of the Virgin Mary, had lived in Nazareth, had preached the message of salvation, had died on the cross, was none other than what he had said he was, the divine Son of God. He had come to give mankind life and "abundant" life—an eternal life hereafter in the kingdom of his Father.

The first converts to Christianity had grasped this truth, this consoling knowledge, and they rejoiced in it "with unutterable and exalted joy." We, too, have grasped this truth; we, too, know that through the Incarnation, death and resurrection of Christ, we have been made heirs to an "inheritance which is unperishable, undefiled and unfading." But do we always let this consoling knowledge, this Christian conviction, govern and regulate our daily lives and actions?

The things of this world are very close to us and hard to ignore. Heaven seems very far away, and may seem to be something we can worry about later. The joys and pleasures of this passing life are very attractive because they surround us so closely now—the thought of the true, unending pleasure and happiness, much as it satisfies and answers to our innate human, intellectual desires and ambitions, can easily be pushed into the background by the hustling and bustling of the present, temporary attractions.

Today, perhaps, more than ever before, the advance of science and technology, that is, the discovery of the laws that govern our created universe and their application to daily living, keep so many so occupied that they have no time to think of the Law-maker, the Creator of all, and the future he has planned for them. They miss the wood because of the trees. They are so busy using and enjoying the earthly gifts God put at their disposal that they ignore the greatest gift of all—the one that will last forever.

"Our faith is more precious than gold": let us never forget these words of St. Peter.

GOSPEL : John 20 : 19–31. On the evening of that day, the first day of the week, the doors being shut where the disciples were, for fear of the Jews, Jesus came and stood among them and said to them, "Peace be with you." When he had said this, he showed them his hands and his side. Then the disciples were glad when they saw the Lord. Jesus said to them again, "Peace be with you. As the Father has sent me, even so I send you." And when he had said this, he breathed on them, and said to them, "Receive the Holy Spirit. If you forgive the sins of any, they are forgiven; if you retain the sins of any, they are retained."

Now Thomas, one of the twelve, called the Twin, was not with them when Jesus came. So the other disciples told him, "We have seen the Lord." But he said to them, "Unless I see in his hands the print of the nails, and place my finger in the mark of the nails, and place my hand in his side, I will not believe."

Eight days later, his disciples were again in the house, and Thomas was with them. The doors were shut, but Jesus came and stood among them, and said, "Peace be with you." Then he said to Thomas, "Put your finger here, and see my hands; and put out your hand, and place it in my side; do not be faithless, but believing." Thomas answered him, "My Lord and my God!" Jesus said to him, "Have you believed because you have seen me? Blessed are those who have not seen and yet believe."

Now Jesus did many other things in the presence of his disciples, which are not written in this book; but these are written that you may believe that Jesus is the Christ, the Son of God, and that believing you may have life in his name.

EXPLANATION : Last Sunday's gospel, also taken from St. John, described the first hint at the resurrection which the Apostles received. Peter and John, convinced that the body had not been taken away, because the winding sheets were left behind, were beginning to believe. But the others were skeptical, the two disciples on the way to Emmaus paid no heed to the women's story, and Thomas refused to believe the testimony of the other ten, even when this present appearance of our Lord had convinced them.

evening of . . . first day : The evening of the Sunday.

the doors being shut . . . : He came through the closed door, which shows the spiritual qualities of the resurrected body (see 1 Cor. 15 : 44–48).

came and stood among them : To prove that he was the Christ who had been crucified and who was now alive once more.

Peace be with you : Jews saluted one another by wishing peace, that is, health and prosperity both in the material and spiritual sense. Here Christ is not only wishing "well-being," especially the spiritual well-being, but he is *giving* it (see 14 : 27).

so I send you : He is now conferring on them the mission he had promised them before his death (see Mt. 4 : 19; Jn. 17 :

18 etc.), which was the continuation of the work of divine salvation inaugurated by himself.

Receive the Holy Spirit: He breathed on them and said these words—the sacramental action. He had promised them the Holy Spirit when he had returned to his Father in glory (7 : 39; 16 : 7). This condition had been fulfilled that Easter morning.

If you forgive . . . sins: Catholic tradition has rightly seen in this act the institution of the Sacrament of Penance.

Thomas, one of the twelve, . . . : He stubbornly refused to believe the word of the other ten Apostles and perhaps of disciples also who may have been with them. He needed personal evidence and the merciful Savior gave him that evidence.

eight days later: For Thomas's sake the risen Jesus appeared again in the very same place and circumstances. He asked Thomas to prove for himself that his body bore the marks of the crucifixion.

Thomas answered: Whether Thomas did touch the sacred wounds we are not told but his statement:

My Lord and my God: Proves how convinced he now was. And his statement goes further in expressing the divine nature of Christ than that of any other person in the four Gospels. "Lord and God" were the words used in the Old Testament to stress the true God "Yahweh Elohim."

Blessed . . . who have not seen: Christ is not belittling Thomas's expression of faith, but rather his slowness in accepting it on the testimony of others. Far greater, therefore, and more meritorious, Christ says, is the faith of all those, including ourselves, who have not had the privilege of seeing the risen Christ with our bodily eyes, but yet have believed in him on reliable testimony.

Many other things: These last two verses were the original ending of John's gospel. Chapter 21 was added later. His reason for writing his gospel was that men might believe that the Jesus who lived and died in Palestine was the promised Messiah and the true Son of God. He who believes this and lives up to his belief will have everlasting life because of what this Jesus has done for all men.

APPLICATION: It may surprise and amaze us that the Apostles were so reluctant to believe that Christ had risen from the dead, to live forever in glory with his Father in heaven. But we must remember that during their two or three years with him they saw nothing in him but a mere man, one with divine powers, but yet a man; certain prophets of the old covenant had some such powers also. Christ had "emptied himself" of his divine nature, and he had foretold his resurrection many times. But that he could be really God, as well as man, was something they could not then grasp, and if he was a mere man death had to be the end.

Their slowness of faith had its value for the future Church and for all of us. If they had been expecting the resurrection, and anxiously looking forward to it, people could say that they imagined it, that they persuaded themselves it had happened. Indeed, there have been men proud of their acuteness of judgement, who have said that the story of the resurrection is a story of mass hallucination, although all the evidence proves the opposite. Their conviction that it could not happen, could not be removed from their minds except by impressive evidence that it had. Hallucination is born in a mind already expecting and hoping for the *imagined fact*.

We can thank the Apostles and especially Thomas, the last to give in, that our faith in the resurrection and divine glorification of Christ is that much the stronger. Our Christianity which would have ended before the first Easter week had passed, if Christ had not risen in glory, spread rapidly to the then known world and is still spreading, because its author was none other than Christ "our Lord and our God." How prophetic were the words of Gamaliel at the meeting of the Sanhedrin which tried to prevent the Apostles from preaching the new Christian faith: "If this plan or work is of men, it will be overthrown; but if it is of God, you will not be able to overthrow it" (Acts 5 : 38–39).

THIRD SUNDAY OF EASTER

FIRST READING: Acts 2 : 14; 22–28. On Pentecost day Peter, standing with the eleven, lifted up his voice and addressed the crowd, "Men of Judea and all who dwell in Jerusalem, let this be known to you, and give ear to my words. Jesus of Nazareth, a man attested to you by God with mighty works and wonders and signs which God did through him in your midst, as you yourselves know—this Jesus, delivered up according to the definite plan and foreknowledge of God, you crucified and killed by the hands of lawless men. But God raised him up, having loosed the pangs of death, because it was not possible for him to be held by it. For David says concerning him. 'I saw the Lord always before me. for he is at my right hand that I may not be shaken; therefore my heart was glad, and my tongue rejoiced; moreover my flesh will dwell in hope. For thou wilt not abandon my soul to Hades, nor let thy Holy One see corruption. Thou hast made known to me the ways of life; thou wilt make me full of gladness with thy presence.' "

EXPLANATION: The crowds that had gathered around the Upper Room were full of amazement and anxious for an explanation. They heard the noise "as of a mighty wind" in that part of the city, and then heard the Apostles speaking foreign languages.

Peter . . . eleven: Peter, whom Jesus had made the Rock on which he was building his Church, was already recognized by the other Apostles and disciples as their official leader and head. It was he, therefore, who addressed the people and explained the events that had happened and were now happening.

Jesus of Nazareth : The name by which he was especially known to the Jews who opposed him. The lowliness of the village from which he came stressed his unimportance in their minds.

attested . . . God : The miracles Jesus had worked "in their midst" (the curing of the man born blind, and the raising of Lazarus from the dead after four days in the tomb, had taken place in and beside Jerusalem), were proofs offered to them by God that Jesus was what he claimed to be—the promised Messiah and more, the real Son of God.

delivered . . . God : The chief priests and the Pharisees "planned" to end Jesus' influence among the people by putting him to death. Judas "planned" to betray him to them at the opportune moment. What they did not know was that the death of Jesus in all its details was "planned" by God from the beginning. "He was delivered up according to the definite plan and foreknowledge of God" (see the account of the agony in the garden in all 4 Evangelists).

You crucified . . . men : Peter tells the Jews (that is, their leaders) that they went so far in their hatred of Jesus that they called on "lawless men," that is, Gentiles (who knew not the law of Moses), to put him to death on the cross.

God . . . up : The resurrection was the crowning act in the drama of the Incarnation. Unwittingly, but nevertheless guiltily, because of their personal, wicked designs, the Jews had helped to carry out God's eternal plan for mankind's salvation.

not . . . for him : The resurrection was part of God's plan for Christ in his human nature. He could not remain dead, since his death was the door to eternal life for all men and he himself was to be the first to come through that door.

David says : Peter now cites Psalm 16 : 8–11, in which it was foretold that Christ could not remain in Hades, the abode of the dead, but would be released from it. Peter goes on to show in the verses that follow (29–36), that David was still in Hades, still in his tomb, and that his words in this Psalm 16 were a prophecy fulfilled in Christ.

APPLICATION : Easter is the season of hope, of encouragement and of consolation for every true Christian. It recalls to his mind the fact of Christ's victory over death—a victory which in God's eternal plan was not for him alone, but for all men who believe in him and try to follow him. The true Christian knows that his bodily or physical death is but a necessary prelude to the new and unending life God has prepared for him. The few verses of St. Peter's sermon, preached to the Jews in Jerusalem on that first Pentecost Day, bring this consoling thought to our minds, and it is a thought which should influence and direct our way of living every day of our lives.

It so affected St. Peter's audience that day that 3,000 joined the Apostles (2 : 41), and this was an audience which up to then paid little or no heed to the "man" who had been crucified, some seven weeks earlier on Mount Calvary.

How much greater should not its impact be on us, who already know who Christ really was, and who know the meaning his resurrection has for us?

However, let us not forget, that in the audience, too, were men who shut their ears and their minds to the facts told by St. Peter, men who continued to oppose Christ and revile him, and who did their utmost to put an end to his faithful followers. But in vain. Christ had triumphed, the Church he had founded would triumph, and millions of his faithful followers down through the centuries, have entered the eternal kingdom which his life, death and resurrection opened to them.

While we have still today, thank God, millions who are striving to follow Christ and to make their way to heaven, we have millions too (apart from those who through no fault of theirs have not heard his "good news," and for whom God will provide), millions who, like those unrepentant Jews of Jerusalem, shut their ears and their minds to the facts of the Incarnation and to its relevance to them.

Death, even eternal death, has, they proclaim, no fears for them; yet in their every action they are proving their love of life by their attachment to the very limited comforts and consolations which the fleeting life of this earth can give them. Are they not in their theories contradicting their own very actions, and contradicting the natural desire to continue living—a desire which the Creator instilled in every intelligent being, and which God arranged to satisfy, through the merciful mystery of the Incarnation?

Charity, true love of God and neighbor, demands that we pray frequently and fervently that God will open the eyes of our fellowmen to the light of the true Christian faith, that they too may profit by the Incarnation, that they too may rise to a life of eternal happiness. As for ourselves, let each one of us be another St. Peter in our own small way, by letting the light of faith, which God has given us, shine brightly before all men in our words and especially in our deeds.

SECOND READING : 1 Peter 1 : 17–21. You invoke as Father him who judges each one impartially according to his deeds; conduct yourselves with fear throughout the time of your exile. You know that you were ransomed from the futile ways inherited from your fathers, not with perishable things such as silver or gold, but with the precious blood of Christ, like that of a lamb without blemish or spot. He was destined before the foundation of the world but was made manifest at the end of the times for your sake. Through him you have confidence in God, who raised him from the dead and gave him glory, so that your faith and hope are in God.

EXPLANATION : On this Epistle see last Sunday's Second Reading.

You . . . Father : When the Apostles asked Jesus to teach them to pray he gave them the "Lord's Prayer," which begins by invoking God as "Our Father." This became one of the liturgical prayers of the Christian assemblies from the very first days of the Church. The Jews in the Old Testament sometimes called Yahweh their father, but in the mouth of Christians it had a new and objectively true meaning, for they knew Christ was their brother, hence they too were children of God.

judges each one : While God is a true loving Father, he is also a just judge, and we prove our true sonship by our actions in relation to him and our neighbor.

conduct . . . exile : We are adopted sons of God here on earth—a period of exile from our real home—but we shall get the inheritance promised us only if we serve God reverently and truly during this period of trial. Fear means reverence and due respect in this context.

ransomed . . . ways : Before their conversion to Christianity they were all pagans or Jews. Neither Judaism nor paganism could ever have made them sons of God and heirs to heaven, but Christ had earned this right and title for them.

not silver . . . blood : Christ assumed human nature, and gladly offered his human life by shedding his blood on the cross, in order to open to us eternal life.

lamb . . . blemish : He who had no sin became a "sin-offering," that is, a true sacrifice for us sinners.

before . . . world : The eternal decree of God, before the universe or man was created, had planned an eternal life for man, the masterpiece of creation, the one creature in the universe who through his spiritual gifts had the "image" of God in him.

manifest . . . times : The whole period of time that passed between creation and the coming of Christ, the completion and perfection of creation, was looked on as a period of waiting, of preparation. Christ's coming marked the end of those periods—"the fulness of time," as St. Paul calls it. No other such world-changing event will ever again come until the end of time.

confidence in God : Because of Christ we have learned of God's infinite love and mercy for us, and it was by raising Christ from the dead that God proved that Christ was his Son in human nature and restored to him the glory of the Godhead of which "he had emptied himself," while living on earth among us.

your faith . . . God : Because of all he has already done for us we can firmly trust and feel secure that we will attain heaven, the reward earned for us by Christ through God's mercy and love.

APPLICATION : St. Peter's message to us today is this : we are sons of God because of his infinite mercy in sending Christ to us as our brother. So we can rightly call God our "Father." But we must behave as true, loyal sons, during our "time of exile" on this earth, for our merciful Father is also the absolutely just God who will judge each one of us "impartially according to our deeds" when we lay down our earthly life.

The fact that we are adopted sons of God, and thus co-heirs of Christ to the eternal kingdom, is the foundation, the title-deed, to our future possession of the promised inheritance. But we must live our lives in accordance with the conditions laid down in those title-deeds. We must follow Christ all through our earthly life if we are to join him in the eternal kingdom.

Our Lord himself put this very emphatically and clearly when he said : "If anyone will come after me, let him deny himself and take up his cross and follow me" (Mt. 16 : 24). This does not mean that life must be one long martyrdom, but it means that we must keep our human passions and unlawful earthly desires under control. Millions of Christians in the past have done this, and nobody could say they lived a miserable life on this earth. There are millions of Christians today who are keeping the laws of God and living as loving and grateful "sons of God," and they should be and are the happiest men and women on earth.

Look around and see the non-practicing Christians; they have more than they can use of the wealth of this world, but they are unhappy because they want more. The sixth and seventh commandments have been long since ignored and forgotten by them, but the troubles of body and mind brought on by their illicit actions remain with them all their earthly lives. They spend their energies striving for financial and political power, only to find they have been chasing rainbows. They may live in luxury, but do they live in peace with their own consciences? They can hardly refuse to admit that one day soon they must leave all they had spent their life acquiring; and their being buried in a gold casket or coffin, in a marble vault, will not guarantee them any future happiness.

Every good Christian realizes what St. Peter tells us today: this life is but a period of exile. We are on our way to our true home, and any trials we have to meet on the way are examinations we have to pass in order to graduate into that everlasting home. But the crown of glory which awaits us is worth a thousand times more than all the crosses and trials this earthly life can inflict on us.

St. Peter reminds us, too, that it was not with gold or silver or any other earthly goods that this future life of happiness was bought for us, but by the life and sufferings of Christ, whom God had "destined before the foundation of the world" to be our mediator and Savior. God thought of us from all eternity—he is still thinking of us and of our true happiness. Surely, we have enough sense, and enough interest in our own welfare, to think of our own future and to live the few years of exile as true, adopted sons of God, and thus make ourselves worthy to be with our heavenly Father for all eternity!

GOSPEL : Luke 24 : 13–25. On the first day of the week, two of the disciples of Jesus were going to a village named Emmaus, about seven miles from Jerusalem, and talking with each other about all the things that had happened. While they were talking and discussing together, Jesus himself drew near and went with them. But their eyes were kept from recognizing him. And he said to them, "What is this conversation which you are holding with each other as you walk?" And they stood still, looking sad. Then one of them, named Cleopas, answered him, "Are you the only visitor to Jerusalem who does not know the things that have happened there in these days?" And he said to them, "What things?" And they said to him, "Concerning Jesus of Nazareth, who was a prophet mighty in deed and word before God and all the people, and how our chief priests and rulers delivered him up to be condemned to death, and crucified him. But we had hoped that he was the one to redeem Israel. Yes, and besides all this, it is now the third day since this happened. Moreover, some women of our company amazed us. They were at the tomb early in the morning and did not find his body; and they came back saying that they had even seen a vision of angels, who said that he was alive. Some of those who were with us went to the tomb, and found it just as the women had said; but him they did not see." And he said to them, "O foolish men, and slow of heart to believe all that the prophets have spoken! Was it not necessary that the Christ should suffer these things and enter into his glory?" And beginning with Moses and all the prophets, he interpreted to them in all the scriptures the things concerning himself.

So they drew near to the village to which they were going. He appeared to be going further, but they constrained him, saying, "Stay with us, for it is toward evening and the day is now far spent." So he went in to stay with them. When he was at table with them, he took the bread and blessed, and broke it, and gave it to them. And their eyes were opened and they recognized him; and he vanished out of their sight. They said to each other, "Did not our hearts burn within us while he talked to us on the road, while he opened to us the scriptures?" And they rose that same hour and returned to Jerusalem; and they found the eleven gathered together and those who were with them, who said, "The Lord has risen indeed, and has appeared to Simon!" Then they told what had happened on the road, and how he was known to them in the breaking of the bread.

EXPLANATION : We have here a delightful and instructive account of an event that happened on the first Easter Sunday. Besides the twelve Apostles, our Lord had seventy-two disciples (as well as many other followers), who accompanied him on his missionary journeys. They came with him to Jerusalem, and witnessed the sad, and, to them, the fatal events of Good Friday. Two of them, having given up all hope, were now returning home depressed and sad.

talking and discussing : They must have found it hard to understand how Jesus, who had worked so many miracles and had even raised the dead to life, could allow his enemies to put him to death.

Jesus . . . them : A third man joined them. They did not recognize him. Jesus had risen in his glorified body, entirely different from that laid in the tomb. He appeared in various visible forms—sometimes recognizable, to convince the Apostles of the truth of his resurrection, sometimes not recognizable, as on this occasion.

What . . . conversation? : The two disciples were amazed that this man could have been in Jerusalem and had not heard what had happened there the previous Friday.

chief . . . him : They had no doubt as to who were responsible for the death of Jesus.

we had hoped : They had the Jewish idea of the Messiah—one who would give Israel a new earthly kingdom. They had lost all hope, now that he had been crucified.

some women : The story of the empty

tomb had reached them before they left Jerusalem. But Christ was dead and, they thought, dead he would remain. Hence, all they had heard left them unimpressed, and they were returning home, thinking perhaps of the months and years they had "wasted" following Jesus.

slow . . . prophets : The stranger now chides them for not paying heed to the prophecies of the Old Testament concerning the Messiah.

was . . . necessary : Because of sin which had entered the world and the wickedness of his contemporary enemies, Jesus had to die as a sinner and malefactor (for the sins of the world) and by his resurrection place the divine seal on his Messiahship and his true sonship of the Father. All this he proved to the two disciples, from the Old Testament prophecies.

they recognize him : Out of true hospitality they constrained him to pass the night with them, and take a meal with them.

took bread . . . them : The "breaking of bread" is a technical term for the Eucharist (see Acts 2 : 42–46; 20 : 7; 1 Cor. 10 : 17). Whether the Eucharist is meant here is disputed, but Luke is certainly using eucharistic language (see Lk. 22 : 19).

they recognized . . . vanished : The moment they recognized him he disappeared—again a proof that he was in his glorified body, not subject to the conditions of an earthly body.

did not . . . burn : They now remember how his conversation with them on the way had set their hearts afire with love for him and for the Father who had sent him.

returned to Jerusalem : Their despair was over; they returned to their vocation, placing themselves under the direction of the Apostles. They found the Apostles already convinced of the resurrection : "the Lord has risen indeed and has appeared to Simon." Their story was only a confirmation of the acknowledged fact.

APPLICATION: There are two thoughts that should sink into our minds on hearing this beautiful and most instructive incident which happened on that first Easter Sunday.

First, the loving kindness of Jesus to two disciples who had lost faith in him, because of his having failed, as they thought, to triumph over his enemies on that dreadful Good Friday. He followed them, like the Good Shepherd he was, and brought them back to the fold.

In the lives of many Christians, and today especially, in the lives of many he has chosen as special disciples, there are moments when the doings and sayings of some who claim to be "masters in Israel" may make them doubt if Christ is still what he claimed to be, if his demands on them are still obligatory and necessary. They are tempted to think Christianity was a human invention, that heaven is a figment of human imagination, that God is dead or paying no heed to them, and they are tempted to go back to the Emmaus of agnosticism or atheism.

The solution for their problem is that given by the risen Jesus to the disciples. What seemed a failure and a tragedy to the disciples was the triumph of God's eternal plan for raising man up to sonship with God himself and an eternal inheritance. God has not failed; Christ has not failed; Christianity has not failed and never will, but there will always be weaklings among us who will fall by the wayside and try to get others to join them to boost their sagging morale. The second thought is closely connected with the first: it is a divine remedy for those who feel their faith growing weak. The two disciples recognized the risen Jesus "in the breaking of bread." We have still the risen Christ present with us every time we join in the celebration of the Eucharist. He is not only at the table, the altar, with us, but in the bread he breaks for us through his ordained minister he is giving himself to us as our spiritual nourishment. He promised to do this (see Jn. 6) and he fulfilled his promise at the Last Supper when he gave the power and the command to his Apostles and their successors to celebrate the Eucharist for his people, for all time.

If we partake regularly and devoutly of this divine nourishment, our faith will be strong enough to resist any doubts our own weak, human minds, or the bad example of Godless surroundings, may cause to arise within us. Our renewed liturgy is a replica of the Emmaus event. We have first the liturgy of the word, in which God's revelation is explained to us, and we then sit at table with our divine Lord—the Word of God made flesh—who gives himself to us under the form of human food—something which only a God, and a loving God, could do.

Christ has called us to be his followers and disciples. He has called us not because he needs us, but because we need him. He has prepared for us a heavenly banquet—a feast of joy and happiness which will last forever. The present eucharistic meal is the means he instituted to help us reach the new Jerusalem which is above. Let us use this means frequently and fervently; in it we shall, like the two disciples, recognize him as our loving, risen Savior and each time we receive him we will return full of the glad tidings that Jesus has risen and conquered death, not only for himself but for all men of goodwill.

FOURTH SUNDAY OF EASTER

FIRST READING: Acts 2:14; 36–41. On the day of Pentecost, Peter, standing with the eleven, lifted up his voice and addressed the crowd, "Let all the house of Israel know assuredly that God has made him both Lord and Christ, this Jesus whom you crucified."

Now when they heard this they were cut to the heart, and said to Peter and the rest of the Apostles, "Brethren, what shall we do?" And Peter said to them, "Repent, and be baptized every one of you in the name of Jesus Christ for the forgiveness of your sins; and you shall receive the gift of the Holy Spirit. For the promise is to you and to your children and to all that are far off, everyone whom the Lord our God calls to him." And he testified with many other words and exhorted them saying, "Save yourselves from this crooked generation." So those who received his word were baptized, and there were added that day about three thousand souls.

EXPLANATION: On the events of the first Pentecost Sunday see the First Readings of the Second and Third Sundays of Easter.

Peter . . . eleven: Peter is already the recognized leader and speaks for the Apostles.

God . . . Christ: Peter fearlessly tells all Jews—"all the house of Israel"—that the man "Jesus whom they crucified," was proved to be both the Messiah (Christ) and God, by God the Father raising him from the dead.

they were . . . heart: Many (not all) of those present felt responsible for the condemnation of Jesus. They accept Peter's declaration that Jesus was the promised Messiah and more. They feel guilty and ask:

Brethren . . . we do?: How can they get pardon for their crime?

Repent . . . baptized: Peter tells them, they must have a change of heart and a change of allegiance. They must become followers of Jesus, members of the society he had founded to carry on his work. This they could do by being baptized "in his name," that is, dedicated to his service. If they do this their sins will be forgiven them and they will receive the gift of the Holy Spirit, just as the Apostles had received him that very day.

promise . . . children: They were the race God had chosen, through whom the blessing of the Incarnation would come to all men. It was therefore offered to them first.

to all . . . calls: But the Incarnation was not for the Jews only, but for the

Gentiles also—"those that are afar off." God planned the Incarnation and its effects for all men. If all men do not respond, the fault is not God's.

from this . . . generation : Peter continues to exhort them to change their hearts and accept Christ as their Messiah and Savior and thus save themselves. The "crooked generation" were the present leaders of the Jews, who were determined to continue in their hatred of and opposition to Christ and his message—his gospel.

about three thousand : This was a great number of converts, which proves the power of the Holy Spirit was active among them. Many of the converts would have been pilgrim Jews who had come from foreign lands for the feast of Pentecost (see 2 : 5–10) and who would be less prejudiced than the upper classes in Jerusalem.

APPLICATION : One of the many proofs of the truth of our Christian religion, is the rapidity with which it spread from Jerusalem over the then known world. Within a generation, before the last of the Apostles died, there was scarcely a town or city in the Middle East, in North Africa, in Asia Minor, Greece and the southern parts of the Roman empire, including its capital Rome, in which the faith of Christ had not a foothold and center. There is no human explanation for this historical fact. Its explanation is from above, and the brief summary of what happened in Jerusalem on that first Pentecost day, read to us today, is proof of this divine intervention.

The change wrought in the Apostles by the descent of the Holy Spirit, as witnessed by St. Peter's fearless accusation of the leaders of the Jews, the effect of Peter's brief exposition of the essence of the Christian faith, as was proved by the conversion of three thousand Jews and the gift of foreign languages given to Galilean fishermen—these things demand more than a natural cause. If an innovator offers men a life of freedom, of pleasure, of plenty without any effort on the part of his followers, he would attract most, if not all, men and women. But Christ demanded that his followers should carry their cross daily, should mortify their senses, should forgive their enemies, should share the little they had with more needy fellowmen—all in all a life which had no attraction for an earthly man. But in return he promised them a future, unending life which would satisfy every rational desire of the human heart. And he proved by his resurrection that he was able to fulfill this promise, because he was the Son of God who had come on earth for this very purpose—namely, to give mankind a share in the eternal kingdom of his Father.

The first Christians so appreciated this eternal reward that the duties and obligations of the Christian faith seemed nothing to them in comparison. They looked forward anxiously to the end of their exile on this earth so that they could be citizens of their heavenly home. Those of them who suffered martyrdom for their faith went gladly to their death, for they were delighted to be a little more like to their divine Master who had won for them their future everlasting happiness.

How does our faith compare with theirs? Do we really appreciate what Christ's life, death and resurrection have won for us? Do we think often and seriously on our future life? Do we make its attainment the true goal and purpose of our exile here below? An honest answer to these questions today will make us take a second look at ourselves, and on our reaction our eternal future may depend.

SECOND READING: 1 Peter 2:20–25. If when you do right and suffer for it you take it patiently, you have God's approval. For to this you have been called, because Christ also suffered for you, leaving you an example, that you should follow in his steps. He committed no sin; no guile was found on his lips. When he was reviled, he did not revile in turn, when he suffered, he did not threaten; but he trusted to him who judges justly. He himself bore our sins in his body on the tree, that we might die to sin and live to righteousness. By his wounds you have been healed. For you were straying like sheep, but have now returned to the Shepherd and Guardian of your souls.

EXPLANATION: On this first Epistle of St. Peter see the Second Reading for the Second Sunday of Easter. In these verses today, St. Peter is giving advice to Christians who were slaves. He tells them to be submissive to their masters with all respect.

if you ... for it: In the first half of this verse he says: "What credit is it, if when you do wrong and are beaten for it you take it patiently?"—in other words, you should take what you deserve. But to take punishment for an offense not committed—this was Christian patience.

you have ... approval: God will reward such an act.

to this ... called: The Christian vocation, the call to follow Christ, is a call to bear the daily crosses patiently.

Christ ... you: In Christ every Christian has his model. He suffered for us, not for any fault of his own, not for any gain for himself.

He ... no sin: The innocent servant of Yahweh, as described by the second-Isaiah, five hundred years earlier, had to bear injuries, insults and bodily sufferings. What a perfect model he was for a suffering slave of that day. "He was (to be) led like a lamb to the slaughter and like a sheep that before its shearers is dumb, he opened not his mouth" (Is. 53:9). St. Peter sees Christ fulfilling to the letter the role of the suffering servant as Isaiah had described the future Messiah.

trusted ... justly: Christ had full confidence in his Father's decisions. He left himself entirely in his hands.

love ... tree: Isaiah had said of him: "He was wounded for our transgressions, he was bruised for our iniquities ... and with his stripes we are healed" (Is. 53:5). It was because of the sins of mankind, and especially because of the spite and hatred of the leaders of the Jews at the time, that Christ was put to death by crucifixion. If the primary purpose of the Incarnation was to make us men adopted sons of God and heirs to heaven, the atonement for the world's sins, which only Christ could make, had to be made to God before man could be worthy of this, his eternal inheritance.

that ... to sin: The death of Christ on the cross obtains pardon for all the sins of mankind provided man asks for that pardon. All Christians in their baptism have symbolically died with Christ, died to sin, and have begun to live the new life of sons of God, living in righteousness.

you were . . . sheep : Before their conversion they were like lost sheep (another reference to Is. 53 : 6), not knowing whence they had come nor whither they were going.

Shepherd . . . souls : Now that they have become Christians their lives, in this world and the next, are under the leadership and protection of the Good Shepherd, a term Christ had used for himself (Jn. 10 : 11, see 10 : 1–17).

APPLICATION : Although the words we have read were addressed by St. Peter to slaves who had become Christians, they have a lesson today for each one of us. Even if we are living in what we may proudly claim to be a "free country" (and not, as millions of our fellowmen are, under a despotic rule which makes their lives in many respects worse by far than that of the slaves in the Roman empire), we too have many things and persons who interfere justly or unjustly with what we claim as our God-given rights. Day after day, we are called on to exercise the great Christian virtue of patience.

To begin with the home, there is often need for the exercise of patience, sometimes to a heroic degree, in our family life. There are nagging wives, suspicious, ill-tempered husbands, disloyal and disobedient children, days of hostile silence or cold-war treatment, cutting and untrue remarks, provocative behavior, false accusations—the list, alas, could go on.

Outside the home, in our dealings with local and state authorities and with our neighbors in general, how many times each week, if not each day, are we not called on to practice Christian patience, recommended by St. Peter to the slaves of his day! For the fact is that free though we may claim to be, our freedom is very limited by the necessity of living in the society of our fellowmen. Even outside the iron and bamboo curtain countries, we all have to live under some form of slavery, benevolent and necessary though it be.

Every man of sense will have to admit that restrictions on his personal liberty and his freedom to do as he pleases, must be accepted if he is to live in peace in the society of others. Where these restrictions are unjust and malicious and we have no legal, peaceful redress, we must practice Christian patience and prayer. St. Peter reminds us of the noble example of innocent suffering given us by our Lord and leader, Christ himself. Our sacrifice will rarely go to that extreme, but even if it should, and it is in the cause of justice, we should be proud to be found worthy to imitate our Divine Master.

We must always be ready, too, to help by word and by deed, a fellowman who is struggling to bear injustices with Christian patience. Today, more than ever before, people are taking a true Christian interest in the sufferings of their fellowmen, wherever they may be. This noble effort is worthy of the assistance and cooperation of every Christian, indeed of every man who claims to be human.

If every Christian family became actively interested in helping a more needy family, at home or abroad, there would be less time for family squabbles and dissensions; their united interest in Christian well-doing would make each one more Christian and more united. If employers and employees, in the relatively prosperous cities and countries, united in a Christian endeavor to help find food and employment for the starving millions in other less fortunate lands, there would be less time for unnecessary local or national disruption of production, which only produces waste and want for themselves and thousands of others.

True Christian charity, which is the mother of patience, need not necessarily begin at home, but its fruits will return a hundredfold to the home and to the society which practices it. If we be true followers of our Good Shepherd, we will help him to feed all his hungry sheep on this earth and in as far as in us lies, we will, by word and example, help to lead them eventually to the eternal pastures he has prepared for them.

GOSPEL : John 10 : 1–10. Jesus said : "Truly, truly, I say to you, he who does not enter the sheepfold by the door but climbs in by another way, that man is a thief and a robber; but he who enters by the door is the shepherd of the sheep. To him the gate-keeper opens; the sheep hear his voice, and he calls his own sheep by name and leads them out. When he has brought out all his own, he goes before them, and the sheep follow him, for they know his voice. A stranger they will not follow, but they will flee from him, for they do not know the voice of strangers." This figure Jesus used with them, but they did not understand what he was saying to them.

So Jesus again said to them, "Truly, truly, I say to you, I am the door of the sheep. All who came before me are thieves and robbers; but the sheep did not heed them. I am the door; if any one enters by me, he will be saved, and will go in and out and find pasture. The thief comes only to steal and kill and destroy; I came that they may have life, and have it abundantly."

EXPLANATION : These ten verses are spoken to the Pharisees and are a continuation of the preceding incident—the curing of the man born blind. The Pharisees, who claimed to be the leaders and the judges of God's people, had tried their best to deny the miracle, then defamed the miracle-worker, Jesus, and cast out the man who had been healed. Jesus tells the Pharisees openly that they are blind leaders and that this blindness is a guilty one (unlike the cured man), having been brought on by their own pride. He now goes on in chapter 10 to say that they are not true shepherds of

Israel—they are thieves and mercenaries who steal and kill. He himself is the true Shepherd, who has come to give life and abundant (real) life.

Truly . . . to you : A phrase frequent in John, which signifies an emphatic repetition of something already stated. He has just told the Pharisees that they are blind leaders.

climbs . . . way : The man who enters the sheepfold stealthily is a thief and a robber, not the shepherd.

He . . . door : He is the real shepherd of the sheep.

the gate-keeper opens : He is known and

willingly admitted.

calls . . . out : He has a name for each of them; they know his voice, therefore, they come to him.

the sheep follow him : Instead of driving them he leads the way and they follow him. This is a sight still to be seen today in Palestine—the shepherd going on ahead and his sheep following in a group behind him.

a stranger . . . follow : They have a natural trust in their own shepherd, and a natural fear of a stranger.

This . . . used : Jesus used this simile of the true shepherd and his flock to drive home his condemnation of the Pharisees, but they did not understand it. They could not see themselves as false shepherds.

I am . . . sheepfold : He now changes the simile somewhat. He, Jesus, is the door through which all his flock will enter the true sheepfold.

all who . . . robbers : This does not include all the leaders of the Jews in the ages gone by, but the present ones who *are* thieves and robbers. They are look-

ing, not for the true welfare of their people, but rather for their own material and political gain.

but . . . heed them : The vast majority of the ordinary people—the poor and the sinners (in the eyes of the Pharisees) —did not belong to their party. Christ's followers during his public life were among the latter, and after the resurrection and the descent of the Holy Spirit they became Christians in their thousands.

If any . . . by me : Whosoever enters through Christ by baptism into the true sheepfold, will be saved. He will be on the way to eternal life.

the thief . . . destroy : The Pharisees fulfilled this to the letter when they thought they could kill and destroy the messianic kingdom forever by putting Christ to death.

have life . . . abundantly : The purpose of the Incarnation, the reason why God the Son became man, was that all men could become heirs to heaven and possess eternal life, life abundantly without limit.

APPLICATION : One of the oldest paintings of Christ, in the Roman catacombs, represents Christ as carrying the injured, straying sheep gently on his shoulders back to the sheepfold. This is an image of Christ which has always appealed to Christians. We have Christ as our shepherd—he tells us so himself in today's gospel—and we do not resent being called sheep in this context. There is something guileless about a sheep, and at the same time a lot of foolishness! But with Christ as our shepherd and the " good shepherd " who is sincerely interested in the true welfare of his flock we have reason to rejoice.

The leaders of the Jews, the Pharisees and Sadducees, were false shepherds who

tried to prevent the people from following Jesus, but they failed. They then killed the shepherd but in vain. He rose from the dead and his flock increased by the thousands and will keep on increasing until time ends.

We surely are fortunate to belong to the sheepfold of Christ—his Church. We surely are blessed to have the Son of God as our Shepherd, who came among us in order to lead us to heaven. Do we fully appreciate our privileged position? Do we always live up to our heavenly vocation? We know his voice, we know what he asks of us, but do we always listen to that voice, do we always do what he asks of us?

There are many among us today who

foolishly think they need no shepherd. They think they know all the facts of life while they are in total ignorance of the most basic fact of all, namely, the very purpose of life. Not that the thought of it does not arise disturbingly before their minds time and time again. But they try to smother that thought and ease their consciences by immersing themselves deeper and deeper in the affairs and the passing pleasures of this temporary life. Alas for them, a day of reckoning lies ahead, a day that is much nearer than they would like to believe. What will be their fate when they meet Christ the Judge, whom they had refused to follow and acknowledge during their days on earth?

This is a misfortune that could happen to any one of us, unless we think often of our purpose and our end in life. We have a few short years, but short though they be, we can earn for ourselves an eternity of happiness during this life. Let the straying sheep boast of their false freedom and of the passing joys they may get in this life—this freedom and these joys are mixed with much sorrow, and will end very soon. We know that if we follow the shepherd of our souls, we are on the way to the true life, the perfect life, the unending life which will have no admixture of sorrow, regret or pain. Where Christ is, there perfect happiness is, and there with God's grace we hope and trust to be.

FIFTH SUNDAY OF EASTER

FIRST READING: Acts 6:1-7. In these days when the disciples were increasing in number, the Hellenists murmured against the Hebrews because their widows were neglected in the daily distribution. And the twelve summoned the body of the disciples and said, "It is not right that we should give up preaching the word of God to serve tables. Therefore, brethren, pick out from among you seven men of good repute, full of the Spirit and of wisdom, whom we may appoint to this duty. But we will devote ourselves to prayer and to the ministry of the word." And what they said pleased the whole multitude, and they chose Stephen, a man full of faith and of the Holy Spirit, and Philip, and Prochorus, and Nicanor, and Timon, and Parmenas, and Nicolaus, a proselyte of Antioch. These they set before the Apostles, and they prayed and laid their hands upon them.

And the word of God increased; and the number of the disciples multiplied greatly in Jerusalem, and a great many of the priests were obedient to the faith.

EXPLANATION : The infant Christian Church in Jerusalem was growing in numbers daily. The converts were helping one another not only spiritually but in the necessities of life as well. Those who had shared with those who had not. There was a daily distribution of food among the poorer people and this required some organisation as the numbers multiplied. It was because of this that the order of the diaconate was introduced by the Apostles.

Hellenists . . . Hebrews : Ever since the time of Alexander and earlier, many Jews lived outside of Palestine. There was scarcely a town of any size in the Greco-Roman empire which did not have a Jewish colony. Greek was the language in daily use among these exiles. Some of them returned to Palestine in later life, when they had saved enough to support themselves there. They were known among the native Jews as "Hellenists" because of their language (Greek), while those who had remained at home, spoke Hebrew (rather Aramaic), and called themselves "Hebrews."

Hellenists murmured : These returned exiles felt their widows and orphans (the needy among them) were not being fairly treated by the Apostles, who were all Hebrews, and their assistants in the daily distribution of food and other necessities. Therefore, they brought their complaints before the Apostles.

give . . . tables : As the Apostles were fully occupied day after day instructing the new converts, they had no time to regulate the fair distribution of charity.

pick . . . you : The Apostles saw the need for some wise, saintly men who would take charge of this important task of looking after the needy and of seeing to it that all were treated fairly. They left the election to the laity.

seven men : The number seven has no symbolic meaning here; seven were judged sufficient for the task. That all seven elected have Greek names would seem to suggest that these deacons were chosen from the Hellenists only; the Hebrews being already provided for.

Stephen : Among the seven elected, Stephen is placed first and described as "full of faith and of the Holy Spirit" —an outstanding Christian evidently, which later events were to prove.

prayed . . . on them : The people, the laity, elected the seven deacons (the name comes from the Greek word *diakonein* meaning "to serve" which was the office given them), but it was the Apostles who conferred the office, and the power to carry it out, on them.

prayed . . . hands : In the Old Testament power was delegated to others by the imposition of the hands of the holders on the heads of those who were chosen to receive the power (see Num. 8 : 10; 27 : 16–23; Dt. 34 : 9). The Apostles are following this same ritual. The first deacons are "ordained" by the imposition of hands and prayer.

numbers . . . Jerusalem : Luke notes again how the Jews of Jerusalem, natives and returned exiles alike, were flocking to join the Christian Church.

great . . . priests : There were hundreds of the priestly caste who served in the temple in turns, usually one week at a time. Most of these were simple, devout men, who had little or nothing to do with the chief priests and Pharisees. On being convinced of the resurrection of Christ, especially by the descent of the Holy Spirit on Pentecost day, they came to believe that Christ was the promised Messiah and the Son of God. Hence, a great many of them joined Christ in his mystical body, the Church.

APPLICATION : The first eight chapters of the book we call the "Acts of the Apostles," describe the birth and the infant days of the Church in Jerusalem. It is an account which should inspire and console us. The little group of Apostles and disciples, who had lost all heart and hope on seeing Christ their leader crucified, regained confidence once they became convinced, during his forty days with them, of his resurrection. They waited ten days for the Holy Spirit whom Christ had promised them on his Ascension day. When they received the Holy Spirit they set out immediately to preach Christ, completely regardless of the consequences this would bring to them. Remember Jerusalem was still governed politically by pagan Romans who saw nothing but folly in the Christian religion. But, worse still, the religious leaders of the citizens of Jerusalem—the Jews—were still the very men who had Christ condemned to the cross, as an impostor and a blasphemer, because "he made himself the Son of God" (Jn. 19 : 7).

It was not human courage that enabled the Apostles, in such surroundings, to preach Christ as Messiah, Son of God, and Savior of the human race. It was the Holy Spirit. And the result was worthy of the cause : within a few weeks, almost half the inhabitants of Jerusalem had become faithful followers of the crucified and risen Christ.

This surprising spread of the faith, something in itself humanly impossible in such or in any circumstances, should surely inspire us with gratitude and love for God's interest in us, and his goodness to us. We still have the same faith as the first Christians of Jerusalem— we are followers of the same Christ who lived and died for us, who rose from the dead and sent the Holy Spirit with his gifts and power on the Church which he had founded. That same power and those same gifts of God's love are with us still today in our Church, leading us kindly and gently to the end he has planned for us from all eternity.

Surely, we Christians have every reason to be grateful to God for having given us the faith. And we should show this gratitude, by our love of neighbor, as the first Christians did, and all true Christians down through the ages have done. We must share with the poor and the needy not only our temporal goods, but especially the divine gift of the true faith. There are many ways today in which we can do our part in spreading the gospel of Christ. That gospel has reached us because zealous Christians down the ages lived the faith and did their share to give it to others.

St. Stephen, one of the deacons mentioned in today's reading, gave his life gladly for Christ a few weeks after his ordination. Stephen's martyrdom may have been a remote cause of preparing Saul's conversion—Saul never forgot the incident and his own part in it. Saul became St. Paul, the great Apostle of the Gentiles and one of the greatest glories of the infant Church.

You may not be called on to have the honor of martyrdom, but you are called to be a saint, an honor which can be earned only by living a life of true love of God and neighbor.

SECOND READING : 1 Peter 2 : 4–9. Come to the Lord, to that living stone, rejected by men but in God's sight chosen and precious; and like living stones be yourselves built into a spiritual house, to be a holy priesthood, to offer spiritual sacrifices acceptable to God through Jesus Christ. For it stands in scripture : "Behold, I am laying in Zion a stone, a cornerstone chosen and precious, and he who believes in him will not be put to shame." To you therefore who believe, he is precious, but for those who do not believe, "The very stone which the builders rejected has become the head of the corner," and "A stone that will make men stumble, a rock that will make them fall;" for they stumble because they disobey the word, as they were destined to do.

But you are a chosen race, a royal priesthood, a holy nation, God's own people, that you may declare the wonderful deeds of him who called you out of darkness into his marvelous light.

EXPLANATION : See the second reading of the Second Sunday of Easter. St. Peter is here reminding the new converts to Christianity, that they must be holy, for they are the living stones out of which the new spiritual temple of God is formed. The cornerstone, the base and binding force of this temple, is the risen Christ. Because of him, and through him, they are able to offer sacrifices which are acceptable to God. Christ, the Son of God, is their High Priest; they are his assistants.

come to the Lord : They have already come to him when they accepted baptism, but they must remain united with him daily by their good deeds.

living . . . men : Christ was and is the true and only foundation on which men can unite with God. He was God-incarnate, uniting the divine with the human, but the leaders of the Jews rejected him.

in God's . . . precious : As proclaimed at the baptism in the Jordan, at the Transfiguration, and proved by the resurrection.

be yourselves built : Christians must be the living material out of which the new temple of God, unlike the temple of Jersualem, built out of ordinary dead stones, is being built. The same idea is in the metaphor of the vine and the branches, and the body built out of living members.

to be . . . priesthood : The temple of Jerusalem was served by the Aaronic priests. They offered sacrifices of animals and fruits of the field to God. Now Christians, through Christ and because of Christ, will offer spiritual sacrifices of daily good works and especially of the Eucharist, the re-offering of Christ's sacrifice on Calvary,—sacrifices acceptable to God because Christ is the chief offerer.

I am . . . stone : St. Peter quotes Isaiah 28 : 16, where the prophet gives God's promise that he will fulfill his promise to David, that he will bring salvation to Zion, Jerusalem. He will build there a lasting temple. The cornerstone will be the Messiah.

to you therefore : To Christians, Christ will be the precious cornerstone, the very foundation of their spiritual temple, but to those who reject him he will be the occasion of their stumbling and falling.

disobey the word : They refused to listen to Christ, and to see the prophecies God had given them down through the centuries, as fulfilled in Christ.

were destined to do : There is no question of predestination here, but simply that the pride and self-sufficiency of the Pharisees led them logically to the rejection of Christ.

But you . . . race : The followers of Christ, Gentiles and Jews, are the new chosen race.

a royal priesthood : The titles given to the Chosen People in the Old Testament are now given to the Church of the New Testament. Christians are all priests because they all take part through Christ's delegate in offering true sacrifice to God. In the Old Testament, the priests were taken from only one of the twelve tribes. They are "a holy nation," made up of all nations; "God's own people," because united with his divine Son in the new spiritual temple.

that you may declare : Their duty and privilege is to tell all men of the great and glorious gift God conferred on them, when he called them out of the darkness of paganism and Judaism into the marvelous light of the faith, in Christ.

APPLICATION : St. Peter's call to his contemporaries is as imperative for us today, as it was for the first Christians. We are called to be saints, in other words, our Christian vocation is a call to take our place in heaven when we end our earthly life. We all know this, but for far too many of us, it is more a subconscious than a conscious thought in our daily lives. While doing the same daily tasks, as the Christians who are striving to become saints, we waste precious months and maybe years, in which we could be storing up treasure in heaven, because we forget God and the purpose of our Christian vocation.

Listen to a simple parable : two young men at the age of twenty went to another country where wages were high, in order to earn enough to buy for themselves comfortable homes and businesses when they returned, after some years. One saved his earnings, sent home his monthly packet and had his house and business set up. The other, attracted by the pleasure and play of the foreign land, squandered his earnings and forgot the purpose which led him to that land. When both returned home, the squanderer and forgetful one realized his mistake, but too late.

St. Peter is speaking to each one of us today. We are called to be saints. We have the means of becoming saints, for Christ has made us his brothers and heirs of heaven. Our part is to offer spiritual sacrifices acceptable to God. These sacrifices consist of our daily actions, dedicated to God by our simple, morning offering. They are acceptable to God because we have been made his adopted children, through Christ becoming man. Away and above our daily actions, which God accepts, we have the weekly (or daily where possible) sacrifice of Christ, the Son of God himself, which we have the privilege of offering, together with Christ's human representative. Just as it was the first offering of himself on Calvary which made us capable of reaching heaven, it is the re-presentation of their initial sacrifices on our altars that blesses all our worldly or daily actions and makes them of value for our eternal life.

Let us never forget it, we are "a chosen race, a royal priesthood, God's own people." What more could God have done for us? And how little he asks in return!

Are we giving him even that little? Is our home a Christian home where the love of God and neighbor reign? Is true justice the guiding rule in our dealings with our fellowmen? Can our non-Christian neighbors recognize us as God's own people?

If we can answer in the affirmative to these questions, we are building ourselves into a spiritual house. We are the true temple of God; we are on the direct road to our true home in heaven. If, unfortunately, we cannot say yes but a sad no to these questions, let us not despair—we are dealing with a Father, not a policeman. He is ever ready to welcome back the repentant sinner; remember the story of the lost sheep, and the prodigal son. If, hitherto, you have ignored the marvelous light of the faith to which God in his goodness has called you, look at it today, and resolve to live by it. It is the only light, the only answer to man's life on earth.

GOSPEL : John 14 : 1–12. Jesus said to his disciples : "Let not your hearts be troubled; believe in God, believe also in me. In my Father's house are many rooms; if it were not so, would I have told you that I go to prepare a place for you? And when I go and prepare a place for you, I will come again and will take you to myself, that where I am you may be also. And you know the way where I am going." Thomas said to him, "Lord, we do not know where you are going; how can we know the way?" Jesus said to him, "I am the way, and the truth, and the life; no one comes to the Father, but by me. If you had known me, you would have known my Father also; henceforth you know him and have seen him."

Philip said to him, "Lord, show us the Father, and we shall be satisfied." Jesus said to him, "Have I been with you so long, and yet you do not know me, Philip? He who has seen me has seen the Father; how can you say, 'Show us the Father?' Do you not believe that I am in the Father and the Father in me? The words that I say to you I do not speak of my own authority; but the Father who dwells in me does his works. Believe me that I am in the Father and the Father in me; or else believe me for the sake of the works themselves.

Truly, truly, I say to you, he who believes in me will also do the works that I do; and greater works than these will he do, because I go to the Father."

EXPLANATION : During the Last Supper, Jesus foretells his proximate departure (through death) from them. He is to be betrayed into the hands of his enemies by one of the Twelve. The eleven faithful ones are deeply saddened —they have not yet grasped that "he must suffer and so enter into his glory" (Lk. 24 : 26). They had not yet realized that he was God, as well as man. So in today's verses, he consoles his Apostles by telling them that his going (his death) is necessary for their future, eternal happiness, but they will see him again when he will come to take them to himself.

believe . . . in me : If they have trust in God and in himself (he puts himself on an equal footing with the Father), and believe in the promises given them in the Old Testament by the prophets and in the New by himself, they will cease to be troubled at his departure.

In my Father's house : His death will open heaven—his Father's house—in which there are many rooms.

I go . . . for you : Heaven will be the eternal abode of the Apostles and for multitudes of others. His death was the key to that eternal abode.

I will come again : At each one's death, at the *Parousia,* the general judgement, and also in the Church when the coming of the Holy Spirit will set it on its way; as he told them before his Ascension: I am with you always; yes, to the end of time (Mt. 28 : 20).

Lord . . . know : Thomas probably speaks for all—they cannot grasp the idea that he should die, and their still Jewish idea of life after death was no consolation or light for them.

I am the way . . . life : Thomas's answer brought forth a statement from Jesus which can be said to summarize the gospel of St. John : Jesus, the Incarnate Son of God, is the one and only *way* to the Father and to eternal life. Without the coming of Christ in our human nature, we could not become adopted sons of God, and co-heirs with Christ of

heaven. He is the *truth* : he is God's Word which is the word of truth itself (see 1 : 9; 14; 17); he is the *life* (see Jn. 4 : 10; 13; 10 : 10), the true everlasting life.

Philip . . . Father : Philip's request shows how little he had learned of the true nature of Christ during his two or more years as his disciple.

He who . . . Father : During his public life, Christ had often declared his close association, in fact, his intimate association, with the Father, in almost identical words (see 7 : 16; 8 : 28; 10 : 38 : "the Father is in me and I in the Father"). He repeated these latter words verbatim now for Philip.

for the . . . works : If Philip would not take his word for it, the miracles, "the works," he had performed should have proved it to him.

He who . . . me : He promises the power of miracles to those who will really admit that he was what he claimed to be—the Son of God made man.

greater . . . Father : These greater works were to be the miraculous spread of Christ's message, the Christian faith after the Ascension and the sending of the Holy Spirit. Christ, during his public mission, had relatively few followers and fewer still who really believed in his claims. But the completion of his mission on earth, in his resurrection and glorification, had to take place before his claims and his doctrines were accepted.

APPLICATION : We may well wonder at the slowness of the Apostles in seeing in Christ nothing more than a man—a great man, a man with power from God, yes, but still a mere man. That he was the Messiah, they were convinced, but their idea of the Messiah was wrong. They thought he would free Israel from foreign domination (Lk. 24 : 21), and set up a new kingdom of God —a prosperous, earthly kingdom with God guaranteeing peace and plenty for all. If, therefore, he allowed his enemies to put him to death, all their hopes would be dashed to the ground. Hence, the mention of his impending death at the Last Supper filled them with dismay and despair.

But we must not judge them too harshly. Christ had indeed often claimed to be God, but his words fell on deaf ears. It was only after his resurrection that they began to understand that he had spoken literally—it was only then they believed he was indeed the Son of God, in human nature.

For us today, the Incarnation is still a mystery, but it is not the "how" that should trouble us, we know that with God all things are possible. It is rather the "why" that should cause us amazement. Why should God go to that length for our sake—mere creatures, and sinful, ungrateful creatures at that? The infinite goodness and the infinite love of God are the answer, but still an answer which is mysterious to us. For we, with our limited capacity for love, can form no idea of infinite love.

God created us "in his own image and likeness" (a very limited likeness, granted) and intended, because of the spiritual faculties he gave us, which enable us to see and enjoy truth and beauty, to give us a share in his eternal life and glory. To do this, the Incarnation of the second Person of the Holy Trinity was God's plan. There must have been other ways of doing this, but God, we can be sure, chose the best way. Even with our limited intelligence, we ourselves can see what a perfect way this was for proving to us the infinite love, goodness and compassion of our Creator.

Sin entered the world of man, as God had foreseen, but notwithstanding this ingratitude on our part, God's Son came in our lowly, human nature and suffered, even though sinless, all the effects of men's sins. He suffered in our name, and because he was God, his sufferings in his human nature made infinite atonement for the sins of all mankind.

His Incarnation had made us his brothers and co-heirs to heaven. His death on the cross wiped out, and gave us the means of wiping out, our sins, so that we would be capable of possessing our inheritance.

Knowing the story of the Incarnation therefore, we know of the love and kindness of God toward us. We need not ask, with Philip, "show us the Father," we have seen him in his riches and wisdom and knowledge of God! "How unsearchable are his judgements and how inscrutable are his ways!" (Rom. 11 : 33).

"What return can I make to the Lord?" All the mortifications and good works of all the holy men and women that ever lived, or will live, would not be adequate a return to God for the miracle of love he has shown toward us. But he accepts the widow's mite, the little acts of love, the little proofs of gratitude, the willing acceptance of the crosses he sends us, to purify us. In one word, all he asks in return is that we try to live our Christian life day after day, ever thanking him for the gift of Christ and the Christian faith.

SIXTH SUNDAY OF EASTER

FIRST READING : Acts 8 : 5–8; 14–17. Philip went down to a city of Samaria, and proclaimed to them the Christ. And the multitudes with one accord gave heed to what was said by Philip, when they heard him and saw the signs which he did. For unclean spirits came out of many who were possessed, crying with a loud voice; and many who were paralyzed or lame were healed. So there was much joy in that city.

Now when the Apostles at Jerusalem heard that Samaria had received the word of God, they sent to them Peter and John, who came down and prayed for them that they might receive the Holy Spirit; for it had not yet fallen on any of them, but they had only been baptized in the name of the Lord Jesus. Then they laid their hands on them and they received the Holy Spirit.

EXPLANATION : Christ had told his Apostles on Ascension day that when they had received the Holy Spirit they should be "his witnesses in Jerusalem and in all Judea and Samaria and to the ends of the earth" (Acts 1 : 6). The martyrdom of Stephen was the beginning of the formal rejection of the new faith by official Jews of Jerusalem (Acts 8 : 1), and of its spread to Judea, Samaria and eventually to Rome itself—the heart of the Empire.

Philip . . . Christ : The Samaritans were mixed, both in race and in religion. Descended from Assyrian planters and Jewish remnants they retained some knowledge of the true God interspersed with pagan liturgies. They expected the Messiah as is clear from the Samaritan woman with whom Jesus spoke (Jn. 4 : 25), and therefore Philip, one of the seven deacons (not the Apostle),

announced to them that the Messiah (the Christ) had come.

multitudes gave heed : They were much more open to the truth than prejudiced and proud Jews of Jerusalem. His miracles also helped to prove that he was speaking the truth.

unclean . . . paralyzed : The deacons possessed the power of miracles promised by Christ to those who would believe in him (Jn. 14 : 12). Healing the mentally and physically sick was proof of divine power and divine mercy.

They . . . John : Normally converts received the Holy Spirit on being baptized (1 : 3; 38; 9 : 17) but here, perhaps because it was the first occasion that the faith had been accepted outside of Jerusalem, the formal act of conferring the Holy Spirit was reserved to the Apostles.

laid . . . them : The laying on of hands

with prayer (verse 14) was the first direct example of the conferring of what was later called the sacrament of confirmation. In the early Church it was usually given with the sacrament of baptism.
received . . . Spirit: Manifested by special charisms or gifts. This is evident from the reaction of Simon Magus who wanted to buy this power (the power of giving these gifts to people) from the Apostles. The first attempt in the Church at buying a divine gift or sacred object. Hence the name simony.

APPLICATION: Although the convert Samaritans did not receive the Holy Spirit with his visible supernatural gifts immediately, nothing but the power of the Holy Spirit, in Philip and in the Christian message he brought to them, could explain the readiness with which they accepted the Christian truth. They were natural enemies of the Jews for centuries and the enmity was returned heartily. They would have no truck with Jerusalem or with any teacher who came from there, yet they listened to Philip and in "multitudes gave heed with one accord" to what he had to tell them. Nothing but the grace of the Holy Spirit can explain their change of attitude.

When the two Apostles came down from Jerusalem and bestowed the Holy Spirit on them his presence in them was made manifest to all, because of the special gifts that accompanied his bestowal in almost all cases of conversion in the early Church.

People may ask why it is that today, when people receive the sacraments of baptism and confirmation the Holy Spirit does not prove his presence in them by any external signs or miracles. St. Augustine answered that very question centuries ago. He said: When one plants a young tree one waters it regularly and stakes it firmly, but as soon as the tree has taken firm root it needs no further care. So it is with the Church, he said. In its infancy it needed miracles and signs to convince those who believed and to convert those who had not yet believed. But when the Church had taken firm root in the Roman Empire which was the known world of that time, there was no further need for the *special* intervention of God. The ordinary graces of the Holy Spirit were sufficient.

And so it is with each one of us. We have received the Holy Spirit with what we call his seven gifts and these are sufficient without any miraculous signs to make us soldiers of Christ. As such, we should be active members of his Church ready to do our duty each day, to live the faith, defend the faith when called on, and even if necessary, to die for it.

But to live our faith to the full and to be able to defend it if called on, we need to learn more and more about the truths of our faith. We need to know first and foremost what it promises us, what it means for our true life. A Christian is still a human being but he is no longer a mere human being—he has been made a brother of Christ and an adopted son of God. He is therefore made a citizen of heaven and his earthly life is but a journey to his native home—to a home which he will never have to leave again. When we look on our earthly life from this heavenly point of view most if not all of what we call the trials and troubles of life cease to be impassable mountain ranges and appear as little hillocks over which we can skip lightly. The true Christian who lets this truth be the guiding light of

G

his life, will be well equipped to answer the questionings and hesitations of those who have not yet received the light of faith, or who, having once had it, lost it or let it die through inertia. The illiterate street sweeper who lives his faith devoutly—who never forgets that God loved him so dearly that he sent his only-begotten Son as man on earth in order to bring him to heaven, is a more convincing theologian than the lukewarm author of learned tomes. Every devout Christian is an apostle. His very way of living, as well as his daily conversation in the home and outside of it, are lights which illumine all around him. He is a living furnace of divine love which warms and softens the heart of the sinners and the unbelievers with whom he comes into contact.

SECOND READING : 1 Peter 3 : 15–18. In your hearts reverence Christ as Lord. Always be prepared to make a defense to anyone who calls you to account for the hope that is in you, yet do it with gentleness and reverence; and keep your conscience clear, so that, when you are abused, those who revile your good behavior in Christ may be put to shame. For it is better to suffer for doing right, if that should be God's will, than for doing wrong. For Christ also died for sins once for all, the righteous for the unrighteous, that he might bring us to God, being put to death in the flesh but made alive in the spirit.

EXPLANATION : St. Peter continues his practical spiritual advice.

reverence . . . Lord : The Christian who becomes a convert because he firmly believed that the Christ who lived, died and rose from the dead a few years previously in Palestine, was in fact the Son of God, must never forget this. He must always honor Christ as Lord, that is, as God, "in his heart." This belief and this reverence for the God-man must be the mainspring of his Christian life.

a defense . . . you : They are Christians from conviction, they must be always ready to defend their faith, to explain to non-Christians what being a Christian means and not only its value in this life but especially its import for the future life.

gentleness . . . reverence : They must treat their questioners with kindness. The questions may often sound even blasphemous, but the true Christian will understand that this comes from ignorance of the facts and he will respect his fellowman even if he holds very wrong opinions.

conscience . . . shame : If Christians live their life devoutly, they may be falsely accused of many things, as they were in those early days by Jews and pagans, but no evil can be proved against them. Their accusers will bring shame on themselves for their false accusations.

better . . . right : If God permits suffering, the Christian who suffers for keeping the law of God will have his reward. The evildoer who suffers can expect no reward from God or men if he is punished for a crime that he committed.

Christ . . . sins : The Christian has the inspiring example of the innocent Christ who suffered the death of the cross for the sins of mankind. He who had no sin was made a sin-offering for us (see 2 Cor. 5 : 21), the "righteous for the uprighteous."

that he might . . . God : The divine purpose of the Incarnation, to make us sons of God and gain access for us to heaven.

put to death . . . spirit : Christ died for us in his human nature and this was the culmination of the perfect obedience of the suffering servant to his Father. In dying he was our representative : "He was pierced through for our faults, crushed for our sins" (Is. 53 : 5). But the Father raised him from the dead and "made him both Lord and Christ" (that is, proved he was God and Messiah) as St. Peter told the Jews on Pentecost day (Acts 2 : 36).

APPLICATION : These first converts to Christianity to whom St. Peter wrote this letter lived in a world which was very similar in many respect to our world of today. There were the self-styled intellectuals who thought they had the solution to all human problems because they had picked up scrips and pieces of the pagan Greek philosophy. There were others whose only thought was to get all they could out of this earthly life and whose motto was : "eat, drink, sleep and be merry, for tomorrow we die." There were the agnostics whose life was one big question-mark, and who refused to accept any answers. There were the "practical" ones, so busy making a good living for themselves that they had no time to question the real meaning of life.

Who can fail to see the similarity between their world and the world in which we live today? While it is true that the number of Christians in our world today is away above that of St. Peter's day, it is true also that the number of the opponents of Christianity has increased accordingly. And what is worse, most of these opponents come from Christian parentage and live in countries that are still called Christian.

Add to this, that many, very many of those we number as Christians are so only in name. Unlike the early Christians whose exemplary lives spread the faith very quickly to their pagan neighbors, our nominal Christians spread disrespect for the very name of Christ and for all he did for mankind.

Let us admit it, this is the kind of world in which we live, but it need not remain so. Each one of us, who is convinced of the truth of his faith, must realize that he has a solemn duty to help bring about this necessary change.

St. Peter tells us in a few words today how this can be done. He reminds us of the basic truth of our Christian religion : God created us for heaven. He sent his Son on earth to earn heaven for us. Our real purpose in this life is to work our passage to our true and everlasting home. This we shall do if we keep ever before our minds that Christ was God who came on earth as a man and suffered torments and death in our name and in our stead, so that we too could rise with him after our lives had ended. If we grasp this basic truth— the only true and satisfactory explanation of our sojourn on this earth—our daily actions will be truly Christian; we will gladly "keep our conscience clear" by following the rules of conduct that Christ has laid down for us.

By so doing we will also be prepared always to give an account, an explanation, to those who ask us why we are

Christians. Our very lives will be of themselves an explanation and an answer to those who are curious about us, and even to those who while openly opposing and maybe deriding us, are gravely doubting in their hearts, whether it is we or they who are wrong. We can change our world, and in the innermost hearts of the vast majority of our "intellectuals," our "agnostics" and our "practical men of the world" there is a desire for change. Christ is calling on us today, through his Apostle St. Peter, to help him call home the prodigal sons and the lost sheep. He suffered for them too. Would we turn a deaf ear to his call for help? Not if we reverence him as our Lord, our God. Not if we love our neighbor whom he has made our brother and co-heir with himself to heaven.

GOSPEL : John 14 : 15–21. Jesus said to his disciples, "If you love me, you will keep my commandments. And I will pray the Father, and he will give you another Counselor, to be with you forever, even the Spirit of truth, whom the world cannot receive, because it neither sees him nor knows him; you know him, for he dwells with you, and will be in you. I will not leave you desolate; I will come to you. Yet a little while, and the world will see me no more, but you will see me; because I live, you will live also. In that day you will know that I am in my Father, and you in me, and I in you. He who has my commandments and keeps them, he it is who loves me; and he who loves me will be loved by my Father, and I will love him and manifest myself to him."

EXPLANATION : Jesus continues his discourse to his disciples during the Last Supper.

will . . . commandments : Again he identifies himself with God the Father : God's commandments are his too.

Father . . . Counselor : He promises them that he will get the Father to send them another Counselor when he leaves them. Here we have the Trinity as three distinct persons, yet as one God.

Spirit of truth : His office will be to teach them all things, and recall to their minds all that he has already taught them (14 : 26).

world cannot receive : The "world" in the bad sense of opposition to Christ and to the truth. Such men cannot receive or know the truth or its Author, the Holy Spirit.

you know . . . you : The Apostles are open to the truth, they and their successors, the Church of God, will have the Holy Spirit dwelling in them.

not . . . desolate : He realizes their anguish at the thought of his leaving them. He promises that he will return to them after the resurrection, and also in his glorious life which the disciples and all his followers, but not the "world" of the unbelievers, will share with him.

I am in the Father : After the resurrection and Pentecost they will forever be convinced of Christ's divinity. They will also understand that through his Incarnation he has made himself one with them and made them one with him—adopted sons of the Father.

keeps . . . commandments : This is the

final proof of love of Christ, and the Father will repay this love for his Son. Christ himself too will repay his loyal follower, and form an intimate acquaintance with him. He will manifest himself to him.

APPLICATION : In this discourse at the Last Supper, which was his last will and testament, our divine Lord promised his Church, through the Apostles, that the Holy Spirit would be with it until the end of time. The Spirit of truth will be directing it and effectively aiding it to preserve the faith, the doctrine, and the morals which Christ taught his Apostles.

Looking back now over almost 2,000 years of the Church's history we can see how this promise has been fulfilled. There were heretics and schismatics who threatened the very continuance of the Church as God's faithful people on earth. There were crises and near catastrophes caused by the human weaknesses of its heads and its members, yet the Church survived and spread and continued to send saints to heaven because of the direct and active aid of the Holy Spirit.

During those two thousand years great empires have risen and fallen. They had large armies and vast wealth and earthly resources at their disposal, yet they disintegrated like all things human. The names of one-time mighty men who ruled over millions are now nothing more than a nuisance for children in their history classes. The large tracts of our globe which they ruled are now divided and known by other names. This was, is, and will be the lot of all merely human enterprises. Today's despots, where they rule with iron hand, will share the same fate.

In the midst of all these upheavals the Church of Christ has continued to flourish because it was directed and sustained by the Holy Spirit, who abides within it. How can we ever show enough gratitude to the three Divine Persons of the Blessed Trinity who planned so lovingly and so efficaciously for our safe journey to heaven? The Father sent his Son as man among us so that we men could become his brothers, and adopted sons of the Father. The Son suffered hardships, insults and misunderstanding during his temporary stay on earth, and ended like a crucified malefactor because of the sins of mankind. But he rose triumphantly from the dead and set up the Church as a society which would bring to men of all races, ages and colors the salvation and exaltation of mankind, which his life and death had won for us.

Knowing only too well the weaknesses and waywardness of human nature, he and the Father sent the Holy Spirit to remain with his Church as its infallible guide until the last man has entered heaven.

This is a very brief summary of what the Blessed Trinity has done, and is continuing to do for us, through the Church. We, the people of God, the chosen race of the New Testament are God's Church on earth. It is for you and me that the Holy Spirit is at work this very day. When he guides the steps of Peter's successor, the Pope, or the deliberations of the bishops, the heirs of the apostolic college, it is for us and for our salvation that he is acting. While we are faithful members of the Church, and of Christ's mystical body, while we remain live branches safely attached to the vine who is Christ, we have nothing to fear; we are on the sure road to heaven, to enjoy eternal happiness with the Father, Son and Holy Spirit whom we shall thank and glorify forever.

THE ASCENSION OF OUR LORD

FIRST READING: Acts 1 : 1–11.   In the first book, O Theophilus, I have dealt with all that Jesus began to do and teach, until the day when he was taken up, after he had given commandment through the Holy Spirit to the Apostles whom he had chosen. To them he presented himself alive after his passion by many proofs, appearing to them during forty days, and speaking of the kingdom of God. And while staying with them he charged them not to depart from Jerusalem, but to wait for the promise of the Father, which, he said, "you heard from me, for John baptized with water, but before many days you shall be baptized with the Holy Spirit."

So when they had come together, they asked him, "Lord, will you at this time restore the kingdom to Israel?" He said to them, "It is not for you to know times or seasons which the Father has fixed by his own authority. But you shall receive power when the Holy Spirit has come upon you; and you shall be my witnesses in Jerusalem and in all Judea and Samaria and to the end of the earth." And when he had said this, as they were looking on, he was lifted up, and a cloud took him out of their sight. And while they were gazing into heaven as he went, behold, two men stood by them in white robes, and said, "Men of Galilee, why do you stand looking into heaven? This Jesus, who was taken up from you into heaven, will come in the same way as you saw him go into heaven."

EXPLANATION : St. Luke begins his second book, called Acts of the Apostles, with a brief description of our Lord's bodily ascension into heaven, after he had given his Apostles their final instructions. He identifies the exact location of this event as Mount Olivet, both here and in his gospel (24 : 50). In Acts he seems to imply that forty days elapsed between the resurrection and ascension. All the other writings of the New Testament assume that the ascension took place immediately after the resurrection, which would be according to the nature of things. This was also the belief of the Church for the first three centuries; the ascension was then closely associated with the resurrection ceremonies. It was only from the fourth century that a special feast of the ascension, forty days after Easter (following the Lucan date), came to be celebrated.

That our Lord, in his glorified body, took his place at the right hand of the Father is the dogmatic and historical fact, and the time, most likely, if not certainly, was resurrection day. Luke's forty days is most likely a round number, not to be taken literally, for our Lord's "appearances" in human form to his disciples. These appearances were repeated over a period of two weeks or so (see Jn. 20 : 19; 26; 21 : 1).

the first book . . . day : In his gospel Luke describes the resurrection, the appearances to two disciples on the road to Emmaus, an appearance to Simon (Peter), an appearance to the eleven Apostles and some disciples (all apparently on the resurrection day), and finally his ascension from the outskirts of Bethany which is part of Mount Olivet.

to them he presented . . . alive : Christ proved he had risen—"he was alive again,"—by his appearances to them over a period of time (see above on the forty days).

while staying . . . depart . . . Jerusalem : They were to wait in Jerusalem to receive the Holy Spirit whom he had promised to send them from the Father, when he had returned to the Father (Jn. 14 : 26; 16 : 6ff).

you . . . be baptized . . . Holy Spirit : The Baptist's baptism with water was an external sign of internal change of heart, the descent of the Holy Spirit will bring about a complete change of mind and heart in the Apostles.

restore the rule of Israel now : The Apostles were still expecting a messianic kingdom for Israel, or perhaps a theocratic kingdom here on earth, to be established when Christ would return in glory.

my witnesses . . . earth : Our Lord's answer seems to be that he understood their question to refer to his second coming, the time of which was a secret God was not revealing. The second part, however, the missionary activity of the Apostles from Jerusalem to the ends of the earth, implied that his kingdom was not for Israel alone and that the second coming was in the far distant future.

lifted up . . . their sight : Each time he appeared to his Apostles, he disappeared again. Luke, perhaps because he is describing the last appearance here, describes his departure as an ascension, as heaven the abode of God, was thought to be above the skies.

why do you stand . . . heaven : This is probably a reprimand for those Christians who, instead of earning their daily bread, were waiting in idleness for the second coming of Christ, at the time Luke was writing (see 2 Thess.).

Jesus who was taken up from you : Their beloved master will return (some day) as Judge of all. In the meantime they had their apostolic life-work to fulfill.

APPLICATION : The ascension or the return of Christ to heaven, in his human but glorified body, is the culmination, the sign and seal of the accomplishment of his salvific mission on earth. He, the Son of God, the second divine Person of the Blessed Trinity, became man, lived and died on this earth so that we men could live with God forever in heaven. By his death on the cross, he reconciled sinful man with his divine Creator. His human death earned for us a share in the divine life. His resurrection is the divine guarantee that we too shall rise again, and his ascension to the Father is the prelude to our entrance into God's everlasting kingdom.

Christ, our Savior, our intimate friend, who suffered hardships, humiliations, and finally the painful and degrading death on the cross for our sakes, while here on earth, is now seated in the place of honor at the right hand of the Father in heaven. He is there as our representative and as our intercessor. He has gone to heaven to prepare a place there for us. He said to his Apostles (and through them to all of us) at the Last Supper : "In my Father's house there are many dwelling places . . . I am going to prepare a place for you and then I shall come back to take you with me, that where I am you also may be" (Jn. 14 : 2–3).

What a consolation, what a source of joy this feast of the ascension is for any true believer! It is the natural desire (indeed the supernatural desire, for it is instilled in our very nature at creation) of every human being to keep on living —death is the negation of everything

we love and have. However, we know that earthly death awaits every one of us. Our human make-up is of its nature mortal. How sad it would be, and how dreadful it must be for those who do not believe in God, if the grave were the final end for us.

We Christians know it is not the end but rather the beginning and today's feast is the reminder of this consoling fact. We shall all leave this world some day soon, but for a true Christian, this thought should be a cause for joy rather than sadness. We leave this valley of tears to go on an eternal holiday. Christ has won this divine heritage for us; he has promised he is preparing a place in his own heavenly home for us and he is helping us on our way there. What have we to fear from earthly death? It is not the entrance to a perpetual prison but rather the door to our eternal happiness.

SECOND READING : Ephesians 1 : 17–23. May the God of our Lord Jesus Christ, the Father of glory, give you a spirit of wisdom and of revelation in the knowledge of him, having the eyes of your hearts enlightened, that you may know what is the hope to which he has called you, what are the riches of his glorious inheritance in the saints, and what is the immeasurable greatness of his power in us who believe, according to the working of his great might which he accomplished in Christ when he raised him from the dead and made him sit at his right hand in the heavenly places, far above all rule and authority and power and dominion, and above every name that is named, not only in this age but also in that which is to come; and he has put all things under his feet and has made him the head over all things for the Church, which is his body, the fulness of him who fills all in all.

EXPLANATION : St. Paul is praying God to give his Ephesian converts an ever deeper insight into the mercy and love of God the Father who made them members of Christ in the Church and called them to share in the divine heri-

tage. They have been made members of the mystical body of which Christ is the Head. The Father raised Christ from the dead and gave him the principal place in heaven. The Church continues daily to increase in numbers and in grace until it completes the fulness (pleroma) of Christ who himself, by his resurrection and ascension, fills and fulfills the divine plan for the universe (see 1 : 10).

God of our Lord Jesus Christ : Paul is praying to the Holy Trinity; to God the Father of Jesus, who is "Lord," i.e. God also, that he may send the Spirit of wisdom on the Ephesian converts.

the hope to which he . . . called you : The real meaning of the Christian faith they have received.

riches . . . inheritance : They have been called to partake in the eternal happiness of the Trinity.

immeasurable . . . of his power : What God does for those who believe in Christ, is to raise them to a supernatural state—to sonship with God—only divine power could do this.

great might . . . accomplished : The resurrection and exaltation of Christ in his human nature was an act of divine power. Christians will also be raised and given a place of honor by the same divine power.

far above . . . dominion : Christ in his human nature is next to God in heaven, above all other creatures.

all things under his feet : The Father has subjected all creatures to Christ, whether past, present or future. Not only man but also all other created beings insofar as they share in the cosmic rebirth brought about by the Incarnation.

APPLICATION : St. Paul reminded the Ephesians nearly nineteen and a half centuries ago of the marvelous generosity and goodness of God who had made them Christians and sharers-to-be in the glory of Christ, which was the eternal glory of God. The words the Apostle wrote to those first converts were written for us also and are as applicable to us today as they were in the year 61 A.D. He prayed that God would enlighten their minds to try to understand and appreciate the marvelous things God had done for them through the Incarnation, death, resurrection and ascension of our Savior, Jesus Christ.

Which of us can say that we really appreciate, as we should, these same marvelous things God has done for us? Because Christ came on earth we have been given the power to go to heaven. As mere creatures we have no such power and not even the slightest claim to any such extraordinary gift. We, as creatures, are by our very nature, mortal. Death on earth should be our final end. But because the infinitely good and generous God wished to raise us up to the status of adopted sons of his, and to make us capable of sharing, in as far as our limited nature could, in his eternal life and happiness, he sent his divine Son on earth to share in our humanity.

This is the mystery of the Incarnation, the mystery of God's love for us, a love of which we are utterly unworthy. Today we are commemorating the final act in this drama of divine love. God the Son, returning to his Father, bearing our human nature and guaranteeing to each one of us that we too, when we leave this earth, will find our true life, our unending life, in the home of the Father with Christ, our true Brother.

Cast your eyes heavenwards today, where Christ now dwells surrounded by millions of our fellowmen, and say to yourself : There is my true home, there is where I shall be forever at peace with God, with neighbor and with myself.

Millions of my fellowmen have already got there. I have the same weaknesses which they had. I have the same strength and helps that they got. Why should I not make it? The one and only person who could stop me from getting to my heavenly home is myself. Could I ever be so foolish? God forbid!

GOSPEL: Matthew 28:16–20. The eleven disciples went to Galilee, to the mountain to which Jesus had directed them. And when they saw him they worshiped him: but some doubted. And Jesus came and said to them, "All authority in heaven and on earth has been given to me. Go therefore and make disciples of all nations, baptizing them in the name of the Father and of the Son and of the Holy Spirit, teaching them to observe all that I have commanded you, and lo, I am with you always, to the close of the age."

EXPLANATION: The event described here happened some days after the resurrection.

Eleven disciples: Judas on realizing his guilt in betraying Christ to the chief priests had committed suicide, and so there were only eleven Apostles left.

to the mountain . . . them: The risen Christ had already appeared to the Apostles in Jerusalem. He evidently arranged with them to meet him later in Galilee, "on a mountain," perhaps the mount of the beatitudes, where he had proclaimed the new law of the new chosen people.

they worshiped him: they reverenced him as God.

but some doubted: As was the case in all his appearances. Christ had risen in a glorious body, not visible to human, earthly eyes. So he took on a human appearance each time he approached them and this appearance was not always the replica of his human appearance before his death—hence the doubts.

All . . . earth: The Father has given him, Christ the Incarnate Son of God, complete power over all creation, as was foretold by Daniel of the "Son of Man,"

the title Jesus used so frequently of himself (see Dn. 7:13–14).

Go . . . nations: Having supreme and universal authority he now delegates part of this power to his Apostles, and to their successors (for it is a delegation and a mission that will last till the end of time).

make disciples: Convert all nations, that is, both Jews and Gentiles to become his disciples, his followers, his chosen people.

baptizing them: This was the specific form for making them disciples, the sacrament of baptism.

Father, Son and Holy Spirit: Christ himself it was who gave the classic trinitarian form of the sacrament of baptism. It has been in use ever since. The newly-converted are thus incorporated into fellowship with the Blessed Trinity. This was the meaning of "into or in the name of" something or somebody. They belonged henceforth to the Father, Son and Holy Spirit.

observe . . . you: The initial incorporation was not enough, the new disciples had to keep the laws laid down by Christ and already given to his Apostles.

lo . . . always: He had appointed a visible head for his Church in the person of Peter (and Peter's successors) but he himself would always be the invisible head of his mystical body. It was from him that the life-blood of grace and glory would flow through that body. It was also through his presence, together with that of the Holy Spirit, that his Church would preserve his teaching free from error for all time.

APPLICATION: As his coming on earth was for our sakes, and as all his actions during his life including the voluntary acceptance of death by crucifixion were for our sakes, so his last thoughts, before ascending in glory to his Father, were for us.

He gave to his Apostles and through them to their successors, the command and the power to bring his message of salvation to all nations and peoples. That day on a hill in Galilee Christ foresaw each one of us here present as his future followers. It was then that the life-giving sacrament of Baptism which made us members of his Church —his mystical body on earth—was instituted. By means of it we were incorporated not only into the Church— the new people of God—but even into the divine family of the Blessed Trinity. We were made brothers of Christ and heirs to heaven.

We didn't know it then, if we were baptized as babies, but that day of our Baptism was the most important day of our lives. From being mere human beings we were changed into superbeings, humans transformed into semi-divine beings in a broad sense, because we were adopted by Christ as his brothers, and therefore by the divine Father as his adopted sons, with an eternal inheritance waiting for us in heaven.

Could even the infinite love of God have done more for us? The Father as Creator gave us the spiritual gifts which will enable us to enjoy an eternal life. The Son bore the humiliation of becoming like us—a creature—in order to raise us above our mere creaturely nature. The Holy Spirit inspires and directs us from Baptism to our last breath toward the goal planned and intended for us.

How do we react to this infinite love and benevolence shown to us? Coldly and ungraciously very often, I am afraid. If any of us were in God's place, and looked down on the millions of Christians any day of any week and saw the ingratitude of the vast majority of these millions on whom he had already conferred such benefits and to whom he was offering infinite unending gifts, would we not feel like dropping all interest in them out of sheer disgust?

Yet God is God and not a limited, small-minded man. He does not forget and ignore us, even though we forget, ignore and insult him much more often than we honor and thank him. But let today, at least, be an occasion when we remember his divine benevolence and thank him from our hearts for having made us Christians and for having given us the privilege of sonship, with heaven as our inheritance. Let us resolve to repeat these acts of thanksgiving much more frequently in the future.

We were made heirs to heaven on our baptismal day, let us never sell our eternal inheritance for the worthless mess of pottage this world offers us in exchange.

SEVENTH SUNDAY OF EASTER

FIRST READING : Acts 1 : 12–14. After Jesus had been taken up into heaven, the Apostles returned to Jerusalem from the mount called Olivet, which is near Jerusalem, a Sabbath day's journey away; and when they had entered, they went up to the upper room, where they were staying, Peter and John and James and Andrew, Philip and Thomas, Bartholomew and Matthew, James the son of Alphaeus and Simon the Zealot and Judas the son of James. All these with one accord devoted themselves to prayer, together with the women and Mary the mother of Jesus, and with his brothers.

EXPLANATION : In these three verses we are given a brief glimpse of how the Apostles, the disciples and the Blessed Mother spent the ten days that elapsed between the Ascension and Pentecost.

after Jesus . . . heaven : According to St. Luke in Acts, Jesus kept appearing to the Apostles and disciples in visible human form for some time (forty days is a round number). Then he led them to the Mount of Olives outside Jerusalem and they saw him ascending to heaven, disappearing from them toward the sky. It was a Jewish idea that the abode of God was above the firmament —the sky. Christ wanted to prove to them that he was returning to the Father; they would see him no more in visible form, now that he had proved to them that he had really risen from the dead.

They . . . Jerusalem : They obeyed Christ's command to stay in Jerusalem until he and his Father sent the Holy Spirit upon them (Lk. 24 : 49).

to . . . room : This was the room in which Christ had eaten the Last Supper with his Apostles and had instituted the Blessed Eucharist. Here the Apostles and some of the disciples had lived ever since that first Holy Thursday.

Peter . . . James : Matthew, Mark and Luke give us a list of the twelve Apostles in their gospels. John mentions only six of them by name but he says they numbered "twelve" (Jn. 20 : 24). In this passage of Acts, Luke names the eleven that remained after Judas's suicide. It is notable that in the three Synoptic gospels Peter is always at the head of the list while Judas is last. Here too Peter is first but Judas is naturally not mentioned.

with . . . prayer : To prepare themselves for the advent of the Holy Spirit they prayed together "with one accord."

the women and Mary : The devout women, like the mother of James and John, and others who had accompanied Jesus and the Apostles on the missionary journeys, as well as the Blessed Mother, were still with the Apostles, catering for their temporal needs.

with his brothers: Brothers and sisters of Jesus have been mentioned many times in the gospels. The terms brother and sister in Hebrew and Aramaic were used for real brothers and sisters as well as for cousins, and for even remote kinsmen. These languages had no word for "cousin" or "relative,"—all who belonged to the one tribe or clan were called and looked on as brothers. It is clear from the infancy narratives of Matthew and Luke that Jesus had no brothers in the strict sense, and could not have because of Mary's plan of virginity. Yet Matthew and Luke spoke of the brothers of Jesus, for they meant cousins or relatives.

APPLICATION: The most important lesson for fervent Christians which these three verses from Acts stress today is the need for prayer, even amidst the most pressing work for God and for our neighbors' salvation. Having but very limited human minds, we might be tempted to wonder why the risen Christ spent so much time (roughly forty days) convincing his Apostles of the fact of his resurrection. He could surely have done this in a few days at the most. Secondly, why the delay in sending the Holy Spirit—ten whole days—when the Apostles had such a gigantic task ahead of them—the bringing of the "good news" to the known world? Their remaining years were so few one would think that every day, every hour, counted—that there was no time for tarrying!

Yet this is how Christ acted, and who was more deeply interested than he in the spread of the message about the salvation he had won for the world? The Apostles and disciples, together with the devout women and Mary the Mother of Jesus, were of course most keenly interested in evangelizing the world. Yet they did not question the wisdom of Christ. They understood the reason for this delay, and they used the time to prepare themselves for the work that lay ahead by fervent prayer in which they all whole-heartedly joined.

This is surely an example for all Christians of all times but maybe an example more necessary than ever today. Since Vatican II a tidal wave of urgency for good works for the neighbor, for dialog, for seminars, for external activities of all kinds, has swept over the Church and has left little, if any, time for personal prayer and personal devotions. There are even those among the most ardent advocates and most active promoters of "aggiornamento" who can see no great value in the lives of the relatively few religious who live an enclosed life, devoted entirely to prayer and intercession with God for their fellowmen. They should come outside their cloisters and help their neighbor, it is said—the implication being that their life of prayer is of little or no help.

Already women religious who spend most of their day teaching children or nursing the sick are urged to spend the little spare time left them which they used to spend in private prayer, in going among the people in order to edify them by showing that they are no different from them! Seminarians too who need the few short years allowed them to prepare for the priesthood are expected to cut down the time they used for study, spiritual reading and meditation, so that they too could go among the people and learn all about human nature from the faults and failings of their less fortunate neighbors!

In the eyes of these modern apostles of progress, the real Apostles and disciples and the Mother of Jesus herself wasted valuable time and—how will they explain it?—it was Christ the Son of God who made them waste this valuable time!

While it is absolutely true that "good works" done for our neighbor are (if done from the right motive) proof of our love for God, "the first and greatest commandment" is still love of God. And if we leave ourselves no time to adore, thank, and petition him for mercy and forgiveness for ourselves and our neighbor what does our love for him mean?

We do not for one moment question the sincerity and zeal of our modern apostles of progress and of the updating of the Church but we wonder if they have got their priorities right. Personal prayer and frequent communion with God in silent meditation are still and always will be the basis of a true Christian life and the only solid foundation on which a true Christian apostolate can be built. The Apostles and their companions who, on the instructions of Christ himself, spent ten days in fervent prayer before beginning their missionary activity, have set us an example we cannot ignore. Their life-long apostolate was successful—ours too will be a success if, and only if, we follow the example they have set us.

SECOND READING: 1 Peter 4:13–16. Rejoice insofar as you share Christ's sufferings, that you may also rejoice and be glad when his glory is revealed. If you are reproached for the name of Christ, you are blessed, because the spirit of glory and of God rests upon you. But let none of you suffer as a murderer, or a thief, or a wrongdoer, or a mischief-maker; yet if one suffers as a Christian, let him not be ashamed, but under that name let him glorify God.

EXPLANATION St. Peter continues his exhortation to the newly-converted in the churches of Asia Minor (see Second Sunday of Easter, Second Reading).

rejoice . . . sufferings: Christ himself had said that all those who would be his followers should imitate him by taking up their cross daily and following in his footsteps. All converts learned this. St. Peter tells them that any sufferings their being Christians brought upon them should be a cause of rejoicing for

it proved that they were close to Christ, helping him to carry his cross.

rejoice . . . revealed: If they have followed him during their earthly life, their meeting with him in his glory at their particular judgement will be an occasion of great rejoicing. Their cross in life will become their crown in heaven.

reproached . . . blessed: If they are insulted and suffer injury because of being followers of Christ, "for the name of Christ," then they are fortunate, because this proves that they are true followers of Christ, and sons of God and heirs to his glory.

murderer . . . wrongdoer : If however they are punished for evil deeds they are no credit to Christ or Christianity —they must never be guilty of such crimes.

suffer as a Christian : This is a cause for glory and rejoicing and :

under that name : He must always live worthy of the name of Christian and in that way he is giving glory to God.

APPLICATION : If there were no future life for us, if we ended like the ox or the horse or the pig in the grave, then Christians would be the silliest of silly men. On the other hand, if all the wonderful gifts which man has and which make him so superior to the dumb beasts, were to end in the grave or in a jar of ashes in a crematorium, how silly would the Creator be, or if we deny a creator, how silly would Evolution (with a capital letter) be which showed such skill in arriving at man the masterpiece of all evolved things, only to let him return to dust : the lowest of the low?

Human reason demands (and the loudest expounders of materialistic evolution have some human reason still left), and revelation proves that there is a future life for man, and that our present life on earth is but a temporary state during which we can earn, through God's goodness to us, a future life of glory and happiness.

The converts to Christianity to whom St. Peter was writing were convinced of this truth, and so are we, today's Christians, and so are many, if not the vast majority, of those who are loudest in their denials of God and of a future life for man. In St. Peter's words therefore, the point for us, as it was for the first Christians, is not that we are destined for a future life but rather how we are to make sure it will be a happy and a glorious future life. St. Peter's advice is that of Christ himself : we will share in his future glory, we will be with him in heaven if we have been true followers of his here below. If we carry the crosses he sends us, or allows to come to us, if we are proud to bear the name of Christian, if we live up to this honorable vocation, then when we lay down our earthly burden, we are assured that our life of glory will begin.

But while we have no doubts whatsoever as to the necessity of the demands that Christianity makes on us, there are few among us who do not find it more than a bit severe on our weak, human nature. It is so hard to be always good, it is so difficult always to resist the temptations that surround us on all sides, it is far from easy to accept cheerfully the trials of life, which, we can argue, do not come from God but from wicked men. All this is perfectly true, for the fact is that human nature is not able to live the Christian life by itself alone. It was never intended to do so, and for that reason Christ, who knew all our weaknesses, and foresaw all our needs, has arranged that his divine grace would be ever in his Church within our reach every day and every moment of our lives.

Living the Christian life then is not the work of mere man. It is the product of human nature aided and elevated to a higher plane by divine grace. The channels through which Christ arranged that his divine grace should reach us are the sacraments and prayer. By baptism we are already made brothers of Christ and raised up to the dignity of adopted sons of God and thus prepared and given a right to all the other graces we need to live our Christian life. Penance properly received removes sin. The Eucharist, toward which all the other sacraments lead and for which they all prepare us, is Christ himself entering into us under the form of bread to be our spiritual nourishment on our heavenly journey. Prayer is ever at our disposal and God listens willingly to all sincere prayer.

The Christian, therefore, who says Christ's demands are too severe has forgotten to avail himself of the aids that Christ gave him. No Christian has to travel alone. He has Christ with him and it is only the disloyal Christian who refuses to travel with Christ, who will meet with him at the road's end not as a loving brother but as a severe judge.

GOSPEL: John 17:1-11. Jesus lifted up his eyes to heaven and said, "Father, the hour has come; glorify thy Son that thy Son may glorify thee, since thou hast given him power over all flesh, to give eternal life to all whom thou hast given him. And this is eternal life, that they know thee the only true God, and Jesus Christ whom thou hast sent. I glorified thee on earth, having accomplished the work which thou gavest me to do; and now, Father, glorify thou me in thy own presence with glory which I had with thee before the world was made.

"I have manifested thy name to the men whom thou gavest me out of the world; thine they were, and thou gavest them to me, and they have kept thy word. Now they know that everything that thou hast given me is from thee; for I have given them the words which thou gavest me, and they have received them and know in truth that I came from thee; and they have believed that thou didst send me. I am praying for them; I am not praying for the world but for those whom thou hast given me, for they are thine; all mine are thine, and thine are mine, and I am glorified in them. And now I am no more in the world, but they are in the world, and I am coming to thee."

EXPLANATION: These eleven verses are part of the priestly prayer of Jesus. He prayed at the Last Supper for himself, for his Apostles and for all those who through the preaching of the Apostles (and their successors) would come to know the true God and his Son. This would be a knowledge which would bind them in a unity of charity like that of the Father and the Son and which is to be consummated in eternal love. We have only the first two parts of this prayer in today's reading.

lifted . . . eyes: The usual attitude of prayer among the Jews.

the hour has come: The moment when he would complete the work for which he came on earth. By accepting the death of the cross, and consummating the work of the perfectly obedient suffering servant, foretold by Isaiah, he was fulfilling his Father's command.

glorify . . . thee : The resurrection and his place at the right hand of the Father were Christ's glorification. This, in turn, would bring glory to the Father, since :

thou . . . flesh : Christ's humiliation in his Incarnation was decreed so that all men (flesh) could have eternal life.

all . . . him : That is : all who will in reality accept Christ, not that some are predestined by the Father : the grace is offered to all but not accepted by all.

this . . . thee : To "know" the Father and Son is to have intimate association with them—to be with them : not a theoretical but a practical experiential knowledge.

I glorified . . . earth : He is speaking as if the sacrifice of Calvary were already completed. The work given him to do in his incarnate state has been accomplished, and has brought external glory to the Father, because all men have been raised to a new status, and have been given access to heaven by means of the Incarnation.

with the glory which I had : He asks the Father to restore to him the divine glory, which was his from all eternity, but of which as St. Paul says "he emptied himself taking the form of a slave" (Phil. 2 : 7) in his Incarnation.

manifested . . . name : Not merely the name, but the nature, the infinite kindness and love of God for mankind. All these he had made known to the Apostles whom God the Father had given him.

that . . . from thee : Jesus is seeing his mission on earth as completed and the Holy Spirit as having come on the Apostles. It was only then that they really grasped that Christ was the Son of God, sent on earth as man by the Father for the salvation of mankind.

not . . . world : The term "world" in John is almost always in the pejorative sense, as all that is evil and opposed to God. He is praying for the Apostles only now, but later on he includes all who will believe in him through the preaching of the Apostles, and he adds that the unity of the Church will move the "world" also to believe in him (17 : 20–21).

I . . . them : The faith of the Apostles and the success of their (and their successors') preaching will add to the external glory of the humanity of Christ in heaven as well as to the divine nature which he shares with the Father and the Holy Spirit.

I am . . . thee : He speaks as if his ascension day were already present.

APPLICATION : The Son of God, Jesus Christ, came on earth and lived among us. He was God in real human nature. This is the mystery of the Incarnation, but the real mystery for us is not how it could be done, but why it was done. The answer is the mystery of God's infinite love for us. God wanted to share his own kingdom of everlasting happiness with mankind. He therefore raised us to the status of adopted sons through this mystery of the Incarnation.

God could have found other ways of bringing us to heaven, we can suppose, but we can be sure he chose the best way. He had created us with human hearts and emotions; he had made us capable of reacting to love and benevolence. In Christ he set before us an example of love and benevolence which should move the hardest heart to gratitude and to a desire to repay in some little way the God who did so much for our sakes.

God wants us to earn heaven for ourselves, aided of course by his grace. Would we enjoy and appreciate it fully if we had played no part in attaining it? Now with Christ as our exemplar and model, and as a living, ever-present example of self-sacrifice for us, the carrying of our personal crosses, the ordinary difficulties of life, should seem almost trivial when compared with what he who was innocent and sinless endured for our sakes. He was born in a stable, grew up in poverty in Nazareth, was often hungry and thirsty, traveled the dusty and rough mule-tracks of Palestine preaching repentance to sinners and calling on all to love God. He was continually heckled by the leaders of the Jews who thought they knew God. They even accused him of being in league with the devil. They finally forced the pagan Roman governor, whom they hated, to crucify him because they hated Christ even more. For three hours he hung in agony on the cross until merciful death finally brought relief.

This was all done for you and for me! He belonged to heaven. He need never have left it. He did not have to earn heaven. He went through all of this to give us the possibility of earning heaven for ourselves. Truly enough most of us have to suffer poverty, pains and sometimes great tribulations during our years on earth. But which of us can say that we are sinless, and if we could say it, that we may not have to thank these very trials and tribulations for keeping us so? Or if we have sinned we can see God in his mercy as using these earthly crosses in order to prepare us for the life of eternal happiness to come.

Sinners or sinless, we are still followers of Christ, and that prayer of his for us at the Last Supper asking his Father "to give eternal life to all who are his" was not said in vain. Unless we deliberately desert him, he will not desert us. He will bring us to the Father, where we will add external glory to the Blessed Trinity, and rejoice forever in the company of Christ who shared our humanity with us so that we could share and enjoy his divinity and humanity in heaven for all eternity.

PENTECOST SUNDAY

FIRST READING: Acts 2:1–11. When the day of Pentecost had come, they were all together in one place. And suddenly a sound came from heaven like the rush of a mighty wind, and it filled all the house where they were sitting. And there appeared to them tongues as of fire, distributed and resting on each one of them. And they were all filled with the Holy Spirit and began to speak in other tongues, as the Spirit gave them utterance.

Now there were dwelling in Jerusalem Jews, devout men from every nation under heaven. And at this sound the multitude came together, and they were bewildered, because each one heard them speaking in his own language. And they were amazed and wondered, saying, "Are not all these who are speaking Galileans? And how is it that we hear, each of us in his own native language? Parthians and Medes and Elamites and residents of Mesopotamia, Judea and Cappadocia, Pontus and Asia, Phrygia and Pamphylia, Egypt and the parts of Libya belonging to Cyrene, and visitors from Rome, both Jews and proselytes, Cretans and Arabians, we hear them telling in our own tongues the mighty works of God."

EXPLANATION: "Pentecost" which means "fiftieth" was the second of the three most important of the annual feasts in the Jewish calendar. It occurred seven weeks after Passover and was primarily a feast of thanksgiving for the harvest: the first-fruits of the wheat crop were offered to God on that day. Later on the giving of the Law to Moses on Mount Sinai was also commemorated on this feast day. All Jewish men, not legitimately impeded, were expected to come to Jerusalem, to the temple, for the feast. Hundreds of Jews from outside of Palestine also came, and the city was usually full to overflowing. It was very fitting therefore that this feastday was chosen for the descent of the Holy Spirit on the Apostles.

The Christian religion was to be universal, and the gift of tongues showed its universality. The law given by God to Moses was for the Jews only; the new law, given by Christ, and confirmed by the power of the Holy Spirit, was for all men. The vast gathering of Jews from Palestine and from all nations was a very suitable occasion on which to proclaim publicly the message of Christ given through the mouth of Peter.

Suddenly . . . a sound came : The Apostles had been told by our Lord to wait in Jerusalem (Lk. 24:49), until the Holy Spirit came on them. They were all in one place, probably the room of the Last Supper where Jesus had appeared to them twice after his resurrection.

like the rush of a mighty . . . : Spirit means breath or wind, so it was fitting the Holy Spirit made his presence felt by the noise of a strong driving wind.

Tongues as of fire appeared : Something that looked like a flame rested on each of them. When God gave the law to Moses, peals of thunder and lightning flashes signified God's presence and made the people tremble (see Ex. 19 : 18ff). The loud noise and the flames signified the presence of the Holy Spirit.

to speak in other tongues . . . : The first signs of the power of the Spirit. They were given foreign languages and a new superhuman courage to proclaim their faith. Hitherto they had sheltered from the Jews.

and at this sound : This sound "like a driving wind" was heard all over the city, and by devout Jews from "every nation under heaven," a pious exaggera-tion and a way of saying that they came from most of the known nations of the Roman empire, which was the whole world then known to the Jews.

each one heard : Each foreigner who spoke the language of the country he came from heard one or other of the Apostles speaking his language.

amazed . . . wondered : Little wonder they were amazed. They had enquired of the local Jews, and knew that the Apostles were simple men, with little education, from Galilee. Where did they learn all these foreign languages?

Parthians . . . : These foreigners say they are from Mesopotamia, Greece, Asia Minor, Egypt and North Africa, Crete and Arabia. There are even Romans present, most of them Jews, but Gentile proselytes also among them.

we hear . . . tongues : This was the cause of their amazement, these simple folk from Galilee speaking all kinds of languages.

the mighty works of God : The Apostles were speaking of Christ, his teaching, and his resurrection. St. Peter develops this theme later (2 : 14ff).

APPLICATION : Pentecost day is called the "birth-day" of the Church. The Apostles had already received the Holy Spirit on Christ's first appearance to them after his resurrection (Jn. 20 : 22). But on Pentecost day the descent of the Holy Spirit was a public manifestation intended to impress and amaze the crowds of local and foreign Jews who thronged Jerusalem on that great festive occasion. The signs and wonders that manifested his coming brought these Jews in huge crowds to the place where the Apostles were staying, and immedi-ately the gift of tongues was used by the Apostles to explain the occurrence.

It was a marvel wrought by God, a necessary consequence of the sojourn of Christ among them. He was the Christ whom the Jews had crucified but whom God had raised from the dead, thus proving he was the promised Messiah and his own beloved Son. Christ had chosen the Apostles to bring his good news to all nations—the good news that all men were once more reconciled to God their Creator, and were now adopted sons of God and heirs to heaven.

Today was the day chosen for the

opening of this mission of the Apostles. That they were backed by the divine power of the Holy Spirit was proved, not only by the gift of tongues but more especially by the change his coming wrought on the Apostles. From this day forward they were men dedicated to one purpose and to one purpose only, to bring the good news, the Gospel of Christ, to the world.

When Peter, representing the eleven, preached Christ, crucified, raised from the tomb by the power of the Father, and now seated at his right hand in heaven, he raised the Christian standard aloft. He and his fellow-Apostles (including Matthias and Paul later) gave their lives gladly to plant it throughout the Roman empire. The remaining twenty-six chapters of the book of Acts and the inspired letters of the Apostles tell the story of the growth of the infant Church. It was brought about by frail and mortal men, turned into spiritual heroes by the power of the Holy Spirit.

Twenty centuries separate us from those heroic men of God, but the truth of their labors is with us still thanks to the same Holy Spirit who has remained with the Church down through the years.

From generation to generation the message and the means of salvation have been handed down, sometimes through periods of peace and evident progress, but more often through years of persecution and apparent near-extermination. The Church survived because men of God valued eternal life, and the Church as the means of reaching it, more than their own comfort or personal safety.

Our own generation too needs men of principle, men of generosity, men who will put the eternal values before personal conveniences or earthly gain. The Church today has her enemies. They shout loud and long—the same centuries-old themes are put to some of the present-day pop music. But we need not fear. The voice of the Holy Spirit is still as strong as it was on that first Pentecost day in Jerusalem. His powers are divine and will never diminish. He is still at the helm of the barque of Peter and will continue to bring millions to the shores of the eternal kingdom as he has done during the past two thousand years.

"Come, Holy Spirit, enkindle in the hearts of the faithful the fire of divine love."

SECOND READING: 1 Cor. 12 : 2–7; 12–13. No one speaking by the Spirit of God ever says "Jesus be cursed!" and no one can say "Jesus is Lord" except by the Holy Spirit.

Now there are varieties of gifts, but the same Spirit; and there are varieties of service, but the same Lord; and there are varieties of working, but it is the same God inspires them all in everyone. To each is given the manifestation of the Spirit for the common good.

But just as the body is one and has many members, and all the members of the body, though many, are one body, so it is with Christ. For by one Spirit we were all baptized into one body—Jews or Greeks, slaves or free— and all were made to drink of one Spirit.

EXPLANATION : The gifts of the Holy Spirit were very evident in the infant Church. This was necessary to prove to the pagans that the Christian religion was from the real God who controlled all things. As pagans they had their local god or gods to whom supernatural powers were often falsely attributed. But the God of the Christians had real powers and they were distributed freely by the Holy Spirit when occasion demanded. St. Paul in this part of his first letter to the Corinthians is emphasizing that these gifts are not given to an individual for his honor or glory but to help to build up the Church.

No one . . . the Spirit : One of the first tests of the genuineness of a gift from the Holy Spirit was conformity with the Christian faith. If any man claimed he was moved by the Holy Spirit to blaspheme Jesus, he was evidently a liar and a fraud. On the other hand he who sincerely professed that Christ was God was moved by the Holy Spirit. Faith is a gift from God.

varieties . . . same Spirit : All the gifts given to the early Christian converts were from the same Holy Spirit and each had its special purpose. It is possible that Paul wished to prevent any temptation for one to boast that he had

a better gift than his neighbor. All were from the same source.

varieties . . . service : The ability to help in administering the affairs of the early Christian communities was a gift of God—each one receiving the gift necessary for his particuar task. Helping the sick, feeding the poor, calling the assemblies together, explaining the faith, powers of healing, are all examples of these different ministries, but they all came from the same God.

given for the common good : These gifts were given for the good of the whole community—to help build up the Church, and so that no one should refuse to use the gift he got or claim it as his own.

The body is one : St. Paul now introduces the simile of the human body made up of many members, to describe the Church of Christ. From this we get the title of "Mystical Body of Christ" to describe the Church.

for by one Spirit : It was the Holy Spirit, sent by Christ on his ascension to heaven to direct and inspire his newly-founded Church, who gave us the grace to become members of Christ's Body.

Jews or Greeks : Meaning all men. Greek stood for Gentile, that was the

rest of the world apart from the Jews.
were baptized : The sacrament instituted by Christ to make men members of his Church, his body.

APPLICATION : These verses of St. Paul are very suitable on this the feast-day of the descent of the Holy Spirit on the Apostles. Not only did he make his presence felt by the external exercise of his powers, on that first Pentecost day, but he continued to do so for some years until the Church had laid solid foundations in the Gentile world.

These gifts of the Spirit were foretold in the Old Testament as signs of the Messiah's arrival (see Joel 3 : 1ff; Acts 2 : 16ff), and were manifested in the early Church in Jerusalem (Acts 2 : 4), Samaria (8 : 17), Ephesus (19 : 6), Rome (Rom. 12 : 6), Galatia (Gal. 3 : 5), and in Corinth. St. Paul has much to say of the gifts given in Corinth because there was evidently some abuse of them or some dissensions because of them in that city.

But for us the important point to bear in mind today on this, the anniversary of the public manifestation of the descent of the Holy Spirit on the Apostles, is the infinite love of God for us, his Chosen People of the new covenant. Through the Incarnation men are empowered to become adopted sons of God; through baptism we become members of Christ's body, his Church. Through the direct reception of the Holy Spirit in the Sacrament of Confirmation, we are made active members of the Christian Church, with all the strength and powers necessary to be effective members, on active service daily, true soldiers of Christ.

Let each one of us take an honest look at himself today, and ask himself : Am I really an active member of the body of Christ? Am I spiritually healthy, living in God's grace and thus helping the whole body to be healthy? Or am I a diseased member, and not only sickly and weak through my personal sins, but spreading that sickness and weakness to my neighboring members by my bad example? But perhaps I can claim I have no very big sins and give no grave scandal, but I am lukewarm in the practice of my religion. I haven't much time for things of that sort. If I am one of these two types—a diseased member or a lukewarm one, I could hardly call myself a soldier of Christ on active service. Deserters and dishonest draft-dodgers are not at the front.

Thank God, a large percentage of Christians do strive to remain healthy members of his mystical body—they may weaken now and then but they call on their divine physician and put things right again. This is as it should be, but is it all that is expected of us?

The Holy Spirit came to us in confirmation with his gifts and graces to enable us to work for the whole Church, for the whole body of Christ. We are made soldiers to form an army that will work together for the protection of our nation and our freedom. No man is put into military uniform in order to look after his own interests. We too are not made soldiers of Christ in order to save our own souls only—we are soldiers in order to help our fellow-Christians and all men in their common fight against sin and Godlessness. We must then take an active part in the battles of the Church, against everything that impedes the practice of the Christian virtues.

There is a place for everyone in the Church's line of battle. We need not search far to find it. We need not be physical or intellectual giants in order to fulfill the role destined for us. What we need is sincerity and a bit of moral courage : sincerity in our belief that it is the future life that counts—the present is only a few years of training; moral courage to face opposition and criticism from enemies and often from false friends. When God and the Holy Spirit are on our side, we need not worry about the opinions or sneers of worldly-minded men. If we are true soldiers of Christ we shall win our battles, not by crushing our enemies but by making them too children of God and our brothers for all eternity.

GOSPEL : John 20 : 19–23. On the evening of the first day of the week, the doors being shut where the disciples were, for fear of the Jews, Jesus came and stood among them and said to them, "Peace be with you." When he had said this, he showed them his hands and his side. Then the disciples were glad when they saw the Lord. Jesus said to them again, "Peace be with you. As the Father has sent me, even so I send you." And when he had said this, he breathed on them, and said to them, "Receive the Holy Spirit. If you forgive the sins of any, they are forgiven; if you retain the sins of any, they are retained."

EXPLANATION : For the explanation of these five verses of St. John, see the second Sunday of Easter. They are repeated here today, the feast of the Holy Spirit, because on that first appear-ance of the risen Lord he conferred the Holy Spirit on the Apostles. Today's feast commemorates the solemn public and publicized conferral of the same Holy Spirit.

APPLICATION : The liturgical cycle, which each year represents to us God's mercy and kindness in our regard, closes today with this great feast of Pentecost —the public solemn descent of the Holy Spirit, the Sanctifier, on the Christian Church. During Advent we try to pre-pare ourselves for the coming of the Son of God to dwell as man among us. Christmas recalls to our minds and hearts that great act of divine love. Lent prepares us for the sufferings endured by Christ during Holy Week on our behalf. Easter is the feast of triumph, Christ's triumph over death, the guaran-tee of our final triumph and union with him in his eternal glory. Pentecost crowns Christ's work among us. The Holy Spirit comes to abide with the Church, directing and effectively aiding its leaders to preserve, explain and spread the gospel of hope and love which Christ had brought on earth. This same spirit helps and aids each member of the Church to live a life of holiness by following the teaching of Christ and by helping his fellowmen to do likewise.

Briefly, this annual series of Church feastdays recalls to our minds the infinite love of the Blessed Trinity for us finite, mortal men. At the same time it shows us the part played by each of the divine Persons in the eternal plan to share with us the perfect peace and the unending happiness which they enjoy in their heavenly kingdom.

God the Father created us with the intention and plan to raise us up to adopted sonship with him. God the Son took human nature so that we might share in the divinity. Representing all men he gave perfect obedience and reverence to the Creator "even unto death on a cross," and thus merited sonship for us. The Holy Spirit, the "fruit of divine love," came from the Father and the Son to bring to perfection the work of our sanctification. Thus the three divine Persons of the Blessed Trinity have cooperated in the great work of infinite love and condescension which opens for us a future of unending happiness, if only we have the common sense to appreciate what has been done for us, and the simple common decency to do in return the few relatively easy little tasks asked of us.

May the Holy Spirit today fill us with gratitude for all that God has done for us.

TRINITY SUNDAY

FIRST READING: Exodus 34 : 4–6; 8–9. Moses rose early in the morning and went up on Mount Sinai, as the Lord had commanded him, and took in his hand two tables of stone. And the Lord descended in the cloud and stood with him there, and proclaimed the name of the Lord. The Lord passed before him, and proclaimed, "The Lord, the Lord, a God merciful and gracious, slow to anger, and abounding in steadfast love and faithfulness." And Moses made haste to bow his head towards the earth, and worshiped. And he said, "If now I have found favor in thy sight, O Lord, let the Lord, I pray thee, go in the midst of us, although it is a stiff-necked people; and pardon our iniquity and our sin, and take us for thy inheritance."

EXPLANATION: Exodus, the second book in the Old Testament, describes the going-out (exit) of the Israelites from the slavery of Egypt under the leadership of Moses whom God appointed as their deliverer. The verses read today describe Moses's second meeting with Yahweh (God) on Mount Sinai. Yahweh had told him to come there again so that he would rewrite the ten commandments on two new tablets of stone. Moses had earlier come down from Sinai to find the people indulging in idolatry, and had broken the first stone tablets on which Yahweh had written the commandments (Ex. 32 : 19).

Moses . . . Sinai : Moses was commanded by God to come up to Mount Sinai again. Notwithstanding the idolatry of the Israelites God was willing to renew the covenant or pact with them— they had been severely punished for their crime, and were repentant (Ex. 32 : 27– 35).

The Lord . . . cloud : No human being could see God, but he spoke to Moses from within a cloud (see 35 : 20).

proclaimed . . . Lord : God assured Moses that he was Yahweh the true God. He had already given this as his name to Moses when sending him to lead the Israelites out of Egypt (Ex. 6 : 3). This name Yahweh means "I am who am," or "I am the Being" implying *the one Self-Existence.*

merciful and gracious : God describes his qualities, insofar as the human words which he had to use could describe him. "Merciful," that is, understanding the needs of man, "and gracious," ready to give aid, kind and sympathetic.

slow to anger : The NEB expresses it better by "long-suffering." God does not get angry quickly or slowly in our human way.

abounding . . . faithfulness : His love for man and his fidelity to any promises he gives man, are boundless and everlasting.

Moses . . . worshiped : Immediately Moses prostrated himself as a sign of respect and reverence.

Lord . . . us : Moses now asks a great favor of Yahweh, namely, that he would accompany them on their journey to the promised land.

although . . . people : Moses admits that his Israelites are unworthy of such a favor, for they are stubborn and rebellious.

our . . . sin : The recent act of idolatry while Moses was on Mount Sinai with Yahweh (Ex. 32) is the reference here.

take . . . inheritance : Make us your own, your Chosen People. This Yahweh did as the following verses show.

APPLICATION : The mystery of the Blessed Trinity—three Persons in one God—was not revealed to the Jews of the Old Testament. They were not yet fit to accept this truth. Surrounded as they were by nations that practiced polytheism (many gods) there would be danger that the Jews would see three Gods in the Trinity—it would look like polytheism to them. Hence it was not revealed to them and therefore we have no Trinitarian text in the Old Testament which could be read on this feast of the Blessed Trinity.

The text chosen gives the basis for its eventual revelation. Yahweh made a covenant with the Israelites. He made them his Chosen People, through whom he would eventually send his divine Son and the Holy Spirit to give man—the whole chosen human race—the possibility and the means of reaching the destination that he had planned for them from all eternity. The covenant made by Yahweh with Moses on Mount Sinai was the preparation for the revelation of the dogma of the Blessed Trinity and its relationship with our salvation.

The Israelites were stubborn, unfaithful and ungrateful to God in spite of all he did for them. Yet God was long-suffering. He put up with them for centuries and in spite of their infidelities he proved himself faithful to his promises. He sent to them (and to us through them) the Messiah—the promised King, Priest and Prophet (teacher) who brought to a happy conclusion the divine plan for mankind.

If the Israelites were stubborn and so often unfaithful, what can we say of ourselves? They were so ungrateful and so forgetful of favors received, but are we not ungrateful and forgetful too of even greater favors? We have a better knowledge of God's love and mercy than the Israelites had. Are we not worse than they? They saw the power of God so often used in their favor; we have seen the weakness of God, as it were, the Son of God who took our human nature and suffered and died for our sakes, and we can and do forget this infinite love of God for us!

Yahweh (the particular name for himself which he gave as a special favor to the Israelites) was with the Chosen People all through their journeying in the desert and eventually he led them by his almighty power into the promised land of Canaan. His divine Son whose name, Jesus, means savior of all men, became one with us in his human nature and, as he promised, is with us daily leading us into the real promised land which he won for us through the humiliation and sufferings which his Incarnation brought on him. Yahweh fed the Israelites in the desert with manna to give them the strength to reach

Canaan. Christ, his Son, has given us his own body and blood under the mysterious form of the Blessed Eucharist to be our spiritual sustenance on our journey to heaven.

Is there really any comparison between what God did for the Chosen People of the Old Testament and what he has done and is daily doing for us— the Chosen People of the new covenant? Yet, how unworthy we prove ourselves of this his infinite love, how ungrateful we so frequently are for this divine interest in our eternal welfare! True, we are dealing with a God of mercy, a God who is long-suffering, a God abounding in steadfast love. But let us not put all these loving qualities of our good God too much to the test. He will never let us down but we could let ourselves down by presuming too much on God's loving kindness and forgetting that he does ask of us certain proofs of our love in return.

One simple resolution on this great feastday would be to promise to make the sign of the cross as an act of dedication and thanksgiving to the loving Father, Son and Holy Spirit, who have already done and are daily continuing to do so much in order to bring us to heaven.

SECOND READING : 2 Cor. 13 : 11–13. Mend your ways, heed my appeal, agree with one another, live in peace, and the God of love and peace will be with you. Greet one another with a holy kiss. All the saints greet you. The grace of the Lord Jesus Christ and the love of God and the fellowship of the Holy Spirit be with you all.

EXPLANATION : These three verses are the conclusion of St. Paul's second letter to the Corinthians. The letter was written during his third missionary journey, 53–58, and probably from Ephesus where he was from 54–57. Paul had much advice and correction to give them and he also praises them. In these last verses he repeats his appeal for unity and fraternal charity and wishes the blessing of the Holy Trinity upon them.

mend . . . ways: They have many defects to correct which are evident from this letter and also from the first epistle. He urges them to pay heed to what he has said in the letter.

agree . . . peace: He begs them to live in harmony and brotherly love, the basis of true peace in the community.

Greet . . . kiss: At the liturgical celebration of the Eucharist they were to give the "pax," the kiss of peace, to one another, and it must not be an empty formula but a true sign of fraternal love. This ancient custom has been reintroduced recently into the Mass.

All the saints greet you: The title "Saints" was sometimes used for the members of the church in the early days. Here it stands for the church in Ephesus or whatever church he wrote from.

The grace . . . all: He ends by invoking the blessings of the three divine Persons on his readers. "The grace of the Lord Jesus Christ": that Jesus was God as well as man was the basic truth of Christianity; "the love of God": God had already proved he loved them by the Incarnation, and by giving them the Christian faith which enabled them to profit by the Incarnation; "fellowship of the Holy Spirit": his indwelling in them which began when they were baptized and was made manifest by many signs, especially among the Corinthian converts (1 Cor. 12). Paul wishes all these blessings of the Trinity on the whole Christian church in Corinth.

APPLICATION: By celebrating the feast of the three divine Persons today, we too are invoking on ourselves the blessings St. Paul invoked on the Corinthian Christians. We need the grace of Our Lord Jesus Christ if we are to reach heaven. He has already put us on the right road by baptism, and has made us receptacles of grace, but that is only the first step although a supernatural one. Every human act we perform in the state of grace—even our eating and drinking, and our daily tasks —is moving us along the road to heaven. But if we lose the divine grace through mortal sin, all our actions, even holy actions, are useless as regards our heavenward journey.

The love of God, the true paternal interest of the Father, as well as the fellowship of the Holy Spirit who is within us, inspiring us to good works, will also be always with us unless we deliberately cut ourselves off from their influence by serious sin.

The Blessed Trinity through Jesus Christ has foreseen this possibility. God knows our weaknesses and our inclination to do what is evil, better than we know them ourselves, and he has provided us with an easy and an accessible remedy. He has left to his Church the Sacrament of Penance in which our sins can be wiped out provided we are sincere in repenting of them. If it should happen that this sacrament is not available, the Church teaches us, following Christ's instruction, that a sincere act of contrition which implies and contains an act of love for God, will likewise blot out our sins and bring us back once more into the family of the Blessed Trinity. In this case however, if and when we get the opportunity of confessing these sins in the Sacrament of Penance, we must do so.

While we see the absolute necessity then of being in God's grace and friendship, in close union with the Holy Trinity, if we are to proceed toward heaven, we see how easy the good and loving God has made this for us. Should anybody be so foolish as to think that sins can keep us from heaven, one glimpse of the past history of the Church will suffice to change his mind. Among the canonized martyrs and saints (to say nothing of the millions of saints who are not officially canonized) for every one adult saint who has preserved his baptismal innocence through life 9,999 had some sins but repented of them and had them forgiven.

It is not sins that will keep us from heaven, but the refusal to repent of them. Let us all take courage then on this great feast of the Blessed Trinity. The three divine Persons want us in

heaven. They have proved this already in the past; they are proving it daily in the Church. If we appreciate what the Blessed Trinity has done and is doing for us, and if we show our sincere gratitude by frequent acts of thanksgiving—a simple "thank you, God," a reverent making of the sign of the cross, a symbol which reminds us of the lengths God went to in order to give us a place in heaven—if we develop this sense of gratitude we need never fear. Should we fall through human weakness, the three Persons are there to help us and put us on the right road to heaven once more.

"The grace of the Lord Jesus Christ, the love of God and the fellowship of the Holy Spirit be with you all" now and forever.

GOSPEL : John 3 : 16–18. Jesus said to Nicodemus, "God so loved the world that he gave his only Son, that whoever believes in him should not perish but have eternal life. For God sent the Son into the world, not to condemn the world, but that the world might be saved through him. He who believes in him is not condemned; he who does not believe is condemned already, because he has not believed in the name of the only Son of God."

EXPLANATION : We have in these verses a part of the conversation that Jesus had with Nicodemus. Nicodemus was a rich Pharisee and a member of the Sanhedrin, the supreme ecclesiastical court of the Jews. He had evidently seen or heard of some of Jesus' miracles and was anxious to learn more about him. He came to Jesus at night for fear evidently of his fellow Pharisees. He did not openly become a follower of Jesus after this conversation, but later on (Jn. 7 : 50–52) he defended Jesus when the Pharisees wanted to condemn him as a

false Prophet. When Jesus died on the cross Nicodemus assisted Joseph of Arimathea in the burial, and supplied a large amount of myrrh and aloes for the embalming of his body (Jn. 19, 39). It is probable that he became a follower of Christ later but there is no record.

God . . . Son : Christ openly tells Nicodemus that the reason why he (Christ) was in the world—the Son of God in human nature—was the infinite love of God for mankind.

whoever . . . life : All those who will accept him and keep his law will have

eternal life. They "should not perish":
this does not mean that they would not
die an earthly death, but that they would
not have an eternal death.

God . . . him: God sent him so that
the whole world, all men, would be
given the means of salvation, that is,
the means of reaching eternal life. His
coming will condemn nobody, but those
who knowingly refuse his offer will condemn themselves. He came "that men
may have life and have it to the full,"

that is to say: eternal life (Jn. 10:10).
who . . . believe: He who willingly shuts
his mind to the evidence.

name . . . God: To believe in the name
is to believe in the person. The Pharisees
and others refused to believe the proofs
of Christ's miracles which showed he
had power from God. He, Christ,
claimed to be the Son of God. Could
God give power to such a blasphemer,
as he would be, if his claim were false?

APPLICATION: Although the Holy
Spirit is not mentioned in this text from
St. John's gospel, the text is included
in the readings for the feast of the
Blessed Trinity because two of the
Persons are mentioned. They are clearly
distinguished one from the other, yet
both are the one God. God the Father
sent God the Son into the world (in
human nature) in order to bring eternal
life within the reach of all men.

While we must admit from the
evidence so clearly given in the story of
our redemption and elevation to adopted
divine sonship, that the three Persons of
the Trinity cooperated in that work, we
cannot claim we understand the mystery
of three Persons in one God. We can
and must admit the fact on the evidence
presented to us, but we must also admit
that our human intellects are too finite
to grasp the essence, the nature of that
fact.

How could it be otherwise? If our
limited minds could grasp the divine
nature and all its qualities it would no
longer be divine—it would be limited
like ourselves. There are many finite
created things in our world which we
cannot fully understand. How then could
we claim that we should be able to
understand the infinite? Of infinity itself

we have only a negative description—
something that has no beginning or no
end. When we get to heaven our minds
will be illuminated with greater graces
but even then there will always be something new in God for us to see and
admire. In the meantime our attitude
toward the Trinity should be one of
sincere gratitude for having placed us on
the road to heaven.

Through the divine graces given us, we
believe that Jesus Christ was the divine
Son whom the Father sent on earth to
give us eternal life. We have accepted
Christ as our master and Savior. We are
striving to follow him by living our
Christian lives. We are assured of his
assistance and of the assistance also of
the Holy Spirit, so that if we play the
part Christ asks of us in the drama of
our salvation, we can wait with serenity
for the final curtain.

The Son and Holy Spirit will sustain
us on our heavenward journey. If we
make use of the aids so thoughtfully left
by Christ in his Church—the true teaching and the sacraments—we shall remain
on the right road. We shall be lifted up
if we fall, spurred on when we grow
weary, and nourished with the divine
food of the Blessed Eucharist—the
manna of the new covenant. Then we

can feel very sure that at the end of our life's journey we shall be ushered into the presence of the Trinity—the Father, Son and Holy Spirit, in whose happy and holy company we shall remain forever.

FEAST OF CORPUS CHRISTI

FIRST READING : Deuteronomy 8 : 2–3; 14–16.   Moses said to the people: "You shall remember all the way which the Lord your God has led you these forty years in the wilderness, that he might humble you, testing you to know what was in your heart, whether you would keep his commandments, or not. And he humbled you and let you hunger and fed you with manna, which you did not know, nor did your fathers know; that he might make you know that man does not live by bread alone, but that man lives by everything that proceeds out of the mouth of the Lord.

"And you shall remember the Lord your God, who brought you out of the land of Egypt, out of the house of bondage, who led you through the great and terrible wilderness, with its fiery serpents and scorpions and thirsty ground where there was no water, who brought you water out of the flinty rock, who fed you in the wilderness with manna which your fathers did not know."

EXPLANATION : Deuteronomy as its Greek title signifies is a repetition in an abbreviated form of the law already given in the first four books of the Old Testament and also a brief résumé of the historical events already narrated in these books. In the four verses read today the reference is to the "manna," the food God gave to his Chosen People during their forty years of wandering in the desert. This reference is made today because the manna has always been looked on as a foreshadowing of the Eucharist, the real heavenly food.
remember . . . years : The author of

Deuteronomy is here purporting to give a speech delivered by Moses to the Chosen People when they had reached Mount Moab on the eastern bank of the Jordan and were about to enter Canaan, "the Promised Land." He wanted them never to forget all God had done for them during the past forty years.
fed . . . manna : We have here a résumé of our loyalty.
fed . . . manna : We have here a resumé of what happened within a few weeks after God had liberated the Israelites from the slavery of Egypt (see Ex. 16). They ran out of food and grumbled

against Moses and against God. God then rained around their camps each night a kind of bread, "fine flakes like hoarfrost on the ground" (Ex. 16: 15). When the people saw it they said: "What is this?", in Hebrew *Man hu,* and that is how this special food given them by God got its name.

not . . . alone: It was not the ordinary bread they had always eaten, yet it was as nourishing as any bread, which showed God could feed his people without the earthly materials which man normally used to feed himself.

word . . . Lord: The power of God had done this. He does not need human aid or earthly materials.

unmindful . . . God: Moses is now reminding them as they are about to enter the "promised land" where they would have all they needed, that they must not forget God's goodness to them in the past. He liberated them from the slavery of Egypt, he miraculously gave them water from the rocks (Ex. 17; Num. 20) and food from the skies.

a food . . . fathers: Hence its name "what is it?" They had never seen a similar kind of food before. According to Wisdom (16:21) the manna "was blended to whatever flavor each one wished," hence our response at Benediction "omne delectamentum in se habentem."

APPLICATION: Abraham, the father and founder of the Chosen People, was told by God to leave his home and pagan surroundings in Mesopotamia and come to a land that he would give to his descendants. Abraham trusted God and came to that foreign land. He and his descendants suffered many hardships before God eventually gave them possession of the Promised Land. Among these sufferings and hardships was the slavery they underwent in Egypt for several generations, until finally God stepped in and liberated them.

Their journey from Egypt to Palestine, or Canaan as it was then called, led through the vast desert of Sinai, an expanse of wilderness without food or water—where they could have perished to a man if their good God had not provided for them. This he did by giving them a special food which fell around their encampments every evening—a food that has ever since been called "manna," expressing the wonderment of the Israelites when they first saw it.

This food, as well as water which burst forth from the rocks at the command of Moses, nourished and sustained them during their forty years' journeying in the desert until they eventually reached home—the land promised to them by God.

That this "manna," this miraculous food from the skies, was a symbol, a foreshadowing, of the more miraculous food from heaven which our divine Lord was to give to us to sustain and nourish us spiritually on our journey toward our eternal promised land, hardly needs emphasizing. Our Lord himself refers to the "manna" given by God to their ancestors in the desert but says that he will give them *the true bread* from heaven (Jn. 6:31ff).

This promise he fulfilled on the night before he was crucified when he took bread, broke and gave it to his disciples, saying: "This is my body, which will be given for you" and taking the cup of wine he said: "This cup is the New Covenant in my blood which will be poured out for you" (Lk. 22:19). God the Son took our human nature, came on earth, in order to make all men not only God's Chosen People, but God's chosen children. By becoming man he raised us to the status of sons of God, heirs to God's kingdom, heaven. To do this he suffered humiliations and torture at the hands of the men he had come to save, but through his death and resurrection he won for us the right to the eternal "promised land."

However, to reach our inheritance we have to journey through the desert of this life, a journey during which we need above all a spiritual nourishment to sustain us and strengthen us to persevere amidst the many difficulties and hindrances our human nature and this earthly world put in our way. Christ, because he was God, because he foresaw our weaknesses and our needs, and because "he loved us to the end," found a way of remaining with us to sustain us on our journey. He left us himself— under the form of food, bread and wine, to nourish us and help us to grow daily stronger in our spiritual, supernatural life and thus be able to reach the eternal home he has prepared for us.

God was surely good to the Israelites —he fed them miraculously in the desert and finally brought them into their "promised land." But how much more generously and more miraculously has he dealt with us? Our promised land is not some strip of earth on which we can enjoy a few years of comfort—it is an everlasting home of peace and joy— it is a sharing in the happiness of the Blessed Trinity. The nourishment he has miraculously provided for us on our journey is not some food to sustain our earthly life, but the body and blood of his divine Son which only he, God, could give us and which only he, a God of infinite love, could think of giving. That we can never thank him enough goes without saying, but we can and we must strive to appreciate this, his greatest of gifts, to his Church and thus to us, by always trying to make ourselves worthy to receive him with the greatest respect and devotion of which we are capable.

SECOND READING : 1 Cor. 10 : 16–17. The cup of blessing which we bless, is it not a participation in the blood of Christ? The bread which we break, is it not a participation in the body of Christ? Because there is one bread, we who are many are one body, for we all partake of the one bread.

EXPLANATION : St. Paul has much to say about the Blessed Eucharist in this first Epistle to the Corinthians. In chapter 11 he corrects abuses that had crept in during the celebration of the Lord's Supper since he had left them. He repeats the account of the institution of the Blessed Eucharist at the Last Supper and the words of consecration which he gives are identical with those in Luke (22 : 19–20) and agree in all essentials with those given in Matthew (26 : 26–29) and Mark (14 : 22–25). In the verses which precede and follow the two verses read today he has warned the Gentile converts to have no part in sacrifices offered to idols (still a common practice among the pagans of Corinth), for Christians take part in the real sacrifice of the body and blood of Christ and are therefore in communion with God. The sacrifices offered by the pagans are sacrifices offered to "demons who are not God. You cannot drink the cup of the Lord and the cup of demons, you cannot share at the table of the Lord and at the table of demons" (verses 20-21).

The cup . . . bless : He inverts the order and begins with the cup. The cup of blessing was the cup of consecrated wine which by the consecration had become the blood of Christ, as he explains later in 11 : 24. Christ said that his blood was the new covenant, that is, the seal which ratified the election of his followers into the new Chosen People. God and Moses had ratified the making of the old covenant with the blood of animals (see Ex. 24 : 1–8) thus electing the Israelites as the Chosen People of the Old Testament. The latter was but a shadow of the new covenant as the means of ratification proves.

participation in . . . Christ : Communion under both species was the practice in the early Church. Those who drank of the consecrated cup received the blood of Christ.

bread . . . break : A loaf or loaves of bread broken up into small portions became the body of Christ by means of the words expressed over them; the words of consecration are given in 11 : 24. That what Christ did at the Last Supper was to be continued is clear from the express command he gave to his Apostles : "do this as a memorial of me" (ibid).

participation . . . body of Christ : When the Christians ate that consecrated bread they were eating the body of Christ. Neither Paul nor his Corinthian converts had any doubts regarding this fact.

because . . . body : All Christians are members of the mystical body of Christ. The participation in the Eucharist, the partaking in the one bread which had become Christ, proved and strengthened the cementing of all Christians into the unity of one body. Lack of true unity was one of the biggest faults of the Corinthian converts. Paul now tells them there can be no divisions, no disunity, among those who are united with Christ and in Christ by their participation in the one body and blood of Christ in the Eucharist.

APPLICATION : The feast of Corpus Christi or the Body of Christ is a commemoration or calling to mind of that extraordinary act of love for us which our Divine Lord performed on the night before he died. Through his divine power he left to his Church, to his followers, the power to re-present again and again the sacrifice of his human nature which he was about to offer to the Father next day on the cross for the salvation and elevation of mankind.

As he could die only once in his being God he was able to do so) that natural body, he ordained (because

this death of his could be repeated time and again under the form of the separation of his precious blood from his body, as happened on Calvary, by means of the separate acts of consecration of bread and wine performed by those to whom he gave this power. This is the meaning of the Eucharist as sacrifice.

It is as true a sacrifice as his death on the cross was, for so he willed it to be. In fact it is the same sacrifice, but under such another form as makes its repetition possible. As God he could do this, he said he was doing it and he gave a command to his Apostles (and through them to their successors) to continue doing it. The follower of Christ who believes he was what he claimed and proved himself to be, God in human nature, is left no room for doubt. Instead he ought to be full of wonder and admiration at the love and thoughtfulness of Christ who has left us a means of giving God infinite honor. We give him this by re-offering in the Eucharistic sacrifice his divine Son's sacrifice of his human life on the cross. Sacrifice was always an essential part of all religions. In the Old Testament God commanded the offerings of animals and fruits of the field. They had value insofar as God accepted them as a sign, a token, of the true sacrifice of infinite value to be offered later by his divine Son.

Our sacrifice of the Mass therefore is a sacrifice which gives infinite honor and glory to God and renews for us all the divine blessings won on calvary.

The Eucharist, the Body of Christ, is also a sacrament, in fact *the* sacrament, he left to the Church. Under the external signs of bread and wine which are a natural bodily nourishment, we are given to eat and drink the body and blood of Christ. They are really present because of the divine power of the consecration pronounced by the celebrant acting in Christ's name. This eucharistic food is for us our spiritual nourishment.

The receiving of Holy Communion, as it is called, is an essential sequence to the offering of Christ in the sacrifice of the Mass. He is present on our altars to re-offer his sacrifice of Calvary; his coming has the added purpose of nourishing us spiritually. When instituting the sacrifice he associated the sacrament with it, when he said of the consecrated bread : "take it and eat," and of the cup : "drink all of you from this." To partake of part of the sacrifices offered by pagans to their gods (and by the Jews to the true God) was looked on as a way of uniting the offerer with God. In the Mass all those present are the offerers, the celebrant alone has the power of consecration, but all are taking part in offering the sacrifice and should therefore take part in the eating of the sacrifice offered.

While the sacrifice of the Mass honors God of itself, our participation puts us in intimate union with God for we take within us Christ who is God. Thus we become the abode of the divine and the recipients of God's most abundant graces. This is what Holy Communion means—union with the holy of holies, intimate union with God.

GOSPEL : John 6 : 51–58. Jesus said to the Jews, "I am the living bread which came down from heaven; if anyone eats of this bread, he will live for ever; and the bread which I shall give for the life of the world is my flesh."

The Jews then disputed among themselves, saying, "How can this man give us his flesh to eat?" So Jesus said to them, "Truly, truly, I say to you, unless you eat the flesh of the Son of man and drink his blood, you have no life in you; he who eats my flesh and drinks my blood has eternal life, and I will raise him up at the last day. For my flesh is food indeed, and my blood is drink indeed. He who eats my flesh and drinks my blood abides in me, and I in him. As the living Father sent me, and I live because of the Father, so he who eats me will live because of me. This is the bread which came down from heaven, not such as the fathers ate and died; he who eats this bread will live for ever."

EXPLANATION : Today's lesson from St. John's gospel is taken from a discourse in which Jesus foretold that he would give his "flesh," his body and blood, to give true life to all who would accept him. The previous day he had worked the "miracle of the loaves": he had fed 5,000 men (the number of women and children not included) with five barley loaves. Because of this, huge crowds followed him to Capernaum, some undoubtedly for more free bread, some because of this astounding miracle. He took this occasion to give a long discourse on the "bread of life"—the bread that would give *eternal* life, and not merely satisfy bodily hunger.

While in the first part of this discourse, verses 26–50, Jesus most likely was speaking of faith in him who had come down from heaven, from the Father, as a necessity for all those who wanted real, eternal life, the section read today seems to speak of Christ as the "bread of life" in the strict Eucharistic sense. Some authors think that this section belongs to the discourse at the Last Supper during which the institution of the Eucharist took place, John does not mention the institution because it

was already so universally known and accepted when he wrote his gospel (between 90 and 100 A.D.). He therefore placed these words of Christ in the discourse at Capernaum. It would seem just as likely that John did not describe the institution of the Eucharist at all because he gave in this section Christ's very clear and definite forecast of its institution, and his readers knew Christ's promise had been fulfilled.

Leaving aside these questions it is generally admitted that this section of Chapter 6 of John refers directly to the fact that Christ's human body—his "flesh" and "blood"—would be the sacrificial victim that would win eternal life for men and at the same time as a sacrament it would be their heavenly food and drink. It was only after the sacrifice on Calvary, and the glorious resurrection, that this truth was really understood; Christ's instructions were faithfully carried out from Pentecost day onward in every Christian community. John's gospel (and the synoptic gospels also, even if written some 30 years earlier) was written when no Christian had the slightest doubt about the meaning of Christ's promise and

Christ's fulfillment of the promise at the Last Supper.

I am ... heaven : In the previous verse he had referred to the "manna," the bread from heaven as the Jews had called the food that Moses had given their fathers in the desert. But their fathers all died, he says. He, Christ, is *living bread*, his "flesh" (his body) will win for them eternal life. His "flesh" will be "given", sacrificed, for the life of the world.

Jews ... disputed : How can this man?" they said. They saw in him a mere man, a man like the prophets of old. He had power from God but he was still a mere man.

truly ... you : He does not solve their difficulty. They could not then grasp the explanation that he was more than *mere* man; he simply repeats his previous statement.

my flesh ... indeed : There is no question here of any metaphorical sense; to eat one's flesh metaphorically in the language of the Jews of that time was to caluminate one; and to drink blood, even mere animal blood, was a heinous crime—the blood belonged to God. So Christ's words had to be taken in a literal sense, but this sense could be understood only after the crucifixion and glorification of Christ. His glorified body still united with his divinity would be the food of eternal life.

abides ... him : The result of Holy Communion would be a real, holy and intimate union between the eucharistic Christ and those who received him sacramentally.

As ... me : As the Father and Son live the one divine life of intimate union, so will those who receive Christ under his eucharistic mode of existence be intimately united with Christ and therefore with the Father also.

bread ... heaven : Unlike the manna of the desert, Christ who has truly come from heaven as the incarnate God, is as bread the source and means of attaining eternal, not merely temporal, life.

APPLICATION : We are told in the verse which follow the part of Christ's discourse read today, that not only the incredulous Jews, but even many of his disciples drew back and no longer went about with him. Jesus said to the twelve : Will you too go away? Simon Peter answered him, "Lord to whom shall we go? You have the words of eternal life" (verses 66–68). Peter did not say he and the other Apostles understood what Christ had said, or that they had no difficulty in accepting his statement. Instead he made the profound act of faith : you have the words of eternal life —if we leave you, if we doubt your word, who else can teach us the truth?

I think we can all repeat today this humble and sincere act of faith which Peter made in Capernaum in that far-off day. Like Peter we cannot say that we can easily understand the mystery of Christ's real presence under the appearance of bread and wine after the words of consecration have been pronounced by the celebrant. But we are certain that Christ said that he was doing this and that he gave a command to his Apostles (and their successors) to continue doing as he had done. We have one big advantage over Peter, we are certain that Christ was God as well as man—Peter was not convinced of this until after the resurrection—and we know that with God all things are possible.

While on earth the God-man Christ

hid his divinity. No one who saw or met him would suspect God was truly present within that human frame. No one could think that the infinite who created the whole universe was within a tiny morsel of that universe, in a human nature. Even his twelve chosen ones to whom he gave many hints and many proofs of his divinity could not bring themselves to admit it, until the resurrection and the coming of the Holy Spirit finally convinced them.

Now, if Christ could hide his divinity under his human nature, it certainly is not impossible for him to hide his divinity and his glorified body, which does not occupy space, under the form of bread and wine. Not only is it not impossible, but if he willed to do so as he clearly stated he did, then it is a fact.

We have a further advantage too over Peter : the two thousand long years of the Church's acceptance of this truth. The "breaking of bread," their term for the celebration of the Holy Eucharist as sacrifice and sacrament, was practiced in the Church from the first day after the descent of the Holy Spirit (Acts 2 : 92), and has been practiced ever since, even by parts of the Church who left the successor of Peter and established a "separate brotherhood."

Admitting the fact then is not our difficulty. Rather our total unworthiness of such love and consideration, and our lack of gratitude in return, are what should give us serious food for thought today. Christ, the Son of God, comes into my home, my heart, every time I receive the Blessed Eucharist! And what kind of a home, what kind of a heart have I prepared for him? Our Sunday Mass is a repetition of the Last Supper—the institution of the Eucharist, which anticipated the death, resurrection, and glorification of the Son of God. Through his death and subsequent glorification he not only made heaven accessible to us, but he left us this crucified and glorified body of his, to be a communal meal for us, his followers, when we are gathered to honor God through him. Do we think of ourselves as being present in that Upper Room in Jerusalem as we come together in our local church to take an active part in the offering of this divine sacrifice for ourselves and for all men?

Sunday Mass and Holy Communion should not be an obligation to be fulfilled but a privilege to perform. An honest look into our hearts and into our attitude would do each one of us a lot of spiritual good and might make many of us find we have an urgent need to turn over a new leaf.

SEVENTH SUNDAY OF THE YEAR

FIRST READING : Leviticus 19 : 1–2; 17–18. The Lord said to Moses, "Say to all the congregation of the people of Israel, You shall be holy; for I the Lord your God am holy.

"You shall not hate your brother in your heart, but you shall reason with your neighbor, lest you bear sin because of him. You shall not take vengeance or bear any grudge against the sons of your own people, but you shall love your neighbor as yourself; I am the Lord."

EXPLANATION : This book gets its name from its contents, which for the greater part deal with matters and laws concerning the worship of God which was conducted by the tribe of Levi; hence the book of "Leviticus." It is the third book in the Old Testament bible, and although it has many very ancient rules and elements which go back to the time of Moses, it was given its final present form after the Babylonian exile (around 500 B.C.). It deals, as we said, with cultic and ceremonial rites and regulations. Chapters 17–26, from which today's reading is taken, form a body of laws commonly called the Law of Holiness. As well as cultic laws, these chapters contain ethical and civic precepts which show the lofty ideals and morals which inspired the sacred author of this section. Some of these moral and religious ideals will be apparent in the four verses read today.

You shall . . . holy : The Lord Yahweh told Moses to give this command to all the people of Israel. They were chosen by God and formed into a special people or nation for no other reason except that through them, and from them would come one day the one who would make all men "holy," that is, adopted sons of God. In the meantime they were to keep the knowledge of the true God alive on earth and make themselves as worthy as possible for this greatest of honors, in which they would (with all men) partake when the Incarnation took place.

for I . . . holy : All the nations and peoples of the time had their local and national gods, but they were neither holy nor could they encourage holiness for they were gods made into man's likeness while Yahweh the true God was holiness itself; his people knew that he had created them in his own likeness not vice-versa, and they should therefore strive to imitate his holiness and goodness.

not hate . . . heart : One of the principal ways of proving their holiness is now put before them. Knowing man's weak nature, and knowing that any man can offend his neighbor, God tells his Chosen People that they must not let any such offense sink into their hearts.

reason . . . neighbor : Instead, they must try to make the offending neighbor see and admit his fault and thus bring him back to true brotherly friendship once more.

bear . . . him : If they refuse to do this, and continue to bear enmity against the offending brother, they themselves become guilty of as grievous a sin.

not take vengeance : The natural inclination of mere human nature is to "get one's own back," to repay the offender in his own coin. This the spiritual man, the man who knows and adores the true God, whose nature is holiness, must not do.

bear any grudge : They must "forgive and forget." Taking vengeance by external acts is wrong, but so is internal hatred or refusal to forgive an offending brother.

your own people : As Yahweh had set them as a "nation apart," a people who were surrounded on all sides by pagan neighbors with whom any contact would endanger the purity of their true religion, the rules of conduct, the laws of charity, he lays down for them apply only to their fellow Israelites. The circumstances of the time and the attraction of the false religions which catered for human weaknesses made this separation necessary.

love your . . . yourself : This law is valid for all time and for all mankind without distinction, but the most the Israelites could be expected to do in those days was to put it into practice among their own people. But note the injunction that should an alien or stranger (a non-Israelite) come to live among them, they were to treat him as one of themselves (19 : 33). The law of brotherly love therefore was universal once the circumstances made its application possible.

neighbor . . . yourself : Do to your neighbor what you would like and want your neighbor to do to you, is the yardstick by which charity is measured.

I am the Lord : Hence these commands. It is not Moses or any human authority who is imposing the obligation of leading a holy life, as shown especially in brotherly love, but God himself, who has the supreme and absolute right to give such orders.

APPLICATION : "You shall be holy : for I the Lord your God am holy." This command given by God to the Israelites seems at first sight impossible of fulfillment for weak, human nature. God is holiness itself, he is holy by his nature, which is divine, while man, even the best of men, seems inclined to unholiness or evil by his very nature. But God did not command the Israelites to be as holy as he is—that would be an impossibility. What he does give them is the reason why they should be as holy as men can be. He is the God of holiness, the God of all perfection, they are his chosen ones. They should therefore strive to achieve such human perfection as would make them worthy of the holy state he has planned for them, namely, adopted sonship.

This same command holds for all men still. We Christians should find it much easier to fulfill, since the Incarnation, which was only very vaguely revealed to the Israelites, has taken place in our history—"before our eyes" as it were. Through the Incarnation, we know God's real purpose for us men. He has made us his adopted sons, he has given us the example of Christ, his divine Son in true human nature, who as man lived a life of perfect holiness, perfect obedience to his heavenly Father. With such an example, and with the clear understanding of what the end and purpose of our journey through life is, we should not find it so hard to strive to make ourselves worthy of the honor and the great future God has in store for us.

We are God's adopted sons. There is an eternity of happiness awaiting us when we end our sojourn here below. The Christian who is convinced of this truth, as every sincere Christian is, will not look on the command to be holy so much as a command, as a necessary preparation for what is to come, a preparation which he gladly undertakes. The bride-to-be who is told by her mother to prepare herself fittingly for her wedding-day would hardly call this a command. We are destined to be brides of Christ for all eternity. We are con-vinced of this, that is why we are Christians. How then could we look on the necessary preparations for our wedding-day, the day of our judgement, as something onerous, something we dislike?

We have seen God's love for us. The Incarnation shows a love which surpasses the wildest hopes or imagination of men. Would we be so mean and so ungrateful as to refuse the puny bit of human love which he asks of us in return? We know for certain what future God has planned for us and earned for us through the God-man Christ—an eternity of happiness with God in heaven. Who would be so foolish, so forgetful of his own best interest, as to let the trifling, fleeting, unsatisfying things of this earth prevent him from reaching such a happy, unending future?

God's call to us to be holy is really not a command but the kind and loving advice of an infinitely loving Father.

SECOND READING : 1 Cor. 3 : 16–23. Do you not know that you are God's temple and that God's Spirit dwells in you? If anyone destroys God's temple, God will destroy him. For God's temple is holy, and that temple you are.

Let no one deceive himself. If anyone among you thinks that he is wise in this age, let him become a fool that he may become wise. For the wisdom of this world is folly with God. For it is written, "He catches the wise in their craftiness," and again, "The Lord knows that the thoughts of the wise are futile." So let no one boast of men. For all things are yours, whether Paul or Apollos or Cephas or the world or life or death or the present or the future, all are yours; and you are Christ's; and Christ is God's.

EXPLANATION : St. Paul continues to instruct and correct his Corinthian converts. One of the abuses he had to correct was the divisions that were arising among them. These he had already referred to (1 : 10–13; see Third Sunday of the Year above) and returns to them briefly in today's reading. The

Christians of Corinth do not belong to the Apostles or preachers who taught them, but to God through Christ. They are, each one of them, nothing less than the temple of God, for the Holy Spirit dwells in them. They must be united therefore, or they cannot be holy, worthy of the divine indwelling. In Christianity they have true wisdom (see last Sunday above), divine wisdom, not the wisdom of this world, which is folly in the eyes of God.

You . . . temple : Both the pagan and the Jewish converts knew what a temple was—the dwelling-place of a God or gods. As Christians they knew, they had been taught, that with baptism the Holy Spirit had come to dwell within them. His presence was proved to them by his many gifts. Should any of them destroy this temple of God, that is, expel the Holy Spirit by sin, then they were destroying themselves, excluding themselves from God. It is not God really who destroys them, but they themselves.

God's temple is holy : As pagans and Jews they recognized this. Now that they are the temples of God they must be holy.

Let . . . himself : Let no one be so foolish as to think that the wisdom of the worldly-wise is better than the divine revelation and knowledge which he has received through the Christian faith. Christianity may seem folly to the worldly pagans, but it is a worthwhile folly.

Wisdom . . . God : The wisest man this world ever knew, if his wisdom and learning began and ended with the things of this world, was nothing but a fool in the sight of God. His wisdom was not only useless but if it prevented him from coming to know God and his own real purpose in life, it was fatal.

It is written : To prove his point Paul quotes rather freely from the Old Testament (Job 5 : 13 and Ps. 94 : 11).

Let . . . men : Paul refers now to the divisions mentioned above. It was not Paul or Apollos or Cephas who gave them the divine wisdom of the Christian faith—it was a free gift of God.

You are Christ's : Through that Christian faith they belong to Christ and Christ belongs to God. Christ was the Son of God in human nature; therefore, they owe everything to God, and not to any human agent or human wisdom. They belong to God.

APPLICATION : Today these words of St. Paul call on each one of us to stop and think of the divine gift God gave us when he made us Christians. We know where we come from, we know where we are going. God created us—be it through evolution or directly, it matters not—and it is to God that we owe the fact that we are here and now on this planet. But great though the gift of earthly life is, it would be, without the hope of a future life, a source of unhappiness for any thinking man. If after all my striving, all my endeavors, all my attempts to collect all the pleasures, wealth and happiness that this life can give, I were convinced that I would end forever in a hole in the ground, in a few years' time, what a cloud of unhappiness would hang over even my happiest day!

But thanks to the divine gift of faith, I know that my few years on this earth are only a period given me to prepare for my future. I know that my earthly death is not the end but the beginning of my real life—a life that will never again end. What a consoling, what an uplifting thought this is, not only in my hours of suffering or trouble but in my moments of greatest happiness. I can see in them a foretaste of what is to come, as I can and should see in my sufferings the divine medicine which will one day bring me back to eternal health.

We have the true wisdom; we know the real truths. Let the world-wise wear out their strength collecting this world's empty packages; let the neo-pagans keep on burying God and straining all their nerves to build a heaven on earth; we know the true value of this world's goods; we know where the true, lasting heaven is, and please God it is there we are going.

But to get there we must never forget that we are God's temple, as St. Paul tells us today. We must keep that temple pure and holy. We belong to God; we are his adopted sons. Let us strive every day of our lives to be worthy of this gratuitous divine honor. We could forfeit and lose this privilege—others have done so before us. God forbid that any of us should find himself among their number when he is called from this life.

GOSPEL : Matt. 5 : 38–48. Jesus said to his disciples, "You have heard that it was said, 'An eye for an eye and a tooth for a tooth.' But I say to you, Do not resist one who is evil. But if anyone strikes you on the right cheek, turn to him the other also; and if anyone would sue you and take your coat, let him your cloak at well; and if anyone forces you to go one mile, go with him two miles. Give to him who begs from you, and do not refuse him who would borrow from you.

"You have heard that it was said, You shall love your neighbor and hate your enemy. But I say to you, Love your enemies and pray for those who persecute you, so that you may be sons of your Father who is in heaven; for he makes his sun rise on the evil and on the good, and sends rain on the just and on the unjust. For if you love those who love you, what reward have you? Do not even the tax collectors do the same? And if you salute only your brethren, what more are you doing than others? Do not even the Gentiles do the same? You, therefore, must be perfect, as your heavenly Father is perfect."

EXPLANATION : Continuing his Sermon on the Mount (according to Matthew) Jesus tells his followers that the Christian law demands much more of them than did the Mosaic law, especially as interpreted by the Pharisees.
You have . . . said : His hearers were all Jews who knew the Old Testament.
An eye . . . eye : This "lex talionis," as it is called, is given in Leviticus 19–20. It sounds very harsh to us today, and we may wonder how God could permit it. But it was rather a restriction on the practices of a primitive society, where there was no central authority or courts of law and where each one took the law into his own hands. So this "lex talionis" prevented men from vindictiveness—the injured could inflict only an injury equal to the one suffered.

But I say to you : Our Lord is now abrogating any permission for revenge allowed by the Mosaic law.

Do not resist . . . evil : A Christian must forgive those who injure him and not retaliate even in the restricted form of the lex talionis. This would seem to exclude one's right to self-defense, except possibly in the case of a threat to one's own life. But even in this case only such defense is permitted as would save one's life, not going as far as taking the unjust aggressor's life. The example Christ gives is a bodily injury, not an attempt on one's life. Furthermore, our Lord is teaching the perfection of Christianity here, as the following examples show.

If one strikes . . . cheek : When one who could retaliate refuses to do so and submits instead to further injury, his example of perfect Christian forbearance will move his unjust aggressor to shame and repentance. In this way the true Christian will have turned an enemy into a brother.

coat . . . as well : Legal persecution. A poor man who cannot pay some debt and has his coat or ordinary daily dress confiscated, should not only yield it up willingly but should offer his cloak (the outer garment which protected him from rain and cold by day and was his covering at night) as well. Only a very hard-hearted creditor would fail to be moved by such a gesture, but the point of the counsel is to give an example of perfect resignation and detachment from any animosity.

mile . . . miles : A case of forced labor or service. Unjust though this enforced labor may be, do not resent it but rather do more than asked.

him who begs : Give alms and loans to those who need them.

love neighbor . . . enemy : The "hate your enemy" was not commanded in the old law, nor is it commanded here. The "hate your enemy" is negative parallelism of "love your neighbor"; the meaning is : "you need not love your enemy."

But I say . . . you : He tells those who would follow him that they must not only love their neighbor but also their enemies.

pray . . . you : Pray for their conversion. He gave an example of this when dying on the cross.

sons of heaven : They will thus prove themselves true Christians, the true adopted sons of God which Christ has come to make of them.

sun . . . rain : God, when sending his gifts, does not give them to the good only.

love . . . you : This is only a natural inclination, it is not the virtue of charity. Even sinners and Gentiles who never heard of God do this.

perfect . . . perfect : True Christians must strive to imitate their infinitely loving, infinitely merciful and forgiving Father. They will fall very, very short of reaching any such perfection, but all God and Christ expect of them is that they will go as far as they can in keeping the Christian mode of life.

APPLICATION : The lesson we have to learn from today's gospel hardly needs any emphasizing. We must, if we are truly Christian, forgive those who offend or injure us. We must love all men, whether they be friends or enemies. G. K. Chesterton says : "We are commanded to love our neighbors and our enemies; they are generally the same people." This is very true for all of us.

It is very easy for me to love (in a theoretical way) all Japanese, Chinese, Russians and most Europeans—they never come in contact with me and never tread on my corns. But it is my neighbors, those among whom I live and work, who are liable to injure me and thus become my enemies.

Charity begins at home, because it is here that it can and should be learned and practiced. It is first and foremost necessary for Christian peace in the home. Husband and wife must learn to understand and tolerate each other's foibles and faults. If one offends in what the other would regard as something serious, the offended one should not demand an apology but should show forgiveness before the other has humbly to apologise. No two persons in the world, not even identical twins, can agree on all things, so it is vain and unrealistic to expect even one's married partner to agree with one in all points. Christian charity alone can cover the multitude of faults of both partners.

If there is peace and harmony between husband and wife, as there will be if both are truly charitable, the children will learn too to be understanding and forgiving. Such a home will be a truly happy home even if it has little of the world's riches.

Our charity must spread from the home to our neighbors—to all those with whom we have contact. It is easy to get on with most people, but in every neighborhood and in every village or town there will always be those who are difficult. There will be the dishonest, the tale-bearers, the quarrelsome, the critic of everyone and everything. It is when we have dealings with such people that all our Christian charity is necessary. Most likely we will never be able to change their ways of acting, but charity will enable us to tolerate their faults and will move us to pray for their eternal welfare.

Life for many, if not for most people, has many dark, gloomy and despairing moments. The man or woman who is moved by true Christian charity can bring a beam of sunshine, a ray of hope, into the lives of these people. Fr. Faber in a booklet on kindness has a poem which we could all learn and practice with great profit for ourselves and for a neighbor in need of kindness. He says:

"It was but a sunny smile,
  And little it cost in the giving,
  But it scattered the night like the
      morning light
  And made the day worth living.

It was but a kindly word,
  A word that was lightly spoken,
  Yet not in vain for it chilled the pain
  Of a heart that was nearly broken.

It was but a helping hand,
  And it seemed of little availing,
  But its clasp was warm, it saved from
      harm
  A brother whose strength was failing."

Try the sunny smile of true love, the kindly word of Christian encouragement, the helping hand of true charity, and not only will you brighten the darkness and lighten the load of your brother but you will be imitating in your own small way the perfect Father of love who is in heaven.

EIGHTH SUNDAY OF THE YEAR

FIRST READING : Isaiah 49 : 14–15. Zion said, "The Lord has forsaken me, my Lord has forgotten me." Can a woman forget her sucking child, that she should have no compassion on the son of her womb? Even these may forget, yet I will not forget you.

EXPLANATION : This is part of the message of consolation that the prophet, second-Isaiah, brought to the Jewish exiles in Babylon when they were on the brink of despair. The exiles thought that God had abandoned them but the prophet tells them emphatically that this is no so.

Zion said : Zion, another name for Jerusalem, is used figuratively here as a personification of the Jewish exiles in Babylon.

my Lord . . . me : Yahweh has abandoned them to their fate; he has lost interest in them.

Can . . . child : The prophet asks them, in God's name, is there a mother so unnatural and so bereft of feeling that she could neglect and abandon her sucking infant, whose very existence depends on her caring for it?

Even . . . forget : It is within the bounds of possibility that there could be mothers who could do this but :

yet . . . you : Yahweh himself declares that even if some unnatural mothers could forget their infants and let them die he will not be so unnatural with his Chosen People, because they are his children, however unworthy of his love and care they have proved themselves to be in the past.

APPLICATION : In human relationships there is no greater love than that of a mother for her baby. It has been proved beyond doubt down through the history of the human race. It is an unselfish love, a love, a dedication that demands and expects nothing in return. The love between husband and wife has of its nature a tinge of selfishness in it—it is at its best a mutual love, which expects and demands an equal response. The love of a child for its parents, when it comes to the use of reason, is inspired by gratitude for past favors and by a self-interested hope for more favors to come. But the love of a mother for her helpless baby is absolutely free of all self-interest, it looks for no return either in the present or in the future.

This is the image that God employs to describe his love for his Chosen People : the love of a mother for the baby at her breast, a love free from all self-interest and prepared to go to any lengths in order to bring his children to the maturity and perfection planned for them.

The exiles, let us hope, believed his word and put their trust in him, but they could not and did not realize or foresee the real lengths to which that unselfish love of God for them would go. The most they hoped for and desired was a return to their native land where peace and plenty would be given them by their kind God. But this was only a tiny part of God's plan for them; we know the full truth now. God's plan was to bring them back to Jerusalem and Judah so that he would fulfill his promise given to Abraham and their ancestors.

In Judah would be born the descendant of Abraham, Judah and David— the Messiah who would bring them, and all who would accept him, to their real homeland, heaven. As we know, God carried out his plan in spite of the stubbornness and disloyalty of those Chosen People to whom he had been not only a kind father but a loving mother all through their history. If some, or many of them, failed to reach their true homeland—the real promised land of eternal peace and plenty—the fault was theirs not God's.

With our greater knowledge today of God's love for us, and of his interest in our true welfare, which the Incarnation has proved, we are much more guilty than the Jews of the Old Testament if we prove disloyal to God and ungrate-ful for all he has done for us. If we allow the things of this world, its pleasures, its wealth, its positions of power (all of which will end for us in a few years), to make us forget God and our own eternal welfare, then we are far worse than the disloyal Jews who knew little about the future life, and who had not before their eyes the example of the Son of God crucified for their sakes.

Yet the sad fact is that there are millions of Christians today, who live unchristian lives; men and women who act and behave as if this world was the beginning and end of everything for them. They forget, or rather do all they can to forget, that there is a future life towards which they are steadily and quickly moving.

However, there is one ray of hope for even the worst of us, and that ray of hope is God's declaration that his love for us is stronger and greater than even that of a mother for the baby at her breast. If we turn to him with true repentance—no matter how numerous or how heinous our past faults were— he will take us back once more to his bosom. He will forgive and forget our past if we will put that past behind us, and from now on serve him as loyal and grateful children. Great sinners in the past have become saints; great sinners in the future will become eternal citizens of heaven. You too, be you a great or a lesser sinner, can end like them, if like them you return truly repentant to the God of love.

SECOND READING: 1 Cor. 4:1–5. This is how one should regard us, as servants of Christ and stewards of the mysteries of God. Moreover it is required of stewards that they be found trustworthy. But with me it is a very small thing that I should be judged by you or by any human court. I do not even judge myself. I am not aware of anything against myself, but I am not thereby acquitted. It is the Lord who judges me. Therefore do not pronounce judgement before the time, before the Lord comes, who will bring to light the things now hidden in darkness and will disclose the purposes of the heart. Then every man will receive his commendation from God.

EXPLANATION: In this letter Paul has already referred to "factions" or divisions which had arisen among his converts. It was nothing very serious— it was rather that some groups boasted of having Paul as their teacher. Others boasted of Apollos, a great orator who came there after Paul had left. Others claimed Cephas, Peter, as their model, while others again claimed Christ as their teacher—as they all could. But a small beginning like this could lead to serious conflict later perhaps. Paul, therefore, condemned them and told them it was the message not the messenger that counted (see Chapters 1–3). In the verses read today Paul stresses this last point and tells them the preachers of the gospel are Christ's servants and no one but Christ and God had a right to pass judgement on them.

servants . . . stewards: The Corinthians must see in their teachers: the true servants of Christ—it is he who appointed and sent them, it is for him, for his gospel that they are primarily working. They are also stewards in that they have charge of God's household. It is their duty to dispense the faith and the sacraments—"the mysteries of God."

found trustworthy: A steward is not free to do his own will, he must manage his master's household and property honestly and according to the orders of his master.

with me . . . you: The Corinthians, therefore, have no right to pass judgement on Paul's actions. Only his master, God, who made him a steward has a right to do this.

not . . . myself: This does not mean that he does not examine his conscience; but he knows that he is incapable of passing a truly objective judgement on his actions, for even though he is not conscious of any wrong-doing or carelessness in his task:

It is the Lord who judges: The Lord is his judge—he will judge objectively without fear or favor.

Therefore . . . time: Do not take the Lord's prerogative, wait until he judges. This applies not only to their judging of Paul but of one another.

things now hidden: God sees all things and will therefore judge with full knowledge of the facts.

purposes . . . heart: The intentions (purpose of the heart) may change the moral value of any act. A good act done with an evil intention becomes evil. An evil act done in ignorance of its evil, can be a good act if the doer intends to do good. An act, indifferent morally in itself, can be a good or an evil act according to the doer's intention.

his . . . God: God will judge justly and each will receive reward or punishment according to his actions.

APPLICATION : The lesson we all must learn from St. Paul today is that we must avoid judging our neighbor— the right to judge belongs to God, who alone is aware of all the facts and circumstances. The strange fact is that there is a deep-rooted inclination in most of us to pass a moral judgement, almost always a condemnatory judgement, on our neighbor's actions. But this is an inclination we must resist, however strong the temptation. What we hear the neighbor say, or what we see him do, may appear evil to us, but even granted that it is evil, ours is not the right to condemn. That remains God's prerogative. As St. Paul tells us, we cannot see the "purpose of the heart." The neighbor's intention, which alone gives moral value to his sayings or doings, is unknown to us, and so our judgement is passed without full knowledge of the facts. It is, therefore, rash.

This prohibition of judging and condemning our neighbor holds for all our neighbors, whether they be above us, below us, or our equals. With our equals, and those below us, we are inclined to be a little more lenient, perhaps because we understand their circumstances better. But as a rule, our severest condemnations are reserved for our superiors. Is it perhaps because we are jealous that they, and not we, hold the higher position, or is it less blameworthy in that we do not understand all the difficulties that they have to contend with? In either case our judgement of them is sinful for we are usurping a right which is not ours.

This does not mean that we must take no interest in our neighbor's spiritual welfare. Though we are not our brothers' judges, we are our brothers' keepers. In all charity, and with true Christian humility and kindness, we must, wherever possible, help our neighbor to avoid offending God. Passing judgement on him and spreading defamatory tales about him is not the Christian approach to charitable help. Instead we must, as far as possible, cover up his failings and try to understand his weaknesses. In this frame of mind we can approach him discreetly, and if he sees our motives are really charitable we may, with God's grace, bring him to realize his mistakes.

Many a broken home, many a lapsed Christian, many an impenitent death could and would have been prevented if neighbors were active in true love of their fellowmen. And if some neighbor or neighbors are condemned when they come to the judgement seat, because we did not do our Christian duty, how can we expect a favorable judgement? We shall be judged not only on what we did but on what we left undone. Resolve today, never again to pass private judgement on your neighbor and his actions. Instead, always resolve to be ready with a word of advice, and of encouragement. Have a fervent prayer for a neighbor who seems in need of spiritual help.

One charitable word of encouragement and counsel given to an apparently erring neighbor will be more likely to help him than pages of condemnation and abuse. We shall be rewarded by God in the first case, whether we succeed or not. We shall be condemned for our judgement in the latter case whether our judgement was true or not, because we usurped God's right.

GOSPEL : Matthew 6 : 24-34. Jesus said to his disciples, "No one can serve two masters; for either he will hate the one and love the other, or he will be devoted to the one and despise the other. You cannot serve God and mammon.

"Therefore I tell you, do not be anxious about your life, what you shall eat or what you shall drink, nor about your body, what you shall put on. Is not life more than food, and the body more than clothing? Look at the birds of the air; they neither sow nor reap nor gather into barns, and yet your heavenly Father feeds them. Are you not of more value than they? And which of you by being anxious can add one cubit to his span of life? And why are you anxious about clothing? Consider the lilies of the field, how they grow; they neither toil nor spin; yet I tell you, even Solomon in all his glory was not arrayed like one of these. But if God so clothes the grass of the field, which today is alive and tomorrow is thrown into the oven, will he not much more clothe you, O men of little faith? Therefore do not be anxious, saying, 'What shall we eat?' or 'What shall we drink?' or 'What shall we wear?' For the Gentiles seek all these things; and your heavenly Father knows that you need them all. But seek first his kingdom and his righteousness, and all these things shall be yours as well.

"Therefore do not be anxious about tomorrow, for tomorrow will be anxious for itself. Let the day's own trouble be sufficient for the day."

EXPLANATION : This is part of the "Sermon on the Mount," a collection of the sayings of Jesus, given in different places and at different times but collected here by St. Matthew in chapters 5–7. They concern the kingdom of God and how it may be attained. The section we read today deals with the things of this world and how we should be detached from them if we wish to be members of God's kingdom on earth and in heaven.

no . . . masters : A slave could be owned by two masters but the situation would be impossible as each would demand his fulltime service.

God and mammon : The two masters that Christ refers to are God and worldly wealth. Each demands fulltime service. If a man loves God, he has no time for mammon. If his heart is set on getting worldly wealth (mammon) he has no time for God.

do . . . on : He tells his disciples and his hearers not to be over-solicitous about their food or their clothing. This does not mean they must not earn their livelihood and wear some clothes, but they must not make themselves slaves to this world's goods.

Look . . . air : The example he gives proves the above point. God feeds the birds because the birds search and search hard for their food. Man must do likewise.

lilies of the field : Their beautiful colors would not keep them warm if they had sensitive bodies to warm. Man needs clothing in most climates and must provide that clothing.

do not be anxious : This is the point Christ is driving home. While we must do our daily chores and do our best to provide for our needs, we must always remember to give God first place in our hearts. If we do this the very daily chores become a prayer and an act of reverence and trust in God who has a divine interest in us.

sufficient . . . day : This was probably a popular proverb and a wise one it is. The parable of the man whose barns were too small to hold all he possessed, and who was on the point of building larger ones, when he was called to the judgement seat, brings this truth out. Yet, we must plan ahead in many ways but we must not be so occupied planning for a wealthy, worldly future that we forget the real future.

APPLICATION : The lesson is evident : God must have first place in our lives, if we really believe in a future, eternal life, as all Christians, and most other sane men do. But we still must earn our living and work our passage through life. What Christ is warning us against is that we must not get so attached to, and so enslaved by, the things of this world, that we neglect God and our own eternal happiness.

Most of us will say : "there is little danger that we shall get enslaved by the wealth of this world—we have so little of it." But a man can get so attached to the little he has and so anxious to increase it, that he can cut God out of his life and forget the one thing necessary. Remember that a man can be drowned as easily in a tub of water as he could be in the deepest point in the Atlantic ocean. It is not the possession of the things of this world that Christ forbids, but letting the things of this world possess us. While we make the wealth and the goods of this earth serve our eternal purpose we can be true followers of Christ, but if we let them enslave us to the exclusion of that purpose then we are indeed on the wrong road.

In the parable of Dives and Lazarus, it was not the possession of much wealth that brought Dives to hell, but the wrong use of it. He lacked charity. He ignored his needy neighbors. He selfishly tried to spend all his wealth on himself. Neither was it the poverty of Lazarus that brought him to Abraham's bosom, but the willing acceptance of his lot. He was unable, through illness, to earn his bread. He got little charity from those who could and should have helped him. Yet he bore with his misfortune patiently and so earned heaven. The fact is, of course, that not all rich men will go to hell. Neither will all beggars go to heaven.

While we work honestly for our living, we have every right to our just wage and have every freedom to spend what we earn on the necessities of life for ourselves and our families. We can also make the normal provisions for the years that may lie ahead. What our Lord is condemning is the inordinate love of riches and the things of this world—a love so inordinate that it leaves us no time, and no desire, to look for, and provide for, our real future—the life that begins when we leave this earth and all that it has.

NINTH SUNDAY OF THE YEAR

FIRST READING : Deuteronomy 11 : 18; 26–28.   Moses said to the people, "You shall lay up these words of mine in your heart and in your soul; and you shall bind them as a sign upon your hand, and they shall be as frontlets between your eyes.

"Behold, I set before you this day a blessing and a curse : the blessing, if you obey the commandments of the Lord your God, which I command you this day, and the curse, if you do not obey the commandments of the Lord your God, but turn aside from the way which I command you this day, to go after other gods which you have not known."

EXPLANATION : The book of Deuteronomy, as its Greek name implies, is a second exposition of the Mosaic law. It gives also many incidents that happened during the journey from Egypt to the mountains of Moab, where the Chosen People could see their promised land to the west of the Jordan. It was in Moab that Moses died. In the book, Moses is portrayed as delivering the discourses that make up the greater portion of the book.

lay . . . mine : Moses is represented in the previous chapters as having reminded the Chosen People of all that Yahweh had done for them in Egypt and during their long journey to Moab. He has warned them of the temptations they would encounter when they entered the Promised Land. They must never forget Yahweh, the true God. If they do, if they follow other gods and bow down before them—"I warn you today, you will most certainly perish." They must, therefore, remember his admonitions.

sign . . . frontlets : The precepts of the law which God had given them through Moses, should be as close to them as the clothes or ornaments they wear. Later the Pharisees interpreted this literally and wore armlets and a band fastened around their foreheads containing the most important words of the law (see Mt. 23 : 3). Christ warned his Apostles against imitating the Pharisees in this as in all the other things they did to attract attention to themselves.

a blessing . . . curse : The Chosen People have a simple choice : If they remain loyal to Yahweh, and keep his commandments, they will be blessed by Yahweh. If they desert him, and turn to false gods, they will bring a curse on themselves, and Yahweh will desert them. Their subsequent history proved the truth of this prophecy and promise.

APPLICATION : The choice which Moses set before the Israelites is the very same choice set before each one of us, when we come to the use of reason. There is this difference that the temporal, earthly blessings, which a faithful service of the true God would bring on the Israelites, were the ones stressed. They had little or no knowledge as yet, of a life of eternal blessings. It would follow—they too would have that eternal life—but this was only very vaguely revealed to them in the promise of the Messiah, who would come at some later date, and make them members of the true kingdom of God.

On the other hand, we have a clear understanding of the blessings and the reward, which a faithful and loyal service of God in this life will earn for us. It is not prosperity, or power, or freedom from pain and sorrow in this life. It is the guarantee that if we accept these trials and troubles, and continue loyal to God, an eternal life of happiness awaits us after we pass through the gates of physical death.

We indeed are fortunate and blessed, that we are living after Christ's coming on earth. He has taught us the true value of life. He has shown us that this earthly life is only a short period, but a valuable one, during which we can prepare ourselves for true and everlasting life. It should be much easier for us, therefore, with such an award awaiting us, to be loyal to God by keeping his commandments, than it was for the Israelites.

They looked for earthly blessings, peace and plenty, during their time on earth. The longer that time lasted, the greater they thought the blessings were. If their crops were poor, and their flocks and herds not increasing as they thought they should, and they saw their pagan neighbors prospering, under the benevolence and power, as they believed, of their pagan gods, they did not hesitate to leave Yahweh and pay their worship to these pagan idols.

We are shocked, surely, at such disloyalty and ingratitude to the true God, who had done so much for them. Before passing judgement on them, however, it would be far more profitable for us to look on our own past, and see how often we have been disloyal to God, when it was a question of a paltry, earthly gain or a passing, personal pleasure. We did not offer sacrifice to pagan idols, maybe, but we made idols of things far less worthy of the name, than even the idols of wood and stone carved by the pagans of Canaan.

The Christian who makes ill-gotten wealth, undeserved power, illicit sexual pleasure, to be his aim in life, has cast the true God and his commandments aside, and has set himself up as the idol he adores. He, as a Christian, knows far more about the infinite goodness of God to him. He knows he is the God who sent his divine Son on earth, to suffer and die for us, so that we could be made heirs to heaven. Furthermore, he knows what the Israelites did not know : that he is swapping eternal happiness for a few short years of very mixed, earthly happiness. There are very few Christians, let us hope, who act so foolishly, and so meanly, in their relations with God. But most of us have moments when we choose the curse instead of the blessing, as Moses put it.

All of us then, must pay heed to these words of Moses. We must keep God and his commandments ever before our eyes. We have to take part in the daily routine of life. We have to earn our livelihood, and do all we can to better ourselves and better the society in which we live. However, our decisions must always be made with God's commandments before our eyes, the thought of what awaits us after death in our hearts.

The Christian who follows this rule of life, will never set up an idol in opposition to the true God. He will rather follow closely in Christ's footsteps on the path which will lead to his eternal reward.

SECOND READING: Romans 3 : 21–25; 28. The righteousness of God has now been manifested apart from law, although the law and the prophets bear witness to it, the righteousness of God through faith in Jesus Christ for all who believe. For there is no distinction; since all have sinned and fall short of the glory of God, they are justified by his grace as a gift, through the redemption which is in Christ Jesus, whom God put forward as an expiation by his blood, to be received by faith. For we hold that a man is justified by faith apart from works of law.

EXPLANATION : St. Paul suffered much in his missionary activity among the Gentiles from Judaizers, that is, half-converted Jews, who held that Gentile converts to Christianity, were obliged to observe all the details of the Mosaic law. Paul emphatically proclaimed that the Mosaic law (with the exception of the ten commandments reconfirmed by Christ) was no longer necessary for salvation. Men are now justified, sanctified, by believing in Christ and following his precepts. The law had indeed served a purpose. It prepared one people, the Jews, for the coming of Christ, but when he came it no longer had any purpose. Christ established a New Covenant, with his blood, a covenant between God and all mankind.

righteousness of God : There is question here not of God's righteousness, justice and sanctity, but of the sanctity and justice which God confers on man by remitting his previous sins. The Pharisees (the Judaizers were their agents) held that a man who kept the law in its

fulness would merit justification or sanctification by his own works. That this is not so Paul now shows by saying : men are made just, made righteous, outside of, and apart from, the law, by God, if they accept Christ and are willing to follow him.

law . . . prophets : As we said above, they prepared the Chosen People for the coming of Christ, but the keeping of the law of itself made no man justified—this belonged to God alone.

there . . . distinction : God's mercy and forgiveness are available now to all men without distinction of race or past history.

all have sinned : All, both Jew and Gentile, have sinned, and no act of their own can remove the guilt of sin.

justified . . . gift : It is only by God's grace, his infinite benevolence and mercy that men's sins are blotted out.

through . . . Jesus : That is, the death of Christ on the cross, the climax of the perfect obedience of the suffering servant (foretold in Second-Isaiah) who, because he had taken our human nature, represented all men. His death made perfect atonement to the Father for the sins of the world, therefore it is because of him that God blots out our sins, as St. Paul puts it to the Corinthians (11 Cor. 3 : 18–19) : "It was God who reconciled us to himself through Christ . . . In other words, God in Christ was reconciling the world to himself, not holding men's faults against them . . . For our sake God made the sinless one (Christ) into sin (sin-sacrifice) so that in him we might become the goodness of God."

whom . . . forward : The Incarnation was planned from all eternity as God's means of raising us up to adopted sonship, and the death of Christ on the cross was necessary because sin had entered into the world. By this death, he atoned for all sins, past, present and future. However, the sinner must apply the merits of the cross to himself, as ordained by Christ, to have his sins remitted by God.

apart . . . law : The observances of the old law have no further part to play in God's plan for men's glorification or justification. Faith in Christ, coupled with a following of Christ in true love of God and neighbor, is the only means by which men can be saved.

APPLICATION : While it is true that these verses of St. Paul which we have read were part of his refutation of the Judaizers, who wanted to impose the whole Mosaic law on Gentile converts, he has a message for all of us Christians today. This message is the infinite and merciful love of God for us. He has proved it by sending his only-begotten Son among us, to make us something much higher than mere mortals, nothing less in fact than his own adopted sons. Christ, the incarnate Son of God, shared our humanity with us so that we could share his divinity with him. He took on himself our created nature, he became one of the human family, so that we could become members, by adoption, of the divine family—the Blessed Trinity. He trod the dusty, rocky, mule-tracks of Palestine, so that we could walk through the rose-paths of heaven. He died the death of a criminal so that we could live forever the life of the just.

Of course, we know all these facts for years. We are familiar with them since our catechism days in primary school. Unfortunately, however, familiarity breeds contempt, even in spiritual things, or if not contempt, loss of interest, at least. It isn't, perhaps, that most of us offend God seriously very often, but, how lukewarm, if not absolutely cold, our gratitude to God is, and our appreciation of all he has done and is daily doing for us! Would each of you ask yourself just now : How many times, since last Sunday, did I really thank God from my heart for the fact that I am alive, and more important : that I shall live forever in perfect happiness, if only I carry out the few rules he has laid down for me?

If your honest answer is "not once" or "very seldom," your faith in God and in his divine Son, whom he sent to make us fit to have eternal life, is not very active, and will perhaps hardly qualify you for that eternal life. However, when dealing with the infinitely merciful God, it is never too late to amend our ways while we still have life in us. It is only when our last breath is drawn that our account is closed and we are found solvent or bankrupt. God's mercy is infinite, but our time for seeking and getting that mercy is very finite. The one and only way of being assured of being in the state of grace, when called, is to try to be in God's friendship every day.

GOSPEL : Matthew 7 : 21-27. Jesus said to his disciples, "Not every one who says to me, 'Lord, Lord,' shall enter the kingdom of heaven, but he who does the will of my Father who is in heaven. On that day many will say to me, 'Lord, Lord, did we not prophesy in your name, and cast out demons in your name, and do many mighty works in your name?' And then will I declare to them, 'I never knew you; depart from me, you evildoers.'

"Every one then who hears these words of mine and does them will be like a wise man who built his house upon the rock; and the rain fell, and the floods came, and the winds blew and beat upon that house, but it did not fall, because it had been founded on the rock. And every one who hears these words of mine and does not do them will be like a foolish man who built his house upon the sand; and the rain fell, and the floods came, and the winds blew and beat against that house, and it fell; and great was the fall of it."

EXPLANATION : These seven verses are the concluding words of the Sermon on the Mount, as given by St. Matthew. Our Lord gives a description of the true disciple who will follow him in truth and in deed.

Not everyone . . . Lord : "Those who called on the name of the Lord" was the usual description of Christians when Matthew wrote his gospel. To be a Christian, it is not enough to profess oneself a Christian; one must live as one.

does . . . Father : The law by which the true Christian must live is the law laid down by Christ in the Sermon on the Mount, which he is just concluding. This law he calls the "will of his Father" who is in heaven.

on that day : Christ is referring to the day of judgement.

did we not . . . name : When the unfaithful Christian finds that he is not being welcomed into heaven, he will begin to enumerate all the miracles he worked in Christ's name. But the possession of the charismata which was common in the infant Church, was no proof that the possessor was himself a true and loyal follower of Christ. St. Paul tells the Corinthians (1 Cor. 13 : 1-3) that if he possessed all the supernatural gifts granted to the Church, but had not true love of God and neighbor, they would profit him nothing, they would not make him a true Christian.

depart . . . evil-doers : Christ will not know them. He will never have known them for they were not members of his flock. He will order them away from his company, that is, from heaven, for they have proved themselves unworthy of it by their evil deeds. They were nominal Christians only. In practice and in reality, they disobeyed Christ and his laws.

Everyone . . . words : He uses a parable now to stress his point. The Christian who heeds his Sermon ("these words") and lives by its teaching, is building his house on a rock, a solid foundation. Difficulties and trials will test him, but he will stand firm, as a house on the rock can withstand the storms and the floods.

Everyone . . . not do them : The nominal Christian may know all the teaching of Christ, but unless he puts it into practice he is building his house on sand. It will fall when the first storm and flood come.

great . . . it : Great surely was the fall of the man who could be in heaven for all eternity but failed, because he found the keeping of the Christian laws for a few short years too onerous.

APPLICATION : To be a Christian, to be called to follow Christ and to become an adopted son of God, and an heir to heaven, is surely a divine gift. There are millions who have not got this call, but, as it is not their fault, God can and will find other ways of bringing them to heaven. They too are heirs to heaven, because of the Incarnation. Having the express call, as we have, and having learned what is expected of us, is only the beginning of our climb to heaven. We must be active, living Christians every day of our lives. We know this, not on the authority of any saint or Apostle, but on the authority of Christ himself.

Nominal Christianity will get no one to heaven, he tells us. Only those who have led their daily lives, according to the rules he laid down, will hear the welcome words on his judgement day : "come you blessed of my Father, possess the kingdom prepared for you." The rules he laid down were summarized by Christ in another place : "Love of God and love of neighbor, on these two commandments stand the whole law and the prophets too" (Mt. 22 : 34–40).

True love of God and true Christian love of neighbor though they may sound easy, will make great and sometimes severe demands on the true Christian. The love of neighbor may be the harder of the two. We have so many reasons for loving God, for thanking and adoring him. But the neighbor, who often seems so unworthy of our charitable help, who is so often ungrateful, how difficult it is for weak nature to continue being kind and helpful to him! Yet it is by our true love of neighbor that we prove our love for God, as St. John tells us, when he says : "Anyone who says 'I love God' and hates his brother is a liar" (1 Jn. 4 : 20). This is strong but true language.

Love of neighbor, and of all neighbors, does not come to us all of a sudden. There are those we naturally like, and those who somehow repel us. It is the latter we must learn to love. This education begins in the home; children will in ninety cases out of a hundred, imitate their parents when they grow up. If children see true respect and reverence for God and his laws put into practice daily in the home, they too will reverence God and his laws, when they leave the home. If they see that their parents are kind in word and deed to the neighbors who are less fortunate, they too will practice true charity when the time comes.

There are millions of nominal Christians in our world today. The blame for this can, in very many, if not most cases, be laid at the door of their parents. What a judgement these parents will have to face! Not only will they have to admit their own personal sins but they will be held responsible for the sins of their children perhaps for several generations to come.

Parents, you have a grave obligation to provide food and clothing and an education for your children. It is your duty to see to it that they can earn a living for themselves in this life. You have a graver obligation still to prepare and educate them, by words and especially by example, so that they can earn their true living—the eternal life God intends for them, the life for which Christ lived and died, so that they might have the true life and have it more abundantly.

But doing this, you will not only be building your own spiritual house on a rock, you will also be laying a solid foundation for the spiritual lives and homes of the generations that will come after you.

TENTH SUNDAY OF THE YEAR

FIRST READING: Hosea 6:3-6. Let us know, let us press on to know the Lord; his going forth is sure as the dawn; he will come to us as the showers, as the spring rains that water the earth. What shall I do with you, O Ephraim? What shall I do with you, O Judah? Your love is like a morning cloud, like the dew that goes early away. Therefore I have hewn them by the prophets, I have slain them by the words of my mouth, and my judgement goes forth as the light. For I desire steadfast love and not sacrifice, the knowledge of God, rather than burnt offerings.

EXPLANATION: Hosea lived in the 8th century B.C. He was a native of the northern kingdom of Israel and preached there about 750–730. The ten northern tribes had broken away from Judah under Solomon's successor, because of the harsh treatment they had received under Solomon. To keep the separation of the two parts of the country complete a political and religious border was set up. The Israelites were forbidden to go up to Jerusalem—the temple of Yahweh their God—so Jeroboam, the first king of the breakaway Israel, set up shrines in the north where Yahweh could be worshiped. Their loyalty to Yahweh did not last long; they took on the worship of Baal and other pagan deities, as well.

Even though they abandoned Yahweh, he did not abandon them. He sent them prophets to remind them and recall them to their duty. The prophets failed and the Israelites ended up slaves to the pagan nations whose gods they worshiped (721 B.C.).

Hosea was one of these prophets. However, neither the kings nor the people heeded the words that Yahweh spoke through him. His marriage, whether real or symbolic, to a prostitute, indicates the infidelity of Israel, who should have been the faithful spouse of Yahweh, but was not. However, Yahweh was willing to take Israel back when the people repented. This happened only centuries later when the remnants of Israel and Judah were united once more under the leadership of Christ, the son of Yahweh, and his representatives.

press . . . Lord : While saying they want to know Yahweh the true God, they show that they think him to be like one of the pagan fertility gods. He comes in the form of "showers and spring rains that water the earth" and makes their land fertile.

What shall . . . Judah : This is anthropomorphism. God is, as it were, deliberating with himself on how he shall deal with them. Although Hosea is speaking in Ephraim (another name for the northern kingdom) he knows Judah (the south) is almost as disloyal.

you love . . . away : Their love for him is unreal; it is as lasting as the morning cloud, or the dew that is dissipated as soon as the sun rises.

I have . . . mouth : Whatever punishment he inflicts on them cannot be said to have come unexpectedly. He had warned them through his prophets— Elijah, Micariah (3 Kgs. 17), Amos, and now Hosea.

my judgement . . . light : His part of the covenant which he made with the Chosen People, will be as steadfast as the sun's light. He has foretold punishment if Israel does not repent. His word is unchangeable. Israel could change but did not.

steadfast . . . sacrifice : Sacrifice offered from true love for God was acceptable and commanded by him, but sacrifice from the disloyal and unfaithful and offered to gain temporal favors, was loathsome to God.

knowledge . . . offerings : A parallelism. What God wants is an intimate knowledge of himself based on love (like marital love), not theoretical knowledge. Burnt offerings coming from a false heart are malodorous, not "sweet-smelling."

APPLICATION : The words we have read from the prophet Hosea were spoken over 2,500 years ago. They describe a situation that then existed. You might ask what that has got to do with us today. Why recall events that happened ages ago? The reason is simple. There are many, far too many Christians, whose religion today is not very different from that of the Israelites. It is a religion of lip-service. God and Christ are practically put on the same level as the many other idols which they have set up in their hearts and homes. While they may attend Mass occasionally or maybe often for social reasons, their worship does not spring from a heart full of love and gratitude to God and Christ. Their hearts are too full of earthly concerns to leave any room for God.

If occasionally, their other idols fail them, or their health or their business profits begin to decline, they then think of God and expect him to step in immediately and put everything right for them. Granted that the mercy of God is infinite, can any Christian who hasn't given a serious thought to God or to his needy neighbor for months, or maybe years expect God to be all attention to his now urgent need? The foolish Israelites turned to Yahweh, asking for showers and spring-rains to grow their crops, when the pagan fertility gods failed them. Yahweh did not listen to them. Their prayers and their burnt-offerings, coming as they did from hearts of stone, which had no room for him, were not acceptable—they were an insult, not an honor.

Then, lest anyone who has neglected God, and has given him no part in his daily life, should try to excuse himself that he didn't realize his negligence, God himself tells us today that he punishes no man without first warning him. "I have hewn them by the prophets, I have slain them by the words of my mouth." This he said of the Israelites, how much

more truly can he say this of any twentieth century Christian? Week after week, we have the word of God read to us, reminding us of our duties of love and gratitude towards God. In various other ways the conscience of the deserter from God is pricked; if he fails to respond, the fault is his. God does his part but we have no idea how long he will continue to play his merciful role. The Israelites continued to test his patience. In the end they ceased to be a nation and became slaves of Assyria : they became what are known as the ten lost tribes. God forbid, that we should ever suffer the same fate—we shall not, if we set about improving our relations with God, today. Let us give him the first place of honor in our hearts, in our homes and in our daily activities. If we do, we can feel assured that he will have a place of honor for us in his kingdom on the judgement day.

SECOND READING : Romans 4 : 18–25. In hope Abraham believed against hope, that he should become the father of many nations; as he had been told, "So shall your descendants be." He did not weaken in faith when he considered his own body, which was as good as dead because he was about a hundred years old, or when he considered the barrenness of Sarah's womb. No distrust made him waver concerning the promises of God, but he grew strong in his faith as he gave glory to God, fully convinced that God was able to do what he had promised. That is why his faith was "reckoned to him as righteousness." But the words, "it was reckoned to him," were written not for his sake alone, but for ours also. It will be reckoned to us who believe in him that raised from the dead Jesus our Lord, who was put to death for our trespasses and raised for our justification.

EXPLANATION : The Judaizers, with the Pharisees, held that carrying out to the letter the works of the Mosaic law, was a necessary means to salvation. St.

Paul refutes them and quotes Abraham as an example of one who was justified (saved) without the works of the law. The law had not been given in Abraham's time. The Christian, who is a real son of Abraham, will be justified by faith in God, who raised Jesus from the dead. This resurrection proved he was the promised Messiah, and the true Son of God, our Redeemer.

In hope . . . hope : Notwithstanding that the promise that God gave to Abraham, seemed impossible of fulfillment, Abraham accepted it. Hope alone gave him the strength to trust in God's word.

father . . . nations : God promised Abraham that he would make him a source of blessing for "all the families of earth" (Gn. 12 : 2-3).

so shall . . . be : "As numerous as the dust of the earth" (Gn. 13 : 16).

He did . . . faith : Even though he realized his great age, and the sterility of Sarah, his wife, he still trusted that God could and would make him the father of numerous descendants.

grew . . . faith : As his conviction of God's power daily grew stronger so did his faith and trust increase.

faith . . . righteousness : It was not the law or its observance (which was not given until some 400 years later) that made Abraham a just man, and a friend of God, but his faith in God and his trust in his promise.

were . . . also : Abraham's faith is the "type" of our Christian faith and he is our father as much, if not more, than he is the father of the Jews.

raised . . . justification : He was put to

to us . . . him : We believe in God the Father, who raised Christ our Lord, his Son, from the dead.

death because of the sins of mankind. The resurrection was the climax of the work of Christ, as Incarnate God, on earth. Through it salvation (eternal life) was made available to all who believe in Christ.

APPLICATION : Abraham is set before us today, in this reading, as an example of a man who had perfect faith. He trusted God's word, God's promise, when all the odds were stacked against him. Even when God kept postponing the fulfillment of his promise—to make him a father—Abraham never doubted that the promise would be fulfilled some-day. It was. Abraham, through Isaac his son, became the father, not only of the Chosen Race, but of all Christians as well.

The faith which our Christian religion demands of us, is not as difficult, or as testing, as was that of Abraham. We believe in God, the Creator and ruler of the universe : our human, natural powers help us to believe this. We believe there are three distinct Persons in that one God : we have God's word for this.

We believe that the Son of God took human nature, and dwelt on this earth among us in order to bring us to heaven. We have human testimony and contemporary eye-witnesses for the fact that the man called Christ, lived in Palestine, that he claimed to be the Son of God and that his miracles crowned by his resurrection, after being crucified, proved his claim. After Christ's ascension, the Holy Spirit, the third Person of the Triune God, was sent by the Father and the Son to strengthen the faith of the Apostles and remain with the Church which Christ founded to carry on his work of redemption.

These are the basic tenets which as Christians we are asked to believe. No human intellect free of prejudice can prove these beliefs wrong, rather they all fit in with what an intelligent mind would expect God, our Creator, to be.

Yet, there are millions of ex-Christians in Europe alone today. Men and women who not alone no longer practice their Christian faith but who actually oppose it and try to tell Christians that they are believers in fairy-tales. But not one convincing argument have they brought forward to prove our faith wrong. If admitting that our immense universe (we have discovered only a part of it, so far) came from an act of will of an infinitely intelligent and benevolent being, whom we call God, is pure imagination, and admitting that this same universe, with its intricate laws and its perfections (including intelligent man), came from a tiny nebula, or little cloud, which had not sense, or reasoning power, is a sign of great intelligence, we can see who is believing in fairy-tales! "A world without meaning or purpose is unlivable-in, and even unthinkable." Man, with his intellectual capabilities, his appreciation of the good and the beautiful, his unlimited desire for happiness should have no higher purpose than to "eat, sleep, drink and be merry" for a few short years on earth, a limited goal which even so, very few can reach, is surely the silliest of all fairy-tales ever told! We are destined for something much more noble, more lasting and obtainable by all. We are destined for an eternal life with the three Persons of the Blessed Trinity, who out of sheer, infinite benevolence made this eternal life available to us.

Let us thank God for our faith and let us show that gratitude by faithfully carrying out any demands it may make on us. Abraham believed in God and trusted in his promise. With much greater reason can we, who have known Christ, believe in our loving Father and trust in his promises. He has adopted us as his sons. Our place in his kingdom is already prepared for us, all we have to do is to move steadily and joyfully toward it.

GOSPEL : Matthew 9 : 9–13. As Jesus passed on, he saw a man called Matthew sitting at the tax office; and he said to him, "Follow me." And he rose and followed him.

And as he sat at table in the house, behold, many tax collectors and sinners came and sat down with Jesus and his disciples. And when the Pharisees saw this, they said to his disciples, "Why does your teacher eat with tax collectors and sinners?" But when he heard it, he said, "Those who are well have no need of a physician, but those who are sick. Go and learn what this means, 'I desire love and not sacrifice.' For I came not to call the righteous, but sinners."

EXPLANATION : These five verses from Matthew's own gospel tell us of his call to be an Apostle of Jesus and how the Pharisees reacted. He does not tell us that it was he who gave the dinner in honor of Jesus at which many of his fellow tax-gatherers and other sinners sat at table with Jesus and his disciples. Luke and Mark tell us this (Lk. 5 : 29 and Mk. 2 : 15). To understand the ire of the Pharisees, it must be recalled that the tax-collectors in Palestine were Jewish agents whom the Romans used to collect the taxes. The Roman system left plenty of room for abuse and injustice. The Romans had to get a certain amount from each district. The agent was free to get all he could, provided he handed in the prescribed amount to the Roman authorities. Because of the frequent injustices, but especially because they cooperated with the hated foreign, pagan rulers, the tax-collectors were despised by nearly all Jews, but especially by the Pharisees.

Matthew . . . tax-office : It seems very probable that Matthew was one of the few honest tax-collectors. Our Lord had not met him before this, but he knew all about him. He knew he would accept the call—he gave it and Matthew, there and then, gave up his job and joined Jesus' disciples.

Why . . . teacher : Already, in fact almost from the beginning of his public ministry, the Pharisees were in opposition to Jesus. They saw him now eating with tax-collectors and sinners. They were shocked. How could he be the Messiah, or even the good man he pretended to be, if he mixed with such disreputable people?

when he heard it : The disciples reported the Pharisees' question to Jesus and his answer was :

Those . . . sick : There is a certain amount of sarcasm in the answer. The Pharisees esteemed themselves as above all sin. They kept the law to the letter. They had no need of a Savior. They could and would get to heaven on their own. The poor tax-collectors and sinners, on the other hand, were only too conscious of their own defects—they were spiritually ill and badly needed a physician.

I desire love and not sacrifice : He tells the Pharisees to go and learn the meaning of that saying, so often used by the prophets to the disloyal Israelites. God wanted them to be loyal to him and his laws. He wanted the sacrifice of their hearts and wills rather than the performance of sacrificial rites, which left their hearts cold and far from him (see Hosea 6 : 6; Amos 5 : 21; Ps. 51 : 16–17).

not . . . righteous : The Pharisees regarded themselves as models of perfection and righteousness. They kept the minutest items of the law and of the rabbinical explanations of it—most of the latter was sheer casuistry. But this very self-esteem and ingrained pride spoiled their many good actions (see the Parable of the Pharisee and the tax-collector, or publican, in the temple, Lk. 18 : 10–14). They too needed a spiritual physician but they did not know this.

APPLICATION : "I came . . . to call sinners" are the words of Christ himself and what consoling words they are for all of us! We have all sinned, or we are all capable of sinning, so what a consolation to know that we are dealing with a divine Judge, who understands our weaknesses and whose desire is the conversion not the condemnation of offenders. "For God so loved the world that he gave his only Son, that whoever believes in him should not perish but have eternal life. For God sent the Son into the world, not to condemn the world but that the world might be saved through him" (Jn. 3 : 16–17).

The call of Matthew to the apostolate, and Christ's partaking of a meal with Matthew and his sinner friends that evening, is a proof of the Lord's forgiving mercy and understanding. Matthew became a faithful follower of Jesus, and gave his life for the spread of the gospel of mercy and divine love. The fellow tax-collectors and sinners, we can feel sure, learned much from that action of Jesus, and that sign of understanding on his part, helped many, if not all of them, to change their lives.

It is the same Christ that we are dealing with. It is the same Christ who has called us to follow him. He knows our human frailties. He knew when he called us that we would trip, many times perhaps, on our upward climb. But he had planned to be ever near us, to lift us up and put us on the road again. He left to his Church, to us, the lovely sacrament of divine mercy, which will wash away each and every sin, if we receive it with true repentance.

The true Christian should really appreciate all that Christ has undergone —the humiliation of the Incarnation, the insults from his enemies, the cruel death on the cross, and all of it so that each one of us, and not just a select few, could get to heaven. What true Christian would be so ungrateful to Christ as to refuse to ask pardon for his sins, and so unmindful of his own eternal future as to risk his all because he is too proud to repent.

The Pharisees acted thus. Their self-esteem and pride would not let them admit that they too were sinners. In fact, their sin, the sin of spiritual pride, was more serious than the sins of weakness for which they despised and condemned their fellow-Jews.

Should there be any Christian among us today whose pride and self-esteem will not let him humbly confess his sins, let him take a look at the crucifix. There he shall see Jesus hanging, dying a slow death on the cross, in order to bring him to heaven. It was our sins that nailed Jesus to the cross, but does Jesus hold it against us? Far from it. Those outstretched arms, amidst all their agonizing pain, are stretched out to welcome us back and to grant us a full pardon for all out past deeds.

Is there any human heart so hardened by pride, as to be able to resist this call to repentance and forgiveness offered by the very victim of his offenses?

ELEVENTH SUNDAY OF THE YEAR

FIRST READING : Exodus 19 : 2–6.   The Israelites set out from Rephidim and came into the wilderness of Sinai, they encamped in the wilderness; and there Israel encamped before the mountain. And Moses went up to God, and the Lord called to him out of the mountain, saying: "Thus you shall say to the house of Jacob, and tell the people of Israel : You have seen what I did to the Egyptians, and how I bore you on eagles' wings and brought you to myself. Now, therefore, if you will obey my voice and keep my covenant, you shall be my own possession among all peoples; for all the earth is mine, and you shall be to me a kingdom of priests and a holy nation."

EXPLANATION : Three months after the Israelites had escaped from Egypt, they came to the desert or wilderness of the Sinai peninsula and they pitched their tents at the foot of Mount Sinai. **Moses . . . to God :** It was on Mount Sinai (called Horeb also), that Moses first encountered Yahweh and received his mission from him to lead his Chosen People out of Egypt. He now ascended this same mountain to get new instructions from Yahweh. He got the Decalogue and the covenant, as the subsequent chapters show. **Jacob . . . Israel :** These are two names for the Chosen People. **what I did to the Egyptians :** He tells Moses to remind the Israelites (and they needed reminding) of the miracles he had worked to set them free from their slavery under the Egyptians. **on eagles' wings :** The journey to Sinai was relatively easy. The expression here is poetic rather than realistic. **brought . . . myself :** They are now under his jurisdiction and care and will be henceforth :

if you . . . covenant : That is, if they obey his commandments and keep the other liturgical and social regulations he is about to lay down for them. **my own . . . peoples :** They shall be God's Chosen People. **all . . . mine :** He is Lord of all creation and of all peoples and he may choose one race for his own special purpose. **kingdom . . . nation :** They shall be dedicated in a very special way to his service. They will all have a part in this service, even though the tribe of Levi is later chosen to represent them at the altar. They will be holy, for they will be serving the true God in the midst of the adorers of idols. They were elected for this purpose, to give honor to the true God and keep his name known on earth until such time as the blessing promised to their father Abraham would bring the knowledge of him to all nations and peoples.

I

APPLICATION : A covenant was a pact, or a solemn agreement, made between two leaders of tribes or nations. Each of the two parties bound themselves by their solemn word to keep their part of the pact, and the covenant was ratified by a special sacrifice offered to their gods whom they called as witnesses. The sacrificial victims were cut in two halves and set some distance apart. The contracting parties walked between the divided victims, signifying that they called on the gods, to cut them in two also, if they violated their solemn promise.

We can understand two human leaders entering into a solemn agreement of this kind, but it was surely an act of infinite condescension and love that God should descend to the level of a mere man, in order to convince the people he was choosing as his own, that he would keep his promises to them.

God promised his Chosen People that he would protect them from all enemies in their journey to Canaan, and that he would establish them there and make them the real owners of that land, and that he would continue to protect and keep them there until his original promise to Abraham was fulfilled. As we know, the Israelites failed again and again to keep their part of the covenant. They broke his commandments and they followed after pagan gods. God punished them often but he took them back once more, each time they repented of their sin. After many lapses and much repentance, the majority of the tribes (10) finally abandoned God. They ceased to have any further part in God's plan for saving mankind. The tribes of Judah and Benjamin in the south were a little more faithful, but they, too,

brought severe punishments on themselves, and only a small remnant was left when the Messiah came to fulfill the promises made "to Abraham and his seed forever."

Christians are also bound by a solemn covenant with God. He has promised to bring us to the promised land of heaven and to give us all the aids and protection we need on the way. That covenant was agreed, not between Moses and God, but between Christ, the Godman, and his heavenly Father. In his human nature he represented us and won for us the right to heaven. The sacrifice he offered to his Father, to ratify the agreement, was not the offering of bulls or sheep, but his own human body offered on the cross. The blood with which the pact or agreement was sprinkled was none other than his own precious life's-blood, which oozed slowly and painfully from his pierced hands and feet on the cross.

Everytime we repeat the words : "this is my blood of the new and everlasting covenant" in the Mass, we are repeating Christ's sacrifice and promising to carry out our part of the agreement, which is to keep his commandments and follow him. He and his heavenly Father will keep their part of it—they will establish us forever in the promised land of heaven—but do we always keep our part?

The Chosen People of old failed, many chosen ones of the new covenant have failed. We, too, could fail. One great help to keep us loyal to our part of the pact, would be to renew our resolutions everytime we assist at Mass, which is a repetition, a re-presentation of the sacrifice of Calvary. The keeping of our baptismal promises may demand sacrifices of us at times, but Christ sacrificed himself for us and our sacrifice will never be as severe as his was.

The rewards promised in the old covenant were temporal blessings. The reward promised to us in the new and everlasting covenant is the life of blessed happiness for all eternity in heaven.

SECOND READING : Romans 5 : 6–11. While we were yet helpless, at the right time Christ died for the ungodly. Why, one will hardly die for a righteous man—though perhaps for a good man one will dare even to die. But God shows his love for us in that while we were yet sinners Christ died for us. Since, therefore, we are now justified by his blood, much more shall we be saved by him from the wrath of God. For, if while we were enemies we were reconciled to God by the death of his Son, much more, now that we are reconciled, shall we be saved by his life. Not only so, but we also rejoice in God through our Lord Jesus Christ, through whom we have now received our reconciliation.

EXPLANATION : In these first chapters of his letter to the Romans, St. Paul is stressing the superiority of the Christian faith over the religion of the Pharisees, which was based on observance of the Mosaic law. In today's verses, he argues from the fact that if God was so good to us as to let his Son die for us while we were yet sinners, we can have the greatest confidence that he will also bring us to heaven when our earthly life ends, because as followers of Christ we are now adopted sons. But, of course, we must keep our part of the contract—this St. Paul develops in the following chapter.

we . . . helpless : Like babies in an orphanage who can make no move towards their adoption until the adopting parents come to take them into their home, mankind could make no move towards adoption by God, until he sent his Son to raise us up, by descending to our level in human nature. Furthermore, because of sin, men were enemies of God, and as only God can forgive sin, mankind was still more helpless.

At . . . time : At the time appointed by God from all eternity ("the fulness of time," Paul calls it in other places), the Incarnation took place (see Eph. 1 : 3–10).

Christ . . . ungodly : We were separated from God, positively by sin and negatively by being as yet mere natural creatures, with no claim on God except the capabilities for a higher life, a share in the divine life, which capability he had given us in creation.

God . . . for us : The infinite love of God stepped in and sent his Son to free us from our sins by his death on the cross, and raise us to the status of adopted sons through his Incarnation. As St. Paul puts it in his letter to the Ephesians : "He destined us in love to be his sons through Jesus Christ according to the purpose of his will . . . In him we have redemption through his blood, the forgiveness of our trespasses, according to the riches of his grace which he lavished upon us " (see Ephesians 1 and 2; also Gal. 4 : 4; Jn. 1 : 12, etc.).

since . . . blood : That God will continue to give us grace to bring us to heaven is therefore much more likely, since he showed his love for us when we were still sinners and not his adopted sons.

not only so : Not only are we assured of the joys of heaven after death, provided we do our part, but we can even now begin to anticipate some of that joy, when we realize that God has become our Father, a loving Father, through the merits of his incarnate Son.

APPLICATION : As Christians, if our Christian faith is really alive in us, we ought to be, and are, the happiest people on earth. We know that God created us, with the purpose and intention of sharing his eternal kingdom of perfect happiness with us when our period of probation and training ends on this earth. We know that God fulfilled that intention of his when he sent his divine Son to become man, to live on earth among us, to die like ourselves, but to die a more cruel death because of the wickedness of sinful men. We know that he rose from the dead, to prove that he had conquered death for all who would believe in him and in his Father who sent him. His resurrection was, as St. Paul puts it, "the *first-fruits* of all who have fallen asleep" (in death), the guarantee that all men who believe in him will rise, like him, to an eternal life of glory.

For true Christians, therefore, the greatest and most disturbing problems of human life on earth are solved. Death, the ever-present menace, the cloud which continually hangs, as the sword of Democles, over the lives of un-believers, is for us not a menace but a friend, not a cloud but a ray of true light, not the end of all things but the beginning, the door to the real life which will have no end.

Look around you, and observe the lives of those who do not believe in God or in Jesus Christ whom he sent. According to their philosophy of life, they will end forever in the grave. What real joy can they find in this life? Even if they were sure of living on this earth for 200 years (they have no guarantee of even 200 days), and if they possessed all the gold in Fort Knox, and had all the pleasures this world can give every day of their lives, they know they must leave all this, and what a sad parting that will be!

But who is there among them who has such a life of unmixed earthly blessings? They have diseases and disasters, disappointments and dissatisfactions to face, just as we have. But we expect and accept these trials of earthly life. We see them as means of preparing us for the real life that is to come. We have our moments of earthly happiness too; they are few and very scattered perhaps in our lives, but they are earnests of the future, unending happiness which awaits us and we thank God for them. We see our trials and troubles, too, as part of our training for the better life. Seen in this light, they become more bearable, if not actually welcome.

We are not forbidden to enjoy the lawful pleasures of life, but we do not make them the purpose of our lives. We enjoy them as one on a train-journey enjoys the scenery from his carriage window. We do not let them hold us back from reaching our fixed destination.

Yes, we Christians, if we are worthy of the name, are the happiest people on this earth. We know that God loves us. He proved it when, through the Incarnation, he made us his adopted sons. We know he has an eternal life awaiting us after death. We understand that this life is a period of preparation for that future life, and aided by God's grace, which is ever available to us, we know we shall reach that eternal goal, let what will happen in this world.

With such an outlook on life and death, with this Christian explanation of man's existence and its accompanying problems—an explanation no humanist philosopher or modern atheist has come up with—not only can we look forward with hope and joy to our future happiness, but even in our present surroundings, "we can rejoice," as St. Paul tells us, "in God through Jesus Christ through whom we have already received our reconciliation."

GOSPEL : Matthew 9 : 36–10 : 8. When Jesus saw the crowds, he had compassion for them, because they were harassed and helpless, like sheep without a shepherd. Then he said to his disciples, "The harvest is plentiful, but the laborers are few; pray therefore the Lord of the harvest to send out laborers into his harvest."

And he called to him his twelve disciples and gave them authority over unclean spirits, to cast them out, and to heal every disease and every infirmity. The names of the twelve Apostles are these : first, Simon, who is called Peter, and Andrew his brother; James the son of Zebedee, and John his brother; Philip and Bartholomew; Thomas and Matthew the tax collector; James the son of Alphaeus, and Thaddaeus; Simon the Cananaean, and Judas Iscariot, who betrayed him.

These twelve Jesus sent out, charging them, "Go nowhere among the Gentiles, and enter no town of the Samaritans, but go rather to the lost sheep of the house of Israel. And preach as you go, saying, 'The kingdom of heaven is at hand.' Heal the sick, raise the dead, cleanse lepers, cast out demons. You received without pay, give without pay."

EXPLANATION : In the first reading for today, God made a covenant or pact with the Israelites, promising that if they would keep their part of the pact, he would make them "a holy nation, his own possession." But they did not. Yet, God kept his promise, and he sent his Son, as St. Paul tells us in the second reading, even though they were sunk in sin and utterly unable to raise themselves above their lowly state.

In the gospel, we are told how Jesus, on seeing the crowds had compassion on them. These crowds were the ordinary, simple folk, who were not only neglected by the priests and Pharisees, but were despised and shunned by them.

like . . . shepherd : These ordinary folk, the vast majority of the Jews of the time, were ignorant of the law, and, in many cases, of the God who gave them the law. Following the example of their leaders, who should have known better, their thoughts were worldly and political. The Messiah they wanted was not one who would earn heaven for them, but one who would set them free from the pagan Roman rule and make them a powerful political nation.

the harvest . . . plentiful : Christ saw that these earthly ambitions of the simple folk were only skin deep. They were ripe for conversion to spiritual ideals.

laborers are few : As yet there were not enough workers to reap this rich harvest, so he tells his disciples to ask God to increase the number of reapers.

called . . . disciples : The twelve Apostles had already been chosen. He now gave them the powers of healing and of exorcism. He sent them out to tell these poor people that salvation was at hand. Their power of working miracles would confirm the truth of their preaching.

Gentiles . . . Samaraitans : Their mission was confined "to the lost sheep of the house of Israel." They were God's Chosen (if unworthy) People, and the messianic message was first to be given to them.

The kingdom . . . hand : The messianic kingdom is called the kingdom of heaven, because its purpose is not to establish any new Jewish kingdom on earth, as the priests and Pharisees expected, but an eternal kingdom in the next world. This is what the Apostles must preach to the people.

Heal the sick : They are to make use of the powers he had just given them, to show the mercy and compassion of God and also to confirm their teaching.

give . . . pay : They must not demand payment for their preaching, or their miracles. They must live on the generosity of their hearers. The gift of miracles was a free gift from God, and the doctrine they were to preach was freely given them by Christ.

APPLICATION : "Jesus had compassion for them." Who were the "crowds" on whom he had compassion? Among them were tax-collectors who cheated, robbers who robbed, murderers who murdered, harlots who lived lives of unchastity, adulterers who violated their marriage vows, nominal believers in God who never went to the temple or honored God in private. These may have been a minority, but there was no town or district in Palestine of that time in which some, or all such sinners, could not be found. Yet Jesus, who read their innermost minds, had pity on them for he saw that most, if not all of these sinners, acted through ignorance and through lack of instruction. They were lost sheep because they had no shepherd to lead them. The exalted opinion of their own sanctity that their official teachers had, caused them to shun the people, lest they be contaminated.

Christ said the harvest of such poor, misguided souls was plentiful and he needed more harvesters. That, indeed, was true in his day, but it is a hundred per cent truer today. Any of our modern larger cities today has a population greater than the whole of Palestine in Christ's day. And the percentage of sinners in these cities would be greater, not less, than the percentage of sinners then in Palestine.

Christ too is unchanged. He still has compassion for today's sinners and wants them to be saved, not lost. But for this he needs "harvesters," apostles, who will help him. Here is where all good Christians, all who really love God and their neighbor, must help. He is not asking us to give up our present occupation, or to leave home and family to become priests or missionaries. The work we can do and which he is asking us to do is on our very doorsteps. In some cases it is inside—in our own homes.

The first movement towards this apostolate to our fellowmen is to show the good example of a truly Christian life. In the home and in our place of employment, example may go unnoticed or sometimes even be ridiculed by the very ones who need it, but with the grace of God, which always accompanies it, it will eventually produce good fruit. There are thousands of men and women in heaven today who owe their salvation, under God, to the good example of a sincere Christian neighbor. After good example, comes good advice. A suggestion, a hint, an encouragement, kindly and charitably offered, may often turn a neighbor from evil ways. This good advice must always be humbly and charitably given. Nobody, a sinner least of all, wants to be lectured or "preached at." St. Francis de Sales, the gentlest of apostles, said that one will catch more flies with a spoonful of honey than with a barrel of vinegar. There are pious Christians who abhor sin so much that they abhor and repel the sinner, as well. In this, they are more pharisaical than Christlike. He abhorred sin, but he still loved the sinner and wanted him saved.

We can also help towards the conversion of sinners and the return of lapsed Christians by joining parish or other societies engaged in this work of God. If we cannot take an active role in these societies, for health or other reasons, we can help them financially to procure literature and other helps that they need. We can rest assured that what we give to God to help our neighbor will return to us with interest. The widow's mite did not go unnoticed.

We have not mentioned the foreign missions, because today, like Christ in today's gospel, we are concerned with the lost sheep of the house of Israel. If Europe and America were once more made truly Christian; if all the lost sheep were brought back to the fold, the conversion of the still-pagan nations would follow quickly. The bad example given by the once-Christian countries has done more to impede the spread of the gospel in pagan lands, than could ever be done by all their own false idols or superstitious practices.

The harvest is plentiful; indeed it is huge. But let not its huge size frighten us. If everyone reaps his own corner, we shall all meet in the centre of the harvest-field some day.

TWELFTH SUNDAY OF THE YEAR

FIRST READING: Jeremiah 20:10-13. I hear many whispering. Terror is on every side! "Denounce him! Let us denounce him!" say all my familiar friends, watching for my fall. "Perhaps he will be deceived, then we can overcome him, and take our revenge on him." But the Lord is with me as a dread warrior; therefore my persecutors will stumble, they will not overcome me. They will be greatly shamed, for they will not succeed. Their eternal dishonor will never be forgotten. O Lord of hosts, who triest the righteous, who seest the heart and the mind, let me see thy vengeance upon them, for to thee have I committed my cause. Sing to the Lord; praise the Lord! For he has delivered the life of the needy from the hand of evildoers.

EXPLANATION: Jeremiah, called at the early age of 23 to the prophetic office, prophesied in Jerusalem during the most critical period of Judah's history. The kings, priests and people were much more interested in politics than in Yahweh, their God. They had been made subject to Babylon and had to pay an annual tax to this foreign power. They were engaged in intrigue with Egypt whose help they sought to set them free. Jeremiah opposed this political scheme, foreseeing that Egypt would not help and that rebellion would bring nothing but the devastation of Judah and exile for its people. Abuses in the temple and in the city reached an alarming point. Jeremiah spoke out fearlessly against the disloyalty of the Chosen People of God, and foretold the destruction of the city and temple, and also the Babylonian exile. Because of this he was imprisoned for a time. Later it was decided to kill him, so he was dropped into a cistern, but a Cushite, a servant of the King Zedekiah, released him, with the King's permission but unknown to the court officials. Eventually, he was forcibly taken down to Egypt and, according to tradition, was murdered there by his own people. In today's four verses, he is referring to the hatred the people and their leaders have for him. He is not afraid because the Lord is on his side.

I hear . . . whispering: On all sides he hears the people murmuring against him, and plotting against him. "Denounce him," they say, "let us denounce him": so far they have not been able to get the king to condemn him. This was before he was imprisoned and later condemned to die in the cistern, but after Pashur, one of the priests and head of the temple police, had him beaten and put in the stocks for a whole night and day.

all . . . friends : It is not only his enemies, the majority of the people, but also his friends who are now against him.

watching . . . fall : They were hoping that he would make some move to prove that he was really an enemy of the people. He was, in fact, their friend, trying to prevent them from opposing Babylon which would cause the ruin of the city, the temple and all of Judah.

he will be deceived : His prophesies will be proved wrong. Egypt may come to their aid against Babylon, as they hoped. Then he can be punished as he deserves.

But the Lord is with me : He knows he is on God's side, as it is the word of God and not his own which he has preached. Therefore, his opponents will fail. They will bring a disgrace on themselves which will never be forgotten. That disgrace will be the ruin of the Temple and of all Judah, and the Babylonian exile. This happened a few years later. Had they listened to his word, which was God's word, this would not have happened.

Lord of hosts : He appeals now to God to let him live to see them receive their just punishment. He deserves this, because he never deserted God, no matter what he had to suffer.

sing to the Lord : He sees his prayer as answered already, and he himself delivered from these evildoers.

APPLICATION : Jeremiah was a representative, and a prophet, of God, who spoke the words of truth to his fellow-Jews. Judah was in a political crisis at the time. They were rebelling against a pagan, foreign power under whose dominion they had fallen because of their disloyalty to their God. They were putting their hopes now in another pagan power, Egypt. They thought Egypt would come to help them repel the threatened Babylonian invasion. God knew this would not come true, and he told Jeremiah to tell them so. It was in God they should trust but he had long since been forgotten. For telling them this truth which he had got from God, Jeremiah was looked on as an enemy of the people. He was punished and hated, and he prayed God to give him the pleasure of seeing them suffer for their wrong political moves, for their disloyalty to God and for the maltreatment he himself had received at their hands.

He lived to see his wish fulfilled. He saw Jerusalem and its temple razed to the ground and the people taken into exile. Naturally, he attributed all this directly to God whereas it was a natural sequence of events. The Egyptians did not feel able to back up the Jewish rebellion and Babylon thus had a free hand and punished the Jews.

While we can understand Jeremiah's natural reactions, we cannot admire them. Calling down God's anger on his enemies is not what our Christian training would see as the act of a holy man. But we must not forget that he was a saint of the Old Testament, when the justice of God was heavily stressed. In the person of the prophet Jeremiah, it was God himself who was despised and punished, and to this, God should surely object and show his disapproval.

We Christians, with the example before us of Christ, the Son of God, praying for pardon for those who crucified him, while he hung dying slowly and painfully on the cross, have a different idea of God. We see that his mercy is as infinite as his justice. Besides, we have his command to forgive our enemies and not only that but also to love them. Unfortunately, there are Christians who, notwithstanding Christ's command and example, find it very hard to forgive enemies. This may be the natural man in them but it is not the act of the supernatural or Christian man.

If such Christians could only bear in mind how much they themselves depend on the mercy of God to reach heaven, they might realize the necessity of forgiving those who injure them. "Blessed are the merciful for they shall obtain mercy," are the words of our Lord. Their opposite : "How unfortunate the unmerciful, for they shall not obtain mercy," is also true. Which of us can bravely face God at the judgement and say : "I don't need any mercy, all I want from you is justice"?

We must then learn the true teaching of today's reading, which is, not to imitate Jeremiah. He was judging by the standards of the Old Testament, where the future life was not thought of and all justice had to be done on this earth. We must follow the example and teaching of our Lord and Savior, who loved all sinners, even those who acted so sinfully and unjustly against himself. We must, as we do, realize that the sufferings and injustices caused us by our neighbors may be, and very often are, God's own way of helping us to be more Christ-like. This will make our attainment of heaven more secure.

Looking back over the history of the Church, one could ask the question : were the persecutors of Christians, who gave us so many martyrs, enemies or friends of the Christian Church? St. Augustine said : "the blood of martyrs is the seed of Christians." Nero, Cromwell and the others were God's gardeners. Whether they received their wages or not, we leave to God.

SECOND READING : Romans 5 : 12–15. Sin came into the world through one man and death through sin, and so death spread to all men because all men sinned—sin indeed was in the world before the law was given, but sin is not counted where there is no law. Yet death reigned from Adam to Moses, even over those whose sins were not like the transgression of Adam, who was a type of the one who was to come.

But the free gift is not like the trespass. For if many died through one man's trespass, much more have the grace of God and the free gift in the grace of that one man Jesus Christ abounded for many.

EXPLANATION : *For explanation and application of these verses of St. Paul* see the first Sunday of Lent, second reading.

GOSPEL : Matt. 10 : 26–33. Jesus said to his Apostles, "Have no fear of men; for nothing is covered that will not be revealed, or hidden that will not be known. What I tell you in the dark, utter in the light; and what you hear whispered, proclaim upon the housetops. And do not fear those who kill the body but cannot kill the soul; rather fear him who can destroy both soul and body in hell. Are not two sparrows sold for a penny? And not one of them will fall to the ground without your Father's will. But even the hairs of your head are all numbered. Fear not, therefore; you are of more value than many sparrows. So every one who acknowledges me before men, I also will acknowledge before my Father who is in heaven; but whoever denies me before men, I also will deny before my Father who is in heaven."

EXPLANATION : In last Sunday's gospel, we read of Jesus sending his twelve Apostles on their first mission to their fellow-Jews, "the lost sheep of the house of Israel." In the verses that follow last Sunday's text (10 : 8–25), he gave them practical advice as to how they should behave (10 : 8–16). Then in 10 : 17–25, he foretold that persecution awaited them, first from the leaders of the Jews, and later from kings and governors, when their mission spread to the Gentile world. In today's pericope, he tells them to proclaim his message fearlessly and openly. They may lose their earthly life for Christ's sake (as they all did except John, who suffered exile and imprisonment), but Christ will be there to welcome them into heaven. He reminds them that God who provides for the smallest of his creatures, will provide for them too.

Have . . . men : Having foretold the sufferings they must expect if they are to preach his gospel to all peoples, he tells them not to fear men, whose power is restricted to this earth only.

nothing . . . revealed : The full truth of Christ's real personality—his divine as well as his human nature—and the purpose of his coming, will be fully revealed later, and the folly of the enemies of

Christ will be seen in its reality, silly pride.

tell . . . dark : Christ had to keep both his Messiahship and his divine nature hidden because of his enemies, the priests and Pharisees, until his preparation and instruction of his disciples were completed. Then he was ready to take the consequences.

utter in the light : At the time appointed, the Apostles are to reveal to the world the person and message of Christ.

kill the body : "the contrast here between body and soul would not be understood by a Semite. It is a Greek concept. The contrast is between the body and the whole person. Man can kill but not destroy someone wholly. God can allow (he does not cause it) someone's total destruction in hell." (*A New Catholic Commentary* ad locum.)

sparrows . . . head : God's providence and his knowledge of the lowest and least valuable of his creatures are surely proof that he will provide and protect men, especially those devoted to his service as the Apostles were.

I . . . acknowledge : Christ states that he will be the intermediary between all men and his Father in heaven. Those

TWELFTH SUNDAY OF THE YEAR • 257

who are loyal to him he will introduce to his Father, those who disown him while they are on earth will be told by him to "depart, I know you not," when their life on earth ends. He will be the universal judge of all men (see Mt. 16 : 27).

APPLICATION : What our Lord said to his Apostles applies to all Christians in the practice of their faith. By the very fact of living our faith openly and fully we are apostles by example. If we are always truthful and faithful to our promises, if we are honest in all our dealings, if as employers we pay a just wage and treat those working for us not as "hands" but as whole men and women, if as employees we give an honest day's work for an honest day's pay, if we live chaste lives whether in single life or in marriage, we are true Christians. Above all, if we have true love of God and show our appreciation of all that he has done for us, and if we prove that love, by helping his other children, our neighbors, we are a light shining in the darkness, because we are helping others to see the true meaning of the Christian religion.

This true light is needed more today perhaps than ever before. Our world is three quarters pagan or neo-pagan. The neo-pagans are those who once were Christians but abandoned their religion, sometimes through their own fault, but more often than not, because of the bad example they were given by their fellow Christians. These are worse off spiritually than the pagans who have never heard of Christ or the true God. These latter have at least some idols, some ancestral deities, to whom they pay respect. The neo-pagans have only themselves to venerate, and they can find little spiritual uplift in this form of religion.

A large majority of today's teenagers, in most so-called Christian countries, have come to despise, or at least to neglect, the religion of their ancestors. In most cases the cause of this is that Christianity was never really put into practice in their own homes. There are cases of very black sheep coming out of very white Christian homes, but these are cases of weak personality—they prefer to follow the mob rather than try to force their way against it. On the whole, the decline of religion among today's youth is due to bad example from their elders.

There is an awakening among Christians, thank God. The ecumenical movement is one good sign. It was not edifying for the young or the old to see Christians, not only separated from one another but engaged in a cold-war with one another. If there is anything each one of us can do with the aid of God's grace, to help bring about a speedy reunion of all Christians, let us do it. The reform of the liturgy, introduced by the Vatican Council, is another help. The interest shown by the people in it is a healthy sign. The more it is studied, and the more sincerely it is practiced, the stronger will our faith be. In today's gospel message, our Lord is asking each one of us to be a fearless apostle. We will be, if we live up to our religion at home and abroad. "Have no fear of men," he tells us, "don't mind what your fellowmen think of you, if you object to obscene language in your work-place. Don't fear what will be thought of you if you say your grace before and after meals in a public restaurant or hotel. Don't take that extra drink just because your companions at the party might ridicule your control . . ."

These acts and many others like them, may seem trivial to some but they are giving testimony to the faith that is in us. Those who scoff at such things at first, may begin later to look into their own hearts, and come to realize what it is to be a man of principle. Eventually they may become men of principle themselves.

Let us remember our Lord's promise: "Everyone who acknowledges me before men, I also will acknowledge before my Father who is in heaven."

THIRTEENTH SUNDAY OF THE YEAR

FIRST READING : 2 Kings 4 : 8–11; 14–16. One day Elisha went to Shunem, where a wealthy woman lived, who urged him to eat some food. So whenever he passed that way, he would turn in there to eat food. And she said to her husband, "Behold now, I perceive that this is a holy man of God, who is continually passing our way. Let us make a small roof chamber with walls, and put there for him a bed, a table, a chair, and a lamp, so that whenever he comes to us, he can go in there."

One day he came there, and he turned into the chamber and rested there. And he said, "What is to be done for her?" Gehazi, his servant, answered, "Well, she has no son, and her husband is old." He said, "Call her." And when he had called her, she stood in the doorway. And he said, "At this season, when the time comes round, you shall embrace a son."

EXPLANATION : Elisha, the disciple and successor of Elijah (2 Kgs. 2 : 1–18), prophesied in Israel during the second half of the eighth century B.C. He worked many miracles and, as happened with Elijah, many legends grew up about his name. By anointing Jehu (842 B.C.) as king of Israel, he helped to bring about the overthrow of Achab's dynasty, which had introduced into Israel the worship of Baal, and had almost paganized the whole northern kingdom.

Today's story shows how Yahweh (God) rewards those who are kind and charitable to his servant.

Shunem : This was a town on the northern side of the rich valley of Esdraelon, which stretches from Mount Carmel to the Jordan. A wealthy and pious woman, who recognized Elisha as a holy man of God, used to invite him in for a meal whenever he passed that way. She later got her husband to build him a hut on the roof of their house,

where he could stay whenever he wished.
What is . . . her : For her charity he felt she should be rewarded, so he asked his servant Gehazi what it was she needed most.

she has no son : Gehazi told him her greatest desire. The prophet sent for her and told her that in a year's time she would have a son in her arms. His prophecy was fulfilled. God had rewarded her.

APPLICATION : It was a minor incident in the life of this prophet, who worked greater miracles, but it is narrated in the Bible to show that God rewards those who are charitable to his friends. This woman recognized Elisha as a man of God, a title then often given to the prophets. She was a believer in God and wanted to show her love for him by helping those who preached his name. Elisha, following his master Elijah, kept the true religion alive amid the paganism which was rampant in Israel, ever since Achab had married a Phoenician princess who tried to convert the country to the worship of the pagan god, Baal.

God rewarded this pious lady of Shunem by granting her the dearest wish of her heart. With reverence for and trust in Yahweh who alone was able to protect and provide for her nation, she was doing what she could to preserve the true religion. Had there been many others like her, Israel—the northern half of the Chosen People—would not have fallen a prey to paganism nor been eventually exterminated by the pagan nations they foolishly imitated. Israel disappeared as a nation, and was erased from the pages of history some hundred years later, when Assyria in 721 overran their land and took the Israelites in a captivity from which they never returned.

This little incident in the life of Elisha is more than a mere story, it is a lesson for all of us. We are living in an age when the true God is being gradually pushed out of the lives of nations and peoples. Men foolishly think that with their modern Baals : science, technology and false philosophy, they can run their countries and this earth without the Creator and Sustainer of the world. Nearly half of our world's rulers deny that there is a God, and a big percentage of the other half's rulers act as if there were no God.

The result is disastrous. We have a world divided into hostile camps. Brother is either at war with brother, or is being trained and armed for a war which must come. There are millions of our fellow-men, fellow sons of God, who have one and the same destiny, one and the same purpose on earth, as their richer brothers, but who are on the brink of starvation. They are often ignored and forgotten by the richer nations, who are fully occupied in arming themselves against one another. Our world today is like a ship manned by sailors who have thrown the navigator, the only one who knew which course to follow, overboard and are now at logger-heads with one another.

We have Atlantic Charters, Pacific Charters, and a plethora of pacts and treaties, but we have torn to shreds the one true charter which can provide peace on earth—the Ten Commandments of God. We are spending millions exploring the craters on the moon, while governments refuse to examine the craters in our cities, the miserable slums unfit for dogs' kennels, where so many of their unfortunate brothers exist in misery and hunger.

Our governments are not solely responsible for this state of affairs. Each one of us must share the blame. Communism was not a mushroom that grew overnight, the soil was prepared and the seed was being sown by generations of disloyal Christians. Our semi-pagan, Western nations have been courting Baals for centuries and gradually ousting God.

We can still save the ship from destruction by taking back the divine navigator. Loyalty to him will produce true brotherhood among the crew, but in order to bring back God to our world, those who believe in him must proclaim their faith and their convictions from the house-tops, through the ballot boxes, through the communications media and through personal sufferings, if needs be.

If those who are still loyal to God do not realize their obligations as regards the running of this world of ours, if they will not exert all the influence they wield to bring God and his law back into the world he created, then like their rulers, and perhaps more than the rulers, who are often inculpably ignorant, they will have to answer for this neglect at the judgement seat of God.

SECOND READING: Romans 6:3-4; 8-11. Do you not know that all of us who have been baptized into Christ Jesus were baptized into his death? We were buried therefore with him by baptism into death, so that as Christ was raised from the dead by the glory of the Father, we too might walk in newness of life. But if we have died with Christ, we believe that we shall also live with him. For we know that Christ being raised from the dead will never die again; death no longer has dominion over him. The death he died he died to sin, once for all, but the life he lives he lives to God. So you also must consider yourselves dead to sin and alive to God in Christ Jesus.

EXPLANATION: To understand Paul's language here, it is necessary to remember that the sacrament of baptism was given by immersion in the early Church. The person being baptized was immersed body and head in a tub, or bath of water, for a few seconds while the words of the form of the sacrament were being pronounced by the minister. This burial in the water symbolized that the catechumen was dead to self and was being buried with Christ. His rising out of the bath of water represented his rising with Christ to a new life of glory.

baptized . . . death: Our baptism symbolized dying with Christ.
as Christ was raised: As the Father raised Christ from the tomb, and gave him a new, everlasting life of glory in his human nature, we too, by baptism, are raised to a new life.
if we . . . Christ: The purpose of baptism was to die to sin and self, and begin a new life in union with Christ.
we know Christ . . . again: His human nature has become immortal.
died . . . God: He died to blot out our sins. His task thus finished "once for

all," he now lives in his human and divine nature with the Father and the Holy Spirit, and this life of glory will last forever.

So you also: Every Christian, in baptism, has died with Christ in order to live with God forever. Through the merits of Christ Jesus and in union with him, he becomes a member of his body, the Church.

APPLICATION: One of the many blessings that have followed from the second Vatican Council is the new rite of baptism. The old rite, in which we all were baptized, was indeed valid. We can have no doubts about that. It made us Christians and followers of Christ. But the new rite emphasizes, more strongly, the essential effects of the sacrament. The presence of a congregation of the faithful, or representatives at least of the community, who welcome the child (or children) to be baptized stresses the fact that baptism makes one a member of the community of Christ, which is the Church—the people of God.

It is the parents of the child, not the God-parents, who now ask for baptism for their child, and they are told by the celebrant that by asking for this, they are openly accepting the responsibility of training them in the practice of the faith. He asks them if they clearly understand what they are undertaking. They answer, "we do." This presupposes previous instruction of the parents, which the preface to the rite prescribes. The celebrant then welcomes the child (or children) into the Christian community and claims them for Christ by signing them with the cross, which he also asks the parents to do.

The "liturgy of the word" (readings from Sacred Scripture) then follows. One of the readings is this very text from St. Paul which is read today. In it, he stresses that we are buried with Christ in baptism (a burial which baptism by immersion so symbolically expresses).

We die with him to sin. Then we rise with him to a new life—the Christian life, which is a life of sonship with God, the beginning of, and the claim to, our eternal life in heaven. Just as Christ in his human nature will live a life of glory forever in the bosom of the Blessed Trinity, so shall we, his brothers, live an eternal life of glory, provided that we do not let sin bring on us spiritual death. We are dead to sin and must endeavor to remain so.

The second reading of the baptismal rite, also from St. Paul, stresses the fact that baptism makes us members of the body of Christ (1 Cor. 12:12). A third reading from 1 Peter points out that, as baptized Christians, we are a royal priesthood, fit to offer spiritual sacrifices acceptable to God, because we are brothers of Christ, his Son. After one of the extracts from the gospel selections has been read, the celebrant gives a homily, explaining the meaning and importance of baptism. Then follows the exorcism. There is no mention of driving the devil out of the baby, as there was in the old rite. The meaning of the prayer is that we are born into a sinful world, and enter into a struggle between good and evil which will go on all our lives.

At the actual baptism it is the parents who bring the child to the font. The prayers recited at the blessing of the font are most instructive as well as inspiring. The renunciation of sin and the profession of faith made by the parents and godparents in the name of the child (or children), comes next. Then follows the actual baptism which, if done by immersion, is most symbolic. However, in most western countries the old custom of pouring the water on the child's head is still, and probably will remain, in use. The anointing of the child with holy oil, chrism, symbolizes that the new Christian is what St. Peter calls a member of a "holy priesthood."

The white garment now put on the baptized and the lighted candle (lit from the Easter candle by the father or godfather) are symbols of the fact that the new Christian is clothed with Christ, "has put on Christ" as St. Paul says. The lighted candle symbolizes the light of faith which is to be kept burning brightly all through life.

A hymn of thanksgiving is sung. The "Our Father" is recited by all present because all Christians are by baptism made adopted children of God. The celebrant then blesses the mother (or mothers), the father (or fathers) and all present. Thus the rite of baptism ends.

When this rite is carried out in the presence of a whole congregation at Sunday Mass, it cannot fail to revive the faith and gratitude to God for that faith in all those present. Christ became man so that we men can become sons of God. Christ died on the cross so that we can have eternal life. These privileges, so far beyond anything we could hope for, are given to us in this great gift of Christ —the sacrament of baptism. Let us strive to be worthy of the honor conferred on us, and reap the reward of our loyalty, when we have successfully finished our days of earthly struggle.

GOSPEL: Matt. 10:37–42. Jesus said to his Apostles, "He who loves father or mother more than me is not worthy of me; and he who loves son or daughter more than me is not worthy of me; and he who does not take his cross and follow me is not worthy of me. He who finds his life will lose it, and he who loses his life for my sake will find it.

"He who receives you receives me, and he who receives me receives him who sent me. He who receives a prophet because he is a prophet shall receive a prophet's reward, and he who receives a righteous man because he is a righteous man shall receive a righteous man's reward. And whoever gives to one of these little ones even a cup of cold water because he is a disciple, truly, I say to you, he shall not lose his reward."

EXPLANATION: In these verses of Matthew, our Lord stresses two points: that the true disciple of Christ must dedicate himself wholly to him, and that whoever is charitable and helpful to a disciple of Christ, or to any of his true followers, will have his reward from God.

loves . . . than me: Christ is not abolishing the fourth commandment, nor the natural love of children for their parents and of parents for their children, but there is a love which is higher, and has a greater claim, than the natural love of family. This is the love of God, and the love of Christ whom the Father has sent.

If, as was the case with the first Christian converts, parents tried to prevent their children, or children tried to prevent their parents, from accepting Christ and following him, then the higher claim had priority.

who does . . . cross : Jesus, foreseeing the carrying of his own cross to Calvary, uses this phrase as a metaphor (for himself it was a reality not a metaphor) to indicate that his true follower must be willing to suffer for his name.

finds . . . lose it : He who refuses to die for him, and thus prolong his earthly life for a few years, will lose his eternal life, and vice-versa, he who accepts death for the cause of Christ, as so many of the early Christians did, will gain eternal life. Our Lord is making it crystal clear to his Apostles, that following him loyally will be no easy road.

he . . . you : He has just told his disciples that they must be ready to face death itself for his sake, when his (Christ's) enemies will want to silence them. In the meantime they will have to preach his message and he now refers to those who will assist them. Granting hospitality and material aid to an Apostle, is the same as granting it to Christ himself, and not only to Christ but to "him who sent him"—his heavenly Father.

prophet . . . ones : These are three names for the same persons—the disciples of Christ. He uses them to emphasize his statement. The Apostles are "prophets," because they speak in the name of Christ —the basic meaning of prophet is one who speaks for another. They are "holy men," because they are dedicated to Christ and the salvation of all men. They are "little ones," for they have no social standing or earthly power; their power comes from on high.

a cup . . . water : Even a charitable act of such a small dimension, if done to a disciple of Christ because he is of Christ, shows that the giver respects Christ. He will be rewarded for it by Christ, and the Father whom he represents.

APPLICATION : In the second part of these words of our Lord, we have the same theme as in the first reading today. The lady of Shunem was rewarded by God, because she was charitable to one whom she recognized as a "man of God." This was in Old Testament times. In the Christian era, all those who co-operate, even in a little way, with the representatives of Christ, will also be rewarded. The reward may not come to them in this life, but if not, it will be all the greater, it will be in the next life.

In the first part, Christ tells his representatives, his delegates the Apostles, and those who succeed them, that they must be prepared to undergo great sacrifices, even death itself, if called on to do so for the sake of Christ. Even though they had only a very vague idea then, of what he meant, when the time came, they remembered his words and gladly suffered imprisonment, hardships, and finally martyrdom for Christ. This shows how the resurrection of Christ, and the descent of the Holy Spirit on them, changed them from worldly weaklings into fearless heroes. They had become convinced that Christ was the Son of God who had come on earth to bring all men to heaven. They came to realize how transitory, and unimportant, the few years of the earthly life were when compared with the eternal life of bliss to follow.

It was not only the Apostles who gave

their lives gladly for Christ. There are thousands of martyrs who, during the first three centuries of the Church, not only accepted but welcomed death for Christ's sake, because they were convinced that it was the door to eternal life, the only life that mattered. Nor did occasions for martyrdom cease when the Church was granted freedom by Constantine, the first convert Roman emperor. Here and there, down through the centuries, the followers of Christ have been persecuted because of their belief in him, and many of us can be proud that we have had among our ancestors men and women who died for the faith.

Today, too, there are still those who are suffering a lingering martyrdom, worse than quick death on the scaffold, because they obey God rather than man. We can help them to persevere, by our prayers. We ourselves, who are free from any overt persecution, must show our gratitude to God for being allowed to practice our religion openly and without fear, by doing just this. We must live according to the convictions of our Christian faith. We are here in this world for a few short years, our real and lasting home is in heaven. We must keep this thought uppermost in our minds, in all our doings and dealings.

As well as carrying out our own personal duties, we must remember the spiritual needs of our fellowmen. They, too, need to go to heaven and anything less will be eternal disaster for them. We may not be able to preach, or teach them the truth of the Christian faith, but we can and must help all those who are doing so.

Remember our Lord's words today: he who receives or gives hospitality and help, to a prophet will have the reward of a prophet. He who helps those who are preaching and teaching the message of salvation, the good news of Christ, at home and abroad, will himself share in the reward of these preachers and teachers. When we get to heaven, one of the many pleasant surprises awaiting us will be the gratitude we will receive from saints we've helped to send to heaven, people we never knew or perhaps thought about. We helped those who thought about them and worked for their salvation, and we thus have a share in their reward.

Remember Christ's promise: even a cup of cold water will not go unrewarded, every little helping hand we give to bring our fellowmen to heaven will help us, too, toward the same goal. Heaven is our real goal in life—it alone will satisfy all our desires and it alone will last forever.

FOURTEENTH SUNDAY OF THE YEAR

FIRST READING: Zechariah 9 : 9–10. Thus says the Lord : Rejoice greatly, O daughter of Zion! Shout aloud, O daughter of Jerusalem! Lo, your king comes to you; triumphant and victorious is he, humble and riding on an ass, on a colt the foal of an ass. I will cut off the chariot from Ephraim and the war horse from Jerusalem; and the battle bow shall be cut off, and he shall command peace to the nations; his dominion shall be from sea to sea, and from the River to the ends of the earth.

EXPLANATION : Zechariah, Haggai and Malachi are the last three of the twelve Minor Prophets (they are called "minor" not because of their importance, but because they wrote less than the four Major Prophets). They returned from Babylon with the exiles about 520 B.C. When the people were depressed, and almost in despair on seeing the city and the temple of Jerusalem in ruins, they encouraged them to rebuild and to settle down. They assured them that there was a great future—the messianic future—in store for the remnant of the Chosen People. We have one of these encouraging messianic prophecies in today's lesson. Whether it was written by a later author (many present-day Scripturists hold that chapters 9–14 are the work of a deutero-Zechariah), makes no difference. It was certainly written long before Christ came and is therefore a prophecy concerning him.

Rejoice . . . Jerusalem : The prophet is calling on the inhabitants of Jerusalem to rejoice and shout with joy for :

your king . . . victorious : their king,

the successor of David, who would sit on David's throne and reign forever over the whole world (2 Sm. 7 : 11–16; Ps. 89), is coming to them victorious, yet :

humble . . . ass : although he will triumph over all his enemies, he will enter Jerusalem not like the conquering eastern kings, but humbly, riding on a donkey. This prophecy was remembered, and on Palm Sunday when Jesus entered Jerusalem riding on a donkey, the populace (but not their leaders) turned out to welcome him as David's successor. "Hosanna to the son of David," they shouted (Mt. 21 : 1–11). They saw the prophecy of Zechariah fulfilled in Jesus on that day, and did as Zechariah had told them—they shouted for joy.

cut off . . . war-horse : He will put an end to war and establish peace among all nations.

dominion . . . sea : His kingdom shall be universal—"from the river," the Euphrates, the most easterly point then known, "to the ends of the earth," the most westerly extreme.

APPLICATION : The fulfillment of the age-old messianic prophecies in the person of Christ, is one of the proofs that Christ was the Messiah—the anointed king, priest and prophet—whom God had promised to send to the Chosen People. Only God can foresee contingent future events, that is, events that need not happen. I can foresee that if I set my alarm clock for 7 a.m. and wind it, it will ring at 7 a.m., but I cannot foresee that I shall be involved in a car-crash next week. The prophets of the Old Testament, illuminated by God, foretold many things concerning the future Messiah. These things were fulfilled in Christ and in no one else. Therefore, he was the one God had promised. These very prophecies were given by God beforehand so that his Messiah would be recognized when he came. And they were referred to by Christ as proofs that he was the promised Messiah (Lk. 24 : 25–27).

Yet, so many of the Chosen People who knew the prophecies and saw them fulfilled in Christ, refused to accept him as such. Today's prophecy is an evident case of this. How can one explain such blindness of intellect and such stubbornness of will? Humanly speaking, God had a difficult time dealing with his Chosen People, and yet he never once deserted them or departed from the promise he had first given to Abraham, and repeated century after century until the "fulness of time" came, and Christ appeared on earth. He fulfilled his promise to them, even though they had again and again proved themselves utterly unworthy of his kindness.

We wonder which should amaze us most : the ingratitude, the hardness of heart, the utter worldliness of the Jews, or the infinite mercy and patience of God, who not only spared and tolerated such a people, but actually loved them to the end. He did not desert them. It was they who deserted him. "He came unto his own but his own received him not" (Jn. 1 : 11).

We have a problem nearer home which can occupy our intellects more profitably than that of the meanness of the Jews toward their loving and merciful God. While the leaders of the Jews rejected Christ as an impostor and a blasphemer, our ancestors—the Gentile nations—accepted him gladly as their Redeemer and as the Son of God, who had become man and who came on earth to bring them to heaven. This is still our faith, and it is still the one and only true explanation of man's life on this earth. We are here to prepare ourselves to merit heaven, the eternal life which Christ has earned for us. That life is the only explanation of why God created us, and the only answer to the human capabilities and natural desires that he instilled in our human nature. God raised us above all his other creatures, because he intended us to pass from this life to a future, everlasting state where perpetual joy and happiness would be our lot.

This is the meaning of the Christian faith which we profess—but how deeply does this conviction really sink into the hearts and minds of the millions who call themselves Christians? If it had sunk into the minds of the leaders of the Christian nations how could one nation be at war with another? How could injustices be rife within a Christian nation if we loved God and loved our neighbor, as the two basic commandments of the Christian faith prescribed? And to come still nearer home : how deeply does our Christian faith affect our daily actions and dealings with our fellowmen? Like many of the Jews on

Palm Sunday, who shouted, "Hosanna to the son of David," but who on Good Friday morning were clamoring for Christ's crucifixion, we too will sing "Hosanna" and "glory to God in the highest" on Sunday, but on Monday morning, we are ready to cheat our employer or our employees! Selfishness takes over and God is forgotten and our neighbor ceases to be our brother.

Thank God, this is not true of most of us. But it is true of far too many, and that is why our world, which was once Christian and is still nominally Christian, is a world of stress and strife where Christian is out to cheat Christian, and nation is out to subdue nation by force of arms, or by political maneuvers.

Can we do nothing about this? Of course we can! We can make our voices heard. But before we preach, we must make sure that we ourselves are practicing what we preach. We must show, by the manner of our daily lives, that getting to heaven is incomparably more important than getting on well, justly or unjustly, in this life.

SECOND READING : Romans 8 : 9; 11–13. You are not in the flesh, you are in the Spirit, if the Spirit of God really dwells in you. Any one who does not have the Spirit of Christ does not belong to him. If the Spirit of him who raised Jesus from the dead dwells in you, he who raised Christ Jesus from the dead will give life to your mortal bodies also through his Spirit who dwells in you.

So then, brethren, we are debtors, not to the flesh, to live according to the flesh—for if you live according to the flesh you will die, but if by the Spirit you put to death the deeds of the body you will live.

EXPLANATION : St. Paul tells the Roman converts to Christianity, that to be a true Christian, to be living at peace with God and on the way to eternal life, one must sternly refuse to follow the sinful desires of human nature.

You are . . . flesh : The convert who has accepted Christ and has been baptized in him, receives the Holy Spirit—the Spirit of the Father and the Son. This Spirit overcomes sin and the evil inclinations of carnal men, and one becomes a "new creation," raised to the status of adopted son.

who does . . . Christ : He is not a true Christian. St. Paul does not mean that the victory of the Spirit is completed once and for all. He knows well (see 1 Cor. 5 and 6) that the Christian life is still a battle-ground and a struggle for many. But he is speaking here of the ideal Christian.

Spirit . . . the dead : The Spirit of God was the author of the resurrection from death of Jesus. He also is our guarantee of final victory over sin in this life and of resurrection to a new and glorious spiritual life, if we try to live according to his directives.

if you live . . . flesh : The Christian who lives a sinful life, and follows the dictates of his carnal nature, will not receive this new eternal life. He will die not only the death of a mortal man, but also a spiritual death. He will not receive the inheritance due to his sonship of God because he did not live as a son of God should.

you will live : The true Christian who controls and subdues his carnal inclinations (and these include all sins), will be transformed at death into a new, living being, having a life that will never end.

APPLICATION : By baptism we were made adopted sons of God, because Christ, in becoming God-Incarnate, made us his brothers. We, therefore, share in the divine life and receive the spirit of God. The first effect of this indwelling of the Spirit in us, is what theologians call, sanctifying grace. As long as we retain this state of grace, we are living in union with the Blessed Trinity, and are moving daily closer to our eternal inheritance. This eternal inheritance is for all men, because Christ's Incarnation was decreed from all eternity so that all men could live forever after their life-span on this earth. People who, through no fault of their own, have not been able to receive baptism or to know of the Christian faith, will be provided for by God, whose power is infinite. St. Paul is writing to Christian converts in this letter and deals only with them.

The man who knowingly and willingly rejects Christ and his teaching, either by refusing to learn of it when he could, or by refusing to live up to his teaching once accepted, cannot expect, and will not get, that eternal life of happiness. This is a truth that should make all of us stop and think. We are Christians by baptism, but are we living according to the Christian rule of life? Are we, at this moment, living in union with the Blessed Trinity, through the sanctifying grace of the Holy Spirit within us?

Though we may be struggling along with many minor lapses in our lives every day, if we are not conscious of any serious offense against God, the answer is yes, because we wipe out those minor lapses everytime we make an act of love of God and beg his pardon for our mistakes and weaknesses. But if we have sinned seriously and have not yet repented of such serious offenses, then we have not the grace of the Holy Spirit in us and we shall have lost our inheritance in heaven if death finds us in this state.

Here it is well to call to mind the infinite mercy of God. St. Paul, as we said, is speaking of the ideal Christian, and therefore does not speak of repentance as he does elsewhere. Christ, our loving Savior, while asking us to carry our cross and follow him daily on the road of self-mortification, knew full well for he was God as well as man, that even the best could fail at times. He therefore left us a sacrament, which can wipe out even grave sins, provided we receive it with true repentance. This sacrament of God's mercy—the Sacrament of Penance—not only wipes out our sins but brings back, to dwell within us once more, the Holy Spirit with his sanctifying grace. And besides, as every instructed Christian knows, if because of circumstances we cannot receive this sacrament, a fervent act of contrition will produce the same effects.

A Christian who continues living a sinful life, without a thought for his eternal welfare, is living in a fool's paradise if he persuades himself that he will get "time yet" for confessing his sins to a priest or to say a fervent act of contrition, and thus put things right with God. Death is always sudden and unexpected, even for one who has spent months ill in hospital. In ninety-nine cases out of every hundred, the desire to live, which is innate in us because we were destined by God for an eternal life, will push the thought of death out of one's mind.

There is one way to remove all the worry as to how death will find us, and that is, to follow St. Paul's advice: to live always ready for death. This is not easy for many of us, but when we think of what is at stake—all eternity in happiness or in misery—it is a small premium to pay for so great a reward.

GOSPEL : Matt. 11 : 25–30. Jesus declared, "I thank thee, Father, Lord of heaven and earth, that thou hast hidden these things from the wise and understanding and revealed them to babes; yea, Father, for such was thy gracious will. All things have been delivered to me by my Father; and no one knows the Son except the Father, and no one knows the Father except the Son and any one to whom the Son chooses to reveal him. Come to me, all who labor and are heavy laden, and I will give you rest. Take my yoke upon you, and learn from me; for I am gentle and lowly in heart, and you will find rest for your souls. For my yoke is easy, and my burden is light."

EXPLANATION : Jesus had just denounced the towns around Galilee. He had worked many miracles in them, yet the people had not believed that he was the Messiah and had not listened to his call to repent of their sins. He said that Chorazin and Bethsaida were full of more hardened sinners than Tyre and Sidon, two pagan cities where God was not known. And Sodom, for all its wickedness, would fare better on the day of reckoning than Capernaum which saw so many miracles and yet was unrepentant. The few who had believed in him, the Apostles and the seventy-two disciples, he compared to innocent children because they repented of any past sins they might have committed and decided to follow him.

from the wise . . . understanding : God has not given the grace of faith and repentance to the Jews who glorified

in their knowledge of the Mosaic law. Their self-esteem made repentance impossible for them. They had all the answers. How could the humble carpenter from Nazareth teach them anything?

revealed . . . babes : Christ thanks his heavenly Father for the gifts of faith and repentance that he has given to the simple fishermen and farmers, the class from which his Apostles and disciples came. Compared with the Scribes and Pharisees, they were but babes as far as knowing the law or having the wisdom of this world was concerned. Yet God had given them a far greater gift, the gift of faith in Christ.

all things . . . Father : The faith, knowledge and power which Christ had given to his Apostles and disciples had been given to him directly by his Father, so it was from the Father, indirectly, that they had received these gifts.

knows the Son . . . Father : The perfect knowledge of each other which the three Persons of the Blessed Trinity have, is infinite and cannot be grasped by any finite mind. But in his human nature Christ shared, to a greater degree than any mere human creature could, the knowledge of his divine Father.

anyone . . . chooses : Christ in his human nature could reveal to those whom he chose, and who accepted his call, an eminently greater knowledge of God the Father (and the Trinity) than any human learning (that of which the Pharisees boasted, for example) could ever give them. So the babes, or simple ones, were really the wise and understanding ones, while the worldly-learned were the babes as far as knowledge of God was concerned.

come . . . laden : The reference is, in the context, to the heavy burden of the complex obligations of the law, and the many additions they had put on to it, which the Scribes and Pharisees were imposing on the ordinary people. Following Christ will be much less difficult and infinitely more rewarding.

Take . . . you : Instead of the yoke of the law (this simile frequently applied to the law by the rabbis, was taken from the heavy wooden bar, to which the plough was attached, and which was put on the necks of a pair of oxen when ploughing), Christ calls on the people to follow him, and promises them that they will find life more peaceful. In following his rule of life, they will be following the will of God, as he, Christ, will reveal it to them. This will be easier and more consoling than trying to keep the Mosaic law, as interpreted by the Scribes and Pharisees.

I am gentle . . . heart : If they come to him they must learn to imitate his gentleness, his kindness, his love of all men, and they must be humble, low in their own estimation, as he was humble, the lowest of the low, in the eyes of men.

APPLICATION : Do we really appreciate the fact that we are Christians, that we know, through Christ's revelation, that the God of heaven, the infinite Creator of the universe, has deigned to call himself our Father, and gives us the right to call him Father? Through that same Christian revelation we also know that he is infinitely merciful and cares for each single one of us more than any human father can care for his child. That he not only put us into this world and provides for us here, but that when our days here come to an end, he has prepared an everlasting abode for us, in his kingdom of peace and happiness.

Think for a moment what our world, or the people in it, were like before Christ came on earth. Ninety-seven per cent of those then on earth adored false gods and offered sacrifices to idols made of wood or stone. Idolatry often made life on earth unbearable and gave no hope whatsoever of any after-life. The remaining three per cent was made up of the Chosen People who had a very limited knowledge of the true God. He had shown mercy and kindness toward them, but they feared him rather than loved him. With rare and notable exceptions, they served him out of self-interest, to get from him temporal gifts, rather than out of real gratitude and love. Their relationship to him was more like that of slaves toward their masters than that of children toward a kind and loving Father. Their life was earth-centered and their ambitions were worldly. He had revealed little or nothing to them about a life after death. The prophets spoke of a great, happy and prosperous age which was to come, when God would send his Messiah, but the most they could hope for in the way of a future life or immortality, was to live on in their descendants, so that, to be childless was one of their greatest disasters.

Pagans and Jews had the same hardships of life to face as we have, and even greater ones. They earned their daily bread with the sweat of brow and body. Their illnesses were more frequent and less bearable than ours, for they had not the medical helps that we have. Death came to young and old then as it does now, but for them it was a final parting from loved ones, and no hope of a future happy meeting served to lighten their sorrow. All their crosses were crushing weights, sent to make life more miserable. Life on earth was passed in gloom and darkness and there was no shining star in the heavens to beckon them on or give them hope.

Surely God is good to us, to put us into this world at this day and age, and give us the light of faith, and the knowledge of God and of his loving plans for us, which make the burdens of this life so relatively light and even so reasonable for us. We still have to earn our bread. We still have sickness and pains. We still have death stalking the earth, but unlike the people before Christ we now see a meaning to all these trials.

The yoke of Christ is not really a yoke but a bond of love, which joins us to him, and through him, to our loving Father in heaven. The rule of life which he asks us to keep, if we are loyal followers of his, is not a series of prohibitions and don'ts. It is rather a succession of sign-posts on the straight road to heaven, making our journey easier and safer. He does ask us to carry our cross daily, that is, to bear the burden of each day's duty, but once the cross is grasped firmly and lovingly it ceases to be a burden.

Ours is a world which is in an all-out search for new idols. It is a world which has left the path marked out by Christ, and forgotten or tried to forget, that man's life does not end with death. To be a Christian and to have the light of faith to guide our steps in this neo-pagan darkness, is surely a gift, and a blessing from God, for which we can never thank him enough. Thank you, God, for this gift. Please give us the grace and the courage to live up to it and to die in the certainty that we shall hear, as we shut our eyes on the light of this world, the consoling words, "come you blessed of my Father, possess the kingdom prepared for you."

FIFTEENTH SUNDAY OF THE YEAR

FIRST READING : Isaiah 55 : 10–11. Thus says the Lord : "As the rain and the snow come down from heaven, and return not thither but water the earth, making it bring forth and sprout, giving seed to the sower and bread to the eater, so shall my word be that goes forth from my mouth; it shall not return to me empty, but it shall accomplish that which I purpose, and prosper in the thing for which I sent it."

EXPLANATION : The prophet second-Isaiah, in the first nine verses of this chapter 55, has been calling on the Chosen People to come to God (Yahweh) : "to seek him while he is still to be found." He begs them to turn back to Yahweh, "who is rich in forgiving," if only the wicked will abandon their evil ways. He goes on to personify the "word of Yahweh which is sent forth, from Yahweh, to accomplish a task, which it does. It is probably here that St. John found the basis of his theology of the Logos—"the Word became flesh" —the idea is later developed in the Wisdom literature (Prov. 8 : 22; Wis. 7 : 22, etc.).

As the rain and snow : The rain and snow produce their good effects by moistening the soil and thus help to grow the crops which give food to man. **so shall . . . be :** In the literal sense here, God's word is the teaching, the advice and admonition he is giving his Chosen People, through his prophet. Following the Wisdom literature, St. John found this term "Word" a most suitable expression to describe the Son of God who took our human nature. He had been with God from all eternity. It was through him that God created all things, "by a word of his mouth." This Word of God was God in his own right, God the Son.

not empty . . . accomplish : The word God spoke through his prophet would produce its effect. It would not be in vain. Some listened and were converted. But it was when the real Word of God came on earth that the real purpose of God was fulfilled. Heaven became the inheritance, not only of the Chosen People, but of all men, and was made available to all who would do the part required of them. The true Word of God did not return to him "empty," but as the "first-fruits" of millions to follow.

APPLICATION : The word of God which came to the Chosen People through the prophets, and the divinely inspired writers, came out of God's loving interest in his people. He wanted to prepare them for the inheritance, the real "promised land," that, when the messianic age (the "fulness of time") came, would be theirs, provided their lives on earth were lived as they should be.

This word of God, this advice and admonition sent through his prophets, though valuable and Godlike, was but a type or shadow of the real Word of God, his divine Son, who came on earth to bring all men to heaven. He carried out the allotted task. He fulfilled his Father's will to the letter, even when this meant a life of suffering and death on a cross on Calvary. He was, in fact, raised from the dead, and returned to heaven victorious, the leader of an innumerable host which will follow him until this earth ceases to be.

As Christians, we are united to the Word of God who became flesh. We are members of his body, the Church. We are his brothers, and with him co-heirs of heaven. God the Father intended all these privileges for us, and Christ, God the Son, earned them for us. The least we can do in return for such favors is to try to be worthy of them, by being loyal to our Christian vocation, and by ever remaining close in love to our Father and to his Son, our brother. To help us live the true Christian life, we still have also the word of God, spoken through the prophets and the inspired writers of the Old and New Testaments. We have in other words, the Holy Bible, the book of books, which, if read with attention and devotion, will not fail to inspire and move us to be grateful and loyal to our divine benefactors, the three Persons of the blessed Trinity.

Every Christian home should have the Holy Bible as one of its most useful and treasured possessions. It should not be an ornament on a book-shelf. It should be read, a page or two daily, by every member of the family. The new rite of Mass gives us three readings from the Bible each Sunday and feastday. These readings have been selected with great care, and each reading has a message, or lesson, for each one of us, to inspire us to greater love of God and of our Christian vocation. We should listen attentively to this "word of God." He is speaking to us through these means. These sacred writings have been preserved down through the centuries for our benefit.

Let us thank our Father in heaven, who deigns to speak to us through the sacred writings, his "inspired word." Let us respect these writings and use them for edification and eventual sanctification but greater ground still for our gratitude is the living Word of God who raised us up from being mere mortals to the status of adopted sonship, by means of his Word, his Son, who became flesh and dwelt among us for a time, in order to bring us in to heaven for all eternity.

SECOND READING: Romans 8 : 18–23. I consider that the sufferings of this present time are not worth comparing with the glory that is to be revealed to us. For the creation waits with eager longing for the revealing of the sons of God; for the creation was subjected to futility, not of its own will but by the will of him who subjected it in hope; because the creation itself will be set free from its bondage to decay and obtain the glorious liberty of the children of God. We know that the whole creation has been groaning in travail together until now; and not only the creation, but we ourselves, who have the first fruits of the Spirit, groan inwardly as we wait for adoption as sons, the redemption of our bodies.

EXPLANATION: In the verses which precede today's reading St. Paul stressed the gift of sonship of God which Christians received, together with the gift of the Holy Spirit, when they were baptized. In verses 16 and 17 he says: "The Spirit himself and our spirit bear united witness that we are children of God. And if we are children we are heirs of God and co-heirs with Christ, sharing his suffering so as to share his glory."
I consider . . . time: That we must suffer with Christ, and in imitation of him, while we are on this earth is a trivial price, Paul says, to pay for the glory that will be ours in the next world.
For the creation . . . sons of God: St. Paul now describes the whole created universe as anxiously waiting for the fulfillment of God's purpose in creating it, namely, the glorification of man. In God's plan this glorification was to be brought about by the Incarnation. The grace given to the first human beings on earth was but a first step toward this end, but when these first human beings refused allegiance to their Creator, the lower creatures, inanimate and animate, lost their purpose which was to serve man and help him attain that end.

creation . . . futility: Serving man who had lost his direction, and was turned away from the end or purpose that God had intended for him, because of his sins, was a futile operation, a reversing of the purpose of all creation.
not . . . will: It was not the lower creatures' fault. They had no power of decision or responsibility. Man's abuse of his free will was the cause of this disorientation.
groaning . . . until now: Paul continues to describe the non-rational creatures as if they were rational. He says they suffered, as it were, the pains of childbirth until man was reborn as a new creature. Then the original purpose for which they were created was restored to them.
we . . . bodies: Although we men, through baptism and the reception of the Holy Spirit, are now once more on the right road toward the inheritance which the Incarnation has won for us, we are still only *on the road*. We have still to reach the end of our journey—the actual possession of the inheritance guaranteed to us which will be ours only after our resurrection.

APPLICATION: God's creation of the world was an act of sheer benevolence. He wished to share his own infinite perfection and happiness with creatures, who could enjoy that perfection and happiness because of the superior gifts with which he endowed them. These creatures were men—the human race. All the other creatures, the inanimate kingdom, plant kingdom, and animal kingdom were intended for man's service while he was on this earth. Man was the masterpiece of God's creative action, and was to be the master of all the lesser creatures.

God's eternal plan for making man a sharer in his own eternal happiness was to be brought about by the extraordinary act of divine love and condescension which we call the Incarnation. God the Son was to become man, unite our human created nature with his divinity, in the historical Jesus Christ, and thus raise man to brotherhood with Christ and sonship of God the Father.

This act of divine love was for all mankind, for the millions who lived and died before Christ came on earth, as well as for the billions who have lived and will live on earth after his coming. Men sinned before he came, men sinned and will sin after his coming, but Christ's death on the cross made infinite atonement to his Father, the good God whom men had offended, so that, if only the sinner repents, all sins are wiped out by God.

Heaven is thus open to all men of good-will. God, who is Love, has infinite ways of reaching the hearts of sinners and bringing them to repentance. But we Christians, who are fully acquainted with all that God has done for us, are obliged to do all in our power to make this loving God, and his plans for their eternal happiness, known to those who are still ignorant of him. Any Christian, who really appreciates what God has done for him, will feel compelled, out of gratitude, to help to bring this knowledge to God's other sons who are still in the darkness of paganism, old or new, but who are God's adopted children even though they are not aware of the fact.

Fidelity and true loyalty to the Christian life and teaching, which it is our privilege to have, are prime factors in helping to spread among those who do not yet possess it, the knowledge of God and his plans for all men. Fervent prayer for the conversion of sinners is another means within the reach of all of us, and a very effective means. Instead of that novena for the health of some relative or for some temporal need which seems so important, let us offer it for the conversion of some unbelievers or sinners that we know, and God will prove himself big enough and generous enough to grant us both requests. When we find life difficult, and cross laid upon cross, let us not forget what St. Paul tells us today : "the sufferings of the present time are not worth comparing with the glory that is to be revealed to us." What are a few years of pain of body or mental unhappiness, when compared with an eternity of peace and happiness in the world to come? We are exiles returning home, and we have to work our passage or earn our way. But we are certain of reaching our happy home, if we work that passage diligently and patiently and cheerfully.

GOSPEL : Matt. 13 : 1–9. Short Form. Jesus went out of the house and sat beside the sea. And great crowds gathered about him, so that he got into a boat and sat there; and the whole crowd stood on the beach. And he told them many things in parables, saying : "A sower went out to sow. And as he sowed, some seeds fell along the path, and the birds came and devoured them. Other seeds fell on rocky ground, where they had not much soil, and immediately they sprang up, since they had no depth of soil, but when the sun rose they were scorched; and since they had no root they withered away. Other seeds fell upon thorns, and the thorns grew up and choked them. Other seeds fell on good soil and brought forth grain, some a hundredfold, some sixty, some thirty. He who has ears, let him hear."

EXPLANATION : Jesus taught his doctrine to the simple uneducated people by means of parables. A parable has been very aptly described as "an earthly story with a heavenly meaning." Jesus used the everyday happenings of which the people were well aware, to bring home to them the Christian message which was concerned with their eternal salvation.

got into a boat : As he sat on the beach of Lake Genesereth, the crowds that gathered were so large that he could not be seen or heard, so he got into a boat and moved out a few yards from the shore. From there he could be seen and heard. This is the parable he told them. Its lesson was clear enough for the majority of those who were anxious to learn. He explained it more fully to the Apostles later (as in the longer form of today's gospel), and declared that many of those who heard him would not see its lesson, because they were unwilling to see it, a fact the prophet Isaiah had already foretold (Is. 6 : 9–10).

a sower . . . sow : A common occurrence every springtime around the Lake of Genesereth.

some seeds . . . path : The path had not been plowed, so the seed remained uncovered and was devoured by the birds.

other . . . ground : Much of the land there was rocky—a thin skin of soil covering the stones. The seeds sprang up but they withered later for want of roots in deep soil.

other . . . thorns : The seeds sprang to life, but the briars and thorns took all the nourishment from the soil, and choked and starved the corn as it tried to grow.

other . . . good soil : There were parts of the field suitable and the seeds produced a hundred per cent yield, or sixty, or thirty according to the difference in the soil.

He who . . . hear : He knows his audience. The lesson is clear to all. He was the sower. The seed was the message of salvation—but many of those listening would not profit by it because of their ingrained hostility. He tells the Apostles they are blessed, fortunate, because they accept him and his teaching. He adds that many lowly men in Old Testament times longed to see and hear him, as the Apostles do, but could not.

APPLICATION : Christ's description of his audience, that day in Galilee, is unfortunately as true today as it was then. His message of salvation has been preached to a great part of the world's population, but the proportion of those who accept it and live up to it, is about the same today as it was then.

There are millions of men and women today, in what was once Christian Europe, who are like the seed sown on the unplowed path. They refuse to accept the message, they have no thought for their future, they are content to end in the grave after their few years of misery and hardship on this planet.

There are others who see the truth and the consolation of the Christian gospel, but when it comes to making sacrifices for it, they give up. The message did not sink into their hearts and minds. They are like the seed which fell on rocky ground because the faith had no deep roots in their lives. Others again, and they are legion, are like the seed that fell among the briars and thorns. They accepted the faith and it took root in them, but later on, "the cares of the world and the delight in riches chokes the word and it proves unfruitful,"—these are our Lord's own words.

The last class of Christians, are like the seed sown on good soil. They not only accept Christ and his teaching, but they live up to it, and, come what may, they are faithful to it. These will produce fruit and will earn for themselves eternal happiness.

Each one of us can look into his own conscience today and discover to which class he or she belongs. The fact that we are here, shows that at least we are still Christians; so we do not belong to the first class—the gospel seed did not fall on the hardened path. But what of the other classes? Are some of us perhaps, like the seed that fell on the rocky ground? While Christianity makes no very difficult demand we are all for it, but when it demands mortification, the curbing of passion, real sacrifices for our neighbor, do we forget our Christian calling then and ignore its precepts? And how does our type of Christianity stand up to the temptations of the world—the desire to get all the enjoyment we can out of this life, licit or illicit, breaking God's commandments weekly or maybe daily? Are we chasing after wealth and power, using all our energies to rise in the world to be above our neighbor by fair or foul means? If the above are our aims in life, our Christianity has been or is being choked out of us.

Let us hope that we all can number ourselves among those Christians who have sown their Christian faith in good soil and who will produce the fruit of eternal life. If we are truly honest with ourselves, the vast majority of us can say that there is a little streak of the stony and thorny ground in our hearts. Our courage must come from the fact that we have a merciful Father, who understands us and who is ever ready to pardon all past faults, if we humbly repent of them.

There are millions of saints in heaven today, enjoying eternal happiness, who had some, if not all, of our present failings. We, too, can be with them one day, provided we do what they did. They repented sincerely and remained God's close friends, until he called them to himself. May the merciful God give us the grace to imitate them while we yet have time.

SIXTEENTH SUNDAY OF THE YEAR

FIRST READING : Wisdom 12 : 13; 16–19. There is no other god besides thee, whose care is for all men, to whom thou shouldst prove that thou has not judged unjustly. For thy strength is the source of righteousness, and thy sovereignty over all causes thee to spare all. For thou dost show thy strength when men doubt the completeness of thy power, and dost rebuke any insolence among those who know it. Thou who art sovereign in strength dost judge with mildness, and with great forbearance thou dost govern us; for thou has power to act whenever thou dost choose. Through such works thou hast taught thy people that the righteous man must be kind, and thou hast filled thy sons with good hope, because thou givest repentance for sins.

EXPLANATION: The Book of Wisdom was written by a Greek-speaking Jew, most probably in Alexandria in Egypt, in the first half of the first century B.C. That he was a Jew is evident : he is loyal to "the God of the Fathers" (9 : 1), and proud to belong to the "holy and blameless race" (10 : 15). He quotes the Old Testament from the LXX, the Greek translation, is well versed in the Greek language and knows something of Greek philosophy. His book was written to commend wisdom which comes from God, the source of all wisdom. In wisdom he created the world and in wisdom he governs it. Wisdom is the basis of all virtue. It is the way to God and to the future life. The present life is but the preparation for the future life in which the virtuous live with God and the wicked are punished (3 : 9–10).

In the verses from this book which we read today, God is supreme governor and judge of all men, not of the Jews

only. He is merciful, forbearing, forgiving and kind.

There is no other . . . thee : The Egyptians, the Greeks and all the other pagan nations had their gods, but the true God is the universal God and has care for all men, Gentiles as well as Jews.

to whom . . . prove : Yahweh is answerable to no other god. He is above them and no one would dare to accuse him of judging unjustly.

strength . . . sovereignty : He is almighty and therefore can be merciful to all, for he is sole ruler over all.

dost . . . strength : If men doubt his almighty power he is able to convince them as he did the Pharaoh, for example, during the Exodus.

rebuke any insolence : He punished his Chosen People, who knew he was almighty and yet dared to disobey and insult him.

in strength . . . mildness : His almighty

K

power notwithstanding, he is mild in his dealings with men.

forbearance . . . govern us : His rule is tolerant and merciful.

thou dost choose : Being the supreme ruler, he is absolutely free to decide when and where to show his power and his mercy.

taught . . . kind : The man who would be holy and righteous knows that he in turn must be kind to his fellowman, as God has been kind to him.

filled . . . hope : The Chosen People, and any others who would recognize the true God, have reasons to hope for their future happiness for :

thou givest . . . sins : The basis of their hope : they all have offended him in many ways but he will forgive repentant sinners.

APPLICATION : The author of this Book of Wisdom had true, sound wisdom and he set out to teach it to his fellow-Jews, who because of the influence of their pagan environment were growing weak in their loyalty to the true God of their fathers. Alexandria was then a thoroughly hellenized city. The philosophy of the great Greek thinkers was influencing the minds of most of its citizens. Great advances, for that day and age, had been made in science, and progress and prosperity in this life were the aims of all, including many Jews. The author reminds his readers that, wise though the philosophers and men of science may think themselves, there is only one who is truly wise, the one who is Wisdom itself and from whom all wisdom comes. This is the God of Israel who is God of all the world. He is almighty, as well as all-wise, and even though he can and may punish those who would challenge his authority, he is all-merciful and ready to forgive those who repent of their folly.

Somebody has said, "the more we change the less change there is." How very like Alexandria of the first century B.C. is our whole world today. Twenty-one centuries have passed since this author wrote his book. The Incarnation has taken place since, and through it the world has learned so much more about the infinite mercy of God and his interest in our true welfare. The coming of the Son of God as a human being on earth, and his death and resurrection, have proved that we were put here for a few years, in order to merit the eternal life which the all-wise and the Almighty has destined for us.

But, just as in Alexandria of old the vast majority of its inhabitants spend their days chasing after the shadows of earthly happiness and prosperity, so the vast majority of the developed world's population today spend their time on similar pursuits. We have new philosophers, inferior in most respects to those of ancient Greece, shouting their earthly wisdom and ignoring, if not denying, the source of all wisdom, the all-wise Creator of all things. We have scientists who have discovered many of the laws of nature and put them to good earthly use, but who ignore the Lawgiver, the sovereign Legislator, who laid down the laws that these scientists discover.

It is, of course, true that the real scientists down through the centuries have recognized that they were but discoveries of the laws of nature made by One more mighty than they. But the pseudo-scientists try to use the laws that are discovered to reject the Lawmaker and ignore his claims on us. "Look what I found in the atom," the pseudo-scientist shouts, while the true scientist says: "Look what God put into the atom."

While we must be grateful for all the progress that science and technology have made in our day (provided they are put at the service of mankind and do not become man's complete master), we must never forget that all these powers of nature are God's gifts to us. They are gifts to help us on our journey to our true home, not shackles to bind us to earth and make us lose the eternal inheritance which God has destined and prepared for us.

True wisdom is the knowledge of God and the recognition of his dominion over us. The truly wise man is the man who knows that he should be grateful to the almighty Creator, who gave him life and who, as Father, has prepared a place for him in an eternal future, on condition that he does his part.

SECOND READING: Romans 8: 26–27. The Spirit helps us in our weakness; for we do not know how to pray as we ought, but the Spirit himself intercedes for us with sighs too deep for words. And he who searches the hearts of men knows what is the mind of the Spirit, because the Spirit intercedes for the saints according to the will of God.

EXPLANATION: Today's verses, from the Epistle to the Romans, are a continuation of last Sunday's second reading. On last Sunday, St. Paul told the Roman converts that they were on the road to eternal life, but only on the road; they still had many obstacles to overcome. By patience, hope and prayer they would arrive safely at their eternal destination. In today's lesson, he tells them, and us, that the Holy Spirit is ever with them to help them.

The Spirit . . . weakness: In baptism the Holy Spirit, the Spirit of the Father and the Son, takes up his abode in us (see second reading fourteenth Sunday above). He will help us all through our lives. He will help us especially in our prayers.

not know . . . we ought: Paul includes himself here and if St. Paul, the great lover of God did not know how to pray properly, how much more true this is of us ordinary Christians.

but the Spirit . . . intercedes: But what we cannot do of ourselves the Holy Spirit can and will do for us.

he who . . . hearts: God the Father, from whom nothing is hidden, will see our good intentions and hear the pious pleadings which the Holy Spirit arouses within us as he prays with us and for us:

the Spirit . . . God: The prayer of the Holy Spirit for Christians (often called "saints" in the early church) will be heard, because it will be entirely conformed to God's will.

APPLICATION: Prayer is an act of adoration of God, of thanksgiving for all past and present favors received, of repentance for past offenses and negligences, and of petition for spiritual and temporal needs. This is an essential activity in our daily lives as Christians. It can be called the very life-blood of a Christian life. But how few, if any, of us can pray as we should. It is a consolation to hear St. Paul say that it was a difficulty for the early Christians who were so fervent, and even for himself who was truly a man of God.

However, his statement that the Holy Spirit is with us, not only in moving us to pray but actually interceding for us personally, is surely a source of encouragement and hope for all of us. We must cooperate with the Holy Spirit. This, in our own poor way, we all try to do, and sometimes succeed, but we know too that, even when we think we have failed, our merciful Father will accept the good will, the good intention.

Our divine Lord tells us we must always pray (Lk. 18 : 1). This would seem to be an impossible demand if by prayer he meant recital of words or formulas. This however, is not what he meant. As we saw above, prayer is an act of adoration, thanksgiving, repentance and petition directed toward God. Our whole life and each single day and hour of it, can and should be such an act. When we make our morning offering, we consecrate our whole day, its recreation as well as its work to the honor and glory of God. Such consecrated action is prayer, and this is how we can always pray.

Besides, we have certain times set apart which we devote exclusively to "prayer" in the strict sense. The most important and most efficacious of these "times of prayer," is when we join with our fellow-Christians in giving true homage and thanksgiving to God, as well as asking for pardon for our faults and failings, and requesting temporal and spiritual benefits. This happens when we devoutly attend the Sunday and Holyday liturgy. Here we are not only witnesses but also active participants at Mass, in re-enacting the most perfect homage and atonement that ever went from this earth to God, the sacrifice which the Son offered to the Father. Devout participation in this sublimest of prayers, is for a true Christian not some obligation to be fulfilled but a privilege out and away above anything we could ever think of claiming for ourselves.

In this sacred liturgical act we have not only the Holy Spirit interceding for us and moving our hearts to true acts of love of God, we also have God the Son offering himself to his Father as a truly acceptable sacrifice in our name and for our sakes. If we participate actively with the celebrant and the whole congregation in this supreme act of adoration, thanksgiving, and atonement, we can be sure that our daily petitions for spiritual and temporal needs will not go unanswered. Our week's work will be sanctified and become a devout prayer. Our daily sufferings will take on a value for eternity, for they will be united to Christ's sufferings and sacrifice on the cross. We will then be living a life of prayer, and the Holy Spirit will be with us, sanctifying our ordinary daily goings and comings.

GOSPEL: Matt. 13:24–30. Short Form. Jesus put before the crowds a parable, saying, "The kingdom of heaven may be compared to a man who sowed good seed in his field; but while men were sleeping, his enemy came and sowed weeds among the wheat, and went away. So when the plants came up and bore grain, then the weeds appeared also. And the servants of the householder came and said to him, 'Sir, did you not sow good seed in your field? How then has it weeds?' He said to them, 'An enemy has done this.' The servants said to him, 'Then do you want us to go and gather them?' But he said, 'No; lest in gathering the weeds you root up the wheat along with them. Let both grow together until the harvest; and at harvest time I will tell the reapers. Gather the weeds first and bind them in bundles to be burned, but gather the wheat into my barn.'"

EXPLANATION: In another parable, or homely story, our Lord warns those who will follow him that they must live with opposition—with evil-doers who will try to impede them in their spiritual journey to heaven. But he consoles them by telling them that if they persevere in spite of this opposition, they will triumph on the day of reckoning.

sowed . . . weeds: The kingdom of heaven on earth, the faithful who will follow Christ and become members of his Church, will be the target of enemies. They will be like the good seed a farmer planted in his field. An enemy of his came at night and sowed the seed of weeds among the good wheat-seeds.

plants . . . appeared also: When the wheat appeared above ground, the weeds came up with it and so deprived the wheat of much of the nourishment it needed. (Actual occurrences of this kind of enemy action were not rare at that time).

did you . . . seed: The farmer's helpers are amazed when they see the weeds appear. They know he has sown wheat seeds only.

an enemy . . . this: The farmer knew the real explanation.

to go . . . them: The servants thought it a good idea to uproot the weeds, and thus give the wheat a chance to grow strong and healthy.

lest . . . wheat: Their idea was good but the farmer foresaw that of necessity some of the wheat stalks would be uprooted also in the process.

grow . . . harvest: The wheat must fight for its life, but it will survive and bear fruit. The reapers will separate the weeds from the wheat at harvest time. The weeds will be burned but the wheat will be gathered into the farmer's barn.

APPLICATION: In the longer form of today's gospel, our Lord added two other short parables which depicted his Church as having a very lowly and very small beginning but, in due course becoming a large and world-wide institution. The Apostles seem to have grasped the lesson of these shorter parables, but they asked him to explain the one about the weeds. According to most present-day commentators, the explanation of the parable is Matthew's own and was not given by our Lord. But, as Matthew's explanation has the guarantee of inspiration behind it, the lesson we are to learn from it is still the same.

The lesson is that in the kingdom of Christ on earth, his Church, there will always be sinners and scandal-givers who will make the Christian life more difficult for Christ's sincere followers. The weeds were among the wheat from the very beginning; one of the twelve, Judas, was a traitor and betrayed our Lord for thirty pieces of silver. The Judaizers, half-converted Jews, caused severe disturbances among St. Paul's Gentile Christians. Heresies troubled the first four centuries of the Church and schisms and divisions later on became a great scandal to those inside and outside the Church.

This state of affairs was foreseen by Christ and is tolerated by God for his own wise purposes. Today's parable is Christ's answer to the question so frequently asked : "Why does God permit evil to triumph so often in this world, why are the wicked allowed to prosper?" The triumph of the wicked is short-lived, the reward of the Christian who suffers from their wickedness is everlasting. The very wickedness and injustices of evil-doers are one of the ways that God uses to perfect his elect. It is only on a battlefield that a true soldier can be proved.

In the parable, the weed does not destroy the wheat. It only makes it more difficult for the wheat to grow to maturity. So it is with the Christian. No one can take his faith from him, but living up to it is made more difficult by the evil influence and bad example of sinners. If some succumb to this evil influence and give up the practice of their faith, the fault is theirs.

God can force no man to serve him.

The patience of the farmer in letting the weed grow on until harvest time, exemplifies the infinite mercy of God toward sinners. The weed could not change its nature, but the sinner can change his ways and God gives him every chance and every help to do this, up to his last moment of life. No sinner will be excluded from heaven because of the sins he committed but because he did not repent of these sins while he had the opportunity.

We must learn a double lesson of patience from this parable. First, to be patient with those who make our spiritual progress more difficult for us—they are actually helping us to be better Christians if we bear with patience the injuries they inflict on us. Second, we must try to imitate the patience God shows in his dealings with sinners. While we must not approve of their evil deeds, or their sins, we must still look on them as our brothers and do all in our power to put them back on the right road to heaven. We can do this by good example, and by fervent prayer for their conversion. This is not easy for human nature, but we can be certain that God will give us the necessary grace and strength to subdue our natural weakness and aversion, if we try to act with charity and true brotherly interest toward our erring fellowmen.

By acting thus, we will not only be helping a weak brother on the rugged road to heaven, we will also be making doubly sure of our own arrival there, for God will never be outdone in generosity.

SEVENTEENTH SUNDAY OF THE YEAR

FIRST READING : 1 Kings 3 : 5; 7–12. At Gibeon the Lord appeared to Solomon in a dream by night; and God said, "Ask what I shall give you." And Solomon said, "O Lord my God, thou hast made thy servant king in place of David my father, although I am but a little child; I do not know how to go out or come in. And thy servant is in the midst of thy people whom thou hast chosen, a great people, that cannot be numbered or counted for multitude. Give thy servant therefore an understanding mind to govern thy people, that I may discern between good and evil; for who is able to govern this thy great people?"

It pleased the Lord that Solomon had asked this. And God said to him, "Because you have asked this, and have not asked for yourself long life or riches or the life of your enemies, but have asked for yourself understanding to discern what is right, behold, I now do according to your word. Behold, I give you a wise and discerning mind, so that none like you has been before you and none like you shall arise after you."

EXPLANATION : Solomon succeeded David as King in Jerusalem in the year 970 B.C. His mother Bethsheba and the prophet Nathan persuaded the aged David to appoint him rather than his elder brother, Adonijah. During his 38 years on the throne, Solomon built the temple of Yahweh in Jerusalem and a sumptuous palace for himself. He developed friendly relations with the neighboring pagan nations; and trade and commerce flourished under his wise direction. Later Jewish traditions credited him with a wisdom which surpassed that of any other sage of any land. While we can perhaps allow for some exaggeration caused by national pride here, the verses we have just read rightly give the credit to God for whatever wisdom Solomon possessed. But it must not be forgotten either, that Solomon in his humility asked God for this so that he might govern wisely, rather than for any material or political gain for himself.

At Gibeon : Gibeon, most probably the present-day Nebi Samivil, six miles north-west of Jerusalem, was an Israelite place of worship ever since the days of the Judges (1 Sm. 7 : 5). The Tent of the Meeting and the altar of sacrifice, were kept there in David's time (1 Ch. 16 : 39; 21 : 39), so it was a legitimate place of worship until the temple was built.

in a dream by night : God often made use of dreams to communicate with his chosen ones (Gn. 20 : 3; 28 : 12; Jgs. 7 : 13).

Ask . . . you give : God gives Solomon a choice of gifts.

Solomon said : The young king realizes how inexperienced he is in governing a kingdom.

a people . . . numbers : The population of Israel at the time is reckoned at about 800,000, but to Solomon and to his contemporaries this number was a huge multitude.

govern the people : He seeks from God "an understanding mind," so that he could always do what was just and best for his subjects.

Because . . . this : The Lord is pleased that Solomon thought of the good of his subjects rather than any personal benefit like long life, or riches, or victory over his enemies, and therefore :

I now . . . your word : God will not only grant him wisdom to govern his people, but will make him the wisest man that ever lived or ever will live. The dream, of course, lost nothing in its telling by Solomon, nor in the retelling of his much later historiographers.

APPLICATION : What particular gift would each one of us ask of God if he spoke to us in a dream tonight and gave us our choice? There are so many pressing needs which we will have at the moment. Many would ask for badly needed health for themselves or for some close relatives. Others would ask for financial help, just to pay off debts and keep the family in comfort, not riches but just enough. Others would wish to be spared to their family for many long years. Some, not many, would ask for the virtue of temperance for themselves, while many would want that virtue for their husbands or sons.

But those who would ask for the gift of true wisdom to govern their earthly lives according to justice and charity would, I fear, be a small percentage. And yet that is the only gift that has eternal value. It is even greater than the gift Solomon asked for and got. He wanted the wisdom to govern others, but he failed pretty badly in governing his own personal life. The really wise man wants to make a success of his own personal life, but that can only be done by regulating his living according to the wisdom God has enshrined in his revelation to us.

If we got all the other gifts mentioned above—a healthy, long life for ourselves and all in the family, a life of comfort free from all financial cares, a life of peace and temperance in the home, with all the other earthly blessings that we think we need thrown in, would the ending of our life-story be necessarily a happy one?

We all like a story to end happily. We do not mind how many scrapes and tight shaves our hero has during the course of the story, but we want him to come out a success in the end. Surely, there is no story of greater interest, or of greater importance to us, than our own life-story, and there can be no story whose happy ending could be more desirable. There is only one happy ending for the story of our life on earth, and it is the attainment of heaven when we die.

If we lived on earth for 200 years, if we never had an ache or pain in that time, if we had all the riches of this world, and all the comforts imaginable which those riches could buy for us, and a life of perpetual peace and plenty, but if we failed to reach heaven what a sad and irreparable conclusion our life-story would have!

Wisdom is the gift we all need—wisdom greater than that of Solomon—the wisdom to govern and direct our own lives according to God's laws. God will not refuse this gift if we ask for it. And having got it we must use it. We are surrounded on all sides by worldly wisdom—the antithesis of what we need.

Today, more than ever perhaps, the stress is on the present—what we can get out of this life. The future life is either denied or ignored. A future there is, and try to forget it as we may, it is drawing nearer daily to each one of us. On the entrance gates of the city cemetery of Rome this truthful inscription stands out in its awful truth: *"Hodie mihi cras tibe"*—"today my fate is decided, tomorrow yours." We can decide our fate today before it is too late. Will we?

SECOND READING : Romans 8 : 28–30. We know that in everything God works for good with those who love him, who are called according to his purpose. For those whom he foreknew he also predestined to be conformed to the image of his Son, in order that he might be the first-born among many brethren. And those whom he predestined he also called; and those whom he called he also justified; and those whom he justified he also glorified.

EXPLANATION : In the readings from St. Paul, which you have heard during the past seven Sundays, the Apostle has been telling the Roman converts to Christianity how vastly superior to the Jewish religion is their Christian religion. The former was only a preparation for the coming of Christ. Now that Christ has come, the preparatory stage has ended. The shadow fades before the reality. The Mosaic Law did not, and could not, give eternal life. Christ's death and resurrection alone could and did.

Christians, therefore, are sure of that eternal life, if they remain faithful to their vocation. Today's three verses tell us that God is doing his part (and will continue to do it), to bring all who accept Christ to glory, that is, to eternal

happiness when they end their earthly life.

in everything . . . good : All God's plans for the human race are for the happiness and perfection of men. He created them and gave them gifts which made them superior to all other earthly creatures, so that they would have eternal life. He made the attainment of that eternal life possible for them, through the Incarnation, which made them brothers of Christ, adopted sons of God.

those who love him : Man must do his part. He has a free will and must show his appreciation of all that God has done for him by thanking God and loving him.

who are called : All men are "called," have received the invitation, to eternal life (and the means of attaining it), but they must love God in order to reach that happy end.

those . . . foreknew : God is eternal, there is no past or future to him. A million years ago, he saw us as we are now and as we will be at the end of our life. He knows from eternity those who will love him and those who will not, but this foreknowledge does not mean any restriction on their freedom of action. God wills that all men should have eternal happiness but, because men are free agents, he cannot make them will to earn that eternal happiness.

conformed . . . his son : The Son of God became man so that we could become sons of God. Through his Incarnation, Christ elevated human nature to the status of adopted sonship with God.

Christ in his human nature is the "first-born," the first to rise from the dead and enter into eternal happiness. All those who accept him and live accordingly will follow him into that eternal happiness—they will become, as it were, other Christs.

those he predestined : Those he foresaw as explained above.

called . . . glorified : His will was that all men should make proper use of the gifts he gave them, and the necessary means were available to all. But in his eternal knowledge he saw those who would use their gifts and accept his aid, and who would therefore follow Christ in this life and die in his peace and love "justified", so reaching eternal glory.

APPLICATION : St. Augustine says, "God created us without our consent or cooperation but he will not (and cannot) save us without our cooperation." This is clear from what St. Paul tells us to-day. God has done, and continues to do, everything that is necessary to bring us to heaven when we die. However, unless we cooperate and do our part, heaven will not be our future abode.

This should make each one of us stop and think! Are we on the right road? Are we truly followers of Christ? Do we love God? Are our prevailing ambitions worldly or other-worldly? We have to take an interest in the affairs of this world but do all our interests end there? Do the ten commandments of God always govern and direct our conduct, or are they often trampled on in our mad rush for some temporal pleasure or gain?

These are questions every Christian should put to himself and honestly answer. We are living in an era which

is daily growing more worldly and more anti-God and anti-Christian. On all sides of us we have bad example, a strong-rushing current of worldliness and immorality, a current difficult to avoid or swim against. But avoid it we must if we really have our real and eternal welfare at heart. What is more, if we love our fellowmen as our Christian faith obliges us to do, we must do all in our power to lead them out of that fatal current and bring them to safety with us. We must be life-guards.

There is a future life, revelation tells us, and our reasoning demands it. That future life will be one of eternal happiness for those who strive to love God in this life, and eternal unhappiness for those who refuse to do this. Ask yourself this question : "If I were to die to-night, to which class would I like to belong?" Tonight may not be the night of our departure from this life, but that departure is nearer to us than any of us think, and the state of our conscience at the moment of our death may depend on the resolutions we make today.

Nobody, not even God himself, can give us eternal life. We must earn it for ourselves. Our Christian faith tells us how.

GOSPEL : Matthew 13 : 44–52. Jesus said to the crowds, "The kingdom of heaven is like treasure hidden in a field, which a man found and covered up; then in his joy he goes and sells all that he has and buys that field.

"Again, the kingdom of heaven is like a merchant in search of fine pearls, who, on finding one pearl of great value, went and sold all that he had and bought it.

"Again, the kingdom of heaven is like a net which was thrown into the sea and gathered fish of every kind; when it was full, men drew it ashore and sat down and sorted the good into vessels but threw away the bad. So it will be at the close of the age. The angels will come out and separate the evil from the righteous, and throw them into the furnace of fire; there men will weep and gnash their teeth.

"Have you understood all this?" They said to him, "Yes." And he said to them, "Therefore every scribe who has been trained for the kingdom of heaven is like a householder who brings out of his treasure what is new and what is old."

EXPLANATION : In this chapter, St. Matthew has a collection of seven parables ("earthly stories with heavenly meanings") spoken by our Lord, probably on different occasions. Teaching through parables was a method commonly practiced by the Jewish rabbis of that time. In the three parables read today, the first two describe the kingdom of heaven as worth more than all the treasures of this earth. The third teaches that accepting Christ or calling him "Lord, Lord," will not merit heaven. "Doing the will of his father," is necessary for salvation.

treasure . . . field : In a country frequently overrun by invaders it was not unusual for people to bury their gold and other precious possessions in tombs, in caves or in the fields when an invader was approaching. It often happened that the owner was killed or disappeared and all knowledge of the hidden treasure disappeared with him. The Dead Sea Scrolls recently found in caves at Qumran were hidden there over 2,000 years ago.

hid it : It is evident that the discoverer was working in another man's field when he found the treasure. To gain legal possession he buys the field from the other. It is also clear that the owner of the field did not own the treasure, or he would not have sold the field. Whether he had more moral right to the treasure is another question, but all the material points of a parable are not set up by a teacher for praise or imitation. In favor of the discoverer is the fact that he did not take away the treasure secretly: instead he bought the field, evidently in order to get legal and honest possession of it.

sells . . . has: This is the lesson. All else that this man had he considered as nothing compared with this treasure. So likewise the kingdom of heaven—the following of Christ to heaven—is incomparably of greater value than all the riches, power and pleasures of this world.

merchant . . . search of pearls: In the previous example the discoverer came on the treasure accidently, here the merchant is actually searching for a treasure. Perhaps the former represent the Gentiles who were not expecting or looking for Christ, while the Jews were, like this merchant, looking forward to his coming.

sold . . . had: Again the same appreciation of what had been found—it was worth more than all other possessions.

every Scribe: Addressing the Apostles who tell him they have understood the lesson of his parables, he tells them they will be "scribes," men of learning, who will have ancient (Old Testament) and modern (Christ's) teaching to give to their hearers. This is exactly what the Apostles did.

APPLICATION: The lesson of these two parables is as true for us today, as it was for those Palestinians to whom Christ spoke. All Christians are called on to imitate these two wise men, and surrender all their earthly possessions if necessary in order to gain eternal life. Does this "giving all" mean that we are all expected to abandon the world and take on the religious vows of poverty, chastity and obedience? There are many who do just this. But it is not the only way, nor the normal way, to purchase the eternal treasure. Heaven is within the reach of all, who follow the ordinary vocations of life and partake of this world's joys and pleasures *within the framework of God's commandments*, but never lose sight of the goal toward which they are moving.

Keeping within the framework of God's commandments is the difficulty. We need not have a vow of obedience, but we must obey all legitimate authority. We may possess the goods of this world, but only such goods as we lawfully and justly acquire. Nor may we withhold all of these from a fellow-man who is in need. We do not have to take a vow of chastity, but yet we must be chaste, we must use the gifts and the pleasure of sex only within the limits set down by God's wise laws.

All of this is not easy for human nature. But we are not relying on weak human nature, we have within our reach in the Church all the spiritual and supernatural aids we need. Our twentieth century, it is true, is so engrossed in chasing after the earthly comforts and pleasures of the body, and so devoid of any spiritual or other-worldly outlook, that even those who know and believe that there is an eternity after death, find it hard to allow their faith and convictions to govern and direct their daily actions. Yet, the evil example of others will never justify our wrong-doing. The commandments of God are still binding, even though they are openly and flagrantly violated by individuals and whole nations today.

Remember this: we shall not be asked at the judgement, "What did your neighbor do?", but "what did you do?" If we lose the pearl of great price in the eternity of happiness God has offered to us—it will not be the fault of others. The fault will be ours and ours only.

We refused to pay the price. We did not think it worth the "paltry all" which we possessed in this life.

EIGHTEENTH SUNDAY OF THE YEAR

FIRST READING : Isaiah 55 : 1–3. Thus says the Lord : "Ho, every one who thirsts come to the waters; and he who has no money, come, buy and eat! Come, buy wine and milk without money and without price. Why do you spend your money for that which is not bread, and your labor for that which does not satisfy? Hearken diligently to me, and eat what is good, and delight yourselves in fatness. Incline your ear, and come to me; hear, that your soul may live; and I will make with you an everlasting covenant, my steadfast, sure love for David."

EXPLANATION : The prophet (second-Isaiah), living among the Jewish exiles in Babylon, utters words of consolation for the despairing exiles. Here he tells them that Yahweh is inviting them to a banquet which he freely gives them. Yahweh alone can provide for their real needs; they are foolish to look elsewhere for consolation or help. If they cooperate he will fulfill the promise he had made to David (cf. 2 Sm. 7 : 14–16; Ps. 2 : 7), the promise of a future Messiah.

Thus says the Lord : The prophet is speaking as God's mouth-piece.

who thirsts : God will not only slake their thirst with water, but he offers them wine, milk and bread—the makings of a banquet for a people suffering from hunger.

without money : All these gifts are free; they will not have to pay for them.

why . . . money : Many of the exiles were inclined to desert Yahweh, their God, because they thought he had failed them. He tells them that trust in any false god is wasted effort.

hear . . . live : He alone can give them life and preserve them as a nation.

an everlasting covenant : If they remain loyal to him he will make a new and everlasting covenant with them. He will fulfill the promise already made to David : he will place a descendant of David on the throne of Judah (the Messiah), one whose reign will last forever.

APPLICATION : It was their own sins, their own disloyalty to Yahweh, that brought the Babylonian Exile on the Jews. In their exile many of them lost all faith and trust in him. Thus, we cannot but be amazed at the infinite forgiveness and mercy of Yahweh. The Jews deserved to be abandoned to the fate they had earned for themselves, but Yahweh did not abandon them. He sent his prophets, Ezekiel and second-Isaiah (so called because his prophecies were joined on to Isaiah by a later editor), and later Haggai and Zechariah, to console and comfort them with the promise that they would return to their native land and survive as a people, until the coming of the Messiah. He would establish an everlasting kingdom and an everlasting pact or covenant.

Infinite mercy and forgiveness towards the exiles were exercised by God not only for the Jews of that time but especially for us Christians. The return of the exiles from Babylon, their re-establishment in Palestine, were all necessary parts of God's plan in preparation for the coming of Christ. Because of the mercy shown to these rebellious Jews we are Christians today. We partake of the banquet which God offered to the Jews in Babylon, through his prophet. It is with us, his Church, 99 per cent Gentile, that he has made the new and everlasting covenant. He has made a pact with us : if we follow Christ and his teaching on earth we shall have the eternal possession of the promised land of heaven.

Today, therefore, we must look on these words of second-Isaiah as the words of God spoken to us. He tells us to come to him and trust in him and he will provide for our real needs. He has an eternal banquet prepared for us. He warns us not to waste our lives and our substance on perishable things—the things of this life, which will not and cannot satisfy our real needs. Let us "hear, that our soul may live"; let us pay heed to his request if we have our own best and true interests at heart. We want to live happily, not for seventy or even a hundred years, but forever; this we can do only by listening to God's word and by putting it into daily practice.

SECOND READING : Romans 8 : 35; 37–39. Who shall separate us from the love of Christ? Shall tribulation, or distress, or persecution, or famine, or nakedness, or peril, or sword? No, in all these things we are more than conquerors through him who loved us. For I am sure that neither death, nor life, nor angels, nor principalities, nor things present, nor things to come, nor powers, nor height, nor depth, nor anything else in all creation, will be able to separate us from the love of God in Christ Jesus our Lord.

EXPLANATION : In the preceding verses of this chapter (see last Sunday), St. Paul has been telling the Roman converts of the blessings and the divine gifts which the faith has brought them. He concludes the chapter with a hymn in praise of God's love for us : "with God on our side," he says, "who can be against us? Since God did not spare his own Son, but gave him up to benefit us all, we may be certain, after such a gift, that he will not refuse anything he can give. When God acquits could anyone condemn? Could Christ Jesus? No, he not only died for us—he rose from the dead and there at God's right hand he stands and pleads for us" (8 : 31-34). Then come today's verses, which are rhetorical questions, showing that there is no power in heaven or on earth that can take away or lessen God's love for us as manifested in Christ, his Incarnate Son.

Who . . . us : Having seen the proofs of God's love in the past, the crowning act of which was the Incarnation, what Christian could even suspect that God's love would now change?

from the love of Christ : This does not mean our love for Christ, but his and the Father's love for us. That will not change; nothing can change it.

tribulation . . . sword : Paul enumerates the many sufferings and hardships a Christian may have to undergo in this life.

more . . . conquerors : Instead of thinking that these sufferings are a proof that God no longer loves us, we should see that they are proof that he does love us, for they are the means used "by him who loves us" to bring us to our eternal perfection and happiness.

neither . . . life : No power in this world nor in heaven is able to take away from us the love of God. He had this love for us, when he sent us his Son in human nature. He still has love for us, for that Son in his human and divine nature is ever at God's right hand pleading for us (verse 34).

APPLICATION : The purpose of this reading from St. Paul in today's Mass is to get us Christians to think for a few moments on the immense, infinite love God has for us. Many, if not all, of us are inclined to pay too much heed to our own weaknesses and to despair of ever reaching heaven. What we forget is that God, the Infinite, the all-loving is on our side, and that he has a positive interest in every single one of us.

Before he created the world we were in God's mind; he had plans for us. Not only did he intend to make man the masterpiece and master of all earthly creatures, but he planned to make him his own adopted son, by means of the Incarnation. This made man a brother of Christ, heir to an eternal life of happiness with him. Only infinite love could think of such a thing; only infinite power could do it. God is both.

God is unchangeable. That infinite love for mankind which made him send his divine Son on earth in order to bring us to heaven, has not weakened or changed. It cannot. He wants every individual of the human race in heaven, and he has done and continues to do all that is necessary for this to be realized. God's love therefore is never withdrawn from us. When we sin we fall out with God, but he does not fall out with us. He still loves us and wants us to return to him. There are sinners who will not ask for forgiveness because of their wrong idea of God. They think he'll be glad to push them down into hell—they do not realize that though he hates sins, he still loves the sinner.

Could a loving mother, whose little son dirties and soils the new suit and shoes she puts on him, forget her love in her displeasure and send him off to an orphanage? How much more impossible is it to imagine the infinitely loving God wishing or wanting the eternal loss of one whom he has made his adopted son?

No, this cannot and will not happen. Troubles and trials during our journey through life are not a sign that God has forgotten or deserted us. Rather are they a proof of his love. The surgeon who uses his scalpel or his knife when our survival needs it is not our enemy but a loving benefactor. So, too, it is with God. If and when he allows earthly troubles and trials, it is in order to help us earn our eternal reward. As St. Paul tells us, the trials of life, instead of separating us from our loving Father, are golden bonds that should unite us more closely with him. "With God on our side who can be against us" (Rom. 8 : 31).

GOSPEL : Matthew 14 : 13–21. When Jesus heard of the death of John, he withdrew in a boat to a lonely place apart. But when the crowds heard it, they followed him on foot from the towns. As he went ashore he saw a great throng; and he had compassion on them, and healed their sick. When it was evening, the disciples came to him and said, "This is a lonely place, and the day is now over; send the crowds away to go into the villages and buy food for themselves." Jesus said, "They need not go away; you give them something to eat." They said to him, "We have only five loaves here and two fish." And he said, "Bring them here to me." Then he ordered the crowds to sit down on the grass; and taking the five loaves and the two fish he looked up to heaven, and blessed, and broke and gave the loaves to the disciples, and the disciples gave them to the crowds. And they all ate and were satisfied. And they took up twelve baskets full of the broken pieces left over. And those who ate were about five thousand men, besides women and children.

EXPLANATION : This reading is St. Matthew's account of the miracle of the multiplication of bread to feed a multitude—a miracle related by the three other Evangelists also. In all four gospels this miracle is seen as a foreshadowing of the eucharistic meal which Christ was to provide miraculously for the multitude of his followers. In St. John this is clearly indicated, for it was the occasion of Christ's discourse on the Eucharist (Jn. 6 : 27–40). In the other gospels certain phrases, like "blessed, broke, gave to his disciples," occur which would remind the readers already familiar with the eucharistic liturgy, of the institution of the Eucharist.

This miracle also brought out the messiahship of Christ, for the miraculous feeding of the hungry was to be one of the gifts of the messianic age. Moses fed the Israelites miraculously in the desert (Ex. 16 : 13–14); the prophet Elisha fed a hundred men miraculously (2 Kgs. 4 : 42–44); the prophets frequently describe the messianic era as one of peace and plenty for everyone. In today's first lesson the second-Isaiah promises that God has prepared a banquet for all his Chosen People; all they have to do is to come to it.

a lonely ... apart : This was some place away from the towns and villages, most likely on the eastern shore of Lake Genesareth, as St. John explicitly states (6 : 1).

healed ... sick : He had come to confer spiritual and eternal benefits on men, but in his mercy he also gave them bodily and temporal benefits.

it was evening : Note that the institution of the Eucharist took place in the evening. The people had remained, attracted by his healing miracles and his preaching, longer than they intended, for they had come without any provisions for a meal.

we ... loaves : Jesus told the Apostles

not to send them away but to give them food. This was impossible, they said, they had barely enough for a meager meal for themselves. This brings out clearly the miraculous nature of Christ's act.

looked ... grave : These are the same actions as at the eucharistic meal during the Last Supper.

five thousand men : A very round number, but greatly exaggerated. Five thousand would have been one third of the population of Galilee at the time. Nevertheless, the number fed was such that nothing but a miracle would explain the fact that all had their fill. And the twelve baskets of remnants were far more than the original five loaves.

APPLICATION : This miracle was an act of kindness and loving thoughtfulness on the part of Christ. He saw the people's need—it was late for them to return to their homes and they had had nothing to eat all day—and he worked a miracle to provide for this need. The miracle also helped to convince the people of Galilee—the news spread around quickly—that he was the expected Messiah, but especially it prepared the way for the announcement of the greatest miracle of all—the miracle of the Eucharist.

As St. John tells us in his version of the story, Jesus referred to this miracle next day in order to introduce his promise of the heavenly bread which he would give them and which was to be his own body and blood, under the form of bread and wine. The bread he miraculously multiplied that day to supply the bodily needs of the Galilean multitude was but a foreshadowing of that heavenly food which he was about to give as spiritual nourishment to the millions who would become his fol-

lowers down through the centuries until the end of time.

The Galileans were grateful to him for providing so kindly and so thoughtfully for their needs. How much more grateful should we not be for the miracle by means of which he has left us himself to be our daily spiritual food? We are grateful, of course, to our loving Lord who not only handed up his body to his enemies to be crucified for us, but through his divine power, arranged that his glorified body, triumphant over death, should remain with us, his Church, forever under the eucharistic species.

Though invisible to mortal eyes, he is as truly present on our altars as he was that day in Galilee, when he miraculously fed the multitude. He is present under the form of bread and wine—so that we can partake of him as spiritual nourishment during our earthly life. Could love go any further? He himself said : "A man can have no greater love than to lay down his life for his friends" (Jn. 15 : 13). Yes, once a man has given his life he has given his all; there is nothing more he can give. But Christ was more than man. He was God as well, and, therefore, he was able not only to lay down his human life for us, but was able and willing to remain with us after death under the eucharistic species: to be our strength and nourishment until we join him in the promised land of heaven.

When we compare our own unworthiness with this, almost incredible, love and thoughtfulness of Christ for us, all we can do is simply to say: "Lord, you know I am not worthy to receive you, but you say you want to come into my poor and untidy home, please make me less unworthy, forgive all my past sins and offences, and give me the grace and strength to be better in future."

NINETEENTH SUNDAY OF THE YEAR

FIRST READING: 1 Kings 19:9; 11–13. Elijah came to a cave, and lodged there; and behold, the word of the Lord came to him, and he said to him, "Go forth, and stand upon the mount before the Lord." And behold, the Lord passed by, and a great and strong wind rent the mountains, and broke in pieces the rocks before the Lord, but the Lord was not in the wind; and after the wind an earthquake, but the Lord was not in the earthquake; and after the earthquake a fire, but the Lord was not in the fire; and after the fire a still small voice. And when Elijah heard it, he wrapped his face in his mantle and went out and stood at the entrance of the cave.

EXPLANATION: The northern tribes broke away from Judah on the death of Solomon (922 B.C.), and formed an independent country which was called Israel. Separated from the temple and the priestly caste (the tribe of Levi which remained with Judah and Benjamin), they gradually lost their knowledge and belief in Yahweh, the true God, as well. During the reign of Ahab (869-850), their seventh King, idolatry became rampant in Israel. Ahab had married a pagan called Jezebel, a daughter of the king of Tyre. She set up a temple to Baal in Samaria and had 400 pagan priests daily at her table. She banished all the prophets of the true God from the country or almost all, for Elijah remained to preserve the true faith and make life miserable for Jezebel.

After his victory over the priests of Baal on Mount Carmel (1 Kgs. 18:16–40) and his execution of 400 of them Elijah decided it was safer to leave Israel to escape the wrath of Jezebel.

He was heading for Mount Sinai, evidently in the hope of meeting Yahweh where Moses had seen him, when the incident narrated in today's reading took place. Remember, Elijah was a holy man of God, who wanted God to be a God of fire and sword for he was waging a one-man war against the queen and her forces.

Elijah . . . cave : He had reached Mount Horeb in Sinai and was resting in a cave when a voice told him to come out and meet Yahweh the Lord. (In verses 10 and 11, not included in the reading, God had asked him why he had run away and he answered that he had run to save his life.)

great . . . fire : In all of these physical proofs of God's might and power, which Elijah felt were needed in Israel, God was not present.

after . . . voice : The CCD translation, "a tiny whispering sound," is more correct. JEB has : "the sound of a gentle breeze," and the NEB : "a low murmuring sound." The contrast is between the roaring and noise of the tornado, the earthquake and fire, and the gentle sound that follows them.

he wrapped . . . mantle : Elijah realized that the gentle sound meant that God was present, so lest he should see him (and die, as was the common belief), he covered his eyes.

In the verses that follow the above, God (Yahweh) tells him to return via Damascus to his country and his work.

APPLICATION : Elijah was a great prophet, a great defender of the true faith in Israel, where a defense was needed—but, being of a fiery, violent nature, he was evidently not quite satisfied with the help God was giving him. He wanted fire and brimstone poured abundantly on all God's enemies, but God did not always see things as Elijah did. When running away in despair, or with the hope of collecting reinforcements in the form of more active cooperation (according to his ideas), on the part of God, he was taught a lesson and, to his credit, he learned it.

Many of us have at least a little of the spirit of the pre-Horeb Elijah in us. When we see wickedness prosper and open opponents of God continuing to live and to thrive, we begin to wish God would step in and show his power by exterminating them, in a way that would prevent others from daring to imitate them. An earthquake could so easily swallow up the leaders of atheistic policy when they all meet in Moscow; and what a blessing for the world and for the true religion! We wonder, perhaps, why God doesn't show his power and his presence in some such way to those who deny his existence.

But, as Christians, we should know better. We have the great advantage (which Elijah lacked) of Christ's teaching on God's mercy. God is the father, and the loving father, of the sinner as well as of the saint. He does not wish the death of the sinner, but that he should be converted and live. He gives his grace to all men; he lets his sun shine on the sinners and the just. He has infinite patience and is ready, up to the last moment, to welcome back the greatest sinner who turns to him. How many saints are in heaven today, who would have been cut down in their sins, if God acted as Elijah and some other devout lovers of God would have him act?

No, the lesson for each one of us

today is that God is especially a God of mercy in his dealings with us. He would have us deal mercifully with our fellowmen who are not serving him or who, worse still, are even denying his existence. Tornadoes of vituperation and abuse, thundering condemnations and threats of fire and brimstone are not the means God uses to bring back his prodigal sons, and they are not the means he wants us, his friends, to use either.

God is to be found in "the tiny gentle breeze," in the kind, charitable understanding word spoken out of a true brotherly heart. In the sinner God sees his child and still loves him. We too should see in the sinner our brother, and we should love him and wish him to reach the happy end God intends for

him. A kindly word will do more to produce his conversion than torrents of abuse and condemnation. There are few of us who have not sinned and offended God during our adult years. How fortunate we were that God was not Elijah's type of God while we were in our sins! He gave us a chance because he was a merciful, understanding God. Let us be merciful and understanding to our brothers who now are what we once were. Let us pray for them and ask God to continue to be merciful towards them. Let us help them kindly and charitably whenever we can. If we are instrumental in bringing back a prodigal son to his loving Father in heaven, we can rest assured that our Father will help us on our road back to him in heaven.

SECOND READING : Romans 9 : 1–5. I am speaking the truth in Christ, I am not lying; my conscience bears me witness in the Holy Spirit, that I have great sorrow and unceasing anguish in my heart. For I could wish that I myself were accursed and cut off from Christ for the sake of my brethren, my kinsmen by race. They are Israelites, and to them belong the sonship, the glory, the covenants, the giving of the law, the worship, and the promises; to them belong the patriarchs, and of their race, according to the flesh, is the Christ, who is God over all, blessed for ever. Amen.

EXPLANATION : In the preceding eight chapters, St. Paul has been telling the Roman converts to Christianity of the blessings Christ, the Messiah, had brought to mankind. Christ was the fulfillment of all God's dealings with the Chosen People of the Old Testament— he was the fulfillment of "the Law and the prophets." Yet the Jews, as a nation, had refused to see Christ as the Messiah who was promised to them by God through their patriarchs and prophets.

This question troubled Paul very much. (It must be remembered that a great many individual Jews had accepted Christianity, among them Paul and the other Apostles.) Paul would gladly have given everything, even his life and his Christian faith, to get them to accept Christ as the fulfillment of the promises. It is of this sorrow of heart that he speaks in the following verses.

I . . . lying : He solemnly declares that what he is about to say is the objective truth. He calls Christ as a witness : "in Christ."

great . . . anguish : In spite of all the sufferings and trouble the Jews had caused him ever since he began his Christian missionary activity (12 or 13 years previously), he still loves them as his brother-Jews, and he has sorrow of heart and anguish because they do not see the gift of God in Christ.

I myself were accursed : Accursed= anathema. Paul says he would be willing to be excluded from Christ—the worst possible fate he could imagine— if, as a people, the Jews who were his brethren and kinsmen by race, would thereby accept Christ.

They are Israelites : Paul gives them the more honorable and religious name of Israelites. God changed Jacob's name to Israel and his descendants inherited that name. The title "Jews" was given them by outside nations, and not always with respect. (Note how the presentday Jews who have established a political nation in Palestine called it "Israel," not "Judah." They are Israelis rather than Jews.)

To them belong : Paul goes on to mention seven of the privileges which Yahweh down through the ages had given to the Israelites, the descendants of Jacob.

1 : sonship : Yahweh adopted them as his sons, his chosen ones (Ex. 4 : 22; Is. 1 : 2).

2 : glory : This was Yahweh's presence manifested by a cloud in the tabernacle, in the desert, and in the temple of Jerusalem built by Solomon (Ex. 40 : 34; 1 Kgs. 8 : 10–11).

3 : covenants : These were the solemn pacts Yahweh made with Abraham (Gen. 15–18), with Jacob (Gen. 32 : 29), and Moses (Ex. 20 : 1–17), this latter being the principal one which formed them into a nation, a Chosen People.

4 : law : The decalog (in Gen. 20 : 1–17).

5 : worship : The cultic laws regulating divine worship of the one true God in the tabernacle and later in the temple of Jerusalem (Gn. 21–31).

6 : promises : Yahweh made promises to Abraham, Jacob, Isaac, Moses and David. They were promises of his special protection and love made to them as his Chosen People and to David of a kingly descendant whose reign would last forever (see Sm. 7 : 11ff).

7 : patriarchs : Abraham, Isaac, Jacob, Judah, distinguished ancestors of the Jews and friends of Yahweh.

the Christ . . . all : The final and crowning gift and privilege, which they unfortunately did not accept or acknowledge, was Christ, the Messiah, who was God as well as man. It was because he claimed to be God as well as man (a claim he proved by his miracles and especially by his resurrection) that they rejected him and handed him over to the Roman authorities to be crucified, "because he has claimed to be the Son of God" (Jn. 20 : 7).

APPLICATION : Like St. Paul we too can and should grieve that God's Chosen People of the Old Testament refused, and still refuse, as a nation to accept the last and greatest of the many gifts he gave them, his Messiah, Christ. For eighteen centuries he treated them as a people apart. He let the other nations go their way, but to them he revealed himself as the true and only God, who made and regulated the whole universe and all it contains. And his reason for this special treatment was that his Son (according to the flesh), whom he was going to send on earth to make all nations his new Chosen People, would be a descendant of Abraham, a member of their race.

While we regret that they are not our brothers in Christ, and while we must always pray that one day they will become our Christian brothers, we must realize that they are a small percentage of those who reject Christ today. There are millions living among us—men and women—who know nothing and care nothing for God or for their own eternal future. If they were not baptized then their parents were, but indifference followed by disbelief has ousted the faith in families, and almost in whole nations, in much of the so-called civilized part of our world.

What is the cause of this? It is the same as that which prevented the Jews of St. Paul's day from accepting Christ : pride and worldliness. The leaders of the Jews, the Pharisees and the priestly caste, could not bear to be taught by Christ. What was he but a country carpenter, while they were doctors of the law! They had nothing to learn, they thought. Our ex-Christians and anti-Christians today think they have all the answers to all questions too. Because they know a little more than their grandparents about the things of this world, they think they can ignore or deny the existence of what does not come within the range of their bodily senses.

As well as being proud, the priests and Pharisees of Paul's day were worldly and politically minded. They looked for a Messiah who would not only set them free from the hated Roman rule, but who would make of their country a world-power. And in this new empire they would, of course, have the seats of honor. Christ's teaching was concerned not with power or wealth in this world but with the eternal joy and happiness that men could obtain for themselves in the next. Our ex-Christians today have no time, and no thought, for God or for Christ's teaching, because they are totally occupied with obtaining the pleasures, the wealth, the comforts of this world. They may not think in terms of world-power for themselves, but they have put themselves completely and entirely in the power of this world. Talk of a future-life is to them sheer folly— the present is what counts : "eat, sleep, drink and be merry" is their motto, their creed. They are reluctant to add "for tomorrow you die"—that might disturb their present bliss!

What should be our reaction to this sad state of so many of our fellowmen? Our first reaction should be a fervent "Thank you, God, for the true faith we have; please give us the grace to live in it until we draw our last breath." Our second thought must be to ask the good God to send the light of faith to the descendants of Abraham, and to re-light it among those Gentiles who have extinguished it. It is not enough for a true Christian that he should live his own life according to the laws of Christ, true charity demands that he be seriously interested in the spiritual welfare of his neighbors.

GOSPEL : Matthew 14 : 22–33. Jesus made the disciples get into the boat and go before him to the other side, while he dismissed the crowds. And after he had dismissed the crowds, he went up into the hills by himself to pray. When evening came, he was there alone, but the boat by this time was many furlongs distant from the land, beaten by the waves; for the wind was against them. And in the fourth watch of the night he came to them, walking on the sea. But when the disciples saw him walking on the sea, they were terrified, saying, "It is a ghost!" And they cried out for fear. But immediately he spoke to them, saying, "Take heart, it is I; have no fear."

And Peter answered him, "Lord, if it is you, bid me to come to you on the water." He said, "Come." So Peter got out of the boat and walked on the water and came to Jesus; but when he saw the wind, he was afraid, and beginning to sink he cried out, "Lord, save me." Jesus immediately reached out his hand and caught him, saying to him, "O man of little faith, why did you doubt?" And when they got into the boat, the wind ceased. And those in the boat worshiped him, saying, "Truly you are the Son of God."

EXPLANATION : In this reading from St. Matthew's gospel we have two miracles worked by our Lord; he walks on the water and calms a storm. The faith and trust of Peter in Christ is greater than that of the other Apostles, but it is as yet not complete and unquestioning.

Christ had spent the day somewhere on the eastern shore of Lake Genesareth. As evening came he told the disciples to return home by boat to the western shore. He himself spent most of the night alone in prayer. The disciples ran into a heavy head-wind and were hardly making any headway—they still hadn't reached the western shore at 3 a.m. Suddenly Jesus came near them, walking on the water. The disciples were terrified; they thought he was a ghost. Jesus told them not to be afraid, that it was he, their Master, who was there. Peter was ready to believe him, but put him to the test. If he really was the Master he could give them the power to walk on the water. Christ gave him the power and while his faith in Christ lasted he walked on the water. But his faith weakened when he saw a large wave approaching, and he then began to sink. He called out to his master : "Lord save me." Christ caught him and lifted him up, remarking that it was the wavering of his faith that caused him to sink. They both got into the boat and immediately the wind ceased. The others in the boat declared then that truly he was the "Son of God." This was not a proclamation of their faith in his divinity —this conviction did not come to them until after the resurrection—but an affirmation that he was the Messiah.

APPLICATION : Our Lord sent his disciples to row across the lake, knowing that they would meet strong, gale-force head-winds and be in danger. He did this because he wanted to strengthen their faith and trust in himself. He intended to come to them at the right moment, working two miracles—walking on the water and calming the storm. This he did and the result was as he had intended—their faith in him was strengthened, they declared he was the Messiah, the Chosen of God. Peter, already the recognized leader, and always the most daring among them, showed himself ready to risk drowning in order to prove his trust and confidence in Christ. While he trusted in Christ, all went well, but when his faith weakened he would have been lost were it not for the outstretched helping hand of his master. This was also a very necessary lesson in the education of Peter and his companions.

For us, too, there is a necessary lesson in this incident. It is that we must continue to trust in Christ and his loving Father, even when God seems to have deserted us. Most of the troubles and trials of our lives are caused by the injustice and lack of charity of our fellowmen. The remainder can be attributed to our own defects and sins or to some weakness in our mental and bodily make-up. But God foresees all these misfortunes, and can prevent them. Instead he lets them take their course, because they can and should be the means of educating us in our knowledge of life's true meaning and they should draw us closer to him.

Christ foresaw the storm and the grave risk his Apostles would run when he sent them off across the lake. But that trial and the grave danger they ran was for their own good, because they learned to realize that he was from God and they could always trust him. Our trials and our earthly ailments are also foreseen by God and permitted by him (even if inflicted on us by a sinful fellowman) so that they will draw us closer to him and help us on the road to heaven.

This they will do, if we accept them and bear with them until he comes to our aid. Our troubles in life are like the growing pains of our youth—they are necessary if we are to arrive at our full stature as sons of God. They form, mold and shape our religious character and bring us closer to God—if we allow them to do so. For the lukewarm Christian who rebels against God because of his earthly sufferings, they can do the opposite. He cannot see the purpose and value of suffering because he has never seriously pondered or grasped the real meaning of this life and God's loving plans for him.

As in the first reading today, God may not be in the tornadoes or earthquakes or roaring fires, nor does he cause them perhaps, but he is ever near to his true children when such calamities occur. He has a purpose in every trial or tribulation which crosses the path of our lives, a purpose always to our eternal advantage if only we will see and accept his will in these trials.

TWENTIETH SUNDAY OF THE YEAR

FIRST READING : Isaiah 56 : 1; 6–7. Thus says the Lord : "Keep justice, and do righteousness, for soon my salvation will come, and my deliverance be revealed. And the foreigners who join themselves to the Lord, to minister to him, to love the name of the Lord, and to be his servants, everyone who keeps the sabbath, and does not profane it, and holds fast my covenant— these I will bring to my holy mountain, and make them joyful in my house of prayer; their burnt offerings and their sacrifices will be accepted on my altar; for my house shall be called a house of prayer for all peoples."

EXPLANATION : The theme of the prophet here (whether he be second- or third-Isaiah does not matter) is the call of the Gentiles to the service of the true God on the great day which is to come. The temple of that future messianic age will be a "house of prayer" for all peoples.

soon . . . come : Evidently the deliverance from Babylon has already taken place. The temple of Jerusalem seems to have been rebuilt, but all that is only a preparation for the real deliverance to come. The Jews are exhorted to be ready for that day by living a just and holy life.

foreigners . . . the Lord : Non-Israelites who accept Yahweh as their God and who keep his law and his covenant will be allowed by God into his temple, and their sacrifices and burnt-offerings will be as acceptable as those of the Israelites. This is a complete reversal of the centuries-old ban on the Gentiles.

a house . . . peoples : The universality of salvation is clearly and emphatically stated. God's house will in future be for all people, not only for Israelites. It will be a "house of prayer," a place where men will worship God, not with external offerings only, but from their heart—offering themselves rather than material gifts. Jesus quoted these words when he drove the worldly-minded moneymakers from the temple (Mt. 21 : 13).

APPLICATION : The liberation of the Jews from the exile of Babylon (538 B.C.) was, like the first liberation from Egypt, seven centuries earlier, but a preparation for the real liberation to come. The promised Messiah would bring this final liberation to all mankind. He would set all men free from the slavery of sin and the estrangement from God which sin brought with it into the world, and he would make them citizens-to-be, not of a small corner of this earth, but of the eternal kingdom of heaven.

This liberation has taken place, and we are the new Chosen People of God. The Christian Church is the new temple of God. It is open to all nations and peoples. It is the place where, through baptism, all men become children of God, brothers of Christ and heirs to the eternal kingdom. But it is a "house of prayer," a place where all must strive to keep God's laws and be loyal subjects of his kingdom on earth, if they want to earn their place in his heavenly kingdom.

While proud of the privileges God had given them, the Jews, God's Chosen People of old, neglected their obligations to him and, content with keeping the external shell of the law, forgot to give God true reverence and gratitude from their hearts. This pride and purely external observance blinded them to the true meaning of God's promises; they were unable to see in Christ the Son of God, which he claimed to be, or the long-promised Messiah. They had grown worldly and politically-minded, and had gradually lost interest in God's eternal kingdom. All they wanted was a worldly kingdom of power and plenty. But Christ's kingdom was "not of this world."

The same fate, alas, has befallen many members of the new Chosen People and it can happen to any one of us. This world and its passing interests can blind us to the real facts of life. We can become so enmeshed in the search for the goods of this earth that we leave ourselves no time or no inclination to think about and prepare for the goods of the after-life. Yet, these are the goods that matter!

The industry and zeal with which many—far too many—Christians, use their energies in amassing the goods and comforts of this world would perhaps be understandable, or at least a little less foolish, if they expected to live on here for seven or eight hundred years. But they cannot guarantee themselves even one hundred. Their zeal and industry are surely misplaced. When they have to leave this world they can take none of its goods with them. All that they can produce at the judgement seat are the virtues or vices they accumulated during life. The millionaire and the beggar will be judged by the same yardstick. We will not be asked for our bank-account; we will be asked to account for the years God has given us in which to earn eternal credit.

Like the Jews of old, many Christians have in the past let the cares and interests of this life blind them to the true purpose of life. To their grief they have now learned what folly this was. Any one of us could make the same mistake. Today's lesson reminds us not to follow in that foolish path and end as they did. If we love and reverence the name of the Lord and keep his commandments, we may enjoy God's gift in this life while making sure of the gift of eternal life, when we are called from this world.

SECOND READING: Romans 11:13–15; 29–32. Now I am speaking to you Gentiles. Inasmuch then as I am an Apostle to the Gentiles, I magnify my ministry in order to make my fellow-Jews jealous, and thus save some of them. For if their rejection means the reconciliation of the world, what will their acceptance mean but life from the dead?

For the gifts and the call of God are irrevocable. Just as you were once disobedient to God but now have received mercy because of their disobedience, so they have now been disobedient in order that by the mercy shown to you they also may receive mercy. For God has consigned all men to disobedience, that he may have mercy upon all.

EXPLANATION : St. Paul, who never forgot that he was a Jew by birth and had been loyal to the Jewish faith until Christ called him, never missed an opportunity to bring his Jewish fellow-nationals to the Christian faith. In every town or village he entered he spoke first of all to the Jews who lived there and, when they rejected him and Christ, he turned to the Gentiles and preached of Christ to them. In spite of this rejection of Christ and the new law by the Jewish nation in the person of their leaders Paul was convinced that as a nation they would yet accept Christ and become obedient to him. Many individuals did in fact become Christians and saints.

Apostle of the Gentiles : It was Christ himself who gave Paul this special apostolate (Acts 9 : 15). That Paul has not forgotten it is clear from Rom. 1 : 5; Gal. 2 : 7–10; Acts 22 : 21.

my fellow-Jews jealous : He hopes his fellow-Jews will notice his success among the Gentiles, which was due to God's mercy, and that some of them will follow the good example of the pagan nations.

life . . . dead : When the Jews rejected Christ and his gospel, the Apostles, Paul amongst them, turned immediately to the Gentiles (they would have preached the gospel to all nations in any case as commanded by Christ in Matt. 28 : 19–20), and the Gentiles thereby were reconciled to God. Eventually, when the Jews as a body will accept Christianity they too will have a new life, the life of the Spirit as opposed to the dead letter of the Mosaic Law.

the gifts . . . God : Paul is convinced that the Jewish nation will eventually accept Christ, because God's call given to them through Abraham, was a call to eternal salvation.

because . . . disobedience : As we saw above, the Gentiles received the Gospel earlier because the Jews rejected it.

by the mercy . . . you : Because of the proofs of God's mercy seen in the lives of the Gentile Christians the Jews will one day accept Christ.

have mercy on all : The Gentile peoples ignored and disobeyed God down through the ages; the Jews ignored and disobeyed Christ (who was God) in recent times. But as God showed his mercy to the Gentiles notwithstanding their long disobedience, so too will he do likewise for the Jews, and thus he will be merciful to all men.

APPLICATION : The lesson for us today in these words of St. Paul is that our Christian faith—the greatest gift in life, the pearl of great price—is a free gift from God. Through it we Gentiles, whose pagan ancestors knew nothing of God, have been brought to know and love the God who created us and who will bring us to heaven through the Incarnation of his only-begotten Son.

This is a gift we must cherish and nourish daily in our lives if we hope to earn the eternal happiness which God intended for us when he gave us this gift. Through the sacrament of baptism we have been made brothers of Christ and heirs to heaven, but if we are to die as brothers of Christ and be worthy of our eternal inheritance, we have to live the years given us on earth as true brothers of this same Christ.

This is no easy task, but neither is it impossible, as is proved by the millions who have gone through the same difficulties before us, and have earned their reward. All those who are now in heaven have one thing in common—their great love for God and true appreciation of his gifts to them. If we can imitate these two basic points we too shall, with God's assured help, make a success of our lives.

A second point we should learn from St. Paul's message to us today, is that we should pray fervently and often for the conversion of the members of the Jewish race. They are really our brothers in God, for their father Abraham was our father too. He was asked to leave his home and his kindred, his family and his country so that God's plan for bringing all the peoples of the world to heaven could be put into action. Abraham's call was the first step in the long journey of preparation for the coming of the Messiah on earth.

For eighteen centuries the direct descendants of Abraham were dear to God, and sometimes they were very near to him. It was through them that God brought Christ and the new covenant to us; it would be fitting now that we, through our prayers and good works, should be instrumental under God, in bringing them to Christ. St. Paul was confident that one day God's mercy would reach out to them and bring them into his new kingdom. Let us help to hasten that day, so that they will become not only our brothers in Abraham but our brothers in Christ, and our fellow-citizens in heaven.

GOSPEL : Matthew 15 : 21–28. Jesus withdrew to the district of Tyre and Sidon. And behold, a Canaanite woman from that region came out and cried, "Have mercy on me, O Lord, Son of David; my daughter is severely possessed by a demon." But he did not answer her a word. And his disciples came and begged him, saying, "Send her away, for she is crying after us." He answered, "I was sent only to the lost sheep of the house of Israel." But she came and knelt before him, saying, "Lord, help me." And he answered, "It is not fair to take the children's bread and throw it to the dogs." She said, "Yes, Lord, yet even the dogs eat the crumbs that fall from their master's table." Then Jesus answered her, "O woman, great is your faith! Be it done for you as you desire." And her daughter was healed instantly.

EXPLANATION : In the first reading for today, we heard the prophet Isaiah foretelling that the expected messianic kingdom was intended not only for the Jews but all nations as well. In this gospel episode St. Matthew (and St. Mark also in 7 : 24–30) tells us how our Lord, moved by the persevering faith of a Gentile woman, answers her prayer and heals her daughter. The only other instance of Jesus' dealing with gentiles is that of his healing the centurion's servant (Mt. 8 : 5–23) at Capernaum. Outside of these two cases all our Lord's preaching and miracles during his public life were for the Jews only. But after his witnessing the faith of the centurion he foretold that the Gentiles would supplant the children of Abraham in the new kingdom which he was about to establish (Mt. 8 : 10–12).

Tyre and Sidon : Two cities in the southern region of Phoenicia. It is not clear whether Jesus was traveling near the border of this part of Phoenicia or had actually crossed into the territory.

a Canaanite woman : Matthew seems to use this term "Canaanite" to stress the paganism of the woman. The Canaanites were the ancient arch-enemies of the Jews and their religion, but that day is gone forever.

Lord, Son of David : Lord equals "Sir," not "God," but the title "Son of David" is messianic. The people of Phoenicia could have heard of Christ's miracles and preaching—this woman certainly had, or she would not have asked for a miracle—and that he was looked on as the Messiah promised of old to the Jews. The title "Son of David" refers to the promise made to David that a son of his would sit on his throne and establish it forever (2 Sm. 7 : 12).

he . . . her : He was thus putting her faith to the test.

disciples . . . him : As the Greek text reads and as our Lord's answer indicates his disciples asked him to grant her the favor she requested.

only . . . Israel : The Messiah was promised to Israel and it was from Israel that his gospel was to spread to all nations. Christ had come on earth for all men, but according to God's pre-arrangement it was to Israel he came. He could have preached in all the principal cities of the Roman empire, but this was not God's plan. His messianic kingdom was to grow from the tiny mustard-seed sown in Palestine.

children's bread . . . dogs : This sounds harsh and uncharitable, but it is only a proverb in common use. The Canaanite woman knew that she was not referred to as a dog. She answered with another proverb.

crumbs . . . table : The dogs—the outsiders—are glad to get the crumbs that fall from their master's table; they do not ask for the children's bread.

great . . . faith : She has proved her faith and trust in him and has, like the centurion (another Gentile), shown greater faith than most of the Israelites.

daughter . . . instantly : He granted her request. Her daughter was healed that very moment.

APPLICATION : There is a lesson, a very necessary one, for all of us in this episode of Christ's public life. It is the necessity of perseverance in our prayers of petition. Prayer is an essential part of our Christian life, and the essential part of prayer is that of adoration and thanksgiving, but prayer of petition has a big part in our daily prayers. We have so many spiritual and temporal needs, needs which we cannot provide by ourselves. Christ himself has told us to ask him for these needs : "ask and you shall receive."

Do we ask with the fervor and perseverance which prove that we have "great faith"? That faith is the proof which Christ needs before he grants our requests. The Canaanite woman of whom we have just heard is for us an example of that deep-seated faith and trust in Christ's power and Christ's goodness. Even though he ignored her she continued to beseech him, and when he answered with what seemed a direct refusal her faith and trust did not waver. She answered his reason for refusal with another statement which showed that the granting of her petition would not in any way interfere with or impede his primary task, his mission to his father's chosen people. This was the proof of great faith which he required. He granted her request.

We must imitate and learn from this pagan mother. Her love for her child made her ready to undergo every hardship or suffering for the restoration to health of her loved one. When we turn to Christ in our needs is our faith in him as sincere and unwavering as was this woman's? No doubt it often is, and yet we do not get the desired answer. As Christians we know that our particular request may not always be for our good, or for the final good of the person for whom we are praying. In that case, the good God will not grant what would be to our eternal disadvantage. But if our prayer is sincere and persevering—we shall always get *an* answer, and one which is better than what we asked for.

How often do we wonder at or perhaps doubt God's mercy when we see, for example, the young father of a family being taken from his loved and helpless ones, notwithstanding the prayers and tears of his wife and children. Where is God's mercy here? Where is his answer to these sincere prayers? But who are we to question God's mercy? The answer is there and often clear enough : that death brings out in his relatives and neighbors virtues which they would otherwise never have had occasion to practice— virtues that will earn for them eternal life.

It is only when we get to heaven—and getting to heaven is our purpose in life— that we shall see how our prayers, sincere and persevering, were answered by God.

TWENTY-FIRST SUNDAY OF THE YEAR

FIRST READING : Isaiah 22 : 19–23. Thus says the Lord to Shebna steward of the household : "I will thrust you from your office, and you will be cast down from your station. In that day I will call my servant Eliakim the son of Hilkiah, and I will clothe him with your robe, and will bind your girdle on him, and will commit your authority to his hand; and he shall be a father to the inhabitants of Jerusalem and to the house of Judah. And I will place on his shoulder the key to the house of David; he shall open, and none shall shut; and he shall shut, and none shall open. And I will fasten him like a peg in a sure place, and he will become a throne of honor to his father's house."

EXPLANATION : Because of the reference to the "key of the house of David" in this text, some Fathers saw in it a messianic prophecy, foretelling the removal from power of the leaders of the Chosen People of the Old Testament, and the transfer of that power to Christ, who in turn handed it to Peter as head of the Church, the new Chosen People. The mention of the key of authority seems to be the reason why this lesson was chosen for today where the Gospel describes the giving of the keys to Peter.
steward . . . household : This steward, called Shebna, was evidently abusing his power by urging the king Hezekiah (716–687) to revolt against Assyria and call Egypt to his aid. Isaiah was totally opposed to this; Judah should trust in her God, not in any pagan help. But she did not, and this is what ultimately led to the total destruction of Judah and Jerusalem a hundred years later.
my . . . Eliakim : This Shebna will be (and was) deposed and in his place a true steward "who shall be a father to . . . the house of Judah" will be appointed by Yahweh ("Thus says the Lord").
key . . . David : He would wear the "key," the sign of authority, over his shoulder.
he shall . . . shut : Nobody but he may use that key. See today's Gospel (Mt. 16 : 19).
like . . . place : He shall be solidly established—"on this rock I will build my Church" (Mt. 16 : 18).
honor . . . house : Here the steward represents Christ rather than Peter. Christ's mission on earth was primarily for the honor and glory of his Father.

APPLICATION : Just as in the days of King Hezekiah, seven hundred years before Christ came on earth, the major-domo, the chief authority (next to the king) in the household, was deposed because of his disloyalty to Yahweh and his worldly ambitions, so also when Christ came the kingdom of God passed from the Chosen People of old and was given to the Gentiles, with Peter as chief steward representing Christ and next to him in authority.

Shebna lost his position because of worldliness and infidelity to God. The Scribes and Pharisees lost their leadership and their place in the new kingdom of God, for the very same reasons. This should surely be a lesson to us. But how many Christians fail to learn this lesson? They forget the exalted position they hold in God's plan, and through their worldliness and disloyalty to God in his earthly kingdom, they put at risk their inheritance in the eternal kingdom.

The incisive saying of Christ : "what does it profit a man if he gains the whole world and loses his life?" is forgotten by many Christians today. They make the possessing of all this world's goods their sole purpose in life. They therefore neglect, and eventually forget, their own best interests, their eternal interests. Could folly be greater? Our world today is full of such foolish people. More than ever before in the two thousand years of Christianity there are ex-Christians who have become atheists in practice if not in theory.

There are many causes for this state of affairs. The basic cause is the reluctance of human nature to accept the need for self-restraint and sacrifice. Man does not like obligations or duties, but he is ever ready to grasp at privilege and freedom. The false doctrine that each one is captain of his own soul, sole master of his own life, is much more attractive to human nature than the call to obedience and submission to the Creator. But the cure for this sad state of our present-day world is much more important than diagnosing its causes. We, practicing Christians, want all our fellowmen to reach heaven; we want them all to recognize what they are, whence they came, and whither they are going. We want them in other words to have their own eternal interests at heart.

Apart from fervent prayer for all our neighbors, whatever their color, creed or non-creed, the next best remedy we can apply to the infidel world, is to give to all men the example of a truly Christian life. Good, practicing Christian parents must hand down to their children untarnished the Christian faith they themselves received from their own parents. They do this especially by good example. Outside of the home, every good Christian must strive to let his non-practicing neighbor see that he lives according to Christ's gospel, and that he appreciates and esteems it.

If each loyal Christian won back three lapsed Christians each year, in thirty years time most of the western countries would be Christian once again! We have heard too many lamentations and condemnations of the paganism which has gripped our present-day society. It is time we were up and doing our part to bring our neighbors back to God and Christ. Sitting and lamenting has not helped; action will.

SECOND READING: Romans 11:33–36. O the depth of the riches and wisdom and knowledge of God! How unsearchable are his judgements and how inscrutable his ways! "For who has known the mind of the Lord, or who has been his counselor?" "Or who has given a gift to him that he might be repaid?" For from him and through him and to him are all things. To him be glory forever. Amen.

EXPLANATION: In the previous chapters of his letter to the Romans, St. Paul has been describing God's love for Jews and Gentiles and his merciful dealings with them. He concludes this section of his letter with a hymn of praise for God's infinite wisdom and mercy—a wisdom and mercy which is away beyond anything we can imagine.

riches ... knowledge: Paul, thinking on the nature, wisdom and knowledge of God, is simply astounded. The nature and the gifts of God are infinite, and therefore no finite mind can grasp or adequately conceive of them. A man *has* human nature, knowledge, wisdom; God *is* the divine nature, the divine knowledge, the divine wisdom.

how ... ways: It is useless for man, therefore, with his limited mind to try to grasp fully the decisions made by God or the wisdom he employed in carrying them out.

who ... counselor: Paul here quotes Isaiah, who declares that no human being is able to understand God's ways, and no man can ever advise him, for God knows all truth—everything is present to him; he does not forecast or guess the future as man has to do.

given ... him: God is dependent on no creature; he is self-sufficient and independent of all creatures.

from him ... through him ... to him: God is the Creator ("from him"), the Sustainer ("through him"), and the final Goal ("to him") of all creation.

glory forever: All creatures must give him honor in all times and places.

APPLICATION: What strange creatures we are! We admire and exalt great scientists, men who have discovered more of the laws of nature than any others who went before them. Yet, we do not stop to admire and praise the One who made all the laws, discovered by science, and millions more as yet undiscovered! We praise and extol great painters who can reproduce in color faces of men and women and beautiful landscapes, but we forget or ignore the maker of these landscapes and the creator of these faces!

Yes, we praise and admire our fellow-creatures who have greater gifts than ordinary men, but we forget the good God from whom these gifts came, and who possessed them to an infinite degree. We fail to praise and admire him. How illogical!

In a very real sense it may be said that no true scientist and no true student of nature has ever been an atheist. Because of the perfection of the natural laws and the proofs of supreme intelligence evident in creation the inference is almost inevitable that some supremely intelligent Being (in other words, God) was the originator and inventor of all this created perfection. It is the pseudo-scientists and the self-styled intelligentsia who fail to see God in his marvelous creation. As some writer put it: "The

L

pseudo-scientist says : 'Look what I found in the atom,' while the scientist says : 'Look what God put into the atom'."

Without being scientists or highly-versed in the intricate nature of created things, we have a knowledge of God sufficient for our purpose in life, because God in his love and mercy revealed himself to us. He has told us he is our Creator, our Sustainer, our Savior, and our Last End, our Goal in life. While with St. Paul we must marvel at, and admire, the infinite wisdom and knowledge of God, we must marvel still more at the infinite love which moved him to reveal himself and his purpose to us.

However, because of that same infinite love of God, we are no longer unworthy creatures : we are finite and limited, but we are still important in God's eyes, because through the Incarnation he has made us his adopted children in order to give us a share in his eternal life. It is because of this relationship that we can approach the infinite God as a loving father, as one who, though infinitely above and beyond us, has a father's interest in our eternal and temporal welfare. We need not fear his infinite power and majesty, for in the Incarnation he has proved to us how he can descend to our level in order to give us a place and make us feel at home in his eternal kingdom.

Today, with St. Paul, let us say from the depths of our hearts : "To the infinitely wise and merciful God may all honor and glory be forever offered by all his adopted children." And may we never fail to thank him for this almost incredible privilege. May we ever show in our daily lives that we appreciate and treasure all he has done and is continuing to do for our temporal and eternal welfare.

GOSPEL : Matthew 16 : 13–20. When Jesus came into the district of Caesarea Philippi, he asked his disciples, "Who do men say that the Son of man is?" And they said, "Some say John the Baptist, others say Elijah, and others Jeremiah or one of the prophets." He said to them, "But who do you say that I am?" Simon Peter replied, "You are the Christ, the Son of the living God." And Jesus answered him, "Blessed are you, Simon Bar-Jona! For flesh and blood has not revealed this to you, but my Father who is in heaven. And I tell you, you are Peter, and on this rock I will build my Church, and the powers of death shall not prevail against it. I will give you the keys of the kingdom of heaven, and whatever you bind on earth shall be bound in heaven, and whatever you loose on earth shall be loosed in heaven." Then he strictly charged the disciples to tell no one that he was the Christ.

EXPLANATION : In this reading from St. Matthew we have St. Peter's profession of faith in the messiahship of Jesus, and the conferring on St. Peter of the gift of infallibility and primacy in the Church which Jesus is establishing.

Caesarea Philippi : This was a city twenty miles north of the Sea of Galilee, built by the Tetrarch Philip about the year 1 A.D.

men . . . is : Jesus asks his disciples what the people are saying about him. He has already worked many miracles and has proved he is more than a prophet. He calls himself the Son of Man, which in Aramaic usage could mean just "a man," but in Jesus' use of it so often there is more than a veiled hint at his messiahship.

they said : The disciples told him what they had heard the people say, and the general impression was that he was one of the prophets or John the Baptist sent back from the dead to prepare for the coming of the Messiah. Evidently the people had not yet recognized him as the Messiah. That he was Elijah the great prophet of the northern kingdom (870–850 B.C.) returned to life, would be based on the words of the prophet Malachi (3 : 23–24). That he was Jeremiah (646–580 B.C.) back from the dead could have come from the vision described in 2 Maccabees (15 : 11–16). And that John the Baptist, who had openly proclaimed himself to be the Precursor of the Messiah, could or should have returned from the underworld to complete his mission, is understandable.

but . . . say : He now wants the opinion of his disciples, who had a much closer acquaintance with him than any of the people.

Simon . . . replied : Peter answers for all the disciples, declaring without any hesitation that they are convinced he is the promised Messiah (translated in Greek as "the Christ"). The added "Son of the living God," not in Mk. (8 : 29) or Lk. (9 : 20), if said by Peter, was not a profession of the divine nature of Christ. It was only after the resurrection that the disciples, Peter included, became convinced of the divine nature of Christ.

At the time the Gospel was written it was part of the creed of all Christians.

flesh and blood : Jesus tells Peter that it was not from human reasoning he had come to acknowledge his messiahship but through divine revelation, from Jesus' Father who is in heaven.

Simon . . . Peter : Jesus addressed the leader of the disciples, first by the name he was known by up to this, "Simon, Son of Jonah"; but Jesus is now naming him "Cepha," a rock, which is translated by "Petros" in the Greek.

and . . . rock : This rock will be the solid foundation of the Church, the community of the new Chosen People which Jesus is about to set up on earth to carry on his work for men. This special privilege is a reward for Simon's confession.

powers of death : The gates of Sheol, the abode of the dead, will be unable to prevent the Church from taking all men from its clutches and giving them eternal life. The old translation "gates of hell" was false as well as misleading.

keys . . . kingdom : The legal possession of the keys of a house was, and is, a sign of power and jurisdiction in that house. See today's first reading.

whatever . . . loose : Jesus goes on to show what this power is. It is a spiritual power by which Peter can impose obligations on people, or remove them. What he does, in virtue of this power, which Jesus is giving him will be approved and ratified in heaven, because it will be a true decision or declaration.

charged the disciples : Jesus did not want the people to know he was the promised Messiah, because their idea of the Messiah was political rather than spiritual, and there was therefore grave danger of an uprising against the ruling Roman authorities if the people thought the Messiah had come.

APPLICATION : Jesus, the true Son of God, became man in order to make all men his brothers and co-heirs with him, to the divine, eternal kingdom. To carry on his divine mission on earth (after he had ascended into heaven), he founded the Church on the twelve Apostles. This Church was to be God's new Chosen People (hence perhaps the twelve Apostles take the place of the heads of the twelve tribes of the Chosen People of old). It was to be made up of all races from all parts of the world. As its mission was to bring the message of salvation to all men, it was to go on until the end of time.

For this Church, this divinely instituted society of human beings, to carry out its mission of helping all men to reach their eternal kingdom, it was necessary to be sure of the road and the aids offered to its members. In other words, the Church should be certain that what it told men to believe and to practice was what God wanted them to believe and to practice. Today's reading from St. Matthew tells us how Christ provided for this necessity. In making Peter the head of the Apostolic College, the foundation-stone of his Church, the guarantor of its stability in the symbol of the keys and the promise that all his decisions would be ratified in heaven, Christ gave him the power of freedom from error when officially teaching the universal Church.

In other words, Peter received the primacy in the Church and the gift of infallibility in his official teaching on matters of faith and morals. As the Church was to continue long after Peter had died, it was rightly understood from the beginning that the privileges given to him and which were necessary for the successful mission of the Church, were given to his lawful successors—the Popes.

This has been the constant belief in the Church from its very beginning. The first Vatican Council solemnly defined this dogma and it was reconfirmed recently in the second Vatican Council. In giving these powers to Peter and to his lawful successors Christ was planning for our needs. In order to preserve and safeguard the right conduct of all its members he provided a central seat of authoritative power in his Church. Through the gift of infallibility he assured us that whatever we were commanded to believe (faith) or to do (morals) would always be what he and his heavenly Father wanted us to believe and to do.

How can we ever thank Christ for these marvelous gifts to his Church, that is, to us? Let us say a fervent : "thank you, Lord; you have foreseen all our needs and provided for them, grant us the grace to do the little part you ask of us in order to continue our progress on the one direct road to heaven."

TWENTY-SECOND SUNDAY OF THE YEAR

FIRST READING : Jeremiah 20 : 7–9. O Lord, thou hast deceived me, and I was deceived; thou art stronger than I, and thou hast prevailed. I have become a laughingstock all the day; everyone mocks me. For whenever I speak, I cry out. I shout, "Violence and destruction!" For the word of the Lord has become for me a reproach and derision all day long. If I say, "I will not mention him, or speak anymore in his name," there is in my heart as it were a burning fire shut up in my bones, and I am weary with holding it in, and I cannot.

EXPLANATION : (On Jeremiah and his difficult mission see the twelfth Sunday of the year). Jeremiah was sent by God "to tear up and to knock down, to destroy and to overthrow" (Jer. 1 : 10). For a man of peace and gentle nature, being continually at war with his own people was a torture of soul which Jeremiah could not avoid. He loved his country, yet he was regarded as a traitor by his own people because, as God's mouthpiece, he had to foretell the dire results that would follow their plan of revolt against the mighty power of Babylon. The grief and torture of soul which his divine mission brought on him was so great that at one time the prophet exclaimed (like Job later) : "a curse on the day when I was born, no blessing on the day my mother bore me" (20 : 14).

In today's reading we hear Jeremiah giving voice to this internal anguish of mind; he hates what he has to say to his people, yet he is compelled by God to say it.

hast deceived me : He feels as if God deceived him when calling him to be his prophet, for God told him, he would "build up and plant" after he had "knocked down and destroyed," but so far he has been knocking down and has done no building. But God's will prevailed for :

stronger than I : God was stronger, and so Jeremiah was compelled to do his will.

laughingstock all day : So far none of his gloomy predictions have come to pass, so the people feel they can despise him and mock him, and this they do all day and every day.

violence . . . destruction : This is the burden of his prophecies, and God delays in fulfilling them.

a reproach . . . derision : Because they think his threats are empty words they laugh at him, and reproach him with disloyalty to his country.

speak . . . name : His natural inclination is to stop being God's mouthpiece and so avoid the reproaches and insults of his fellow-citizens, but :

in my heart . . . fire : He cannot cease to be God's prophet. The power of God within him, moving him to speak, is overpowering. He cannot retain the words of God, he must speak them, for God is mightier than he. The prophet Amos expressed similar feeling and conviction (Am. 3 : 3–8).

APPLICATION : Among all the prophets of the Old Testament Jeremiah is the one who most closely resembled Christ in his sufferings. Other prophets were martyred by their own people, but the whole public life of Jeremiah was one long drawn-out martyrdom. He loved his country and his countrymen, but he had to forewarn them of the fate which would follow from their worldliness and their worldly politics. For this they hated and derided him, and, refusing to listen to God's warning, which he spoke to them, they went headlong toward the destruction of Jeremiah, of Jerusalem with God's temple, and the slavery of exile.

Christ too loved his country and his fellow-Jews. The aim of his mission was to bring them into the new kingdom of God on earth from which they would pass in due course, to God's eternal kingdom. However, they were more interested in worldliness and worldly politics than in their eternal happiness. They refused to see in him the Messiah whom God had promised to their forefathers. They rejected his message as not being from God. They mocked and insulted him during his mission among them, and they ended up by having the pagan Romans nail him to the cross. Christ loved his fellow-Jews notwithstanding their insults and their rejection of him. Sitting on Mount Olivet one day shortly before his crucifixion, "he shed tears over the city and said : If you had only understood . . . the message of peace! but alas it is hidden from your eyes . . . your enemies will not leave one stone standing on another within you, because you did not recognize your opportunity when God offered it (Lk. 19 : 41–44). And again : "Jerusalem, Jerusalem, you that kill the prophets and stone those that are sent to you! How often have I longed to gather your children (your inhabitants) as a hen gathers her brood under her wings, but you refused" (Lk. 13 : 34).

Jeremiah's sufferings, endured because he was God's chosen prophet, should encourage us to bear whatever sufferings the practice of our Christian religion may bring on us. To those around us who ignore God, we too are prophets of God, if we put our Christian faith into daily practice. Christian living is a clear message from God, to those whose lives are totally engrossed in this world. In our daily lives we are God's mouthpieces, preaching the true purpose of life by our actions. We may be mocked and derided for this, but it must not prevent us from carrying out our Christian duty—the giving of good example to our neighbor, whether he accepts it or not.

Like Jeremiah and like our Savior Christ, we must continue to love our neighbors even if they revile and mock us because of our fidelity to God. They especially need our love and our prayers. They are putting their eternal welfare in jeopardy. Our good example, together with our prayers, may be the means God has ordained to bring them to heaven. Let us not be found wanting in this mission, given by God to each one of us. If we are loyal to our faith, during our short spell on earth, we shall merit eternal happiness for ourselves and for those who were influenced by our exemplary lives.

SECOND READING: Romans 12:1-2. I appeal to you therefore, brethren, by the mercies of God, to present your bodies as a living sacrifice, holy and acceptable to God, which is your spiritual worship. Do not be conformed to this world but be transformed by the renewal of your mind, that you may prove what is the will of God, what is good and acceptable and perfect.

EXPLANATION: In the preceding eleven chapters of his letter St. Paul has expounded the blessings and the benefits Christ and Christianity have brought to all men. God's goodness to the descendants of Abraham, the Chosen People of the Old Testament, was marvelous but it was only a shadow, a preparation, for the Christian dispensation. Paul now tells the Roman Christians (converts, for the most part, from paganism) that they must prove themselves worthy of this great favor, they must live truly Christian lives.
I appeal . . . God: Having reminded them of the mercies God has shown them, he now begs them to prove themselves generous in their self-giving.
bodies . . . sacrifice: Their bodies, that is, themselves. They are to offer themselves to God as living victims. The Jewish and pagan sacrifices consisted of dead animals. The Christian worships and honors God by living his daily life in God's love and grace—"doing all for the glory of God." That is worship according to the Spirit—the higher nature of man.
conformed . . . world: They must not follow the standard of the ungodly, the earthly, but instead:
be transformed: They must change the outlook they had on life before their conversion and have a new purpose, a spiritual end in life, which raises them above passing earthly interests.
that . . . prove: In your lives you may experience that you are doing what is "good, acceptable and perfect," which means: you are carrying out God's will, in order one day to become perfect.

APPLICATION: These words were written over nineteen hundred years ago, but they are as obligatory for us and as instructive for us today as they were for the Roman converts of the year 58 A.D. We have the very same Christian life to live as they had. We have the self-same road to travel to heaven and the same marvelous mercies of God to be grateful for. Therefore, we have the same obligation of showing our gratitude to the good God who called us to be followers and co-heirs of his divine Son.

St. Paul tells us how we are to show that gratitude to God. He tells us we must live our lives as true Christians, that is, our daily lives must conform to the will of God. The prime motive in all our actions must ever be the honor and glory of God. When we do this our lives are living sacrifices, we are offering ourselves daily to God. Because God accepts our offering this makes our Christian lives good and acceptable and perfect in his sight.

Is not this too high a standard to set for a weak mortal? How can a man be always thinking of God when he has so many earthly cares and worries which demand his attention? The answer is, of course, that it is exactly by attending to our earthly worries and problems, and by carrying out our duties faithfully, that we honor God. He does not ask us or want us to be always on our knees saying "Lord, Lord." He wants us to work honestly and faithfully and from the right motive.

While we must not imitate the foolish ones who try to make their heaven in this world neither must we despise this world. It is God who gave it with all its products so that we could use it as the testing-ground in which we are to earn our eternal happiness. God does not forbid us to possess and to use the goods of this world : it is precisely for our use that he put them there. It is the abuse, not the lawful use, of this world's goods that is wrong; it is not the possession of earthly goods, but the folly of allowing earthly goods to possess us, that is forbidden.

It is God's will for all Christians that they should always remember to be dedicated to his service by their baptism. They are destined for heaven, and they will reach their destination by justly and honestly using the things of this life, as means to that end and not as ends in themselves.

GOSPEL : Matthew 16 : 21–27. Jesus began to show his disciples that he must go to Jerusalem and suffer many things from the elders and chief priests and scribes, and be killed, and on the third day be raised. And Peter took him and began to rebuke him, saying, "God forbid, Lord! This shall never happen to you." But he turned and said to Peter, "Get behind me, Satan! You are a hindrance to me; for you are not on the side of God, but of men."

Then Jesus told his disciples, "If any man would come after me, let him deny himself and take up his cross and follow me. For whoever would save his life will lose it, and whoever loses his life for my sake will find it. For what will it profit a man, if he gains the whole world and forfeits his life? Or what shall a man give in return for his life? For the Son of man is to come with his angels in the glory of his Father, and then he will repay every man for what he has done."

EXPLANATION : Immediately after Peter's confession that Jesus is the promised Messiah (see last Sunday's Gospel), our Lord tells his disciples that even though he is the Messiah— in fact because he is the Messiah, he has to undergo humiliations, suffering and violent death at the hands of the Jewish authorities in Jerusalem. But he will be raised from the dead on the third day and the victory of the Jewish authorities will be short-lived.

Peter . . . him : Peter, again spokesman for all the disciples, could not imagine his Master, who had such divine power, suffering anything much less death, at the hands of his enemies. The disciples still looked on Christ as a man with divine power, but sent to set up a new earthly kingdom of David—a kingdom which would overcome all enemies, whether pagan Romans or obstinate Jewish leaders. They had not yet grasped the spiritual nature of the kingdom he was establishing. Little wonder then that Peter argued with Jesus; it must have seemed to him that Jesus was joking—how could one who raised the dead to life be himself put to death?

Get . . . Satan : The word Satan in Aramaic, the language used by Christ, means an obstacle, an impediment, not the demonic connotation it now has. Christ tells Peter he is trying to impede God's plan, because God's plan was that Christ should suffer and die in order to earn victory and eternal life for all men.

not . . . of God : Therefore, Peter's outlook (and that of the other disciples)

was a worldly one. He wanted his Master to be a success in this life, whereas God was planning for the eternal life.

take . . . cross : Having silenced Peter (but not having convinced him, as Peter's behavior during our Lord's Passion shows), Jesus goes on to tell his disciples (and the people Mk. 8 : 34) what he expected from his followers. They must imitate him and be ready to suffer any hardship rather than deny him.

save . . . lose it : The follower of Christ who denies his Christian faith in order to save himself from sufferings and temporal death, shall earn for himself eternal death and vice-versa.

gains . . . world : All the possessions, pleasures, and power that this world has to offer, are as nothing compared with the happiness and joy of eternal life.

What . . . give : There is no treasure on earth capable of buying eternal life. Christ has shown us how we can acquire it through God's mercy and infinite goodness : by faithfully following Christ and willingly suffering the hardships of this life for his sake.

come . . . father : Christ refers now to the day of judgement, when as God and man he will come again to reward the good and punish the wicked.

APPLICATION : By becoming man—equal to us in all things save sin—the Son of God joined our human nature to the divine and so made all men his brothers and adopted sons of the Father. From all eternity this was God's plan for mankind. But because sin had entered into the world before the Incarnation took place, the Son of God in his human nature had to suffer the violent death of the cross at the hands of sinners. In this very suffering he became the Lamb of God who took away the sins of the world, as the second-Isaiah had foretold in his "suffering servant" prophecies (Is. 53 : 1–7; 42 : 1–9 etc). His death, because he was God as well as man, was a sacrifice, an atonement, of infinite value, and therefore obtained forgiveness from the Father for all the sins of the human race.

In foretelling his sufferings and death, which took place some months later, Christ intended to prepare his disciples and other followers for what he knew would be for them a severe crisis of faith. He also took occasion from it to remind his disciples, and all others who would follow him, of what their attitude to suffering and death should be. He told them, and us too, that we must be ever ready to accept sufferings in this life, and even an untimely death if that should be demanded of us, rather than deny our Christian faith.

To prove their loyalty to their faith in Christ thousands of Christians in the early Church, and thousands more during persecutions in later centuries, gladly took him at his word and went joyfully to their martyrdom. It is to be hoped that, aided by God's grace, we would all be ready to imitate their example, if called on to prove our fidelity to Christ and our Christian faith. But at the moment what Christ expects and asks of us is that we should bear the sufferings and hardships of daily life cheerfully and gladly for his sake.

This daily carrying of our Christian cross can be, and is for many, a prolonged martyrdom. Poverty, ill-health, cruelty and hardheartedness met with in the home and in one's neighbors, are heavy crosses which only a truly Christian shoulder can bear. But, if we were offered health, happiness, peace, wealth and power for the next fifty or seventy years on this earth, in exchange for an eternal heaven after death, what rational one among us would accept that offer?

Christians know that this life is a period of training, which makes us ready hereafter to receive the eternal reward which Christ has won for us. Every trainee knows that one must endure certain hardships and sufferings in order to merit graduation into one's chosen profession or trade. On our Christian graduation day we shall, please God, hear the welcome words : "Well done good and faithful servant; because you have been faithful in small things, I will trust you with greater, come and join in your Master's happiness" (Mt. 25 : 21). May God grant that every one of us will hear these words of welcome.

TWENTY-THIRD SUNDAY OF THE YEAR

FIRST READING : Ezekiel 33 : 7–9. Thus says the Lord : "You, son of man, I have made a watchman for the house of Israel; whenever you hear a word from my mouth, you shall give them warning from me. If I say to the wicked, O wicked man, you shall surely die, and you do not speak to warn the wicked to turn from his way, that wicked man shall die in his iniquity, but his blood I will require at your hand. But if you warn the wicked to turn from his way, and he does not turn from his way; he shall die in his iniquity, but you will have saved your life."

EXPLANATION : Ezekiel, one of the four major prophets of the Old Testament, prophesied from 593–571 B.C. In 597 he was deported by Nebuchadnezzar from Jerusalem to Babylon together with king Joachin of Judah and most of the nobles of the country. Some four years after arriving in Babylon, God appointed him to speak to his fellow-exiles. The burden of his preaching was that Judah had brought this exile on herself by her infidelity to Yahweh, her God. Worse was still to come. Jerusalem and its temple (which had been desecrated by unworthy priests) would be razed; Judah would cease to exist as a country and all the able-bodied people would be carried as slaves to Babylon. As he (and Jeremiah also) had foretold, all this happened in 587.

Then, in the latter half of his ministry, he began to console the exiles and to promise them that, having undergone their just punishment, they would be restored to their homeland. A new

Jerusalem and a new temple would be built. The people purified by the exile would serve God with a new heart and a new spirit. The heart of stone which they had up to now would be replaced by a heart of flesh (see 11 : 18–19). This part of the prophecy was not completely fulfilled until the coming of Christianity.

Today's quotation from Ezekiel gives us the warning which God gave to his prophets. As God's representatives they have a grave responsibility for their people's salvation.

You . . . man : God calls him "man" to emphasize that he is his servant and agent and must therefore obey God his Master.

watchman . . . Israel : The image is of a sentry placed on a hill-top, or some elevated place, at the time of a threatened invasion. The sentry's task is to give warning to his fellow-citizens the very moment he sees any signs of invasion.

word . . . mouth : The prophet must

make known to the people immediately whatever message God gives him to deliver.

you . . . wicked : God tells his prophet to warn the sinner of the certain damnation that will follow if he does not mend his ways. If the prophet does not do so the sinner will die in his sins, but the prophet will have to share in his damnation.

you . . . your life : On the other hand if the prophet gives God's warning to the sinner and the latter still dies in his sins, the prophet will not bear any responsibility for that man's damnation.

APPLICATION : As Christians we are all God's prophets, God's representatives. We have been given the right and the obligation of letting the light of our faith shine before all men. Whenever the occasions arise we are bound to help our fellowmen on the road to heaven by our good example and charitable advice. This grave obligation falls first on parents in the home. Parents must realize that their children came from God and are destined to return to him. Woe to the parents who give bad example to their children—they will be responsible not only for their own sins but for the sins of the children they led astray.

Today, unfortunately, many of our teenagers seem to have lost interest in the things of God and in their own eternal happiness. Many outside influences are blamed for this, but in ninety per cent of the cases of teenage laxity in faith and morals, the basic cause can be traced to lax and careless parents. The child who grows up in a home where God and his laws are venerated and obeyed, where Christianity is truly lived, will retain this reverence for God and for the Christian faith which his parents taught him.

Parents, therefore, have a terrible responsibility—the eternal welfare of their children is placed in their hands. If through the fault of the parents children miss the eternal happiness prepared for them by God, those parents are certainly risking their future happiness also. There are exceptions, of course; a black sheep can be found among the whitest flock.

Outside of the home all Christians are bound by charity to help their fellowmen. Whether pagan or Christian they are also adopted sons of God and their brothers in Christ. This help is given first and foremost by the good example of a true and upright Christian life. There are thousands in heaven because the example of a good-living neighbor moved them to think seriously of their eternal destiny. We must all be ready, too, to give charitable and kindly advice to an erring neighbor when and where this will have a chance of success. A zealous and truly charitable Christian will find the right occasion for such advice, and his evident charity and kindness will touch and soften even a hardened sinner.

Yes, we Christians are watchmen, sentinels, placed on elevated places to give warning of approaching danger to our brothers, and help our fellow-citizens even if they pay no heed to the warning signal. Nor must we grow tired or despondent because our Christian zeal may often be in vain. Ezekiel carried out his mission of charity for twenty-three years, and Jeremiah for fifty, even though most of their fellow-Jews paid no heed to their words.

Today's lesson is read to remind us

of the grave obligation God places on us. He himself could change the hearts of the lax and the incredulous, but he respects men's freedom. What is more important, he wants to give us a share in the reaping of his harvest. It is only in heaven that we shall realize how much our own salvation depended on the zeal and charity with which we helped our neighbors reach their eternal home.

SECOND READING : Romans 13 : 8–10. Owe no one anything, except to love one another; for he who loves his neighbor has fulfilled the law. The commandments, "You shall not commit adultery, You shall not kill, You shall not steal, You shall not covet," and any other commandment, are summed up in this sentence, "You shall love your neighbor as yourself." Love does no wrong to a neighbor; therefore love is the fulfilling of the law.

EXPLANATION : In the first seven verses of this chapter St. Paul urged the Christian converts of Rome to obey all lawful civil authority. He now turns to the obligation each Christian has of loving his neighbor.

owe . . . love : The obligation of loving all men binds Christians always and everywhere. This love of brother is not to be restricted to our fellow Christians. It was not so among the Jews (Lev. 19 : 18).

fulfilled the law : If one truly loves his neighbor (all neighbors) he cannot violate any of the commandments of the second table of the Decalog. That the love of God comes first is understood; Paul is referring here solely to love of neighbor as he proved by the precepts of the Decalog which he quotes.

adultery . . . murder : Commandments five to ten inclusive are divine precepts regulating our duties and obligations toward our neighbor.

summed up . . . sentence : The man who truly loves his neighbor will not kill him, will not steal his wife or his goods, will not covet his neighbor's goods or wife. "Love does no wrong to a neighbor."

fulfilling of the law : Our Lord himself said to the Pharisees that loving God, and loving neighbor as oneself, fulfills the whole law and the prophets (Mt. 22 : 34–40). St. Paul (who presupposes love of God as an obligation which all Christians carry out), says here that the Christian who exercises love of neighbor not only negatively but also positively, fulfills the law—three parts of the Decalog that relate to one's neighbor.

APPLICATION : Love of neighbor was the hall-mark of Christianity from the very beginning. This love of neighbor presupposed love of God, for if God is not known and loved there can be no basis, no motive for true love of neighbor, which is charity. It's a divine virtue, distinct from natural human love. Human love is based on natural affection as among the members of a family or self-interest, and is always in a closed circuit. Charity extends to the whole human race—nobody can be excluded, for every human being is a child of the same God, the Father of all. Our Christian religion commands us to love all men with a practical love, a love that is ready and glad to help a fellowman in temporal or spiritual need.

There are some among us who would persuade us that even though we ignore or deny God, we can and must love and help our neighbor. This is one of the many substitutes for true religion today. In reality it is the retention of the basic tenet in Christianity, while Christ the founder is discarded. Christian humanism, or fraternal charity, is a supernatural virtue; humanism without Christ is human self-deception. Our natural instincts *may* keep us attached to and interested in the temporal affairs of our family, but what can make us interested in the temporal success of those who are complete strangers to us? To a practicing Christian no man is a complete stranger. We are brothers in Christ, adopted children of God. Our principal interest in all men is not a temporal but a spiritual one. We want them to get to heaven, but to do so they sometimes need a helping hand in this life. Again true Christian charity urges us

to encourage a fellowman suffering from some incurable disease, so that he may bear his sufferings patiently and willingly, thus supplying "what is wanting in the sufferings of Christ" for his own and others' sanctification. Such encouragement would be inhuman in the extreme for humanists who ignore or deny a future life. In such circumstances the defenders of euthanasia are much more humane.

There is no substitute for the Christian law of fraternal charity, just as there is no substitute for the Christian religion. We love our neighbor because God, through Christ's coming on earth, has made us all his children and wants us to be happy with him forever. Because we love God we must do all in our power to see his wish fulfilled. It is love of God then which alone can move us to a disinterested and true love of neighbor. St. John tells us that our love of God can be judged by our active love of neighbor: "if anyone says he loves God and hates (does not love) his brother, he is a liar" (1 Jn. 4:20). How strong, how sincere, is our love of God? The answer depends on how strong, how sincere, is our love of neighbor.

GOSPEL : Matthew 18 : 15–20.   Jesus said to his disciples : "If your brother sins against you, go and tell him his fault, between you and him alone. If he listens to you, you have gained your brother. But if he does not listen, take one or two others along with you, that every word may be confirmed by the evidence of two or three witnesses. If he refuses to listen to them, tell it to the Church; and if he refuses to listen even to the Church, let him be to you as a Gentile and a tax collector. Truly, I say to you, whatever you bind on earth shall be bound in heaven, and whatever you loose on earth shall be loosed in heaven. Again I say to you, if two of you agree on earth about anything they ask, it will be done for them by my Father in heaven. For where two or three are gathered in my name, there am I in the midst of them."

EXPLANATION :   True Christian charity obliges a Christian not only to help his neighbors in their temporal and spiritual needs by alms and by prayer but also to correct an erring brother if his sins are public. If the erring brother refuses the charitable correction, Matthew then outlines what the duty of the Church is. It has power to forgive sin but that power can be effective only if the sinner repents and decides to give up his sinful way of living. He then mentions the efficiency of community prayer (as contrasted with one's private prayer), for Christ is present in the Christian community.

brother . . . you : The words "against you" are textually doubtful and the context here excludes them. There is question, not of a personal offense received, but of unchristian behavior which is bringing scandal in its train.

between you and him : Out of love of God and love of the erring neighbor the Christian who knows of the public sin must speak privately to this sinner and try to get him to realize the evil of his conduct.

if . . . to you : If he heeds your kind warning, he will change his way of living and you will have put him back on the right road to heaven.

one . . . others : In the old law two or three witnesses were necessary for a conviction, one person was not enough. Here the sinner is to be officially reproved, but still in private, to save his good name. If this fails then the Church —the local Christian community—is to act.

if he refuses . . . listen : If he does not repent when officially and publicly told to do so by the Church, he is to be excommunicated (see 1 Cor. 5 : 1–5 where St. Paul excommunicated a public sinner). This process of expelling from the society a member who gave grave scandal was practiced by the Jews and was adopted by the Christian Church, but only after the steps prescribed above.

whatever you bind : The power of the keys given to Peter, and each local church authority (as in this context), is the juridical basis for expelling a member.

again . . . you : This statement of Christ is probably out of context here but is indirectly connected with the preceding counsel inasmuch as it shows the spiritual value and efficiency of community action. The heavenly Father will answer all community prayers, for Christ is present in every community. This does not mean that private prayers will not be answered, but only that community prayer is guaranteed as more efficacious.

APPLICATION : Unfortunately, there are far too many Christians today who pay no heed to the serious obligation of encouraging an erring brother to give up his sinful ways. They shrug it off by saying : "I have more than enough to do to keep myself from sin" or "am I my brother's keeper?" The answer is in this lesson we have just read. We *are* our brothers' keepers, and even if we have many temptations and inclinations to sin we shall not overcome them if we have no time to think of our neighbours' need.

There are, alas, millions of lapsed or luke-warm Christians who could and would have been active members of Christ's mystical body if their neighbors had fulfilled this grave obligation which Christ has imposed on us all. They are now a source of scandal to the weaker and youthful members of the Church, and an impediment to the possible acceptance of the faith by non-Christians. Would the Reformation, which has caused whole countries of the western world to lose almost all faith in Christ and indeed in God, have had such disastrous effects, if those who remained within the Church had put this law of fraternal charity into practice? However, it is no use crying over spilt milk! Let us see our present-day obligations and what we are doing to help our neighbors retain their Christian faith and practice. How much of the indifference to religion which the youth of today seems to be showing is due to lack of parental control and example? How many children of Christian families grow up as practical pagans because their Christian faith meant little or nothing to their parents? It is in the home that the religion of the next generation is firmly established or lost. When parents are loyal to their faith in their daily lives, their children will, as a rule, be loyal to it too; where parents are careless and lax their children will be still more careless and more lax.

Parents! the first neighbors and fellow-Christians whom you must kindly and charitably correct are your own children. Their future salvation and your own too will depend on how well you fulfill this obligation. Parents who are obedient to Christ in this will find time and many opportunities to have a charitable word of help for an erring neighbor outside their household. On the other hand, the lax parents, who give little or no thought to getting to heaven or to their children getting there in God's good time, will hardly bother with their neighbor's salvation. Thus this cancer of infidelity and irreligion grows and spreads.

Let each one of us look into his past conduct in relation to this law of charity. Have we really tried to help our fellow-men on the road to heaven? Have we given them the good example of a truly Christian way of living? Have we offered advice and encouragement when it was needed, and correction in private where that was possible? If so "we have gained our brother." We have brought a prodigal son back to a loving Father and that loving Father will repay us a hundred-fold in this life and especially in the next.

TWENTY-FOURTH SUNDAY OF THE YEAR

FIRST READING: Sirach 27:30–28:7. Anger and wrath, these are abominations, and the sinful man will possess them. He that takes vengeance will suffer vengeance from the Lord, and he will firmly establish his sins. Forgive your neighbor the wrong he has done, and then your sins will be pardoned when you pray. Does a man harbor anger against another, and yet seek for healing from the Lord? Does he have no mercy toward a man like himself, and yet pray for his own sins? If he himself, being flesh, maintains wrath, who will make expiation for his sins? Remember the end of your life, and cease from enmity, remember destruction and death, and be true to the commandments. Remember the commandments, and do not be angry with your neighbor; remember the covenant of the Most High, and overlook ignorance.

EXPLANATION: On Sirach, the author of these verses, see the Feast of the Holy Family (Sunday in the Octave of Christmas). In the verses read today, Sirach tells us that we must forgive our neighbor if we want God to forgive us our own sins. We must be merciful if we hope to obtain mercy from God. We must not seek revenge on a neighbor lest God should take vengeance on us. If we remember our end in life we will keep God's commandments and we will not be angry with a neighbor who offends us.
Anger and wrath: Only a sinful man can be angry with a neighbor because of some offense the neighbor has committed against him.
takes vengeance: The man who repays his neighbor in kind must expect God to do likewise to him.
establish his sins: God will hold his sins against him because, instead of forgiving his neighbor, he took vengeance on him.
Forgive . . . neighbor: If you forgive your neighbor then God will listen to your request for forgiveness. "Forgive us our trespasses as we forgive those who trespass against us."
harbor . . . mercy: How foolish is he who bears anger in his heart against a neighbor and refuses merciful forgiveness, and yet expects God to forgive and blot out his own effenses against God!
maintains . . . expiation: The angry man's sins will not be forgiven because God does not listen to a man who is angry with his neighbor.
remember . . . your life: Although Sirach, like the Jews of his day, had no clear idea of the future life, he emphasizes the importance of the state of one's conscience at the moment of death. In

7 : 36 he says, "In everything you do remember your end and you will never sin," and in 11 : 28, "call no man fortunate before his death, it is by his end that a man will be known." In this verse today he tells the man who is still at enmity with his neighbor to meditate on his end (his death) and he will then see what folly it is for him to be angry with any man.

the commandments : God commanded the Jews to love God and to love their neighbor.

covenant . . . High : The infinite God condescended to make a pact, a covenant, with the sinful Israelites. Because of this covenant, again and again he forgave them their sins of neglect and disloyalty. Surely a mere man must forgive a fellowman, an equal, who has offended him, if God the Creator is so merciful as to forgive us miserable, sinful creatures!

APPLICATION : Is there one among us here who does not need and cannot profit by the advice of this saintly author? He lived about two hundred years before Christ came on earth. He had not the advantage of the example of God's infinite love and mercy which was manifested in the Incarnation and practiced to a sublime degree by the Incarnate Son of God. But he can put all of us to shame by his deep understanding of the law of charity and mercy which he placed before his fellow-Jews.

We have seen God's infinite mercy and forgiveness in sending his Son to raise us up to the dignity of adopted sonship, when we were sunk in sin. We have seen with what superhuman patience Christ put up with the offenses and insults of the leaders of those he had come to save. We cannot forget his prayer for forgiveness, offered to his Father as he slowly and painfully died on the cross. This was a prayer for the very ones who had so unjustly and cruelly condemned him to that death.

We Christians, who claim to follow and to imitate Christ, are absolutely dependent on the mercy and forgiveness of God to obtain salvation. Yet we can forget our leader and our faith when a fellow sinner offends us. We turn on our unfortunate fellowman and use every means in our power to "get our own back," to wreak vengeance upon him. We forget the command and the example Christ has given us, and we think only of our own offended pride. By so doing we are gravely offending the infinite God because we are violating one of his basic commandments.

While we expect mercy and forgiveness from the infinite God whom we have offended, we often refuse a brother even a small measure of mercy and forgiveness. This is unchristian, unreasonable, and it is fatal for us, if we persevere in this state of mind. St. John says : "To hate your brother is to be a murderer, and murderers as you know do not have eternal life in them (1 Jn. 3 : 15). While we are heaping just punishment, as we think, on our fellowman who offended us, it is on ourselves that we are heaping the more serious punishment; we are excluding ourselves from God's mercy and God's eternal kingdom.

"Forgive your neighbor . . . and your sins will be pardoned when you pray," the saintly Sirach tells us today. Our divine Lord repeated this divine counsel when he told his disciples, and us, to say : "Forgive us our trespasses as we forgive those who trespass against us."

Let the Christian who continues to refuse forgiveness to those who offended him never say that prayer, because what he is saying is, " God do not forgive me as I don't forgive my neighbor." This is calling God's curse down on his own head. God forbid that any one of us could be so foolish as to let our offended pride prevent us from obtaining God's forgiveness. Our own offenses against God should make us humble enough to be ready to forgive any offense committed by a neighbor against us. We should not only forgive, but should also be ready to follow our Savior's example and to pray to our heavenly Father saying, "God, please forgive all those who have offended and injured us, they did not know what they were doing."

SECOND READING : Romans 14 : 7–9. None of us lives to himself, and none of us dies to himself. If we live, we live to the Lord, and if we die we die to the Lord; so then, whether we live or whether we die, we are the Lord's. For to this end Christ died and lived again, that he might be Lord both of the dead and of the living.

EXPLANATION : In these three verses Paul emphasizes the fact that through our baptism we have been made members of Christ's mystical body, we have become brothers of Christ, intimately united with him in his death and resurrection. Whether living or dead (for death is but the beginning of the new eternal life) we belong to Christ. It was for this purpose, to unite all men closely to himself not only in this life but especially in the next, that Christ became man and "dwelt among us."

lives to himself : As baptized Christians we belong to Christ. We are no longer mere earthly creatures. Our earthly death will not be the end; it will not separate us from Christ, rather it will unite us forever with him.

Christ died and lived again : It was to make us heirs of heaven, that Christ died and rose from the dead—the guarantor of our resurrection.

Lord . . . living : Not only those still on earth, but also all those who have died in God's friendship, belong to Christ. He is the Lord of all, for he has conquered death. He has earned eternal life for all men.

APPLICATION : In these short verses St. Paul reminds the Romans, and us too, of the fundamental privilege which the Incarnation has conferred on us. Too often, perhaps, the Incarnation has been equated with the redemption in the restricted sense of making atonement for our sins. By his life and death Christ did atone for all the sins of the world. But he did something much more basic for our welfare : he fulfilled God's plan for our elevation to adopted sonship. When the Son of God took our human nature that human nature was united with the Godhead and we became brothers of Christ. We were given a share with God's real Son in the Father's kingdom. We ceased to be creatures only; we became intimately associated with Christ and therefore with God. Our earthly death (which would have been the end for us if God in his infinite generosity had not decreed otherwise) cannot now separate us from Christ and God. By his victory over death—his resurrection—Christ has obtained a resurrection for all men.

Today, St. Paul's words recall this joyful truth to our minds. We are no longer individual creatures with a few years to live on earth : we have an eternity of life and of happiness awaiting us when we die. Death has no longer any terrors for a true Christian. As the preface of the requiem mass says : "by death life is not taken away but is changed." Our earthly death is the door through which we enter into eternal life. Therefore, instead of being an occasion for grief and tears it should be an occasion for rejoicing. It means not that someone has left this earth and lost this temporal life but that one

of Christ's brothers has reached heaven and gained heaven and gained eternal life and happiness.

If we meditate more often on the basic effect which the Incarnation has had on us—raising us up to sonship with God and the possibility of an eternal life in God's kingdom, we will be able to face the trials of life with greater courage; we will resist temptations to sin more strongly—for sin alone can prevent us from gaining possession of our eternal heritage—and we will see in our earthly death not a disaster but the welcome call of God to become a chosen member of his heavenly household.

If we live a truly Christian life, we live to the Lord and if we die in God's grace, as we shall if we have lived a truly Christian life, we die in the Lord. What more could the infinite love of God do for us? The little he asks us to do in return is a trifling wage to pay for such an eternal reward.

GOSPEL : Matthew 18 : 21–35. Peter came up and said to him, "Lord, how often shall my brother sin against me, and I forgive him? As many as seven times?" Jesus said to him, "I do not say to you seven times, but seventy times seven.

"Therefore the kingdom of heaven may be compared to a king who wished to settle accounts with his servants. When he began the reckoning, one was brought to him who owed him ten thousand talents; and as he could not pay, his lord ordered him to be sold, with his wife and children and all that he had, and payment to be made. So the servant fell on his knees, imploring him, 'Lord, have patience with me, and I will pay you everything.' And out of pity for him the lord of that servant released him and forgave him the debt. But that same servant, as he went out, came upon one of his fellow servants who owed him a hundred denarii; and seizing him by the throat he said, 'Pay what you owe.' So his fellow servant fell down and besought him, 'Have patience with me, and I will pay you.' He refused and went and put him in prison till he should pay the debt. When his fellow servants saw what had taken place, they were greatly distressed, and they went and reported to their lord all that had taken place. Then his lord summoned him and said to him, 'You wicked servant! I forgave you all that debt because you besought me; and should not you have had mercy on your fellow servant, as I had mercy on you?' And in anger his lord delivered him to the jailers, till he should pay all his debt. So also my heavenly Father will do to every one of you, if you do not forgive your brother from your heart."

EXPLANATION : Our Lord had been teaching the disciples how necessary it was to be ever ready to forgive their fellow-men who injured them. Peter, always the interpreter of the group, asks if seven times would not be enough to forgive an enemy; anyone who offended more often than that could hardly deserve forgiveness! Christ tells him there is no limit to the forgiveness we must be ready to give our neighbor. He then tells a parable to bring out the lesson : unless we forgive our neighbor God will not forgive us. If we take revenge on an offending neighbor God will take revenge on us.

seven times : This was much in Peter's estimation.

seventy times seven : Our Lord indicates times without number when he uses this figure.

kingdom . . . compared : All Christ's parables were intended to illustrate and exemplify the "kingdom of heaven" which has two phases, the Church here on earth and the eternal kingdom where all the faithful will be gathered together forever. This parable deals with the Church here on earth. We shall be forgiven our sins by the merciful God if we are merciful to our fellowmen who offend us. But God will not forgive the Christian who refuses to forgive his fellowman.

out of pity . . . debt : The king, being very merciful, forgave a servant a huge debt of ten thousand talents—over a million dollars in present-day currency —a debt he could never pay.

seizing . . . throat : As he was leaving the king's presence freed from this huge debt, he met a fellow-servant, who owed him the paltry sum of a hundred pennies, and demanded immediate payment under pain of manhandling.

have patience . . . you : The fellow-servant asked for mercy but he got none; instead he was cast into the debtors' prison.

I forgave you . . . fellow-servant : The king, being informed of what the first servant had done, was angry with him and cast him into prison because, having pleaded for and obtained a great mercy himself, he refused even a small mercy to his fellowman.

my heavenly . . . to you : Christ applies the lesson of the parable to his followers. If they do not forgive their brothers, God will not forgive them. Their sins are far more grievous, as they are committed against God, and thus greater than any offense a fellowman can commit against his brother.

APPLICATION : On reading or hearing this story of the merciless servant, each one of us would rightly judge him a mean, low type of man, a heartless man, who puts himself outside the pale of mercy. He throttled his fellow-servant for a paltry debt of ten dollars, and would not listen to the poor man's plea for mercy. When we hear what the king did to this heartless servant we heartily approve and say : "It served him right, he got what he richly deserved."

We had better stop and think for a moment today and reflect that we ourselves may be that merciless servant described in the parable. Every time we have sinned mortally we have incurred an unpayable debt to God. Each time we have received absolution we have come out of God's courtroom as free men. A weight greater than a million dollar debt has been lifted from our shoulders. A fate worse than generations of earthly imprisonment—that is, eternal slavery—has been spared us because of God's loving, infinite mercy. How then can it happen that we could be so heartless, mean, and foolish as to refuse to forgive a neighbor for some offense he has committed against us?

Yet it happens, and it may be that there are some among us here today who continue to have enmity in their hearts against neighbors who offended them. In their hard-heartedness they cannot get themselves to forgive and forget. Are these not following in the footsteps of the merciless servant? Will they not receive the punishment of the merciless servant—a punishment richly deserved? This will be the fate of all unforgiving Christians; they will meet an unforgiving God when they are called to settle their accounts.

That day has not yet come for us. We still have time to put our affairs in order. We still can forgive all our enemies from our heart. If we do not, we are cutting ourselves off from the possibility of having our own sins and offenses forgiven by God. We have the solemn word of our divine Lord for this in the lesson he draws from the parable : "So also my heavenly Father will do to every one of you (that is, deliver us up to eternal slavery) if you do not forgive your brother from your heart."

TWENTY-FIFTH SUNDAY OF THE YEAR

FIRST READING : Isaiah 55 : 6–9. "Seek the Lord while he may be found, call upon him while he is near; let the wicked forsake his way, and the unrighteous man his thoughts; let him return to the Lord, that he may have mercy on him, and to our God, for he will abundantly pardon. For my thoughts are not your thoughts, neither are your ways my ways, says the Lord. For as the heavens are higher than the earth, so are my ways higher than your ways and my thoughts than your thoughts."

EXPLANATION : On second-Isaiah, see eighteenth Sunday of the year. In this text the prophet urges the Chosen People to seek Yahweh, to come close to him in friendship. To do this the sinner must abandon his evil ways. He need not fear : Yahweh is "rich in forgiving," he will forgive all sins of a repentant sinner. Though he is infinite and transcendent, yet he can and does come close to and is a true friend of all who seek him. He is a personal God, not an abstract idea.

while . . . found : God is ever there, but our span of life is very limited and it is only while we are on this earth that we can get God's grace, pardon and friendship. He is near us now as a kind father and a loving benefactor. Let us approach him while we have time.

forsake his ways : To approach near to God the sinner must give up his evil deeds, evil thoughts and intentions for :

have . . . him : If the sinner does not repent of his sins, even the infinitely loving God cannot have mercy on him, but if he repents God will most gladly do his part, he "will abundantly pardon."

my thoughts not your . . . : There were among the Chosen People sinners who thought their sins were so bad that not even God could forgive them. The Lord himself says that this is not so, for his mercy, understanding and love are infinite. In comparison, our mercy and love are limited and puny.

my ways . . . ways : Even though God made man to his own image and likeness, God is not like man—he is infinitely superior and man has not the capacity to understand the workings of God's mind. His thoughts are not like our thoughts, his manner of acting is not like ours.

APPLICATION : There are (and there always have been) intelligent people in our world who, because of the transcendence and infinity of God, cannot imagine him as a true friend of mortal man—a Father who takes a personal interest in man's spiritual and temporal concerns. For them, therefore, the idea of man praying to God is utter folly. The trouble with such people is that because of their preconceived idea of God's infinity and transcendence they cannot admit that he has revealed himself to us.

Through the revelation he gave to the Patriarchs and prophets God has told us many things we need to know about himself and about our purpose in life. He has also sent his divine Son as man to prove to us the interest, love and mercy he has in abundance for us all. Yes, God is infinite, supreme and away beyond any idea we can form of him. The important concept of himself which revelation and the Incarnation impress on our minds is that he is at the same time a loving Father who wants to share his eternal happiness with his adopted children—all mankind.

He is transcendent and infinite in his nature, but in his relations with us he is a father and the truest friend we could ever have. If the Jews knew this before the Incarnation (today's exhortation of the prophet shows that they did) how much more clearly and more convincingly is it not known to us, after Christ's coming on earth. "He did not spare his own son but gave him up for us all" (Rom. 8 : 32). Can any Christian have the slightest doubt of God's personal interest in him? We may not always understand God's ways of acting and be tempted to ask: "Why should the innocent suffer, why should cruel tyrants live and prosper, why should the father or mother of a young family die? and so on. Our faith and our conviction that as a loving Father God is ever acting for our good, should allay these doubts.

God is ever near us then in this life, and if we remain near to him while on this earth we can trust in his love and goodness to keep us near him forever in heaven.

SECOND READING : Philippians 1 : 20–24; 27. Now as always Christ will be honored in my body, whether by life or by death. For to me to live is Christ, and to die is gain. If it is to be life in the flesh, that means fruitful labor for me. Yet which I shall choose I cannot tell. I am hard pressed between the two. My desire is to depart and be with Christ, for that is far better. But to remain in the flesh is more necessary on your account. Only let your manner of life be worthy of the gospel of Christ.

EXPLANATION : Philippi, a Roman colony, and important town of Macedonia, was the site of the first Christian church in Europe. During his second missionary journey (50–54 A.D.), St. Paul, in a vision, was called by a Macedonian to come over from Asia (across the Dardanelles) to bring them the gospel (Acts 16 : 9). This Paul did and in a short while he had a flourishing church in Philippi. The Philippians were the only people from whom he accepted financial help for his missionary work, for he dreaded being accused of preaching for personal gain, and he must therefore have been on very intimate terms with them. St. Paul wrote the letter, from which today's reading is taken, from a prison cell in Rome (61–63 A.D.), or possibly Ephesus (56 A.D.). It is a friendly letter, giving some news of his work to the converts in Philippi, warning them against certain enemies of the faith and exhorting them to remain humble.

Christ . . . body : Paul does not yet know whether his imprisonment will end in his death (execution) or liberation, but in either case it will be for the honor and glory of Christ. His death will honor Christ, for he freely accepts it, and if he is liberated he will continue to spread the name and the gospel of Christ.

live . . . gain : If he continues to live it will be a life spent for and in Christ.

If he is put to death it will mean reaping his eternal reward—a great personal gain surely.

choose, I cannot tell : He is in a dilemma : both prospects are attractive to him. However, "to depart and be with Christ . . . is far better," he says, therefore more preferable. Yet "to remain is more necessary on your account" : the needs of his newly-converted and the needs of so many others not yet converted make it necessary that he should continue to live and preach the gospel.

let your . . . Christ : For their part, no matter what happens to himself, the Philippians by their daily manner of living, must prove themselves worthy of the blessings of Christianity.

APPLICATION : The Church has chosen these verses of St. Paul to remind us that as Christians our whole life and our very death must be for Christ and in Christ. St. Paul's life, which was so completely dedicated to Christ, is set before us as a model—a model, however, which most of us can only imitate from afar. While we are not asked to give up home and family and go among the pagans to bring Christ to them, we are expected to live our Christian lives daily in the love and grace of God and Christ.

This, of course, is not as easy as it sounds. This world and its attractions are very close to us. We are hemmed in by worldly interests and cares. We seem to have little time for thinking and planning for the world to come, or for the things of God. Yet, Paul's life was a very busy one too. He had to eat and sleep and by the work of his hands provide for his bodily upkeep. He had worries in plenty—worries and cares for his newly-converted, worries caused by

enemies who tried hard to impede the spread of the gospel. He had trials and sufferings, including scourgings and stonings and two or three gaol-terms.

This surely was no life of leisure. From 39 A.D., the year of his conversion, to 69 A.D.—thirty years, Paul labored incessantly to make Christ and his message known to all men. He established Christian communities in most of the principal centers of Syria, Asia Minor, and Greece. He did much to spread and build up the Church in Rome, and, between his release from his Roman imprisonment (620 A.D.) and his death in 69, probably went as far as Spain. He was especially successful among the pagan peoples and has been called the Apostle of the Gentiles because of this.

St. Paul is, therefore, our model in a special way. It was through him that the faith reached our Gentile ancestors and eventually came to us. The best way we could thank him, the way that would give him greatest joy, would be to try to love Christ and to live every day of our lives for Christ. This will not mean that we must spend all day long on our knees or in Church; it will mean faithfully fulfilling the duties of our vocation in life out of love for God and Christ.

Paul's vocation in life was to preach the gospel, the good news of salvation, to as many as possible. Our duty is to live according to that gospel and thus earn the eternal salvation put within our reach by the Incarnation. If we do this faithfully by living in peace and charity, loving God and neighbor, we too are missionaries, for our good example will move many to imitate us. "Let your manner of life be worthy of the gospel of Christ," St. Paul said to the Philippians. This exhortation is repeated to us in today's reading. It is by our daily manner of living we prove that we appreciate what Christianity means to us; it is by carrying out our daily tasks for the honor and glory of God, that we can show we are worthy of the divine gift of the faith which Christ has given to us through his great apostle St. Paul.

GOSPEL : Matthew 20 : 1–16. Jesus spoke this parable to his disciples : "The kingdom of heaven is like a householder who went out early in the morning to hire laborers for his vineyard. After agreeing with the laborers for a denarius a day, he sent them into his vineyard. And going out about the third hour he saw others standing idle in the market place; and to them he said, 'You go into the vineyard too, and whatever is right I will give you.' So they went. Going out again about the sixth hour and the ninth hour, he did the same. And about the eleventh hour he went out and found others standing; and he said to them, 'Why do you stand here idle all day?' They said to him, 'Because no one has hired us.' He said to them, 'You go into the vineyard too.' And when evening came, the owner of the vineyard said to his steward, 'Call the laborers and pay them their wages, beginning with the last, up to the first.' And when those hired about the eleventh hour came, each of them received a denarius. Now when the first came, they thought they would receive more; but each of them also received a denarius. And on receiving it they grumbled at the householder, saying, 'These last worked only one hour, and you have made them equal to us who have borne the burden of the day and the scorching heat.' But he replied to one of them, 'Friend, I am doing you no wrong; did you not agree with me for a denarius? Take what belongs to you, and go; I choose to give to this last as I give to you. Am I not allowed to do what I choose with what belongs to me? Or do you begrudge my generosity?' So the last will be first, and the first last."

EXPLANATION : Our Lord used many parables—stories about everyday affairs, well-known to his hearers—to illustrate or bring out a spiritual message.

The spiritual truth our Lord wanted to teach all the Jews, but especially the Pharisees, was that the life of eternal happiness is a sheer gift of God's generosity. It cannot be earned by any man. The fact that the Jews were the Chosen People of God up to then was no guarantee that their future was assured, and the fact that other nations were heathens and sinners hitherto was no impediment to their entrance into heaven provided they turned to God and his Son.

early . . . to hire : It was customary for workers to assemble at daybreak in the squares of cities and towns, where farmers and vine-growers would hire them for a day's work. The hours of day mentioned in the story would equal 6 a.m., 9 a.m., 12 noon, 3 p.m., and 5 p.m. Work ended at 6 p.m.

agreed . . . laborers : He made a contract with the first men he hired at 6 a.m. to work the full day for a denarius. This was the standard wage at the time.

whatever is right : The workers who came at 9 a.m., 12, 3 p.m. and 5 p.m. did not demand a contract (they could not, as part of the day was gone), but the hirer promised them a just wage.

beginning . . . last : The hirer told his steward to call the workers together and to pay first the ones who had worked only one hour. This was done so that the full-day workers would see those who had worked only one hour getting a full day's pay. Had they themselves been paid first they would have gone off and not noticed what happened.

us who . . . burden : They felt they should get twelve denarii if those who had worked only one hour got a denarius.

did you . . . me : The hirer shows there is no injustice. They got their full day's pay as agreed upon.

begrudge . . . generosity : If he gave a full day's pay to those who hadn't worked a full day, this simply was generosity on his part. The money was his to do with as he pleased. He was not unjust to those who grumbled.

so . . . first : Christ now applies the lesson : those who up to now had not been God's Chosen People were being called to that privilege, while the Jews (especially their leaders) would find themselves excluded because they rejected the Messiah whom God sent them. It was not God who excluded them, they excluded themselves.

APPLICATION : The call to the vineyard (to the Church), through God's gift of faith and the sacrament of baptism, is a gift for which we can never sufficiently thank God. If we remain in the vineyard and labor honestly, that is, if we cooperate with the actual graces God is continually giving us, we are assured of reaching heaven when our earthly days are ended. The work we have to do in God's vineyard is the fulfilling of the duties of our state in life. By carrying out these duties faithfully and honestly we are doing the will of God and earning heaven. The greater part of our day and indeed of our life, will be taken up with tasks of themselves worldly, but these tasks when done in the state of grace and with the intention of honoring God, have a supernatural value. For this we have to thank God for his goodness and generosity.

He could have made the attainment of heaven so much more difficult. He could have demanded extraordinary mortifications and renunciations and the reward (heaven) would still be exceedingly great. Instead he allows us to live our everyday life, to enjoy the love and friendship of our family and friends, to satisfy the natural desires of our bodies, within the commandments, and yet to merit a supernatural reward while so doing. As he tells us through St. Paul : "whether you eat or drink or whatever else you do, do all to the glory of God (1 Cor. 10 : 31).

Looking back on our past life, how many years have we really given to God since we came to the use of reason? Those school years, the time spent learning a trade or profession, the weeks, months, years working in an office or factory or farm, the hours among the pots and pans in the kitchen—have we earned some credit in heaven for all of this, or is it all crossed off our pay-sheet through lack of right intention or through sin?

If so, those years are lost to us. We were "idle" all that time. Today's parable, however, should give us new hope and courage. It may be the sixth or the ninth or even the eleventh hour of our life but we can still earn heaven if we listen to God's call and set to work diligently in his vineyard. If we put our conscience right with God today and resolve to be loyal to him from now on he will be as generous to us, as the parable promises.

TWENTY-SIXTH SUNDAY OF THE YEAR

FIRST READING : Ezekiel 18 : 25–28. Thus says the Lord : "You say, 'The way of the Lord is not just.' Hear now, O house of Israel : Is my way not just? Is it not your ways that are not just? When a righteous man turns away from his righteousness and commits iniquity, he shall die for it; for the iniquity which he has committed he shall die. Again, when a wicked man turns away from the wickedness he has committed and does what is lawful and right, he shall save his life. Because he considered and turned away from all the transgressions which he had committed, he shall surely live, he shall not die."

EXPLANATION : A notion very prevalent among the Jews, all through their history, was that the sins of parents were punished in their children. Even the Apostles had not rid their minds of this erroneous opinion. When they saw the man who was born blind they asked their Master : "Rabbi, who sinned this man or his parents, that he was born blind?" (Jn. 9 : 1–2). Ezekiel tells his audience that each man is responsible for his own sins. As each man has a free-will, the good man may foolishly turn to sin, and likewise the sinner may repent and live a good life.

Thus . . . Lord : This is an expression found frequently in the prophets to show that it is not their own thoughts but God's word they are speaking.

way . . . not just : Because they had convinced themselves that God punished a man for sins he did not commit, they held that God was acting unjustly, which would be so if that opinion of theirs were true. But it is :

your ways . . . just : They each had their own sins, they walked the way of injustice, and it was for their own sins, therefore, that they were punished.

he shall die : The prophet was most probably not thinking of eternal death here, as the Jews had only very vague ideas of the future life, but an early death was usually looked on as a punishment for sins just as a long life on earth was deemed a reward for virtue.

wicked . . . away : As the saintly man can become a sinner, so can the sinner become a saint, and thus save himself from an early death.

APPLICATION : There is something frightening, but yet something very necessary, for each one of us in this reading today. Each one of us is responsible to God for every one of his actions. In the presence of our fellowmen we are very much inclined to blame others for our wrongdoings, or at least to share the blame with them. But when our actions are judged by God we stand alone, in compete isolation from all others. While it is true that the bad example of parents, or of companions, may play a part in our guilt, it is our will, our personal decision, and not that bad example, that produces a sin. On the other hand, we may be the children of saintly parents and our companions through life may be exemplary Christians, but unless we willingly and knowingly act like them we will not reach heaven. Each man, therefore, is fully responsible for his own actions, and the just God will punish or reward each individual according to his actions.

While it is depressing and disconcerting to learn that the good and holy can turn from God and commit sin, this very thought should make us vigilant and watchful over ourselves and our actions.

Knowing our weakness and our general inclination to do what is wrong, should help us to look for help where it can be found—in the bountiful mercy of God. He will never desert the man who is sincerely anxious to serve him. On the other hand, the word of God telling us through the prophet, that a sinner may turn away from his wickedness, should be a great consolation for most of us who have often offended God. God holds no enmity against sinners. He is ever ready to take them back to his bosom. He sends grace after grace to them to help and encourage them to come back to the source and the author of eternal life.

There is not, and there never was, a man on earth who did not want to live on forever if possible. We believers know it *is* possible because God has told us that he has arranged it so for us. Eternal life, "where tears will be wiped away and death will be no more," is awaiting each one of us after our earthly death, on the one condition that we die in God's friendship. As we do not know the moment death will strike us, our only guarantee of dying in God's friendship is that we live in that friendship always. This we could never do on our own but we are not on our own. God is ever with us to strengthen us, and to pardon and lift us up again, if through human weakness we stumble on the road. Christ has left to his Church the sacrament of reconciliation, by the use of which the greatest sinner can be restored to God's friendship, if he repents and resolves to mend his ways.

If any Christian dies in his sins and forfeits eternal happiness, he can blame nobody but himself. If, during his time on earth, he refused to accept the mercy and forgiveness God offered him so often, he must now accept the sentence of condemnation which the just judge has to impose on him.

SECOND READING: Philippians 2:1–11. If there is any encouragement in Christ, any incentive of love, any participation in the Spirit, any affection and sympathy, complete my joy by being of the same mind, having the same love, being in full accord and of one mind. Do nothing from selfishness or conceit, but in humility count others better than yourselves. Let each of you look not only to his own interests, but also to the interests of others. Have this mind among yourselves, which was in Christ Jesus, who, though he was in the form of God, did not count equality with God a thing to be grasped, but emptied himself, taking the form of a servant, being born in the likeness of men. And being found in human form he humbled himself and became obedient unto death, even death on a cross. Therefore God has highly exalted him and bestowed on him the name which is above every name, that at the name of Jesus every knee should bow, in heaven and on earth and under the earth, and every tongue confess that Jesus Christ is Lord, to the glory of God the Father.

EXPLANATION: On the Philippians see last Sunday's second reading. In today's extract from this letter, St. Paul is urging his new converts to live in the unity of love and mutual charity. Each one must esteem his neighbor as of more importance than himself and be ready to help him in every way. In doing this, they are only imitating (from afar) their Savior Christ Jesus who although Creator became a creature, though Master he made himself a slave —all for love of us. For this, God exalted him at the resurrection and placed him—the Incarnate God—at his right hand, in the principal place of glory in heaven, to be revered and honored by all angels and men forever.

If . . . encouragement: Paul appeals to his converts to live in true Christian love and unity: through their participation in Christ, through their love for God, their fellowship in the Holy Spirit, and their affection for himself as their Apostle.

selfishness or conceit: They must put the interests of their neighbors before their own interests. They must never put themselves first.

Have . . . yourselves: Paul has a model

for humility and putting others before themselves. He now recommends (as something they had already learned) the humiliation of Christ. It was for love of us, for our benefit, that Christ became man. He hid his divinity and became "like us in all things save sin." He goes on then to describe this humiliation of the Son of God.

though . . . God : Though his nature was divine :

emptied himself : He did not think he should not deprive himself (for a while) of the external honor due to his divine sonship. He hid his divine glory while not ceasing to be God.

taking . . . servant : He took on human nature, the nature of one of his creatures, by being born of a human mother.

humbled . . . death : He became not only the obedient servant of the Father, but submitted himself even to spiteful men who put him to death.

on a cross : This was the cruelest and most shameful of deaths at that time— the very nadir in humiliation for one who was God.

God has . . . him : St. Paul had previously taught the truths of the sufferings, death and resurrection of Jesus, so he does not go into details here.

name . . . name : From his lowly status of the suffering servant he is once more given back to his status of divine glory. He is, therefore, above every other being, so that all creatures must revere him as they revere God. He is God. He was always God. What lay hidden during his earthly sojourn is now manifest once more, and the assumed human nature partakes in the divine glory.

Jesus . . . Father : The divinity of him who appeared on earth as a mere man is now made manifest once more. The God-man, Jesus Christ, who brought external glory to his eternal Father through his earthly mission of love, is now next to the Father in heaven (see Is. 45 : 23).

APPLICATION : The basic dogma of our Christian religion is that Christ, who was born of the Virgin Mary in Bethlehem, spent his childhood and youth in Nazareth, traveled through the valleys and over the hills of Palestine preaching the good news of their eternal salvation to men, that he was the Son of God in human nature. During his public life he often claimed to be the Son of God. Because this title has often been given to men, however, and because he was so really human, even his closest disciples did not understand this claim in its real, strict meaning. His enemies noted the claim, but not believing it either, they looked on it as a blasphemous statement and used it as a justification for crucifying him; "we have a law," the Jews replied to Pilate, "and according to that law he ought to die, because he has claimed to be the Son of God" (Jn. 19 : 7).

His resurrection from the dead changed the Apostles and his other followers. His appearance to them convinced them that he was indeed the real Son of God, who had taken human nature in order to raise mankind up to divine sonship and to take away the sins of the world through his sufferings and death. From Pentecost day their one and only mission in life was to bring this good news—the gospel of Christ—to all men. This they faithfully did, in spite of persecutions, sufferings and martyrdom, for what could a shortening of earthly life mean to men who looked forward anxiously to an eternal life!

We of the twentieth century have the

same faith which inspired and sustained the first-century Apostles. That faith is solidly built on the same unchangeable truth. In order to carry out the divine Father's plan to raise mankind to a superhuman status, the status of adopted sonship on earth, Christ the Son of God, took human nature. That adopted sonship was to be followed after death, by a sharing in the eternal kingdom of God. This is the central truth of our Christian religion. This is the basic motivation of our Christian lives. Our kingdom is not of this world; we are living and working for the kingdom prepared for us by God's eternal and infinite love.

God grant that we will never forget this truth, never cease to thank our divine Lord for all he has done for us. The only true and acceptable thanks we can offer him, is our true appreciation of the honor he has conferred on us through his Incarnation. We are children of God, on our way to our real and lasting home. Our loving Savior has not only opened the door to that eternal home for us, he has shown us very clearly the way to get there and has given us all the helps we need on the way. All he asks of us is to follow the map he gave us and to use the means he left to us. Could we be so ungrateful to our divine benefactor and so forgetful of our own eternal interests as to refuse to do that little? God forbid!

GOSPEL : Matthew 21 : 28–32. Jesus said to the chief priests and the elders of the people, "What do you think? A man had two sons; and he went to the first and said, 'Son, go and work in the vineyard today.' And he answered, 'I will not'; but afterward he repented and went. And he went to the second and said the same; and he answered, 'I go, sir,' but did not go. Which of the two did the will of his father?" They said, "The first." Jesus said to them, "Truly, I say to you, the tax-collectors and the harlots go into the kingdom of God before you. For John came to you in the way of righteousness, and you did not believe him, but the tax-collectors and the harlots believed him; and even when you saw it, you did not afterward repent and believe him."

EXPLANATION : This is the first of three parables which Matthew places in the same context because they have the same basic teaching. Christ is telling the leaders of the Jews that the fact that they were God's Chosen People, and that they were proud of their observance of the law of Moses, is not a guarantee that they will possess the kingdom of God. Rather, because of their pride and their refusal to obey God's call to repentance, they will exclude themselves, while the tax-collectors and sinners, whom they despised, will repent of their sins and will be accepted into God's kingdom.

chief . . . elders : The leaders of the Jews prided themselves on their strict observance of the letter of the Mosaic law while they failed dismally in keeping its basic motive true : love of God and neighbor.

A man had two sons : Our Lord now puts them a question in the form of a story or parable. It's a question, which if their pride could allow, would make them see the folly of their ways.

I will not . . . go : This son refused at first to work for his father, but later repented and went to work in the father's vineyard. The second was prompt in promising obedience, but failed to carry out that promise.

which . . . two : The temporary refusal of the first was blameworthy, but was forgiven because of the subsequent change of mind. The prompt "yes" of the second was valueless because of the failure to put it into execution.

They said : The leaders gave the correct answer but refused to see any lesson for themselves in it. Christ brings out the lesson.

tax-collectors and harlots : Of all sinners those two classes were most despised by the leaders of the Jews. Christ tells the leaders that these very sinners will be sharers in God's kingdom, while their own false pride will not let them share in it.

John . . . righteousness : John the Baptist preached repentance to prepare his fellow-Jews for the new kingdom of God. The tax-collectors and harlots listened to his advice and followed it. Most of them became followers of Christ. But the priests and elders did not listen to John (see Matt. 3 : 7ff; Jn. 1 : 19), not even after they saw the conversion of the public sinners. They were, therefore, condemning themselves in condemning the second son. Like him, they pretended to be fully interested in their Father's business, but in practice they did their own will. Whereas the first son (first, because the Chosen People came later in the history of the human race) refused to do his father's will he later realized how wrong this was and set about obeying. He represented the public sinners and the Gentiles.

APPLICATION : This parable was primarily intended to show up the hypocrisy of the chief priests and elders of the Jews, and the perilous position in which they stood in relation to God and heaven. It is, however, a warning against hypocrisy for all time. Lip service of God will not merit heaven. Nominal Christians are not working in the Lord's vineyard. At any moment they may be called from this life, and what defense can they offer the just judge? Will they dare to offer the flimsy excuses with which they try to silence their consciences now : "we didn't realize how sinful we were"; "we were too occupied with family and personal cares to have time for our spiritual duties"; "we were led astray by bad example"; "we didn't like to be different from others"; "we were going to put things right"? Who will dare to offer such excuses at the judgement seat? Their utter futility will then be apparent in all its nakedness.

However, we are still on earth, and while we are the door of God's mercy is wide open to us. If in the past we said, "I will not go into your vineyard", we still have time to reverse that sinful decision. Not only can we with God's grace turn over a new leaf, but we can completely wipe out the sinful pages of our life's story written up to now. Remember that what God in his mercy did for the tax-collectors and harlots in the parable, the Matthews, the Mary Magdalenes, the Augustines, the Margarets of Cortona, the Matt Talbots and the millions of unknown penitents who are now saints in heaven he can also

M

do for you.

We answered the call to God's vineyard by accepting baptism and membership of his Church. If we have grown lax in our fervor and refused to do the tasks allotted to us, we still have time, thanks to God's mercy and patience, to put things right. Today, look into your conscience and see how much of your past life you have given to God and how much you have kept for yourself. If you were called tonight to render an account to the Lord, would the balance sheet be in your favor? Is our corner of the vineyard producing abundant crops, or is it perhaps filling up with weeds, briers and brambles? If the latter, then we will say a heartfelt: "Thank you, God, for not calling us to judgement today. We will begin right now to understand our sinful past, so that our corner of your vineyard will be in good order when you do call us. Thank you, Lord, for your mercy. God grant that we shall never abuse it."

TWENTY-SEVENTH SUNDAY OF THE YEAR

FIRST READING : Isaiah 5 : 1–7. Let me sing for my beloved a love song concerning his vineyard. My beloved had a vineyard on a very fertile hill. He digged it and cleared it of stones, and planted it with choice vines; he built a watchtower in the midst of it, and hewed out a winevat in it; and he looked for it to yield grapes but it yielded wild grapes.

And now, O inhabitants of Jerusalem and men of Judah, judge, I pray you, between me and my vineyard. What more was there to do for my vineyard, that I have not done in it? When I looked for it to yield grapes, why did it yield wild grapes?

And now I will tell you what I will do to my vineyard. I will remove its hedge, and it shall be devoured; I will break down its wall, and it shall be trampled down. I will make it a waste; it shall not be pruned or hoed, and briers and thorns shall grow up; I will also command the clouds that they rain no rain upon it. For the vineyard of the Lord of hosts is the house of Israel, and the men of Judah are his pleasant planting; and he looked for justice, but behold, bloodshed; for righteousness, but behold, a cry!

EXPLANATION : Under the image of a wine-grower who had done everything he could to make his vineyard fertile and productive, the prophet describes God's care for and interest in his Chosen People. God's vineyard produces wild grapes (useless for making wine) instead of real grapes. Israel and Judah failed to carry out the will of him who had made them what they were. They produced bloodshed instead of justice, and a rebellious outcry in place of true obedience. God's vineyard had failed him.

my beloved . . . hill : The prophet speaks of Yahweh as his beloved. He describes him as a wine-grower who had done so much to make his vineyard—his Chosen People—a people who would serve him loyally by living virtuously, but it was all in vain.

it yielded wild grapes : His people produced vices, not virtues.

between . . . vineyard : God now challenges the Chosen People of that day, asking them if he had failed in any way to make them a holy people, a people of virtue. There is only one answer : "no."

what I will do : He will remove all protection from his vineyard; he will leave it a prey to its enemies, and so it will be laid waste and desolate.

house of Israel . . . Judah : At the time Isaiah wrote this poem (about 740 B.C.), Israel, although separated from Judah, was still in existence. However, it soon (721) met with the fate Yahweh said he would allow because of its infidelity. Judah survived for some hundred odd years, but it too was laid waste by its pagan enemies, because of the wild grapes of sin it continued to produce.

APPLICATION : This image of a vineyard, carefully laid out and cared for by its owner, expressed very vividly the Chosen People's relationships with God. It was a self-evident image in a wine-growing country, and is repeated in today's gospel. The Chosen People of Isaiah's day were well aware of all that God had done for them in the past. Ever since the call of Abraham (about 1800 B.C.), and especially since the Exodus (1300 B.C.), their history was handed down from generation to generation and was one continuous reminder of God's benevolence towards them. But the return they made for this divine benevolence and love was a reluctant, cold service at its best, and a complete forgetfulness of him and his past favors at its worst.

However, this reading from Isaiah was not put before us today to have us say how deserving the Jews were of the fate their disloyalty brought on them, but rather that we, the new Chosen People of God, might apply this word of God to ourselves. If God did so much for his Chosen People of the Old Testament, how incomparably greater is the benevolence and love he has shown us Christians? The love God showed his Chosen People was but a shadow, a foretaste, of the love he has shown to his chosen ones of the New Testament. He sent his prophets to reveal himself and his message to the Jews; to us he sent his own divine Son, in human nature, to live and die among us and prove his love for us. He gave the land of Canaan to the Jews to be their homeland; through the Incarnation he has made us heirs of his own eternal kingdom of heaven. In spite of the overflowing love which God has shown us, how ungrateful we Christians can be and are! How often do we not only forget him, but positively offend him through our sinful attachment to the goods and pleasures of this world. How often must our heavenly Father have said of Christians whom he had adopted as sons: "what more was there to do for my vineyard, that I have not done for it?" When he expected loving gratitude and generosity from his privileged children, he received instead cold indifference and disloyalty from so many of them. Sunk in their own selfishness, they did not recognize their divine benefactor. Over-interested as they were in this world, they had no time for God's interests or their own true interest. They sold their eternal inheritance for a mess of earthly pottage.

Such Christians are the vineyard which the heavenly Father says he will lay waste and destroy. There is a dire threat in it for the worst of us. But if we heed the warning, the merciful Father will remove his threat and will take us back once more as his beloved children.

SECOND READING: Philippians 4:6–9. Have no anxiety about anything, but in everything by prayer and supplication with thanksgiving let your requests be made known to God. And the peace of God, which passes all understanding, will keep your hearts and your minds in Christ Jesus.

Finally, brethren, whatever is true, whatever is honorable, whatever is just, whatever is pure, whatever is lovely, whatever is gracious, if there is any excellence, if there is anything worthy of praise, think about these things. What you have learned and received and heard and seen in me, do; and the God of peace will be with you.

EXPLANATION: On the Philippians and St. Paul's relationship with them, see 25th Sunday above. In the excerpt taken from this epistle today, Paul is encouraging his converts to put their full trust in God. Fervent prayer of thanksgiving and petition will keep their hearts and minds on Christ. They should live exemplary Christian lives, following the teaching and the example of their Apostle. Their reward will be peace of mind in this life and everlasting peace in the world to come.

your requests . . . God: Paul exhorts them to put away all anxiety for temporal and spiritual affairs. The God who called them to the Christian faith is ever close to them. All they have to do is to make their requests to him with confidence, thanking him for all he has already done for them and asking for the further helps they need.

peace of God: Their close union with God, through prayer, will bring them peace on earth—a foretaste of the true, everlasting peace of heaven.

passes all understanding: Our finite minds cannot form any adequate idea of what the eternal peace of God is, but while on this earth true fidelity to, and love of Christ, brings the true Christian a measure of this peace.

whatever . . . just: The Apostle now recommends to them a whole set of natural virtues which were admired by the pagan Greeks (at least in theory). Grace builds on nature: the practice of the natural virtues will help them in their

Christian vocation, and will attract others as well.

learned . . . do : He had taught them the Christian faith by word and the example of his life. If they have learned this lesson and put it into practice, "the God of peace will be with them," that is, the God who is the source of eternal peace and salvation will be ever near to them, helping them on their road to heaven.

APPLICATION : These words of encouragement and comfort which St. Paul wrote to his converts in Philippi, have encouragement and comfort too for us Christians of today. The world and its ways have changed since, but the road to heaven has not altered and human nature has not changed. Getting to heaven was then a strenuous upward climb, there were many worldly attractions which tempted men to linger on the way or turn off the main road. It is no different today. Keeping the Christian law is still something which is beyond the power of weak human nature, if left to itself. But it is not left to itself. By baptism we are made members of Christ's mystical body and have the channels of divine grace open to us. All we have to do is to switch on the current of grace, and St. Paul tells us how to do this today.

He tells us to make our needs known to God through prayer and supplication with thanksgiving. The primary purpose of prayer is adoration—man recognizes God as his creator and benefactor and pays him homage. The second end of prayer is thanksgiving—the creature shows gratitude to God for the many gifts he has so gratuitously received. It is only when a man has fulfilled these two obligations, that he can ask God for further spiritual and temporal favors. This is, as St. Paul tells us today, the true prayer that will bring us the peace of God—peace of mind in this life and eternal peace and happiness in the life to come—for it will keep us united closely with our brother, Christ, who is ever interceding for us in heaven.

The true Christian life is a life of continual prayer. Our Lord himself told his disciples that they should pray continually (Lk. 18 : 1). But many will object : how can we do this, we have so many cares and distractions in life; earning our livelihood is a full-time occupation, where can we find time for prayer? The answer is, of course, that our daily chores are prayers if offered to God. Using the muscles and brawn of our bodies in manual labor, or the gifts of intellect and mind in office or professional work, is and should be a way of thanking God for giving us these gifts. And, done with the intention of thanking him, these daily occupations give honor and glory to God.

Prayer is not only the few moments of each day or each week which we spend on our knees; it is the dedication of our whole life to God, our recreation and rest as well as our labor. Our life was thus dedicated to God in our baptism, but we need to renew that dedication again and again during our lives. Today we are reminded to renew that dedication once more. It is of the essence of a Christian life, it is through the daily prayer of our work and recreation, interspersed and activated by verbal or oral prayer in the home or in church, that we can earn the peace of God which surpasses all human understanding. It is the guarantee of our happiness in this life and the next.

GOSPEL : Matthew 21 : 33–43. Jesus said to the chief priests and elders of the people, "Hear another parable. There was a householder who planted a vineyard, and set a hedge around it, and dug a wine press in it, and built a tower, and let it out to tenants, and went into another country. When the season of fruit drew near, he sent his servants to the tenants, to get his fruit; and the tenants took his servants and beat one, killed another, and stoned another. Again he sent other servants, more than the first; and they did the same to them. Afterward he sent his son to them, saying, 'They will respect my son.' But when the tenants saw the son, they said to themselves, 'This is the heir; come, let us kill him and have his inheritance.' And they took him and cast him out of the vineyard, and killed him. When therefore the owner of the vineyard comes, what will he do to those tenants?" They said to him, "He will put those wretches to a miserable death, and let out the vineyard to other tenants who will give him the fruits in their seasons."

Jesus said to them, "Have you never read in the Scriptures: 'The very stone which the builders rejected has become the head of the corner; this was the Lord's doing, and it is marvelous in our eyes'? Therefore I tell you, the kingdom of God will be taken away from you and given to a nation producing the fruits of it."

EXPLANATION : On parables see 25th Sunday above. Our Lord tells this parable or story of the vineyard to his opponents, "the chief priests and elders of the people," to show them that even though they were God's Chosen People in the past they have forfeited any claim to the new kingdom of God because of their disloyalty and disobedience to him. They were given a vineyard to cultivate, but they claimed it as their own, and not only refused to give any return to the true owner but murdered the owner's son when he was sent to reason with them. The Jews were chosen by God to prepare the world for the coming of Christ; they not only failed in their appointed task but they put Christ to death when he came, thus excluding themselves from his new kingdom, the Church, where they would be replaced by the Gentile nations.

planted a vineyard : The vineyard as an image of God's kingdom on earth often occurs in the Old Testament (see Is. 5 : 1–7; 27 : 1–7; Ps. 80 : 8–16; Jer. 2 : 21). Our Lord had Is. 5 : 1–7 (today's first reading) before his mind when speaking this parable.

hedge . . . tower : The owner of the vineyard did everything necessary to make it fertile and productive.

went . . . country : He gave the tenants time to produce the grapes.

sent his servants : He sent them to collect the wine or its value. God sent his prophets to his Chosen People, generation after generation, calling on them to produce fruits of penance and prepare themselves for the coming Savior.

beat . . . stoned : Instead of listening to God's word they maltreated and sometimes killed his innocent messengers (see Mt. 23 : 37 where Our Lord himself says : "Jerusalem . . . you that kill the prophets and stone those who are sent to you . . .").

he . . . son : The householder in the parable thought they would respect his son, but instead they killed him. God, the owner of Israel's vineyard, had no doubts as to the reception his only Son would receive from the leaders of the Jews, but in his infinite mercy he gave them this last opportunity to atone for their past. Our Lord himself was not telling these leaders that he was the Son of God and that he knew what they had planned to do with him. But they refused to listen.

what will . . . tenants? : Christ now asks them what the owner would do to such tenants. They answer correctly : he will put them to a miserable death, and let his vineyard to other tenants who will give him the fruits. Now, unless this answer was given by the disciples, it is clear, if the leaders gave it, that they did not apply the lesson to themselves. In their pride they perhaps could not see themselves in the role of dishonest tenants in God's vineyard.

stone . . . rejected : Christ now quotes two verses from Psalm 118 to leave no doubt in their minds that the parable applied to themselves. They were rejecting Christ, who would become the cornerstone, the source of strength, stability and unity among the various races who would form his new kingdom. **Therefore I tell you :** He now repeats in crystal-clear language the truth he wished to convey to them. The Gentiles will become God's new Chosen People— his elect of the Old Testament had failed him.

APPLICATION : There are two leading thoughts that come to the mind of any true believer on hearing this parable : the infinite goodness, patience and mercy of God in his dealings with mankind, and the unsounded depths of wickedness and ingratitude to which men can sink. To his Chosen People of the Old Testament God had given a fertile and fully-equipped vineyard : his revelation, his protection, a homeland of their own in Canaan, and all this in order to prepare them for the future Messiah, who would bring them an eternal home in God's own kingdom. All he asked in return was their co-operation.

But they had other plans; they wanted their kingdom on earth. Yet God was patient with them; again and again he pardoned their infidelities. He sent them prophet after prophet to recall them to their senses, but they maltreated these messengers of God and refused to heed their warnings.

Then "the fullness of time" came and he sent his divine Son on earth in human form. He took his human nature from one of their race, lived among them and preached his gospel of love and peace to them. He tried to soften their hard hearts, and made them the final offer of the Father's mercy and pardon. But instead of accepting God's offer of mercy the chief priests and elders only made it an occasion of an even greater sin. To their crimes of infidelity and injustice they added the murder of God's Messiah and Son.

In God's plan of love and mercy the tragedy of Calvary turned out to be the great " triumph of failure." That death brought life to the world and opened the gates of God's eternal kingdom for all nations and races. The Gentiles rallied around the standard of Christ. A new vineyard was set up in which all men could work for their Father in heaven and for their own eternal interests.

We Christians today are the successors of the first Gentile followers of Christ. We too have been called to work in God's vineyard. Are we working honestly and devotedly? Are we producing the grapes and the wine that our divine Master expects of us? If our answer is "yes, I am living a true Christian life, I am working for God's honor and glory and for my own eternal salvation," then we can say a heartfelt "thank you" to our merciful Father, and ask him to keep us ever on this right path. But if our answer is "no," then let us pay heed to today's lesson. What happened to the chief priests and elders can and will happen to unfaithful Christians if they persevere in their infidelity and disobedience. But we can still put ourselves right with God. Let us do it today; tomorrow may be too late.

TWENTY-EIGHTH SUNDAY OF THE YEAR

FIRST READING : Isaiah 25 : 6–10. On this mountain the Lord of hosts will make for all peoples a feast of fat things, a feast of wine on the lees, of fat things full of marrow, of wine on the lees well refined. And he will destroy on this mountain the covering that is cast over all peoples, the veil that is spread over all nations. He will swallow up death for ever, and the Lord God will wipe away tears from all faces, and the reproach of his people he will take away from all the earth; for the Lord has spoken. It will be said on that day, "Lo, this is our God; we have waited for him, that he might save us. This is the Lord; we have waited for him; let us be glad and rejoice in his salvation." For the hand of the Lord will rest on this mountain.

EXPLANATION : Isaiah carried out his prophetic mission in Jerusalem from 742 to about 700 B.C. He spoke strongly against the disloyalty and worldliness of the Chosen People of his day. He also foretold many things concerning the messianic age that was to come. In today's reading he describes under the image of a great banquet, the blessings, the contentment and happiness that the messianic kingdom will bring. It will take place in Sion (Jerusalem) and it will be for all peoples, not for the Chosen People of the Old Testament only. It will be much more than an earthly banquet because death and tears will have been conquered. Those taking part in it will "rejoice in God's salvation" : they will know they have been saved by God forever.

on this mountain . . . feast : The victory banquet will be held in Jerusalem. Christ won his messianic victory on Mount Calvary in that city and it was there that his messianic kingdom had its first beginnings on Pentecost Day.

covering . . . peoples : The Messiah, God's Son and representative, will remove the veil of darkness and sorrow that covered all peoples until then.

swallow . . . forever : By his physical death the Messiah has conquered forever the spiritual death of mankind. Our physical death is now the doorway to everlasting life.

the Lord . . . spoken : This is the Lord's promise, not that of Isaiah.

this . . . God : Both Jew and Gentile will together recognize the true God. It is he who has brought them the salvation they had been expecting.

the hand . . . Lord : The power of God will be manifested in Jerusalem. This prophecy was fulfilled when the new covenant, the new Jerusalem, the new Chosen People, the Church, was formally manifested on the first Pentecost day.

APPLICATION : Seven hundred years or so before Christ came on earth the prophet Isaiah described the result of that coming under the image of a bountiful banquet in which those taking part would find everlasting happiness and contentment. He was referring, of course, to heaven, the second and final stage of the messianic kingdom. There all tears will be wiped away, there death will no longer have sway. There every desire for what is good and what is perfect will be satisfied, and man's natural desire for perfect happiness will be fulfilled.

What the prophet foretold Christ brought to pass. He who was God's Son took our human nature. He made us his brothers and co-heirs with him of heaven, thus fulfilling God's plan for mankind. God intended that we should share his eternal kingdom of happiness when we die. This we can now do because through the Incarnation of his Son we have been made his adopted sons.

Heaven, therefore, is ours for the taking. God the Father intended it for us, God the Son has earned it for us, God the Holy Spirit is ready at every moment of our lives to assist us to obtain it. We have very few descriptions of heaven in our revelation, because our minds are incapable of grasping its infinite happiness and perfection. St. Paul's negative description is perhaps the best we can get. He had been given a vision of heaven but he said he could not describe it in human language, nor could anyone, while still alive on earth, understand him even if Paul could describe it. He says that "no (human) eye has seen, no human ear has heard, no human mind can grasp all that God has prepared for those who love him" (1 Cor. 2 : 9).

Negative though our descriptions are,

we can form a sufficient picture of it to make us want to reach it. Who would not want to have : eternal freedom from all cares and worries; eternal freedom from pain, sickness and death; eternal union with all friends and relatives and with all the saints of God, the eternal company of Mary the Virgin Mother, and the assured and lasting friendship and love of Christ our Savior in his human nature, and to crown all, the beatific vision of God in the three divine persons?

Is it any wonder that many saints, including St. Paul himself, longed to put off this mortal life so that they could be in the happy possession of heaven! Unfortunately for ourselves, we ordinary Christians do not give enough thought to heaven. If we meditated more often on the future life, we would see this world for what it is—a journey, a very short journey, often unpleasant and difficult, but a journey by means of which we can reach that future home if we travel as God wants us. Too many of us mistake this world for the future one. We try to get our perfect happiness here on earth even though the most thoughtless among us shall have to leave this world. Not even the merciful God himself can take us into his eternal banquet unless we have traveled through this world on the path he has laid down for us, or repented of our sins if we have strayed from that path.

SECOND READING : Philippians 4 : 12–14; 19–20.

I know how to be abased, and I know how to abound; in any and all circumstances I have learned the secret of facing plenty and hunger, abundance and want. I can do all things in him who strengthens me.

Yet it was kind of you to share my trouble. And my God will supply every need of yours according to his riches in glory in Christ Jesus. To our God and Father be glory for ever and ever. Amen.

EXPLANATION : As we said above in the 25th Sunday of the year, the Philippians were the only converts from whom St. Paul accepted any financial help. He is thanking them here for some such assistance which he must surely have needed for he was in prison when he wrote this letter. He assures them that God will reward them for the charitable aid given him.

be abased, and . . . abound : Paul has trained himself to accept the ups and downs of life. He was often hungry and even starving (see 2 Cor. 11 : 23–29). He sometimes had all he needed—this was for him abundance.

can do . . . me : His secret was that he had put his complete trust in Christ and was firmly convinced that Christ would not abandon him in his trials.

to share my trouble : By coming to his aid they had shared his trouble with him, they had carried part of his load with and for him.

God . . . supply : God in his generosity will repay them. He will help them in their needs as they helped Paul. This will be specially true in their spiritual needs, as the reference to "glory in Christ Jesus" implies.

glory . . . ever: He gives praise and glory to God our Father; we are his adopted sons, brothers of Christ, and this glory will be given to God for all eternity.

APPLICATION: The generous unsolicited aid which the Christian converts of Philippi gave to St. Paul should be an example and encouragement to all Christians to help in the spread of the gospel. We have St. Paul's word for it that such generosity will not go unrewarded in this life and the next. What is given for God's work for our fellowmen is not lost but invested—it will reap an abundant harvest perhaps when we least expect it. Our surest and most direct entry to heaven is when we help to bring as many of our fellowmen as we can with us. The "loner" who excludes others from his life and prayer is a non-starter in the heavenly journey.

There is another important lesson too for all of us in today's few short verses from St. Paul. It is our need for a complete and unquestioning trust in God and the firm conviction that he is regulating all the affairs of our lives. Our Lord himself tells us: "can you not buy two sparrows for a penny? And yet not one falls to the ground without your Father knowing. Why, every hair in your head has been counted. So there is no need to be afraid, you are worth more than hundreds of sparrows" (Mt. 10 : 29).

St. Paul had learned this lesson well and put it into daily practice. He faced trials and troubles as gladly as he faced peace and plenty, for he was convinced that God allowed all these things to happen for his salvation and for the spread of God's kingdom, the Church. We too must learn this lesson. We must have complete confidence in God. Our whole lives are in his capable hands. If he allows temporal or spiritual trials to assail us, he has a good purpose in so doing. We may not see that purpose, but we can be certain it is there. If the little sparrow is under his care how much more so are not we—his chosen children. If the hairs of our head are numbered by God, how much more so are not our daily sorrows and joys his concern?

To make a statue from a lump of stone the sculptor has to chip and cut and hew. If the stone could object, it would most likely tell that sculptor how unjust and unmerciful he was. But when the statue is finished that which was once a lump of rough stone will be a thing of beauty and dignity on a pedestal for all to see. God is the perfect Sculptor. He intends to place us on an everlasting pedestal of glory. To do this he has to cut and hew and chip away at us all through our life. Those of us who realize God's divine plan for us will, instead of complaining, thank him for the infinite love which makes him take such pains to make us what we ought to be.

GOSPEL : Matthew 22 : 1–14. Jesus spoke to the chief priests and elders of the people in parables, saying, "The kingdom of heaven may be compared to a king who gave a marriage feast for his son, and sent his servants to call those who were invited to the marriage feast; but they would not come. Again he sent other servants, saying, 'Tell those who are invited, Behold, I have made ready my dinner, my oxen and my fat calves are killed, and everything is ready; come to the marriage feast.' But they made light of it and went off, one to his farm, another to his business, while the rest seized his servants, treated them shamefully, and killed them. The king was angry, and he sent his troops and destroyed those murderers and burned their city. Then he said to his servants, 'The wedding is ready, but those invited were not worthy. Go therefore to the thoroughfares, and invite to the marriage feast as many as you find.' And those servants went out into the streets and gathered all whom they found, both bad and good; so the wedding hall was filled with guests.

"But when the king came in to look at the guests, he saw there a man who had no wedding garment; and he said to him, 'Friend, how did you get in here without a wedding garment?' And he was speechless. Then the king said to the attendants, 'Bind him hand and foot, and cast him into the outer darkness; there men will weep and gnash their teeth.' For many are called, but few are chosen."

EXPLANATION : The Jews as a whole, and the Pharisees especially, judged that because the Messiah was to come from their race, they were therefore assured not only of a place in his kingdom but the leading positions in it. This parable was intended to show them that because of their ungodliness, their pride, and their earthly attachments, they were about to forfeit not only all the privileges they hitherto had as God's Chosen People on earth, but, worse still, they were to have no place in his heavenly kingdom because they willfully excluded themselves from the new Israel which he was founding, the Church, which was to be the gateway to heaven (see Lk. 14 : 16–24).

To check any inclination to self-glory on the part of the sinners and Gentiles, "those from the highways and byways" who will supplant the Pharisees in the new kingdom, our Lord adds a warning on the necessity of proving oneself worthy of this great invitation, in the parable of the wedding garment.

The kingdom of heaven : Because the Jews had many erroneous ideas concerning the Messiah, and the kingdom he would set up, Christ found it necessary to describe the true nature of his kingdom by means of parables. The false expectations of a Messiah who would set up a universal kingdom of earthly power and glory with Israel in the seat of government were not going to be abandoned without a fight. But Christ in his divine wisdom found a means of conveying the as yet unpalatable truth in language which would be crystal clear to the well-disposed, once the realization of his true nature and mission had erased forever from their minds the false prejudices of the past. In his parables

Christ shows that his kingdom will not be one of earthly power and splendor which comes ready-made from heaven, but must rather grow on earth from humble beginnings amid obstacles and opposition.

A king . . . son : This was a very special celebration to which it was an honor to be invited. The king here is God the Father, the son is Christ, and the marriage is between Christ and his spouse, the Church.

servants . . . invited : The invitations had been sent out sometime previously, and evidently had been accepted. But when the wedding day was at hand those invited refused to come. Ever since the call of Abraham (about 1800 B.C.—see Gen. 18 : 18), the Jews had been called to the messianic kingdom. That call had been repeated by the prophets and sacred writers of the Old Testament down through their history, but when Christ came "He came unto his own, and his own received him not" (Jn. 1 : 11).

Again he sent . . . servants : With great forbearance the king overlooked the insult and tried once more to move them to a sense of propriety. The first servants were the prophets, the second were the Apostles. These latter announced that the wedding feast was ready, the kingdom of God was at hand.

But they made light . . . business : Some of the invited just ignored the invitation, and went about their own personal affairs; they had no time for the king or his kingdom. Others were even worse; they maltreated the servants, and even put them to death. The Acts of the Apostles tell of the fulfillment of these words.

King . . . angry : The murder of the servants did not go unpunished. The king sent his armies to destroy the murderers and burn their city. This prophecy of Christ, in the form of a parable, was fulfilled in the year 70 A.D., when Jerusalem was burned to the ground by the Romans under Titus.

those . . . not worthy : It was not the king who excluded them; they made themselves unworthy because of their worldliness and wickedness.

Go therefore . . . as you find : Since the elite of the city have excluded themselves, others must be found to fill the banquet chamber. Therefore the servants are told to go to the crossroads, very likely the roads leading from the country to the city, and bring in all they could find. These people would be unimportant, at least in the minds of the city magnates, country folk, strangers, and stragglers.

gathered . . . good : The king's messengers (the Apostles) went into the crossroads and byways of the pagan world, and announced the king's banquet (the founding of the Church). These people listened and came gladly to the marriage feast. They accepted Christianity and became the new Chosen People instead of the Pharisees. As a result, "the marriage was filled with guests." We should note that it was God's plan to call the Gentiles to his Church, no matter how the Pharisees reacted to his gospel. Here the emphasis is on the rejection of the Pharisees and their being supplanted by the despised Gentiles.

a man . . . garment : According to most commentators on the gospel this is a new parable, but one closely connected with the first, insofar as there were bad and good among those called from the crossroads. This second parable explains what will happen to the bad who are called and remain bad.

Friend . . . garment? : Evidently each guest was expected to wear a special, easily obtained, garment for the occasion; for if it had been difficult to obtain, the king would not have been angry with one who had been called in off the byway. The lack of such a garment, therefore, showed a lack of respect and appreciation on the part of the delinquent.

he was speechless : The guilty one had no defense; his guilt was evident and inexcusable. Now the call to the Church given to the Gentiles is a tremendous privilege. Even if most of them were " bad," that is, entirely unworthy of such an honor, they could make themselves worthy, and many did. They could all easily obtain the wedding garment, the necessary grace, to make them acceptable to the Lord; but some failed in this. The mention of one unworthy person in the parable is taken to represent all failures. Numbers are used only to clarify the lesson intended.

cast . . . darkness : A wedding feast was no place for an improperly and disrespectfully dressed person. Heaven is not for those who have not made themselves worthy by penance and the acquisition of virtue. The binding of hands and feet signifies that there is no escape from the sentence of the king. The exterior darkness and the weeping and gnashing of teeth indicate the loss of happiness and the pain of separation from God.

many . . . chosen : All get sufficient grace from God to attain to eternal salvation; but some, as is clear from the parable, fail to cooperate with the grace and are thus, through their own fault, excluded from the banquet of the "elect."

APPLICATION : How foolish the Pharisees were in not listening to our Lord's warnings. He gave them every opportunity to turn away from the false path which their pride had chosen for them. His divine heart was ever ready to embrace them if only they would say "mea culpa." "Jerusalem, Jerusalem, you who kill the prophets, and stone them that are sent to you, how often would I have gathered together your children, as the hen does her chickens under her wings, and you would not?" (Mt. 23 : 37). "God created us without our cooperation," says St. Augustine, "but he cannot save us unless we cooperate."

We too could make the Pharisees' mistake. We have the invitation to the wedding feast; in fact, we are already in the banquet hall, since our baptism; but are we wearing the wedding garment of virtue and grace? If not, we are no better off than those who rejected the invitation. The king may come in at any moment and cast out those who are not properly dressed. Being a member of the Church on earth is a wonderful privilege, and a sure guarantee that we will reach heaven, if we do what is expected of us. But the same obstacles which prevented the Pharisees from entering the kingdom—love of this world, its wealth and its pleasures—can impede us too, unless we are on our guard. The world with its allurements is very close to us; heaven seems very far away. Thus we must be prepared to do violence to our ordinary inclinations, to go against them whenever and wherever "the things that are Caesar's" tend to blot out or make us forget "the things that are God's."

This implies a daily carrying of the cross, a daily struggle against our evil inclinations, a daily endeavor to acquire true love of God and neighbor. This may sound superhuman, but Christ did not ask anyone to do the impossible. He led the way, and millions have followed him to eternal glory. He has called us too and has placed within our easy reach in his Church all the grace we need. If we fail to use these divine helps, if we are found without the wedding garment, we will have no one to blame but ourselves. We have been called with the many. We can be among the "chosen."

TWENTY-NINTH SUNDAY OF THE YEAR

FIRST READING : Isaiah 45 : 1; 4–6. Thus says the Lord to his anointed, to Cyrus, whose right hand I have grasped, to subdue nations before him and ungird the loins of kings, to open doors before him that gates may not be closed : For the sake of my servant Jacob, and Israel my chosen, I call you by your name. I surname you, though you do not know me. I am the Lord, and there is no other, beside me there is no God; I gird you, though you do not know me, that men may know, from the rising of the sun and from the west, that there is none beside me; I am the Lord, and there is no other.

EXPLANATION : The prophet, second-Isaiah, who lived in Babylonia with the exiled Jews, tells us, in God's own words, that he is the God, not only of the Jews, but of history and of the whole world. Cyrus, who had become king of the Medes and the Persians, later extended his rule to include Syria, Babylon, Egypt. God declares that it was he who so exalted him "for the sake of Jacob," that the Jewish exiles could return to Judah and rebuild God's temple in Jerusalem. God calls him his "anointed," his Messiah (a title given to the kings, prophets and priests of the Chosen People but never elsewhere to a pagan), because he was to be God's agent in the liberation of the Jews. Cyrus carried out God's plan, he set the Jewish exiles free, giving them permission to rebuild their temple and city, and returning to them the gold and silver vessels which Nebuchadnezzar had taken from the temple. God adds that because he so raised up a king "who did not know him" all men would learn that he alone was God of the whole world.

Thus . . . Lord: The prophet declares that it is not he but God himself who is making the following statement.

right . . . grasped : The kings of Babylon on the day of their coronation grasped the hand of their pagan god, Bel-Mahduk. God is indicating that Cyrus is his king, it is for God's purpose that he is being crowned.

to . . . gates : God claims Cyrus's campaigns successful.

Jacob . . . Israel : Cyrus was raised up so that God's Chosen People would be set free and his plans for the Incarnation, by which all men would be "raised up," could come to fulfillment.

name . . . surname : God not only knows Cyrus by name, he gives him also a further title (surname), Messiah or "the anointed of God."

beside me . . . no God : He alone is God of the universe. All other gods are false imitations.

you . . . me : Cyrus was a pagan, an adorer of false gods. He did not know the true God, but the true God was able to use him as his agent. From this all men should learn that the power of the God of Israel was universal because he was God of all creation.

APPLICATION : God is indeed the lord of the universe. As he used the pagan king Cyrus in the sixth century B.C., so is he using the neo-pagans of today to carry out his divine plans for mankind. Cyrus did not know the true God and was unaware that he was co-operating with him, and neither do today's atheists realize that they are helping to fulfill the plans of the very God whose existence they theoretically or practically deny. They will earn no merit for their unwilling cooperation, but nevertheless, willy nilly, they are agents under God's command. They would wish to expel God from the universe he created, and from the minds of men. Their puny efforts not only will be in vain but, unknown to themselves, they are helping God in his overall plan for his world. God will still be master of his world when they are dead and long forgotten.

How foolish can we become! Because we know much more about the laws that govern our planet, there are men who say we can run it now without any help from any god. God was only an invention of the ages of ignorance, when man did not know the true nature of things!

We do not need him now! Can any scientist, any really learned man, admit for a moment that these laws of nature which science has discovered, were made by blind chance? Does not a law need a lawmaker, one who has a purpose in view and decides how that purpose can best be achieved? The intricate, complicated laws that govern not only this earth and all that exists in it, but all of the wider universe which we have so far discovered, do these not demand not only a superior mind but a superhuman mind?

We have still much more to learn about the nature and purposes of created things. But even when we know all there is to know about our universe, we can only admit that we have found what was put in that universe by God. True science should lead to God, not away from him.

We Christians, thank God, are not depending on science or on the laws of nature to learn of God's existence. We have his revelation. We know he is more than a legislator, a lawmaker; he is a loving Father who put us on earth and gave us all there is for our use. This is not the home he has prepared for us, it is only a place of transit. Let us use it, gratefully, to help us reach our eternal home. Unlike Cyrus and all those others who unwittingly and unwillingly co-operate with God, let us give him a cheerful, willing service. "God loves the cheerful giver."

SECOND READING: 1 Thessalonians 1:1–5. Paul, Silvanus, and Timothy, to the church of the Thessalonians in God the Father and the Lord Jesus Christ: Grace to you and peace. We give thanks to God always for you all, constantly mentioning you in our prayers, remembering before our God and Father your work of faith and labor of love and steadfastness of hope in our Lord Jesus Christ. For we know, brethren beloved by God, that he has chosen you; for our gospel came to you not only in word, but also in power and in the Holy Spirit and with full conviction.

EXPLANATION: This is the first written document of the whole New Testament. St. Paul converted some Jews and many Gentiles in Thessalonica (northern Greece) in the summer of 50 A.D., during his second missionary journey. From there he went on to Athens and Corinth (Acts 17:1–10), where he wrote this letter early in 51 A.D. He had had good news from the church in Thessalonica in the meantime (his companion Timothy had gone back there on a visit), hence the very friendly tone of the letter. In the five verses read today, Paul praises his converts for their fidelity to God and to Christ his Son and tells them how they are ever in his prayers so that they would continue faithful to the call God had given them, a call proved by the many gifts of the Holy Spirit bestowed on them.

the church . . . Thessalonians: Paul is writing to the assembly of Christians in Thessalonica not to any individual. The word church is a translation of the Greek *ekklesia* which means an assembly of people called to a meeting. In the Old and New Testaments *ekklesia* means a religious assembly. From the very beginning Christian converts met each week to celebrate the Eucharist—the "breaking of bread" (Acts 2:42 etc.)—and to hear the preaching of the gospel. This meeting was later fixed for each Sunday, thus to recall Christ's resurrection.

God . . . Christ: The divinity of Christ and his equality with the Father are accepted truths among the converts, and need no stressing.

Grace . . . peace: Paul uses this wish for his readers in almost all his epistles. Grace means God's loving bounty and blessing, and peace means contentment of conscience and harmony with one's neighbors. The salutation resembles closely the words of blessing that Yahweh instructed Aaron to pronounce over the assembly (see Nm. 6:22–27, especially 26: "may Yahweh uncover his face to you and bring you peace").

you . . . prayers: Paul and his co-workers Silvanus and Timothy, are constantly thanking God for the active, living faith of the Thessalonians and are always asking God to keep them that way forever.

beloved by God : They are God's friends, God's chosen, and this was proved by the outpouring of the gifts of the Holy Spirit when they accepted the gospel. They were not converted by Paul's preaching alone, but especially by the manifest will and power of God.

APPLICATION : We, today, have the self-same faith as the Thessalonians of the year 50 A.D. All the gifts of the Holy Spirit given to them to prove that the Christian faith which St. Paul taught them, was true, were given also for our sakes. We, like them, know that God is our loving Father, that Jesus Christ is his divine Son who became man in order to bring us to heaven. We know that the Holy Spirit, the Third Person of the Blessed Trinity, is in the Christian Church today, helping its members, just as he was with the infant Church in St. Paul's day. His presence may not be accompanied by as many external signs and charisms but it is no less powerful and active.

We have the same faith then, and the same true purpose in life as had the Thessalonians. But is that faith as sincere and as active as it was in the daily lives of those first Christians? If St. Paul were to write a letter to the assembly or congregation gathered here today, could he thank God for our "work of faith" our "labor of love" and our "steadfastness of hope in our Lord Jesus Christ"? Does our Christian faith influence and affect every action of each day, its work as well as its recreation, its difficulties as well as its pleasures? Or is it, as the Sunday missal was, something locked away in a bookcase, to be brought out on Sunday morning? Is the keeping of the ten commandments and of the precepts of the Christian religion a "labor of love" or a load on our shoulders which if carried at all, is done so with reluctance? Is our hope in the future life which Jesus Christ won for us, and promised to us, the guiding star of our lives, the yardstick with which our earthly plans are measured and ruled?

These five verses from St. Paul's first letter to the converts of Thessalonica are chosen by the Church today, not for us simply to admire such great faith, hope and charity in the first converts but that we would try to imitate them. What they did we too can do. What Christ expected of them, he expects of us too. What he promised them he is promising to us, but on condition that like them we live a life of faith, a life of hope and a life of charity.

GOSPEL : Matthew 22 : 15-21. The Pharisees went and took counsel how to entangle Jesus in his talk. And they sent their disciples to him, along with the Herodians, saying, "Teacher, we know that you are true, and teach the way of God truthfully, and care for no man; for you do not regard the position of men. Tell us, then, what you think. Is it lawful to pay taxes to Caesar, or not?" But Jesus, aware of their malice, said, "Why put me to the test, you hypocrites? Show me the money for the tax." And they brought him a coin. And Jesus said to them, "Whose likeness and inscription is this?" They said, "Caesar's." Then he said to them, "Render therefore to Caesar the things that are Caesar's, and to God the things that are God's."

EXPLANATION : The Pharisees were a religious sect of Jews which originated in the second century B.C. Their aim was to keep the Mosaic law in all its minutiae, and the many strict interpretations of it handed down by tradition, to which indeed they added many more ever stricter ones. At the time of Christ they had many followers among the elite but as their very name Pharisee (which means separated) indicated, they kept strictly aloof from the ordinary people. They specially despised "sinners" —those who did not observe the strict letter of the law as interpreted by them; and the tax-collectors, who were often though not always, unjust in their exaction of the taxes they collected.

The Pharisees opposed Christ almost from the very beginning of his public preaching because he "came to call sinners" and associated freely with sinners and tax-collectors. They were in opposition to the Herodians and the Sadducees, two other contemporary Jewish sects. Nevertheless, they were willing to join hands with them in their desire to silence Christ. They used the Sadducees to get Christ crucified; here in today's text, they used the Herodians to try to trap Jesus in his teaching.

Pharisees . . . counsel : They thought they had a golden opportunity to put an end to Christ's mission.

disciples . . . Herodians : The leaders did not come to Christ themselves, they sent their students who would appear to be humbly seeking information. Their purpose in getting Herodians (admirers of Herod Antipas of Galilee, who most probably were friends and spies for the Roman authorities) to form part of the delegation would, they thought, make Christ's answer an offense to one or the other party. If he answered that it was lawful to pay the Roman taxes, he would offend the Pharisees and ninety per cent of the Jews, who would then refuse to listen to him. If he said it was wrong to pay Roman taxes then the Herodians would report him to the Roman authorities and an end would be put to his mission.

Teacher . . . truthfully : With such words of flattery they thought that they could fool Jesus. They failed.

aware . . . malice : He understood perfectly the reason for this delegation. They had not come to seek knowledge, but to "put him to the test," to get him to condemn himself no matter whether he said "yes" or "no."

hypocrites : A synonym for Pharisees in all languages ever since; they pretended outwardly to be strictly religious, whereas in their hearts they were lacking in true religion, love of God and neighbor, and true humility.

whose . . . inscription : Roman money was then legal in Palestine, a mere province of Rome. The right to mint coinage was and still is a sign of sovereignty.
Caesar's : His questioners had no hesitation in recognizing the coin, they had been using it daily, they could not get enough of it.
render to Caesar : If the coinage you use is Caesar's and you accept it without question, then why object to returning some of this coinage to him? Christ does not solve the juridicial question as to Rome's right to rule Palestine, but he tells his questioners that they accept Rome's rule "de facto" when they accept the Roman coinage.
the things . . . God's : Those sent had not asked for any religious advice but Christ gives it to them. He tells them to serve God as he has a right to be served, with sincerity and humility.

APPLICATION : Notwithstanding the malicious intention the Pharisees had in putting this question to our Lord, they did us all a good turn by getting his answer. That answer is forceful and final. It lays down a norm which solves for all time the problems that can arise from our dual citizenship on this earth.

God's plan for man on earth was that he should live in the society of his fellowmen. Society must be governed, there must be authority which will direct the actions of the component members toward the common good, which common good is principally, though not exclusively, the material welfare of the members as a whole. As his ultimate end, however, man has his spiritual welfare. This government, this temporal power to rule and direct the human groups or societies or states, comes, therefore, from God for it is his will that such societies should exist. The answer of our Lord explicitly restates this fundamental norm of the divine natural law. "Give to Caesar what is Caesar's"; the state authorities have a right to the obedience and cooperation in all things that tend to the material welfare of the state, provided always the spiritual welfare of the members is not impeded by the rulers' demands.

As a partly spiritual being man is destined to be a citizen of a spiritual eternal kingdom, and while on this earth he has the duty and the possibility of preparing himself for citizenship in that kingdom. And since this kingdom is of a higher and much more important nature, man's primary aim in life must be to reach that kingdom. He must, in other words, find out and fulfill his duties toward God; he must "give to God what is God's."

This dual citizenship of man and the dual obligations that arise from it are the common knowledge of all from the natural law but are made more explicit still in divine revelation of which today's answer, given by Christ to the Pharisees, is a precise and perfect résumé. We have duties to God and duties to our country and the fulfilment of the latter is part of the fulfillment of the former. We Christians have no doubts as to our obligations under these two headings. We fulfill our duties to God by being faithful, loyal, active members of the spiritual kingdom, the Church, which Christ established on earth in order to lead us to our eternal kingdom. We fulfill our duties to our country by loyally obeying the just laws of the State, by paying all lawful taxes, and by contributing our share, whenever called on, toward the common good.

Both St. Peter (1 Pet. 2 : 13–14) and St. Paul (Rom. 13 : 1–7), stressed the obligation on the early Christians of being an example to all in their loyalty as citizens of the state. The same necessity obliges us too. We who know the divine, positive and natural law so much better than many others, must help to enlighten those others by our faithful observance of these laws. And our loyalty, too, will give the lie to those enemies of the faith who, in their ignorance and foolish opposition to things spiritual, are only too ready to think that loyalty to our Church and our God must of necessity make us disloyal to our country. History already has given the lie to such calumnies, for the loyal Christian has ever been the loyal citizen, but we must keep on writing such history in glaring lights of daily deeds, for there are, and there always will be, those enemies who cannot read history books.

THIRTIETH SUNDAY OF THE YEAR

FIRST READING : Exodus 22 : 21–27. Thus says the Lord : "You shall not wrong a stranger or oppress him, for you were strangers in the land of Egypt. You shall not afflict any widow or orphan. If you do afflict them, and they cry out to me, I will surely hear their cry; and my wrath will burn, and I will kill you with the sword, and your wives shall become widows and your children fatherless.

"If you lend money to any of my people with you who is poor, you shall not be to him as a creditor, and you shall not exact interest from him. If ever you take your neighbor's garment in pledge, you shall restore it to him before the sun goes down; for that is his only covering, it is his mantle for his body; in what else shall he sleep? And if he cries to me, I will hear, for I am compassionate."

EXPLANATION : When God brought the Israelites out of Egypt he made a covenant or pact with them on Mount Sinai. In this pact he promised to bring them into the promised land and to be ever with them, provided they, on their part, kept certain rules of conduct which are written down in the "Book of the Covenant" in Exodus 19 : 1–24 : 18. The verses read to us today cover the Israelites' duties toward strangers (non-Israelites), widows and orphans and the poor in general. They are a practical application of the law of charity in their dealings with their neighbors.

not wrong . . . him : The "stranger" was one who for some reason had become a "displaced person" and had come to live among the Israelites. They were to treat him with justice and charity, remembering that they themselves had been displaced persons in Egypt. This obligation of respect for the stranger is often repeated in the Old Testament.

widow . . . orphan : Dire punishments are foretold for those who would afflict widows or orphans—those who have lost their protector and breadwinner. God will be their avenger.

lend money . . . people : Loans to their needy brethren were to be given free of interest, but interest was allowed on loans to strangers.

garment in pledge : The only pledge or earnest a poor man could give to get a loan from a neighbor was his mantle which protected him from the cold by day, and served as his blanket at night. Israelites must return this pledge each night when it is most needed. They are commanded to have compassion on their fellowman as God has compassion on all.

APPLICATION : The law of fraternal charity, the obligation to love their neighbor, was imposed by God on the Israelites from their very beginning as a people. For the most part, down through their history, they practiced it among themselves only. That was due to the fact that they lived apart from their pagan neighbors lest they should be tempted to follow the pagans' false gods. But as the first precept of charity mentioned today shows, they were to be just and charitable also to any pagan who came to live peaceably among them.

Whether the Israelites kept these precepts of charity or, more often than not, ignored them is not our concern today. What must strike us in today's reading is the merciful condescension of God. He legislates for those of his human creatures who need help and protection (the stranger, widows, orphans, the poor). From the very beginning of his self-revelation to man, he showed that he was the kind Father of all men. He created man for an eternal life, but man's bodily needs during his mortal existence on earth were also his concern.

That he could provide for all men's needs is beyond doubt; he could so arrange things that there would be no displaced persons, no widows, orphans, poor; but he chose this other way, so that men could cooperate with him and thus work their way to the eternal life.

Just think for a moment. If everyone on earth had perfect health, had all he needed of this world's goods, had absolute security and peace, would God be loved and praised by everybody, or rather would he be completely forgotten and ignored in such an earthly paradise? God does not need any love or thanks from us. It is through showing him love and thanks that we can earn our place in heaven, and it is by loving and helping our neighbor that we can prove our love for God and our gratitude to him for all he has given, and has promised to give us.

He has therefore allowed the trials and troubles of life, which naturally follow from our mortal and temporal existence on earth, to take their course. The needy and the poor, who are very often in the majority, have a golden opportunity of learning patience and trust in God. For many these very trials bind them to God. Without them they would not reach heaven. On the other hand, the succor and help which the more fortunate can give to their fellowmen in need, are some of their greatest opportunities for thanking God and keeping close to him.

Meditate today on the commandment of fraternal charity. Are you just and kind to the stranger, of whatever race, religion or color, who is in your neighborhood? Do you help the needy as much as you could? Do you thank God for giving you this opportunity for showing your real love for him? If you are one of the many who are so much in need of so many earthly things, do you try to realize that God has reason for asking us to bear these earthly sufferings? You were in his divine plan from all eternity; you are very much in his divine plan just now. If you co-operate willingly with him, you will see his eternal plan brought to realization in you before very long. Not only will you be saved but you will have been the instrument which enabled others to reach their salvation.

SECOND READING: 1 Thessalonians 1 : 5–10. You know what kind of men we proved to be among you for your sake. And you became imitators of us and of the Lord, for you received the word in much affliction, with joy inspired by the Holy Spirit; so that you became an example to all the believers in Macedonia and in Achaia. For not only has the word of the Lord sounded forth from you in Macedonia and Achaia, but your faith in God has gone forth everywhere, so that we need not say anything. For they themselves report concerning us what a welcome we had among you, and how you turned to God from idols, to serve a living and true God, and to wait for his Son from heaven, whom he raised from the dead, Jesus who delivers us from the wrath to come.

EXPLANATION : On this epistle see the second reading of last Sunday. St. Paul in today's six verses continues to praise the Thessalonians, not only for accepting the faith in difficult circumstances, but for the wonderful example their Christian life had already given to most of Greece.

kind . . . to be : Paul had Timothy, Silas and most probably Luke (Acts 16 : 11), with him when he preached the gospel in Thessalonica. They suffered for their faith and were eventually driven from the city but not before they had many Gentile converts and some Jewish ones.

imitators . . . Lord : The converts met with opposition and suffered at the hands of the Jewish community, but they gladly accepted their sufferings in imitation of Paul and of Christ who had died for them.

your faith . . . forth : The spirit with which the Thessalonians accepted and lived the faith was an example and an encouragement to the other young Christian communities in Greece.

turned . . . idols : They left their false gods when Paul told them of the true God.

wait . . . heaven : That is, the second coming of Christ as judge of the universe.

raised . . . dead : Christ in his human nature had gone to heaven, having been raised from the dead by God the Father.

from . . . to come : Christ it is, who gives all men the chance of repenting of their sins and of avoiding God's punishment of the unrepentant on the judgement day.

APPLICATION : What the good example of a truly Christian life did in the early Church it also has done down through the ages and can still do today. But how few Christians today really give this good example! In spite of the neo-paganism of our age there is still a longing for God in the hearts of the vast majority of those who pretend, or try to persuade themselves, that they can do without him. What they need is a Christian neighbor who is truly Christian, the man who will live by and stand up for his Christian principles no matter what the cost. There are, thank God, some such Christians, but they are too few and far between. We need millions of such sincere, active Christians to stem the flood of materialism and worldliness which has been let loose on us in recent times.

The anti-God world of today, and it is not all behind iron or bamboo curtains, is a reaction to the failure of Christians in the past to live their Christianity. Communism would never have arisen if the justice and charity of the Christian faith had been practiced in the countries where it arose. Religion was called the "opium of the people" because Christian rulers and the divided Christian Church used religion as a cover for their injustices toward, and exploitation of, the working class, the vast majority of the people. In Marxist theory God "became" only the projection of human ideals of love, peace, justice and power—and Marx pushed people to cease worshiping the ideal and grab the power to make these qualities come true in their own lives. God had been rejected before then—philosophically by Feuerbach (accepted quite uncritically by Marx) and by working people because of illiteracy combined with an identification of God and a Church aligned with capitalist oppressors.

When the founders of communism wrongly thought that God wanted the majority of men to be serfs and slaves on this earth in order to get to heaven, they naturally abandoned such a God and such a heaven. But they and their followers have not found a substitute for heaven nor a replacement for God, yet they are still seeking happiness. Many, even most of them, know that true and lasting happiness cannot be found on this earth. It is, therefore, our duty to show them the way to this true happiness and the only way this can be done is by the good example of our own Christian life.

An old proverb and a wise one says : "If each man would sweep in front of his own house we would have clean streets." We as individuals cannot convert the world but each one of us can do his part in his own neighborhood. There are those around us who are looking for the light and the truth. We have that light and truth to give them— the truth of our Christian faith. If put sincerely into daily practice this faith will be a shining light to those who are in the darkness of disbelief. Would we refuse that help to our fellowmen, and through that refusal risk losing our own as well as our brother's eternal salvation?

GOSPEL : Matthew 22 : 34—40. When the Pharisees heard that Jesus had silenced the Sadducees, they came together. And one of them, a lawyer, asked him a question, to test him. "Teacher, which is the great commandment in the law?" And he said to him, "You shall love the Lord your God with all your heart, and with all your soul, and with all your mind. This is the great and first commandment. And the second is like it, You shall love your neighbor as yourself. On these two commandments depend the law and the prophets."

EXPLANATION : In this section of his gospel (21 : 23—22 : 46), Matthew, after describing Christ's triumphal entry into Jerusalem on the Sunday before his crucifixion, gives us a series of the attempts made by his enemies, the Pharisees and Sadducees, to catch Jesus in some legalistic or political error. Today's question concerned the greatest commandment in the law of Moses. They had many disputes among themselves as regard this question. Christ's clear-cut answer was that the two commandments of love of God and neighbor were the essence of the Old Testament and the basis for the New Testament. This was not only an answer for the Pharisees but an answer and a rule of life for all of us for all time.

silenced the Sadducees : In the preceding verses (23–33) the Sadducees, who denied the resurrection of the dead, thought to show how impossible it was by relating the case of the woman who had, successively, several husbands. Christ showed them that the resurrection was not a return to the same mode of life that men lived while on earth. He added that if scripture called God, the God of Abraham, Isaac and Jacob, there must be a resurrection for these patriarchs for "God is God not of the dead but of the living."

lawyer . . . question : Many of the Pharisees had the title "lawyer" because they had made a special study of the Mosaic law.

Teacher : "Rabbi" was a title of honor given to a teacher of the law. They knew that Christ claimed the right to interpret the law (see Mt. 5 : 20–48) but as he was not one of their sect they would not concede any such right to him. So the title "rabbi" given him by the lawyer was insincere.

the great commandment : The intention of the question, as related in this context by Matthew, was not to get the correct answer but rather to get the wrong one.

love . . . as yourself : True love of God is the first and greatest of the commandments, but the "second is like it": true love of neighbor. The measure of that love is the love one bears toward oneself.

on these two . . . prophets : The man who truly and sincerely keeps these two laws fulfills all that God demands of him. While almost all Pharisees would agree that love of God was the greatest of the commandments, not many would agree that the love of neighbor was like it, equally binding with it, but they did not dare argue this point with Christ.

APPLICATION : The Pharisees may not have had evil intentions when asking Christ the question as to the greatest commandment. But they have done us a good service by getting this crystal clear answer from him. In this answer he tells us that the man who loves God and neighbor fulfills all his obligations, and carries out all the duties that God's self-revelation in "the law and the prophets" imposes on him. God revealed himself to us in the Old Testament as our Creator and divine benefactor. He had no need of us, since he is infinitely perfect in himself, but out of his infinite goodness he wished to share his eternal kingdom of happiness with mankind and so he created us. That we should love such a benefactor and be grateful to him is not asking much of us; such love should surely be the spontaneous reaction of a rational being, and yet there were and there are many who fail to acknowledge any such obligation.

No Christian, worthy of the name, can ever be among such thoughtless and thankless people. We have greater proofs of God's love for us than "the law and the prophets" gave to the Israelites. We have the added proofs of God's infinite interest in us brought to us by the Incarnation. We have been raised to the sublime status of adopted sons of God.

Where Christians can, and too often do fail, is in their true love of neighbor. Yet Christ says that this commandment is like the first. Love of neighbor is an essential part of our obligations toward God. If we fail in this we fail in our love for God, for we refuse to carry out this sacred duty. If we do not recognize our neighbor as our brother, we do not recognize God as our Father and we do not love him. As St. John puts it : "anyone who says : 'I love God' and hates (does not love) his neighbor is a liar" (1 Jn. 3 : 20).

Let each one of us ask himself today how seriously he takes this law of fraternal charity and how faithfully he carries it out. Not all of us may be able to give material help to a neighbor in need but the poorest of us can spare a kindly word, an encouraging word, for a neighbor weighed down with cares and troubles. All of us can pray for a neighbor who needs spiritual and temporal help. Most of us can deny ourselves some unnecessary luxuries in order to give a needed loaf of bread to a hungry fellowman, while those who have an abundance of this world's goods need not look far afield to find cases and causes worthy of their Christian charity.

Remember that whatever spiritual or material help is given out of true charity to a neighbor in need, is given to God, and whatever is given to God is soundly invested in heaven, and heaven pays handsome dividends.

In the Apostolic Letter of May 1971, the Pope has spelled out the way in which we can and should act to give the example of Christian living to the modern world. It involves a study of social problems, prayer to the Holy Spirit about them, reflection on how the gospel applies to them, and then real political commitment to change.

THIRTY-FIRST SUNDAY OF THE YEAR

FIRST READING: Malachi 1 : 14–2 : 2; 8–10. I am a great King, says the Lord of hosts, and my name is feared among the nations.

And now, O priests, this command is for you. If you will not listen, if you will not lay it to heart to give glory to my name, says the Lord of hosts, then I will send the curse upon you. You have turned aside from the way; you have caused many to stumble by your instruction; you have corrupted the covenant of Levi, says the Lord of hosts, and so I make you despised and abased before all the people, inasmuch as you have not kept my ways but have shown partiality in your instruction.

Have we not all one father? Has not one God created us? Why then are we faithless to one another, profaning the covenant of our fathers?

EXPLANATION: The book which now has the name Malachi is most probably the work of an anonymous prophet —the last of the prophets sent to the Chosen People—who preached (and wrote down what he preached) in Jerusalem about the year 450. The Jews returned from Babylon in 538. In 515 the new temple of Jerusalem was rebuilt. Moved by the preaching of two prophets Haggai and Zechariah, the returned exiles were zealous in their observance of God's law, and the liturgical rules of the temple were carried out faithfully. But when this prophet Malachi spoke, a change for the worse had come about. Both people and priests had grown lax. Marriage with neighboring Gentiles, strictly forbidden by the Mosaic law, was becoming very frequent, and the temple priests were lax and negligent in their liturgical services. In the verses read today the prophet chastises and threatens the priests of the temple.

great king . . . feared: God deserves the respect and honor given to the greatest of earthly kings—he is the great king. That his name is feared among the nations is a prophecy in line with the preceding verse 11, where it is said that he will be universally recognized and honored.

O priests . . . upon you: In verses 6–13, the prophet has listed the offenses that the priests have committed in their liturgical services. They have offered lame, diseased and even stolen animals as sacrifices to the Lord—strictly forbidden in Lev. 22 : 17–25. They have polluted the altar of sacrifice, "the table of the Lord." The prophet offers those sinful priests an opportunity to repent and change their ways. If they will not, God threatens to send the curse upon them, that is, the opposite of the blessings a worthy priest receives.

stumble . . . instruction : It is not so much a question of teaching false doctrine, but rather one of bad example which led the laity to disrespect God.

corrupted . . . Levi : God chose the tribe of Levi to serve the temple and to live by the fruits of this service (Dt. 18 : 1-8), but those priests to whom the prophet now speaks have not been faithful to their part of the covenant that God made with their ancestors. Unless they change their ways, they will be punished, "despised and abased before all the people."

all one Father : This verse introduces the prophet's condemnation of mixed marriages and is not directly connected with the priests' offenses.

profaning the covenant : It is not the universal fatherhood of God that is stressed here. The point is that God, the true God and Creator, is the father of all Jews. Therefore the descendants must keep the pact that God made with their ancestors. They are all children of the same family and of the same God.

APPLICATION : This first reading for today has been chosen because of its similarity to today's gospel. Like the Pharisees in the time of Christ the priests of the temple in Malachi's day were the leaders to whom the people looked for guidance and example. Both failed the people miserably.

Those priests to whom God spoke through his prophet had made a mockery of religion. They cheated (or tried to cheat) God and led the people to do likewise. Their service of the temple was dishonest and purely external; they brought the true religion into disrepute. They did not teach the law of God to their people for their own faith and belief were lukewarm, if not altogether lost.

In spite of all this infidelity, God was able to preserve the true faith in a remnant of his people, until the time came to fulfill the purpose for which he had chosen them : the coming of Christ. God can tolerate unworthy human helpers. His plans cannot be frustrated by them, but unfortunately, those unfaithful servants can and do frustrate their own true purpose in life.

There is perhaps a very apposite application of that sad period of the Jewish history to present-day, disturbing happenings in the Church. We read of priests and people who not only question the authority and the teaching of the Church of God, but who abandon their vocation and their faith, to the great scandal of devout believers. But we should not be scandalized. These defections did not happen overnight. They were long in preparation through the lukewarm faith and practice of past generations in many countries, through worldliness in some high places, through lack of sound education in things spiritual and through the all-pervading materialism which embraces today's world.

Nevertheless, God is still in his world and his plans for our eternal welfare will not be thwarted by the desertion of some of his weak helpers. What he did in the days of Malachi he is doing again today. He is using these upheavals to strengthen and fortify the faith and practice of his true followers. We have a part to play here and it is a big part. Each one of us must live our faith to the full. There are millions waiting for our good example, millions who are groping in the dark to find their purpose in life. We can light their way for them by the faithful fulfillment of our baptismal covenant with God.

SECOND READING : 1 Thessalonians 2 : 7–9; 13. We were gentle among you, like a nurse taking care of her children. So, being affectionately desirous of you, we were ready to share with you not only the gospel of God but also our own selves, because you had become very dear to us.

For you remember our labor and toil, brethren; we worked night and day, that we might not burden any of you, while we preached to you the gospel of God.

And we also thank God constantly for this, that when you received the word of God which you heard from us, you accepted it not as the word of men but as what it really is, the word of God, which is at work in you believers.

EXPLANATION : On the Thessalonians and this letter see twenty-ninth Sunday above.

gentle ... nurse : Paul continues to show his love and esteem for his converts in Thessalonica. He reminds them of how kind and gentle he was when preaching the gospel to them.

share ... selves : He thought so highly of them that as well as giving them the Christian faith he was willing, if necessary, to give himself, his very life, for them.

our labor and toil : Paul made a very special point of not seeking or accepting financial assistance from his converts. The Philippians were the only exception to this rule. He was a tent-maker and earned his living at that trade. He often had to work at night when his day had been spent preaching.

not ... men : The people of Thessalonica accepted the Christian faith, not because Paul or anybody else preached it, but because it was God's revelation. Unlike the Greek philosophies which came from men, the author of the truths of faith was God. This the Thessalonians knew because the gifts of the Holy Spirit which they received convinced them of the fact (1 : 5).

is at work in you : The Christian revelation is active in their daily lives. It is not some theoretical knowledge which one can learn without being affected by it. It revitalizes one's everyday life.

APPLICATION: We, too, have accepted the Christian faith as God's word, God's revelation to us. We know it is not a human philosophy invented by man : it is instead the theological truth concerning God's plan for man and his realization of that plan among us. The Old Testament tells us of God's plan for us; the New Testament describes how the coming of Christ as man put that plan into action. God's love was frequently proved in the Old Testament.

Calvary was the final irrefutable proof of it.

Today, our world is full of man-made philosophies which offer solutions for all the problems of this life, but man's greatest problem is not life but death. No human philosophy solves this problem. It is only through God's revelation that we can understand death, and see in it not an end to our activities, but the door to eternal, unending activity and life.

If we are true Christians, like the Thessalonians, this revealed knowledge of God's purpose for us, must influence our whole lives and every action of each day. We are moving steadily and quickly toward that doorway which opens into eternal life. While most of our daily activities are concerned with the material and transient things of this life, they are, or should be made spiritual stepping-stones which help us to cross over to the shores of eternity. Their value can be made eternal if they are done with the right intention.

Look back over your own past life and judge if your ordinary daily occupations were a help toward heaven. They were a help, an essential help, if they were done with the intention of honoring God and earning eternal life. They were at best time lost, or else that were done for some worldly, personal ambition which excluded God and his purpose for you. The hour or two out of the 168 hours of each week which we spend in prayer will not be sufficient to earn heaven for us; in fact, they too will be time lost, unless our Christian faith puts spiritual life and values into the remaining 166 hours.

Let us imitate the Thessalonians today; let us have our Christian faith "at work in us" every hour of our lives. Our lives will still be very ordinary, but if they are lived with the proper and right intentions, they will have an extraordinary end, they will end in the eternal life of happiness that God in his goodness has prepared for us.

GOSPEL : Matthew 23 : 1–12. Jesus said to the crowds and to his disciples, "The scribes and the Pharisees sit on Moses' seat; so practice and observe whatever they tell you, but not what they do; for they preach, but do not practice. They bind heavy burdens, hard to bear, and lay them on men's shoulders; but they themselves will not move them with their finger. They do all their deeds to be seen by men; for they make their phylacteries broad and their fringes long, and they love the place of honor at feasts and the best seats in the synagogs, and salutations in the market places, and being called rabbi by men. But you are not to be called rabbi, for you have one teacher, and you are all brethren. And call no man your father on earth, for you have one Father, who is in heaven. Neither be called masters, for you have one master, the Christ. He who is greatest among you shall be your servant; whoever exalts himself will be humbled, and whoever humbles himself will be exalted."

EXPLANATION : In the preceding two chapters of Matthew's gospel the Scribes and Pharisees had been in controversy with Jesus. They were trying to trip him up by saying something which would turn the people or the Roman authorities against him. Having silenced them, he now tells the people and his disciples, what the Scribes and Pharisees really are. Their teaching may be sound, although it is too rigorous, but their way of life, based as it is on personal pride and ambition, vitiates and ruins any merit their teaching could earn for them.

sit . . . seat : They are professors, teachers of the old law given to the Chosen People through Moses.

not . . . do : He tells the people to follow their teaching but not their example for "they preach but do not practice."

heavy burden : It has been said that they had surrounded the law of Moses with such a thick hedge of extra precepts, made mostly by themselves, that nobody could get near the Mosaic law to keep it!

not . . . finger : They tried to impose their burdensome laws on the ordinary people but they themselves would not even attempt to keep them.

to be . . . men : Pride was their predominant sin.

phylacteries . . . fringes : A phylactery was a small receptacle containing the main precepts of the Mosaic law which was attached to the arm or forehead as Ex. 13 : 9 prescribed. The fringes were colored cords sewn on each of the corners of one's cloak to remind one of the law he had to keep. The Pharisees wore larger phylacteries and longer fringes than the other Jews.

best seats . . . synagogs : At feasts they always sought the seats of honor nearest the host and the principal places in the synagogs.

salutations . . . rabbi : They sought recognition everywhere and the honorable title of "rabbi" (teacher).

you . . . called : Christ tells his disciples not to seek any such adulation—all Christians have but one teacher, Christ, and neither must they be called "father" —a title also given to the Pharisees, for Christians have but "one Father who is in heaven."

greatest . . . servant : The disciples were to minister and serve the Christian community and not to be served or ministered to by others.

exalts . . . humbled : The man who thinks humbly of himself will be respected by God and by his followers, while the proud man's folly will be despised by God and man.

APPLICATION : As this picture of the Pharisees is painted by none other than Christ himself, we can have no doubt but that the description given is the truth and nothing but the truth. In spite of their great knowledge of "the law and the prophets"—the divine revelation God had given to the Chosen People—and of their many strict observances of that law, they were not pleasing to God. All their good works and all their learning were spoiled by the vice of pride which made them seek earthly glory for themselves and prevented them from giving glory or thanks to God. Their religion was an empty external cloak which they used to attract attention and honor to themselves. Internally, they were so full of their own importance that there was no room for God in their hearts.

Our divine Lord warned his disciples, and through them all of us, to avoid that pernicious vice of pride. It should not be hard for any true Christian to avoid this vice. We know that every material and spiritual talent we have has been given us by God, so we must give glory to God for any gifts we possess and not to ourselves. St. Paul reminds us of this fact when he asks us : "What have you that you have not received, and if you have received it why glory in it as if it were your own?" We owe everything we have to God and we should use all the gifts he has given us for his honor and glory, and for that purpose alone.

Do we always do this? Are we never tempted to look down on our less fortunate brothers? If we have got on well in our temporal affairs do we attribute our success to our own skill and hard work or do we thank God for the opportunities he gave to us and not to others. If, aided by God's grace, we are keeping his commandments, do we show contempt for those who give in to temptations which we did not have to meet? The best of us can profit from an examination of conscience along these lines. If our external observance of the Christian rule of life is motivated solely by love and gratitude to God all is well. But if our hearts are far from God and our motives in our religious behavior is self-glorification, we are in a dangerous position. The sinners and harlots of Christ's day repented and were received into his kingdom; the Pharisees, unable to repent, were left outside.

THIRTY-SECOND SUNDAY OF THE YEAR

FIRST READING : Wisdom 6 : 12–16. Wisdom is radiant and unfading, and she is easily discerned by those who love her, and is found by those who seek her. She hastens to make herself known to those who desire her. He who rises early to seek her will have no difficulty, for he will find her sitting at his gates. To fix one's thoughts on her is perfect understanding, and he who is vigilant on her account will soon be free from care, because she goes about seeking those worthy of her, and she graciously appears to them in their paths, and meets them in every thought.

EXPLANATION : The book of Wisdom was written after the year 150 B.C. It is the latest of the Old Testament books and was, by a common literary device of the time, attributed to Solomon. It was written in Greek, hence its exclusion from the Jewish Canon. It was also written in Egypt after the LXX Greek translation of the Old Testament was made (hence after 150), because that translation is used by the anonymous author. He was a pious Jew living in Egypt who had meditated deeply on God's revelation as contained in the Jewish sacred books. His purpose was to strengthen the faith of his fellow-Jews who were exposed to the worldly Greek philosophies of that time. No Jew need envy the wisdom of the pagan philosophers, because he himself has true wisdom in his sacred scripture, a wisdom which regulates not only this life but the next.

wisdom . . . unfading : Wisdom is personified here as in Proverbs, Job, Baruch, and Sirach. It is not a "person" separate from Yahweh but a literary personification of one of his attributes. It is, therefore, always bright and never loses its value.

discerned . . . found : The author says this wisdom is easily recognized by those who love the truth, and easily found by all who seek true knowledge.

sitting . . . gates : The man who searches for true wisdom and really desires it will not have far to seek. The pagan philosophers labored hard and long to knit their earthly wisdom into some system. But for a sincere Jew every page of the Old Testament radiated the true wisdom of knowledge of God and of self.

those worthy of her : This divine wisdom is never denied to those who are "worthy" and who are honest in their quest.

meets . . . thought : Wisdom is ever present to the man who seriously thinks on life and its meaning and value.

N

APPLICATION: If you were driving along an open road and stopped to give a hitch-hiker a ride and to ask him where he was going and he told you he did not know, nor did he know where he came from, you might be wise not to take him with you. He might be dangerous. There are many men and women on the road of life today who do not know, or at least declare that they do not know, where they came from or whither are they bound. Their journey is only from the cradle to the grave, they say, and their purpose in life is to fit into those few short years all the pleasures and joys that this lowly earth has to give. They have enclosed themselves in mental ghettoes mostly of their own making. They refuse to open their minds to the light of true widom, lest it should disturb their consciences and their earthly plans.

Nor are they content to sit alone in their self-made cave of darkness; they want others to join them, like the tailless fox in the fable. Hence the flood of pagan philosophy and false propaganda to prove to all that man has no purpose in this life except to cram into it all the pleasure and plenty he can. From this it appears that our so-called cultured and enlightened society is, if anything, even worse than the pagan society of Egypt of the second century B.C., against which the author of Wisdom warned his fellow-Jews. At least the Egyptians of that day did not have twenty centuries of Christianity to learn from, nor the clear teaching on the meaning of life which Christ's life, death and resurrection brought to the world. This true knowledge, this divine wisdom is within reach of any person of ordinary intelligence who wishes to know the basic facts of life and death that concern him personally.

We Christians who have all the knowledge we need, not only as to our purpose and end in life, but also as regards the ways and means available to us to reach that end, must not be selfish in grasping this widom to ourselves. We must do everything we can to make our fellowmen study and learn this same divine wisdom. God has planned heaven for them; he expects us to help him in bringing them there. We must first and foremost live our own lives in strict conformity with the divine wisdom given us so generously by God. Then we must be ready to advise and instruct a neighbor who is on the wrong road, whether from ignorance or malice. As individuals we may not be sufficiently versed in our theology to stand up and refute the pagan philosophies of atheists and others, but we can help by aiding the societies engaged in this work. Where there is a will there is a way. Where there is true love of God, a way will be found to prove that love for God, by helping a neighbor.

The Christian who shares his wisdom and knowledge with his needy neighbor is the true Christian whose personal wisdom will be ever "radiant and unfading."

SECOND READING: 1 Thessalonians 4:13–18. We would not have you ignorant, brethren, concerning those who are asleep, that you may not grieve as others do who have no hope. For since we believe that Jesus died and rose again, even so, through Jesus, God will bring with him those who have fallen asleep. For this we declare to you by the word of the Lord, that we who are alive, who are left until the coming of the Lord, shall not precede those who have fallen asleep. For the Lord himself will descend from heaven with a cry of command, with the archangel's call, and with the sound of the trumpet of God. And the dead in Christ will rise first; then we who are alive, who are left, shall be caught up together with them in the clouds to meet the Lord in the air; and so we shall always be with the Lord. Therefore comfort one another with these words.

EXPLANATION: The Thessalonians were much preoccupied with the question of Christ's second coming as judge of the world. At the time of their conversion they evidently expected his coming in the near future, and even though they believed in the resurrection of the dead, they seemed to hope to escape death by the early arrival of Christ in the *parousia*. Some of their members had died in the meantime. They were worried over this, and questioned Paul about it, through Timothy who had visited them.

may not grieve: Unlike the pagans who had no hope in a resurrection from the dead, the Thessalonian converts must not grieve over the death of their relatives or friends. They will one day rise again to the glorious life.

Jesus . . . rose: The resurrection of Jesus from the dead is the proof and the guarantee of our resurrection. He is "the first-fruits of all who have fallen asleep" (1 Cor. 15:20).

we who are alive: Paul seems to include himself among those who will still be living when the *parousia* takes place, but this is probably a literary device, for Christ, as Paul knew (see 5:2), did not give any indication as to when this would be. In his parables he implied it would not be for a long time (see Lk. 12:43; Mt. 25:5; 19). Paul tells the Thessalonians that those who are alive will have no advantage over those who are dead when Christ returns.

with a cry . . . trumpet: The description here follows the apocalyptic literature of the time—the basic truth is:

we shall . . . Lord: All his faithful followers will have eternal life with Christ when they finish their allotted time on this earth.

APPLICATION: We have many philosophies which try to solve the problems of man's life on this earth but no human philosophy has found a satisfactory solution for the problem of man's death. Materialists may hold that our world had no rational Creator and that all that is came about by mere chance. They must surely be taken aback by the perfection (especially the intelligent mind) which this blind chance brought to man. But it leaves them in the unhappy state of having only a few short years to enjoy the irrepressible desire for happiness which his intelligence creates in him. Such an accident of fate was surely very blind and cruel to man. The sapling oak we plant is far better off because it will be there two hundred years after we are gone and it will never have a moment of worry in its long life.

On the other hand, those who admit a rational Creator but deny a future life for man, make that Creator very irrational and cruel. He has put the qualities and desires for lasting happiness in man but makes their fulfillment impossible if earthly death is man's final end. Man is evidently the master and masterpiece of all creation but if real life ends for him after a few short years he is in a worse position than that of all the rest of creation. Such a Creator would be not a benefactor but a cruel jester.

Human philosophy, if properly used, can lead the way to solving man's greatest problem, but it is only in Christian revelation that the full and true answer to the problem of earthly death is found. We are fortunate to have that knowledge. We know that just as and because Christ rose from the dead, we too shall rise again in glorified bodies, or rather as glorified persons, to live on forever in God's kingdom in heaven. There all tears, all pains, all worries will be ended forever, and all our desires will be completely fulfilled in the beatific vision of God. Even though our bodies will not be the same as those we had on earth, we shall be able to identify one another and to enjoy one another's company in God's presence, and this happy state will never have an end.

What a consoling thought! No wonder it is that the great saints of God were willing to undergo any hardship in this life in order to reach that happy state. If we would meditate and ponder over our future life a little more often, we should be better able to take the "slings and arrows" of the fortunes of this life in our stride as the saints did. Death is not something to be feared by the man who believes in God and lives up to that belief. It is a welcome departure from sorrow and an arrival at the abode of eternal peace.

GOSPEL: Matthew 25:1-13. Jesus spoke this parable to his disciples. "Then the kingdom of heaven shall be compared to ten maidens who took their lamps and went to meet the bridegroom. Five of them were foolish, and five were wise. For when the foolish took their lamps, they took no oil with them; but the wise took flasks of oil with their lamps. As the bridegroom was delayed, they all slumbered and slept. But at midnight there was a cry, 'Behold, the bridegroom! Come out to meet him.' Then all those maidens rose and trimmed their lamps. And the foolish said to the wise, 'Give us some of your oil, for our lamps are going out.' But the wise replied, 'Perhaps there will not be enough for us and for you; go rather to the dealers and buy for yourselves.' And while they went to buy, the bridegroom came, and those who were ready went in with him to the marriage feast; and the door was shut. Afterward the other maidens came also, saying, 'Lord, lord, open to us.' But he replied, 'Truly, I say to you, I do not know you.' Watch therefore, for you know neither the day nor the hour."

EXPLANATION: To impress the supreme need of vigilance, our Lord tells a story which shows that some of his followers who have been chosen to play a special role in the nuptials of Christ with his Church will forfeit their place at the eternal nuptials in heaven through carelessness and not positive malice.

The image of a marriage to describe Christ's union with his Church was easily understood by his hearers. God's union with the Chosen People of the Old Testament was frequently compared to a marriage, God being the spouse, Israel the bride (cf. Canticle of Canticles; Is. 54; 2 Cor. 11:2; Eph. 5:25–32).

the kingdom . . . maidens: The reference is to the second coming of Christ in glory, to judge all mankind. On that day his kingdom will be completed; the kingdom on earth, the preparatory period in his Church, will end, and the eternal triumphal kingdom in heaven will begin. The story he now tells illustrates what will happen on that day to some of those whom he had chosen, and to whom he had given every facility to reach their one and only goal.

ten maidens: A wedding among the Jews at the time of Christ was preceded by a week of feverish preparations on the part of the bride assisted by her chosen attendants, unmarried maidens of her own age. The wedding feast generally took place in the bridegroom's house. He, accompanied by his companions, "friends of the bridegroom," came to the bride's house about sunset. Having received his bride from her parents or guardians, a procession was formed, and with music and joyful chant the wedding group went to the bridegroom's home, for the wedding feast, which would last all night and perhaps even for days. The invited guests were generally numerous, the relatives and friends of both families, as well as the outstanding people of the neighborhood; and oriental hospitality could not exclude casual acquaintances and strangers should they drop in. The expenses were not as formidable as one might think, for each guest donated flour, cheese, wine, and other useful items, instead of an expensive gift.

In his parable our Lord describes the fate of very special guests, the intimate friends of the bride, who gladly accepted the invitation and went to a lot of trouble to prepare for the occasion, and yet, through carelessness, were found unworthy to share in the festivities.

took . . . lamps : The chosen bridesmaids had to carry lighted lamps in the bridal procession, which always took place at night. All ten came to the bride's home in good time, dressed for the occasion and carrying the necessary lamps. These lamps were generally small, shallow earthenware or bronze vessels which held enough oil to burn for a few hours.

five . . . wise : The number ten was held in high honor among the Jews, and so there were generally ten bridesmaids to accompany a bride on her wedding procession. The folly of the five is shown below.

took . . . them : They came to the bride's home early in the day. They remembered to take their lamps but forgot to take a supply of oil with them. This supply was carried in a small vessel or jar when one was going on a journey, as it would be almost impossible to keep the oil from spilling out of the saucerlike lamps. The wise bridesmaids realized that they were going as torchbearers in this bridal procession and took a supply of oil for their lamps.

the bridegroom . . . delayed : Having gathered in the bride's home, there was much chatter and talk at first; everybody was happy and excited. The foolish as well as the wise looked forward eagerly to the great wedding feast in which they would participate, but as the night wore on they all gradually grew tired until finally they fell into a sound sleep.

Behold . . . bridegroom : About midnight a watchman, stationed outside the house to give warning as soon as he saw the bridegroom's party approaching, shouted : "Behold, he comes; get ready to meet him."

then all . . . lamps : The wise maidens poured in oil and lighted the wicks. The foolish ones just lighted the wick and only when the flame flickered and died did they realize their foolish negligence.

give us . . . oil : Now they try to borrow what they should have provided for themselves.

wise answered . . . yourselves : This answer may sound unkind and uncharitable, but it was only another proof of the wise bridesmaids' prudence.

while . . . buy : For want of any better solution to their problem, the five foolish bridesmaids went out in search of a dealer from whom they could purchase some oil. In the meantime the procession was formed, and went to the bridegroom's home. The door was shut, and the celebration began.

the other maidens came : After a long search, perhaps in vain at that late hour, they reached the bridegroom's house. Relying on the fact that they were the chosen friends of the bride, the foolish virgins beseeched the bridegroom to let them enter.

But he replied . . . you : Their claim to admission was not substantiated by the facts. The bride had selected them as her attendants, but they had proved themselves unworthy of this honor; they had not prepared themselves for the privilege offered them. Thus the bridegroom does not acknowledge them.

watch . . . hour : The conclusion to be drawn from this story by the disciples is this : the time of arrival of our Lord as judge of the universe—the day on which the eternal wedding feast of Christ with his elect will begin—is as uncertain as was the hour of arrival of the bridegroom in the story. There is but one sure way to be found ready on that all-important moment—constant preparedness.

APPLICATION : Although commentators and writers have found difficulty in explaining many of the details in this parable, the general lesson is clear enough. Our Lord described an incident that happened or could have happened at a wedding festival in order to bring home to his listeners the need for being ever vigilant and ready in his service if they wish to avoid the calamity of being excluded from the heavenly and eternal nuptials on the last day. In the other parable in which our Lord uses a wedding feast to describe his kingdom, the lesson concerns those who refused the invitation and will not come to the wedding. Here it concerns those who gladly accepted the invitation.

The ten bridesmaids, or maidens, in the parable represent all Christians. On receiving the sacrament of baptism, the Christian starts on the road to heaven; he gets his invitation to the heavenly nuptials but this is only the beginning. From the moment he comes to the use of reason he is expected to prepare himself, by living according to the law of God, for the great moment when the call will go forth : "Behold the bridegroom! Come to meet him." This moment will be, first, at the hour of death for each individual when each one's eternal fate will be decided, and again at the general judgement of the human race. During their lifetime all are invited to the heavenly wedding, and all have the necessary means to get ready. But, like the foolish bridesmaids, many will fail to make use of these means and will realize their folly when it is too late. Sad, but true.

A certain number of those for whom Christ died on the cross, and to whom he gave the gift of his revelation and offered all the helps they needed, will never reach heaven because they exchanged their heavenly birthright for a mess of earthly pottage. That the foolish bridesmaids in the parable lost a golden opportunity through their negligence is evident and we can all sympathize with them up to a point, but the thoughts of very few will turn to the bride and groom who were so seriously insulted by this act of negligence on the part of chosen friends.

So too, every Cristian lost is a grievous insult to the God who created and redeemed him. Christians have received the fullness of God's revelation, and have been offered a special place in his marriage festival; they have received a privileged invitation not given to others. Is it not a serious and deliberate insult to God not to comply with the conditions of that generous offer?

Providing themselves with oil was the obligation imposed on the bridesmaids in the parable. It was surely a trivial condition when compared with the reward offered them : a very special place at the marriage feast. The obligations imposed on us Christians are surely trivial too when compared with the reward offered us in return : an eternity of happiness in heaven. It seems incredible that there are many among us this very day who, like the foolish bridesmaids, doze and sleep contentedly holding empty lamps in their hands, while at any moment they may be awakened by : "Behold, the bridegroom comes! Go forth to meet him." It will be too late then to do anything; even their best friends cannot help them. Each one must stand before the judge just as he is; there can be no borrowing of the oil of merit from others and there will be no time to buy any.

Now is the time for all of us to say: "Lord, Lord, open to us," open to us the doors of your mercy and kindness. Open to us the eyes of our understanding that we may see our defects and remedy them while there is yet time.

It is up to us now to decide, aided by God's grace, where we shall be found on the last day—with the wise bridesmaids or with the foolish.

THIRTY-THIRD SUNDAY OF THE YEAR

FIRST READING: Proverbs 31:10–13; 19–20; 30–31. A good wife who can find? She is far more precious than jewels. The heart of her husband trusts in her, and he will have no lack of gain. She does him good, and not harm, all the days of her life. She seeks wool and flax, and works with willing hands. She puts her hands to the distaff, and her hands hold the spindle. She opens her hand to the poor, and reaches out her hands to the needy. Charm is deceitful, and beauty is vain, but a woman who fears the Lord is to be praised. Give her of the fruit of her hands, and let her works praise her in the gates.

EXPLANATION: The book Proverbs is a collection of wise sayings and wise religious precepts to govern the daily lives of lovers of wisdom and of God. The book was attributed to Solomon because he was looked on as the patron and inspirer of wisdom in Israel. Though some of the wise sayings of the book may have come down by oral tradition from Solomon, most of the material contained in it comes from later sources and the language and style point to a post-exilic (after 500 B.C.) date for its final composition.

The verses chosen for today's reading are taken from the last half of the last chapter of the book and are a hymn in praise of the ideal wife. This is somewhat unusual in the Old Testament where women played a rather minor role in public, civic or religious life. But the anonymous author of this section rightly saw to it that the part that a wise, prudent and industrious wife plays in a man's life, and hence in the life of the nation, deserved to be stressed and admired.

precious . . . jewels: The ideal wife is

far more precious to a man than all the jewels he could collect.

trusts in her : The husband of the good wife can put all his trust in her; the care and management of his home is in safe and capable hands.

no . . . gain : Not only will she not waste his property, she will add to it by her industry.

wool . . . hands : Weaving cloth and knitting were the sparetime occupations of women in those days and for centuries after. The "good" wife will not only provide the material and the garments needed in her household but will have some for sale (v. 24).

opens . . . poor : The good wife will provide for her own family but will have enough to help her needy neighbors.

charm . . . beauty : A foolish man may select a wife because of her charm or beauty, but these are really false criteria on which to base such an important decision.

a woman . . . Lord : The ideal wife who will really enrich her husband is the woman who has the true religion and whose life is motivated by her faith.

praises . . . gates : Each gate (sometimes there were more than one) of a city in Palestine was a place where the commercial and legal business of the city was carried on. The products of her industry as seen in her husband's dress (v. 23) and in the wares she has for sale in the marketplace will earn for the ideal wife, the esteem and praise of the public.

APPLICATION : While it is possible that it is "wisdom" (the theme of his book) that the author of Proverbs is personifying here in his praise of the ideal wife, the fact remains that what is said is eminently true of a faithful wife. Such a woman, faithful to God, to her husband and children, is more valuable to a man than all the gold, silver and pearls he could ever collect. With an ideal wife of this kind and thank God for it, the vast majority of wives are of this kind, a man can safely leave his home and his possessions in her care. He is free to devote all his energies to providing the necessities of life. In this provision the ideal wife can and will lend a helping hand, as Proverbs and history tell us. Even within the walls of her home a faithful, zealous wife will find time to do work that will supplement the weekly income.

A wise old saying tells us that : "the hand that rocks the cradle rules the world," that is, the mothers of families are those who regulate and stabilize this world's affairs. If this is true of all good mothers, it is doubly true of Christian and religiously-minded mothers, for these not only rule this world but play a very big part in arranging and deciding men's fate in the world-to-come. Read the lives of most of our greatest canonized saints and see the important and even decisive role their mothers played in their sanctification. St. Monica comes to mind. She spent years in prayer and self-mortification beseeching God to give the grace of conversion to her heretical and morally lax son, Augustine.

She followed him all the way from Carthage in North Africa to Milan in Italy to try to move him, as she was trying to move God, by her tears and entreaties. She succeeded, and the result : St. Augustine, the great doctor of the Church.

What is true of so many of our canonized saints is surely true of the millions of noncanonized saints who are today enjoying the bliss of heaven because of the influence their mothers had on their lives.

Christian mothers, try never to forget the absolutely necessary role you have been given by God in his plan for populating heaven. He has made you necessary for producing citizens of this world but that was only the preliminary step to making them citizens of heaven. In this task the mother must play the essential role. It is at your knees that your

children will learn about their Father in heaven. It is in your home from your example and advice that they will learn to serve that heavenly Father during their lives and so reach their eternal home where you will be joyfully awaiting them.

Charm and beauty are trivial and passing possessions but the woman who fears, that is faithfully serves, the Lord is a precious treasure which will last forever.

SECOND READING : 1 Thessalonians 5 : 1-6. As to the times and the seasons, brethren, you have no need to have anything written to you. For you yourselves know well that the day of the Lord will come like a thief in the night. When people say, "There is peace and security," then sudden destruction will come upon them as travail comes upon a woman with child, and there will be no escape. But you are not in darkness, brethren, for that day to surprise you like a thief. For you are all sons of light and sons of the day; we are not of the night or of darkness. So then let us not sleep, as others do, but let us keep awake and be sober.

EXPLANATION : St. Paul continues his discussion of the *parousia,* the second coming of Christ as judge of mankind. See last Sunday's second reading. Today he tells his Thessalonian converts that they know as much as he does about the time of that second coming. He had already told them in his preaching what our Lord himself had said about it : that it would be unexpected; it would come "like a thief in the night." However, this need not frighten them, they would be prepared because they were living their Christian faith every day.

times and seasons : This is an eschatological phrase which meant the moments of divine intervention in human affairs (see Dn. 2 : 21). Here the reference is to the second coming and they knew that

the time of its happening had not been revealed.

like . . . night : Our Lord had used this very expression to tell his disciples that his second coming would be sudden and unexpected (see Mt. 24 : 36–43).

peace and security : In those days robber gangs frequently raided towns and cities. Because of the period of quiet it was foolish to conclude that there was no need to bar and lock their doors.

you . . . darkness : The second coming of Christ would be in the darkness of night only for those who were not living and working in the light of the faith. The Thessalonians had no dark night in this sense, they were always loyal to their faith.

sleep . . . do : It is while a man sleeps

that the thief enters. No burglar dares to break in while the householder is up and about. So Paul urges his converts to be always "up and about" in the spiritual sense. Then the second coming of Christ will be a joyful event because they will be ready to receive him.

APPLICATION : The *parousia* or second coming of Christ has not yet taken place and we still have no idea as to when it will be. But what has taken place, ever since the days of the Thessalonians, is that Christ has come to billions of men and women at the moment of their death to decide their eternal fate. This is what concerns each one of us today—the moment when we will meet Christ as our judge. In God's wise providence this most important moment of our earthly lives is hidden from us.

Many of us will say : "why does God not tell us when our death will take place so that we properly could prepare ourselves?" Would we in fact, or could we do so? God knows our weak nature infinitely better than we do. How many of us would postpone our conversion and continue to enjoy the illicit joys of life until the last week before our appointed moment of death? And granted the infinite mercy of God who has accepted death-bed conversions, how many of us would be able to turn to God sincerely and honestly after such a life?

Furthermore God has allotted a life's work to each one of us. He has given a certain number of talents to each and expects us to produce spiritual fruits with these talents. What of the years wasted if we left our conversion to the last week? The inspector who finds a factory-worker laboring diligently each time he comes to the workshop, but finds no end product during the remaining hours of the day, could hardly be expected to keep that worker in his employment and reward him handsomely! Our service of God is a labor of love and gratitude for all he has done for us. It is not slave labor controlled by the taskmaster's whip. We serve God, we keep his commandments because we love him and we are trying to repay a little the infinite kindness he has showered upon us.

The fact, therefore, that the moment of our death is hidden from us is a blessing for even the best of us—it keeps us on our toes—and a necessity for the lazy and luke-warm among us. Our own self-interest in the future life, and the uncertainty of the moment of final decision, will spur us on to love and thank God and to endeavor to remain ever in his friendship.

This is what St. Paul urges his converts to do; it's his message for us today. We have the light of the gospel—the illumination of the true faith. If we continue to live in that light, to lead our lives under that illumination, death's advent cannot be in the darkness. We shall be spiritually prepared for it.

GOSPEL : Matthew 25 : 14–30. Jesus spoke this parable to his disciples : "The kingdom of heaven will be as when a man going on a journey called his servants and entrusted to them his property; to one he gave five talents, to another two, to another one, to each according to his ability. Then he went away. He who had received the five talents went at once and traded with them; and he made five talents more. So also, he who had two talents made two talents more. But he who had received the one talent went and dug in the ground and hid his master's money. Now after a long time the master of those servants came and settled accounts with them. And he who had received the five talents came forward, bringing five talents more, saying, 'Master, you delivered to me five talents; here I have made five talents more.' His master said to him, 'Well done, good and faithful servant; you have been faithful over a little, I will set you over much; enter into the joy of your master.' And he also who had the two talents came forward, saying, 'Master, you delivered to me two talents; here I have made two talents more.' His master said to him, 'Well done, good and faithful servant; you have been faithful over a little, I will set you over much; enter into the joy of your master.' He also who had received the one talent came forward, saying, 'Master, I knew you to be a hard man, reaping where you did not sow, and gathering where you did not winnow; so I was afraid, and I went and hid your talent in the ground. Here you have what is yours.' But his master answered him, 'You wicked and slothful servant! You knew that I reap where I have not sowed, and gather where I have not winnowed? Then you ought to have invested my money with the bankers, and at my coming I should have received what was my own with interest. So take the talent from him, and give it to him who has the ten talents. For to everyone who has will more be given, and he will have abundance; but from him who has not, even what he has will be taken away. And cast the worthless servant into the outer darkness; there men will weep and gnash their teeth.' "

EXPLANATION : This is another of the parables or stories which Jesus told to illustrate and emphasize the teaching on the kingdom of heaven that he gave to his disciples. The point of the story here (as in Lk. 19 : 12–27, very likely the same parable in slightly different words), is that we shall be judged by God according to the use we make of the gifts he gave us.

man . . . journey : The businessman is described as going abroad. He divided his money among his servants so that they would use it profitably while he was away.

five . . . one talent : He gave different amounts to each for the servants were not all of equal business acumen.

hid . . . money : While the servants who received the five and the two talents used them wisely and doubled their holdings, the third servant left his talent unused— buried in the ground.

settled accounts : On his return, the master, a real businessman, questioned each servant as to what use he had made of the money given him, and what profit he had gained.

faithful . . . little : Those who had acted wisely were praised and told there was much more coming to them because they had used the "little" he had lent them so wisely and well.

joy . . . master : Henceforth they would not be servants or slaves but would have an honored place in their master's household.

he . . . talent : Finally the servant who had not used the talent or money given him tried to excuse his negligence by saying that he knew how hard and demanding the master was and therefore did not risk investing his money in case he should lose it.

wicked . . . servant : The master knew the real reason why this servant did not invest his talent. It was sinfulness and sloth. He said he knew the master was demanding and exacting, but he knew he was safe during the master's absence, and probably had convinced himself that the master would never return. Now his troubles begin.

take . . . him : The talent he had left lying idle is taken from him and given to one of the honest and willing servants. Because of his refusal to earn anything for a master he called hard and exacting, he is not admitted to the master's household. The fact that the master leaves the original talents plus what they had earned with them and also rewards them so highly (bringing them into his own household) proves that he was not in fact a hard, exacting master but a kind and generous one.

to everyone who has : The generous master (God) will not be outdone in generosity. Those who are loyal to him will be greatly rewarded, while the disloyal will lose even the original gifts given them because they abused them or did not use them as they should.

outer darkness : Instead of being received in the household of the master the unfaithful servant will be cast into the "outer darkness", a metaphor to describe the lot of those who exclude themselves from heaven.

weep and gnash : This describes the grief and bitter disgust for themselves which will torture those who have missed their real purpose in life.

APPLICATION : The lesson of this parable, like all the teaching of the gospel, is as applicable to us today as it was to the first generation of Christians. In its relation to Christ and to his divine Father our world today is very similar to first century Palestine. Christ and God have opponents and followers. Their opponents today have the very same reasons that moved the Pharisees and leaders of the people in Christ's day. They want their messianic kingdom here on earth, a kingdom of pleasure and plenty; they want no limits set to their freedom to follow their own earthly inclinations. Their pride in their own self-exalted dignity will not let them bow the head to any deity or divine authority which does not conform to their standards. Like the Pharisees they keep on trying to convince themselves that Christianity is not true, that Christ will not reign, that there will be no day of reckoning.

Yet with all their efforts to get rid of Christ and God, the small inner voice of conscience is not completely silenced. It has the nasty habit of reminding them of their folly. They have their troubled moments when the epicurean motto "eat, drink, sleep and be merry" does not somehow ring true.

For the followers of Christ who are sincere in their efforts, the parable has a message of encouragement and consolation. At times the road we have to travel seems strewn with obstacles, our battles seem never-ending, yet God has provided each one of us with the necessary helps to ensure the final victory. These helps are given according to each one's need. Those servants in the parable who received five and two talents used them faithfully and successfully. He who received one talent needed only one, and could have succeeded with it had he been a faithful servant.

Eternal happiness is the divine reward for an earthly service faithfully rendered. The false excuse of the third servant is repeated in many forms among us still:

"God is too austere, he could not expect me to make such sacrifices. I have to provide for myself; his promises and threats may be only empty words. He may never return to demand a reckoning, to settle accounts with us." These and all other such excuses are proved false in this parable.

God is a kind Father who has our eternal interests at heart. He does expect us to make the necessary sacrifices. He showed us the way on Calvary. When working for God we are really providing for our own future; his external glory and our eternal salvation are the fruits of the same labor. He will certainly return to settle accounts—it will then be too late to make any changes. Let us be wise and make the changes now while we have time and then our books will be in order on the day of reckoning.

THIRTY-FOURTH SUNDAY OF THE YEAR
SOLEMNITY OF CHRIST THE KING

FIRST READING : Ezekiel 34 : 11–12; 15–17. Thus says the Lord God : "Behold, I, I myself, will search for my sheep, and will seek them out. As a shepherd seeks out his flock when some of his sheep have been scattered abroad, so will I seek out my sheep; and I will rescue them from all places where they have been scattered on a day of clouds and thick darkness. I myself will be the shepherd of my sheep, and I will make them lie down, says the Lord God. I will seek the lost, and I will bring back the strayed, and I will bind up the crippled, and I will strengthen the weak, and the fat and the strong I will watch over; I will feed them in justice.

"As for you, my flock, thus says the Lord God : Behold, I judge between sheep and sheep, rams and he-goats."

EXPLANATION : On Ezekiel see the 23rd Sunday of the year. The prophet was called by God to instruct and console the Jewish exiles in Babylonia. This exile and all the hardships it brought on the people was caused by infidelity and disloyalty to God on the part of their kings and leaders. They were the "shepherds of Israel" but they "fed themselves rather than the flock" entrusted to them by God (see verses 1–10 of this 34th chapter). Now God promises, through Ezekiel, that he himself will be his people's shepherd. He will care for them; he will rule them in peace and justice. He will be the new David (v. 23). He will replace the unfaithful shepherds who brought this calamity (the exile) on the Chosen People.

search . . . sheep : Like a true shepherd he will go after any lost sheep (see the parable of the Lost Sheep Lk. 15 : 3–10).
rescue . . . places : God's flock had been scattered far from their homeland because of their own sins but especially because of the sins of their leaders. But God would bring them back home once more, a reference to the return from Babylonia.
I will . . . justice : The new kingdom of his Chosen People will be one of justice and therefore of peace. In it the crippled and the weak will be looked after and provided for, as well as the fat and the strong.
judge . . . sheep : God will punish those

(the leaders) who exploited the weak and he will reward their victims. Those leaders were he-goats in their abuse of power, not rams to protect the weak. God will distinguish the wicked from the good.

APPLICATION : In his infinite love and kindness God consoled and encouraged the Jewish exiles in Babylonia through the prophet Ezekiel. He told them that they would return to their own country where they would once more be a Chosen People directly under his divine care. The earthly rulers he had placed over them had failed in their duty. Now he himself would be their ruler and he would rule mercifully, kindly and justly.

He described the relationship between his people and himself under the image of a flock of sheep and its shepherd. It's an image often found in the Old Testament. That God was referring to the future messianic kingdom, to the new Chosen People, is evident from the fact that our divine Lord, the Messiah, applied this passage of Ezekiel to himself in John 10 : 1–18. Speaking to the Pharisees whose pride and prejudice had blinded them so that they could not see him as the promised Messiah, Jesus told them that he was the true "shepherd" who would lay down his life for his sheep. He had come, he said, so that his sheep might have life and have it to the full (eternal life). There were other sheep who up to then did not belong to God's fold (referring to the Gentiles) but those too he would lead to life, they would eventually be one flock and one shepherd.

This prophecy given by God over 500 years before Christ came on earth was fulfilled to the letter in Christ, as Christ himself declared and as history has proved. The Son of God came on earth as man to give all men eternal life. He founded the new sheepfold, the new Chosen People, the kingdom of God on earth, to prepare for entry into heaven all who will enter its gates. We are fortunate to belong to that kingdom. We have a king who has proved his love by dying for us in order to give us life. By his sufferings our wounds were healed; by his death on the cross he has conquered death; by his resurrection he has made our physical death the doorway that leads to everlasting life.

SECOND READING : 1 Corinthians 15 : 20–26; 28. Christ has been raised from the dead, the first fruits of those who have fallen asleep. For us by a man came death, by a man has come also the resurrection of the dead. For as in Adam all die, so also in Christ shall all be made alive. But each in his own order : Christ the first fruits, then at his coming those who belong to Christ. Then comes the end, when he delivers the kingdom to God the Father after destroying every rule and every authority and power. For he must reign until he has put all his enemies under his feet. The last enemy to be destroyed is death. When all things are subjected to him, then the Son himself will also be subjected to him who put all things under him, that God may be everything to everyone.

EXPLANATION : Some members of the Christian Church in Corinth evidently denied or were doubtful about the resurrection of all men from the dead. This denial or doubt would spring from the philosophy of Plato, then common in Greece. Plato held that all men were originally spiritual beings, "souls," who lived in the presence of the all-perfect, but because some offended in some way, they were put into bodies and had to suffer with these bodies on earth. If they proved themselves worthy, they would at death shed these bodies and return to their happiness. Because of this erroneous philosophy many Greeks found it difficult to accept the Christian dogma of the resurrection of the whole man, body included (see Acts 17 : 32). Paul devotes the whole of chapter 15 of this letter to convince his converts that all men would rise again after death. His central proof is that Christ rose from the dead, as trustworthy witnesses proved. If Christ had not risen, there would have been no redemption. Christianity would never have begun much less continued to exist. But Christ did rise and so will all those united with him by baptism.

Today's extract from this chapter, however, has been chosen not because of the doctrine it contains on the resurrection, but because of the reference to the kingship of Christ. It was Christ who founded the new kingdom of God on earth and he will reign over it until the final victory is won, namely, when the last man on earth to be saved has been safely included in God's kingdom. Then Christ, as man, will hand over the kingdom and all kingship to God the Creator and Father of all.

Christ . . . first-fruits : Christ's resurrection is the proof and the guarantee of resurrection from the dead. Christ is the first-fruits not only because he was the first in time to rise, but because his resurrection is the cause and the guarantee of the resurrection of all others. "First-fruits" is a cultic term, the offering of the first fruits of the harvest by the Jews was the symbol of the dedication of the entire harvest to God.

then . . . coming : When Christ comes the second time to judge mankind all those who belong to Christ by baptism, and by a life faithful to their baptismal promises, will rise from the dead.

delivers . . . God : All those faithful to Christ will be handed to the Father to enter into his eternal kingdom.

he . . . feet : In the period which intervenes between his resurrection and the end of the world, Christ the Son of God Incarnate is king of all mankind. It is by their final loyalty to Christ or by their disloyalty to him that men will prove themselves worthy or unworthy to enter God's eternal kingdom. At his second coming his royal majesty will be made evident to all.

enemy . . . death : With the resurrection of the dead "on the last day" Christ's victory will be complete. Death itself will have been conquered.

the Son . . . subjected : On the day of final victory, Christ as man will, together with all God's adopted children, render homage to God. In heaven Christ as God will reign over the heavenly king-dom together with the Father and the Holy Spirit while as man he will occupy the first place next to the Trinity.

God may . . . everyone : God is first cause and final end of all creation, but in a special way he is the final and only real end of mankind. The plan of God's love for human destiny began with creation, continued through revelation and culminated in the supreme act of love, the Incarnation. At the end of time this plan will be made manifest to all men—to those who in life refused to believe it as well as to the believers who will be enjoying the beatific vision of their heavenly Father.

APPLICATION : It is very fitting that the Church should dedicate the last Sunday of the liturgical year to honoring Christ, her founder and Savior, as King of the universe. Through the divine intervention, in the Incarnation of the Son of God in human history, mankind has been raised to the sonship with God which was planned before creation began. The sins of the world have been atoned for, and men are made citizens of God's kingdom on earth with the promise of citizenship in the eternal kingdom if they do the little that is expected of them while they are on earth.

All this we owe to Christ the Son of God "who emptied himself" of his divine glory and deigned to become man so that we mortals could become sons of God. We close our liturgical year, therefore, with a feastday which honors Christ as man and we give him the highest title a man can have as we proclaim him our King. Although this title was introduced only in recent times by Pius XI, its meaning and understanding go back to the very beginning of Christianity. St.

Paul tells us in today's reading that Christ began his triumphant reign at the moment of his resurrection and that it will continue on earth until his last opponent is overcome. That will be on the day of the final judgement. Christ's kingdom on earth will then pass into the Father's eternal kingdom of heaven, where Christ as God will reign in majesty together with the Father and Holy Spirit.

We have every reason, therefore, to rejoice in Christ today and to render him all the gratitude and glory of which our human nature is capable. We have the great blessing of being members of his kingdom after death. Christ lived and died for us. He lived to teach us the truth and show us the way to heaven. He died to conquer our death and earn for us eternal life. He rose from the dead to prove he had overcome sin and death and to open the gates of heaven for us. Christ is "the way, the truth and the life." If we follow him we are following the king who can lead us to victory.

Let us thank our Savior for all he has

done for us. Our thanks will be sincere only if we renew our pledge of loyal service to him. Earthly kings regulate the temporal lives of their subjects, Christ is preparing for us an unending life. Earthly kings sometimes reward their outstanding subjects; Christ has promised an everlasting reward to all who serve him—the lowly of the world as well as the highest in the land. Only those who refuse to have him to reign over them—those who have no king but Caesar—will fail to receive his reward.

Christ is our king in this world. Let us make sure that he will be our king for all eternity by doing our best to be his loyal subjects here on earth.

GOSPEL: Matthew 25:31–36. Jesus said to his disciples, "When the Son of man comes in his glory, and all the angels with him, then he will sit on his glorious throne. Before him will be gathered all the nations, and he will separate them one from another as a shepherd separates the sheep from the goats, and he will place the sheep at his right hand, but the goats at the left. Then the King will say to those at his right hand, 'Come, O blessed of my Father, inherit the kingdom prepared for you from the foundation of the world; for I was hungry and you gave me food, I was thirsty and you gave me drink, I was a stranger and you welcomed me, I was naked and you clothed me, I was sick and you visited me, I was in prison and you came to me.' Then the righteous will answer him, 'Lord, when did we see thee hungry and feed thee, or thirsty and give thee drink? And when did we see thee a stranger and welcome thee, or naked and clothe thee? And when did we see thee sick or in prison and visit thee?' And the King will answer them, 'Truly, I say to you, as you did it to one of the least of these my brethren, you did it to me.' Then he will say to those at his left hand, 'Depart from me, you cursed, into the eternal fire prepared for the devil and his angels; for I was hungry and you gave me no food, I was thirsty and you gave me no drink, I was a stranger and you did not welcome me, naked and you did not clothe me, sick and in prison and you did not visit me.' Then they also will answer, 'Lord, when did we see thee hungry or thirsty or a stranger or naked or sick or in prison, and did not minister to thee?' Then he will answer them, 'Truly, I say to you, as you did it not to one of the least of these, you did it not to me.' And they will go away into eternal punishment, but the righteous into eternal life."

EXPLANATION: Speaking to his disciples, Jesus describes his second coming as that of a king arriving in all his majesty and sitting on his kingly throne to judge all mankind. A king he is, and as a king he will judge rightly and authoritatively. There will be no appeal against his sentence. Let us hope that

that day of judgement will be a day of triumph for the vast majority. For some it will be a day of rude awakening to the realities of life, which they managed to hide from themselves in earthly life.

all the nations : The men of all nations and of all times will be gathered together before Christ the king seated on his throne. Each will receive his reward or his punishment according to his merits or demerits.

as . . . separates : There will be no need for discussion or proofs, all the facts will be an open book not only to Christ but to all men. Those who have been loyal subjects—the sheep—will be placed at Christ's right hand; the disloyal—the goats—on his left. The right hand is considered the place of honor.

inherit . . . kingdom : This is the glad news for the loyal : they are to enter into the kingdom of the Father—an eternal life of happiness.

prepared . . . world : God's plan from all eternity was to share his kingdom with mankind. He gave men the right to this inheritance through his Incarnation.

for I was hungry : The whole stress here is on the law of fraternal charity—love of neighbor. There are other obligations and duties in life but true love of neighbor is a proof of true love of God. Therefore, he who truly loves God will keep all his laws.

"I was hungry, thirsty, naked, sick, in prison," Christ says, identifying himself with the members of his mystical body. Those on his right, the saved, express surprise in order to bring out Christ's answer. When they acted charitably toward their neighbor they did so for love of God and Christ, otherwise their actions would have no merit for heaven.

Depart from me : Those on the king's left hand are excluded from the new kingdom of heaven. In reality, they excluded themselves by their failure in fraternal charity.

eternal . . . angels : Jesus is using the eschatological terminology then current among the Jews. Those who fail in their life's purpose—those who refuse to love God and neighbor—will not enter heaven but will join Satan and the angels who followed him, in some place of punishment. This punishment will be permanent just as the joys of heaven for the "saved" will be eternal.

APPLICATION : Christ himself in this description of the last judgement, describes his role as that of a king. He will "sit on a glorious throne." As a "king" he will pronounce judgement on all mankind; he will separate the good from the bad. His decision will be final and forever. This gospel reading, therefore, reminds us of the Kingship of Christ who "humiliated himself" in the Incarnation for our sakes, but was raised again to glory by the Father and so gave all men the possibility and means to raise themselves to eternal glory.

This gospel reading brings out also the very necessary lesson which we must learn if we are to serve Christ as faithful subjects while on earth and so come into our eternal kingdom when we die. We serve him, he tells us himself today, by serving his needy members. These we will always have with us, so that we shall never be short of the opportunity to show our love and gratitude to Christ.

The hungry, sick, naked, imprisoned provide us with opportunities for serving Christ. If there are none of these in our immediate neighborhood, there are millions in other parts of our world today and we need not search far for means of helping them. There are hundreds of associations dedicated to serving those in need of the corporal works of mercy. Let us be as generous as our means will allow in our donations to one or other of these associations.

Let us not forget either, that our Lord's reference to his needy members was not restricted to those in bodily need only. There are many of our fellow-men, Christians and non-Christians, who are hungry and thirsty for spiritual things; others are spiritually sick through worldliness and sin; many others who are so imprisoned in their own earthly ambitions that they have no time to think of their future life. To help such neighbors out of their difficulties, self-inflicted or not, is to serve Christ. He wants all men for heaven. He came on earth for that purpose. He expects us to cooperate with him in bringing them there, and he gives us these opportunities so that we can prove our love for him now on earth and later for all eternity, rejoice with those we helped.

On this feast of Christ our King, let us renew our pledge of loyalty to him, and so that this pledge will not be an empty formula, let each one of us resolve to study once more the spiritual and corporal works of mercy and see how well we put them into practice. If we have failed in the past, let us resolve to begin again today. Many of us may feel that we ourselves need all we can get for our bodily needs, and those of our families. If that is really so, Christ will understand it, but this will not excuse us from carrying out the spiritual works of mercy. The fervent prayer; the sincere Christian advice for an erring neighbor; the prudent counsel to parents in disagreement or to parents neglecting their children's Christian upbringing; these works of charity, aided by God's grace, can work miracles. They have done so time and time again in the past; they will do so again in the future.

Let us help one another by bearing one another's burdens. This is what Christ asks of us. This is how we can prove ourselves loyal and grateful subjects. This is what we will be judged on when we meet him on our last day. If we love our neighbor with an active and practical love for Christ's sake, we are thereby loving God, and are keeping "the two greatest commandments on which the whole law and the prophets depend."

FEAST OF THE ASSUMPTION OF THE BLESSED VIRGIN MARY

FIRST READING: Revelation 11:19; 12:1–6; 10. God's temple in heaven was opened, and the Ark of his Covenant was seen within his temple. And a great portent appeared in heaven, a woman clothed with the sun, with the moon under her feet, and on her head a crown of twelve stars; she was with child and she cried out in her pangs of birth, in anguish for delivery. And another portent appeared in heaven; behold, a great red dragon, with seven heads and ten horns, and seven diadems upon his heads. His tail swept down a third of the stars of heaven, and cast them to the earth. And the dragon stood before the woman who was about to bear a child, that he might devour her child when she brought it forth; she brought forth a male child, one who is to rule all the nations with a rod of iron, but her child was caught up to God and to his throne, and the woman fled into the wilderness, where she has a place prepared by God. And I heard a loud voice in heaven, saying, "Now the salvation and the power and the kingdom of our God and the authority of his Christ has come."

EXPLANATION: On the authorship and literary style of the Book of Revelation see the Second Sunday of Easter (153, Cycle C). The apocalyptic literature was full of imagery and visions which need not be taken in the literal and objective sense. In these verses, taken from Revelation today, John is describing the beginning of the messianic era, in which the powers of evil, represented by a dragon, would fight bitterly to hinder the victory of the Messiah. This dragon tries to kill the Messiah at birth but fails. The Messiah fulfills his mission and triumphantly reaches the throne of God. The woman, representing Mary the mother of Christ, and also the Church, will likewise triumph. When the dragon has been conquered the reign of God and of Christ will begin.

God's temple in heaven: In a vision John sees God's throne in heaven. In his earthly Temple in Jerusalem the Ark of the Covenant was his throne. At the time of the Babylonian exile Jeremiah hid this Ark in a cavern in Mount Nebo and it was not to be rediscovered until the messianic era had come (see Mc. 2: 4–8). John is very probably referring to this.

a woman clothed with the sun . . . twelve

stars : John has before his mind both Mary the virgin Mother of Christ the Messiah, and the Church, the new Chosen People of God. The pangs of childbirth refer to the sufferings of the early Church, as does the later flight into the desert. The sun covering the heavenly woman, with the moon under her feet and the twelve stars as her diadem, are images which together attempt to describe the glory of Mary, the mother of the triumphant Messiah. The twelve stars also symbolize the twelve tribes of Israel whose place is taken by the new Israel with the twelve Apostles as its leaders. Thus it applies to the Church.

dragon . . . ten horns : These are apocalyptic images to describe the opponents of the messianic kingdom. Isaiah refers to Rahab and the dragon who were hacked to pieces by the Lord (Is. 51 : 9) and Leviathan the writhing serpent whom the Lord will punish with his powerful sword (Is. 27 : 1). The fourth beast in Daniel's vision has ten horns (Dn. 7 : 7). John draws on these images to describe the opponents of the Messiah and his kingdom, the Church.

dragon stood before the woman : He meant to devour the woman's child at birth. Herod comes to our mind here, but so do the Sanhedrin, and Saul before his conversion, and the Roman emperors who did everything possible to destroy and devour the infant Church.

to rule . . . nations : He was to be King of the world, a King who would be as a shepherd over his flock.

with . . . iron : There is a reference here to psalm 2 where the Messiah is said to break the power of the impenitent pagan nations with a rod of iron, and so win freedom for his Chosen People.

caught up : John moves directly from the birth of the Messiah to his ascension. In Acts (1 : 2; 11; 22) the ascension is described as a "taking up," a "taking away from" the Apostles. It was God the Father who took him up to heaven.

woman fled into the wilderness : St. John is here speaking of the infant Church which had to go through its period of persecution and formation just as the Chosen People of old had to go through their desert before entering the promised land. This was God's plan and therefore a success. The blood of the martyrs became the seed of Christians.

kingdom . . . God : When Constantine the Roman Emperor became a Christian (311 A.D.) freedom was eventually given to God's kingdom on earth.

authority of his Christ : Christ's authority as head of the Church was then publicly admitted.

APPLICATION : This text from the Book of Revelation or Apocalypse was chosen for the feast of the Assumption of Our Lady, because of the close link between Christ our Messiah and Savior and his blessed Mother. John stresses it in these verses. In God's plan for our elevation to divine sonship by adoption, Mary was chosen from all eternity to be the Mother of his divine Son's human nature. She was thus intimately connected with her son in the carrying out of this divine plan. As this plan was to be opposed by sin, and by Satan, the head and representative of all sinners, it was to be expected that opposition would concentrate on his blessed Mother, as well as on her offspring, Christ the Messiah.

In chapter three of Genesis this opposition was already foretold in the poetic description of the first sin of disobedience, attributed to the wiles of Satan. God said to the serpent, who represented Satan, as the Dragon in Revelation does, "I will put enmity between you and the woman, between your offspring and hers" (Gn. 3 : 15). St. John in his apocalyptic imagery, describes this opposition. We know from the Gospel story how Mary suffered with her divine Son. The culmination of that suffering was the three hours of incredible and indescribable agony she had to bear while her beloved one slowly shed his life's blood on the cross.

Today, on the feast of our Blessed Mother's triumph, we can omit the tragic events of her life and, like St. John, pass quickly to the victorious outcome of the struggle between the Dragon and the Messiah, a victory in which Mary had played her part. In return she received a reward far exceeding any earthly pains which she had endured.

Today the Church celebrates Mary's assumption into heaven which took place immediately after her death. She was then given the same glorified existence which her divine Son's human nature had been given by the Father at his moment of death, and which all the elect will be given at their moment of resurrection. We believe that, after Christ, she has occupied the next highest place of glory in heaven from the moment that her earthly life ended. This has been the constant belief of the Church from the very beginning, a belief confirmed and guaranteed by the infallible declaration of Pope Pius XII in 1950.

Mary was Mother of Christ, the God-man and our Savior. She cooperated with him in his salvific mission. She suffered, as we saw above, because of our sins. She saw her beloved Son suffer and die on the cross for our sins. She is now enjoying eternal glory in heaven. Is it likely that she could lose interest in us, her other children who are brothers of Christ? No, her divine Son has not lost interest in us and therefore his blessed Mother cannot fail to be interested in our eternal welfare. We can feel certain that she will intercede for us if we ask her, and we can rest assured that her intercession will not be ignored.

Let us honor her today in the manner in which she wants us to honor her, that is, by thanking God for all the graces which he conferred on her, graces which flowed from her privileged position as Mother of Christ. Her immediate assumption into heaven was the crowning grace and the divine reward which the infinitely loving God conferred on the woman whom he had chosen to cooperate in the messianic mission of his beloved Son. For having been made sons of God and heirs to heaven we owe a debt of thanks, after God, Father, Incarnate Son and Holy Spirit, to the Mother of God and our Mother.

SECOND READING: 1 Corinthians 15:20-27. Christ has been raised from the dead, the first fruits of those who have fallen asleep. For as by a man came death, by a man has come also the resurrection of the dead. For as in Adam all die, so also in Christ shall all be made alive. But each in his own order: Christ the first fruits, then at his coming those who belong to Christ. Then comes the end, when he delivers the kingdom to God the Father after destroying every rule and every authority and power. For he must reign until he has put all his enemies under his feet. The last enemy to be destroyed is death. "For God has put all things in subjection under his feet."

EXPLANATION: In this chapter of his first letter to his Corinthian converts St. Paul is proving that we shall all rise one day from the dead. Evidently some of the converts were doubting this. St. Paul refutes this false idea by reminding them that one of the basic doctrines of the Christian faith, which they had accepted, was Christ's resurrection. For his proofs of this basic fact of the faith see verses 1–11 of this fifteenth chapter. See also the Sixth Sunday of the Year.

the first fruits . . . fallen asleep: As the appearance of the first fruits was a sign and proof that the rest would follow, so the resurrection of Christ was a proof that all men would be raised from the dead one day. In the New Testament death is often compared to a sleep (see Jn. 11:11; Acts 7:60; 13:16; 1 Cor. 7:29; 11:30, etc.). This figure of speech was so common among the early Christians that the Greek word "koimeterion", which meant a dormitory or sleeping-place, came to mean the Christian burial-place. Hence our English word "cemetery."

In Adam all die: St. Paul accepted the literal interpretation of Genesis 3:5–19, and so Adam's physical (not spiritual) death was a punishment for his disobedience. This punishment was incurred by all his descendants.

In Christ . . . alive: Christ by his death and resurrection has earned for all men, all the descendants of Adam, a resurrection from death. As St. Paul says later in this chapter, our risen bodies will be different from our present bodies: "What is sown (buried) in the earth as a perishable thing is raised imperishable, sown in humiliation, it is raised in glory; sown in weakness, it is raised in power, sown as an animal body it is raised as a spiritual body" (15:42–43).

at his coming . . . belong to Christ: Christ has already risen. At the **parousia,** or second coming of Christ, at the end of time, all those who belong to him, that is, those who were loyal to him in life, will rise in glory as he did. He does not say what will happen to those who were disloyal.

destroying . . . rule: Having completed his salvific mission as the Incarnate Son of God, and having brought all the elect to the glory of the eternal life, he will have conquered all evil. He will then hand over the kingdom he has won to the Father.

he must reign: The end of the world will see the end of his kingdom on earth. All his opponents will be subjected to him, if not willingly, then to their own eternal loss. All his elect will be transferred to the heavenly kingdom of his Father.

APPLICATION : St. Paul says in the verse that immediately precedes today's reading (15 : 19) : "If it is for this life only that we had hope in Christ, we of all men are most to be pitied." How true this is! If all were to end for us in the grave how foolish we would be to deprive ourselves of any of the pleasure, power or wealth of this life! What folly it would be for any man to mortify himself, to keep laws that were restricting his personal liberty, to waste time on prayer and other practices which produced no earthly pleasure or gain! In other words, being a Christian would mean taking on oneself unpleasant obligations which earned nothing for us but the grave!

However, St. Paul proves in this same chapter that there is a life beyond the grave, an eternal life which Christ has won for us and which God has planned for us from all eternity. We shall all rise from the dead and enter into this new life. Christ's own resurrection is the proof that this will be so. We have another proof of this basic truth of our faith in the feast we are celebrating today. This proof has been infallibly defined by the successor of St. Peter, the head of the Church.

Our blessed Lady, Mother of Christ and our Mother, has been raised from the dead and is now in heaven in a glorified state next to the Incarnate Son of God who is her Son also. The blessed Mother is one of us, a mere creature who was made of flesh and blood as we are. She differs from us in this, that because of her honored and most special relationship with God's Incarnate Son she received greater graces than any other human being, and she cooperated with these graces. If we cooperate with them each one of us is guaranteed enough graces and favors to win our

own resurrection to the eternal life.

As the resurrection or assumption of our blessed Lady is a further proof and guarantee that we too shall one day rise in triumph from our graves, so also is it a source of greater confidence and hope for each one of us. She, our Mother, is in heaven. She is interested in each one of us. She has influence with her Son and with the Holy Trinity. She will use that influence on our behalf if we ask her. This fact of her power of intercession has been proved again and again down through the history of the Church. She has obtained material blessings for thousands. The spiritual blessings she has obtained for those devoted to her are innumerable. They will be known to all only on the last day.

Today, then, let us thank God first and foremost for the Incarnation, for sending his Son on earth as a man in order to lift us up to sonship with his Father. Then let us thank him for choosing this human Mother—one of ourselves—for his Incarnate Son, and for giving her all the graces necessary for the position he gave her in life. She suffered with her divine Son on Calvary and that suffering was for us. She, like her beloved Son, wants us in heaven. She is able and willing to help us to get there. At the wedding feast in Cana she successfully interceded with him to save a bridal pair from temporary embarrassment. Will she not be even more successful still in her intercession to save all her devoted children from eternal embarrassment, now that she is with her Son in heaven?

All that is needed is trust and confidence on our part. Let us ask her today, on this great feast of her triumph, to be ever watching over us, directing and encouraging us to persevere in our loyalty to her divine Son. Let us resolve to follow her example and climb our Calvary as she climbed hers. If we do so, the day is not far distant when we too will rise from the dead and join her and him in the home prepared for us through the Incarnation and the infinite love of God.

GOSPEL : Luke 1 : 39–56. Mary arose and went with haste into the hill country, to a city of Judah, and she entered the house of Zechariah and greeted Elizabeth. And when Elizabeth heard the greeting of Mary, the babe leaped in her womb; and Elizabeth was filled with the Holy Spirit and she exclaimed with a loud cry, "Blessed are you among women, and blessed is the fruit of your womb! And why is this granted me, that the mother of my Lord should come to me? For behold, when the voice of your greeting came to my ears, the babe in my womb leaped for joy. And blessed is she who believed that there would be a fulfillment of what was spoken to her from the Lord."

And Mary said, "My soul magnifies the Lord, and my spirit rejoices in God my Savior, for he has regarded the low estate of his handmaiden. For behold, henceforth all generations will call me blessed; for he who is mighty has done great things for me, and holy is his name. And his mercy is on those who fear him from generation to generation. He has shown strength with his arm, he has scattered the proud in the imagination of their hearts, he has put down the mighty from their thrones, and exalted those of low degree; he has filled the hungry with good things, and the rich he has sent empty away. He has helped his servant Israel, in remembrance of his mercy, as he spoke to our fathers, to Abraham and to his posterity for ever." And Mary remained with her about three months, and returned to her home.

EXPLANATION : The Angel Gabriel told Mary that she was to be the mother of the Messiah. Mary's big problem was how this could be, because she intended to remain a virgin. The Angel told her that God's power would do this, because the son whom she would conceive and give birth to would be the Son of the Most High. As a proof of this power of God the Angel tells her that her cousin Elizabeth, who was barren and then quite advanced in years, had conceived, and was already in her sixth month "for God's promises can never fail."

Mary accepted the Angel's word saying : "I am the maidservant of the Lord, let it be done unto me as you say." The Incarnation took place at that moment.

Mary's first thought was to visit, congratulate and help Elizabeth. Without hesitation she left for Elizabeth and Zechariah's house, which was in the hill country of Judah about five miles west of Jerusalem, a four days' journey from Nazareth.

Elizabeth . . . filled with the Holy Spirit : On hearing Mary's greeting, Elizabeth was inspired by the Holy Spirit and proclaimed Mary as the most blessed of all women and Mother of God. She feels how unworthy she is that the Mother of her Lord (God) should visit her. John the Baptist, the baby in her womb, also recognized the presence of the Son of God and of his Mother, and leaped in Elizabeth's womb.

Mary said : We have now what we know as the "Magnificat," Mary's hymn of praise to God, who is about to fulfill the messianic promises which he had made to Abraham and his descendants. The Son of God has become man so that all men could become sons of God. It is very likely that Mary did not compose this hymn verbatim as St. Luke gives it. However, it certainly expresses her feelings. There is gratitude for the infinite love and mercy of God toward the humble and lowly. These will be filled with good things (the fruits of the Incarnation) while the selfish and proud will not share in his generosity. She realizes how unworthy she is of the great things he has done for her. She prophesies that all ages will call her blessed because God, through his mighty power, had made her Mother of his Incarnate Son.

She remained with her : Although St. Luke does not say so expressly, it is evident that Mary remained until the Baptist was born, so that she could be of help and comfort to her cousin.

APPLICATION : "All ages to come shall call me blessed" was a prophecy uttered by our Lady and was not a boast. She who was chosen by God to be the Mother of his Incarnate Son, saw in herself nothing but a maidservant, completely and entirely unworthy of the dignity conferred on her. Elizabeth had called her "blessed among women" but Mary attributes this blessedness to the "greatness of the Lord" who had "looked on his servant in her lowliness." She had no doubts about her own unworthiness and her unfitness for the dignity conferred on her by God, but she recognized how great, how sublime that dignity was. She had been made the Mother of God.

Her prophecy has been fulfilled from the very first days of the Church. She has been given the highest place among all of God's creatures—Queen of Angels and Queen of all Saints—right through the history of Christianity. In giving her this place of honor above all other angelic or saintly creatures, we are but following God's own initiative—he made her the Mother of his divine Son and gave her all the graces which that position of unparalleled dignity demanded. When we honor her it is really his infinite love for, and his unbounded generosity towards, the human race that we are honoring. It was for us men and for our salvation that the Son of God came down from heaven. It was for us that he chose Mary as his Mother. She was but the human intermediary in God's plan of salvation for mankind.

Today's feastday of God's Mother and ours is the climax and crowning of all the other graces and honors which God conferred on her. The assumption or the transferring of our blessed Lady to heaven, in her glorified but identical, total personality, immediately after her death on earth, was not only the triumph of Mary but a triumph for all humanity. Where the Mother is, there will be all her loyal children. She played a large part in the redemption work of her divine Son on earth. She continues in heaven to play a very effective part in applying the fruits of that redemption to all her children. If we follow Mary we are following Christ. If we remain close to the Mother we can never wander away from her Son. If we put ourselves under the mantle of her protection, Christ will shelter us from the enemies of our salvation. If we call on her to intercede for us our petitions will be answered by Christ.

This climax of all God's gifts to Mary —the assumption into heaven, not of her separated soul, but of her total person, is a gift which God has ready for all of us, provided we imitate Mary on earth and be loyal to her Son and God's Son. We cannot expect the same degree of heavenly glory which is hers, but we shall be perfectly happy with what we shall receive. All eternity will not be long enough for us to thank the Blessed Trinity, Christ in his humanity and his Blessed Mother who did so much to save us.

FEAST OF THE IMMACULATE CONCEPTION

FIRST READING: Genesis 3 : 9–15; 20. After Adam had eaten of the tree, the Lord God called to the man, and said to him, "Where are you?" And he said, "I heard the sound of thee in the garden, and I was afraid, because I was naked; and I hid myself." He said, "Who told you that you were naked? Have you eaten of the tree of which I commanded you not to eat?" The man said, "The woman whom thou gavest to be with me, she gave me fruit of the tree, and I ate." Then the Lord God said to the woman, "What is this that you have done?" The woman said, "The serpent beguiled me, and I ate." The Lord God said to the serpent, "Because you have done this, cursed are you above all cattle, and above all wild animals; upon your belly you shall go, and dust you shall eat all the days of your life. I will put enmity between you and the woman, and between your seed and her seed; it shall bruise your head, and you shall bruise its heel."

The man called his wife's name Eve, because she was the mother of all living.

EXPLANATION: In the preceding verses (2 : 4—3 : 8) the Yahwehistic source of this part of Genesis has described the temptation of the woman (later called Eve) by the serpent. She succumbs and tempts the man (haadam). As soon as they had disobeyed God's command given in 2 : 16–17, they realized their guilt and tried to hide from God.

where are you : God knows where he is, but he wants them both to come forward and admit their guilt.

afraid because I was naked : This answer implies that because of their disobedience, concupiscence of the flesh had now entered the world of humans. In their state of innocence it had no place in their lives (as 2 : 25 clearly states : "the man and his wife were both naked and they felt no shame").

eaten . . . to eat : They had eaten of what was called the "tree of knowledge of good and evil" and were therefore conscious of evil. They had disobeyed a test of obedience which God had given them and they now felt a sense of guilt.

the woman . . . with me : Not only has man lost his friendship with God but his love and friendship for his wife has changed. He throws the blame on her, while at the same time blaming God for giving her to him, "you put her here with me!"

the serpent beguiled : The woman in turn puts the blame on the serpent, who had certainly tempted her, although she was free to reject his suggestion.

said to the serpent : It is clear from God's condemnation of the serpent that there is more than an irrational animal in question. Some of the punishment applies to the animal, some to a rational

being hidden in and symbolized by the serpent.

cursed . . . cattle : Because of his poisonous fangs all other animals avoid the serpent.

upon your belly you shall go : This and "dirt you shall eat" is a symbol of humiliation for an intelligent being, not for the animal who was made as a crawling creature and appears to eat dirt but does not.

enmity between you and the woman : A perpetual hatred will exist between the tempter and the woman (Eve in the context), between his (seed) offspring (followers and helpers) and the woman's (seed) offspring, that is, all mankind.

It shall bruise your head : The Hebrew word for seed (offspring) is singular, hence *he* will strike could be used here.

bruise its heel : The image of the serpent, while it means the tempter, is still used. In this struggle the descendants of the woman will have the victory, for the serpent's head is his most vulnerable part. The seed of the woman will also suffer but not fatally.

Eve . . . mother of all living : In the preceding verses the Hebrew word used for "woman" was "ishah" derived from man = "ish." Now we are told that the man changed her name to "Hawwah," Heva in Latin, Eve in English, and the reason is because it is from her that the human race, the living = "Hay" will spring.

APPLICATION : "I will put enmity between you and the woman and between your offspring and hers." These words of God addressed to the serpent, the evil tempter, immediately after the sin of disobedience committed by the first parents, have been called the proto-

Evangelium or "first good news" of hope for the human race. These verses from the Book of Genesis have been chosen for today's feast day, that of the Immaculate Conception of Mary, because she was chosen by God to be the human Mother of his Incarnate Son, and was conceived free from any stain of the sin handed down from the first parents. From the first moment of her human existence she was "full of grace" and God's "highly favored daughter."

In Mary, therefore, this "first good news" had its first fulfillment. Satan had no part in her. The serpent had lost his power in her case. This was because of the privileged position God had allotted to her. She was to be the Mother of the long-expected Messiah—Savior, who would finally crush the serpent's head.

This victory, already won in the moral sense, had still to be won on the physical plane. As foretold by this first prophecy and promise of eventual salvation for the human race, the serpent could still inflict pain and suffering. Using his offspring, his human agents, he had Christ condemned as a criminal to the cruel death of the cross. Christ's blessed Mother suffered with him. She stood beneath the cross during his three hours of death-agony. She knew that he was the innocent victim of Satan's wiles, and of the sins of mankind. She had to listen to the jeers and the insults of those very men whom he had come to save, and for whom he was laying down his life.

Yes, the serpent could and did use his poisonous fangs but they failed to save him from defeat. The sufferings of Jesus and of his blessed Mother were the very means foreseen by God to con-quer sin and Satan, and to win eternal life and freedom for all the children of Eve. Satan unwittingly played the chief role in his own undoing. Calvary was the stage where the "triumph of failure" was enacted. The death of the Savior brought eternal life to men.

If Eve was given her name because she brought all living human beings into this world, how much more so can Mary be called the source of life for all men? Eve brought men into a world of misery, a world of suffering, a world of sin. Mary brought Christ our Savior, the author of eternal life into this world. Through him she brought to all those who will become his brothers through faith, and therefore her children, the assurance of an everlasting life of happiness, joy and unending peace and love.

We honor our sinless Mother on this great Feast of her Immaculate Conception. Though we are sinners, let us ask her to spread her mantle of purity and grace over us. She loves us because she suffered with her beloved Son for us. She wants his triumph on Calvary to be as full and complete as possible. She is able and willing to help us to gain the victory which he won for us. All that is needed is that we turn to her as humble suppliants. She will pray for us sinners now and especially at the hour of our death.

SECOND READING: Ephesians 1:3–6; 11–12. Blessed be the God and Father of our Lord Jesus Christ, who has blessed us in Christ with every spiritual blessing in the heavenly places, even as he chose us in him before the foundation of the world, that we should be holy and blameless before him. He destined us in love to be his sons through Jesus Christ, according to the purpose of his will, to the praise of his glorious grace which he freely bestowed on us in the Beloved.

In him, according to the purpose of him who accomplishes all things according to the counsel of his will, we who first hoped in Christ have been destined and appointed to live for the praise of his glory.

EXPLANATION: From his prison in Rome (about 63 A.D.) St. Paul wrote this letter to his converts in Ephesus. He had preached the Gospel to them some eight years previously and the Christian message had since spread to the neighboring cities and towns. The purpose of this letter was to recall to their minds the basic Christian truths and to encourage them to remain faithful followers of Christ.

Blessed be the God and Father: St. Paul has taught the doctrine of the Blessed Trinity to his Ephesian converts (Jews and Gentiles). They have accepted it without question, although for Jewish converts especially this was not easy.

of our Lord Jesus Christ: The Jesus who had lived and died recently in Palestine was "Christ," that is, the promised "Messiah." Furthermore, he was "Lord," that is, God. We have, therefore, in this single verse the doctrine of the Trinity, God the Father, God the Son (the Holy Spirit is mentioned later on) and the doctrine of the Incarnation. Jesus, the man they all knew about, was also God, the Son of God the Father.

blessed us in Christ: Through Christ, that is, through the Incarnation of his Son, God the Father had bestowed every spiritual blessing in the heavens (where the Christians would receive their full reward) on the Ephesian Christians.

chose us in him: Through the medium of the Incarnation, Christians (and all men of good will) have been predestined by the Father to share in eternal happiness.

before . . . the world: As Scotus teaches, God's plan for sharing heaven with us by making us his adopted sons through his divine Son's Incarnation was from all eternity, and not a remedy necessary because of men's sins.

through . . . Christ: Through his Son's adoption of our human nature we were predestined to be elevated to the status of adopted sons of God. The prayer which we say in the Mass points to this: "through this mystery of water and wine may we come to share in the divinity of Christ who humbled himself to share in our humanity."

according . . . will: The only explanation of this infinite generosity on the part of God the Father toward us mere creatures is his will and pleasure.

glorious . . . Beloved: Unending praise and thanksgiving should be man's response and reaction to the favor which the Father, in the mystery of the Incarnation, has planned for us through his beloved Son.

In him . . . appointed: St. Paul is referring first to the Jewish converts. While they were still Jews they were the first to have hope in Christ the Messiah. They praised God for his mercies. Then in the following verse (13) he addresses the Gentiles: "you too . . . became incorporate in Christ. . . "

APPLICATION : The Christo-centric doctrine of St. Paul expressed above occurs too in all of his greater Epistles, especially in the captivity Epistles (Colossians, Ephesians, Philippians). It is closely connected with the Feast of the Immaculate Conception which we are celebrating today. God planned from all eternity to make man, the masterpiece and master of creation, his adopted son, and heir to his own eternal happiness. He was to bring this about through his divine Son's adoption of our human nature. Man would then become a brother of Christ and therefore a son of God by adoption. Christ, the Son of God in human nature, the God-man, is the pivotal point in all of God's creative activity. In him, through him, and for him all creation came into existence. In him and through him all mankind, the whole human race, was destined for eternal life.

But man, realizing the many gifts which he had, and forgetting the one who gave them to him, grew proud of his own capabilities and wanted to be his own master. He rebelled and sin came into the world. Despicable and mean as it was on the part of man, it did not stop God from carrying out his eternal plan. The Incarnation could still have taken place. When the "fullness of time" as St. Paul calls it, was approaching, he called Abraham from his pagan homeland and made him the Father and Founder of a Chosen People. This People would prepare the world for the fulfilling of the "mystery" which he had planned from all eternity.

As the prophecies given to his Chosen People had foretold, Christ was to be born of a virgin, a descendant of Abraham and of David. She was a virgin and intended to remain a virgin. Today's Gospel makes that clear. When told by the angelic messenger, whom God sent to her, that the conception of this child would take place through the power of the Most High she humbly accepted the role to which God had appointed her.

Mary the virgin of Nazareth, the humblest of the humble who would have been the last to expect any such dignity, became the Mother of Christ. She thus played the leading human part in the fulfillment of God's eternal plan for the human race. As she said herself : "God who is mighty has done great things for me." When he chose her, before time began, for this sublime dignity of motherhood of his Incarnate Son, he decreed to preserve her free from any stain of the sin committed by the First Parents. She was conceived "Immaculate," pure and free from any human stain. She was "our tainted nature's solitary boast," as the Protestant poet Wordsworth puts it.

This befits one who was to bear for nine months in her womb the world's greatest mystery; God's greatest gift to humanity, the Son of God clothed in human nature, Christ, God and Man. He was the perfect man and God as well. His Mother, the creature who was nearest and dearest to him, was the most perfect of creatures—the most favored daughter of God.

O

Had sin not entered the world, hers would still be the highest dignity that a creature could be given—the Motherhood of God. Her preservation from the stain of sin was but a consequence of that dignity. But in the imperfect, sinful world into which she was born it was an added, lustrous gem in her crown of glory.

We congratulate the Immaculate Mother of Christ and our Mother on this special privilege of exemption from the guilt which all of Eve's children incurred and incur. While doing so let us turn with gratitude to the God and Father of our Lord Jesus Christ. He chose her and prepared her to be the proximate means through which he was to give us every blessing in heaven.

We shall all be saints in heaven one day enjoying unending happiness. For this we give thanks to the infinitely loving Father, to the Holy Spirit, to God's incarnate Son, and to the Immaculate Virgin Mother who played and still plays such a big part in bringing us to our eternal heritage.

GOSPEL : Luke 1 : 26–38. The angel Gabriel was sent from God to a city of Galilee named Nazareth, to a virgin betrothed to a man whose name was Joseph, of the house of David; and the virgin's name was Mary. And he came to her and said, "Hail, full of grace, the Lord is with you!" But she was greatly troubled at the saying, and considered in her mind what sort of greeting this might be. And the angel said to her, "Do not be afraid, Mary, for you have found favor with God. And behold, you will conceive in your womb and bear a son, and you shall call his name Jesus. He will be great, and will be called the Son of the Most High; and the Lord God will give to him the throne of his father David, and he will reign over the house of Jacob forever; and of his kingdom there will be no end."

And Mary said to the angel, "How can this be, since I have no husband?" And the angel said to her, "The Holy Spirit will come upon you, and the power of the Most High will overshadow you; therefore the child to be born will be called holy, the Son of God. And behold, your kinswoman Elizabeth in her old age has also conceived a son; and this is the sixth month with her who was called barren. For with God nothing will be impossible." And Mary said, "Behold, I am the handmaid of the Lord; let it be to me according to your word." And the angel departed from her.

EXPLANATION : In these thirteen verses St. Luke gives us a brief account of what we call the Annunciation or the message of the Angel Gabriel to Mary. He told her that she was to be the Mother of the Messiah, Son of the Most High. When the angel solved the problem concerning her virginity, she humbly accepted the role that God had planned for her. At that moment of acceptance the Incarnation took place. The Son of God began his human life in the chaste womb of the Blessed Virgin.

Angel Gabriel: He is the same divine messenger who had announced the birth of the Baptist to Zechariah (Lk. 1 : 11) and the seventy weeks of years to Daniel (Dn. 9 : 21).

city . . . named Nazareth: A hamlet of no importance, never mentioned in the Old Testament, and not held in much esteem by Jesus' contemporaries (Jn. 1 : 46).

a virgin betrothed to . . . Joseph: A young girl of marriageable age which also meant at that time physical virginity. Although she was betrothed to Joseph, with his consent, she could have an intention of perpetual virginity. Many scriptural writers hold this view even though it would have been an unusual intention in Palestine at that time.

The virgin's name was Mary: Luke's repetition of the qualification "virgin" seems to imply something more than the fact that she was as yet unmarried.

Hail . . . grace: The CCD translation of the Greek: "Rejoice O highly favored daughter" brings out the angel's meaning better than the old form "Hail, full of grace." He is bringing her great good news. It is a time for rejoicing, and he tells her that she is a highly favored daughter of God, a statement that must have surprised one so humble as she.

The Lord is with you: As the sequel shows, this implies some special prerogative, the divine maternity. God is working through her to fulfill his messianic prophecies.

she . . . be: Because of her lowly opinion of herself she wondered at this greeting. What was she but an unknown young girl engaged to an unknown car-penter in an unknown and despised village? Why should she be favored by God?

do not . . . Mary: The angel notices her amazement and goes on to explain.

favor with God: He has already told her that she is God's favorite daughter. Now he explains why.

conceive . . . and bear a Son . . . Jesus: There is a reflexion of the Immanuel prophecy here. Isaiah says: "the virgin is with child and will soon give birth to a son whom she will call Immanuel" (Is. 7 : 14). It was the father's right to name his child. Here Mary, and the virgin mother in Isaiah, name the child. This would seem to exclude human paternity. The angel gives Mary the name which means "Yahweh (God) will save." Immanuel means "God is with us." Jesus was God Incarnate.

Great . . . Son of the Most High: The angel now describes the Son to be born of Mary in messianic terms (see Is. 9 : 6; Dn. 7 : 14) especially in

throne of . . . David: This refers to the prophecy which Nathan made to David, that he would have a successor on his throne and that throne would be established forever (2 Sm. 7 : 13; 17).

over the house of Jacob forever: The house of Jacob refers to the Chosen People. Mary's Son will reign forever over a Chosen People of Jews and Gentiles. It will be more than an earthly kingdom, it will have no end.

since I . . . husband: Unlike Zechariah (1 : 18) she does not doubt the word of the angel but admits that she cannot understand how a virgin, while remaining a virgin, can be with child.

Holy Spirit . . . Most High . . . overshadow you: God's power will do this. As shown in the Old Testament, there are reminiscences of God's power and presence here (see Gen. 1 : 2, the Spirit of God hovered over the waters before creation began; the Tabernacle was covered with a cloud to show the presence of God (Ex. 40 : 35), and so was the newly-built Temple of Jerusalem (1 Kgs. 8 : 10)).

be called . . . the Son of God : The title Son of God means more than the Messiah here. The child will be conceived by the action of God *hence* he "will be" the true "Son of God."

your kinswoman Elizabeth : The angel tells Mary of Elizabeth's good fortune as a proof of God's power and a guarantee that God's power would be forth-coming in her own case. She had not asked for a proof.

I am the handmaid of the Lord : She had been chosen to be Mother of the Lord, Mother of Christ, God's Son, but she fully realized her lowliness and her nothingness in relation to God. However, she accepted what God had willed for her; with the help of his grace she would fulfill his wishes.

Let it be done to me as you say : I accept whatever God wants of me : A fitting close to an interview between the humble Mother of God and God's angelic messenger.

APPLICATION : God planned to bestow an eternal, heavenly life on men, the highest of the creatures whom he placed on this earth. This heavenly life will be supernatural, quasi-divine. We shall still be human beings, creatures of God, finite in our powers, but we shall be free from all defects to which our human lives on earth are subject. Death and all its preliminaries and consequences will have no further place in that heavenly life. There will be no more sicknesses or ailments, no more mental or physical pains, no more partings from relatives and friends; "all tears shall be wiped away."

There will be no more vices, hatred, jealousy, anger, lust, deception, egoism, pride and prejudice. All the evils that make the life of man a burden for himself and for his neighbor on this earth, will remain in our graves when we rise from the dead.

Not only will all evil and sources of evil be removed but we shall have all that is good. First and foremost, with the grace of the beatific vision, we shall see, in a limited but satisfying way, the glory and the beauty and the perfection of the Blessed Trinity. As the Triune God is infinite, there will be something new for us to enjoy in him for all eternity. Next we shall converse with and enjoy Christ glorified, who has brought about our glorification.

Finally, we shall be in the intimate company of our blessed Mother who has played such an important part in the drama of our redemption and our glorification. We, her children, for whom she suffered so much will then be able to render her the praise and the thanks that she deserves from us.

Today, on this great feast of her Immaculate Conception, let us turn to her with hope and confidence. We are commemorating the graces and blessings which God gave her to fit her for the dignity he had chosen for her. She, like her divine Son, wants all of us in heaven. Like any human mother she wants nothing but the best for her children. But, as in any human family, the children must cooperate. Otherwise, all the

Mother's desires and hopes will be in vain.

If we expect to be in heaven with her we must try to imitate her on earth. Above all she was humble and unselfish, pride had no part in her make-up. She was chaste and pure to a degree we cannot expect to reach. But even if from afar, each of us in his or her own vocation in life, can follow her. Chastity, the proper use and respect for God's gift of sex, can and must be practiced, not only in a life of virginity consecrated to God's service but also in the married state. Obedience was another of her outstanding virtues. She welcomed and carried out the will of God even when it meant offering her beloved and only Son on the altar of the cross for our sakes. Those humble, submissive words of hers: "Let it be done to me as you say" should be always in our hearts and ready on our lips, when God asks some sacrifice of us.

Love of God and neighbor were the main-spring of her life. Her unhesitating acceptance of motherhood of the Savior of the human race proves both her love for God and her fellowman. Most of us have much lee-way to make up if we wish to come in any way near to her in the practice of these basic commandments. In heaven, we have a most powerful advocate, a Mother who loves us with a love greater than the love that any earthly mother can have for her child. If we call on her she will hear our prayer. When we begin to stumble on our upward climb she will stretch out her hand to steady us. When we fall and injure ourselves, she will lift us up and heal the wound if only we ask her. Even if, as sometimes happens, we should turn our back on her and on her divine Son, she will not turn her back on us. She will be praying and waiting patiently for our return.

With such a Mother, the Immaculate Virgin Mary, in heaven, looking down on us, what true Christian can ever have any doubt about safely reaching heaven?

FEAST OF ALL SAINTS

FIRST READING: Revelation 7 : 2–4; 9–14. I, John, saw an angel ascend from the rising of the sun, with the seal of the living God, and he called with a loud voice to the four angels who had been given power to harm earth and sea, saying, "Do not harm the earth or the sea or the trees, till we have sealed the servants of our God upon their foreheads." And I heard the number of the sealed, a hundred and forty-four thousand sealed, out of every tribe of the sons of Israel.

After this I looked, and behold, a great multitude which no man could number, from every nation, from all tribes and peoples and tongues, standing before the throne and before the Lamb, clothed in white robes, with palm branches in their hands, and crying out with a loud voice, "Salvation belongs to our God who sits upon the throne, and to the Lamb!" And all the angels stood round the throne and round the elders and the four living creatures, and they fell on their faces before the throne and worshiped God, saying, "Amen! Blessing and glory and wisdom and thanksgiving and honor and power and might be to our God for ever and ever! Amen."

Then one of the elders addressed me, saying, "Who are these, clothed in white robes, and whence have they come?" I said to him, "Sir, you know." And he said to me, "These are they who have come out of the great tribulation; they have washed their robes and made them white in the blood of the Lamb."

EXPLANATION: St. John here describes two visions which he had of the elect on earth and of the countless numbers of martyrs in heaven. The chosen ones of God on earth are the new Israel, the successors of the twelve tribes. They are about to suffer persecution. Marked with the seal of God on their foreheads, they will be given the supernatural strength to bear their sufferings. In the second vision he sees the huge crowd, countless numbers in heaven wearing white robes as a sign of their victory over their enemies. They surround the throne of God and the "Lamb", Christ, and sing their praises. **seal of the living God:** A sign or mark that indicates those who are loyal to the true God, the living God. **the four angels:** Described in 7 : 1 as standing at the four corners of the earth, holding back the winds which would destroy the earth.

do not harm . . . till : The four angels are commanded to prevent destruction until God's chosen ones are marked with God's seal. This would give them the strength to persevere.

I heard the number : John could not count them but he was told their number, a symbolic number : the twelve tribes multiplied by twelve and then by a thousand. One hundred and forty-four thousand, that is an immense number.

from . . . tongues : He now sees the countless numbers of saints in heaven.

before . . . the Lamb : They stand in the presence of the throne of God and before the Lamb, the paschal lamb who is the Savior Jesus Christ. He is the suffering servant of Isaiah who was led like a lamb to the slaughter (see Ex. 12; Is. 53 : 7; Jn. 1 : 29).

salvation . . . God . . . the Lamb : They are singing the praises of God and of his Incarnate Son who brought them salvation.

elders . . . four living creatures : The elders represent the saints in praising and worshiping God. The number twenty-four is probably taken from the twenty-four priestly classes in I Chronicles 24 : 1–9.

Four living creatures : These are the four animals in Revelation which symbolize the noblest (the Lion), the strongest (the Bull), the swiftest (the Eagle) and the wisest (the Man) of God's creatures. From the second century these four animals have been taken as symbols of the four Evangelists.

worshiped God : All the inhabitants of heaven adore, worship and praise God.

washed their robes . . . in the blood of the Lamb : Having suffered for Christ and shared in his crucifixion, they are now in glory with him.

APPLICATION : This vision of St. John is chosen for today's reading in order to encourage us to persevere in our Christian faith. Firstly, those on earth (ourselves) have to be prepared to meet opposition in our Christian lives. From the very beginning Christ had his followers and opponents. Christ, the innocent lamb, was "led to the slaughter and opened not his mouth." As our representative and Savior he saw that the perfect obedience which he was to give to his Father demanded that his enemies' wicked plans should be carried out. Likewise, during the first three centuries of the Church thousands of his followers had to give their lives for his sake and for their faith. In the intervening centuries, up to and including our own day,

thousands have been put to death because of their loyalty to Christ.

If not for most of us today, at least for many, it is not a quick martyrdom that is threatening us, but a subtle persecution which is trying to make us disloyal to Christ and to our Christian principles. Under various pretexts the enemies of Christ and of God are trying to undermine our faith. Open atheism is not the most dangerous of these enemies. Few sane men can be convinced that there is no God or nothing for man but the grave. That is the fate only of the dumb beast. The dangerous enemy is the one who, in theory, admits that there is a God and a future life, but that what we do in this life has no connexion with God or our future. We are free agents, they say. We can and should do what we like. Why should we accept any restrictions on our personal liberty? Why keep the commandments? Why control our natural instincts? We should get all the pleasure and wealth we can in this life and the next will look after itself.

Today, we are reminded that every Christian on earth and everyone who wants to go to heaven must face opposition. But St. John tells us that the followers of Christ are given the necessary graces to face and overcome this opposition. Their foreheads are imprinted with the seal of the servants of God. Try to remember this when the advocates of earthly pleasures, the agents of the powers of evil, are using their wiles to make you forget that you are God's chosen servant. His grace is there for the taking. The Christian who perseveres is he who lives his daily life at peace with God and neighbor, drawing on the sources of God's grace—prayer and the sacraments.

Another source of encouragement for us today, on this the feast day of all of God's saints, is the countless numbers John saw in heaven. These countless numbers were men and women of flesh and blood like ourselves. They had the same weaknesses, the same human inclinations, the same faults and failings in many cases as we have. They never forgot God, they never gave up trying to live the Christian life. They died at peace with God and so went to heaven. Many good-living Christians would almost laugh if they were told that they will be

saints. Yet, that is what they will be. The reason why they would laugh at this statement of fact is the wrong idea that some spiritual writers have given us of the essence of a saint. The few saints who are canonized by the Church, and whose lives are written to encourage and inspire us, were exceptional individuals. We have no written lives of the ordinary men and women who were not exceptional in any way but who lived in God's friendship and died in his grace. They now are saints in heaven.

Christ died to save all mankind. His death on the cross was not for St. Paul or St. Augustine or St. Francis only. It was for plain Mrs. Murphy and Franz Allesmanner and Signora Benvenuta also. They didn't work miracles or do anything extraordinary, but they fully lived the very ordinary, humdrum daily Christian life. Thanks to God's infinite mercy and thanks to the Lamb of God who takes away the sins of the world, there are countless saints in heaven today. One day soon you and I, please God, will increase their number. There are close relatives of each one of us in heaven. Let us ask them and all the other millions today to intercede for us. We are anxious to get to heaven and we are anxious to do the things that will get us there. Each day we have to meet much opposition. This will obtain for us God's grace and "we shall overcome." We too will be saints in heaven praising and thanking the good God who brought us there.

SECOND READING : 1 Epistle of John 3 : 1–3. See what love the Father has given us, that we should be called children of God; and so we are. The reason why the world does not know us is that it did not know him. Beloved, we are God's children now; it does not yet appear what we shall be, but we know that when he appears we shall be like him, for we shall see him as he is. And everyone who thus hopes in him purifies himself as he is pure.

EXPLANATION : The Apostle and Evangelist St. John wrote this letter to the Churches of Asia Minor to encourage them to remain faithful to Christ who was the Son of God. There were heretics and heresies arising here and there. There were proud men who questioned the divinity of Christ and the true love of God for mankind. In the verses read today he tells them (his readers) and us that God has made us his children and that if we live as true children we shall see him in heaven later on as he is.

what love the Father has . . . us : The love of God for man is the central theme of all John's writings. Through that love God has sent his Son to become "flesh," to become one of us. Because Christ the Son of God is one of us, we have become brothers of Christ and therefore sons, "children," of God.

the world does not know us : The enemies of God, the followers of evil are the "world" for John. They cannot recognize Christians as children of God for they do not recognize Christ as the true Son of God.

what we shall be : John states that we are God's children now. What we shall

be, that is, what changes will take place in us, when we leave this earth, John says he does not know. It has not been revealed. We shall still be the same individuals, the same "we" both now and in the hereafter. But we shall be changed so that we can "see God as he is" and live an eternal life.

we shall be like him : This much John knows : we shall be like God in some limited way. St. Paul says we shall be spiritual bodies, we shall be transformed, the corruptible will become incorruptible, the mortal in us will become immortal (1 Cor. 15 : 53).

for we shall see him as he is : We shall be in God's presence in the future life. We shall never be able to comprehend God, for our knowledge will still be finite, but, with the aid of the grace of the beatific vision, we shall more and more understand God's infinite qualities for all eternity.

Everyone who . . . hopes : Because he wants to reach heaven and spend an eternity of happiness with God, every true Christian must strive to keep himself "pure," that is, free from *all* sins (not impurity only).

APPLICATION : We are celebrating the Feast of all Saints, that is, of the millions of men and women who are today in heaven. St. John's words are intended to help us to persevere in our heavenward journey. The great, en-

couraging thought that John puts before us is the fact that God the Father has already placed us more than half-way on our road to heaven by making us his adopted children through the Incarnation. No father can forget his children.

He is every ready to protect, help and guide them. Could the heavenly, all-powerful, all-loving Father forget his children? Their adoption caused the humiliation of his beloved Son in taking human nature and the sacrifice of that same beloved Son on the cross of Calvary.

A human father can be inhuman and desert and neglect his human children. God can never be unGodlike. He cannot change his nature which is Love itself. He cannot forget us, his adopted children. This is surely an encouragement for us. At times we may find the uphill climb to heaven hard. But if we remember the all-loving, omnipotent Father who is watching over us, we can never despair, no matter how dark our nights of struggle and sorrow may seem.

We must never forget that a loving father may have to appear severe at times in order to be truly kind. The human father has to correct his child at times. He has to make him learn obedience, to do things necessary for his health and soundness of body. If he is to prepare him to face life and earn his living he has to make him study his lessons, a thing most children would gladly avoid. Most of this discipline can appear cruel to the unthinking child. Instead it is true love and kindness.

So it is with our heavenly Father's dealings with us. We would all love to be free from all temptations, free from all anxieties, free from all physical pain but our loving Father sees otherwise. He sends us these messengers of his love in order to prepare us to face our

true life and earn for ourselves an eternal living in the future. When we are looking down from heaven on the troubles and misfortunes that we thought no kind God should let us suffer, we shall see their purposes. We shall heartily thank God for having provided them to help us on our way to heaven.

The reward for a few years of very limited suffering here on earth will be an eternity of happiness in the company of God and all his saints. As St. John says, we have only a limited revelation as to the nature of our existence in heaven, but we have enough knowledge of heaven to make us exert all our endeavors to get there. We shall be in the presence of God, the source and author of all that is good and enjoyable. We shall see the Son of God in his human nature. In him we shall understand the love of God for us which brought about the Incarnation and all that it entailed for Christ of humiliations and sufferings for our sake. We shall be in the company of our blessed Mother and all our fellow human beings who will be intimately united with us in singing the praises of God, our common Father. Added to these joys will be the certainty that this state of happiness will last forever. Never again shall anxiety or suffering enter our lives. Pain, death and separation from those we love will never again cast a shadow on our existence. We shall feel safe with God for all eternity.

God grant that every one of us will meet in this happy state some day in the future!

GOSPEL: Matthew 5:1–12. Seeing the crowds, Jesus went up on the mountain, and when he sat down his disciples came to him. And he opened his mouth and taught them, saying:

"Blessed are the poor in spirit, for theirs is the kingdom of heaven. Blessed are those who mourn, for they shall be comforted. Blessed are the meek, for they shall inherit the earth. Blessed are those who hunger and thirst for righteousness, for they shall be satisfied. Blessed are the merciful, for they shall obtain mercy. Blessed are the pure in heart, for they shall see God. Blessed are the peacemakers, for they shall be called sons of God. Blessed are those who are persecuted for righteousness' sake, for theirs is the kingdom of heaven. Blessed are you when men revile you and persecute you and utter all kinds of evil against you falsely on my account. Rejoice and be glad, for your reward is great in heaven."

EXPLANATION: These verses we read today from St. Matthew's Gospel are what we call the "Beatitudes." The name comes from the Latin word "beatus=blest" with which each of the sayings begins. In the Old Testament the term "blest" or "happy" was understood of material happiness, earthly prosperity, but as a reward for carrying out the law. As given here in Matthew the statements made by Christ mean the following: the blessedness and happiness which are in store for those who do what is right and put up with sufferings and injustices are the spiritual blessings and happiness of God's eternal kingdom. Hence the suitability of these verses for today's feast day. The saints have their blessed state of eternal happiness because they carried out what is recommended in the "Beatitudes."

poor in spirit . . . heaven: That is, those who are really poor, through no fault of their own. Such were the vast majority of the people of the Roman Empire at the time. It is not so much the lack of temporal wealth that Matthew emphasizes, but the servile conditions under which they had to live. Christ says that they will be rich and independent in the kingdom of God later in heaven.

mourn . . . comforted: This refers in general to all who have heavy burdens to bear such as pain and grief, in this world. In particular it may refer to the pious Jews of that day who grieved over the lowly state of Israel which was caused by the sins of the Chosen People. Their sorrow will be changed to joy because the messianic kingdom has arrived. Our Lord applied the words of Isaiah to himself, words in which the prophet foretold that the humble, the broken-hearted, the prisoners, the mourners would all be comforted and freed when the Messiah would come (see Is. 61:1–3 and Lk. 4:18–21).

who hunger and thirst for righteousness: Those who are anxious to serve God truly. The Pharisees boasted of their holiness because they kept the letter of the Old Law. Christ insisted that his followers must do better than that. They must serve God in spirit and truth. The law of the love of God and neighbor covers much more than the letter of the commandments (see Mt. 5:20–6:34). Those who will fulfill God's law sincerely and truly will have their

FEAST OF ALL SAINTS • 417

abundant reward in the next life.

Blessed . . . mercy : Compassion for one's neighbor, and a willingness to help him in his need, is one of the basic principles of the law of charity which is so much stressed by Christ. Those who are really merciful and kind to their neighbor will find that God will deal mercifully and kindly with them.

pure . . . shall see God : The true service of God is not the external ritual of purity by ablutions which the Pharisees stressed, but the service given by a sincere God-loving heart. Our Lord quotes Isaiah to the Pharisees whom he calls hypocrites: "well did Isaiah prophesy of you. This people pays me lip service, but their heart is far from me. They do me empty reverence making dogmas out of human precepts" (see Is. 29 : 13 and Mt. 15 : 7–9). Those who

follow Christ's teaching will "see God," that is, they will be in his kingdom in heaven.

peacemakers . . . sons of God : Those who foster love among men by settling quarrels are true Christians. Peace was a mark of the messianic age and was the special gift of Christ to his disciples (Jn. 14 : 27).

persecuted for righteousness' sake : Those who suffer because of their love for God and for their loyalty to Christ his Son, will have the eternal reward of heaven, God's kingdom.

revile . . . account : This is an expansion of the previous beatitude, but those who suffer all these false accusations and insults do so because of their fidelity to Christ, who is God as well as man. Their reward in heaven will be great.

APPLICATION : The eight Beatitudes are a résumé of the Christian charter. They are the boundaries within which the Christian life is successfully lived. We are celebrating today the Feast of All Saints, that is, of all those who have lived their Christian life according to the ideals that Christ placed before them in the Sermon on the Mount. They have succeeded. They have reached heaven because they followed the rules which Christ laid down for them. They loved God and they showed that love in their daily living. They kept his commandment not only according to the letter but in spirit and in truth.

They bore the trials and troubles of life patiently, as part of God's plan for their sanctification. They loved their neighbor and proved it by their deeds of charity and mercy. They forgave

those who persecuted and injured them. They lived in peace with God and with their neighbor. They helped to promote peace among their fellowmen wherever and whenever they could.

Some of the saints whose feasts we are celebrating today were outstanding in their sanctity. They lived their lives of mortification far beyond what was required of them. They loved God with an intensity that is not expected of ordinary mortals. They served their neighbor with a life-long dedication. They set an example and made an impression on the life of their contemporaries which will never be forgotten. God be thanked for such noble examples of saintly Christians!

But there are millions of others in heaven, saints of God also, who did nothing except their ordinary Christian duties. They did this sincerely and willingly. Their names are not inscribed in the Church's Martyrology but they are written in the "Book of Life" in heaven. Most of us can only admire the first group from afar and thank God for the graces which their very saintly lives obtained, and are still obtaining, for the Church of God. However, we can all feel a little more confident today because of the lesser saints. What they did, we can do. Where they succeeded we too can succeed. With the help of God's grace and the assistance of the major and minor saints in heaven we will and we shall succeed.

Heaven is the eternal home that God has planned for all men of goodwill. It was to raise us up to sonship with God that Christ came down and lived and died as a man on earth. It was to help us on the way that he founded the Church and gave her the sacraments that sinners and weak mortals would need on their road to heaven. God knows the material of which we are made. He knows too how to make something far greater out of that same weak material. He has done so already with millions of very ordinary human beings. He is doing it daily and will continue to do it.

All that is needed is that we put ourselves in his hands. That he fashioned Adam out of a lump of clay may be a fact or a poetic description. What he can and will make out of me is a saint, a citizen of the kingdom of eternal happiness if only I will let him. May God give me the sense and the grace to do just that, so that when I close my eyes in death, I shall see God and become one of the millions of saints whose feast I am honoring today. So be it.